GMAT

Focus Edition
Unofficial Guide 2023

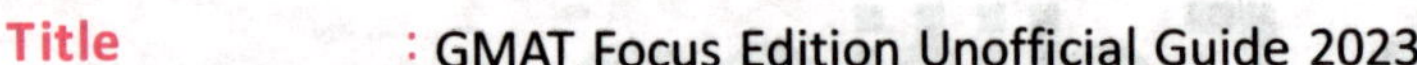

Title : GMAT Focus Edition Unofficial Guide 2023

Language : English

Editor's Name : CL Editorial Team

Copyright © : 2023 CLIP

No part of this book may be reproduced in a retrieval system or transmitted, in any form or by any means, electronics, mechanical, photocopying, recording, scanning and or without the written permission of the Author/Publisher.

Typeset & Published by :

Career Launcher Infrastructure (P) Ltd.

A-45, Mohan Cooperative Industrial Area, Near Mohan Estate Metro Station, New Delhi - 110044

Marketed by :

G.K. Publications (P) Ltd.

Plot No. 9A, Sector-27A, Mathura Road, Faridabad, Haryana-121003

ISBN : **978-93-56812-58-1**

Printer's Details : Printed in India, New Delhi.

For product information :

Visit *www.gkpublications.com* or email to *gkp@gkpublications.com*

Foreword

Welcome to the "GMAT Focus Edition - Unofficial Guide 2023" book - a comprehensive and specialized resource designed to sharpen your skills and elevate your performance on the Graduate Management Admission Test (GMAT).

The GMAT is a gateway to countless opportunities in the world of business and management. It demands not only a solid grasp of fundamental concepts but also the ability to apply that knowledge strategically. The book has been meticulously crafted to provide you with precisely what you need - a focused and expertly curated collection of content to maximize your potential on this critical exam.

In this book, you will find a streamlined and potent selection of practice questions, thoughtfully organized to cover all sections of the GMAT Focus Edition: Quantitative, Verbal, and Data Insight. Each question has been handpicked to represent the diverse array of challenges you are likely to encounter on test day.

Recognizing that time is a valuable asset in your preparation, this edition emphasizes efficiency. As you progress through these pages, you will find that every question, every explanation, and every strategy has been fine-tuned to provide the most impactful learning experience.

The authors of the "GMAT Focus Edition" are experts in their fields, each with a deep understanding of the GMAT and a passion for helping aspiring business leaders like you to succeed. They have poured their expertise and dedication into crafting a resource that goes beyond the norm, guiding you through each question with clarity and precision.

While this book is a powerful tool, it is only one part of your journey. Your success on the GMAT will also depend on your commitment, perseverance, and the belief that you have what it takes to excel. Embrace the challenges presented within these pages, and let each question be an opportunity to refine your thinking, hone your skills, and push the boundaries of your abilities.

Remember that the GMAT is not just about achieving a score; it is a stepping stone toward your dreams and aspirations. Embrace the process of learning, celebrate every step forward, and allow this experience to shape you into the future leader you envision.

As you embark on this transformative journey, know that you are not alone. Countless individuals have faced the GMAT before you, and many more will follow. Let the "GMAT Focus Edition" be your ally, guiding you with expertise and encouragement as you navigate the path to success.

On behalf of the authors and the entire team behind this book, I extend my best wishes for your GMAT preparation. May your dedication, hard work, and focus on excellence propel you toward a bright and prosperous future.

Best Wishes!

Content

Introduction to the GMAT

Introduction to GMAT

The GMAT (Graduate Management Admission Test) is a standardized exam that is used to assess the readiness of prospective students for graduate-level business programs. The exam evaluates various skills that are important for success in a business school, such as Data insight, quantitative reasoning, and verbal reasoning. The GMAT is accepted by thousands of graduate-level business programs worldwide, and it is typically taken by individuals who are seeking admission to MBA (Master of Business Administration) programs or other business-related master's degree programs. The exam is administered in English, and it is offered year- round at test centers around the world.

The GMAT score is used in admission decisions by more than 7,000 graduate management programs, at approximately 2,300 graduate business schools worldwide. It helps you gauge, and demonstrate to schools, your academic potential for success in graduate-level management studies.

Let's start with the basics. The GMAT is, among other things, an endurance test. It is a computerized test, consisting of 135 minutes of multiple-choice math, verbal, and data insights questions.

Taking the GMAT helps you stand out in the admissions process; and demonstrate your readiness and commitment to pursuing graduate management education. Schools use GMAT scores to help them select the most-qualified applicants because they know that candidates who take the GMAT are serious about earning a graduate business degree; and it's a proven predictor of a student's ability to succeed in his or her chosen program.

Format of GMAT

The GMAT exam is designed to assess the critical reasoning and data literacy skills that are essential for success in business school and beyond.

The GMAT has three sections:

- **Quantitative Reasoning:** This section tests your ability to solve math problems using a variety of methods, including basic arithmetic, algebra and data analysis.
- **Verbal Reasoning:** This section tests your ability to read critically and understand complex text. It includes questions that test your reasoning and reading comprehension skills.
- **Data Insights:** This section tests your ability to interpret and analyze data. It includes questions that test your ability to understand graphs, charts, and tables.

Each section of the GMAT is 45 minutes long, for a total test time of 2 hours and 15 minutes. There is one optional 10-minute break after the Quantitative Reasoning section.

The scores for the GMAT are reported on a scale of 205 to 805, with a 10-point increment. The scores for each section are also reported separately.

The GMAT is a valuable tool for students who are preparing for business school. It can help you assess your strengths and weaknesses in the critical reasoning and data literacy areas, and it can give you a good idea of how you would perform on the actual GMAT exam.

Here is a table summarizing the format of the GMAT:

Section	Time	Number of Questions
Quantitative Reasoning	45 minutes	21 questions
Verbal Reasoning	45 minutes	23 questions
Data Insights	45 minutes	20 questions

Section Order

The GMAT allows you to choose the order in which you take the three sections. You can choose to take the Quantitative Reasoning section first, the Verbal Reasoning section first, or the Data Insights section first.

There are a few factors to consider when choosing your section order. First, you should consider your strengths and weaknesses. If you are stronger in quantitative reasoning, you may want to take that section first. If you are stronger in verbal reasoning, you may want to take that section first.

Second, you should consider your timing. If you know that you tend to get tired towards the end of the exam, you may want to take the Data Insights section first, as it is the shortest section.

Finally, you should consider your personal preference. Some people prefer to start with the section that they are most confident in, while others prefer to start with the section that they are least confident in.

Here are some tips for choosing your section order:

- Consider your strengths and weaknesses. If you are stronger in quantitative reasoning, you may want to take that section first. If you are stronger in verbal reasoning, you may want to take that section first.

- Consider your timing. If you know that you tend to get tired towards the end of the exam, you may want to take the Data Insights section first, as it is the shortest section.

- Consider your personal preference. Some people prefer to start with the section that they are most confident in, while others prefer to start with the section that they are least confident in.

Ultimately, the best way to choose your section order is to experiment and see what works best for you. Try taking a practice test with different section orders and see how you do.

Quantitative Aptitude

Chapter 1

Number Properties

Number Properties is a topic that is tested in the Quantitative Reasoning section of the GMAT. It is a broad topic that covers various concepts related to numbers, such as prime numbers, divisibility, fractions, decimals, integers, and their properties.

Here are some key concepts related to Number Properties that you should be familiar with for the GMAT:

- **Prime numbers :** A prime number is a positive integer greater than 1 that has no positive integer divisors other than 1 and itself.
- **Divisibility :** An integer a is divisible by an integer b if there exists an integer c such that a = bc. For example, 15 is divisible by 3, since $15 = 3 \times 5$.
- **Factors :** A factor of an integer a is any integer that divides a without leaving a remainder. For example, the factors of 12 are 1, 2, 3, 4, 6, and 12.
- **Multiples :** A multiple of an integer a is any integer that is the product of a and another integer. For example, the multiples of 3 are 3, 6, 9, 12, and so on.
- **Even and odd numbers :** An even number is an integer that is divisible by 2 without leaving a remainder, while an odd number is an integer that is not divisible by 2 without leaving a remainder.
- **Fractions and decimals :** Fractions represent a part of a whole, while decimals represent a number that has been divided by a power of 10.

Divisibility Rules

If there is no remainder when integer x is divided by integer y, then x is said to be divisible by y. Put another way, divisible means you can evenly divide the bigger number by the smaller number. For example, 10 is divisible by 5.

Some useful divisibility rules are mentioned below:

Divisibility rule for 2 : A number is divisible by 2 if its unit's digit is even. For example, 138 is divisible by 2 as unit digit is even, which is 8, whereas 1,234,567 is odd, as 7 is odd.

Divisibility rule for 3 : A number is divisible by 3 if the sum of its digits is divisible by 3. For example, 4,317 is divisible by 3 because $4 + 3 + 1 + 7 = 15$ and 15 is divisible by 3.

Divisibility rule for 4 : A number is divisible by 4 if its last two digits is divisible by 4. For example, 1,728 is divisible by 4 because 28 is divisible by 4, but 25,618 is not divisible by 4 because 18 is not divisible by 4

Divisibility rule for 5 : A number is divisible by 5 if its unit's digit is divisible by 5. For example, 75 and 80 are divisible by 5, but 77 and 83 are not.

Divisibility rule for 6 : A number is divisible by 6 if the number is divisible by both 2 and 3. If the unit's digit is even and the sum of the digits divisible by 3, then the number is divisible by 6. For example, 48 is divisible by 6 since it is divisible by 2 (it ends with an 8, which is even) AND by 3 (4 + 8 = 12, which is divisible by 3).

Divisibility rule for 8 : A number is divisible by 8 if its last three digits compose a three-digit number that is itself divisible by 8. For example, 23,456 is divisible by 8 because 456 is divisible by 8, whereas 23,556 is not divisible by 8 because 556 is not divisible by 8.

Divisibility rule for 9 : A number is divisible by 9 if the sum of its digits is divisible by 9. For example, 4,185 is divisible by 9 since the sum of its digits is 4 + 1 + 8 + 5 = 18, which is divisible by 9.

Divisibility rule for 10 : A number is divisible by 10 if its units digit is zero. For example, 670 is divisible by 10, but 675 is not.

Divisibility rule for 11 : A number is divisible by 11 if the difference between the sum of its odd-placed digits and the sum of its even-placed digits is divisible by 11. For example, 5,181 is divisible by 11 because (5 + 8) - (1 + 1) = 11, which is divisible by 11

Divisibility rule for 12 : Rule of 3 and 4 both; i.e. if sum of digits divisible by 3 and the last two digits divisible by 4, then the number is divisible by 12. For example, 1,732 is divisible by both 3 and 4, hence divisible by 12

Example : Is the integer 7,256 divisible by 8?

Solution : To determine whether 7,256 is divisible by 8, we need to check whether its last three digits are divisible by 8, as per the divisibility rule for 8. The last three digits of 7,256 are 256, which is divisible by 8 since it is a multiple of 8. Therefore, 7,256 is divisible by 8.

Answer : Yes.

Example : Is the integer 4,809 divisible by 3?

Solution : To determine whether 4,809 is divisible by 3, we need to check whether the sum of its digits is divisible by 3, as per the divisibility rule for 3. The sum of the digits of 4,809 is 4 + 8 + 0 + 9 = 21, which is divisible by 3. Therefore, 4,809 is divisible by 3.

Answer : Yes.

Remainders

If an integer cannot be divided evenly by another integer, the integer that is left over at the end of division is called the remainder. Thus, remainders must be integers.

Example : When 7 is divided by 2, remainder is 1.

Every division has four parts :

1. The dividend is the number being divided. In $7 \div 2$, the dividend is 7.

2. The divisor is the number that is dividing. In $7 \div 2$, the divisor is 2.

3. The quotient is the number of times that the divisor goes into the dividend completely. The quotient is always an integer. In $7 \div 2$, the quotient is 3 because 2 goes into 7 three (1) times completely.

4. The remainder is what is left over if the dividend is not divisible by the divisor. In $7 \div 2$, the remainder is 1.

Note : A remainder is always smaller than the divisor.

Example : 17 divided by 3 is 5 with a remainder of 2.

The relation between dividend, divisor, quotient and remainder is :

Dividend = divisor × Quotient + Remainder

Example :

100 divided by 3 is 33 remainder 1, since $100 = (33)(3) + 1$.

100 divided by 25 is 4 remainder 0, since $100 = (4)(25) + 0$.

80 divided by 100 is 0 remainder 80, since $80 = (0)(100) + 80$.

The remainder r is 0 if and only if dividend is evenly divisible by divisor.

Example : Since 32 divided by 8 yields a remainder of 0, 32 is divisible by 8. So 8 is a divisor or factor of 32, and 32 is a multiple of 8.

Example : What is the remainder when 3^{17} is divided by 7?

Solution: To find the remainder when 3^{17} is divided by 7, we can use the concept of cyclicity of remainders. Since the divisor is 7, we need to find the remainders when 3 is divided by 7, 3^2 is divided by 7, 3^3 is divided by 7, and so on, until we identify a pattern.

3^1 divided by 7 leaves a remainder of 3.

3^2 divided by 7 leaves a remainder of 2.

3^3 divided by 7 leaves a remainder of 6.

3^4 divided by 7 leaves a remainder of 4.

3^5 divided by 7 leaves a remainder of 5.

3^6 divided by 7 leaves a remainder of 1.

3^4 divided by 7 leaves a remainder of 3. ...

We can see that the remainders repeat in a pattern of length 6. Therefore, we can find the remainder when 3^{17} is divided by 7 by dividing the exponent 17 by 6, which gives a quotient of 2 and a remainder of 5. This means that the remainder when 3^{17} is divided by 7 is the same as the remainder when 3^5 is divided by 7.

3^5 divided by 7 leaves a remainder of 5, as we can see from the pattern above.

Therefore, the remainder when 3^{17} is divided by 7 is 5.

Answer : 5.

Factors and Multiples

Multiples

Multiples are numbers that can be obtained by multiplying a given number by any integer. For example, the multiples of 3 are 3, 6, 9, 12, 15, and so on.

Multiples are an important concept that is tested on the GMAT, particularly in the areas of number properties and algebra.

Example : What is the sum of all the even multiples of 7 that are less than 100?

(a) 392

(b) 294

(c) 394

(d) 492

(e) 494

Solution : To solve this question, we need to find the even multiples of 7 that are less than 100 and add them up. We can do this by multiplying 7 by each even integer from 2 to 14 (since 7 times 16 is greater than 100):

Even multiples of 7 : 14, 28, 42, 56, 70, 84, 98

Sum of even multiples of 7 : $14 + 28 + 42 + 56 + 70 + 84 + 98 = 392$

Therefore, the answer is (a) 392

Factors

The factors, or divisors, of a number are the positive integers that divide the given number without a remainder (or a remainder of 0).

An integer, x, is a factor of another integer, y, if y is divisible by x. So, in other words, y = nx, where y, n and x are all integers.

The positive factors of 60 are 1, 2, 3, 4, 5, 6, 10, 12, 15, 20, 30, and 60.

Important points :

- 1 and (–1) are divisors of every integer.
- Every integer is a divisor of itself.
- Every integer is a divisor of 0, except, by convention, 0 itself.

Here are some important rules:

- If x is a factor of y and y is a factor of z, then x is a factor of (y+z).
- If x is a factor of y and y is a factor of z, then x is a factor of z.
- If x is a factor of y and y is a factor of x, then or x = y or x = – y.

Example : What is the sum of the factors of 48?

(a) 60

(b) 78

(c) 96

(d) 124

(e) 144

Solution : To find the sum of the factors of 48, we first need to determine all the factors of 48. We can do this by finding the prime factorization of 48:

$$48 = 2^4 \times 3^1$$

To find all the factors, we need to determine all possible combinations of the prime factors. For example, the factors of 48 include 1, 2, 3, 4, 6, 8, 12, 16, 24, and 48.

The sum of these factors is :

$$1 + 2 + 3 + 4 + 6 + 8 + 12 + 16 + 24 + 48 = 124$$

Therefore, the answer is (d) 124

Finding Number of factors

Let $n = a^p \times b^q \times c^r$, where a, b and c are prime factors of n and p, q and r are their powers.

The number of factors of n will be expressed by the formula $(p + 1)(q + 1)(r + 1)$.

Example : How many positive factors does 540 have?

(a) 12

(b) 16

(c) 18

(d) 20

(e) 24

Solution : To solve this question, we need to determine how many positive integers divide evenly into 540. We can do this by finding the prime factorization of 540:

$$540 = 2^2 \times 3^3 \times 5$$

To find the number of factors, we can count the number of ways to choose exponents for each prime factor, and then multiply those counts together.

Number of factors of 540 = $(2 + 1) \times (3 + 1) \times (1 + 1) = 24$

Therefore, the answer is (e) 24.

HCF / LCM

HCF / GCD (Highest Common Factor / Greatest Common Divisor)

The greatest common divisor (GCD), also known as the greatest common factor (GCF), or highest common factor (HCF), of two or more non-zero integers, is the largest positive integer that divides the numbers without a remainder.

Example: the greatest common divisor of 30 and 75 is 15. This is because the positive divisors of 30 are 1, 2, 3, 5, 6, 10, 15, and 30, and the positive divisors of 75 are 1, 3, 5, 15, 25, and 75. Thus, the common positive divisors of 30 and 75 are 1, 3, 5, and 15, and the greatest of these is 15.

To find the HCF / GCD, you will need to do prime-factorization. Then, multiply the common factors (pick the lowest power of the common factors)

Example: To find HCF of 4 and 6

Solution: Prime factorisation of 4 is 2^2

Prime factorisation of 6 is 2×3

Lowest power of 2 is 1 and lowest power of 3 is 1, hence HCF is $2^1 \times 3^1 = 2 \times 3 = 6$

Example: HCF of 63 and 72

$63 = 7 \times 3 \times 3 = 3^2 \times 7$

$72 = 2 \times 2 \times 2 \times 3 \times 3 = 2^3 \times 3^2$

$HCF = 3^2 = 9$

Important points:

- Every common divisor of a and b is a divisor of HCF (a, b).
- $a \times b = HCF(a, b) \times LCM(a, b)$

Example: What is the highest common factor (HCF) of 72 and 90?

(a) 3

(b) 6

(c) 9

(d) 12

(e) 18

Solution: To solve this question, we need to find the factors of both 72 and 90, and then identify the highest factor that is common to both. First, we can find the prime factorizations of 72 and 90:

$72 = 2^3 \times 3^2$

$90 = 2^1 \times 3^2 \times 5$

To find the HCF, we need to identify the lowest power of the prime numbers involved. In this case, the only prime factor that appears in both is 2, with the lowest power of 2 being 2^1 and lowest power of 3 is 3^2. The highest common factor of 72 and 90 is therefore $2^1 \times 3^2 = 18$.

Option (e) is correct.

LCM (Least Common Multiple)

The least common multiple of two nonzero integers a and b is the least positive integer that is a multiple of both a and b.

Example : Least common multiple of 30 and 75 is 150. This is because the positive multiples of 30 are 30, 60, 90, 120, 150, 180, 210, 240, 270, 300, etc., and the positive multiples of 75 are 75, 150, 225, 300, 375, 450, etc.

Thus, the common positive multiples of 30 and 75 are 150, 300, 450, etc., and the least of these is 150.

LCM of two numbers ranges: Larger no $\leq$ LCM $\leq$ Product of two Numbers

To find the LCM, you will need to do prime-factorization. Then multiply all the factors (pick the highest power of the common factors).

Example : LCM of 24 and 36

24 : $2 \times 2 \times 2 \times 3$

36 : $2 \times 2 \times 3 \times 3$

LCM : $2 \times 2 \times 2 \times 3 \times 3 = 72$

Example : What is the smallest positive integer that is a multiple of 9 and a multiple of 14?

(a) 54

(b) 126

(c) 162

(d) 252

(e) 378

Solution : To solve this question, we need to find the LCM (least common multiple) of 9 and 14. We can do this by listing out the multiples of each number and finding the first one they have in common:

Multiples of 9 : 9, 18, 27, 36, 45, 54, 63, 72, 81, 90, 99, 108, 117, 126, 135, 144, 153, 162, 171, 180, 189, 198, 207, 216, 225...

Multiples of 14 : 14, 28, 42, 56, 70, 84, 98, 112, 126, 140, 154, 168, 182, 196, 210, 224, 238, 252, 266, 280, 294, 308, 322, 336, 350...

The first multiple that they have in common is 126, so the answer is (b) 126.

Example : What is the least common multiple (LCM) of 12, 18, and 30?

(a) 180

(b) 360

(c) 540

(d) 720

(e) 900

Solution : To solve this question, we need to find the prime factorizations of all three numbers and then identify the smallest number that contains all the factors with their highest power. The prime factorizations of 12, 18, and 30 are:

$12 = 2^2 \times 3^1$

$18 = 2 \times 3^2$

$30 = 2 \times 3^1 \times 5^1$

To find the LCM, we need to take the highest power of each prime factor that appears in any of the three numbers. In this case, we need to take 2^2 (the highest power of 2), 3^2 (the highest power of 3), and 5^1 (the only power of 5). Multiplying these together, we get :

$\text{LCM} = 2^2 \times 3^2 \times 5^1 = 180$

Therefore, the answer is (a) 180.

Positive and Negative

Some GMAT questions gives importance on whether the numbers involved are positive or negative. These properties are especially important when Picking Numbers on a Data Sufficiency question. If both positives and negatives are permissible for a given question, make sure to check for both possibilities.

A positive number is a real number that is greater than zero.

A negative number is a real number that is smaller than zero.

Zero is not positive, nor negative.

Properties of Positive and Negative :

Multiplication:

positive × positive = positive

positive × negative = negative

negative × negative = positive

Division:

positive / positive = positive

positive / negative = negative

negative / negative = positive

Properties of Zero

Adding or subtracting zero from a number does not change the number.

Example: $12 \times 0 = 0$

Division by zero is undefined.

Properties of 1 and –1

Multiplying or dividing a number by 1 does not change the number.

Multiplying or dividing a number by – 1 changes the sign.

The sum of a number and – 1 times that number is equal to zero.

The reciprocal of a number between 0 and 1 is greater than the number itself.

Example: The reciprocal of $\frac{2}{3}$ is $\frac{3}{2}$.

Decimals

The decimal number system is based on representing numbers using powers of 10. The place value of each digit corresponds to a power of 10. For example, the digits of the number 7,532.418 have the following place values.

7	,	5	3	2	.	4	1	8
Thousands		Hundreds	Tens	Ones of Units		Tenths	Hundredths	Thousandths

$$7{,}532.418 = 7(1{,}000) + 5(100) + 3(10) + 2(1) + \frac{4}{10} + \frac{1}{100} + \frac{8}{1000}$$

In scientific notation, a decimal is expressed as a number with only one nonzero digit to the left of the decimal point, multiplied by a power of 10. To convert a number expressed in scientific notation to regular decimal notation, move the decimal point by the number of places equal to the absolute value of the exponent on the 10. Move the decimal point to the right if the exponent is positive and to the left if the exponent is negative.

Example: In scientific notation, 231 is written as 2.31×10^2, and 0.0231 is written as 2.31×10^{-2}.

To multiply decimals, multiply the numbers as if they were integers and then insert the decimal point in the product so that the number of digits to the right of the decimal point equals the sum of the numbers of digits to the right of the decimal points in the numbers being multiplied, the multiplicands.

Example: If $0.75x = 2.25$, what is the value of x?

(a) 1

(b) 2

(c) 3

(d) 4

(e) 5

Solution: To solve this question, we can start by isolating x on one side of the equation. We can do this by dividing both sides of the equation by 0.75:

$$0.75x = 2.25$$

$$x = \frac{2.25}{0.75}$$

$$x = 3$$

Therefore, the answer is (c) 3.

Problem Solving

1. A straight wire one centimetre in length was cut into smaller pieces by cutting on every third and fourth. Which of the following is the range of all the lengths of smaller wire pieces, in centimetre?

(a) $\frac{1}{6}$ and $\frac{1}{4}$ only

(b) $\frac{1}{4}$ and $\frac{1}{3}$ only

(c) $\frac{1}{6}, \frac{1}{4},$ and $\frac{1}{3}$

(d) $\frac{1}{12}, \frac{1}{6},$ and $\frac{1}{4}$

(e) $\frac{1}{12}, \frac{1}{6},$ and $\frac{1}{3}$

2. All 7 students of a class received their scores on math test. All of them got at least a score of 1. At most three of the students received the same score, and no two of the remaining students got the same score. What is the least possible sum of the scores of the seven students?

(a) 7

(b) 13

(c) 17

(d) 22

(e) 28

3. In an increasing sequence of 12 consecutive integers, the sum of the first 6 integers is 594. What is the sum of the last 6 integers in the sequence?

(a) 630

(b) 625

(c) 620

(d) 615

(e) 610

4. Kevin has an odd number of cards with him. All his cards are either white or green. He placed all his cards on the table alternating between white and green. If the first card is white, and the total number of cards is x, how many of cards were white?

(a) $\frac{(x+1)}{2}$

(b) $\frac{(x-1)}{2}$

(c) $\left(\frac{x}{2}\right)+1$

(d) $\left(\frac{x}{2}\right)-1$

(e) $\left(\frac{x}{2}\right)$

5. If w, x, y, and z are prime factors of 3315 such that $w < x < y < z$, then what is the value of y?

(a) 3

(b) 5

(c) 11

(d) 13

(e) 17

6. If m is a multiple of 18, but not a multiple of 12, which of the following CANNOT be an integer?

(a) $\frac{m}{6}$

(b) $\frac{m}{7}$

(c) $\frac{m}{8}$

(d) $\frac{m}{26}$

(e) $\frac{m}{81}$

7. If x and y are integers such that $1 < x < y$, then which of the following CANNOT be a multiple of either x or y?

I. $x - 1$

II. $y - 1$

III. $xy - 1$

(a) I only

(b) II only

(c) III only

(d) I and II only

(e) I, II and III

8. When a number is divided by 10,000, the remainder is 41. What is the remainder when the same number is divided by 1,000?

(a) 0

(b) 1

(c) 4

(d) 21

(e) 41

9. If $x = 0.9999$, $y = \sqrt{0.9999}$, and $z = (0.9999)^2$, which of the following is correct?

(a) $x > y > z$

(b) $x > z > y$

(c) $y > x > z$

(d) $y > z > x$

(e) $z > x > z$

10. If $5p + 13q = 61$; where p and q are positive integers, what is the value of pq?

(a) 2

(b) 10

(c) 12

(d) 14

(e) Cannot be determined

11. If $x = 85n$, and $y = 95n$, where n is prime, what is the greatest common factor of x and y ?

(a) 5

(b) n

(c) $5n$

(d) $1{,}615n$

(e) $1{,}615n^2$

12. How many numbers from 4 to 501, inclusive are NOT divisible by 7?

(a) 69

(b) 70

(c) 71

(d) 427

(e) 428

13. If a and b are positive integers, which of the following can be the remainder of $\frac{a}{b}$, if $\frac{a}{b} = 3.75$?

(a) 1

(b) 2

(c) 4

(d) 8

(e) 12

14. What is the units digit of

$$(13^{49} \times 12^{49}) + (17^{39} \times 25^{34})\ ?$$

(a) 1

(b) 2

(c) 3

(d) 6

(e) 9

15. How many even numbers between 1 and 400 are divisible by 17 but not by 11 ?

(*a*) 9

(*b*) 10

(*c*) 11

(*d*) 12

(*e*) 20

16. A shopkeeper sold his first 50 books at the price of \$60 per book and the rest at \$50 per book. If he collected \$25,000 at the end of the day, how many books did he sell?

(*a*) 270

(*b*) 310

(*c*) 440

(*d*) 490

(*e*) 520

17. What is the value of $6 + |-3 - (12 - (-8 + 12))|$?

(*a*) 12

(*b*) 14

(*c*) 16

(*d*) 17

(*e*) 19

18. If $A = 12! + 14! + 6$, which of the following numbers is NOT a factor of A?

(*a*) 1

(*b*) 2

(*c*) 3

(*d*) 5

(*e*) 6

19. John has 18 pencils, 27 erasers, and 45 sharpeners. He wants to distribute these items among a few students such that each student gets the same number of pencils, erasers, and sharpeners. How many items does each student get if John wishes to distribute the items to the maximum number of students?

(*a*) 3

(*b*) 9

(*c*) 10

(*d*) 45

(*e*) 90

20. How many numbers that are squares of prime numbers have the sum of their factors equal to 133 ?

(*a*) One

(*b*) Two

(*c*) Three

(*d*) Eleven

(*e*) Twelve

Answer Key

1. (*d*)	6. (*c*)	11. (*c*)	16. (*d*)
2. (*c*)	7. (*e*)	12. (*d*)	17. (*d*)
3. (*a*)	8. (*c*)	13. (*e*)	18. (*d*)
4. (*a*)	9. (*c*)	14. (*a*)	19. (*c*)
5. (*d*)	10. (*d*)	15. (*b*)	20. (*a*)

Answer Explanations

1. (d)

Number line with markings at $0, \frac{1}{4}, \frac{1}{3}, \frac{1}{2}, \frac{2}{3}, \frac{3}{4}, 1$

The markings represent the points at which the wire is cut. As the wire is cut at 5 points, 6 pieces are cut. Possible lengths

$$\left(\frac{1}{4}\right) - 0 = \frac{1}{4}$$

$$\left(\frac{1}{3}\right) - \left(\frac{1}{4}\right) = \frac{1}{12}$$

$$\left(\frac{1}{2}\right) - \left(\frac{1}{3}\right) - \frac{1}{6}$$

$$\left(\frac{2}{3}\right) - \left(\frac{1}{2}\right) = \frac{1}{6}$$

$$\left(\frac{3}{4}\right) - \left(\frac{2}{3}\right) = \frac{1}{12}$$

$$1 - \left(\frac{3}{4}\right) = \frac{1}{4}$$

2. (c) To determine the least possible sum of the seven scores, the smallest possible scores should be given to each score. Let the three students who received the same score, get a score of 1 each. Let the fourth student gets a score of 2, fifth student gets a score of 3, sixth student gets a score of 4, and the seventh student gets a score of 5.

Hence, the total sum of the scores = $1 + 1 + 1 + 2 + 3 + 4 + 5 = 17$

Hence, the answer is (c).

3. (a) Let the first six number be $(x + 1), (x + 2), (x + 3), (x + 4), (x + 5)$ and $(x + 6)$.

So, the last six numbers will be $(x + 7), (x + 8), (x + 9), (x + 10), (x + 11)$, and $(x + 12)$.

Sum of the first six numbers is $6x + 21$

Sum of the last six numbers is $6x + 57$

Difference between the two sums

$$= (6x + 57) - (6x + 21) = 36$$

Hence, the sum of the last six numbers will be $594 + 36 = 630$

The answer is (a).

4. (a) Since there is an odd number of cards and the first card is white, the last card must be white. Hence, there is one more white card than green cards.

If the number of white cards is w, then the number of green cards is $w - 1$.

So, the total number of cards is $w + (w - 1)$.

$\Rightarrow \quad w + (w - 1) = x$

$\Rightarrow \quad 2w - 1 = x$

$\Rightarrow \quad 2w = x + 1$

$\Rightarrow \quad w = \frac{(x+1)}{2}$

The answer is (a).

5. (d) $3315 = 3 \times 5 \times 13 \times 17$

Hence, the four prime numbers are 3, 5, 13, and 17.

As y is the second greatest of the four numbers, $y = 13$

The answer is (d).

6. (c) Minimum possible value of m is 18 as m is multiple of 18.

$18 = 2 \times 3 \times 3$

Hence, m must have at least one 2 and two 3s.

Also, m is not a multiple of 12.

$12 = 2 \times 2 \times 3$

Hence, m must have less than two 2s.

$\Rightarrow$ m has exactly one 2.

(*a*) If m = 18, then $\frac{m}{6}$ is an integer.

(*b*) If m = 18 × 7, then $\frac{m}{7}$ is an integer.

(*c*) For $\frac{m}{8}$ to be an integer, m must have at least three 2s, which is not allowed.

(*d*) If m = 18 × 13, then $\frac{m}{26}$ is an integer.

(*e*) If m = 18 × 9, then $\frac{m}{81}$ is an integer.

The answer is (c).

7. **(e)** A multiple is always greater than equal to divisor.

x – 1 is smaller than both x and y, hence, it CANNOT be the multiple of either x or y.

Hence, I must be among the answer choices.

So, eliminate (A), (C), and (D)

Also, xy is a multiple of both x and y, hence, xy – 1 CANNOT be a multiple of either x or y.

Hence, the answer is (e).

8. **(c)** Say the number is where is the quotient, a positive integer. Since is divisible by 1,000, the question comes down to whether 41 is divisible by 1,000. Since 41 is not divisible by 1,000, the remainder would be 41 only.

9. **(c)** Note that the base number 0.9999, is less than 1. Remember that...

(1) n^{th} root of a number less than 1 is always greater than the number itself; so $0.9999 < \sqrt{0.9999}$.

(2) Squares, cubes, and other high value powers of a number less than 1 are always smaller than the number itself; so, $0.9999 > (0.9999)^2$.

It means that $z < x < y$.

Opposite is true for a number greater than 1.

You may take a convenient number.

Say $x = \frac{1}{4}, y = \sqrt{\frac{1}{4}}, \& z = \left(\frac{1}{4}\right)^2$.

Thus, $x = \frac{1}{4}, y = \frac{1}{2}, \& z = \frac{1}{16}$.

Thus, $z < x < y$.

10. **(d)** Looking at the linear equation 5p + 13q = 61, we may presume that the values of *p* and *q* are indeterminable as there are two unknown variables and only one equation is given; however, it is not so. We have the second condition given in the question: '*p* and *q* are positive integers'. Let's make use of it.

The equation 5p + 13q = 61 can be written as $p = \frac{61 - 13q}{5}$. Since *p* is a positive integer, (61 – 13q) must be divisible by 5. Let us plug in some positive integers for *q*, and see for what value of q, (61 – 13q) is a multiple of 5.

For q = 1, $p = \frac{61 - 13 \times 1}{5} = \frac{48}{5}$ (not an integer); So, we discard the probable value of q as 1.

For q = 2, $p = \frac{61 - 13 \times 2}{5} = \frac{35}{5} = 7$ (an integer); So, we take the value of q as 2, and p would be 7 and pq = 7 × 2 = 14.

There is no need to check further as the value of pq would be a finite number; however, for your curiosity, we find that for $q = 3$, $p = \frac{61 - 13 \times 3}{5} = \frac{22}{5}$ (not an integer).

For *q* = 4, $p = \frac{61 - 13 \times 4}{5} = \frac{9}{5}$ (not an integer). There is no need to deep dive as for larger values of q, p would be negative. So, we get pq = 7 × 2 = 14.

11. (c) Greatest common factor among numbers is also called HCF or GCD. The question asks us to find out the HCF of $85n$ and $95n$. Since $85n = 17 \times 5 \times n$ and $95n = 19 \times 5 \times n$ have '5' and 'n' common, the HCF would be $5 \times n = 5n$ or the greatest common factor of x and y is '$5n$'.

Alternatively,

$x = 17 \times 5 \times n;$

$y = 19 \times 5 \times n;$

HCF = 5n (Common between x and y)

The answer is $5n$.

12. (d) There are a total of ([501 – 4) + 1] = 498 numbers under consideration.

The first number, within 4 and 501, divisible by 7 is 7, and the last number is 497.

So, there are total of $\left[\frac{497-7}{7}+1\right] = 71$ numbers divisible by 7.

So, the total numbers, not divisible by 7 from 4 to 501 = 498 – 71 = 427.

13. (e) So, we have $\frac{a}{b} = 3.75$.

Thus, $a = 3.75b = 3b + 0.75b$

$$a = 3b + \frac{3b}{4}$$

Given a and b are positive integers, and since for the fraction $\frac{3b}{4}$, 3 and 4 are co-prime to each other, b must be a multiple of 4. So, the reminder for $\frac{a}{b}$ must be a multiple of 3. Or, the set of remainders would be {3, 6, 9, 12, ..., 150, ...}.

For example: Say, $\frac{a}{b} = 3.75 = \frac{15}{4}$. Reminder = 3; however, say, $\frac{a}{b} = 3.75 = \frac{750}{200}$. Reminder = 150.

Among the options, only 12 is the multiple of 3, therefore, the remainder could be 12.

14. (a) The units digit of 13^{49} is the same as that of 3^{49}; it is governed by the digit at the units place.

The same logic works for the other numbers too.

Thus, the question is equivalent to finding the units digit of $(3^{49} \times 2^{49}) + (7^{39} \times 5^{34})$.

Since the exponents of 3 and 2 are the same, we can write $3^{49} \times 2^{49}$ as $(3 \times 2)^{49} = 6^{49}$

We know that the units digit of 6 raised to any positive integer exponent is always 6.

Similarly, for $7^{39} \times 5^{34}$, we observe that 7^{39} is odd and 5^{34} has units digit of 5 (since the 5 raised to any positive integer exponent is always 5).

Thus, the units digit of $(7^{39} \times 5^{34})$ is essentially an odd number multiplied with 5, which is always 5, irrespective of any odd number being multiplied to.

Hence, the units digit of $(13^{49} \times 12^{49}) + (17^{39} \times 25^{34})$ is the units digit of the sum of 6 and 5, equals to 1.

15. (b) Since we need even numbers divisible by '17', we should look at numbers

$17 \times 2, 17 \times 4, 17 \times 6, 17 \times 8, 17 \times 10 \ldots$

The last number, less than 400, divisible by '17' is $391 = 17 \times 23$

Since we need even numbers, the last multiple of '17' would be

$17 \times (23 - 1) = 17 \times 22.$

Thus, the required set of numbers: 17×2, 17×4, 17×6, 17×8, ... 17×22, i.e., 11 numbers

However, we do not want numbers divisible by '11'.

In the above set, there is only one multiple of '11' i.e. 17×22

Thus, we need to exclude it.

Hence, the number of required numbers = $11 - 1 = 10$.

16. **(d)** Let number of books sold by the shopkeeper = n

Total sum collected

= Sum collected from 50 books + Sum collected from the remaining books

$\Rightarrow \quad 25{,}000 = 50 \times 60 + (n - 50) \times 50$

$\Rightarrow \quad 25{,}000 = 3{,}000 + 50n - 2{,}500$

$50n = 25{,}000 - 500$

n = 490 books

17. **(d)** $6 + |-3 - (12 - (-8 + 12))|$

$= 6 + |-3 - (12 - 4)|$

$= 6 + |-3 - 8| = 6 + |-11|$

$= 6 + 11$

$= 17$

18. **(d)** We can write 12! + 14! + 6 as (1.2.3.4.5.6 ... 12) + (1.2.3.4.5.6 ...12.13.14) + (1.2.3).

Thus, each term of A : 12!, 14!, and 6 is divisible by 1, 2, 3 and 6; thus, the correct answer is 5 as the third term of A, 6, is not divisible by 5.

19. **(c)** The maximum number of students among whom the items can be distributed would be the HCF of 18, 27 and 45 = 9. HCF – Highest Common Factor-implies that John cannot have a greater common factor from them (18, 27, and 45) compared to itself, i.e., 9.

Thus, John can distribute these items to a maximum of 9 students so that each student gets the same number of items.

In such an event, each student gets $\frac{18}{9} = 2$ pencils; $\frac{27}{9} = 3$ erasers; and $\frac{45}{9} = 5$ sharpeners.

Thus, each student gets $2 + 3 + 5 = 10$ items.

20. **(a)** Let the number (s) be a^2, where a is a prime number.

The factors of a^2 are 1, a and a^2.

Thus, we have

$1 + a + a^2 = 133$

$\Rightarrow \quad a + a^2 = 132$

$\Rightarrow \quad a^2 + a - 132 = 0$

$\Rightarrow \quad a^2 + 12a - 11a - 132 = 0$

$\Rightarrow \quad a(a + 12) - 11(a + 12) = 0$

$\Rightarrow \quad (a - 11)(a + 12) = 0$

$\Rightarrow \quad a = 11 \text{ or } -12$

Since a is a prime number, we have a = 11

Hence, we have only one such number.

You may cross check this. For $a^2 = 121$, we have factors 1, 11, & 121, and their sum $= 1 + 11 + 121 = 133$.

Data Sufficiency

1. What is the remainder when x is divided by 20?

I. x is a multiple of 2.

II. x is a multiple of 5.

(a) Statement (I) ALONE is sufficient but statement (II) ALONE is not sufficient.

(b) Statement (II) ALONE is sufficient but statement (I) ALONE is not sufficient.

(c) BOTH statements TOGETHER are sufficient, but NEITHER statement ALONE is sufficient.

(d) EACH statement ALONE is sufficient.

(e) Statements (I) and (II) TOGETHER are not sufficient.

2. Is $\frac{x}{9}$ an integer?

I. $\frac{x}{909909}$ is an integer.

II. $\frac{x}{567}$ is an integer.

(a) Statement (I) ALONE is sufficient but statement (II) ALONE is not sufficient.

(b) Statement (II) ALONE is sufficient but statement (I) ALONE is not sufficient.

(c) BOTH statements TOGETHER are sufficient, but NEITHER statement ALONE is sufficient.

(d) EACH statement ALONE is sufficient.

(e) Statements (I) and (II) TOGETHER are not sufficient.

3. How many of the three positive different integers X, Y and Z are divisible by 7?

I. The product of X, Y and Z is divisible by 3, but only Z in divisible by 21.

II. Each of the three positive integers is divisible by 3, but only Z is divisible by 21.

(a) Statement (I) ALONE is sufficient but statement (II) ALONE is not sufficient.

(b) Statement (II) ALONE is sufficient but statement (I) ALONE is not sufficient.

(c) BOTH statements TOGETHER are sufficient, but NEITHER statement ALONE is sufficient.

(d) EACH statement ALONE is sufficient.

(e) Statements (I) and (II) TOGETHER are not sufficient.

4. Sapna runs a friendship club on the 10th floor of a multi-storeyed building. The left in this building has a different stop sequence on different days of the week. On which days of the week should Sapna keep her club open, if the club members visit the club only on those days when the lift stops at the 10th floor?

I. The lift stops on only odd-numbered floors on Monday, Tuesday and Wednesday.

II. The lift stops on floors divisible by 3 or 5 on Thursday and Friday.

(a) Statement (I) ALONE is sufficient but statement (II) ALONE is not sufficient.

(b) Statement (II) ALONE is sufficient but statement (I) ALONE is not sufficient.

(c) BOTH statements TOGETHER are sufficient, but NEITHER statement ALONE is sufficient.

(d) EACH statement ALONE is sufficient.

(e) Statements (I) and (II) TOGETHER are not sufficient.

5. If $P > Q$, what is the value of P and Q?

I. LCM of P and Q is 42 and HCF of P and Q is 6.

II. Product of P and Q is 1764.

(a) Statement (I) ALONE is sufficient but statement (II) ALONE is not sufficient.

(b) Statement (II) ALONE is sufficient but statement (I) ALONE is not sufficient.

(c) BOTH statements TOGETHER are sufficient, but NEITHER statement ALONE is sufficient.

(d) EACH statement ALONE is sufficient.

(e) Statements (I) and (II) TOGETHER are not sufficient.

6. If both Sonu and Mohit started running simultaneously, find the distance traveled by Sonu.

I. Sonu and Mohit are running towards each other and their speeds are in the ratio 1 : 4 respectively.

II. Sonu and Mohit were initially separated by a distance of 420 m in a straight road, and finally they were together.

(a) Statement (I) ALONE is sufficient but statement (II) ALONE is not sufficient.

(b) Statement (II) ALONE is sufficient but statement (I) ALONE is not sufficient.

(c) BOTH statements TOGETHER are sufficient, but NEITHER statement ALONE is sufficient.

(d) EACH statement ALONE is sufficient.

(e) Statements (I) and (II) TOGETHER are not sufficient.

7. If a, b and c are digits, is $(a + b + c)$ a multiple of 9? [A digit can be one of the integers 0, 1, 2, 3, 4, 5, 6, 7, 8, 9.]

I. The three digit number abc is a multiple of 9.

II. $[(a \times b) + c]$ is a multiple of 9.

(a) Statement (I) ALONE is sufficient but statement (II) ALONE is not sufficient.

(b) Statement (II) ALONE is sufficient but statement (I) ALONE is not sufficient.

(c) BOTH statements TOGETHER are sufficient, but NEITHER statement ALONE is sufficient.

(d) EACH statement ALONE is sufficient.

(e) Statements (I) and (II) TOGETHER are not sufficient.

8. If X and Y, both are 2-digit integers, is $\frac{(X-Y)}{9}$ an integer?

I. X and Y have the same two digits, but in reverse order.

II. The tens' digit of X is 2 more than the units' digit, and the tens' digit of Y is 2 less than the units' digit.

(a) Statement (I) ALONE is sufficient but statement (II) ALONE is not sufficient.

(b) Statement (II) ALONE is sufficient but statement (I) ALONE is not sufficient.

(c) BOTH statements TOGETHER are sufficient, but NEITHER statement ALONE is sufficient.

(d) EACH statement ALONE is sufficient.

(e) Statements (I) and (II) TOGETHER are not sufficient.

9. How many books does Gautam have?

I. No. of books Gautam has is less than the square root of 100.

II. The number of books Gautam has, is divisible by both 2 and 3.

(*a*) Statement (I) ALONE is sufficient but statement (II) ALONE is not sufficient.

(*b*) Statement (II) ALONE is sufficient but statement (I) ALONE is not sufficient.

(*c*) BOTH statements TOGETHER are sufficient, but NEITHER statement ALONE is sufficient.

(*d*) EACH statement ALONE is sufficient.

(*e*) Statements (I) and (II) TOGETHER are not sufficient.

10. X, Y, Z are three different positive odd integers. Is (X + Z) divisible by 8?

I. $Y - X = 4$

II. $Z - Y = 4$

(*a*) Statement (I) ALONE is sufficient but statement (II) ALONE is not sufficient.

(*b*) Statement (II) ALONE is sufficient but statement (I) ALONE is not sufficient.

(*c*) BOTH statements TOGETHER are sufficient, but NEITHER statement ALONE is sufficient.

(*d*) EACH statement ALONE is sufficient.

(*e*) Statements (I) and (II) TOGETHER are not sufficient.

11. Four points a, y, x, and b are on the number line such that $a < y < x < b$. What is the value of $\frac{(b-y)}{(y-a)}$?

I. x is halfway between a and b

II. y is halfway between a and x

(*a*) Statement (I) ALONE is sufficient but statement (II) ALONE is not sufficient.

(*b*) Statement (II) ALONE is sufficient but statement (I) ALONE is not sufficient.

(*c*) BOTH statements TOGETHER are sufficient, but NEITHER statement ALONE is sufficient.

(*d*) EACH statement ALONE is sufficient.

(*e*) Statements (I) and (II) TOGETHER are not sufficient.

12. M and N are two-digit numbers, what is the sum of M + N?

I. M and N have the same digits.

II. M and N have the same digits, but in reverse order.

(*a*) Statement (I) ALONE is sufficient but statement (II) ALONE is not sufficient.

(*b*) Statement (II) ALONE is sufficient but statement (I) ALONE is not sufficient.

(*c*) BOTH statements TOGETHER are sufficient, but NEITHER statement ALONE is sufficient.

(*d*) EACH statement ALONE is sufficient.

(*e*) Statements (I) and (II) TOGETHER are not sufficient.

13. Is $O < x < 1$?

I. $x^2 \leq x$

II. $x^3 < 0$

(*a*) Statement (I) ALONE is sufficient but statement (II) ALONE is not sufficient.

(*b*) Statement (II) ALONE is sufficient but statement (I) ALONE is not sufficient.

(*c*) BOTH statements TOGETHER are sufficient, but NEITHER statement ALONE is sufficient.

(*d*) EACH statement ALONE is sufficient.

(*e*) Statements (I) and (II) TOGETHER are not sufficient.

14. What is the value of the two-digit integer x?

I. The sum of the digits of x is 5.

II. x is divisible by 5.

(a) Statement (I) ALONE is sufficient but statement (II) ALONE is not sufficient.

(b) Statement (II) ALONE is sufficient but statement (I) ALONE is not sufficient.

(c) BOTH statements TOGETHER are sufficient, but NEITHER statement ALONE is sufficient.

(d) EACH statement ALONE is sufficient.

(e) Statements (I) and (II) TOGETHER are not sufficient.

15. Is $xy < 8$?

I. $x < 2$ and $y < 4$

II. $x^2 < 4$ and $y^2 < 16$

(a) Statement (I) ALONE is sufficient but statement (II) ALONE is not sufficient.

(b) Statement (II) ALONE is sufficient but statement (I) ALONE is not sufficient.

(c) BOTH statements TOGETHER are sufficient, but NEITHER statement ALONE is sufficient.

(d) EACH statement ALONE is sufficient.

(e) Statements (I) and (II) TOGETHER are not sufficient.

16. If a and b are positive single digit integers, is $3(10^a) + b$ divisible b 9?

I. $a = 4$

II. $b = 6$

(a) Statement (I) ALONE is sufficient but statement (II) ALONE is not sufficient.

(b) Statement (II) ALONE is sufficient but statement (I) ALONE is not sufficient.

(c) BOTH statements TOGETHER are sufficient, but NEITHER statement ALONE is sufficient.

(d) EACH statement ALONE is sufficient.

(e) Statements (I) and (II) TOGETHER are not sufficient.

17. If a and b are integers, is $a + b + ab$ an odd number?

I. a is an even number

II. $a + b$ is an odd number

(a) Statement (I) ALONE is sufficient but statement (II) ALONE is not sufficient.

(b) Statement (II) ALONE is sufficient but statement (I) ALONE is not sufficient.

(c) BOTH statements TOGETHER are sufficient, but NEITHER statement ALONE is sufficient.

(d) EACH statement ALONE is sufficient.

(e) Statements (I) and (II) TOGETHER are not sufficient.

18. If x, y, and z are positive integers such that $x^3 y^5 = z$, what is the value of x ?

I. $z = 1944$

II. $y = 3$

(a) Statement (I) ALONE is sufficient but statement (II) ALONE is not sufficient.

(b) Statement (II) ALONE is sufficient but statement (I) ALONE is not sufficient.

(c) BOTH statements TOGETHER are sufficient, but NEITHER statement ALONE is sufficient.

(d) EACH statement ALONE is sufficient.

(e) Statements (I) and (II) TOGETHER are not sufficient.

19. If x, y, and z are integers, is xyz divisible by 6?

I. xyz is a multiple of 3

II. x, y, and z are consecutive

(*a*) Statement (I) ALONE is sufficient but statement (II) ALONE is not sufficient.

(*b*) Statement (II) ALONE is sufficient but statement (I) ALONE is not sufficient.

(*c*) BOTH statements TOGETHER are sufficient, but NEITHER statement ALONE is sufficient.

(*d*) EACH statement ALONE is sufficient.

(*e*) Statements (I) and (II) TOGETHER are not sufficient.

20. How many of the 10 consecutive integers are multiples of 7?

I. When the greatest of the 10 integers is divided by 7, the remainder is 3

II. The median of the 10 integers is 12.5

(*a*) Statement (I) ALONE is sufficient but statement (II) ALONE is not sufficient.

(*b*) Statement (II) ALONE is sufficient but statement (I) ALONE is not sufficient.

(*c*) BOTH statements TOGETHER are sufficient, but NEITHER statement ALONE is sufficient.

(*d*) EACH statement ALONE is sufficient.

(*e*) Statements (I) and (II) TOGETHER are not sufficient.

21. When $4^a + 1$ is divided by 5, what is the remainder?

I. a is an odd number

II. a is a multiple of 3

(*a*) Statement (I) ALONE is sufficient but statement (II) ALONE is not sufficient.

(*b*) Statement (II) ALONE is sufficient but statement (I) ALONE is not sufficient.

(*c*) BOTH statements TOGETHER are sufficient, but NEITHER statement ALONE is sufficient.

(*d*) EACH statement ALONE is sufficient.

(*e*) Statements (I) and (II) TOGETHER are not sufficient.

22. If x and y are prime numbers, what is the value of x?

I. $x^3 y^2$ is an even number

II. y is an odd number

(*a*) Statement (I) ALONE is sufficient but statement (II) ALONE is not sufficient.

(*b*) Statement (II) ALONE is sufficient but statement (I) ALONE is not sufficient.

(*c*) BOTH statements TOGETHER are sufficient, but NEITHER statement ALONE is sufficient.

(*d*) EACH statement ALONE is sufficient.

(*e*) Statements (I) and (II) TOGETHER are not sufficient.

23. If a and b are integers, is a + b an odd number?

I. $b = 7a + 3$

II. $b = 2a - 7$

(*a*) Statement (I) ALONE is sufficient but statement (II) ALONE is not sufficient.

(*b*) Statement (II) ALONE is sufficient but statement (I) ALONE is not sufficient.

(*c*) BOTH statements TOGETHER are sufficient, but NEITHER statement ALONE is sufficient.

(*d*) EACH statement ALONE is sufficient.

(*e*) Statements (I) and (II) TOGETHER are not sufficient.

24. What is the value of a + b + 1 ?

I. $a^3 + b^3 + 1 = 3ab$

II. $a^2 - 2ab + b^2 > 0$

(*a*) Statement (I) ALONE is sufficient but statement (II) ALONE is not sufficient.

(*b*) Statement (II) ALONE is sufficient but statement (I) ALONE is not sufficient.

(*c*) BOTH statements TOGETHER are sufficient, but NEITHER statement ALONE is sufficient.

(*d*) EACH statement ALONE is sufficient.

(*e*) Statements (I) and (II) TOGETHER are not sufficient.

25. If a > 1, is M > N? (M and N are positive numbers.)

I. $M = (a - 1)(a^2 + a + 1)$

and $N = (a + 1)(a^2 - a + 1)$

II. $M = a \times N$

(*a*) Statement (I) ALONE is sufficient but statement (II) ALONE is not sufficient.

(*b*) Statement (II) ALONE is sufficient but statement (I) ALONE is not sufficient.

(*c*) BOTH statements TOGETHER are sufficient, but NEITHER statement ALONE is sufficient.

(*d*) EACH statement ALONE is sufficient.

(*e*) Statements (I) and (II) TOGETHER are not sufficient.

26. a, b and c are 3 digits of a number 'abc', which is a multiple of 3.

Find (a + b + c).

I. a = 3, b = 4

II. c is an odd number.

(*a*) Statement (I) ALONE is sufficient but statement (II) ALONE is not sufficient.

(*b*) Statement (II) ALONE is sufficient but statement (I) ALONE is not sufficient.

(*c*) BOTH statements TOGETHER are sufficient, but NEITHER statement ALONE is sufficient.

(*d*) EACH statement ALONE is sufficient.

(*e*) Statements (I) and (II) TOGETHER are not sufficient.

27. If a, b and c are consecutive integers, in increasing order, what is the value of a?

I. b = a + c

II. ac = –1

(*a*) Statement (I) ALONE is sufficient but statement (II) ALONE is not sufficient.

(*b*) Statement (II) ALONE is sufficient but statement (I) ALONE is not sufficient.

(*c*) BOTH statements TOGETHER are sufficient, but NEITHER statement ALONE is sufficient.

(*d*) EACH statement ALONE is sufficient.

(*e*) Statements (I) and (II) TOGETHER are not sufficient.

28. What is the average of 3 consecutive odd integers?

I. One of the integers is –1.

II. The sum of 2 of the integers is 4.

(*a*) Statement (I) ALONE is sufficient but statement (II) ALONE is not sufficient.

(*b*) Statement (II) ALONE is sufficient but statement (I) ALONE is not sufficient.

(*c*) BOTH statements TOGETHER are sufficient, but NEITHER statement ALONE is sufficient.

(*d*) EACH statement ALONE is sufficient.

(*e*) Statements (I) and (II) TOGETHER are not sufficient.

29. If $n = p + r$, where n, p and r are positive integers and n is odd, is $p = 2$?

I. p and r are prime numbers.

II. $r \neq 2$

(*a*) Statement (I) ALONE is sufficient but statement (II) ALONE is not sufficient.

(*b*) Statement (II) ALONE is sufficient but statement (I) ALONE is not sufficient.

(*c*) BOTH statements TOGETHER are sufficient, but NEITHER statement ALONE is sufficient.

(*d*) EACH statement ALONE is sufficient.

(*e*) Statements (I) and (II) TOGETHER are not sufficient.

30. If p is an integer between 10 and 100, what is the value of p?

I. One of p's digits is 3 more than the other, and sum of its digits is 9.

II. $p < 50$

(*a*) Statement (I) ALONE is sufficient but statement (II) ALONE is not sufficient.

(*b*) Statement (II) ALONE is sufficient but statement (I) ALONE is not sufficient.

(*c*) BOTH statements TOGETHER are sufficient, but NEITHER statement ALONE is sufficient.

(*d*) EACH statement ALONE is sufficient.

(*e*) Statements (I) and (II) TOGETHER are not sufficient.

31. A, B, C are positive but unequal integers and $A < B < C$. Is $C - A$ even?

I. $A \times B \times C$ is odd.

II. $AB + BC + CA$ is even.

(*a*) Statement (I) ALONE is sufficient but statement (II) ALONE is not sufficient.

(*b*) Statement (II) ALONE is sufficient but statement (I) ALONE is not sufficient.

(*c*) BOTH statements TOGETHER are sufficient, but NEITHER statement ALONE is sufficient.

(*d*) EACH statement ALONE is sufficient.

(*e*) Statements (I) and (II) TOGETHER are not sufficient.

32. A two-digit number is mistakenly written in the reversed order of the digits. The difference between original number and reversed number is divisible by 9. What is the original two-digit number?

I. The digits of the number are odd.

II. The sum of the digits of the number is divisible by 16.

(*a*) Statement (I) ALONE is sufficient but statement (II) ALONE is not sufficient.

(*b*) Statement (II) ALONE is sufficient but statement (I) ALONE is not sufficient.

(*c*) BOTH statements TOGETHER are sufficient, but NEITHER statement ALONE is sufficient.

(*d*) EACH statement ALONE is sufficient.

(*e*) Statements (I) and (II) TOGETHER are not sufficient.

33. Is X an even integer? [Where 'n' and 'p' are integers.]

I. $X = (n + p)^2$

II. $X = 2n + 10p$

(*a*) Statement (I) ALONE is sufficient but statement (II) ALONE is not sufficient.

(*b*) Statement (II) ALONE is sufficient but statement (I) ALONE is not sufficient.

(*c*) BOTH statements TOGETHER are sufficient, but NEITHER statement ALONE is sufficient.

(*d*) EACH statement ALONE is sufficient.

(*e*) Statements (I) and (II) TOGETHER are not sufficient.

34. is p divisible by 35?

I. p is divisible by 15.

II. p is divisible by 14.

(*a*) Statement (I) ALONE is sufficient but statement (II) ALONE is not sufficient.

(*b*) Statement (II) ALONE is sufficient but statement (I) ALONE is not sufficient.

(*c*) BOTH statements TOGETHER are sufficient, but NEITHER statement ALONE is sufficient.

(*d*) EACH statement ALONE is sufficient.

(*e*) Statements (I) and (II) TOGETHER are not sufficient.

35. If $Ax = Bx$, is $A = B$?

I. $A + x = B + x$

II. x is a non-negative integer

(*a*) Statement (I) ALONE is sufficient but statement (II) ALONE is not sufficient.

(*b*) Statement (II) ALONE is sufficient but statement (I) ALONE is not sufficient.

(*c*) BOTH statements TOGETHER are sufficient, but NEITHER statement ALONE is sufficient.

(*d*) EACH statement ALONE is sufficient.

(*e*) Statements (I) and (II) TOGETHER are not sufficient.

36. Is $\frac{49}{x}$ an integer?

I. x is an odd integer

II. $10 < x < 20$

(*a*) Statement (I) ALONE is sufficient but statement (II) ALONE is not sufficient.

(*b*) Statement (II) ALONE is sufficient but statement (I) ALONE is not sufficient.

(*c*) BOTH statements TOGETHER are sufficient, but NEITHER statement ALONE is sufficient.

(*d*) EACH statement ALONE is sufficient.

(*e*) Statements (I) and (II) TOGETHER are not sufficient.

37. Is the product of 14 integers in Set negative?

I. Set L has at most 7 negative integers.

II. Set L has at least 7 positive integers.

(*a*) Statement (I) ALONE is sufficient but statement (II) ALONE is not sufficient.

(*b*) Statement (II) ALONE is sufficient but statement (I) ALONE is not sufficient.

(*c*) BOTH statements TOGETHER are sufficient, but NEITHER statement ALONE is sufficient.

(*d*) EACH statement ALONE is sufficient.

(*e*) Statements (I) and (II) TOGETHER are not sufficient.

38. If $x = \frac{a}{b}$, is x an integer?

I. a is a multiple of 10.

II. b is a divisor of 10.

(*a*) Statement (I) ALONE is sufficient but statement (II) ALONE is not sufficient.

(*b*) Statement (II) ALONE is sufficient but statement (I) ALONE is not sufficient.

(*c*) BOTH statements TOGETHER are sufficient, but NEITHER statement ALONE is sufficient.

(*d*) EACH statement ALONE is sufficient.

(*e*) Statements (I) and (II) TOGETHER are not sufficient.

39. If z is a positive integer, what is the remainder when z is divided by 4?

I. The remainder when z is divided by 8 is 2.

II. The remainder when z is divided by 12 is 6.

(*a*) Statement (I) ALONE is sufficient but statement (II) ALONE is not sufficient.

(*b*) Statement (II) ALONE is sufficient but statement (I) ALONE is not sufficient.

(*c*) BOTH statements TOGETHER are sufficient, but NEITHER statement ALONE is sufficient.

(*d*) EACH statement ALONE is sufficient.

(*e*) Statements (I) and (II) TOGETHER are not sufficient.

40. Is the number of divisors of a^4 greater than the number of divisors of b^2?

I. b = 4

II. a = 3.

(*a*) Statement (I) ALONE is sufficient but statement (II) ALONE is not sufficient.

(*b*) Statement (II) ALONE is sufficient but statement (I) ALONE is not sufficient.

(*c*) BOTH statements TOGETHER are sufficient, but NEITHER statement ALONE is sufficient.

(*d*) EACH statement ALONE is sufficient.

(*e*) Statements (I) and (II) TOGETHER are not sufficient.

Answer Key

1. (*e*)	**11.** (*c*)	**21.** (*a*)	**31.** (*a*)
2. (*d*)	**12.** (*a*)	**22.** (*c*)	**32.** (*e*)
3. (*b*)	**13.** (*b*)	**23.** (*a*)	**33.** (*b*)
4. (*e*)	**14.** (*c*)	**24.** (*c*)	**34.** (*c*)
5. (*a*)	**15.** (*b*)	**25.** (*d*)	**35.** (*e*)
6. (*c*)	**16.** (*b*)	**26.** (*c*)	**36.** (*b*)
7. (*a*)	**17.** (*b*)	**27.** (*d*)	**37.** (*e*)
8. (*a*)	**18.** (*a*)	**28.** (*c*)	**38.** (*c*)
9. (*c*)	**19.** (*b*)	**29.** (*c*)	**39.** (*d*)
10. (*c*)	**20.** (*d*)	**30.** (*c*)	**40.** (*c*)

Answer Explanations

1. (e) Neither statements I and II alone nor taken together can give remainder as remainder will vary according to the numbers.

   The answer is (e).

2. (d) From statement I, since x is divisible by 909909 and 909909 is divisible by 9.

   ∴ x is also divisible by 9.

   Hence statement I alone is sufficient.

   From statement II, since x is divisible by 567 which is also divisible by 9.

   ∴ x is also divisible by 9.

   Hence statement II alone is also sufficient.

   The answer is (d).

3. (b) From statement I, Only Z is divisible by 21, we cannot conclude that X and Y cannot be divisible by 7.

   Hence, statement I alone is not sufficient.

   From statement II - Since, each of X, Y and Z is divisible by 3 and only Z is divisible by 21, so only Z is divisible by 7.

   Hence, statement II alone is sufficient.

   The answer is (b).

4. (e) Combining both statements, we cannot find the days because we don't have data on Saturday and Sunday.

   The answer is (e).

5. (a) From statement I, since HCF and LCM of P and Q are 6 and 42 respectively, so each of them must be greater than or equal to 6 and less than or equal to 42.

   Product of P and Q = LCM × HCF

   $$= 42 \times 6 = 252.$$

   By factorizing, the value of P and Q must be 42 and 6.

   From statement II,

   Product of P and Q = 1764.

   Multiple values of P and Q are possible.

   Hence, statement II alone is not sufficient.

   The answer is (a).

6. (c) From statement I, only ratio of their speed is given, nothing can be said about the distance.

   Hence, statement I alone is not sufficient.

   From statement II, the initial distance between them was 420 m and finally they meet to each other. But in which direction they travelled to meet other is not given.

   Hence, statement II alone is also not sufficient.

   Using both the statements together, we can say that distance travelled by Sonu

   $$= \frac{1}{5} \times 420 = 84\text{m}.$$

   The answer is (c).

7. (a) The three digit number abc is (100 × a) + (10 × b) + c. If abc is a multiple of 9, then there is an integer k such that 9k = (100 × a) + (10 × b) + c. Divide this equation by 9 and you have

   $$k = \left(\frac{100}{9} \times a\right) + \left(\frac{10}{9} \times b\right) + \frac{c}{9}$$

   $$= \left(11a + \frac{a}{9}\right) + \left(b + \frac{b}{9}\right) + \frac{c}{9}$$

   $$= 11a + b + \left(\frac{a}{9} + \frac{b}{9} + \frac{c}{9}\right)$$

$= 11a + b + \frac{a+b+c}{9}$

[Or if number is multiple of 9 its sum of digits has to be multiple of 9].

Hence, statement I alone is sufficient.

Statement II is not sufficient since choosing a = 0 = b and c = 9 makes II valid and (a + b + c) is 9 but choosing a = 4 = b and c = 2 also makes II valid with (a + b + c) equal to 10.

Hence, statement II alone is not sufficient.

The answer is (a).

8. (a) From statement I, it follows that if X = 10a + b, then Y = 10b + a (where a and b are each digits from 1 to 9)

X – Y = 10a + b – (10b + a) = 9(a – b)

$\therefore \quad \frac{(X-Y)}{9} = a - b$, which is an integer.

Even if a = b, that is when our numbers are 55, 66, 77 or any other such number, $\frac{(X-Y)}{9} = 0$, which is still an integer.

Hence, statement I alone is sufficient.

From statement II, consider the example if X = 53 and Y = 35, then X – Y = 18, which is divisible by 9; however, if X = 53 and Y = 46, then X – Y = 7, which is not divisible by 9.

Hence, statement II alone is not sufficient.

The answer is (a).

9. (c) From statement I, Number of books < 10.

Hence, statement I alone is not sufficient.

From statement II, Number of books = 6, 12, 18 and so on.

Hence, statement II alone is also not sufficient.

Combining both statement, we get number of books = 6.

The answer is (c).

10. (c) Neither of the statements independently gives the answers.

Combining the two we have the information that Z > Y > X and the difference between Z and X is 8. So X + Z = 2X + 8. For this to be divisible by 8, X must be a multiple of 4 (or) an even number, which violates the condition given.

The answer is (c).

11. (c) **Considering statement (I) alone :**

$x = \frac{(a+b)}{2}$

No information about y

INSUFFICIENT Eliminate AD

Considering statement (II) alone :

$y = \frac{(a+x)}{2}$

No information about b

INSUFFICIENT Eliminate B

Considering both the statements together :

$x = \frac{(a+b)}{2}$ and $y = \frac{(a+x)}{2}$

$\Rightarrow \quad y = \frac{(3a+b)}{4}$

So,

$$\frac{(b-y)}{(y-a)} = \{b - \left(\frac{(3a+b)}{(4)}\right)\}\{\left(\frac{(3a+b)}{(4)}\right) - a\}$$

$$= \frac{\{4b-(3a+b)\}}{\{(3a+b)-4a)\}} = \frac{3(b-a)}{3(b-a)} = 1$$

Sufficient The answer is (c).

12. (a) **Considering statement (I) alone :**

If M = 12 and N = 21, then M + N = 12 + 21 = 33

if M = 31 and N = 13, then M + N = 31 + 13 = 44

INSUFFICIENT Eliminate AD

Considering statement (II) alone :

If M = 12 and N = 21, then M + N = 12 + 21 = 33

If M = 31 and N = 13, then M + N = 31 + 13 = 44

INSUFFICIENT Eliminate B

Considering both the statements together :

If M = 12 and N = 21, then M + N = 12 + 21 = 33

If M = 31 and N = 13, then M + N = 31 + 13 = 44

Insufficient The answer is (e).

13. (b) **Considering statement (I) alone :**

if x = 0, then $x^2 \leq x$. Is 0 < x < 1? No

If x = 0.5, then $x^2 \leq x$. Is 0 < x < 1? Yes

INSUFFICIENT Eliminate AD

Considering statement (II) alone :

If x3 < 0, then x < 0

SUFFICIENT The answer is (b).

14. (c) **Considering statement (I) alone :**

x can be 14, 41, 50 and many others.

INSUFFICIENT Eliminate AD

Considering statement (II) alone :

x can be 10, 15, 20 and many more, INSUFFICIENT Eliminate B

Considering both the statements together :

Possible values of x are 14, 23, 32, 41, and 50.

Only 50 is a multiple of 5.

SUFFICIENT The answer is (c)

15. (b) **Considering statement (I) alone :**

If x = 1 and y = 3, then xy < 8. Yes

If x = –3 and y = –4, then xy > 8. No

INSUFFICIENT Eliminate AD

Considering statement (II) alone :

If $x^2 < 4$ and $y^2 < 16$, then –2 < x < 2 and –4 < y < 4

Hence, –8 < xy < 8

SUFFICIENT The answer is (b).

16. (b) For a number to be divisible by 9, the sum of the digits must be divisible by 9.

Possible values for $3(10^a)$ = 30 or 300 or 3000 or 30000 or any such number with 0s at the end.

Hence, the sum of digits of $3(10^a)$ + b would be 3 + b

As b is a single digit number, 3 + b would be divisible by 9 if b = 6

Considering statement (I) alone :

if a = 4, then $3(10^a)$ + b = 30000 + b

Hence, the sum of digits is 3 + b

If b = 1, then $3(10^a)$ + b is not divisible by 9

If b = 6, then $3(10^a)$ + b is divisible by 9

INSUFFICIENT Eliminate AD

Considering statement (II) alone :

If b = 6, then $3(10^a)$ + b would be any number such as 30 + 6 or 300 + 6 or 3000 + 6 or any such number. Hence, the sum of the digits will always be 9, which is divisible by 9.

SUFFICIENT The answer is (b).

17. (b) For a + b + ab to be odd, either all a, b, and ab must be odd or exactly one of the three must be odd.

Considering statement (I) alone :

If a is even, then ab is also even.

Let b also be even.

Then a + b + ab = even + even + even = even

If a is even, then ab is also even.

Let b be odd.

Then a + b + ab = even + odd + even = odd

INSUFFICIENT Eliminate AD

Considering statement (II) alone :

If a + b is odd, then only of the two – a or b – is odd.

If a is odd and b is even, then ab is even.

Hence, a + b + ab = odd + even + even = odd

If a is even and b is odd, then ab is even.

Hence, a + b + ab = even + odd + even = odd

SUFFICIENT The answer is (b).

18. **(a)** If (C) look like the obvious answer, be more careful.

Considering statement (I) alone :

If z = 1944, then $x^3y^5 = 1944$

$1944 = 2^3 3^5$

Hence, $x^3y^5 = 2^3 3^5$

So, x = 2 and y = 3

SUFFICIENT Eliminate BCE

Considering statement (II) alone :

If y = 3, there still are 2 unknowns and only equation.

INSUFFICIENT The answer is (a)

19. **(b)** A number is divisible by 6 only if the number is divisible by both 2 and 3.

Considering statement (I) alone :

If xyz is an even multiple of 3, then it is divisible by both 2 and 3 and hence, by 6.

If xyz is an odd multiple of 3, then it is not divisible by both 2 and 3 and hence, is not divisible by 6. INSUFFICIENT Eliminate AD

Considering statement (II) alone :

If x, y, and z are consecutive integers, then xyz is a multiple of both 2 and 3, hence, 6.

SUFFICIENT The answer is (b).

20. **(d)** **Considering statement (I) alone :**

The largest number of the list could be 10 or 17 or 24 or any other number that leaves a remainder of 3 when the number is divided by 7.

If the greatest number in the list is 10, then the list is as follows: 1, 2, 3, 4, 5, 6, 7, 8, 9, 10. Only one of these numbers is divisible by 7. If the greatest number in the list is 17, then the list is as follows: 8, 9, 10, 11, 12, 13, 14, 15, 16, 17.

Only one of these numbers is divisible by 7.

SUFFICIENT Eliminate BCE.

Considering statement (II) alone :

If the median of 10 consecutive integers is 12.5, then the two numbers must be 12 and 13.

Hence, the list of numbers is 8, 9, 10, 11, 12, 13, 14, 15, 16, and 17.

Only one of these numbers is divisible by 7.

SUFFICIENT The answer is (d).

21. **(a)** **Considering statement (I) alone :**

If a is odd, then 4^a is a number that ends in 4 always. Hence, $4^a + 1$ will always end in 5. Any number that ends in 5 is always divisible by 5 i.e it leaves a remainder of 0.

SUFFICIENT Eliminate BCE

Considering statement (II) alone :

If a = 3, then $4^a + 1$ is 64 + 1 = 65. It leaves a remainder of 0 when divided by 5.

If a = 6, then $4^a + 1$ is 4096 + 1 = 4097. It leaves a remainder of 2 when divided by 5.

INSUFFICIENT The answer is (a)

22. (c) **Considering statement (I) alone :**

If x^3y^2 is an even number, then at least one of x or y is an even number. But, no information about either of the numbers.

INSUFFICIENT Eliminate AD

Considering statement (II) alone :

No information about x.

INSUFFICIENT Eliminate B

Considering both the statements together :

If x^3y^2 is an even number and y is an odd number, then x must be an even prime number.

Hence, the value of x is 2.

SUFFICIENT The answer is (c)

23. (a) **Considering statement (I) alone :**

If a is even, then b is odd. Hence, a + b is odd

If a is odd, then b is even. Hence, a + b is odd.

SUFFICIENT Eliminate BCE

Considering statement (II) alone :

If a is even, then b is odd. Hence, a + b is odd

If a is odd, then b is odd. Hence, a + b is even.

INSUFFICENT The answer is (a).

24. (c) From statement I, we can say that either $a + b + 1 = 0$ or $a = b = 1$.

Hence, statement I alone is not sufficient.

From statement II, $a^2 - 2ab + b^2 > 0 \Rightarrow (a - b)^2 > 0 \Rightarrow a \neq b$

Hence, statement II alone is also not sufficient.

Using both the statements, we get that

$a + b + 1 = 0$

The answer is (c).

25. (d) **From statement I :** $M = a^3 - 1$ and $N = a^3 + 1$

$\Rightarrow$ N > M (if a > 1, then $a^3 + 1 > a^3 - 1$).

Hence, statement I alone is sufficient.

From statement II : M = a N

$$\Rightarrow \frac{M}{N} = a > 1$$

$\Rightarrow$ M > N.

Hence, statement II alone is also sufficient.

The answer is (d).

26. (c) From statement I, a = 3, b = 4

For 'abc' to be divisible by 3, a + b + c should be divisible by 3. Thus, 'c' can be 2, 5, 8

Hence statement I alone is not sufficient.

From statement II, nothing is given about a and b.

Hence statement II alone is also not sufficient.

Using both the statements together, we get a = 3, b = 4 and c = 5.

The answer is (c).

27. (d) From statement I, a + 1 = a + a + 2

$\therefore$ a = –1

Hence statement I alone is sufficient.

From statement II, a (a + 2) = – 1

$\therefore$ a = –1

Hence statement II alone is also sufficient.

The answer is (d).

28. (c) From statement I, we get

a − 2	a	a + 2
(−1)	1	3
−3	(−1)	1
−5	−3	(−1)

All 3 cases we get '−1'

So we do not know what the average.

Hence statement I alone is not sufficient.

From statement II, we can say that the numbers are

−1, 1, 3 or 1, 3, 5.

Hence statement II alone is also not sufficient.

Using both the only possibility is −1, 1, 3 and hence we can find the average.

The answer is (c).

29. (c) Since n is odd, it follows that either p is odd and r is even or p is even and r is odd.

From statement I, with the fact that 2 is the only even prime number, it can be concluded that p = 2 or r = 2; but additional information is needed to decide which one of these two alternative holds.

Hence, statement I alone is not sufficient.

From statement II, r ≠ 2. But this alone is not sufficient.

By combining both we can find the value of p.

The answer is (c).

30. (c) Let X and Y (X > Y) are the digits of p.

From statement I,

X = Y + 3 and X + Y = 9, by solving we get X = 3 and Y = 6. There are two possible values of numbers 36 and 63.

Hence, statement I alone is not sufficient.

From statement II, it is not sufficient because it only say that p is less than 50.

Hence, statement II alone is also not sufficient.

By combining both we can say that p = 36.

The answer is (c).

31. (a) From statement I, since A × B × C is odd, so each of A, B and C is odd.

So, C − A = even. (odd − odd = even)

Hence, statement I alone is sufficient.

From statement II, it can be deduced that at least two among A, B, C, are even. So the value of C − A may be even or odd.

Hence statement II alone is not sufficient.

The answer is (a).

32. (e) From statement I, multiple values of the number are possible.

Hence statement I alone is not sufficient.

From statement II, the possible values of the number are possible and 97 and 79.

Hence statement II alone is also not sufficient.

Even using both the statements together, we do not get any unique value of the digits of the number. The number can be 79 or 97.

The answer is (e).

33. (b) As even integer is an integer divisible by 2.

From statement I, n + p may be even or not, depending upon value of p and n.

Hence, statement I alone is not sufficient.

From statement II, Since 2n + 10p

$= 2(n + 5p).$

$X^2 = 4(n + p)^2$ which is even.

Hence, statement II alone is sufficient.

The answer is (b).

34. (c) For p to be divisible by 35, p must be divisible by each prime factor of 35. The prime factor s of 35 are 5 and 7.

Question rephrased: Is p divisible by 3 and 7 both?

Let's see each statement one by one.

Considering Statement (I) alone:

Since p is divisible by 15, p must be divisible by each prime factor of 15, i.e., 3 and 5. However, we are not certain that p is divisible by 7, too. Insufficient.

Hence, eliminate A/D.

Considering Statement (II) alone

Since p is divisible by 14, p must be divisible by each prime factor of 14, i.e., 2 and 7. However, we are not certain that p is divisible by 5, too. Insufficient.

Hence, eliminate B.

Statement (I) and (II) together:

From Statement 1, we know that p is divisible by 5 and from Statement 2, we know that p is divisible by 7. Sufficient.

The correct answer is Option (c).

35. (e) Given that Ax = bx, it seems that it is self-sufficient to conclude that A = B. We can divide both sides by x and get A = B. However, it is not so. What if $x = 0$? In that case, A & B need not necessarily be equal.

Example: $3 \times 0 = 4 \times 0$. So, the question boils down to whether $x \neq 0$.

Let's see each statement one by one.

Considering Statement (I) alone:

Given that $A + x = B + x$, we can cancel x from both sides and get A = B. However, $x = 0$ is still a possible value. Insufficient.

Hence, eliminate A/D.

Considering Statement (II) alone:

The information means that x can be 0 or a positive integer. x = 0 is still a possible vale. Insufficient.

Hence, eliminate B.

Statements (I) and (II) together:

Even both statements together are insufficient.

The correct answer is Option (e).

36. (b) $\frac{49}{x}$ can be an integer only if x is one among $\pm 1, \pm 7$ or ± 49, i.e., x is a factor of 49.

Considering Statement (I) alone:

Knowing that x is an odd number is not sufficient since x can be $\pm1, \pm3, \pm7, \pm11, \pm49$, etc. This statement alone is not sufficient.

Hence, eliminate A/D.

Considering Statement (II) alone:

Given that $10 < x < 20$, we know that x lies between 10 and 20. $\frac{49}{x}$ cannot be an integer since $\frac{49}{x}$ can be an integer only if $x = \pm1$, ±7 or ± 49.

Hence this statement alone is sufficient.

Hence, eliminate C/E.

The answer is (b).

37. (e) For the product of 14 integers to be negative, no integer must be equal to 0, and there must be an odd number of negative integers in the list because even number of integers makes the product positive.

Let's see each statement one by one.

Considering Statement (I) alone:

Set L has at the most 7 negative integers.

This statement alone is not sufficient because we do not know whether there is an integer 0 in the set and whether there are an odd or even number of negative integers.

Statement 1 alone is not sufficient.

Hence, eliminate A/D.

Considering Statement (II) alone :

Set L has at least 7 positive integers.

Again, this statement alone is not sufficient because we do not know whether there is an integer 0 in the set and whether there are an odd or even number of negative integers.

Statement 2 alone is not sufficient.

Hence, eliminate B.

Considering Statement (I) and (II) together:

Let us take two cases to analyze.

(1) There are 7 negative, and 7 positive integers. It means the product would be negative. The answer is Yes.

(2) There are 6 negative, and 8 positive integers. It means the product would be positive. The answer is No.

Since we do not get the unique answer, statements (I) and (II) together are not sufficient.

The answer is (e).

38. (c) **Considering Statement (I) alone :**

We are not given any information about b; for example, if a = 10 and b is 3, then x is not an integer; however, if a = 10, and b is 2, then x is an integer. No unique value.

Hence Statement (I) alone is not sufficient.

Considering Statement (II) alone :

Statement (II) alone is also insufficient because of no information about a.

Take a couple of test values.

Case 1 : Say a = 35; since b is a divisor of 10, let us assume b = 2. We get $x = \frac{a}{b} = \frac{35}{2}$, not an integer.

Case 2 : Say a = 40, and b = 2, then $x = \frac{a}{b} = \frac{40}{2} = 20$, an integer

We do not get a unique answer, hence Statement 2 alone is not sufficient

Hence, eliminate B.

Statements (I) and (II) together :

In the light of both statements, Case 1 discussed in Statement (II) in not applicable; thus, x must be an integer. Sufficient.

The answer is (c).

39. (d) **Considering Statement (I) alone :**

Statement 1 implies that z = 8a + 2, where a is a positive integer. Since 8a is divisible by 4, the remainder of (8a + 2) when divided by 4 will be 2. Statement (I) alone is sufficient.

Hence, eliminate B/C/E.

Considering Statement (II) alone :

Statement (II) implies that z = 12a + 6 $\Rightarrow$ z = 12a + 4 + 2. Since 12a and 4 are divisible by 4, the remainder of [(12a + 4) + 2] will be 2. Statement (II) alone is also sufficient.

Hence, eliminate A.

The answer is (d).

40. (c) Let us first understand the counting of divisors of any number, say, p^n.

Case1: If p is a prime number, then the number of divisor of, $p^n = (n + 1)$

Case 2: If p is a composite number, say, p = st; where s and t are prime numbers. thus, $p^n = s^n t^n$, then the number of divisors of, $p^n = (n + 1)^2$

Considering Statement (I) alone:

Statement 1 tells us only about the value of b and is therefore insufficient. Let's take two cases.

- **Case 1 :** Say

  a = 2; the number of divisors of

  $a^4 (=2^4) = 4 + 1 = 5$.

  The number of divisors of

  $b^2 (=4^2 = 2^4) = 4 + 1 = 5$. The answer is No.

- **Case 2 :** Say

  a = 4; the number of divisors of $a^4 (= 4^4 = 2^8) = 8 + 1 = 9$.

  The number of divisors of

  $b^2 (= 4^2 = 2^4) = 4 + 1 = 5$. The answer is Yes.

No unique answer. Insufficient.

Hence, eliminate A/D

Considering Statement (II) alone :

Statement 2 only tells us about a and is therefore insufficient. Let's take two cases.

- **Case 1 :** Say

  b = 9; the number of divisors of $a^4 (=3^4) = 4 + 1 = 5$.

  The number of divisors of

  $b^2 (= 9^2 = 3^4) = 4 + 1 = 5$. The answer is No.

- **Case 2 :** Say

  b = 1; the number of divisors of

  $a^4 (=3^4) = 4 + 1 = 5$.

  The number of divisors of $b^4 (- 1^2 = 1) = 1$.

  The answer is Yes.

  No unique answer. Insufficient.

Hence, eliminate B.

Considering Statements (I) and (II) together:

Both statements combined are sufficient as we know the values of both a and b.

In DS questions, it is not necessary to calculate the answer if you are satisfied that you will get the unique answer.

For the sake of your curiosity, let's calculate the answer.

- Number of divisors of $a^4 (= 3^4) = 4 + 1 = 5$
- Number of divisors of $b^2 (= 4^2 = 2^4) = 4 + 1 = 5$

We see that the number of divisors of a^4 is equal, not greater than the number of divisors of b^2. The answer is No - a unique answer. Sufficient.

The answer is (c).

Chapter 2

Arithmetic

Most of the Quantitative questions you will see on the GMAT involve arithmetic to some extent. The GMAT frequently increases the difficulty level of questions by combining various topics, such as absolute value, inequalities, exponents, and fractions, and often incorporating these topics into questions that involve algebra, geometry, or proportions.

This chapter will guide you through the basics and give you practice applying arithmetic concepts to GMAT questions ranging from the simple to the most advanced.

Classification of Numbers

Numbers can be classified into various categories based on their properties and characteristics. Here are some common classifications of numbers:

- **Real numbers :** These are all the rational and irrational numbers combined. Every number on the number line is a real number.
- **Rational numbers :** These are numbers that can be expressed as a ratio of two integers, i.e., numbers that can be written in the form a/b, where a and b are integers and b is not equal to zero. For example, $\frac{1}{2}, \frac{3}{4}, -\frac{2}{3}$, etc. are all rational numbers.
- **Natural numbers :** These are the counting numbers 1, 2, 3, 4, 5, ... and so on.
- **Whole numbers :** These are the natural numbers and zero (0), i.e., 0, 1, 2, 3, 4, 5, ... and so on.
- **Integers :** These are the whole numbers and their negatives, i.e., ..., -3, -2, -1, 0, 1, 2, 3, ... and so on.
- **Irrational numbers :** These are numbers that cannot be expressed as a ratio of two integers, and they have non-repeating, non-terminating decimal expansions. Examples of irrational numbers include pi (π) and the square root of 2.

Real Numbers

All numbers on the number line. All of the numbers on the GMAT are real.

The set of real numbers consists of all rational numbers and all irrational numbers.

The real numbers include all integers, fractions, and decimals. The set of real numbers can be represented by a number line called the real number line.

Real numbers can be positive, negative, or zero. They can be expressed as either a terminating decimal (such as 0.5, –1.75, or 3.0) or a non-terminating, non-repeating decimal (such as pi, the square root of 2, or 0.33333...)

Integers

All of the numbers with no fractional or decimal parts: in other words, all multiples of 1. Negative numbers and 0 are also integers.

The integers are the numbers 1, 2, 3, and so on, together with their negatives, −1, −2, −3, . . . , and 0. Thus, the set of integers is {. . . . , −3, −2, −1, 0, 1, 2, 3, . . .}.

The positive integers are greater than 0, the negative integers are less than 0, and 0 is neither positive nor negative. When integers are added, subtracted, or multiplied, the result is always an integer

Here are some general facts regarding multiplication of integers.

- The product of two positive integers is a positive integer.
- The product of two negative integers is a positive integer.
- The product of a positive integer and a negative integer is a negative integer.

Rational Numbers

All of the numbers that can be expressed as the ratio of two integers (all integers and fractions).

A fraction is a number $\frac{a}{b}$, of the form where a and b are integers and $b \neq 0$. The integer a is called the numerator of the fraction, and b is called the denominator.

For example, $\frac{-7}{5}$ is a fraction in which is the numerator is −7 and 5 is the denominator Such numbers are also called rational numbers.

Irrational Numbers

All real numbers that are not rational, both positive and negative. All the numbers that can be written as non-terminating, nonrepeating decimals are non-rational, so they are called the "irrationals". Examples would be square root of two or the number pi.

Root 2 is 1.41421356237. . . , and it can be shown that this decimal does not terminate or repeat.

Another example is 0.010110111011110111110. . . , which has groups of consecutive 1's separated by a 0, where the number of 1's in each successive group increases by one. Since these two decimals do not terminate or repeat, they are not rational numbers. Such numbers are called irrational numbers.

Few properties of Real Numbers

- $a + b = b + a$
- $a \times b = b \times a$
- $(a + b) + c = a + (b + c)$
- $(a \times b) \times c = a \times (b \times c)$
- $a\,(b + c) = ab + bc$
- $1 \times a = a$
- $\frac{a}{1} = a$
- $a \times 0 = 0$
- $a + 0 = a$
- $\frac{a}{a} = 1$ (excluding 0)
- $a + (-b) = a - b$
- $a - (-b) = a + b$
- $(a) \times (b) = ab$
- $(-a) \times (-b) = ab$
- $\frac{(a)}{(b)} = \frac{a}{b}$
- $\frac{(-a)}{(-b)} = \frac{a}{b}$
- $(-a) \times (b) = -ab$
- $(a) \times (-b) = -ab$
- $\frac{(-a)}{(b)} = \frac{-a}{b}$
- $(a) \times (-b) = -ab$

Odd/Even Numbers

The terms odd and even apply only to integers.

Odd numbers are integers that are not divisible by 2. An odd number is an integer of the form $n = 2k + 1$, where k is an integer.

Even numbers are integers that are evenly divisible by 2, i.e., divisible by 2 without any remainder. An even number is an integer of the form $n = 2k$, where k is an integer.

Odd and even numbers may be negative; 0 is an even number.

Rules for Odds and Evens

Odd ± Odd = Even   Odd × Odd = Odd

Even ± Even = Even   Even × Even = Even

Odd ± Even = Odd   Odd + Even = Even

Division of two integers can result into an even/odd integer or a fraction.

Example : If the product of two consecutive even numbers is 168, what is the sum of these two numbers?

Solution : Let's start by using algebra to represent the two consecutive even numbers:

Let x be the smaller even number.

Then $x + 2$ is the next even number, since it is two more than x.

Now we can use the given information to write an equation :

The product of these two numbers is 168, so we have: $x(x + 2) = 168$

To solve for x, we can first simplify the equation by expanding the product on the left-hand side:

$$x^2 + 2x = 168$$

Next, we can rearrange the terms to get a quadratic equation in standard form:

$$x^2 + 2x - 168 = 0$$

We can factor this quadratic equation as follows:

$$(x - 12)(x + 14) = 0$$

From this factorization, we see that there are two possible solutions:

x = 12, which gives x + 2 = 14

x = –14, which gives x + 2 = –12

We can eliminate the negative solution, since we are looking for two consecutive even numbers. Therefore, the two numbers are 12 and 14.

To check that these are indeed the correct numbers, we can verify that their product is 168:

$$12 \times 14 = 168$$

Finally, we can find the sum of these two numbers:

$$12 + 14 = 26$$

Therefore, the sum of the two consecutive even numbers whose product is 168 is 26.

Prime Numbers

A Prime number is a natural number with exactly two distinct natural number divisors: 1 and itself. In other words, a prime number has no positive integer divisors other than 1 and itself.

Therefore, 1 is not a prime, since it only has one divisor, namely 1. The number 2 is the first prime number and the only even prime.

A number n > 1 is prime if it cannot be written as a product of two factors a and b, both of which are greater than 1 then n = ab.

The GMAT expects test takers to recognize the prime numbers up to 50. They are 2, 3, 5, 7, 11, 13, 17, 19, 23, 29, 31, 37, 41, 43, and 47.

Note :

- Only positive numbers can be primes.
- There are infinitely many prime numbers.
- All prime numbers except 2 and 5 end in 1, 3, 7 or 9
- All prime numbers above 3 are of the form 6n - 1 or 6n + 1, because all other numbers are divisible by 2 or 3.
- Any nonzero natural number can be factored into primes, written as a product of primes or powers of primes.

Prime Factorization

The prime factorization of a number is the expression of the number as the product of its prime factors. No matter how you factor a number, its prime factors will always be the same.

Any nonzero natural number can be factored into primes, written as a product of primes or powers of primes.

Example : $36 = 6 \times 6 = 2 \times 3 \times 2 \times 3 = 2^2 \times 3^2$

$12 = (2)(2)(3) = (2^2)(3)$

$14 = (2)(7)$

$81 = (3)(3)(3)(3) = 3^4$

$338 = (2)(13)(13) = (2)(13^2)$

$800 = (2)(2)(2)(2)(2)(5)(5) = (2^5)(5^2)$

$1{,}155 = (3)(5)(7)(11)$

Note :

If n is a positive integer greater than 1, then there is always a prime number p with $n < p < 2n$.

An integer greater than 1 that is not a prime number is called a composite number. The first ten composite numbers are 4, 6, 8, 9, 10, 12, 14, 15, 16, and 18.

Example : Find the prime factorization of 72.

Solution : To find the prime factorization of 72, we can start by dividing it by the smallest prime number, which is 2 :

$$72 \div 2 = 36$$

Now we have 36, which is an even number and can be divided by 2 again:

$$36 \div 2 = 18$$

Continuing in this way, we can divide by 2 repeatedly until we can no longer do so:

$$18 \div 2 = 9$$

At this point, we cannot divide by 2 anymore, so we need to try the next smallest prime number, which is 3:

$$9 \div 3 = 3$$

Now we have 3, which is a prime number, so we have found the prime factorization of 72:

$$72 = 2 \times 2 \times 2 \times 3 \times 3$$

Therefore, the prime factorization of 72 is $2 \times 2 \times 2 \times 3 \times 3$, which can also be written as $2^3 \times 3^2$

Example : What is the largest prime factor of 84?

Solution : To find the prime factors of 84, we can start by dividing it by 2, since it is even:

$$84 \div 2 = 42$$

Now we have an even number, so we can divide it by 2 again:

$$42 \div 2 = 21$$

21 is odd, so it is not divisible by 2. We can now try dividing it by the next smallest prime number, which is 3:

$$21 \div 3 = 7$$

7 is a prime number, so we have found all the prime factors of 84. They are 2, 2, 3, and 7.

To find the largest prime factor, we can simply look at the list of prime factors and choose the largest one, which is 7.

Therefore, the largest prime factor of 84 is 7.

Percentages

GMAT questions will often require that you convert among percents, decimals, fractions, and ratios.

percent is just another word for "per one hundred."

The term percent means per hundred, or hundredths. Percents are ratios that are often used to represent parts of a whole, where the whole is considered as having 100 parts.

1 percent means 1 part out of 100 parts, or $\frac{1}{100}$

32 percent means 32 parts out of 100 parts, or $\frac{32}{100}$

50 percent means 50 parts out of 100 parts, or $\frac{1}{2}$

Note : that the part is the numerator of the ratio and the whole is the denominator. Percents are often written with the % symbol; fractional and decimal equivalents are often used as well but without the % symbol

Example : If the whole is 20 and the part is 13, you can find the percent as follows.

$$\frac{\text{Part}}{\text{whole}} = \frac{13}{20} = 0.65 = 65\%$$

To make a percent from a decimal or fraction, multiply by 100%. Since 100% means 100 hundredths, or 1, multiplying by 100% will not change the number.

Example : $0.17 = 0.17 \times 100\% = 17\%$

To drop a percent, divide by 100%. Once again, dividing by 100%, which is equivalent to 1, will not change the number.

Example : $32\% = 0.32$

Example : 15 is 60% of what number?

Solution : Use the decimal equivalent of 60%. Because 60% of some number z is 15, multiply z by the decimal equivalent of 60%, or 0.6.

$$0.6z = 15$$

$$z = 25$$

Example : A store is having a 20% off sale on all items. If a dress originally costs \$50, what is the sale price?

Solution : To find the sale price, we need to subtract the discount from the original price:

Discount = 20% of \$50 = 0.20 × \$50 = \$10

Sale price = Original price – Discount = \$50 – \$10 = \$40

Therefore, the sale price of the dress is \$40.

Common Fraction-to-Percent Equivalents

$\frac{1}{20} = 5\%$ $\frac{1}{11} = 9\frac{1}{11}\%$ $\frac{1}{10} = 10\%$ $\frac{1}{9} = 11\frac{1}{9}\%$

$\frac{1}{8} = 12\frac{1}{2}\%$ $\frac{1}{6} = 16\frac{2}{3}\%$ $\frac{1}{5} = 20\%$ $\frac{1}{4} = 25\%$

$\frac{1}{3} = 33\frac{1}{3}\%$ $\frac{1}{2} = 50\%$ $10\% = \frac{1}{10}$ $12\frac{1}{2}\% = \frac{1}{8}$

$16\frac{2}{3}\% = \frac{1}{6}$	$20\% = \frac{2}{10} = \frac{1}{5}$	$25\% = \frac{2}{8} = \frac{1}{4}$	$33\frac{1}{3}\% = \frac{2}{6} = \frac{1}{3}$
$30\% = \frac{3}{10}$	$37\frac{1}{2}\% = \frac{3}{8}$	$50\% = \frac{3}{6} = \frac{1}{2}$	$40\% = \frac{4}{10} = \frac{2}{5}$
$50\% = \frac{4}{8} = \frac{2}{4} = \frac{1}{2}$	$66\frac{2}{3}\% = \frac{4}{6} = \frac{2}{3}$	$50\% = \frac{5}{10} = \frac{1}{2}$	$62\frac{1}{2}\% = \frac{5}{8}$
$83\frac{1}{3}\% = \frac{5}{6}$	$60\% = \frac{6}{10} = \frac{3}{5}$	$75\% = \frac{6}{8} = \frac{3}{4}$	$70\% = \frac{7}{10}$
$87\frac{1}{2}\% = \frac{7}{8}$	$80\% = \frac{8}{10} = \frac{4}{5}$	$90\% = \frac{9}{10}$	$100\% = \frac{10}{10} = 1$

Percentage Change

When dealing with percent increase and percent decrease, always be careful to put the amount of increase or decrease over the original whole, not over the new whole

General formula for percent increase or decrease, (percent change):

$$\text{Percent Change} = \frac{(\text{Final} - \text{Original}) \times 100\%}{\text{Original}} = \frac{(\text{Change})}{(\text{Original})} \times 100\%$$

When a quantity changes from an initial positive amount to another positive amount, for example, an employee's salary that is raised, you can compute the amount of change as a percent of the initial amount. This is called percent change. If a quantity increases from 600 to 750, then the percent increase is found by dividing the amount of increase, 150, by the base, 600

Example : The price of a book increased from \$20 to \$25. What is the percentage change in price?

Solution : To find the percentage change, we need to first find the difference between the old and new prices, and then divide that difference by the old price. We can express this as a formula:

$$\text{Percentage change} = \frac{(\text{new price} - \text{old price})}{\text{old price}} \times 100\%$$

Plugging in the values given in the problem, we get :

$$\text{Percentage change} = \frac{(\$25 - \$20)}{\$20} \times 100\% = \frac{\$5}{\$20} \times 100\% = 0.25 \times 100\% = 25\%$$

Therefore, the percentage change in the price of the book is 25%. This means that the price increased by 25% from its original value of $20.

Interest

Interest rate questions rely on three important pieces of information: (1) the principal, or the amount initially invested; (2) the interest rate, or the rate at which the investment grows; and (3) the time period during which the investment accrues interest.

Simple Interest

Simple interest = Principal x Interest rate × Time, where "principal" is the starting amount and "rate" is the interest rate at which the money grows per a given period of time (**note :** express the rate as a decimal in the formula).

$$V = P\left(1 + \frac{rt}{100}\right)$$

Simple interest is based only on the initial deposit, which serves as the amount on which interest is computed, called the principal, for the entire time period. If the amount P is invested at a simple annual interest rate of r percent, then the value V of the investment at the end of t years is given by the formula

Example : If $8,000 is invested at 6% simple annual interest, how much interest is earned after 3 months?

Solution : Since the annual interest rate is 6%, the interest for 1 year is (0.06)($8,000) = $480. There are 12 months in a year, so the interest earned in 3 months is $\left(\frac{3}{12}\right)(\$480) = \$120$.

Example : John borrowed $5,000 from a bank for 3 years at an annual interest rate of 6%. How much interest will he pay at the end of the 3 years?

Solution : The formula for simple interest is:

Interest = Principal × Rate × Time, where Principal is the initial amount borrowed, Rate is the interest rate per year, and Time is the duration of the loan in years.

Plugging in the values given in the problem, we get :

Interest = \$5,000 x 0.06 x 3 = \$900

Therefore, John will pay \$900 in interest at the end of the 3-year period.

Compound Interest

In the case of compound interest, interest is added to the principal at regular time intervals, such as annually, quarterly, and monthly. Each time interest is added to the principal, the interest is said to be compounded. After each compounding, interest is earned on the new principal, which is the sum of the preceding principal and the interest just added. If the amount P is invested at an annual interest rate of r percent, compounded annually, then the value V of the investment at the end of t years is given by the formula :

Final Amount = Principal × [1 + (interest/c)]^{nt}

where n is the number of times compounded and t is the number of years

Example : If \$10,000 is invested at 10% annual interest, compounded semiannually, what is the balance after 1 year?

Solution : Since the interest is compounded semi-annually (every 6 months), the interest rate for each 6-month period is 5%, which is half of the 10% annual rate. Thus, the balance after the first 6 months would be 10,000 + (10,000)(0.05) = \$10,500. For the second 6-month period, the interest is calculated on the \$10,500 balance at the end of the first 6-month period. Thus, the balance after 1 year would be 10,500 + (10,500)(0.05) = \$11,025.

The balance after one year can also be expressed as $10{,}000\left(1+\frac{0.1}{2}\right)^2$ dollars.

Example : Mary invests \$10,000 in a savings account that pays 4% interest compounded annually. How much money will she have after 5 years?

Solution : The formula for compound interest is:

$$A = P\left(1+\frac{r}{n}\right)^{nt}$$

where A is the final amount, P is the initial principal, r is the annual interest rate, n is the number of times the interest is compounded per year, and t is the number of years.

Plugging in the values given in the problem, we get:

$$A = \$10{,}000\left(1+\frac{0.04}{1}\right)^{(1\times 5)}$$

$$A = \$10{,}000(1.04)^5$$

Ratio

A ratio is a comparison of two quantities by division.

The ratio of one quantity to another is a way to express their relative sizes, often in the form of a fraction, where the first quantity is the numerator and the second quantity is the denominator.

For example, if there are 2 apples and 3 oranges in a basket, we can say that the ratio of the number of apples to the number of oranges is $\frac{2}{3}$ or that it is 2 to 3 or that it is 2:3. Like fractions, ratios can be reduced to lowest terms.

Example : Joe is 16 years old and Mary is 12. The ratio of Joe's age to Mary's age is 16 to 12.

A ratio represents the proportional relationship between quantities or numbers. A ratio can compare either a part to another part or a part to a whole.

Example : The ratio of domestic sales to foreign sales of a certain product is 3 : 5. Then the ratio of the domestic sales to total sales is 3 : 8

One type of ratio can readily be converted to the other only if all the parts together equal the whole and there is no overlap among the parts.

Some GMAT questions deal with ratios that have three or more terms. Always represent them with colons (e.g., $x:y:z$).

Example : If the ratio of men to women to children in a room is 4:3:2, then

Ratio of men : total people = 4 : 9

Ratio of women : total people = 3 : 9 = 1 : 3

Ratio of children : total people = 2 : 9

A proportion is an equation relating two ratios; for example, $\frac{9}{12} = \frac{3}{4}$. To solve a problem involving ratios, you can often write a proportion and solve it by cross multiplication.

Important Points:

If $\frac{a}{b} = \frac{c}{d}$, then:

- **Invertendo :** $\frac{b}{a} = \frac{d}{c}$
- **Alternendo :** $\frac{a}{c} = \frac{b}{d}$
- **Componendo :** $\frac{(a+b)}{b} = \frac{(c+d)}{d}$
- **Dividendo :** $\frac{(a-b)}{b} = \frac{(c-d)}{d}$

Example : A recipe calls for a ratio of 3 cups of flour to 2 cups of sugar. If you want to make the recipe with 6 cups of flour, how much sugar do you need?

Solution : We can use proportions to solve this problem. If we know that the ratio of flour to sugar is 3:2, we can set up the following proportion:

3 cups flour / 2 cups sugar = 6 cups flour / x cups sugar

where x is the unknown amount of sugar needed.

Cross-multiplying, we get :

3 cups flour x x cups sugar = 6 cups flour x 2 cups sugar

Simplifying, we get :

$$3x = 12$$

$$x = 4$$

Therefore, if you want to make the recipe with 6 cups of flour, you need 4 cups of sugar.

Rate and Work

Most rate problems involve conversions from one rate to another. These are best handled by multiplying the various rates so that measurements cancel.

Rate is defined as the amount of work done in a given amount of time.

When a job involves two or more people, then we can add their individual rates, but not the Time.

Combined work questions present you with information about different people or machines that can perform the same job in different amounts of time.

When dealing with multiple rates, be sure to express rates in equivalent units. If a person takes A hours to complete a job, and a second person takes B hours to complete the same job. If both of them work together (at their respective rates), then time required (T) to complete the same job is given as:

$$\frac{1}{T}=\frac{1}{A}+\frac{1}{B}$$

or,

$$T=\frac{AB}{(A+B)}$$

Example: If John can complete a job in 6 hours and Jack can complete the same job in 4 hours, how long will it take them to complete the job if they work together?

Solution: We can use the formula :

Rate × Time = Work, where Rate is the work done per unit of time, Time is the duration of work, and Work is the total amount of work that needs to be done.

Let's assume that the total work is 1 unit. Then we can find the individual rates of John and Jack:

John's rate = $\frac{1}{6}$ units per hour Jack's rate = $\frac{1}{4}$ units per hour

If they work together, their combined rate is the sum of their individual rates:

Combined rate = John's rate + Jack's rate = $\frac{1}{6}+\frac{1}{4}=\frac{5}{12}$ units per hour

Now we can use the formula again to find the time it takes for them to complete the job together:

$$\text{Rate} \times \text{Time} = \text{Work}$$

$$\left(\frac{5}{12}\right) \times \text{Time} = 1$$

$$\text{Time} = \frac{12}{5} \text{ hours}$$

Therefore, it will take John and Jack 2.4 hours, or 2 hours and 24 minutes, to complete the job if they work together.

Example : A group of 6 workers can complete a construction project in 12 days. How many workers are needed to complete the same project in 8 days?

Solution : Let's start by finding the total amount of work required for the project. If a group of 6 workers can complete the project in 12 days, then their combined rate is : $\frac{1}{12}$ of the project per day per worker

Multiplying by the number of workers, we get the rate for the group: $6 \times \frac{1}{12} = \frac{1}{2}$ of the project per day

So, the amount of work required for the project is 1.

Now, we can use the formula :

Amount of work = Rate × Time × Number of workers

To find how many workers are needed to complete the project in 8 days.

Since we want to complete the same amount of work in a shorter time, we need to increase the rate. Let's call the new number of workers needed "x". The rate for this new group is:

$x \times$ Rate per worker = $\frac{x}{2}$ of the project per day

The time is 8 days, so we can set up the equation:

$$1 = \left(\frac{x}{2}\right) \times 8$$

Simplifying, we get:

$$x = 4$$

Therefore, we need 4 workers to complete the same construction project in 8 days.

Speed Time Distance

The GMAT often uses scenarios involving multi-part journeys in order to ask questions about "average rates."

$$\text{Distance} = \text{Speed} \times \text{Time}$$

$$\text{Speed} = \frac{\text{Distance}}{\text{Time}}$$

$$\text{Time} = \frac{\text{Distance}}{\text{Speed}}$$

For any multi-part journey,

$$\text{Average Speed} = \frac{\text{Total distance traveled}}{\text{Total time taken}}$$

Example : If a car travels at an average speed of 70 kilometers per hour for 4 hours, how many kilometers does it travel?

Solution : Since distance = rate × time, simply multiply 70 km/hour × 4 hours. Thus, the car travels 280 kilometers in 4 hours.

Example : A car travels 240 km in 4 hours. What is the average speed of the car?

Solution : We can use the formula : $\text{Speed} = \frac{\text{Distance}}{\text{Time}}$ to find the average speed of the car.

Plugging in the given values, we get : $\text{Speed} = \frac{240}{4}$ km/hours = 60 km/hour

Therefore, the average speed of the car is 60 km/hour.

Relative speed

The concept of relative speed can appear in some GMAT questions, particularly in problem-solving questions related to rates and time.

It's important to remember that in relative speed problems, you need to pay attention to the direction of the movement, as well as the speed. When two objects are moving in opposite directions, you need to add their speeds to find their relative speed. When two objects are moving in the same direction, you need to subtract their speeds to find their relative speed.

Overall, understanding the concept of relative speed and knowing how to apply it to different types of problems can be a useful skill to have for the GMAT.

Example : Two trains are traveling towards each other on parallel tracks. Train A is traveling at a speed of 50 km/hour and train B is traveling at a speed of 60 km/hour. If the distance between the trains is 500 km, how long will it take for the two trains to meet?

Solution : Since the two trains are traveling towards each other, we need to find their relative speed. To do this, we add their speeds:

Relative speed = Speed of train A + Speed of train B = 50 km/hour + 60 km/hour = 110 km/hour

Now we can use the formula :

$$\text{Distance} = \text{Speed} \times \text{Time}$$

To find the time it takes for the two trains to meet. Let's call this time "t". Since the trains are moving towards each other, the combined distance they cover is the sum of their initial distances:

Distance = Distance of train A + Distance of train B = 500 km + 500 km = 1000 km

Plugging in the values, we get:

$$1000 \text{ km} = 110 \text{ km/hour} \times t$$

Solving for "t", we get:

t = 9.09 hours (rounded to two decimal places)

Therefore, it will take approximately 9.09 hours for the two trains to meet

Problem Solving

1. Jack has 80 pens out of which 45 percent are blue. He must purchase 82 new pens, how many of them must be blue such that he has 50 percent of all the pens after the purchase?

(*a*) 36

(*b*) 45

(*c*) 50

(*d*) 55

(*e*) 51

2. A trader makes a profit equal to the selling price of 12 articles on selling 84 articles. What is the percentage profit?

(*a*) 25

(*b*) 14.28

(*c*) 16.67

(*d*) 20

(*e*) 12.5

3. The salary of A is 20% more than the salary of B, which in turn is 25% more than the salary of C. By what percent is the salary of C less than the salary of A?

(*a*) 33.33

(*b*) 40

(*c*) 47.5

(*d*) 50

(*e*) 30

4. Helix University declared its annual results and it followed a trend that first 2500 results had m% distinction holders and the rest had n% of them. If 3700 results yielded 788 distinction holders and 5000 results yielded 1100 distinction holders, find the value of 'n'.

(*a*) 18

(*b*) 20

(*c*) 22

(*d*) 24

(*e*) 26

5. Adam incurred a loss by selling a TV set for Rs. 4,280. Bob earned a profit by the same percentage when he sold a similar TV set for Rs. 4,720. At what price (in Rs.) should the TV set be sold to make a profit of $16\frac{2}{3}\%$?

(*a*) 5250

(*b*) 4950

(*c*) 5400

(*d*) 5512

(*e*) 5521

6. Nancy sold his ipod to Trixy at a loss of 12%. After using it for a few days, Trixy sold it off to her friend, Megan at a profit of 20%. Had Megan bought it directly from Nancy spending the same amount, what would have been the profit for Nancy?

(*a*) 1.2%

(*b*) 4.2%

(*c*) 5.6%

(*d*) 8%

(*e*) 6.5

7. Sam went to the shop with Rs. 300 to buy flour. The price of flour has fallen down by 15%, so he could buy an extra of 3 kg. What was the approximate original price of one kilo flour?

(*a*) Rs. 15

(*b*) Rs. 17.65

(*c*) Rs. 20.25

(*d*) Rs. 13.04

(*e*) Rs. 16.15

8. A trader, who has 90 units of an article, makes a profit equals the cost price of 12 units of the article on selling 50 units of it. If the profit made on selling the rest of units of the article equals the cost price of 10 units, then what is the percentage profit of the trader?

(*a*) 55.55

(*b*) 24.44

(*c*) 23.33

(*d*) 22.22

(*e*) 25.22

9. A container contains a mixture of wine and water in the ratio 1 : 3. What percentage of the mixture should a butler replace with another mixture that contains wine and water in the ratio 3 : 1 in order to make 100% profit by selling the resultant mixture at the price of the pure wine ? (Assume the cost price of water is negligible)

(*a*) 20

(*b*) 25

(*c*) 50

(*d*) 100

(*e*) 75

10. The ratio of the speeds of top three position holders in a marathon is 2 : 4 : 5. Find the ratio of their respective ratio of time to speed.

(*a*) 10:5:4

(*b*) 100:25:16

(*c*) 10:25:16

(*d*) 20:12:9

(*e*) 25:16:20

11. A 30% milk-water solution is mixed with another n% milk-water solution to get a 45% final solution. Every five parts of this solution has two parts of 30% milk-water solution. What is the value of 'n' ?

(*a*) 48

(*b*) 52

(*c*) 55

(*d*) 67.5

(*e*) 50

12. Prakash and Ajay started a business with initial investments in the ratio of 2 : 5 respectively. After 4 months, Ajay pulled out of the business and 2 months later, Niraj joined it by investing 40% less than Ajay. At the end of the year, they made a profit of Rs. 46,500. What is the share of profit for Ajay?

(*a*) Rs. 18,000

(*b*) Rs. 16,500

(*c*) Rs. 15,000

(*d*) Rs. 13,500

(*e*) Rs. 18,500

13. A milkman mixes milk and water in the ratio 9 : 1 respectively and sells the mixture at the cost price of milk. But while selling the mixture, he uses a measurement of 950 ml instead of 1 liter. If water comes free of cost, then the percentage profit made by the milkman is

(*a*) 16.37

(*b*) 17.37

(*c*) 17.96

(*d*) 16.96

(*e*) 14.28

14. The ratio of two numbers is 5 : 6. If the ratio becomes 4 : 5 on subtracting 3 from both the numbers, what is the absolute difference between the two numbers?

(*a*) 1

(*b*) 2

(*c*) 4

(*d*) 5

(*e*) 3

15. A, B and C started a business in partnership, with an investment of Rs. 60,000 by each. B withdrew one-third of his capital after four months, whereas C withdrew two-thirds of his capital after eight months. At the end of the year, the profit share of C was Rs. 2,100. What was the total amout (in Rs.) of profit in the business at the end of the year?

(*a*) 6600

(*b*) 9900

(*c*) 7200

(*d*) 6900

(*e*) 6500

16. A shopkeeper mixed two varieties of tea costing Rs. 280 per kg and Rs. 360 per kg. If he sells the mixture at Rs. 330 per kg by making 10% profit, then what is the quantity of tea costing Rs. 280 per kg in the mixture of 68 kg?

(*a*) 17 kg

(*b*) 34 kg

(*c*) 48 kg

(*d*) 51 kg

(*e*) 46 kg

17. A container contains 10 liters of water-milk solution, with water and milk in the ratio 2 : 3. X liters of the solution is taken out and replaced with X + 2 liters of water. If the ratio of water to milk in the resulting solution is 3 : 2, then find the value of X.

(*a*) 4

(*b*) 1

(*c*) 3

(*d*) 2

(*e*) 5

18. Raghu invests a sum of money with the bank at a certain rate of simple interest. He receives a sum of Rs. 645 at the end of the fourth year and Rs. 690 at the end of the fifth year. Find the amount invested by him.

(*a*) Rs. 465

(*b*) Rs. 500

(*c*) Rs. 555

(*d*) Rs. 180

(*e*) Rs. 395

19. A man purchases 11 pencils for Rs. 10 and sells 10 pencils for Rs. 11. How much profit or loss does he make?

(*a*) 11.33%

(*b*) 11%

(*c*) 21%

(*d*) 9.09%

(*e*) 25%

20. A timber merchant uses a weight of 950 g for weighing 1 kg of timber. If he gives a discount of 5% on the marked price which is 20% more than his cost price, then the percentage profit made by the merchant is

(*a*) 25

(*b*) 20

(*c*) 22

(*d*) 21

(*e*) $16\frac{2}{3}$

21. A sum of Rs. 20,000 is invested in three schemes, which offer simple interest at rates (in p.a.) of 2%, 3% and 4% respectively, in the ratio 5 : 8 : 7. What is the effective annual rate of interest?

(*a*) 3%

(*b*) 3.1%

(*c*) 3.2%

(*d*) 2.9%

(*e*) 2.5%

22. A milkman mixes water and milk in the ratio 2 : 23 and sells the mixture at Rs. 48/liter. If the cost price of milk and water is Rs. 48/liter and Rs. 10/liter respectively, the percentage profit made by the milkman is

(*a*) 6.23

(*b*) 6.76

(*c*) 6.33

(*d*) 6.50

(*e*) 5.00

23. A shopkeeper mixes Basmati rice costing Rs. 28/kg and Sabarmati rice costing Rs. 32/kg in the ratio 5 : 3. What must be the marked price per kg of the mixture, so that the shopkeeper gains 10% even after allowing a discount of 2%?

(*a*) Rs. 32.50

(*b*) Rs. 33.50

(*c*) Rs. 33.11

(*d*) Rs. 32.00

(*e*) Rs. 35.00

24. Three vessels A, B and C, whose capacities are in ratio 3 : 4 : 5 are full up to the brim with alcohol-water solution of concentration 40%, 55% and 75% respectively. If the contents of the three vessels are poured into a new vessel D, then find the concentration of alcohol in D.

(*a*) 50%

(*b*) 56%

(*c*) 59.6%

(*d*) 66%

(*e*) 62.5%

25. A, B and C together started a joint venture. The amount invested by A was one-third of the amount invested by B and the amount invested by C was half of the amount invested by B. B withdrew the amount invested by him after some time. If the profit at the end of year was distributed in the ratio 2 : 4 : 3, then after how many months did B withdraw his investment?

(*a*) 6

(*b*) 3

(*c*) 8

(*d*) 2

(*e*) 5

26. What is the value of the ratio of the larger value of x and the smaller value of x if $x^2 - 3\sqrt{x} + 2 = 0$?

(a) $\frac{2}{1}$

(b) $\frac{3}{1}$

(c) $\frac{4}{1}$

(d) $\frac{9}{2}$

(e) $\frac{5}{1}$

27. A 90-ml mixture of water and spirit is prepared and left outside for a fixed time; 30 ml of the mixture is evaporated. If 10 ml of only water is left outside, 2 ml of water evaporates at the same time, and if 10 ml of only spirit is left outside, 6 ml of spirit evaporates at the same time. What is the ratio of water to spirit by volume in the mixture?

(a) 1:2

(b) 1:4

(c) 2:3

(d) 1:1

(e) 2:1

28. At company X, one-tenth of the male staff and one-fourth of the female staff play sports. If the number of males is half that of females, what fraction of the staff plays sports?

(a) $\frac{1}{3}$

(b) $\frac{1}{4}$

(c) $\frac{1}{5}$

(d) $\frac{1}{6}$

(e) $\frac{1}{7}$

29. If a factory worker rejects 0.07% of spanners as defective, how many spanners does he examine to reject 700 spanners?

(a) 7

(b) 49

(c) 100

(d) 10,000

(e) 1,000,000

30. If a sum of money becomes four times of itself in 15 years, what is the simple rate of interest per annum?

(a) 10%

(b) 20%

(c) 22%

(d) 25%

(e) 30%

31. On sunny days, 10 equally efficient laborers can build a 100-meter-long wall in 5 days; a company ordered them to build a 220-meter-long wall. If a laborer can perform 10% faster on a cloudy day as compared to a sunny day, how many equally efficient laborers are required to complete this job in 5 cloudy days?

(a) 10

(b) 20

(c) 22

(d) 40

(e) 50

32. If a and b are positive integers and c and d are negative integers, and each of them ends with the digit 2, what is the units digit of $(a + b + c + d)$?

(a) 0

(b) 1

(c) 2

(d) 3

(e) 4

33. If a decimal number 65.4n7 rounded to the nearest tenth is less than 65.5, how many values can n take?

(a) Two

(b) Three

(c) Four

(d) Five

(e) Six

34. If n is even, which of the following CANNOT be odd?

I. $4n + 9$

II. $5n - 4$

III. $5n^4 + 3$

(a) I only

(b) II only

(c) III only

(d) I and II

(e) All three

35. If n is an even integer, which of the following is an odd integer?

(a) $n^2 + 4$

(b) $5n^2 - 5$

(c) $3n^3 - 4$

(d) $3n - 4$

(e) $5n^2 + 4$

36. A 90-ml mixture of water and spirit is prepared and left outside for a fixed time; 30 ml of the mixture is evaporated. If 10 ml of only water is left outside, 2 ml of water evaporates at the same time, and if 10 ml of only spirit is left outside, 6 ml of spirit evaporates at the same time. What is the ratio of water to spirit by volume in the mixture?

(a) 1 : 2

(b) 1 : 4

(c) 2 : 3

(d) 1 : 1

(e) 2 : 1

37. At company X, one-tenth of the male staff and one-fourth of the female staff play sports. If the number of males is half that of females, what fraction of the staff plays sports?

(a) $\frac{1}{3}$

(b) $\frac{1}{4}$

(c) $\frac{1}{5}$

(d) $\frac{1}{6}$

(e) $\frac{1}{7}$

38. What is the value of $\sqrt{11}$ percent of $11\sqrt{11}$?

(a) 0.121

(b) 1.1

(c) 1.21

(d) 1.331

(e) 11

39. If a factory worker rejects 0.07% of spanners as defective, how many spanners does he examine to reject 700 spanners?

(a) 7

(b) 49

(c) 100

(d) 10,000

(e) 1,000,000

40. If a sum of money becomes four times of itself in 15 years, what is the simple rate of interest per annum?

(*a*) 10%

(*b*) 20%

(*c*) 22%

(*d*) 25%

(*e*) 30%

41. Simple interest on a certain sum for 5 years at 5% per annum is one-fourth of the compound interest on $10,000 for 3 years at 10% per annum. What is the sum put on simple interest?

(*a*) $3,331

(*b*) $4,000

(*c*) $4,444

(*d*) $5,000

(*e*) $5,555

42. How many numbers between 10 and 10,000 have the digit '6' in the units place and the digit '3' in the tens place?

(*a*) 91

(*b*) 99

(*c*) 100

(*d*) 191

(*e*) 999

43. A book seller increased the price of a book by 40%. If he sold the book at a discount of 20%, what was his actual profit percentage?

(*a*) 10%

(*b*) 12%

(*c*) 22%

(*d*) 20%

(*e*) 40%

Answer Key

1. (*b*)
2. (*c*)
3. (*a*)
4. (*d*)
5. (*a*)
6. (*c*)
7. (*b*)
8. (*b*)
9. (*c*)
10. (*b*)
11. (*c*)
12. (*c*)
13. (*d*)
14. (*e*)
15. (*d*)
16. (*d*)
17. (*d*)
18. (*a*)
19. (*c*)
20. (*b*)
21. (*b*)
22. (*b*)
23. (*c*)
24. (*c*)
25. (*c*)
26. (*c*)
27. (*e*)
28. (*c*)
29. (*e*)
30. (*b*)
31. (*b*)
32. (*a*)
33. (*d*)
34. (*b*)
35. (*b*)
36. (*e*)
37. (*c*)
38. (*c*)
39. (*e*)
40. (*b*)
41. (*a*)
42. (*c*)
43. (*b*)

Answer Explanations

1. **(b)** Number of blue pens before purchase

$$= 45\% \times 80 = 36$$

Total number of pens after purchase

$$= 80 + 82 = 162$$

Number of blue pens out of the total pens

$$= 50\% \times 162 = 81$$

Number of blue pens required from the purchase

$$= 81 - 36 = 45$$

The correct answer is option (b)

2. **(c)** Let the selling price of one article be Rs. x.

Hence, the percentage profit

$$= \frac{12x}{84x - 12x} \times 100 = 16.67.$$

3. **(a)** Let salary of A, B, C be a, b, c

$$a = 1.2\,b = \frac{6}{5} \times b$$

$$b = 1.25\,c = \frac{5}{4} \times c$$

$$\text{so, } a = \frac{6}{5} \times \frac{5}{4} \times c = \frac{3}{2} \times c$$

$$\frac{a}{c} = \frac{3}{2}$$

means if a = 3 then c = 2

c is less than a by $\frac{1}{3}$ or 33.3%

Option (a) is correct.

4. **(d)** The two equations can be written as m% of 2500 + n% of

(3700 – 2500) = 788

$\Rightarrow$ 25m + 12n = 788 ...(i)

and m% of 2500 + n% of (5000 – 2500)

= 1100

$\Rightarrow$ 25m + 25n = 1100 ...(ii)

Subtracting (i) from (ii), we get

13n = 312

$\Rightarrow$ n = 24.

5. **(a)** Let the cost price of the TV set be Rs. x.

It is given that:

Loss percentage for Govind = Profit percentage for Bob

$$\Rightarrow \frac{x - 4280}{x} = \frac{4720 - x}{x}$$

$$\Rightarrow x = \frac{4280 + 4720}{2} = 4500$$

Therefore, cost price of the TV set

= Rs. 4,500

To earn a profit of $16\frac{2}{3}\%$, selling price of the TV set

$$= 4500 + 16\frac{2}{3}\% \text{ of } 4500 = \text{Rs. } 5{,}250.$$

6. **(c)** Let the CP of the ipod be Rs. 100.

Then SP of the ipod for Nancy = CP for Trixy = Rs. 88

Again, CP of the ipod for Megan = SP for Trixy = 1.2 × 88 = Rs. 105.6

In case, Megan had bought the ipod directly from Nancy, the profit for Nancy

$$= \frac{105.6 - 100}{100} \times 100 = 5.6\%$$

7. **(b)** Since the price of flour has decreased by 15%, so Sam saved 15% of Rs. 300 = Rs. 45.

With this savings, he bought 3 kilos of flour.

∴ New price of 1 kilo of flour = Rs. 15

Therefore, original price of 1kg of flour

$$= \frac{15}{0.85} \approx \text{Rs. } 17.65.$$

8. (b) Let the cost price of 90 units of article be Rs. 90.

Selling price of 90 units of article

= Selling price of 50 units of article + Selling price of 40 units of article

$= 62 + 50 = \text{Rs. } 112.$

The profit percentage

$$= \frac{112-90}{90} \times 100 = 24.44.$$

9. (c) In order to make a profit of 100%, quantity of wine in the resultant mixture should be twice of the initial quantity, which means ratio of wine and water in the resultant mixture will be 1 : 1.

Let the required percent be k.

$$\therefore \frac{1\times\left(\frac{100-k}{100}\right)+3\times\left(\frac{k}{100}\right)}{3\times\left(\frac{100-k}{100}\right)+1\times\left(\frac{k}{100}\right)} = \frac{1}{1}$$

$\Rightarrow$ $k = 50.$

10. (b) Let the distance be LCM (2,4,5) i.e. 20 units. Therefore, the respective ratio of the time taken by them = 10 : 5 : 4.

$$\text{Hence, the ratio} = \frac{10}{2} : \frac{5}{4} : \frac{4}{5} = 100 : 25 : 16.$$

11. (c) **Using allegation :**

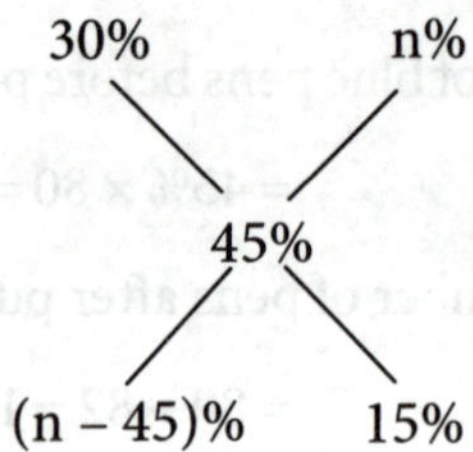

i.e 2 : 3

$$\text{Therefore, } \frac{n-45}{15} = \frac{2}{3} \text{ or } n = 55.$$

12. (c) Let the initial investments of Prakash and Ajay be Rs. 2k and Rs. 5k respectively.

Total investment of Prakash = 12 × 2k = Rs. 24k

Ajay = 4 × 5k = Rs. 20k

Niraj = 6 × 0.6 × 5k = Rs. 18k

∴ Ratio of profit sharing for Prakash, Ajay and Niraj

= 24 : 20 : 18 = 12 : 10 : 9

Therefore, Ajay's share of profit

$$= \frac{10}{12+10+9} \times 46500$$

= Rs. 15,000.

13. (d) Let the total volume of the mixture be 10x litres. The profit percentage

$$= \frac{\frac{1000}{950} \times 10x - 9x}{9x} \times 100 \approx 16.96$$

14. (e) Let the two numbers be 5x and 6x.

$$\therefore \frac{5x-3}{6x-3} = \frac{4}{5}$$

$\Rightarrow$ $x = 3.$

Hence, the absolute difference = 18 – 15 = 3

15. (d) Let the total profit be Rs. x.

The ratio of investments of A, B and C

= (60000 × 12) : (60000 × + 40000 × 8) : (60000 × 8 + 20000 × 4)

= 9 : 7 : 7.

$$\therefore \quad \frac{7}{9+7+7} \times x = 2100$$

$$\Rightarrow \quad x = 6900.$$

16. (d) Let the quantity of tea costing Rs. 280 per kg in the mixture be x kg.

$$\text{Cost price of the mixture} = \frac{330}{1.1} = \text{Rs. } 300$$

$$\frac{x \times 280 + (68 - x) \times 360}{68} = 300$$

$$\Rightarrow \quad x = 51.$$

17. (d) The volume of the new solution

= 10 + 2 = 12 liters

The quantity of water in the new solution

$$= \frac{2}{5} \times 10 - \frac{2}{5} X + (x+2) = 12 \times \frac{3}{5}$$

$$\Rightarrow \quad X = 2$$

18. (a) Simple interest on Rs. 645 for 1 year

= 690 – 645 = Rs. 45

Simple interest for 4 years

= 45 × 4 = Rs. 180

∴ Principal = 645 – 180 = Rs. 465.

19. (c) Suppose the person bought 11 × 10 pencils.

$$\text{CP of 110 pencils} = \frac{10}{11} \times 110 = \text{Rs. } 100$$

$$\text{SP of 110 pencils} = \frac{10}{11} \times 110 = \text{Rs. } 121$$

$$\therefore \text{percentage profit} = \frac{121 - 100}{100} \times 100 = 21\%.$$

20. (b) Let the CP of timber be Rs. 1000/kg.

Actual CP for the timber merchant = Rs. 950 (since he uses a false weight of 950 gm)

Marked price = 1.2 × 1000 = Rs. 1200

$$\text{SP} = 1200\left(1 - \frac{5}{100}\right) = \text{Rs. } 1140$$

Profit = Rs. 1140 – 950 = Rs. 190

$$\text{Profit percentage} = \frac{190}{950} \times 100 = 20.$$

21. (b) The amounts invested at the rates of 2%, 3% and 4% come out to be Rs. 5000, Rs. 8000 and Rs. 7000 respectively. Total interest earned

$$= \left(\frac{5000 \times 2 \times 1}{100} + \frac{8000 \times 3 \times 1}{100} + \frac{7000 \times 4 \times 1}{100}\right)$$

= Rs. 620

Hence, the effective rate of interest

$$= \frac{620 \times 100}{20000} = 3.1\% \text{ p.a.}$$

22. (b) Since the ratio of water and milk in the mixture is 2 : 23, their respective percentages will be 8% and 92%. Cost price of 1 liter adulterated milk

= (0.92 × 48 + 0.08 × 10) = Rs. 44.96

Selling price = Rs. 48

Hence, profit percentage

$$= \frac{3.04}{44.96} \times 100 = 6.76\%$$

23. (c) Average price of mixture

$$= \frac{28 \times 5 + 32 \times 3}{8} = \text{Rs.}29.5/\text{kg.}$$

The selling price, in order to gain 10% must be $29.5 \times 1.1 = \text{Rs. } 32.45$

Let the marked price be Rs x/kg.

$\Rightarrow \quad 0.98 \times x = 32.45$

$\Rightarrow \quad x = 33.11.$

24. (c) Let the capacities of the vessels be 3, 4 and 5 litres respectively.

$\Rightarrow$ The concentration of alcohol in vessel D

$$= \frac{3 \times 40 + 4 \times 55 + 5 \times 75}{3 + 4 + 5} = \frac{715}{12} = 59.6\%$$

25. (c) The amounts invested by A, B and C are in the ratio 2 : 6 : 3.

Let the number of months after which B withdrew his amount be x.

$\therefore \quad 2 \times 12 : 6 \times x : 3 \times 12 = 2 : 4 : 3$

$\Rightarrow \quad x = 8.$

26. (c) This is indeed a quadratic equation, though it does not look like one as we do not see a squared term; however, the equation can be solved by applying the concept of quadratic equation.

Say $\sqrt{x}$ = y, then the equation becomes $y^2 - 3y + 2 = 0$. It is a quadratic equation. Let's solve this.

$y^2 - 3y + 2 = 0$

$y^2 - 2y - y + 2 = 0$

$y(y - 2) - 1(y - 2) = 0$

$(y - 2)(y - 1) = 0$

So, $y = 2$ or 1.

$\sqrt{x} = 2$ or 1

$x = 4$ or 1

Thus, the ratio of the larger value of x and the smaller value of $x = \frac{4}{1}$.

27. (e) Let w be the volume of water and s be the volume of spirit in the mixture; thus, $w + s = 90$.

2 ml of water evaporates out of 10ml at the given time;

$\Rightarrow$ evaporated water percentage

$= 20\% = 0.2.$

Hence, from the mixture of 90 ml, water evaporated = $0.2w$ ml.

Also, 6 ml of spirit evaporates out of 10 ml at the given time;

$\Rightarrow$ evaporated spirit percentage = 60% = 0.6.

So, the volume of spirit evaporated = $0.6s$ ml.

Now we have,

$0.2w + 0.6s = 30$; given that the evaporated mixture volume is 30 ml.

We also know that $w + s = 90$.

Solving the above two simultaneous equations, we get $s = 30$ and $w = 60$

$\Rightarrow \quad w : s = 2 : 1$

The correct answer is Option (e).

28. (c) Since the number of male staff is half that of female staff, it means that 2M = F.

Let us assume that the total number of staff is 300. Therefore, the number of male staff = 100 and the number of female staff = 200. We chose 300 because it is a convenient figure; you may choose any number.

Number of male staff that play sports

$= \frac{100}{10} = 10$

Number of female staff that play sports

$= \frac{200}{4} = 50$

Total staff that play sports = 10 + 50 = 60

The fraction of the staff that play sports

$= \frac{60}{300} = \frac{1}{5}$

29. (e) Say, the worker examines x number of spanners.

So, 0.07% of $x = 700$

$\Rightarrow \quad x = \frac{700}{0.07\%} = \frac{700}{\frac{0.07}{100}}$

$= \frac{700 \times 100}{0.07} = 1{,}000{,}000$ spanners.

30. (b) Let the sum P be \$100, so it becomes A = Amount = 4 × \$100 = \$400 in $t = 15$ years

Thus, SI = 400 – 100 = \$300

We know that $SI = \frac{p \times r \times t}{100}$

$\Rightarrow \quad r = \frac{SI \times 100}{P \times t}$

$r = \frac{300 \times 100}{100 \times 15} = 20\%$

31. (b) On sunny days, 10 laborers can build a 100-meter-long wall in 5 days.

Therefore, one laborer can build $\frac{100}{10}$

= 10-meter-long wall in 5 days.

If a laborer can perform 10% faster on a cloudy day, then he can build 10 × 1.1 = 11 meter long wall in 5 days.

Number of laborers required to build a 220-meter-long wall in 5 cloudy days

$= \frac{220}{11} = 20$

32. (a) The integers $a,b,c,$ and d can have any number of digits; however, for this question, it is not important to know how many digits each integer has as while adding the integers, we first add units digits, so the addition of unit digits of $a,b,c,$ and d would be $2 + 2 + (-2) + (-2) = 4 - 4 = 0$.

Alternatively, you can assume some values for a, b, c, and d. Say $a = 2{,}452$, $b = 32$, $c = -82$, and $d = -2$. It is clear that the units digit of the sum of a, b, c, and d would be 0.

The correct answer is Option (a).

33. (d) Note that n must be less than '5' for if n were '5' or greater than 5, the tenth digit '4' of the number 65.4n7 would be rounded off to '5' ('4' is increased by 1) and the number would be '25.5'.

So, to keep the number less than '65.5', the set of values of n = {0, 1, 2, 3, 4}. So n can have five values.

Note that we must not start rounding off from the right-most digit, i.e., '7'. Had you done this way, since '7' is greater than '5', you would round up n to $(n + 1)$. Thus, the set of values of n + 1 = {0, 1, 2, 3, 4} and the set of values of n = {0, 1, 2, 3}. So n would have four values, which is incorrect.

The correct answer is Option (d).

34. **(b)** The question is if **n** is even, which of the following CANNOT be odd?

Results of the product of Even and Odd numbers

- Even × Even = Even
- Even × Odd = Even
- Odd × Odd = ODD

It must be noted that if there is only one even number, the product is even; whereas, if the product of two numbers is Odd, then both the numbers must be Odd.

Let us look at the options one by one.

1. $4n + 9$: In this option, 4 and n are even, whereas 9 is odd.

   So, $4n + 9$ = even × even + odd = even + odd = odd.

   Thus, $(4n + 9)$ is an odd number.

II. $5n - 4$: In this option, 4 and n are even, whereas 5 is odd.

   So, $5n - 4$ = odd × even − even = even − even = even.

   Thus, $(5n - 4)$ is an even number. **correct answer.**

III. $5n^4 + 3$: In this option, n is even, whereas 5 and 3 are odd. Any positive exponent of an even number is also an even.

   So, $5n^4 + 3$ = odd × even + odd

   = even + odd = odd.

   Thus, $(5n^4 + 3)$ is an odd number.

The correct answer is Option (b).

35. **(b)** The efficient approach to solve this question is by assuming a convenient value for the even integer n. Say $n = 2$. You may also choose 0; note 0 is an even number.

Let's take each option one by one by plugging-in the value of $n = 2$. You may even choose 0.

(*a*) $n^2 + 4 \Rightarrow 2^2 + 4 = 4 + 4 = 8$, an even number

(*b*) $5n^2 - 5 \Rightarrow 5 \times 2^2 - 5 = 20 - 5 = 15$, an odd number : correct answer

(*c*) $3n^3 - 4 \Rightarrow 3 \times 2^3 - 4 = 24 - 4 = 20$, an even number

(*d*) $3n - 4 \Rightarrow 3 \times 2 - 4 = 6 - 4 = 2$, an even number

(*e*) $5n^2 + 4 \Rightarrow 5 \times 2^2 + 5 = 20 + 4 = 24$. an even number

The correct answer is Option (b).

36. **(e)** Let w be the volume of water and s be the volume of spirit in the mixture; thus, $w + s = 90$.

2 ml of water evaporates out of 10ml at the given time;

⇒ evaporated water percentage

$= 20\% = 0.2.$

Hence, from the mixture of 90 ml, water evaporated $= 0.2w$ ml.

Also, 6 ml of spirit evaporates out of 10 ml at the given time;

⇒ evaporated spirit percentage

$= 60\% = 0.6.$

So, the volume of spirit evaporated

$= 0.6s$ ml.

Now we have,

$0.2w + 0.6s = 30$; given that the evaporated mixture volume is 30 ml.

We also know that $w + s = 90$.

Solving the above two simultaneous equations, we get $s = 30$ and $w = 60$

$\Rightarrow \quad w:s = 2:1.$

37. (c) Since the number of male staff is half that of female staff, it means that 2M = F.

Let us assume that the total number of staff is 300. Therefore, the number of male staff = 100 and the number of female staff = 200. We choose 300 because it is a convenient figure; you may choose any number.

Number of male staff that play sports

$$= \frac{100}{10} = 10$$

Number of female staff that play sports

$$= \frac{200}{4} = 50$$

Total staff that play sports = 10 + 50 = 60

The fraction of the staff that play sports

$$= \frac{60}{300} = \frac{1}{5}$$

38. (c) We have to get the value of $\sqrt{11}$ percent of $11\sqrt{11}$.

$\sqrt{11}$ percent of $11\sqrt{11} = \sqrt{11}\,\%$ of $11\sqrt{11}$

$$\frac{\sqrt{11} \times 11\sqrt{11}}{100} = \frac{11^2}{100} = 1.21$$

39. (e) Say, the worker examines x number of spanners.

So, 0.07% of $x = 700$

$$\Rightarrow \quad x = \frac{700}{0.07\%} = \frac{700}{\frac{0.07}{100}}$$

$$= \frac{700 \times 100}{0.07} = 1{,}000{,}000 \text{ spanners.}$$

40. (b) Let the sum P be \$100, so it becomes A

= Amount = 4 × \$400 in $t = 15$ years

Thus, SI = 400 – 100 = \$300

We know that $SI = \frac{p \times r \times t}{100}$

$$\Rightarrow \quad r = \frac{SI \times 100}{P \times t}$$

$$r = \frac{300 \times 100}{100 \times 15}$$

$$r = 20\%.$$

41. (a) Let's first compute compound interest.

We know that $CI = P\left[\left(1 + \frac{r}{100}\right)^n - 1\right]$;

where CI = Compound interest; P = Principal (Sum); r = Rate of interest; n = Number of compounding (time)

$$CI = 10{,}000\left[\left(1 + \frac{10}{100}\right)^3 - 1\right]$$

$$= 10{,}000\left[\left(\frac{11}{10}\right)^3 - 1\right]$$

$$= 10{,}000\left[\frac{1{,}331}{1{,}000} - 1\right]$$

$$= 10{,}000\,[1.331 - 1]$$

$$CI = 10{,}000 \times 0.331 = \$3{,}331$$

So, Simple interest = $\frac{1}{4}$ of Compound interest

We know that $SI = \frac{p \times r \times t}{100}$; where

SI = Simple interest; P = Principal (Sum); r = Rate of interest; n = time (in years)

$$SI = \frac{P \times 5 \times 5}{100} = \frac{1}{4} \times 3{,}331$$

P = \$3,331, upon simplification.

42. (c) There is only 'one' two-digit number having the digit '6' in the units place and the digit '3' in the tens place, i.e., 36.

Of the three-digit numbers with the units and tens digits 6 and 3, respectively, the hundreds digit may be chosen from '1' to '9' in 9 ways. Thus, there are 'nine' such three-digit numbers.

Of the four-digit numbers with the units and tens digits 6 and 3, respectively, the thousands digit may be chosen from '1' to '9' in 9 ways and the hundreds digit may be chosen from '0' to '9' in 10 ways. Total number of ways of choosing the two digits. Thus, there are 90 such four-digit numbers.

There is no five-digit number having the digit '6' in the unit's place and the digit '3' in the tens place since the last number is 10,000, which is the least possible five-digit number.

Thus, we have such numbers.

43. (b) Let x be the initial price of a book.

After the 40% increase, the new price would be $\left(x+\frac{40}{100}\times x\right)=1.4x$.

After discount, the price would be $1.4x-1.4x\times\left(\frac{20}{100}\right)$

or $1.4x\times(1-0.2)=1.12x$.

Therefore, the actual profit percentage

$$=\left[\frac{(1.12x-x)}{x}\right]\times 100\% = 12\%.$$

Data Sufficiency

1. If m and n are both greater than 0, what is the value of m?

   I. m is 200% of n.

   II. $m \times n = z^2$, where z is a positive integer.

   (*a*) Statement (I) ALONE is sufficient but statement (II) ALONE is not sufficient.

   (*b*) Statement (II) ALONE is sufficient but statement (I) ALONE is not sufficient.

   (*c*) BOTH statements TOGETHER are sufficient, but NEITHER statement ALONE is sufficient.

   (*d*) EACH statement ALONE is sufficient.

   (*e*) Statements (I) and (II) TOGETHER are not sufficient.

2. If x and y are positive and $\frac{x}{y}$ is greater than 110 percent, is x greater than 35?

   I. $y > 35$

   II. $x = 10 + y$

   (*a*) Statement (I) ALONE is sufficient but statement (II) ALONE is not sufficient.

   (*b*) Statement (II) ALONE is sufficient but statement (I) ALONE is not sufficient.

   (*c*) BOTH statements TOGETHER are sufficient, but NEITHER statement ALONE is sufficient.

   (*d*) EACH statement ALONE is sufficient.

   (*e*) Statements (I) and (II) TOGETHER are not sufficient.

3. Which one is greater in a stationary shop: the total number of pens and pencils, or the number of sharpeners?

   I. The ratio of the number of sharpeners to the number of pens to the number of pencils in the shop is 33 : 17 : 21.

   II. The total number of sharpeners, pens, and pencils in the shop is 142.

   (*a*) Statement (I) ALONE is sufficient but statement (II) ALONE is not sufficient.

   (*b*) Statement (II) ALONE is sufficient but statement (I) ALONE is not sufficient.

   (*c*) BOTH statements TOGETHER are sufficient, but NEITHER statement ALONE is sufficient.

   (*d*) EACH statement ALONE is sufficient.

   (*e*) Statements (I) and (II) TOGETHER are not sufficient.

4. What is the number of type 2 widgets produced if the total number of widgets produced is 20,000?

   I. If the number of type 1 widgets produced is higher by 10% and that of type 2 is lower by 6%, the total production remains the same.

   II. The ratio in which type 1 and type 2 are produced is 2 : 3.

   (*a*) Statement (I) ALONE is sufficient but statement (II) ALONE is not sufficient.

   (*b*) Statement (II) ALONE is sufficient but statement (I) ALONE is not sufficient.

   (*c*) BOTH statements TOGETHER are sufficient, but NEITHER statement ALONE is sufficient.

   (*d*) EACH statement ALONE is sufficient.

   (*e*) Statements (I) and (II) TOGETHER are not sufficient.

5. What is the profit percentage made by the shopkeeper?

   I. Selling price of 100 eggs is Rs. 120.

   II. Cost price is two-thirds of the selling price.

   (*a*) Statement (I) ALONE is sufficient but statement (II) ALONE is not sufficient.

   (*b*) Statement (II) ALONE is sufficient but statement (I) ALONE is not sufficient.

   (*c*) BOTH statements TOGETHER are sufficient, but NEITHER statement ALONE is sufficient.

(*d*) EACH statement ALONE is sufficient.

(*e*) Statements (I) and (II) TOGETHER are not sufficient.

6. Steve's running speed is what percent of his walking speed?

I. Steve takes 40 minutes to walk from his home to the office and return home running.

III. Steve takes 30 minutes to run from his home to the office and return home running.

(*a*) Statement (I) ALONE is sufficient but statement (II) ALONE is not sufficient.

(*b*) Statement (II) ALONE is sufficient but statement (I) ALONE is not sufficient.

(*c*) BOTH statements TOGETHER are sufficient, but NEITHER statement ALONE is sufficient.

(*d*) EACH statement ALONE is sufficient.

(*e*) Statements (I) and (II) TOGETHER are not sufficient.

7. Amy travels from Stop X to Stop Y, and Betty travels from Stop Y to Stop X. At what time do they meet on the way?

I. Amy starts at 10:00 am, and Betty starts at 1 : 00 pm.

II. Amy takes 10 hours to reach Stop Y, and Betty takes 5 hours to reach Stop X.

(*a*) Statement (I) ALONE is sufficient but statement (II) ALONE is not sufficient.

(*b*) Statement (II) ALONE is sufficient but statement (I) ALONE is not sufficient.

(*c*) BOTH statements TOGETHER are sufficient, but NEITHER statement ALONE is sufficient.

(*d*) EACH statement ALONE is sufficient.

(*e*) Statements (I) and (II) TOGETHER are not sufficient.

8. A car leaves City A at 1:00 p.m. and travels towards City B at a speed of 100 kilometers per hour. Another car leaves City A after some time. At what time will the second car overtake the first?

I. The distance between the cities is 400 kilometers, and the second car leaves at 2:00 p.m.

II. The distance between the cities is 400 kilometers, and speed of the second car is 1.5 times that of the first.

(*a*) Statement (I) ALONE is sufficient but statement (II) ALONE is not sufficient.

(*b*) Statement (II) ALONE is sufficient but statement (I) ALONE is not sufficient.

(*c*) BOTH statements TOGETHER are sufficient, but NEITHER statement ALONE is sufficient.

(*d*) EACH statement ALONE is sufficient.

(*e*) Statements (I) and (II) TOGETHER are not sufficient.

9. A and B start from their homes at the same time, move at their respective uniform speeds towards each other, and meet at Point X. If A were late by t minutes, they would have met at Point Y. What is the value of t ?

I. A and B move at speeds of 6 kilometers per hour and 12 kilometers per hour, respectively.

II. The distance between the points X and Y is 1.2 kilometers.

(*a*) Statement (I) ALONE is sufficient but statement (II) ALONE is not sufficient.

(*b*) Statement (II) ALONE is sufficient but statement (I) ALONE is not sufficient.

(*c*) BOTH statements TOGETHER are sufficient, but NEITHER statement ALONE is sufficient.

(*d*) EACH statement ALONE is sufficient.

(*e*) Statements (I) and (II) TOGETHER are not sufficient.

10. How long would it take 7 men and 3 women to paint a wall with dimensions of 30 feet by 80 feet, if all men and all women work at their respective uniform rates?

I. Fifteen men can paint a wall with dimensions of 15 feet by 90 feet in 9 hours.

II A 20-square-foot wall can be painted by two men in 1 hour or by one women in 2 hours.

(a) Statement (I) ALONE is sufficient but statement (II) ALONE is not sufficient.

(b) Statement (II) ALONE is sufficient but statement (I) ALONE is not sufficient.

(c) BOTH statements TOGETHER are sufficient, but NEITHER statement ALONE is sufficient.

(d) EACH statement ALONE is sufficient.

(e) Statements (I) and (II) TOGETHER are not sufficient.

11. If pq and r are even, is $(p + r)$ even?

I. q is even.

II. p and q are integers.

(a) Statement (I) ALONE is sufficient but statement (II) ALONE is not sufficient.

(b) Statement (II) ALONE is sufficient but statement (I) ALONE is not sufficient.

(c) BOTH statements TOGETHER are sufficient, but NEITHER statement ALONE is sufficient.

(d) EACH statement ALONE is sufficient.

(e) Statements (I) and (II) TOGETHER are not sufficient.

12. Steve's running speed is what percent of his walking speed?

I. Steve takes 40 minutes to walk from his home to the office and return home running.

II. Steve takes 30 minutes to run from his home to the office and return home running.

(a) Statement (I) ALONE is sufficient but statement (II) ALONE is not sufficient.

(b) Statement (II) ALONE is sufficient but statement (I) ALONE is not sufficient.

(c) BOTH statements TOGETHER are sufficient, but NEITHER statement ALONE is sufficient.

(d) EACH statement ALONE is sufficient.

(e) Statements (I) and (II) TOGETHER are not sufficient.

13. Amy travels from Stop X to Stop Y, and Betty travels from Stop Y to Stop X. At what time do they meet on the way?

I. Amy starts at 10:00 am, and Betty starts at 1:00 pm.

II. Amy takes 10 hours to reach Stop Y, and Betty takes 5 hours to reach Stop X.

(a) Statement (I) ALONE is sufficient but statement (II) ALONE is not sufficient.

(b) Statement (II) ALONE is sufficient but statement (I) ALONE is not sufficient.

(c) BOTH statements TOGETHER are sufficient, but NEITHER statement ALONE is sufficient.

(d) EACH statement ALONE is sufficient.

(e) Statements (I) and (II) TOGETHER are not sufficient.

14. The bill for a Dutch dinner was shared equally among friends. What was the bill amount for the Dutch dinner?

I. Each of them paid $21.

II. If there were one more friend at the dinner, each would have paid $20.

(a) Statement (I) ALONE is sufficient but statement (II) ALONE is not sufficient.

(b) Statement (II) ALONE is sufficient but statement (I) ALONE is not sufficient.

(c) BOTH statements TOGETHER are sufficient, but NEITHER statement ALONE is sufficient.

(*d*) EACH statement ALONE is sufficient.

(*e*) Statements (I) and (II) TOGETHER are not sufficient.

15. A car leaves City A at 1:00 p.m. and travels towards City B at a speed of 100 kilometers per hour. Another car leaves City A after some time. At what time will the second car overtake the first?

I. The distance between the cities is 400 kilometers, and the second car leaves at 2:00 p.m.

II. The distance between the cities is 400 kilometers, and speed of the second car is 1.5 times that of the first.

(*a*) Statement (I) ALONE is sufficient but statement (II) ALONE is not sufficient.

(*b*) Statement (II) ALONE is sufficient but statement (I) ALONE is not sufficient.

(*c*) BOTH statements TOGETHER are sufficient, but NEITHER statement ALONE is sufficient.

(*d*) EACH statement ALONE is sufficient.

(*e*) Statements (I) and (II) TOGETHER are not sufficient.

16. If *s* is a positive integer, is *s* a prime number?

I. $\frac{21}{s}$ is an integer.

II. $\frac{47}{s}$ is an integer.

(*a*) Statement (I) ALONE is sufficient but statement (II) ALONE is not sufficient.

(*b*) Statement (II) ALONE is sufficient but statement (I) ALONE is not sufficient.

(*c*) BOTH statements TOGETHER are sufficient, but NEITHER statement ALONE is sufficient.

(*d*) EACH statement ALONE is sufficient.

(*e*) Statements (I) and (II) TOGETHER are not sufficient.

17. What is the present age of Jasmine?

I. The ratio of the present ages of Jasmine and Katy is 2:3.

II. The sum of the present ages of Jasmine and Katy is 40 years.

(*a*) Statement (I) ALONE is sufficient but statement (II) ALONE is not sufficient.

(*b*) Statement (II) ALONE is sufficient but statement (I) ALONE is not sufficient.

(*c*) BOTH statements TOGETHER are sufficient, but NEITHER statement ALONE is sufficient.

(*d*) EACH statement ALONE is sufficient.

(*e*) Statements (I) and (II) TOGETHER are not sufficient.

18. A and B start from their homes at the same time, move at their respective uniform speeds towards each other, and meet at Point X. If A were late by *t* minutes, they would have met at Point Y. What is the value of *t*?

I. A and B move at speeds of 6 kilometers per hour and 12 kilometers per hour, respectively.

II. The distance between the points X and Y is 1.2 kilometers.

(*a*) Statement (I) ALONE is sufficient but statement (II) ALONE is not sufficient.

(*b*) Statement (II) ALONE is sufficient but statement (I) ALONE is not sufficient.

(*c*) BOTH statements TOGETHER are sufficient, but NEITHER statement ALONE is sufficient.

(*d*) EACH statement ALONE is sufficient.

(*e*) Statements (I) and (II) TOGETHER are not sufficient.

19. How long would it take 7 men and 3 women to paint a wall with dimensions of 30 feet by 80 feet, if all men and all women work at their respective uniform rates?

I. Fifteen men can paint a wall with dimensions of 15 feet by 90 feet in 9 hours.

II. A 20-square-foot wall can be painted by two men in 1 hour or by one woman in 2 hours.

(*a*) Statement (I) ALONE is sufficient but statement (II) ALONE is not sufficient.

(*b*) Statement (II) ALONE is sufficient but statement (I) ALONE is not sufficient.

(*c*) BOTH statements TOGETHER are sufficient, but NEITHER statement ALONE is sufficient.

(*d*) EACH statement ALONE is sufficient.

(*e*) Statements (I) and (II) TOGETHER are not sufficient.

20. John and Christian invested their money in a bank at 10% interest rate per annum. By how much, in dollars, Christian's investment was greater than John's investment?

I. After one year Christian earned \$50 more than John.

II. If the interest rate were 12%, Christian would have earned \$60 more than John.

(*a*) Statement (I) ALONE is sufficient but statement (II) ALONE is not sufficient.

(*b*) Statement (II) ALONE is sufficient but statement (I) ALONE is not sufficient.

(*c*) BOTH statements TOGETHER are sufficient, but NEITHER statement ALONE is sufficient.

(*d*) EACH statement ALONE is sufficient.

(*e*) Statements (I) and (II) TOGETHER are not sufficient.

21. To cover a particular distance, a man calculated that he would arrive on time if he traveled the first half of the distance at 20 miles per hour and the remaining half at a greater speed. What is the total distance the man traveled?

I. The man traveled the second half of the distance at 40 miles per hour and reached his destination on time.

II. Had the man traveled the second half of the distance at 30 miles per hour, he would have reached his destination 15 minutes late.

(*a*) Statement (I) ALONE is sufficient but statement (II) ALONE is not sufficient.

(*b*) Statement (II) ALONE is sufficient but statement (I) ALONE is not sufficient.

(*c*) BOTH statements TOGETHER are sufficient, but NEITHER statement ALONE is sufficient.

(*d*) EACH statement ALONE is sufficient.

(*e*) Statements (I) and (II) TOGETHER are not sufficient.

Answer Key

1. (*e*)	**7.** (*c*)	**13.** (*c*)	**19.** (*b*)
2. (*a*)	**8.** (*c*)	**14.** (*c*)	**20.** (*d*)
3. (*a*)	**9.** (*c*)	**15.** (*c*)	**21.** (*c*)
4. (*d*)	**10.** (*b*)	**16.** (*c*)	
5. (*b*)	**11.** (*e*)	**17.** (*c*)	
6. (*c*)	**12.** (*c*)	**18.** (*c*)	

Answer Explanations

1. (e) **Considering statement 1 alone :**

$m = 200\% \times n$

$m = 2n$

Not sufficient to get the single numerical value of m.

Eliminate A/D

Considering statement 2 alone :

$m \times n = z^2$, where z is a positive integer

Not sufficient to get the single numerical value of m

Eliminate B.

Considering statement 1 & 2 together :

Since from statement (1) m = 2n then from statement (2) $2n \times n = z^2$

$2n^2 = z^2$

Taking square root on both sides

Hence, $z = \sqrt{2} \times n$

We still cannot get the single numerical value of m. Insufficient.

Eliminate C.

The correct answer is option (e)

2. (a) It is given that $\frac{x}{y} > 1.1$

As y is positive, $x > 1.1y$

Considering statement 1 alone :

when $y > 35, x > 35$

Sufficient

Eliminate B/C/E

Considering statement 2 alone :

$x = 10 + y$

x could be greater than or less than 35.

Insufficient

The correct answer is option (a)

3. (a) **Considering statement 1 alone :**

The ratio of the number of sharpeners to the number of pens to the number of pencils in the shop is 33 : 17 : 21

So, the number of sharpeners are 33x, number of pens are 17x and number of pencils are 21x, where x is an integer

Hence, the total number of pens and pencils $= 17x + 21x = 38x$

The number of sharpeners are 33x

Sufficient

Eliminate B/C/E

Considering statement 2 alone :

The total number of sharpeners, pens, and pencils in the shop is 142.

Total number of three items is only given which is not sufficient to answer the question. Insufficient

The correct answer is option (a)

4. (d) Let the number of type 2 widgets produced be x. The number of type 2 widgets produced = 200 – x. From statement I,

$$(20000 - x) \times \frac{10}{100} = x \times \frac{6}{100}$$

$$\Rightarrow 2000 - \frac{x}{10} = \frac{3x}{50}$$

$\Rightarrow 2000 = \frac{8}{50}x$

$\Rightarrow x = \frac{2000 \times 50}{8} = 150 \times 50 = 12500.$

Hence, statement I alone is sufficient. From statement II, type 2 widgets

$= 20000 \times \frac{3}{5} = 4000 \times 3 = 12000.$

Hence, statement II alone is also sufficient.

The answer is (d).

5. (b) From statement I, nothing is given about the cost price. Hence statement I alone is not sufficient.

From statement II,

$CP = \frac{2}{3}SP$

$\Rightarrow \quad SP = 1.5\,CP$

Profit percentage is 50.

Hence statement II alone is sufficient.

The answer is (b).

6. (c) Let the time Steve takes to walk from his home to office be w minutes.

Let the time Steve takes to run from his home to office be r minutes.

Considering Statement 1 alone:

$r + w = 40$ ...(i)

Since the individual values of r and w are not known, the answer cannot be determined. – Insufficient

Hence, eliminate A/D.

Considering Statement 2 alone :

$r + r = 30$

$\Rightarrow \quad r = 15$ ...(ii)

However, there is no information about w. – Insufficient

Hence, eliminate B.

Considering Statements 1 and 2 together:

Using (i) and (ii):

$w = 40 - 15 = 25$ ...(iii)

Thus, the ratio of Steve's running and walking speeds is inverse of the times taken while running and walking, respectively (since the distance is constant)

$= 25 : 15 = 5 : 3$

Thus, the required percent

$= \frac{5}{3} \times 100\% = 166.7\%$ – Sufficient

The answer is (c).

7. (c) **Considering Statement 1 alone:**

There is no information about the ratio of the speeds of Amy and Betty. – Insufficient

Hence, eliminate A/D.

Considering Statement 2 alone:

There is no information about the times Amy and Betty start their respective journeys.- Insufficient

Hence, eliminate B.

Considering statements 1 and 2 together:

We know that the ratio of the times taken by Amy and Betty to cover the same distance

$= 10 : 5 = 2 : 1$

Thus, the ratio of the speeds of Amy and Betty is the inverse of the ratio of their speeds as the distance is constant.

$= 1 : 2$

Let us assume the speeds of Amy and Betty to be x miles per hour and $2x$ miles per hours.

Thus, the distance between the stops X and Y = $10 \times x = 10x$ miles or $5 \times 2x = 10x$ miles.

Since Amy started 3 hours before Berry, the distance covered by Amy from 10:00 am to 1:00 pm

Since Amy started 3 hours before Betty, the distance covered by Amy from 10:00 am to 1:00 pm

$= 3 \times x = 3x$ miles

Thus, the remaining distance

$= 10x - 3x = 7x$ miles

At 1:00 pm, both Amy and Betty are traveling towards each other.

Thus, their relative speed = $x + 2x = 3x$ miles per hour; relative speed would the sum of their speeds as they are traveling in opposite directions. Thus, time taken to meet

$$= \frac{7x}{3x} = 2.33 \text{ hours}$$

= 2 hours 20 minutes

Thus, the meeting time is 2 hours 20 minutes past 1:00 pm, i.e., 3:20 pm. – Sufficient.

The answer is (c).

8. (c) Let the first car be X and the second car be Y.

Speed of Car X is 100 kmph

The question asks us to find the time when Car Y overtakes Car X.

To answer this, we need to know the speed of Y and the time it departs from City A.

Let's see each statement one by one.

Considering Statement 1 alone:

Statement 1 only gives the time of departure of Y from City A, hence this statement alone is not sufficient.

Hence, eliminate A/D.

Considering Statement 2 alone:

Statement 2 only gives the speed of Y, which is $1.5 \times 100 = 150$ kmph, but not departure time; hence this statement alone is not sufficient.

Hence, eliminate B.

Considering statements 1 and 2 together:

Since Statement 1 gives the departure time of Car Y and Statement 2 gives its speed, statements 1 and 2 together are sufficient. There is no need to calculate the answer as this is a DS question.

For the sake of completeness, let's compute the time.

Since both cars are moving in the same direction, their relative speed = 150 – 100 = 50 kmph. Since Car Y departed after 1 hour, it has to cover = $1 \times 100 = 100$ kilometers (Distance covered by Car X in 1 hour) at a speed of 50 kmph. Thus, Car Y will take $\frac{100}{50} = 2$ hours to overtake Car X.

The answer is (c).

9. (c) Let us assume that A and B meet at 12:00 at Point X.

Since A was late by *t* minutes, we need to find out the time when A would reach X. The difference between this time and 12:00 would give us the value of *t*.

Considering Statement 1 alone:

We have no information about the position of the new meeting point, Y, with respect to the earlier meeting point, X. – Insufficient

Hence, eliminate A/D

Considering Statement 2 alone:

We have no information about the speeds of A and B. - Insufficient

Hence, eliminate B.

Considering statements 1 and 2 together:

We know that Y is 1.2 km away from X (Y is closer to A than to X since A was late).

Since B was on time, he must have reached X at 12:00 (actual meeting time).

Time taken by B to travel 1.2 km to reach point Y

$= \frac{1.2}{12} = 0.1 \text{ hours} = 6 \text{ minutes.}$

Thus, B reaches Y at 12:06 pm.

Since A and B meet at point Y, A was also at Y at 12:06 pm.

Time taken by A to cover 1.2 km to reach X

$= \frac{1.2}{6} = 0.2 \text{ hours} = 12 \text{ minutes.}$

Thus, A reaches X at 12:06 + 12 min.

= 12:18 pm.

Thus, we observe that A reaches X 18 minutes later than when he was supposed to reach.

Thus, we have $t = 18$ - Sufficient.

The answer is (c).

10. (b) **Considering Statement 1 alone:**

There is no information about the working rate of women. So, this is insufficient.

Hence, eliminate A/D.

Considering Statement 2 alone:

We have

An area painted by 2 men in 1 hour is the same as that painted by 1 woman in 2 hours. Thus, the efficiencies of men and women are the same.

Thus, we have

To paint the 20 square feet wall, 2 men take 1 hour

Thus, to paint (30 × 80) or 2,400 square feet wall, time taken by 2 men

$= \frac{1}{20} \times 2{,}400 = 120 \text{ hours}$

So, the question: *How long would 7 men and 3 women take to paint a wall having dimensions 30 feet by 80 feet? becomes...*

How long would (7 + 3 = 10) men take to paint a wall having dimensions of 2,400 square feet?

Note: Working rate of one man = Working rate of one women

Thus, to paint 2,400 square feet, time taken by 10 men

$= 120 \times \frac{2}{10} = 24 \text{ hours}$ – Sufficient

Hence, eliminate C/E.

The answer is (b).

11. (e) Given that r is even, we can write the question as : Is (p + even) even?

It will depend on the nature of p; if p is even, (p + even) would be even, else not even (odd or fraction).

From the information pq = even we cannot ascertain that p is even or odd. p can have any value even/odd/fraction. Let's see.

1. $p = \frac{1}{2}$ & $q = 4 \Rightarrow pq = \frac{1}{2} \times 4 = 2$, even
2. $p = 1$ & $q = 4 \Rightarrow pq = 1 \times 4 = 4$, even
3. $p = 2$ & $q = 4 \Rightarrow pq = 2 \times 4 = 8$, even

Question rephrased: Is p even?

Let's see each statement one by one.

Considering Statement 1 alone :

All the three cases discussed above are applicable; p can be even, odd, or fraction. Insufficient.

Hence, eliminate A/D.

Considering Statement 2 alone :

Case 2 and 3 discussed above are applicable; p can be even or odd. Insufficient.

Hence, eliminate B.

Statements 1 and 2 together :

Even both statements together are insufficient. Case 2 and 3 discussed above are applicable; p can be even or odd.

The correct answer is Option (e).

12. (c) Let the time Steve takes to walk from his home to office be w minutes.

Let the time Steve takes to run from his home to office be r minutes.

Considering Statement 1 alone :

$r + w = 40$ ...(i)

Since the individual values of r and w are not known, the answer cannot be determined. – Insufficient

Hence, eliminate A/D.

Considering Statement 2 alone :

$r + r = 30$

$\Rightarrow r = 15$ ...(ii)

However, there is no information about w. - Insufficient

Hence, eliminate B.

Considering statements 1 and 2 together :

Using (i) and (ii):

$w = 40 - 15 = 25$ ...(iii)

Thus, the ratio of Steve's running and walking speeds is inverse of the times taken while running and walking, respectively (since the distance is constant)

$= 25 : 15 = 5 : 3$

Thus, the required percent

$= \frac{5}{3} \times 100\% = 166.7\%$ - Sufficient

The answer is (c).

13. (c) **Considering Statement 1 alone :**

There is no information about the ratio of the speeds of Amy and Betty. – Insufficient

Hence, eliminate A/D.

Considering Statement 2 alone :

There is no information about the times Amy and Betty start their respective journeys.- Insufficient

Hence, eliminate B.

Considering statements 1 and 2 together :

We know that the ratio of the times taken by Amy and Betty to cover the same distance $= 10 : 5 = 2 : 1$

Thus, the ratio of the speeds of Amy and Betty is the inverse of the ratio of their speeds as the distance is constant. $= 1 : 2$

Let us assume the speeds of Amy and Betty to be x miles per hour and $2x$ miles per hour.

Thus, the distance between the stops X and Y $= 10 \times x = 10x$ miles or $5 \times 2x = 10x$ miles.

Since Amy started 3 hours before Betty, the distance covered by Amy from 10:00 am to 1:00 pm $= 3 \times x = 3x$ miles

Thus, the remaining distance $= 10x - 3x = 7x$ miles at 1:00 pm, both Amy and Betty are traveling towards each other.

Thus, their relative speed $= x + 2x = 3x$ miles per hour; relative speed would the sum of their speeds as they are traveling in opposite directions

Thus, time taken to meet

$= \frac{7x}{3x} = 2.33$ hours = 2 hours 20 minutes

Thus, the meeting time is 2 hours 20 minutes past 1:00 pm, i.e., 3:20 pm. – Sufficient.

The answer is (c).

14. (c) Say k friends had the dinners, sharing equally.

Considering Statement 1 alone :

Bill of the dinner = $21k ...(i)

However, the value of k is unknown. - Insufficient

Hence, eliminate A/D.

Considering Statement 2 alone :

Bill of the dinner = $20 $(k + 1)$ ...(ii)

However, the value of k is unknown. -Insufficient.

Hence, eliminate B.

Statement 1 and 2 together :

From (i) and (ii), we have

$21k = 20 (k + 1)$

$k = 20$

The bill amount = $21k = 21 \times 20$

= $420 – sufficient.

The answer is (c).

15. (c) Let the first car be X and the second car be Y.

Speed of Car X is 100 kmph

The question asks us to find the time when Car Y overtakes Car X.

To answer this, we need to know the speed of Y and the time it departs from City A.

Let's see each statement one by one.

Considering Statement 1 alone :

Statement 1 only gives the time of departure of Y from City A, hence this statement alone is not sufficient.

Hence, eliminate A/D.

Considering Statement 2 alone :

Statement 2 only gives the speed of Y, which is $1.5 \times 100 = 150$ kmph, but not departure time; hence this statement alone is not sufficient.

Hence, eliminate B.

Considering Statements 1 and 2 together :

Since Statement 1 gives the departure time of Car Y and Statement 2 gives its speed, statements 1 and 2 together are sufficient. There is no need to calculate the answer as this is a DS question.

For the sake of completeness, let's compute the time.

Since both cars are moving in the same direction, their relative speed = 150 – 100 = 50 kmph. Since Car Y departed after 1 hour, it has to cover = $1 \times 100 = 100$ kilometers (Distance covered by Car X in 1 hour) at a speed of 50 kmph. Thus, Car Y will take $\frac{100}{50} = 2$ hours to overtake Car X.

The answer is (c).

16. (c) **Considering Statement 1 alone:**

If $\frac{21}{s}$ is an integer, s can be any factor of 21 : 1, 3, 7, or 21. While 3 and 7 are prime numbers, 1 and 21 are not. No unique answer. This statement is insufficient.

Hence, eliminate A/D.

Considering Statement 2 alone :

If $\frac{47}{s}$ is an integer, s can be any factor of 47: 1, or 47. While 47 is a prime number, 1 is not. No unique answer. This statement is insufficient.

Hence, eliminate B.

Considering statements 1 and 2 together :

s = 1 is the only common value for both statements; a unique value; hence both statements together are sufficient.

The answer is (c).

17. (c) **Considering statements 1 alone:**

Given : $\frac{\text{Jasmine's age}}{\text{Katty's age}} = \frac{2}{3}$

For any ratio based problems, we take the ratio as follows:

Let Jasmine's age = $2k$ and Katty's age = $3k$

We cannot say anything about Jasmine's age since $2k$ can be anything say 2, 4, 6, 8, etc.

This statement alone is not sufficient.

Considering Statement 2 alone :

Sum of present ages = 40

Jasmine's age could be anything. This statement alone is not sufficient.

Hence, eliminate B.

Considering Statement 1 and 2 together :

From Statement 1, Jasmine's age = $2k$ and Katty's age = $3k$

From Statement 2, sum of ages = 40

Hence, $2k + 3k = 40 \Rightarrow 5k = 40 \Rightarrow k = 8$

Jasmine's age = $2k = 16$

Statements 1 and 2 together are sufficient.

The answer is (c).

18. (c) Let us assume that A and B meet at 12:00 at Point X.

Since A was late by t minutes, we need to find out the time when A would reach X. The difference between this time and 12:00 would give us the value of t.

Considering Statement 1 alone :

We have no information about the position of the new meeting point, Y, with respect to the earlier meeting point, X. - Insufficient

Hence, eliminate A/D.

Considering Statement 2 alone :

We have no information about the speeds of A and B. - Insufficient

Hence, eliminate B.

Considering statements 1 and 2 together :

We know that Y is 1.2 km away from X (Y is closer to A than to X since A was late).

Since B was on time, he must have reached X at 12:00 (actual meeting time).

Time taken by B to travel 1.2 km to reach point Y = $\frac{1.2}{12}$ = 0.1 hours = 6 minutes.

Thus, B reaches Y at 12:06 pm.

Since A and B meet at point Y, A was also at Y at 12:06 pm.

Time taken by A to cover 1.2 km to reach X = $\frac{1.2}{6}$ = 0.2 hours = 12 minutes.

Thus, A reaches X at 12:06 + 12 min. = 12:18 pm.

Thus, we observe that A reaches X 18 minutes later than when he was supposed to reach.

Thus, we have $t = 18$ - Sufficient

The answer is (c).

19. **(b)** **Considering Statement 1 alone :**

There is no information about the working rate of women. So, this is insufficient.

Hence, eliminate A/D.

Considering Statement 2 alone :

We have

An area painted by 2 men in 1 hour is the same as that painted by 1 woman in 2 hours.

Thus, the efficiencies of men and women are the same.

Thus, we have

To paint the 20 square feet wall, 2 men take 1 hour

Thus, to paint (30 × 80) or 2,400 square feet wall, time taken by 2 men

$= \frac{1}{20} \times 2{,}400 = 120$ hours.

Thus, to paint 2,400 square feet, time taken by 10 men

$= 120 \times \frac{2}{10} = 24$ hours - Sufficient

Hence, eliminate C/E.

The answer is (b).

20. **(d)** Let $\$x$ be the amount of money invested by Christian and $\$y$ be the money invested by John. We have to find out the value of $\$(x-y)$.

Considering Statement 1 alone :

$\Rightarrow$ 10% of x – 10% of $y = 50$

$\Rightarrow$ $0.1x - 0.1y = 50$

$\Rightarrow$ $x - y = 500$; Christian's investment was greater than John's by \$500.

Statement 1 alone is sufficient. The correct answer would be between A/D.

Considering Statement 2 alone :

$\Rightarrow$ 12% of x – 12% of $y = 60$

$\Rightarrow$ $0.12x - 0.12y = 60$;

$\Rightarrow$ $x - y = 500$; Christian's investment was greater than John's by \$500.

Statement 2 alone is also sufficient.

The answer is (d).

21. **(c)** Let the total distance be $2d$ miles.

Time taken to cover d miles at 20 miles per hour $= \frac{d}{20}$ hours

Considering Statement 1 alone :

Time taken to cover the remaining d miles at 40 miles per hour

$= \frac{d}{40}$ hours

However, there is no information regarding the actual time taken. - Insufficient

Hence, eliminate A/D.

Considering Statement 2 alone :

We know that if the man traveled the remaining distance at 30 miles per hour, he would have reached his destination 15 minutes or $\frac{1}{4}$ hours late.

Time taken to cover the remaining d miles at 30 miles per hour

$= \frac{d}{30}$ hours.

However, there is no information regarding the actual time taken. - Insufficient

Hence, eliminate B.

Considering statements 1 and 2 together :

$\frac{d}{30} - \frac{d}{40} = \frac{1}{4}$

$\Rightarrow$ $d = 30$

Thus, the total distance

$= 2d = 60$ miles. – Sufficient.

The answer is (c).

Chapter 3

Algebra

Algebra is a significant component of the GMAT, which tests your ability to solve problems using algebraic concepts. Here are some important topics in algebra that are frequently tested on the GMAT:

- **Linear equations and inequalities :** You should be able to solve linear equations and inequalities, graph them on a coordinate plane, and use them to solve word problems.
- **Quadratic equations :** You should be able to solve quadratic equations using the quadratic formula, factoring, and completing the square.
- **Functions :** You should be able to understand the concept of a function and evaluate functions for specific inputs.
- **Exponents and radicals :** You should be able to simplify expressions with exponents and radicals, and solve equations involving them.
- **Absolute value :** You should be able to work with absolute values and solve equations and inequalities that involve them.

It's important to note that these topics are not exhaustive, and there may be other algebraic concepts that are tested on the GMAT. Additionally, some GMAT questions may involve more than one algebraic concept, so it's important to be able to recognize when to use different algebraic tools to solve a problem.

Linear Equations

Linear Equations are equations in which all the variables are raised to the first power. To solve such an equation, you'll need to perform operations on both sides of the equation in order to get the variable you're solving for alone on one side.

A linear equation is an equation involving one or more variables in which each term in the equation is either a constant term or a variable multiplied by a coefficient. None of the variables are multiplied together or raised to a power greater than 1. For example, $2x + 1 = 7x$ and $10x - 9y - z = 3$ are linear equations, but $x + y^2 = 0$ and $xz = 3$ are not.

Here are some examples of linear equations:

$3x + 2 = 11$

$5y - 7 = 3y + 11$

$2z + 4 = 10 - 3z$

$0.5a - 1 = 2.5$

$-2b + 3 = -7b - 1$

Example : Find the value of x in the equation $3x - 5 = 7$.

Solution : We can solve for x by isolating it on one side of the equation. To do this, we'll add 5 to both sides of the equation to get:

$$3x - 5 + 5 = 7 + 5$$

Simplifying, we get:

$$3x = 12$$

Now we can isolate x by dividing both sides of the equation by 3:

$$\frac{3x}{3} = \frac{12}{3}$$

Simplifying, we get:

$$x = 4$$

Therefore, the value of x that satisfies the equation $3x - 5 = 7$ is 4.

There are two ways of solving the equation: Substitution method and elimination method.

Substitution Method

The substitution method is one way to solve a system of linear equations. In this method, we solve one of the equations for one variable in terms of the other variable, and then substitute that expression into the other equation. This creates a new equation with only one variable, which can be solved. Once we find the value of one variable, we can use that value to solve for the other variable.

Here's an example of how to solve a system of linear equations using the substitution method:

1. Solve the first equation for one variable in terms of the other. For example, if the equations are:

$$2x + 3y = 7$$

$$4x - y = 1$$

   We can solve the second equation for y :

$$y = 4x - 1$$

2. Substitute the expression we just found for the variable into the other equation. In this case, we substitute $y = 4x - 1$ into the first equation:

$$2x + 3(4x - 1) = 7$$

3. Simplify the equation and solve for the variable:

$$2x + 12x - 3 = 7$$

$$14x = 10$$

$$x = \frac{10}{14} = \frac{5}{7}$$

4. Use the value we just found for x to find the value of y. We can use either of the original equations to do this. Let's use the second equation:

$$4x - y = 1$$

$$4\left(\frac{5}{7}\right) - y = 1$$

$$y = 4\left(\frac{5}{7}\right) - 1$$

$$y = \frac{15}{7} - \frac{7}{7}$$

$$y = \frac{8}{7}$$

So the solution to the system of linear equations is $x = \frac{5}{7}, y = \frac{8}{7}$.

Example : Solve the system of equations using the substitution method:

$$2x + y = 10\, x - y = 4$$

Solution : To use the substitution method, we need to solve one of the equations for one of the variables, and then substitute the resulting expression into the other equation. Let's solve the second equation for "y":

$$x - y = 4$$

$$y = x - 4$$

Now we can substitute this expression for "y" into the first equation:

$$2x + y = 10$$

$$2x + (x - 4) = 10$$

Simplifying, we get :

$$3x - 4 = 10$$

Adding 4 to both sides, we get:

$$3x = 14$$

Dividing both sides by 3, we get:

$$x = 4.67$$

Now that we know the value of x, we can substitute it back into the expression we found for "y":

$$y = x - 4$$

$$y = 4.67 - 4$$

$$y = 0.67$$

Therefore, the solution to the system of equations is:

$$x = 4.67$$

$$y = 0.67$$

Elimination Method

The elimination method is another way to solve a system of linear equations. In this method, we add or subtract the equations in such a way that one variable is eliminated, and then we solve for the other variable. We can then substitute the value we found into one of the equations to solve for the other variable.

Here's an example of how to solve a system of linear equations using the elimination method:

1. Rewrite the equations in standard form:

$$2x + 3y = 7$$

$$4x - y = 1$$

2. Multiply one or both equations by a constant to make the coefficients of one of the variables opposite in sign. In this case, we can multiply the second equation by 3 to make the coefficient of y in both equations opposite:

$$2x + 3y = 7$$

$$12x - 3y = 3$$

3. Add the equations to eliminate one of the variables:

$$2x + 3y = 7 \text{ and } 12x - 3y = 3$$

$$14x = 10$$

4. Solve for the remaining variable:

$$14x = 10$$

$$x = \frac{10}{14} = \frac{5}{7}$$

5. Substitute the value we just found for x into one of the original equations to find the value of the other variable. Let's use the first equation:

$$2x + 3y = 7$$

$$2\left(\frac{5}{7}\right) + 3y = 7$$

$$\frac{10}{7} + 3y = 7$$

$$3y = 7 - \frac{10}{7}$$

$$3y = \frac{49}{7} - \frac{10}{7}$$

$$3y = \frac{39}{7}$$

$$y = \frac{13}{7}$$

So the solution to the system of linear equations is $x = \frac{5}{7}, y = \frac{13}{7}$.

Types of Solutions

If a system of linear equations is given as:

$$a_1x + b_1y + c_1 = 0$$

$$a_2x + b_2y + c_2 = 0$$

There are three types of solutions possible for this pair of linear equations:

- **Unique solution :** It means only one point (x, y) will satisfy both the equations. So the graph for the system of linear equations will be intersecting lines. Unique solution is possible when $\frac{a_1}{a_2} \neq \frac{b_1}{b_2}$
- **Infinite solutions :** It means all points (x, y) satisfies either of the equations. So the graph for the system of linear equations will be coincident lines. This is possible when $\frac{a_1}{a_2} = \frac{b_1}{b_2} = \frac{c_1}{c_2}$
- **No solution :** It means that these equations have no point in common. So the graph for the system of linear equations will be parallel lines. This type of solution is possible when $\frac{a_1}{a_2} = \frac{b_1}{b_2} \neq \frac{c_1}{c_2}$

Quadratic Equations

A quadratic equation is a polynomial equation of degree 2, which means that the highest power of the variable in the equation is 2. The general form of a quadratic equation is:

$ax^2 + bx + c = 0$, where a, b, and c are constants and x is the variable.

To solve a quadratic equation, we need to find the values of x that satisfy the equation.

We can use the quadratic formula to find the solutions of a quadratic equation. The quadratic formula is:

$$x = \frac{\left(-b \pm \sqrt{(b^2 - 4ac)}\right)}{2a}$$

where the symbol ± means "plus or minus", and the square root is only defined for non-negative values.

To use the quadratic formula, we first need to identify the values of a, b, and c in the quadratic equation. Then, we substitute those values into the formula to find the values of x.

Example, consider the quadratic equation:

$$2x^2 + 3x - 5 = 0$$

Here, a = 2, b = 3, and c = -5. Substituting these values into the quadratic formula, we get:

$$\frac{\left(-3 \pm \sqrt{(3^2 - 4(2)(-5))}\right)}{2(2)}$$

Simplifying this expression, we get:

$$x = \frac{\left(-3 \pm \sqrt{49}\right)}{4}$$

$$x = \frac{(-3 \pm 7)}{4}$$

So, the solutions of the quadratic equation $2x^2 + 3x - 5 = 0$ are:

$$x = \frac{(-3+7)}{4} = \frac{1}{2}$$

Example : Solve the quadratic equation $2x^2 + 3x - 5 = 0$ using the quadratic formula.

Solution : The quadratic formula is:

$\frac{\left(-b \pm \sqrt{(b^2 - 4ac)}\right)}{2a}$, where a, b, and c are the coefficients of the quadratic equation $ax^2 + bx + c = 0$.

Using this formula, we can find the solutions to the given quadratic equation.

First, we identify the coefficients :

$$a = 2$$

$$b = 3$$

$$c = -5$$

Now we can substitute these values into the quadratic formula and simplify:

$$x = \frac{\left(-b \pm \sqrt{(b^2 - 4ac)}\right)}{2a}$$

$$x = \frac{\left(-3 \pm \sqrt{(3^2 - (4)(2)(-5))}\right)}{2(2)}$$

$$x = \frac{\left(-3 \pm \sqrt{(49)}\right)}{4x}$$

$$x = \frac{(-3 \pm 7)}{4}$$

So the solutions to the quadratic equation are:

$$x = \frac{(-3+7)}{4} = \frac{1}{2}$$

$$x = \frac{(-3-7)}{4} = -\frac{5}{2}$$

Therefore, the solutions to the quadratic equation $2x^2 + 3x - 5 = 0$ are $x = \frac{1}{2}$ and $x = -\frac{5}{2}$

Splitting the Middle Term

Splitting the middle term is a method used to factorize quadratic expressions of the form $ax^2 + bx + c$, where a, b, and c are constants.

The method involves finding two numbers whose sum is equal to b, the coefficient of the x-term, and whose product is equal to a times c, the product of the first and last coefficients. We then rewrite the quadratic expression as a sum of two terms using these two numbers, and then factorize the expression by grouping the terms.

Here are the steps to use the splitting the middle term technique to factorize a quadratic expression:

1. Write the quadratic expression in the standard form $ax^2 + bx + c$.
2. Identify the values of a, b, and c.
3. Find two numbers whose sum is equal to b, the coefficient of the x-term, and whose product is equal to a times c, the product of the first and last coefficients.
4. Rewrite the quadratic expression as a sum of two terms, using the two numbers found in step 3.
5. Factorize each of the two terms separately.
6. Rearrange the terms to obtain the factorized form of the quadratic expression.

Lets understand with an example:

Factorise : $2x^2 + 7x + 3$.

1. Write the quadratic expression in the standard form $ax^2 + bx + c : 2x^2 + 7x + 3$.
2. Identify the values of a, b, and c : $a = 2, b = 7, c = 3$.
3. Find two numbers whose sum is equal to b, the coefficient of the x-term, and whose product is equal to a times c, the product of the first and last coefficients. In this case, we need to find two numbers whose sum is 7 and whose product is $2 \times 3 = 6$. The two numbers are 6 and 1.

4. Rewrite the quadratic expression as a sum of two terms, using the two numbers found in step 3:

$$2x^2 + 7x + 3 = 2x^2 + 6x + x + 3$$

5. Factorize each of the two terms separately:

$$2x^2 + 6x = 2x(x + 3) \quad x + 3 = 1(x + 3)$$

6. Rearrange the terms to obtain the factorized form of the quadratic expression:

$$2x^2 + 7x + 3 = (2x + 1)(x + 3)$$

Therefore, the quadratic expression $2x^2 + 7x + 3$ can be factorized as $(2x + 1)(x + 3)$ using the splitting the middle term method.

Example : Factor the quadratic expression $x^2 + 5x + 6$ using the method of splitting the middle term.

Solution : To factor the expression $x^2 + 5x + 6$ using the method of splitting the middle term, we need to find two numbers that multiply to 6 and add to 5. Those numbers are 2 and 3. Therefore, we can rewrite the expression as:

$$x^2 + 2x + 3x + 6$$

Now we can group the terms as follows:

$$(x^2 + 2x) + (3x + 6)$$

We can factor out the greatest common factor from each group:

$$x(x + 2) + 3(x + 2)$$

Notice that both groups have a factor of $(x + 2)$. We can factor this out:

$$(x + 2)(x + 3)$$

Therefore, the factored form of the quadratic expression $x^2 + 5x + 6$ is $(x + 2)(x + 3)$.

Discriminant Formula & Nature of Roots

The discriminant is a formula used to determine the nature of the roots of a quadratic equation. The quadratic equation is of the form $ax^2 + bx + c = 0$, where a, b, and c are constants.

The discriminant formula is given by:

$$D = b^2 - 4ac$$

If the discriminant is positive (i.e., $b^2 - 4ac > 0$), then the quadratic equation has two distinct real roots.

If the discriminant is zero (i.e., $b^2 - 4ac = 0$), then the quadratic equation has one real root.

If the discriminant is negative (i.e., $b^2 - 4ac < 0$), then the quadratic equation has two imaginary roots.

The discriminant formula can also be used to find the roots of a quadratic equation

Using the quadratic formula :

$$\frac{\left(-b \pm \sqrt{(b^2 - 4ac)}\right)}{2a}$$

If the discriminant is positive, then the square root in the quadratic formula is a positive real number, so the equation has two distinct real roots. If the discriminant is zero, then the square root is zero, so the equation has one real root, which is repeated. If the discriminant is negative, then the square root is an imaginary number, so the equation has two complex conjugate roots.

The roots of the quadratic equation is generally denoted by α and β.

where, $\alpha = \frac{\left(-b + \sqrt{D}\right)}{2a}$ and, $\beta = \frac{\left(-b - \sqrt{D}\right)}{2a}$

Sum & Product of Roots

The sum of the roots of a quadratic equation of the form $ax^2 + bx + c = 0$ can be found using the following formula:

Sum of roots = $-\frac{b}{a}$

Here, "a", "b", and "c" are the coefficients of the quadratic equation.

For example, consider the quadratic equation $2x^2 + 5x - 3 = 0$.

The sum of the roots can be found using the formula:

Sum of roots = $-\frac{b}{a}$

Substituting the coefficients into the formula, we get:

Sum of roots = $-\frac{5}{2}$

Therefore, the sum of the roots of the quadratic equation $2x^2 + 5x - 3 = 0$ is $-\frac{5}{2}$.

Product of roots = $\frac{c}{a}$

Here, "a", "b", and "c" are the coefficients of the quadratic equation.

For example, consider the quadratic equation $2x^2 + 5x - 3 = 0$.

The product of the roots can be found using the formula:

Product of roots = $\frac{c}{a}$

Substituting the coefficients into the formula, we get:

Product of roots = $\frac{(-3)}{2}$

Therefore, the product of the roots of the quadratic equation $2x^2 + 5x - 3 = 0$ is $\frac{-3}{2}$.

Inequality

In the context of the GMAT (Graduate Management Admission Test), inequality typically refers to mathematical inequalities, which are used to express relationships between two values that are not equal.

The GMAT often tests students' abilities to solve and manipulate inequalities, particularly in the Quantitative section of the exam.

Inequalities can be represented using symbols such as < (less than), > (greater than), ≤ (less than or equal to), and ≥ (greater than or equal to). To solve inequalities on the GMAT, you typically need to isolate the variable on one side of the inequality sign and determine the range of values that satisfy the inequality.

Example, if you are given the inequality $3x - 5 > 7$, you would start by adding 5 to both sides to isolate the variable:

$$3x - 5 + 5 > 7 + 5$$

$$3x > 12$$

Then, you would divide both sides by 3 to solve for x:

$$x > 4$$

This tells you that the range of values for x that satisfy the inequality is all numbers greater than 4.

When you multiply or divide an inequality by a negative number on both sides, the inequality sign changes!!

Inequalities can involve variables and are similar to equations, except that the two sides are related by one of the inequality signs instead of the equality sign used in equations. For example, the inequality $4x - 1 \leq 7$ is a linear inequality in one variable, which states that "4x – 1 is less than or equal to 7."

When the same constant is added to or subtracted from both sides of an inequality, the direction of the inequality is preserved and the new inequality is equivalent to the original.

When both sides of the inequality are multiplied or divided by the same nonzero constant, the direction of the inequality is preserved if the constant is positive but the direction is reversed if the constant is negative. In either case, the new inequality is equivalent to the original.

Example : Solve the inequality $2x - 5 > 7$.

Solution : To solve the inequality $2x - 5 > 7$, we need to isolate "x" on one side of the inequality symbol. We can do this by adding 5 to both sides of the inequality:

$$2x - 5 + 5 > 7 + 5$$

Simplifying, we get:

$$2x > 12$$

Now we can isolate "x" by dividing both sides of the inequality by 2:

$$\frac{2x}{2} > \frac{12}{2}$$

Simplifying, we get:

$$x > 6$$

Therefore, the solution to the inequality $2x - 5 > 7$ is $x > 6$. This means that any value of "x" that is greater than 6 will satisfy the inequality

Absolute Value / Modulus

In mathematics, the absolute value (or modulus) of a real number is the non-negative value of that number without regard to its sign. It is denoted by two vertical bars on either side of the number.

For example, the absolute value of 5 is written as $|5|$, which is equal to 5, and the absolute value of -3 is written as $|-3|$, which is also equal to 3.

More formally, if x is a real number, then its absolute value is defined as:

$$|x| = \{x, \text{if } x >= 0; -x, \text{if } x < 0\}$$

The absolute value of a number represents its distance from zero on the number line. For instance, |5| represents the distance of 5 units from zero on the number line, while |–3| represents the distance of 3 units from zero, in the opposite direction.

Here are some examples of absolute value:

|5| = 5 The absolute value of 5 is 5 since 5 is a positive number.

|–3| = 3 The absolute value of –3 is 3 since the distance of –3 units from zero on the number line is 3 units in the opposite direction.

|0| = 0 The absolute value of 0 is 0 since 0 is equidistant from both positive and negative numbers on the number line.

|4 – 7| = |–3| = 3 The absolute value of the difference between 4 and 7 is 3 since the distance between 4 and 7 units on the number line is 3 units in the opposite direction.

|–2.5| = 2.5 The absolute value of –2.5 is 2.5 since 2.5 is the distance of 2.5 units from zero on the number line.

Example : Solve the inequality $\frac{(3x+1)}{(2x-3)} \leq 2$.

Solution : To solve the inequality $\frac{(3x+1)}{(2x-3)} \leq 2$, we need to isolate "x" on one side of the inequality symbol.

First, we can simplify the left-hand side of the inequality by multiplying both sides by the denominator (2x – 3):

$$\frac{(3x+1)}{(2x-3)} \leq 2$$

$$(3x + 1) \leq 2(2x - 3)$$

Simplifying, we get:

$$3x + 1 \leq 4x - 6$$

Now we can isolate "x" by subtracting 3x and adding 6 to both sides of the inequality:

$$3x + 1 - 3x + 6 \leq 4x - 6 - 3x + 6$$

Simplifying, we get:

$$7 \leq x$$

Therefore, the solution to the inequality $\frac{(3x+1)}{(2x-3)} \leq 2$ is $x \geq 7$. This means that any value of "x" that is greater than or equal to 7 will satisfy the inequality

Exponents / Radicals

An exponent is a mathematical operation that indicates how many times a number or variable should be multiplied by itself. The exponent is represented as a superscript number to the right of the base number or variable. For example, in the expression 2^3, 2 is the base and 3 is the exponent.

The exponent tells you how many times the base should be multiplied by itself. In the example above, 2^3 means 2 multiplied by itself three times, which is equal to $2 \times 2 \times 2 = 8$.

Exponents can also be written using negative numbers and fractions. When an exponent is negative, it indicates that the base should be divided by itself the number

of times specified by the absolute value of the exponent. For example, $\frac{1}{(2^3)} = \frac{1}{8}$.

When an exponent is a fraction, it represents a root of the base. For example, $2^{(1/2)}$ represents the square root of 2, which is approximately 1.414. Similarly, $2^{(1/3)}$ represents the cube root of 2, which is approximately 1.259.

When negative numbers are raised to powers, the result may be positive or negative.

For example, $(-3)^2 = (-3)(-3) = 9$, while $(-3)^5 = (-3)(-3)(-3)(-3)(-3) = -243$.

Important Points :

- For all nonzero numbers a, $a^0 = 1$.
- The expression 0^0 is undefined.
- For all nonzero numbers a, $a^{-1} = \frac{1}{a}$.
- If n is an even integer, then $(-1)^n = 1$.
- If n is an odd integer, then $(-1)^n = -1$.

Few exponents' rules are stated below :

$a^p \times a^q = a^{(p+q)}$	$\sqrt{a} \times \sqrt{b} = \sqrt{(ab)}$
$\frac{a^p}{a^q} = a^{(p-q)}$	$\frac{\sqrt{a}}{\sqrt{b}} = \sqrt{\frac{a}{b}}$
$(a^p)^q = a^{pq}$	$x\sqrt{a} + y\sqrt{a} = (x+y)\sqrt{a}$
$a^p \times b^p = (ab)^p$	$\sqrt{x} = x^{\frac{1}{2}}$
$x^0 = 1$	$x^{-a} = \frac{1}{x^a}$

Example : Simplify the expression $\frac{(2^{(3x+2)}) \times 8^{(x-1)}}{(16^{(x+1)})}$

Solution : We can start by rewriting 8 and 16 in terms of powers of 2:

$$8 = 2^3\ 16 = 2^4$$

Substituting these values into the expression, we get:

$$\frac{\left(2^{(3x+2)} \times 2^{(3(x-1))}\right)}{(2^{(4(x+1))})}$$

Simplifying, we get:

$$\frac{2^{(3x+2+3x-3)}}{2^{(4x+4)}}$$

Combining like terms, we get:

$$\frac{2^{(6x-1)}}{2^{(4x+4)}}$$

Now we can use the rule of exponents that states $a^{(m-n)} = \frac{a^m}{a^n}$ to simplify the expression:

$$\frac{2^{(6x-1)}}{2^{(4x+4)}} = \frac{2^{(6x-1-(4x+4))}}{2^{(2x-5)}}$$

Therefore, the simplified form of the expression $\frac{\left(2^{(3x+2)} \times 8^{(x-1)}\right)}{\left(16^{(x+1)}\right)}$ is $2^{(2x-5)}$

Arithmetic Progression

An arithmetic progression (AP) is a sequence of numbers in which each term after the first is obtained by adding a constant value to the preceding term. This constant value is called the common difference of the AP. In other words, an arithmetic progression is a sequence of numbers where the difference between any two consecutive terms is the same.

Example : find the 10th term and sum of first terms of the following sequence of numbers: 2, 5, 8, 11, 14, ...

This is an arithmetic progression because the common difference between any two consecutive terms is 3. The first term of the sequence is 2, and each subsequent term is obtained by adding 3 to the previous term.

The nth term of an arithmetic progression can be found using the following formula:

$$a_n = a_1 + (n - 1)d$$

where a_n is the nth term of the AP, a_1 is the first term, d is the common difference, and n is the position of the term in the sequence.

The sum of the first n terms of an arithmetic progression can be found using the following formula:

$$S_n = \left(\frac{n}{2}\right)(a_1 + a_n)$$

where S_n is the sum of the first *n* terms, a_1 is the first term, a_n is the nth term, and n is the number of terms in the sequence.

Here is an example of an arithmetic progression :

2, 5, 8, 11, 14, 17, 20, 23, 26, 29, ...

In this sequence, the common difference between any two consecutive terms is 3. The first term of the sequence is 2, and each subsequent term is obtained by adding 3 to the previous term.

Using the formulas for arithmetic progressions, we can find the nth term and the sum of the first *n* terms of this sequence. For example:

- The 10th term of the sequence is $a_{10} = a_1 + (10 - 1)d = 2 + 9 \times 3 = 29$.
- The sum of the first 7 terms of the sequence is

$$S_7 = \left(\frac{7}{2}\right)(a_1 + a_7) = \left(\frac{7}{2}\right)(2 + 20) = 77.$$

Example : Find the 10th term of an arithmetic sequence where the first term is 3 and the common difference is 4.

Solution : To find the 10th term of an arithmetic sequence, we can use the formula: $a_n = a_1 + (n-1)d$, where a_n is the nth term, a_1 is the first term, n is the term number, and d is the common difference.

Substituting the values given in the problem, we get:

$$a_{10} = 3 + (10 - 1)4$$

Simplifying, we get:

$$a_{10} = 3 + 36$$

$$a_{10} = 39$$

Therefore, the 10th term of the arithmetic sequence is 39

Example : The sum of the first 10 terms of an arithmetic sequence is 145 and the sum of the next 5 terms is 90. Find the first term and the common difference of the sequence.

Solution : Let's denote the first term of the arithmetic sequence as "a" and the common difference between consecutive terms as "d". We know that the sum of the first 10 terms is 145, so we can use the formula for the sum of an arithmetic series to get:

$$S_{10} = \left(\frac{10}{2}\right)(2a + (10\text{-}1)d) = 145$$

Simplifying, we get:

$$5(2a + 9d) = 145$$

$$2a + 9d = 29 \text{ (Equation 1)}$$

Similarly, we can use the sum of the next 5 terms (which is given as 90) and the formula for the sum of an arithmetic series to get:

$$S_{15} = \left(\frac{15}{2}\right)(2a + (15\text{-}1)d) = 235$$

Simplifying, we get :

$$15a + 105d = 470 \text{ (Equation 2)}$$

Now we can solve this system of equations to find the values of "a" and "d". First, we can use Equation 1 to solve for "a" in terms of "d":

$$a = \frac{(29 - 9d)}{2}$$

Substituting this expression for "a" into Equation 2, we get:

$$15\left[\frac{(29-9d)}{2}\right]+105d=470$$

Simplifying, we get :

$$-45d+435=0$$

$$d=9$$

Substituting this value of "d" back into Equation 1 to solve for "a", we get:

$$2a+9(9)=29$$

$$2a=-58$$

$$a=-29$$

Therefore, the first term of the arithmetic sequence is -29 and the common difference between consecutive terms is 9

Functions

The GMAT often tests students' abilities to understand and apply mathematical functions, particularly in the Quantitative section of the exam.

The domain of a function is the set of all possible input values for which the function is defined. In other words, it is the set of all x-values that can be plugged into the function to obtain a valid output.

For example, consider the function $f(x)=\frac{1}{(x-2)}$. The denominator of this function cannot be equal to zero, so $x-2$ cannot be equal to zero. Therefore, the domain of the function is all real numbers except $x = 2$.

The range of a function is the set of all possible output values that the function can produce. In other words, it is the set of all y-values that are obtained when the function is evaluated at all possible x-values in its domain.

For example, consider the function $f(x) = x^2$. To find the range of this function, we can analyze the behavior of the function as x varies.

Some common types of functions that are tested on the GMAT include:

- Linear functions: Functions of the form $f(x) = mx + b$, where m and b are constants.
- Quadratic functions: Functions of the form $f(x) = ax^2 + bx + c$, where a, b, and c are constants.
- Exponential functions: Functions of the form $f(x) = ab^x$, where a and b are constants.

Example : Let $f(x) = 2x - 1$ and $g(x) = x^2$. Find the value of $f(g(3))$.

Solution : To find $f(g(3))$, we need to first find the value of $g(3)$. Since $g(x) = x^2$, we have:

$$g(3) = 3^2 = 9$$

Now we can use this value to find $f(g(3))$. Since $f(x) = 2x - 1$, we have:

$$f(g(3)) = f(9) = 2(9) - 1 = 17$$

Therefore, $f(g(3)) = 17$

Example : Let $f(x) = 2x + 3$ and $g(x) = x^2 - 5$. Find the value of $(f \text{ of } g)(2)$.

Solution : To find the value of $(f \text{ of } g)(2)$, we need to first find the value of $g(2)$, and then use that value to find the value of $f(g(2))$. Since $g(x) = x^2 - 5$, we have:

$$g(2) = 2^2 - 5 = -1$$

Now we can use this value to find $f(g(2))$. Since $f(x) = 2x + 3$, we have:

$$f(g(2)) = f(-1) = 2(-1) + 3 = 1$$

Therefore, $(f \text{ of } g)(2) = f(g(2)) = 1$.

Problem Solving

1. For what value of x is $|x - 4| + 1$ less than zero?

(a) 0

(b) 1

(c) 3

(d) 4

(e) There is no such value of x

2. $|-x| \geq 5$ and $xy^2 < 0$, which of the following is a possible value of x?

(a) –6

(b) –3

(c) –1

(d) 0

(e) 6

3. If $|x| + |y| > |x + y|$, then which of the following must be true?

(a) $y < 0$

(b) $x > 0$

(c) $y > 0$

(d) $xy > 0$

(e) $xy < 0$

4. If $|x + 3| = 5$ and $|y + 5| = 3$, then what is the greatest possible value of x + y?

(a) –16

(b) –10

(c) 6

(d) 0

(e) 10

5. If $xy < 0$, and $\frac{a}{x} + \frac{b}{y} < xy$, then which of the following must be true?

(a) $ax + by < (xy)^2$

(b) $ax + by < 1$

(c) $ax + by > (xy)^2$

(d) $a + b > xy$

(e) $ax > -by$

6. The first three terms of an arithmetic sequence are 20, 23, and 26. What is the 70th term of the sequence?

(a) 69

(b) 127

(c) 207

(d) 227

(e) 272

7. The sequence S is defined by $S_n = 3(S_{n-1}) - 2$ for each integer n^3 2. If S1 = 2, what is the value of S5?

(a) 2

(b) 4

(c) 10

(d) 28

(e) 82

8. If $\frac{2^2 < x}{(2^6 - 2^4)} < 2^3$, which of the following is x?

(a) 8

(b) 16

(c) 128

(d) 232

(e) 600

9. If $5^k - 5^{k+1} + 5^{k-1} = 5^k \times m$, what is the value of m?

(a) $\frac{-19}{5}$

(b) $\frac{-5}{19}$

(c) 0

(d) $\frac{5}{19}$

(e) $\frac{19}{5}$

10. Which of the following is greater than 10^5?

(a) 2^{13}

(b) 2^{14}

(c) 2^{15}

(d) 2^{16}

(e) 2^{17}

11. If $-2 < x < 4$ and $-3 < y < 2$, then which of the following must be true for $x - y$?

(a) $-4 < x - y > 2$

(b) $1 < x - y < 7$

(c) $1 < x - y < 4$

(d) $-4 < x - y < 2$

(e) $-4 < x - y < 7$

12. If $|x + 3| > 5$, what are the possible values of x?

(a) $-5 < x < 5$

(b) $-3 > x$ and $x > 3$

(c) $-8 < x < 2$

(d) $x < -8$ and $x > 2$

(e) $-3 < x < 3$

13. How many integer integer values satisfy $|x| > 3$?

(a) 0

(b) 1

(c) 3

(d) 5

(e) Infinitely many

14. An art class of 20 students took a final exam and ten of the students scored between 78 and 86 in the exam. If s is defined as the scores of the ten students, which of the following describes values of s?

(a) $|s - 82| = 4$

(b) $|s + 82| = 4$

(c) $|s - 82| < 4$

(d) $|s - 82| > 4$

(e) $|s + 82| > 4$

15. If $0 < x < 1$, which of the following must be true?

I. $x^7 < x^5$

II. $x^7 + x^6 < x^5 + x^4$

III. $x^6 + x^7 < x^4 + x^5$

(a) None of the above

(b) I only

(c) II only

(d) I and II only

(e) I, II, and III

16. Sandy estimates that there are p pens in a box. Many who knows the actual number of pens in the box, notes that the actual number, n, is within 10 pens (inclusive) of Sandy's estimate. Which of the following inequalities represents the relationship between Sandy's estimate and the actual number of pens in the box?

(a) $n+10 \le p \le n-10$

(b) $p-10 \le n \le p+10$

(c) $n \le p \le 10n$

(d) $\frac{p}{10} \le n \le 10p$

(e) $10-p \le n \le 10+p$

17. If $7^{4x} = 49$, what is possible value of $(7^{x-1})^2$?

(a) 49

(b) 21

(c) 7

(d) $\frac{1}{7}$

(e) $\frac{1}{49}$

18. In a sequence, $a_{n+1} = 2 \times a_n$. If $a_7 - a_6 = 96$, then what is the value of a_7?

(a) 48

(b) 96

(c) 98

(d) 192

(e) 198

19. If $x = 2^{y+1}$, then in terms of x, 4^y is

(a) x

(b) $\frac{x}{2}$

(c) x^2

(d) $\frac{x^2}{2}$

(e) $\frac{x^2}{4}$

20. If $(32)^{\frac{1}{x}} = 2^{5x}$, then what is the value of x?

(a) –1

(b) 1

(c) Both (a) & (b)

(d) 0

(e) Cannot be determined

21. The sum of the first three terms of an arithmetic progression is 30 and their product is 750. Find the 5th term of the A.P?

(a) 25

(b) –5

(c) 25 or –5

(d) –10

(e) 10

22. The midpoints of the sides of a square of length 15m are joined to form another square. Midpoints of the newly formed square are joined to form another square and the process continues indefinitely. Find the sum of the areas (in m^2) of all the squares.

(a) 60

(b) 225

(c) 450

(d) 600

(e) 900

23. If $(24)^{4(4+x)} = \frac{(16)^{8-x}}{(81)^{3x-y}}$, then find the value

(a) –1

(b) 0

(c) 1

(d) –2

(e) 2

24. $x^2 \times y^3 = 147$, where x and y are positive real numbers. Find the minimum value of 6x + 7y.

(*a*) 35

(*b*) 70

(*c*) $5\sqrt{7}$

(*d*) 49

(*e*) 40

25. The number of detergent cakes product by a machine increased by 400 every month. Total number of detergent cakes produced by the machine in 2 years is 153600. What is the number of detergent cakes produced by the machine in 8th month?

(*a*) 4600

(*b*) 4400

(*c*) 5000

(*d*) 5200

(*e*) 4800

26. $(x-2)^2 + (x-1)^2 + x^2 + (x+1)^2 + (x+2)^2 = ?$

(*a*) $5x^2$

(*b*) $5x^2 + 10$

(*c*) $x^2 + 10$

(*d*) $5x^2 + 6x + 10$

(*e*) $5x^2 - 6x + 10$

27. If x is directly proportional to y. If x = 8 then y = 2, what is x when y = 4?

(*a*) 10

(*b*) 16

(*c*) 32

(*d*) 64

(*e*) 128

28. In a class of 12 students, there are three times as many girls as boys. How many girls are there in the class?

(*a*) 3

(*b*) 4

(*c*) 6

(*d*) 8

(*e*) 9

29. The sum of the square of a number and its reciprocal is thrice the difference of the square of the number and its reciprocal. How many different rational value(s) of the number is/are possible?

(*a*) 1

(*b*) 2

(*c*) 3

(*d*) 4

(*e*) 0

30. What is the number that is one-third of two-fifth of three quarters of 760?

(*a*) 114

(*b*) 86

(*c*) 76

(*d*) 38

(*e*) 95

31. Milind bought 3 apples, 4 bananas and 7 guavas together for Rs. 86. Had he bought 13 guavas, 6 apples and 7 bananas together, it would have coasted him Rs. 164. Find the cost of 5 bananas, 4 apples and 9 guavas together.

(*a*) 104

(*b*) 112

(*c*) 125

(*d*) 150

(*e*) 115

32. There are some mangoes with Panchu and Chhakku. If Chhakku were to give 20 mangoes to Panchu, Panchu would have twice as many mangoes as left with Chhakku; whereas if Panchu were to give 40 mangoes to Chhakku, Chhakku would have thrice as many mangoes as left with Panchu. The number of mangoes with Chhakku is

(a) 76

(b) 60

(c) 72

(d) 68

(e) 80

33. Find the smallest root of the equation

$2x^3 + 5x^2 + 3x = 0$

(a) 0

(b) –1

(c) –2

(d) $-\frac{3}{2}$

(e) 1

34. If $x^2 < x$, then what can be the value of x?

(a) 2

(b) 1

(c) $\frac{23}{5}$

(d) $\frac{5}{23}$

(e) –2

35. If $-6 \le a \le 5$ and $8 \le b \le 11$, what is the least possible value of $|a - b|$?

(a) –17

(b) –2

(c) 0

(d) 3

(e) 17

36. If $5x - 7 \ge 3x + 9$ which of the following must be true?

(a) $x < 7$

(b) $x > 7$

(c) $x < 8$

(d) $x > 8$

(e) $x > 9$

37. If $|x| > 5$, which of the following CANNOT be the value of x?

(a) 6

(b) 12

(c) 1

(d) –6

(e) –8

38. If 'x' is a real number and $\frac{9}{x-6} > -x$, find the range of 'x'.

(a) $x \in [0, 6]$

(b) $x \in (9, \infty)$

(c) $x \in (6, \infty)$

(d) $x \in (3, \infty)$

(e) $x \in (4, \infty)$

39. If x and y are two integers such that $-3 < x < 8$ and $-5 < y < 4$, then find the least possible value of $8x - x(2 - 4y)$.

(*a*) 0

(*b*) –70

(*c*) –36

(*d*) 70

(*e*) 36

40. A function is defined as $f(x) = \dfrac{x^2 - 5x + 6}{x^2 + 9x + 20}$.

If $f(x) < 0$, find the range of x.

(*a*) $(-5,-4) \cup (2,3)$

(*b*) $[-5,-4] \cup (2,3)$

(*c*) $[-5,-4] \cup (2,4)$

(*d*) $[-5,-4] \cup [2,3]$

(*e*) None of these

41. If $|x - 2| = 9$ and $|y + 9| = 8$, then find the minimum possible value of xy. [where, x and y are real numbers]

(*a*) –11

(*b*) –207

(*c*) –187

(*d*) –154

(*e*) None of these

42. Given that $a < b < c$ and a, b, and c are all positive, consider the following inequalities:

I. $\dfrac{ab}{c} > b + a$

II. $a - b < b - c$

III. $\dfrac{b}{a} < \dfrac{c}{b}$

Which of the following inequalities is always true?

(*a*) I Only

(*b*) II Only

(*c*) I and III

(*d*) II and III

(*e*) None of these

43. What is the value of n, if the sum of consecutive odd numbers from 1 to n equals 256?

(*a*) 17

(*b*) 27

(*c*) 29

(*d*) 31

(*e*) 33

44. What is the value of the ratio of the larger value of x and the smaller value of x if $x^2 - 3\sqrt{x} + 2 = 0$?

(*a*) $\dfrac{2}{1}$

(*b*) $\dfrac{3}{1}$

(*c*) $\dfrac{4}{1}$

(*d*) $\dfrac{9}{2}$

(*e*) $\dfrac{5}{1}$

45. What is the value of x if $-6x^{\frac{1}{4}} + x^{\frac{1}{2}} + 9 = 0$?

(a) 3

(b) 9

(c) 27

(d) 81

(e) 243

46. If [x] is the greatest integer less than or equal to x, what is the vallue of [–2.1] + [2.7] + [6.3]?

(a) 1

(b) 2

(c) 3

(d) 4

(e) 5

47. If $x^2 - xy = -6$, $y^2 + xz = 12$, $z^2 + 26$, and $xy + xz - yz = 5$, what is the value of $x^2 + y^2 + z^2$?

(a) 8

(b) 13

(c) 27

(d) 32

(e) 30

48. A showroom has a few bikes, cars, and buses. The number of bikes and cars is three times the number of buses. There are more cars than bikes or buses. If cars and bikes together have a total of 100 tries and horns, how many bikes are there in the showroom? (Assume that each car has one horn and four tires, and each bike one horn and two tires.)

(a) 5

(b) 8

(c) 10

(d) 14

(e) 17

49. If $a = \sqrt{17} + \sqrt[3]{9} + \sqrt{2}$, which of the following must be true?

(a) $a > 7$

(b) $6 < a < 7$

(c) $|a| < 5$

(d) $a < -7$

(e) $|a| < 6$

50. If $a^3 - a^2 - a + 1 = 0$, how many unique values does a have?

(a) None

(b) One

(c) Two

(d) Three

(e) Four

51. Which of the following inequalities correctly expresses the inequality $\frac{5x-1}{-6} \leq \frac{1-2x}{3}$?

(a) $x \geq -1$

(b) $x \geq 1$

(c) $-1 \leq x \leq 1$

(d) $x \leq 0$

(e) $x \geq 0$

52. If $6 < x < 12$ and $y = x + 4$, what is the maximum possible integer value of $(x + y)$?

(a) 22

(b) 24

(c) 26

(d) 27

(e) 28

53. If $f(x) = 4x - 7$, for what values of x, does $4f(x) - 3 = f(2x - 6)$?

(a) 0

(b) $\frac{1}{2}$

(c) 1

(d) $\frac{3}{2}$

(e) 2

54. If $f(x) = x(x + 3)$, what is the value of $f(f(x))$?

(a) $x(x + 3)$

(b) $[X(x + 3)]^2$

(c) $x(x + 3)(x^2 + 3x + 3)$

(d) $x(x + 3)(x + 4x)$

(e) $x(x + 3)(x + 6x)$

55. If $\frac{x}{2} - \frac{y}{3} = -4$ and $x - \frac{y}{2} + 7 = 0$, what is the value of xy?

(a) –24

(b) –12

(c) 12

(d) 14

(e) 24

56. Aunt Mary is giving chocolates to each of her nephews and nieces. She has 40 chocolates. If Jack gets 4 more than Katherine, Bob gets 12 fewer than Susanne, and Susanne gets 4 more than Jack, and Katherine gets 4 more than Bob, how many chocolates does Katherine get?

(a) 2

(b) 4

(c) 6

(d) 8

(e) 10

57. If $f(a) = f(a^3)$, which of the following must be true?

(a) $f(9) = [f(3)]^2$

(b) $f(27) = f(3)$

(c) $f(3) = -f(81)$

(d) $f(1) = 9f(-1)$

(e) $f(0) = 1$

58. What is the sum of the series 1 + 2 + 3 ……………… + 199?

(a) 10,500

(b) 19,200

(c) 25,452

(d) 19,900

(e) 20,100

Answer Key

1. (*e*)	16. (*b*)	31. (*b*)	46. (*e*)
2. (*a*)	17. (*d*)	32. (*d*)	47. (*c*)
3. (*e*)	18. (*d*)	33. (*d*)	48. (*c*)
4. (*d*)	19. (*e*)	34. (*d*)	49. (*a*)
5. (*c*)	20. (*c*)	35. (*d*)	50. (*c*)
6. (*d*)	21. (*c*)	36. (*e*)	51. (*a*)
7. (*e*)	22. (*c*)	37. (*c*)	52. (*d*)
8. (*d*)	23. (*b*)	38. (*c*)	53. (*a*)
9. (*a*)	24. (*a*)	39. (*b*)	54. (*c*)
10. (*e*)	25. (*a*)	40. (*a*)	55. (*a*)
11. (*d*)	26. (*b*)	41. (*c*)	56. (*d*)
12. (*d*)	27. (*b*)	42. (*e*)	57. (*b*)
13. (*e*)	28. (*e*)	43. (*d*)	58. (*d*)
14. (*c*)	29. (*e*)	44. (*c*)	
15. (*e*)	30. (*c*)	45. (*d*)	

Answer Explanations

1. (e) Minimum possible value of $|x - 4|$ is 0.

   Hence, minimum possible value of $|x - 4| + 1$ is $0 + 1 = 1$.

   So, the answer is (e).

2. (a) If you picked (e), you fell for a trap.

   If $xy^2 < 0$, then $x < 0$

   Eliminate answer choices (d) and (e).

   If $x = -1$, then $|-x| = |-(-1)| = 1$, which is not more than 5.

   If $x = -3$, then $|-x| = |-(-3)| = 3$, which is not more than 5.

   If $x = -6$, then $|-x| = |-(-6)| = 6$, which is more than 5.

   Hence, the answer is (a).

3. (e) Let $x = 3$ and $y = 2$, then $|x| + |y| = |3| + |2| = 5$ and $|x + y| = |3 + 2| = 5$.

   So, $x > 0$ and $y > 0$ doesn't work.

   Let $x = 3$ and $y = -2$, then $|x| + |y| = |3| + |-2| = 5$ and $|x + y| = |3 - 2| = 1$.

   So, $x > 0$ and $y < 0$ works. Hence, $xy < 0$.

   Let $x = -3$ and $y = 2$, then $|x| + |y| = |-3| + |2| = 5$ and $|x + y| = |-3 + 2| = 1$.

   So, $x < 0$ and $y > 0$ works.

   Let $x = -3$ and $y = -2$, then $|x| + |y| = |-3| + |-2| = 5$ and $|x + y| = |-3 - 2| = 5$.

   So, $x < 0$ and $y < 0$ doesn't work. Hence, $xy < 0$.

   The answer is (e).

4. (d) If $|x + 3| = 5$, then $x = 2$ or -8

   If $|y + 5| = 3$, then $x = -2$ or -8

   Hence, there are four possible values of $x + y$.

   If $x = 2$ and $y = -2$, then $x + y = 0$

   If $x = 2$ and $y = -8$, then $x + y = -6$

   If $x = -8$ and $y = -2$, then $x + y = -10$

   If $x = -8$ and $y = -8$, then $x + y = -16$

   Hence, the answer is (d)

5. (c) If $\frac{a}{x} + \frac{b}{y} < xy$, then $\frac{ax + by}{xy} < xy$

   As $xy < 0$, multiplying it will change the sign

   $\Rightarrow ax + by > (xy)^2$

   The answer is (c)

6. (d) In a arithmetic sequence, each term increases or decreases by a constant difference.

   n^{th} term of an AP $= a + (n - 1)d$

   Here, $a = 20$, $n = 70$, and $d = 3$

   So, 70th term of the AP $= 20 + (70 - 1)3$

   $= 20 + 207$

   $= 227$

   The answer is (d)

7. (e) $S2 = 3S1 - 2 = 3 \times 2 - 2 = 4$

   $S3 = 3S2 - 2 = 3 \times 4 - 2 = 10$

   $S4 = 3S3 - 2 = 3 \times 10 - 2 = 28$

   $S5 = 3S4 - 2 = 3 \times 28 - 2 = 82$

   The answer is (e)

8. **(d)** $\frac{2^2 < x}{(2^6 - 2^4) < 2^3}$

$\frac{2^2 < x}{(2^4 - (2^2 - 1)) < 2^3}$

$\frac{2^2 < x}{(2^4 \times 3) < 2^3}$

$\frac{2^6 < x}{3 < 2^7}$

Only $\frac{232}{3}$ is between 2^6 and 2^7

So, the answer is (d).

9. **(a)** $5^k - 5^{k+1} + 5^{k-1} = 5^k \times m$

$5^k(1 - 5 + \frac{1}{5}) = 5^k \times m$

$-4 + \frac{1}{5} = m$

$m = -\frac{19}{5}$

The correct answer is (a).

10. **(e)** The answer is (a).

$10^5 = 10^3 \times 10^2$

(a) $2^{13} = 2^{10} \times 2^3$

$2^{10} > 10^3$, but $2^3 < 10^2$.

(b) $2^{14} = 2^{10} \times 2^4$

$2^{10} > 10^3$, but $2^4 < 10^2$.

(c) $2^{15} = 2^{10} \times 2^5$

$2^{10} > 10^3$, but $2^5 < 10^2$.

(d) $2^{16} = 2^{10} \times 2^6$

$2^{10} > 10^3$, but $2^6 < 10^2$.

(e) $2^{17} = 2^{10} \times 2^7$

$2^{10} > 10^3$, and $2^7 < 10^2$

So, $2^{17} > 10^5$.

Hence, the answer is (e).

11. **(d)** To solve questions asking about the range, it is a good idea to consider all possible values for all the variables.

There could be 4 possibilities.

1. $x = -2$ and $y = -3 \Rightarrow x - y = -2 - (-3) = 1$
2. $x = 4$ and $y = -3 \Rightarrow x - y = 4 - (-3) = 7$
3. $x = -2$ and $y = 2 \Rightarrow x - y = -2 - 2 = -4$
4. $x = 4$ and $y = 2 \Rightarrow x - y = 4 - 2 = 2$

Range means minimum value and maximum value

From the possible values above, the minimum value is–4 and the maximum value is 7

Hence, $-4 < x - y < 7$

So, the answer is (d).

12. **(d)** If $|x + 3| > 5$, then

Case 1 : If $x + 3 > 0$, then

$x + 3 > 5$

$\Rightarrow \quad x > 2 \quad$ ...(i)

Case II : If $x + 3 < 0$, then

$x + 3 < -5$

$x < -8 \quad$ ...(ii)

Hence, the answer is (d)

13. **(e)** If $|x| > 3$, then $x > 3$ or $x < -3$.

Hence, there are infinitely many integers that work for $|x| > 3$.

The answer is (e)

14. (c) The ten students scored between 78 and 86. So, $78 < s < 86$.

So, we can eliminate answer choice (a) and (b).

Now, we need to simplify the other two answer choices.

If $|s - 82| < 4$, then

$-4 < s - 82 < 4$

$78 < s < 86$

Hence, the answer is (c).

15. (e) If $0 < x < 1$, then $x > x^2 > x^3 > x^4$.......

Hence, $x^7 < x^5$

Eliminate (A) and (C)

As $x^7 < x^5$ and $x^6 < x^4$, then $x^7 + x^6 < x^5 + x^4$

Eliminate (B)

Same way III also works.

The answer is (e).

16. (b) Sandy's estimate is p

His estimate is within 10 pens of the actual number

The actual number is n

Hence, $p - 10 \le n \le p + 10$

The answer is (b).

17. (d) We need to find value of $(7^{x-1})^2 = (7^{2x-2})^2$

$= 7^{2x} \times 7^{-2} = \frac{7^{2x}}{7^2}$ It is given

$7^{4x} = 49$

Taking square root on both the sides.

$7^{2x} = +$ or $- 7$ (but, -7 is not possible as options are positive)

Hence, value of $\frac{7^{2x}}{7^2} = \frac{7}{7^2} = \frac{1}{7}$

The correct answer is option (d).

18. (d) It is given that,

$a_{n+1} = 2 \times a_n$.

when $n = 6$; $a_7 = 2 \times a_6$

Substituting this value in $a_7 - a_6 = 96$

$2 \times a_6 - a_6 = 96$

$a_6 = 96$

As $a_7 = 2 \times a_6 = 2 \times 96 = 192$

The correct answer is option (d).

19. (e) $x = 2^{y+1}$,

$x = 2^y \times 2^1$

$2^y = \frac{x}{2}$

$4^y = \frac{x^2}{4}$

The correct answer is option (e).

20. (c) $(32)^{\frac{1}{x}} = 2^{5x}$,

$(2^5)^{\frac{1}{x}} = 2^{5x}$,

$(2^5)^{\frac{5}{x}} = 2^{5x}$,

Hence, $\frac{5}{x} = 5x$

$x^2 = 1$

$x = 1$ or $- 1$

The correct answer is option (c).

21. (c) Let the three terms of the arithmetic progression be

(a – d), a and (a + d)

$\therefore \quad a - d + a + a + d = 30$

$\Rightarrow \quad a = 10$

Also, $(a - d) \times a \times (a + d) = 750$

$\Rightarrow \quad 10^2 - d^2 = 75$

$\Rightarrow \quad d = 5 \text{ or } -5$

Hence, $t_5 = 10 + 3 \times 5 \text{ or } 10 + 3 \times (-5)$

$\Rightarrow \quad t_5 = 5 \text{ or } -5$

The correct answer is option (c).

22. (c)

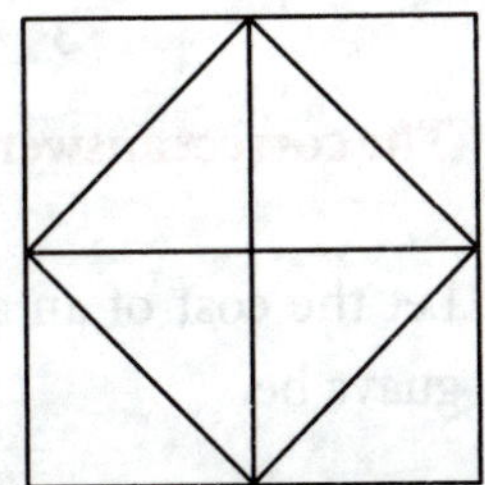

Area of inner square will be half of the immediate outer square.

$$= 15 \times 15\left(1 + \frac{1}{2} + \frac{1}{4} + \frac{1}{8} + ...\right)$$

$$= \frac{225}{1 - \frac{1}{2}} = 450$$

Hence, the required area = 450 m².

The correct answer is option (c).

23. (b) $2^{48 + 12x} \times 3^{16 + 4x} = 2^{32 - 4x} \times 3^{4y - 12x}$

$\Rightarrow \quad 48 + 12x = 32 - 4x$

$\Rightarrow \quad x = -1$

$\therefore \quad 16 - 4 = 4y + 12$

$\Rightarrow \quad y = 0.$

24. (a) The minimum value of 6x + 7y can be found by using A.M ³ G.M. inequality.

$$\therefore \frac{\frac{6x}{2} + \frac{6x}{2} + \frac{7y}{3} + \frac{7y}{3} + \frac{7y}{3}}{5}$$

$$\geq \left(\frac{6x}{2} . \frac{6x}{2} . \frac{7y}{3} . \frac{7y}{3} . \frac{7y}{3}\right)^{\frac{1}{5}}$$

$$\Rightarrow 6x + 7y \geq 5\left(3^2 . \frac{7^3}{3^3} x^2 y^3\right)^{\frac{1}{5}}$$

$$\Rightarrow 6x + 7y \geq 5\left(\frac{343}{3} .147\right)^{\frac{1}{5}}$$

$$\Rightarrow 6x + 7y \geq 35$$

Hence, the minimum value of expression is 35.

The correct answer is option (a).

25. (a) The number of detergent cakes product every month

will form an arithmetic progression.

Let 'a' be the number of detergent cakes produced by the machine in the first month.

$\therefore$ First term = a and common difference, d = 400

2 years = 24 months

$$S_n = \frac{n}{2}[2a + (n - 1)d]$$

$$\Rightarrow \quad 153600 = \frac{24}{2}[2a + (24 - 1)400]$$

$$\Rightarrow a = 1800$$

$$T_n = a + (n - 1)d$$

Where T_n is the number of detergent cakes produced in n^{th} month.

$\therefore \quad T_5 = 4600.$

The correct answer is option (a).

26. (b) $(x-2)^2+(x-1)^2+x^2+(x+1)^2+(x+2)^2$

Using the formulas :

$(a+b)^2 = a^2+b^2+2ab$, and

$(a-b)^2 = a^2+b^2-2ab$

$(x^2-2x-2x+4)+(X^2-1x-1x+1)(x^2)$
$+(x^2+1x+1x+1)$
$+(x^2+2x+2x+4)$

Simplifying :

$(x^2+4)+(x^2+1)+(x^2)+(x^2+1)+(x^2+4)$

Hence, $5x^2+10$

The correct answer is option (b)

27. (b) When x is directly proportional to y, it means that x = ny, where n is a constant

Or In other words, $\frac{x}{y}=n$, where n is a constant.

Hence, $\frac{x_1}{y_1}=\frac{x_2}{y_2}$

Plugging in values :

$\frac{8}{2}=\frac{x_2}{4}$

$x_2 = 16$

The correct answer is option (b).

28. (e) Let, number of boys be m

Number of girls = 3m

Note that we are solving for 3m

Note that we are solving for 3m

$3m+m=12$

$4m=3$

$3m=9$

The correct answer is option (e).

29. (e) Let the number be x.

$$\therefore \quad x^2+\frac{1}{x}=3\left(x^2-\frac{1}{x}\right)$$

$$\text{or} \quad x^2+\frac{1}{x}=3\left(\frac{1}{x}-x^2\right)$$

$$\Rightarrow \quad x^3+1=3x^3-3 \text{ or } x^3+1=3-3x^2$$

$$\Rightarrow \quad x=\sqrt[3]{2} \text{ or } x=\sqrt[3]{\frac{1}{2}}$$

Hence, no rational value of the number is possible for the given condition.

The correct answer is option (e)

30. (c) The required is $\frac{1}{3}\times\frac{2}{5}\times\frac{3}{4}\times 760=76.$

The correct answer is option (c)

31. (b) Let the cost of an apple, a banana and a guava be

Rs. a, Rs. b and Rs. g respectively.

According to given question,

$$3a+4b+7g=86 \quad \text{...(i)}$$

$$6a+7b+13g=164 \quad \text{...(ii)}$$

Subtracting (ii) from (i), we get

$$3a+3b+6g=78$$

$$\text{or} \quad a+b+2g=26 \quad \text{...(iii)}$$

Adding (i) and (iii), we get

$$4a+5b+9g=112$$

Therefore, cost of 5 bananas, 4 apples and 9 guavas is Rs. 112.

The correct answer is option (b)

32. (d) Let the number of mangoes with Panchu and Chhakku be x and y respectively.

$\therefore \quad x + 20 = 2(y - 20)$

$\Rightarrow \quad x - 2y = -60 \quad ...(i)$

and, $\quad 3(x - 40) = y + 40$

$\Rightarrow \quad 3x - y = 160 \quad ...(ii)$

Solving (i) and (ii), we get, x = 76 and y = 68.

The correct answer is option (d)

33. (d) $2x^2 + 5x^2 + 3x = x(2x + 3)(x + 1) = 0$

$\Rightarrow x = 0, -1 - \frac{3}{2}$

Hence, the smallest root is $-\frac{3}{2}$.

The correct answer is option (d)

34. (d) $x^2 < x$

$x^2 - x < 0$

$x(x - 1) < 0$

Zeros of the upward parabola (as the coefficient of x^2 is positive) are 0 and 1.

Hence, $x(x - 1)$ is less than 0 when $0 < x < 1$

The correct answer is option (d)

35. (d) Try each of the four extremes for value of $|a - b|$

$|-6 - 8| = 14$

$|-6 - 11| = 17$

$|5 - 8| = 3$

$|5 - 11| = 6$

Hence, $3 \le |a - b| \le 17$

The correct answer is option (d)

36. (e) $5x - 7 \ge 3x + 9$

Simplifying :

$2x \ge 16$

$x \ge 8$

(e) is correct

The correct answer is option (e)

37. (c) If $|x| > 5$, then $x > 5$ or $x < -5$

Therefore, x cannot be 1

The correct answer is option (c)

38. (c) $\frac{9}{x - 6} > -x$

$\Rightarrow \quad \frac{9}{x - 6} + x > 0$

$\Rightarrow \quad \frac{9 + x^2 - 6x}{x - 6} > 0$

$\Rightarrow \quad \frac{(x - 3)^2}{(x - 6)} > 0 \quad ...(i)$

Since numerator is a square, therefore, it is always positive.

To satisfy (i), $x > 6$

The correct answer is option (c)

39. (b) $8x - x(2 - 4y) = 6x + 4xy = 2x(3 + 2y)$

$= 2 \times 7 \times [3 + 2 \times (-4)] = -70.$

The correct answer is option (b)

40. (a) $\frac{x^2 - 5x + 6}{x^2 + 9x + 20} < 0$

$\Rightarrow \quad \frac{(x - 2)(x - 3)}{(x + 4)(x + 5)} < 0$

$\Rightarrow \quad \frac{(x - 2)(x - 3)(x + 4)(x + 5)}{(x + 4)^2 (x + 5)^2} < 0$

$\Rightarrow \quad (x - 2)(x - 3)(x + 4)(x + 5) < 0$

$\Rightarrow \quad x \in (-5, -4) \cup (2, 3)$

The correct answer is option (a)

41. (c) $|x-2|=9$

$\therefore\quad x-2=\pm 9$

$\therefore\quad x=11 \text{ or } x=-7$

$|x+9|=8$

$\therefore\quad y+9=\pm 8$

$\therefore\quad y=-1 \text{ or } y=-17$

$\therefore$ Minimum possible value of xy

$= 11\times(-17) = -187$

The correct answer is option (c)

42. (e) I. ab > cb + ca. Not true

II. 2b > a + c. Not necessarily true

Take a - 9, b = 3 and c = 1

III. Similarly $b^2 > ac$ is not necessarily true.

The correct answer is option (e)

43. (d) Consecutive odd integers from 1: 1, 3, 5, 7, 9,....

We see that there is a constant gap of '2' between consecutive terms of the above series and hence, it constitutes an arithmetic progression.

The sum of terms is given as:

$$\left[\frac{\text{First term}+\text{Last term}}{2}\right]\times(\text{Number of terms})$$

In the above arithmetic progression, the first term is '1' and the last term is 'n'.

Since we start with '1' (an odd number) and end with 'n', another odd number, the number of terms in the series $=\frac{n-1}{2}+1=\frac{n+1}{2}$; (for example: for the series: 1, 3, 5, 7, 0; the number of terms $=\frac{9-1}{2}+1=5$)

Thus, we have

$$\left[\frac{\text{First term}+\text{Last term}}{2}\right]\times(\text{Number of terms})=\text{Sum}$$

$$\left(\frac{1+n}{2}\right)\times\left(\frac{n+1}{2}\right)=256$$

$$\Rightarrow\quad \left(\frac{n+1}{2}\right)^2=256$$

$$\Rightarrow\quad \frac{n+1}{2}=16$$

$$\Rightarrow\quad n=31$$

The correct answer is Option (d).

44. (c) This is indeed a quadratic equation, though it does not look like one as we do not see a squared term; however, the equation can be solved by applying the concept of quadratic equation.

Say $\sqrt{x}=y$, then the equation becomes $y^2 - 3y + 2 = 0$. It is a quadratic equation. Let's solve this.

$$y^2-3y+2=0$$

$$y^2-2y-y+2=0$$

$$y(y-2)-1(y-2)=0$$

$$(y-2)(y-1)=0$$

So, $y = 2$ or 1.

$\sqrt{x} = 2$ or 1

$x = 4$ or 1

Thus, the ratio of the larger value of x and theh smaller value of $x=\frac{4}{1}$.

The correct answer is option (c)

45. (d) This is indeed a quadratic equation, though it does not look like one as we do not see a squared term: however, the equation can be solved by applying the concept of a quadratic equation.

Say $x^{\frac{1}{4}} = y$, then the equation becomes $-6y + y^2 + 9 = 0$. It is a quadratic equation.

Let's solve this.

$$y^2 - 6y + 9 = 0$$
$$y^2 - 2 \times 3 \times y + 3^2 = 0$$
$$(y - 3)^2 = 0$$

So, $y = 3$

$\Rightarrow$ $x^{\frac{1}{4}} = y = 3$

$x = 3^4 = 81$

The correct answer is option (d)

46. (e) Set of integers less than –2.1 are {–3, –4, –5,...}; among them, the greatest is –3, so, [–2.1] = –3.

Similarly, set of integers less than 2.7 are {2, 1, 0, –1,...}; among them, the greatest is 2, so, [2.7] = 2.

Similarly, set of integers less than 6.3 are {6, 5, 4,...}; among them, the greatest is 6, so, [6.3] = 6.

So, (–2.1] + [2.7] + [6.6] = –3 + 2 + 6 = 5.

The correct answer is option (e)

47. (c) Simply add three equations, we get $x^2 - yz + y^2 + xz + z^2 + xy = 32$

$\Rightarrow$ $(x^2 + y^2 + z^2) + (xy + xz - yz) = 32$

Replace the value of $xy + xz - yz = 5$ in the equation, we get

$$(x^2 + y^2 + z^2) + 5 = 32$$

$\Rightarrow$ $x^2 + y^2 + z^2 = 27$

The correct answer is option (c)

48. (c) Let x be the number of bikes, y the number of cars, and z the number of buses.

Total numbers of tires and horns

= Number of horns in bikes and cars

+ Number of tires in bikes

+ Number of tires in cars

$\Rightarrow$ $100 = 1 \times (x + y) + 2 \times x + 4 \times y$

$\Rightarrow$ $100 = 3x + 5y$

$\Rightarrow$ $100 - 5y = 3x$

$\Rightarrow$ $5(20 - y) = 3x$

We see that on the left-hand side, we have 5, a prime number; similarly, on the right-hand side, we have another 3, a prime number. For the equality to hold true, (20 – y) must be a multiple of 3, and x must be a multiple of 5. Also, it is given that y > x, picking a few numbers, we get two pairs of probable values of x, and y: (5, 17) and (10, 14).

Also given that (x + y) = 3z;

If we plug in x = 5, and y = 17 in (x + y) = 3z, we get $5 + 17 = 3z = 22 \Rightarrow z = \frac{22}{3}$, not an integer.

The number of buses must be an integer. This pair of values is not possible. If we plug in x = 10, and y = 14 in (x + y) = 3z, we get 10 + 14 = 3z ⇒ z = 8, in integer. This pair of values is possible.

Therefore, only the second pair will work. So, x = number of bikes = 10.

The correct answer is option (c)

49. (a) So, we are given that $a = \sqrt{17} + \sqrt[3]{9} + \sqrt{2}$. Note that $\sqrt{17}$ will be slightly greater than 4, which is the square root of the nearest perfect square number (16) to 17. Similarly, the cube root of 9 will be slightly greater than 2, which is the cube root of the nearest perfect cube number (8) to 9. And the square root of 2 will be slightly greater than 1.

Since a is the sum of these three numbers, i.e., (number greater than 4) + (number greater than 2) + (number greater than 1), it must be bigger than 7.

$[a > \{(4 + 2 + 1) = 7\}]$

The correct answer is option (a)

50. **(c)** We have $a^3 - a^2 - a + 1 = 0$

$\Rightarrow \quad a^2(a - 1) - 1\,(a - 1) = 0$

$(a - 1)\,(a^2 - 1) = 0$

$(a - 1)\,(a - 1)\,(a + 1) = 0$

$\Rightarrow \quad a = \pm 1$

There are only two possible values of a : 1 and –1. The answer is: "Two'. Seeing a cubic equation, one must not jump to a conclusion that the variable will necessarily have three values.

The correct answer is option (c)

51. **(a)** So, we have $\frac{5x-1}{-6} \le \frac{1-2x}{3}$.

$\frac{5x-1}{-6} \le \frac{1-2x}{3}$ can be written as

$-\frac{5x}{6} + \frac{1}{6} \le \frac{1}{3} - \frac{2x}{3}$

$-\frac{5x}{6} + \frac{2x}{3} \le \frac{1}{3} - \frac{1}{6}$

$\frac{-5x + 4x}{6} \le \frac{2-1}{6}$

$\Rightarrow -x \le 1$; cancelling 6 from both the sides and simplifying

$\Rightarrow x \ge -1$; multiplying both sides by –1.

Notes the sign reversal of the inequality; when a negative number is multiplied or divided, the inequality reverses its sign.

The correct answer is option (a)

52. **(d)** We know that $6 < x < 12$ and $y = x + 4$.

$x + y = x + x + 4 = 2x + 4$; so basically, we have to calculate the maximum possible value of $(2x + 4)$.

$6 < x < 12$ can be written as $12 < 2x < 24$ and then as $(12 + 4) < (2x + 4) < (24 + 4)$

$\Rightarrow 16 < 2x + 4 < 28 \Rightarrow 16 < x + y < 28$.

It is clear that the maximum possible integer value of $(x + y)$ would be 27.

Had you done in the following way, the answer would be wrong.

The greatest possible integer value of $x = 11$, and the greatest possible integer value of $y = 11 + 4 = 15$, then the answer would been $11 + 15 = 26$, which would have been wrong. We must not assume that x and y are integers. They are real numbers.

The correct answer is option (d)

53. **(a)** Since $f(x) = 4x - 7$, we have $f(2x - 6) = 4 \times (2x - 6) - 7 = 8x - 24 - 7 = 8x - 31$; by replacing x with $2x - 6$ in $f(x) = 4x - 7$.

Now, $4f(x) - 3 = f(2x - 6) \Rightarrow 4 \times (4x - 7) - 3 = 16x - 31$; substituting the values of $f(x) = 4x - 7$.

Again, $4f(x) - 3 = f(2x - 6)$, substituting the value of $4f(x) - 3$ and $f(2x - 6)$

We get $16x - 31 = 8x - 31 \Rightarrow 8x = 0 \Rightarrow x = 0$.

The correct answer is option (a)

54. (c) Replacing the value of f(x) for x, we get f(f(x))

$= [x(x+3)] \times [\{x(x+3)+3\} = x(x+3)$

(x^2+3x+3): The correct answer is C.

Alternate approach

Plug in any value for x; say, $x = 2 \Rightarrow f(x) = x(x+3)$

$\Rightarrow f(x) = 2 \times (2+3) = 10.$

Hence, $f(f(x)) = f(x)(f(x)+3) = 10 \times (10+3) = 130.$

Now, plug in x = 2 in the options; only option (c) equals 130, correct answer.

The disadvantage of this approach is that you might have to try all the options to match 130. It may consume more time.

The correct answer is option (c)

55. (a) So, for the given two linear equations $\frac{x}{2} - \frac{y}{3} = -4$ and $x - \frac{y}{2} + 7 = 0$, we have to find out the values of x and y to get the value of xy.

Let's name the two equations.

$$\frac{x}{2} - \frac{y}{3} = -4 \quad ...(1)$$

$$x - \frac{y}{2} + 7 = 0 \quad ...(ii)$$

Let's multiply equation (2) by $-\frac{1}{2}$ and transposing 7 other side. We get

$$\frac{x}{2} - \frac{y}{3} = -4 \quad ...(1)$$

$$-\frac{x}{2} + \frac{y}{4} = \frac{7}{2} \quad ...(2)$$

Adding the two equations, we get

$$\frac{x}{2} - \frac{y}{3} - \frac{x}{2} + \frac{y}{4} = -4 + \frac{7}{2}$$

$$-\frac{y}{3} + \frac{y}{4} = -\frac{1}{2}$$

$$-\frac{y}{12} = -\frac{1}{2}$$

$$y = 6$$

Let's plug-in the value of y in equation (1) to get the value of x.

$$\frac{x}{2} - \frac{6}{3} = -4 \quad ...(1)$$

$$\frac{x}{2} - 4 + 2 = -2$$

$$x = -4$$

So, $xy = -4 \times 6 = -24$

The correct answer is option (a)

56. (d) We use the initial letter of each name to represent the number of chocolates each kid gets.

Therefore,

- $J = K + 4$
- $B = S - 12$
- $S = J + 4$
- $K = B + 4$

We have four simultaneous equations with four variables. It may be time-consuming to solve this question by the traditional approach. The optimum approach is to plug in the values from the options. But which option should you try first? If you start plugging in from options (a), (b), (c) onwards, then you may lose more time in case the answer is (d) or (e).

The best way to plug-in is to try option (b), and then (d). It is called the B/D plug-in approach for problem solving questions. Under this approach, the values in the options must be arranged in ascending order from options (a) through (e).

Option (b) : If K = 4; J = 8' S = 12; B = 0. This option cannot be the answer as total number of candies, 4 + 8 + 12 + 0 = 24, not equal to 40. As 24 < 40, it means that the answer must be greater than 4, hence answer must not be option A or B. Let's try option (d).

Option (d) : If K = 8; J = 12; S = 16; B = 4. This option is the correct answer as the total number of chocolates, 8 + 12 + 16 + 4 = 40 = actual total number of chocolates.

The advantage with B/D plugging in approach is that if the value in Option (d) had been less than 40, then Option (e) must be the correct answer. We must not calculate the value for option (e); whereas, if the value in Option (d) had been more than 40, then option (c) must be the correct answer. So, merely by trying with only two option values (b & d), we can cover all the five options.

The correct answer is option (d)

57. **(b)** Since we only know one property of the function but not the actual function, the absolute value can't be evaluated.

Let us see each option one by one. Note this is a must be true question; thus, the correct option must be true for all values.

(*a*) $f(9) = f(9^3) = f(729)$;

$f(3) = f(3^3) = f(27)$;

$[f(3)]^2 = [f(27)]^2$

f(729) may or may not be equal to $[f(27)]^2$.

Hence, option (a) is discarded.

(*b*) $f(27) = f(3)$

$f(3) = f(3^3) = f(27)$

Hence, the correct answer is option (b).

(*c*) $f(3) = -f(81)$

We know that f(3) is f(27), but f(3) may or may not be equal to – f(81).

Hence, option (c) is discarded.

(*d*) $f(1) = 9f(-1)$

f(1) may or may not be equal to 9f(−1).

Hence, option (d) is discarded.

(*e*) f(0) = 1 may or may not be true as we don't know the absolute value of the function.

Hence, option (e) is discarded.

58. **(d)** Given numbers are in arithmetic series as the difference between the numbers is constant (=1). The sum of the arithmetic series is given by $\frac{n}{2} \times$ (first term + last term)

Total number of terms = 199

Sum of arithmetic series

$$\frac{199}{2} \times (199 + 1) = 19{,}900$$

Data Sufficiency

1. Is $|x| > |y|$?

   1. $x > y$
   2. $y < 0$

   (a) Statement (1) ALONE is sufficient but statement (2) ALONE is not sufficient.

   (b) Statement (2) ALONE is sufficient but statement (1) ALONE is not sufficient.

   (c) BOTH statements TOGETHER are sufficient, but NEITHER statement ALONE is sufficient.

   (d) EACH statement ALONE is sufficient.

   (e) Statements (1) and (2) TOGETHER are not sufficient.

2. What is the value of x?

   1. $4|x - 4| = 16$
   2. x is a non-negative integer.

   (a) Statement (1) ALONE is sufficient but statement (2) ALONE is not sufficient.

   (b) Statement (2) ALONE is sufficient but statement (1) ALONE is not sufficient.

   (c) BOTH statements TOGETHER are sufficient, but NEITHER statement ALONE is sufficient.

   (d) EACH statement ALONE is sufficient.

   (e) Statements (1) and (2) TOGETHER are not sufficient.

3. Does $x = 2$?

   1. x is an integer.
   2. $-x|x| \geq 4$

   (a) Statement (1) ALONE is sufficient but statement (2) ALONE is not sufficient.

   (b) Statement (2) ALONE is sufficient but statement (1) ALONE is not sufficient.

   (c) BOTH statements TOGETHER are sufficient, but NEITHER statement ALONE is sufficient.

   (d) EACH statement ALONE is sufficient.

   (e) Statements (1) and (2) TOGETHER are not sufficient.

4. Is $x > y$?

   1. $|x| > |y|$
   2. $x + y > 0$

   (a) Statement (1) ALONE is sufficient but statement (2) ALONE is not sufficient.

   (b) Statement (2) ALONE is sufficient but statement (1) ALONE is not sufficient.

   (c) BOTH statements TOGETHER are sufficient, but NEITHER statement ALONE is sufficient.

   (d) EACH statement ALONE is sufficient.

   (e) Statements (1) and (2) TOGETHER are not sufficient.

5. Is $|x| > |y|$?

   1. $x + y > 0$
   2. $x > y$

   (a) Statement (1) ALONE is sufficient but statement (2) ALONE is not sufficient.

   (b) Statement (2) ALONE is sufficient but statement (1) ALONE is not sufficient.

   (c) BOTH statements TOGETHER are sufficient, but NEITHER statement ALONE is sufficient.

   (d) EACH statement ALONE is sufficient.

   (e) Statements (1) and (2) TOGETHER are not sufficient.

6. Is $x > y$?

   1. $|x| + |y| > |x + y|$
   2. $|x| > |y|$

(*a*) Statement (1) ALONE is sufficient but statement (2) ALONE is not sufficient.

(*b*) Statement (2) ALONE is sufficient but statement (1) ALONE is not sufficient.

(*c*) BOTH statements TOGETHER are sufficient, but NEITHER statement ALONE is sufficient.

(*d*) EACH statement ALONE is sufficient.

(*e*) Statements (1) and (2) TOGETHER are not sufficient.

7. Is $x > 0$?

1. $|x|y > x|y|$
2. $xy < 0$

(*a*) Statement (1) ALONE is sufficient but statement (2) ALONE is not sufficient.

(*b*) Statement (2) ALONE is sufficient but statement (1) ALONE is not sufficient.

(*c*) BOTH statements TOGETHER are sufficient, but NEITHER statement ALONE is sufficient.

(*d*) EACH statement ALONE is sufficient.

(*e*) Statements (1) and (2) TOGETHER are not sufficient.

8. If $x > |y| > z$, then which of the following must be true?

I. $x + y > 0$

II. $y + z > 0$

III. $x + y > |y| + z$

(*a*) None of the above

(*b*) I only

(*c*) I and II only

(*d*) III only

(*e*) I, II, and III

9. What is the value of x?

1. $x = -|x|$
2. $x^2 = 9$

(*a*) Statement (1) ALONE is sufficient but statement (2) ALONE is not sufficient.

(*b*) Statement (2) ALONE is sufficient but statement (1) ALONE is not sufficient.

(*c*) BOTH statements TOGETHER are sufficient, but NEITHER statement ALONE is sufficient.

(*d*) EACH statement ALONE is sufficient.

(*e*) Statements (1) and (2) TOGETHER are not sufficient.

10. If $a + b + c > 0$, is $a > 1$?

1. $a > b + c + 1$
2. $b + c + 1 < 0$

(*a*) Statement (1) ALONE is sufficient but statement (2) ALONE is not sufficient.

(*b*) Statement (2) ALONE is sufficient but statement (1) ALONE is not sufficient.

(*c*) BOTH statements TOGETHER are sufficient, but NEITHER statement ALONE is sufficient.

(*d*) EACH statement ALONE is sufficient.

(*e*) Statements (1) and (2) TOGETHER are not sufficient.

11. Is $|x - 50| < |70 - x|$?

1. $70 - x > x - 50$
2. $x < 60$

(*a*) Statement (1) ALONE is sufficient but statement (2) ALONE is not sufficient.

(*b*) Statement (2) ALONE is sufficient but statement (1) ALONE is not sufficient.

(*c*) BOTH statements TOGETHER are sufficient, but NEITHER statement ALONE is sufficient.

(*d*) EACH statement ALONE is sufficient.

(*e*) Statements (1) and (2) TOGETHER are not sufficient.

12. How many cards does Adam have currently?

1. If Adam receives three more cards from his friend then he will have at least 20 cards.
2. If Adam gives three of his cards to a friend, then Adam will have fewer than 15 cards.

(*a*) Statement (1) ALONE is sufficient but statement (2) ALONE is not sufficient.

(*b*) Statement (2) ALONE is sufficient but statement (1) ALONE is not sufficient.

(*c*) BOTH statements TOGETHER are sufficient, but NEITHER statement ALONE is sufficient.

(*d*) EACH statement ALONE is sufficient.

(*e*) Statements (1) and (2) TOGETHER are not sufficient.

13. Roger has 25 pens and 30 erasers. What is the total cost of the 25 pens and 30 erasers?

1. The price of each pen is 3 times the cost of each eraser.
2. The total cost of one pen and 2 erasers in $5.

(*a*) Statement (1) ALONE is sufficient but statement (2) ALONE is not sufficient.

(*b*) Statement (2) ALONE is sufficient but statement (1) ALONE is not sufficient.

(*c*) BOTH statements TOGETHER are sufficient, but NEITHER statement ALONE is sufficient.

(*d*) EACH statement ALONE is sufficient.

(*e*) Statements (1) and (2) TOGETHER are not sufficient.

14. If $3x + 5y = 17$, what is the value of x?

1. y is a positive integer
2. $x = 4y$

(*a*) Statement (1) ALONE is sufficient but statement (2) ALONE is not sufficient.

(*b*) Statement (2) ALONE is sufficient but statement (1) ALONE is not sufficient.

(*c*) BOTH statements TOGETHER are sufficient, but NEITHER statement ALONE is sufficient.

(*d*) EACH statement ALONE is sufficient.

(*e*) Statements (1) and (2) TOGETHER are not sufficient.

15. In a sequence of terms $a_n = 3 \times a_{n-1}$, where, n is an integer greater than 1, what is the value of a_4?

1. $a_1 = 3$
2. $\frac{a_2}{a_n} = 3^{10}$

(*a*) Statement (1) ALONE is sufficient but statement (2) ALONE is not sufficient.

(*b*) Statement (2) ALONE is sufficient but statement (1) ALONE is not sufficient.

(*c*) BOTH statements TOGETHER are sufficient, but NEITHER statement ALONE is sufficient.

(*d*) EACH statement ALONE is sufficient.

(*e*) Statements (1) and (2) TOGETHER are not sufficient.

16. What is value of x?

1. $2x - y = 5x + 2y$
2. $2(x - y) = 8 - 2y$

(*a*) Statement (1) ALONE is sufficient but statement (2) ALONE is not sufficient.

(*b*) Statement (2) ALONE is sufficient but statement (1) ALONE is not sufficient.

(*c*) BOTH statements TOGETHER are sufficient, but NEITHER statement ALONE is sufficient.

(*d*) EACH statement ALONE is sufficient.

(*e*) Statements (1) and (2) TOGETHER are not sufficient.

17. What is the value of x?

1. $2x + 5y = 12$
2. $15y = 26 - 6x$

(*a*) Statement (1) ALONE is sufficient but statement (2) ALONE is not sufficient.

(*b*) Statement (2) ALONE is sufficient but statement (1) ALONE is not sufficient.

(*c*) BOTH statements TOGETHER are sufficient, but NEITHER statement ALONE is sufficient.

(*d*) EACH statement ALONE is sufficient.

(*e*) Statements (1) and (2) TOGETHER are not sufficient.

18. If $0 < xy < xz$, is $x < 0$?

1. $z < 0$
2. $y > z$

(*a*) Statement (1) ALONE is sufficient but statement (2) ALONE is not sufficient.

(*b*) Statement (2) ALONE is sufficient but statement (1) ALONE is not sufficient.

(*c*) BOTH statements TOGETHER are sufficient, but NEITHER statement ALONE is sufficient.

(*d*) EACH statement ALONE is sufficient.

(*e*) Statements (1) and (2) TOGETHER are not sufficient.

19. Is $x \neq 1$?

1. $(3x - 2)^2 = x^2$
2. $(3x - 2)^2 = x$

(*a*) Statement (1) ALONE is sufficient but statement (2) ALONE is not sufficient.

(*b*) Statement (2) ALONE is sufficient but statement (1) ALONE is not sufficient.

(*c*) BOTH statements TOGETHER are sufficient, but NEITHER statement ALONE is sufficient.

(*d*) EACH statement ALONE is sufficient.

(*e*) Statements (1) and (2) TOGETHER are not sufficient.

20. If x, y and z are positive, and $x^2 + z^2 = 313$, what is the value of $(y - x - z)$?

1. $y^2 + z^2 = 244$
2. $x^2 + y^2 = 269$

(*a*) Statement (1) ALONE is sufficient but statement (2) ALONE is not sufficient.

(*b*) Statement (2) ALONE is sufficient but statement (1) ALONE is not sufficient.

(*c*) BOTH statements TOGETHER are sufficient, but NEITHER statement ALONE is sufficient.

(*d*) EACH statement ALONE is sufficient.

(*e*) Statements (1) and (2) TOGETHER are not sufficient.

21. What is the value of a?

1. $2a + 3b = 12$
2. $8a + 12b = 48$

(*a*) Statement (1) ALONE is sufficient but statement (2) ALONE is not sufficient.

(*b*) Statement (2) ALONE is sufficient but statement (1) ALONE is not sufficient.

(*c*) BOTH statements TOGETHER are sufficient, but NEITHER statement ALONE is sufficient.

(*d*) EACH statement ALONE is sufficient.

(*e*) Statements (1) and (2) TOGETHER are not sufficient.

22. If $a > 1$, and $b > 1$, is $a > b$?

1. $\sqrt{a} > b$
2. $\sqrt{b} < a$

(a) Statement (1) ALONE is sufficient but statement (2) ALONE is not sufficient.
(b) Statement (2) ALONE is sufficient but statement (1) ALONE is not sufficient.
(c) BOTH statements TOGETHER are sufficient, but NEITHER statement ALONE is sufficient.
(d) EACH statement ALONE is sufficient.
(e) Statements (1) and (2) TOGETHER are not sufficient.

23. If x is a two-digit number; where a is tens digit and b is units digit, what is the value of x?

1. $a + b = 10$
2. $a - b = 4$

(a) Statement (1) ALONE is sufficient but statement (2) ALONE is not sufficient.
(b) Statement (2) ALONE is sufficient but statement (1) ALONE is not sufficient.
(c) BOTH statements TOGETHER are sufficient, but NEITHER statement ALONE is sufficient.
(d) EACH statement ALONE is sufficient.
(e) Statements (1) and (2) TOGETHER are not sufficient.

24. If $x = 100^{\frac{b}{a}}$, where a ¹ 0, is x an integer?

1. $\frac{b^6}{a^6}$ is an integer
2. $a - 2b = 0$

(a) Statement (1) ALONE is sufficient but statement (2) ALONE is not sufficient.
(b) Statement (2) ALONE is sufficient but statement (1) ALONE is not sufficient.
(c) BOTH statements TOGETHER are sufficient, but NEITHER statement ALONE is sufficient.
(d) EACH statement ALONE is sufficient.
(e) Statements (1) and (2) TOGETHER are not sufficient.

25. Is $a^5 - b^2 - c^2 < 0$?

1. $ab > 0$
2. $bc > 0$

(a) Statement (1) ALONE is sufficient but statement (2) ALONE is not sufficient.
(b) Statement (2) ALONE is sufficient but statement (1) ALONE is not sufficient.
(c) BOTH statements TOGETHER are sufficient, but NEITHER statement ALONE is sufficient.
(d) EACH statement ALONE is sufficient.
(e) Statements (1) and (2) TOGETHER are not sufficient.

26. If $a^2 - ab = a^2 - b^2$ what is the value of c such that $a \neq b$?

1. $c = 3 - a$
2. $b = c^3$

(a) Statement (1) ALONE is sufficient but statement (2) ALONE is not sufficient.
(b) Statement (2) ALONE is sufficient but statement (1) ALONE is not sufficient.
(c) BOTH statements TOGETHER are sufficient, but NEITHER statement ALONE is sufficient.
(d) EACH statement ALONE is sufficient.
(e) Statements (1) and (2) TOGETHER are not sufficient.

27. What is the value of positive integer x?

1. x^3 is a perfect square
2. $x^2 = x$

(a) Statement (1) ALONE is sufficient but statement (2) ALONE is not sufficient.

(b) Statement (2) ALONE is sufficient but statement (1) ALONE is not sufficient.

(c) BOTH statements TOGETHER are sufficient, but NEITHER statement ALONE is sufficient.

(d) EACH statement ALONE is sufficient.

(e) Statements (1) and (2) TOGETHER are not sufficient.

28. Is $a > b$?

1. $a < b^4$
2. a and b are negative integers.

(a) Statement (1) ALONE is sufficient but statement (2) ALONE is not sufficient.

(b) Statement (2) ALONE is sufficient but statement (1) ALONE is not sufficient.

(c) BOTH statements TOGETHER are sufficient, but NEITHER statement ALONE is sufficient.

(d) EACH statement ALONE is sufficient.

(e) Statements (1) and (2) TOGETHER are not sufficient.

29. What is the value of the expression $12x^2 + 18y^2$?

1. $x = 3$
2. $3y^2 + 2x^2 = 14$

(a) Statement (1) ALONE is sufficient but statement (2) ALONE is not sufficient.

(b) Statement (2) ALONE is sufficient but statement (1) ALONE is not sufficient.

(c) BOTH statements TOGETHER are sufficient, but NEITHER statement ALONE is sufficient.

(d) EACH statement ALONE is sufficient.

(e) Statements (1) and (2) TOGETHER are not sufficient.

30. John is 10 years younger than his cousin. How old will John be in 20 years?

1. Five years ago, John's cousin was twice as old as John.
2. If John's cousin were born 5 years earlier, she would, at present, be twice as old as John.

(a) Statement (1) ALONE is sufficient but statement (2) ALONE is not sufficient.

(b) Statement (2) ALONE is sufficient but statement (1) ALONE is not sufficient.

(c) BOTH statements TOGETHER are sufficient, but NEITHER statement ALONE is sufficient.

(d) EACH statement ALONE is sufficient.

(e) Statements (1) and (2) TOGETHER are not sufficient.

31. What is the value of a?

1. $a^2 - a - 6 = 0$
2. $(a + 5)$ is a prime number

(a) Statement (1) ALONE is sufficient but statement (2) ALONE is not sufficient.

(b) Statement (2) ALONE is sufficient but statement (1) ALONE is not sufficient.

(c) BOTH statements TOGETHER are sufficient, but NEITHER statement ALONE is sufficient.

(d) EACH statement ALONE is sufficient.

(e) Statements (1) and (2) TOGETHER are not sufficient.

32. If $a + 3|b| = 50$, what is the value b?

1. $3|b| = a - 20$
2. $|b| + \frac{a}{3} = \frac{50}{3}$

(a) Statement (1) ALONE is sufficient but statement (2) ALONE is not sufficient.

(b) Statement (2) ALONE is sufficient but statement (1) ALONE is not sufficient.

(c) BOTH statements TOGETHER are sufficient, but NEITHER statement ALONE is sufficient.

(*d*) EACH statement ALONE is sufficient.

(*e*) Statements (1) and (2) TOGETHER are not sufficient.

33. What is the value of a^3?

1. $a^2 = 3a + 4$
2. $a^3 - 4a^2 = 4 - a$

(*a*) Statement (1) ALONE is sufficient but statement (2) ALONE is not sufficient.

(*b*) Statement (2) ALONE is sufficient but statement (1) ALONE is not sufficient.

(*c*) BOTH statements TOGETHER are sufficient, but NEITHER statement ALONE is sufficient.

(*d*) EACH statement ALONE is sufficient.

(*e*) Statements (1) and (2) TOGETHER are not sufficient.

34. For all integers x, the function f is defined by $f(x) = (c)^{\frac{6}{x}}$, where c is a constant. What is the value of f(1)?

1. $f(2) = 125$
2. $f(3) = 25$

(*a*) Statement (1) ALONE is sufficient but statement (2) ALONE is not sufficient.

(*b*) Statement (2) ALONE is sufficient but statement (1) ALONE is not sufficient.

(*c*) BOTH statements TOGETHER are sufficient, but NEITHER statement ALONE is sufficient.

(*d*) EACH statement ALONE is sufficient.

(*e*) Statements (1) and (2) TOGETHER are not sufficient.

35. Is $x < 0$?

1. $-x = |-x|$
2. $x^2 = 16$

(*a*) Statement (1) ALONE is sufficient but statement (2) ALONE is not sufficient.

(*b*) Statement (2) ALONE is sufficient but statement (1) ALONE is not sufficient.

(*c*) BOTH statements TOGETHER are sufficient, but NEITHER statement ALONE is sufficient.

(*d*) EACH statement ALONE is sufficient.

(*e*) Statements (1) and (2) TOGETHER are not sufficient.

36. Is $x > y^3z$?

1. $wx > yz$
2. $y = 1$

(*a*) Statement (1) ALONE is sufficient but statement (2) ALONE is not sufficient.

(*b*) Statement (2) ALONE is sufficient but statement (1) ALONE is not sufficient.

(*c*) BOTH statements TOGETHER are sufficient, but NEITHER statement ALONE is sufficient.

(*d*) EACH statement ALONE is sufficient.

(*e*) Statements (1) and (2) TOGETHER are not sufficient.

Answer Key

1. (*e*)
2. (*e*)
3. (*a*)
4. (*c*)
5. (*c*)
6. (*e*)
7. (*a*)
8. (*b*)
9. (*c*)
10. (*b*)
11. (*d*)
12. (*e*)
13. (*e*)
14. (*b*)
15. (*a*)
16. (*b*)
17. (*e*)
18. (*d*)
19. (*c*)
20. (*c*)
21. (*e*)
22. (*a*)
23. (*c*)
24. (a)
25. (*e*)
26. (*b*)
27. (*b*)
28. (*e*)
29. (*b*)
30. (d)
31. (*c*)
32. (*e*)
33. (*b*)
34. (*b*)
35. (*c*)
36. (*c*)

Answer Explanations

1. (e) **Considering statement (1) alone :**

Let x = 3 and y = 2

So, |x| = 3 and |y| = 2

Is |x| > |y|? Yes

Let x = -2 and y = -3

So, |x| = 2 and |y| = 3

Is |x| > |y|? No

INSUFFICIENT

Eliminate AD.

Considering statement (2) alone :

Let x = 3 and y = –2

So, |x| = 3 and |y| = 2

Is |x| > |y|? Yes

Let x = –2 and y = –3

So, |x| = 2 and |y| = 3

Is |x| > |y|? No

INSUFFICIENT

Eliminate B.

Considering both statement together:

Let x = 3 and y = -2

So, |x| = 3 and |y| = 2

Is |x| > |y|? Yes

Let x = –2 and y = –3

So, |x| = 2 and |y| = 3

Is |x| > |y|? No

INSUFFICIENT

The answer is (e).

2. (e) **Considering statement (1) alone :**

If $4|x - 4| = 16$, then $|x - 4| = 4$

So, either $x - 4 = 4$ or $x - 4 = -4$

$\Rightarrow$ x = 8 of x = 0

INSUFFICIENT

Eliminate AD.

Considering statement (2) alone :

If x is non-negative integer, x can take any value greater than equal to 0.

Considering both the statements together:

From statement (1), we get that x = 0 or 8.

Statement (2) allows both the values.

INSUFFICIENT

The answer is (e).

3. (a) **Considering statement (1) alone:**

Just knowing that x is an integer doesn't help.

INSUFFICIENT

Eliminate AD.

Considering statement (2) alone :

If $-x|x| \geq 4$, then $x < 0$

If $x < 0$, then $x \neq 2$.

SUFFICIENT The answer is (b).

4. (c) **Considering statement (1) alone:**

Let x = 3 and y = 2,

then |x| > |y|

Is $x > y$? YES

Let $x = -4$ and $y = -3$,

then $|x| > |y|$

Is $x > y$? NO

INSUFFICIENT

Eliminate AD.

Considering statement (2) alone :

If $x + y > 0$, then $x > -y$

Let $x = 2$ and $y = -1$,

then $x > -y$

Is $x > y$? YES

Let $x = 3$ and $y = 4$, then $x > -y$

Is $x > y$? NO

INSUFFICIENT

Eliminate B

Considering both statements together :

Let $x = 3$ and $y = 2$,

then $|x| > |y|$ and also $x > -y$

Is $x > y$? YES

Let $x = 3$ and $y = -2$, then $|x| > |y|$ and also $x > -y$

Is $x > y$? YES

SUFFICIENT

The answer is (c).

5. (c) **Considering statement (1) alone :**

If $x = 2$ and $y = 1$, then $x + y > 0$

Is $|x| > |y|$? YES

If $x = 2$ and $y = 3$, then $x + y > 0$

Is $|x| > |y|$? NO

INSUFFICIENT

Eliminate AD.

Considering statement (2) alone :

If $x = 2$ and $y = 1$, then $x > y$

Is $|x| > |y|$? YES

If $x = 2$ and $y = -3$,

then $x > y$ Is $|x| > |y|$? NO

INSUFFICIENT

Eliminate B.

Considering both statements together:

If $x = 2$ and $y = 1$, then $x + y > 0$ and $x > y$ Is $|x| > |y|$? YES

If $x = 2$ and $y = -1$, then $x + y > 0$ and $x > y$

Is $|x| > |y|$? YES

SUFFICIENT

The answer is (c).

6. (e) **Considering statement (1) alone :**

For $|x| + |y| > |x + y|$, at least one x or y must be negative.

If $x = 3$ and $y = -2$, then $|x| + |y| > |x + y|$

Is $x > y$? YES If $x = -3$ and $y = 2$, then $|x| + |y| > |x + y|$

Is $x > y$? NO

INSUFFICIENT

Eliminate AD.

Considering statement (2) alone :

If $x = 3$ and $y = -2$, then $|x| > |y|$

Is $x > y$? YES If $x = -3$ and $y = 2$, then $|x| > |y|$

Is $x > y$? NO

INSUFFICIENT

Eliminate B.

Considering both statements together :

If $x = 3$ and $y = -2$, then $|x| > |y|$ and $|x| + |y| > |x + y|$

Is $x > y$? YES If $x = -3$ and $y = 2$, then $|x| > |y|$ and $|x| + |y| > |x + y|$

Is $x > y$? NO

INSUFFICIENT

The answer is (e).

7. (a) **Considering statement (1) alone :**

If $x > 0$ and $y > 0$, then $|x|y = x|y|$.

So, both can't be positive.

If $x < 0$ and $y < 0$, then $|x|y = x|y|$.

So, both can't be negative.

If $x < 0$ and $y > 0$, then $|x|y > x|y|$. Is $x > 0$? NO

If $x > 0$ and $y < 0$, then $|x|y < x|y|$.

These values are not allowed.

SUFFICIENT.

Eliminate BCE.

Considering statement (2) alone :

If $xy < 0$, then either can be negative.

INSUFFICIENT

The answer is (a).

8. (b) If $x = 4$, $y = 3$, and $z = 2$, then $x + y > 0$, $y + z > 0$, and $x + y > |y| + z$.

If $x = 4$, $y = -3$, and $z = 2$, then $x + y > 0$, $y + z < 0$, and $x + y < |y| + z$.

Hence, the answer is (b).

9. (c) **Considering statement (1) alone :**

If $x -|x|$, then x can take any negative value.

INSUFFICIENT Eliminate AD

Considering statement (2) alone :

If $x^2 = 9$, then $x = 3$ or $- 3$

INSUFFICIENT

Eliminate B

Considering both statements together:

Only $x = - 3$ works for both the statements.

SUFFICIENT

The answer is (c).

10. (b) If $a + b + c > 0$, then $b + c > -a$

Considering statement (1) alone :

If $a > b + c + 1$, then $a > - a + 1$

So, $2a > 1$

Hence, $a > 0.5$

INSUFFICIENT Eliminate AD

Considering statement (2) alone :

If $b + c + 1 < 0$, then $b + c < -1$

If $a + (b + c) > 0$, then $a > 1$

SUFFICIENT The answer is (b).

11. (d) If $x = 60$, then $|x - 50| = |70 - x|$

If $x > 60$, then $|x - 50| > |70 - x|$

If $x < 60$, then $|x - 50| < |70 - x|$

Considering statement (1) alone :

If $70 - x > x - 50$, then $120 > 2x$

$\Rightarrow x < 60$

SUFFICIENT

Eliminate BCE

Considering statement (2) alone :

If $x < 60$, then $|x - 50| < |70 - x|$

SUFFICIENT

The answer is (d).

12. (e) Let the number of cards that Adam have is c.

Considering statement (1) alone :

$c + 3 = 20$

$\Rightarrow$ $c = 17$

INSUFFICIENT

Eliminate AD

Considering statement (2) alone :

$c - 3 \leq 20$

$\Rightarrow$ $c \leq 18$

INSUFFICIENT

Eliminate B

Considering both the statements together :

$17 \leq c \leq 18$

Hence, c can be 17 or 18.

INSUFFICIENT

The answer is (e).

13. (e) Let the cost of each pen be p and the cost of each eraser be *e*.

Considering statement (1) alone :

$p = 3e$

INSUFFICIENT

Eliminate AD

Considering statement (2) alone :

$p + 2e = 5$

INSUFFICIENT

Eliminate B

Considering both the statement together

$p = 3e$ and $p + 2e = 5$

$\Rightarrow$ $3e + 2e = 5$

$\Rightarrow$ $e = 1$

If $e = 1$, then $p = 3$

INSUFFICIENT

The answer is (e).

14. (b) **Considering statement (1) alone :**

No information about x

INSUFFICIENT

Eliminate AD

Considering statement (2) alone :

If $x = 4y$ and $3x + 5y = 17$, then $3(4) + 5y = 17$

$\Rightarrow$ $y = 1$

If $y = 1$, then $x = 4$

SUFFICIENT

The answer is (b).

15. (a) $a_1 = 3$

The sequence is : 3, 9, 27, 81, ... so the fourth term is 81.

Sufficient. Eliminate B/C/E

Considering statement 2 alone: $\frac{a_2}{a_n} = 3^{10}$

Since we don't know how many terms are there are there in the sequence, value of n cannot be calculated.

Insufficient.

The correct answer is option (a)

16. (b) **Considering statement 1 alone :**

$2x - y = 5x + 2y$

$-3x = 3y$

$x = -y$

Value of x cannot be calculated. Insufficient

Eliminate A/D.

Considering statement 2 alone :

$2(x - y) = 8 - 2y$

$2x - 2y = 8 - 2y$

$2x = 8$

$x = 4$

Sufficient

17. (e) **Considering statement 1 alone :**

$2x + 5y = 12$

As x and y can have infinite values. Statement (1) is insufficient

Eliminate A and D.

Considering statement 2 alone :

$4y = 12 - 6x$

As x and y can have infinite values, Statement (2) is insufficient

Eliminate B.

Considering statement 1 and 2 together:

Now the equations $2x + 5y = 12$ and $6x + 15y = 26$ are equivalent equations.

If we multiply both sides of the equation $3x + 2y = 6$ of Statement (1) by 3, we will obtain the equation $6x + 4y = 12$. Therefore, there is only one equation given.

Hence, we cannot determine value of x. Insufficient

The correct answer is option (e).

18. (d) Since xy is positive, means that signs of both x and y are the same. Similarly, zx is positive means that signs of both x and y are the same.

Considering statement 1 alone :

As z is negative, therefore, x is negative. So, $x < 0$

Sufficient

Eliminate B/C/E.

Considering statement 2 alone :

It is given that $y > z$ and we know from question stem that $xy < xz$.

When both sides of the inequality $y > z$ is multiplied by x, it reverses sign only when x is negative.

So, $x < 0$

Sufficient

The correct answer is option (d).

19. (c) **Considering Statement 1 alone :**

$(3x - 2)^2 = x^2$

$\Rightarrow (3x - 2)^2 - x^2 = 0$

$\Rightarrow \{(3x - 2) - x\}\{(3x - 2) + x\} = 0$

$\Rightarrow (2x - 2)(4x - 2) = 0$

$\Rightarrow \quad x = 1 \text{ or } \frac{1}{2}$

Thus, we obtain two values of x:1 and $\frac{1}{2}$.

Thus, Statement 1 is not sufficient to answer the question since the answer may be Yes or No.

The correct answer would be among B/C/E.

Considering Statement 2 alone :

$(3x-2)^2 = x$

$\Rightarrow \quad 9x^2 - 12x + 4 = x$

$\Rightarrow \quad 9x^2 - 13x + 4 = 0$

$\Rightarrow \quad 9x^2 - 9x - 4x + 4 = 0$

$\Rightarrow \quad 9x(x-1) - 4(x-1) = 0$

$\Rightarrow \quad (9x-4)(x-1) = 0$

$\Rightarrow \quad x = \frac{4}{9}$ or 1.

Thus, we obtain two values of x : 1 or $\frac{4}{9}$.

Thus Statement 2 is not sufficient to answer the question since the answer may be Yes or No.

The correct answer would be between C/E.

Statements 1 and 2 together :

Combining both the statements, we get x = 1.

Hence, we get the answer by combining statements 1 and 2 and the answer is No- a unique answer

The correct answer is Option (c).

20. (c) **Considering Statement 1 alone :**

The statement has only two variables y and z. Hence Statement 1 alone is not sufficient to find the value of $(y - x - z)$.

Hence, eliminate A/D.

Considering Statement 2 alone :

The statement has only two variables x and y. Hence Statement 2 alone is not sufficient to find the value of $(y - x - z)$.

Hence, eliminate B

Statements 1 and 2 together :

If we subtract equation (2): $x^2 + y^2 = 269$ from equation (1): $y^2 + z^2 = 244$, we get $x^2 - z^2 = 25$.

We also have $x^2 + z^2 = 313$. We can solve these two equations to get x and z and then put these values in equations (1) or (2) to find the value of v. We must keep in mind that x, y, & z are positive, so we need not care about the negative values of the variables.

In DS questions, if you are sure of getting the unique value, you need not necessarily calculate the value.

Hence statements 1 and 2 together are sufficient.

The correct answer is Option (c).

21. (e) **Considering Statement 1 alone :**

We cannot find out the unique value of a as the linear equation has two variables. So, it is insufficient. Hence, eliminate A/D.

Considering Statement 2 alone :

As with Statement 1, we cannot find out the unique value of a as the linear equation has two variables. So, it is insufficient.

Hence, eliminate B.

Statement 1 and 2 together :

You may notice that if we simplify (divide both sides by 4) the equation : $8a + 12b = 48$ in Statement 2, we get the equation: $2a + 3b = 12$ in statement 1. Therefore, we do not really have two distinct equations. Indirectly we are provided only one linear equation. We cannot find the unique value of a.

Both statements together are insufficient.

The correct answer is Option (e).

22. (a) **Considering Statement 1 alone :**

Squaring on both sides we get $a > b^2$. Since $b > 1$, we have $b^2 > b$.

$\Rightarrow a > b^2 > b$. Therefore, a will always be greater than b. This statement alone is sufficient.

Hence, eliminate B/C/E.

Considering Statement 2 alone :

Squaring both the sides we get $b < a^2$. Though we can apply the tactic that we applied in Statement 1, we cannot compare a and b. Let's apply for the sake of understanding. Since $a > 1$, we have $a^2 > a$. From $a^2 > a$ and $b < a^2$, we cannot compare a and b.

Alternatively, ...

Take a couple of test values.

Case 1 : Say $a = 4$ and $b = 3$.

We see that $3^3 > 4$, and $a > b$.

The answer is Yes.

Case 2 : Say $a = 2$ and $b = 3$.

We see that $3^3 > 2$, and $a < b$.

The answer is No.

No unique answer, hence, Statement 2 alone is not sufficient.

Hence, eliminate B.

The correct answer is Option (a).

23. (c) **Considering Statement 1 alone :**

So $x = [ab]$, where a and b are tens and units digits, respectively.

Now to know the value of x, we need to know both a and b.

Now $a + b = 10$.

We can't find the unique value of x since there are numerous possibilities x could be 37, 73, 82, 28, etc; x is not unique.

This statement alone is not sufficient.

Hence, eliminate A/D.

Considering Statement 2 alone :

Like Statement 1, we need to know the value of x we need to know the values of a and b.

$a - b = 4$ is not sufficient to find the unique values of a and b.

This statement alone is not sufficient.

Hence, eliminate B.

Considering statements 1 and 2 together :

Now we have,

$a + b = 10$

$a - b = 4$

Solving we have $a = 7$, $b = 3$. Therefore the value of x is 73.

The answer is (c).

24. (a) **Considering Statement 1 alone:**

$x = 100^{\frac{b}{a}}$ is an integer only if $\frac{b}{a}$ is a non-negative integer or $\frac{1}{2}$.

$\frac{b^6}{a^6}$ is an integer, but $\frac{b}{a}$ not necessarily be.

Let's see a couple of examples.

Case 1 : Say $\frac{b^6}{a^6} = 2^6 \Rightarrow \frac{b}{a} = 2$. The answer is Yes.

Case 2 : Say $\frac{b^6}{a^6} = 2 \Rightarrow \frac{b}{a} = \sqrt[6]{2}$. The answer is No.

No unique answer, hence Statement 1 alone is not sufficient.

Hence, eliminate A/D.

Considering Statement 2 alone :

$$a - 2b = 0 \Rightarrow \frac{b}{a} = \frac{1}{2}$$

$$\Rightarrow x = 100^{\frac{b}{a}} = 100^{\frac{1}{2}} = 10, \text{ an integer}$$

This statement alone is sufficient.

Hence, eliminate C/E.

The answer is (a).

25. (e) We have to find out whether $a^5 - b^2 - c^2 < 0$. We can rewrite it as $a^5 < b^2 + c^2$. Since b and c, each are squared, the right-hand side of the inequality would always be non-negative. The inequality would be true if a is negative. However, if a is positive or 0, the answer would be interminable as i it will then depend on the values of a, b, and c.

Considering Statement 1 alone :

Given ab > 0, a and b can be both negative or both positive. We cannot conclude anything about the nature of a. This statement alone is insufficient.

Hence, eliminate A/D.

Considering Statement 2 alone :

Given bc > 0. b and c can be both negative or both positive. We cannot conclude anything about the nature of a. This statement alone is insufficient.

Hence, eliminate B.

Considering statements 1 and 2 together :

Even after combining both statements, we cannot conclude anything about the nature of a.

The answer is (e).

26. (b) The term $a^2 - ab = a^2 - b^2$ simplifies to either a = b or $(a - b) = (a + b)(a - b)$

$\Rightarrow a = a + b \Rightarrow b = 0$, Since $a \neq b$, $b = 0$

Considering Statement 1 alone :

We cannot determine the value of c since we don't know the value of a. This statement is insufficient.

Hence, eliminate A/D.

Considering Statement 2 alone :

Since $c^3 = b$, and $b = 0 \Rightarrow c = 0$. This statement is sufficient.

Hence, eliminate C/E

The answer is (b).

27. (b) **Considering Statement 1 alone :**

There are infinite such positive integer values for x that make x^3 a perfect square. For example: 1, 4, 64, etc. If $x^3 = 1, x = 1$; 1 is a perfect square. Similarly, if $x^3 = 64, x = 4$; 64 is a perfect square. No unique answer for x. This statement is insufficient.

Hence, eliminate A/D.

Considering Statement 2 alone :

$x^2 = x$ is true for x = 0 or 1. Since x is positive integer, x = 1; a unique answer. This statement is sufficient.

Hence, eliminate C/E.

The answer is (b).

28. (e) **Considering Statement 1 alone :**

If $a < b^4$, we can't determine if a and b are fractions or integers. If say a = 3, and b = 2, $a < b^4 \Rightarrow 3 < 2^4 \Rightarrow 3 < 16$ then a > b. The answer is Yes. If say a = 2, and b = 3, $a < b^4 \Rightarrow 2 < 3^4 \Rightarrow 2 < 81$ then a < b. The answer is No. No unique answer. This statement is insufficient.

Hence, eliminate A/D.

Considering Statement 2 alone :

Again, we don't the values for a and b. This statement is insufficient.

Hence, eliminate B.

Considering Statement 1 and 2 together :

If say a = –3, and b = –2, $< b^4 \Rightarrow -3 < (-2)^4$ $\Rightarrow -3 < 16$ then a < b. The answer is No. If say a = –2, and b = –2, and b = –2, $a < b^4 \Rightarrow$ $-2\ (-3)^4 \Rightarrow -2 < 81$ then a > b. The answer is Yes. No unique answer. Even both statements together are insufficient.

The answer is (e).

29. (b) **Considering Statement 1 alone:**

Statement 1 gives only the value of x. Hence Statement 1 alone is not sufficient

Hence, eliminate A/D.

Considering Statement 2 alone :

Multiplying $3y^2 + 2x^2 = 14$ by 6 gives $12x^2 + 18y^2 = 84$, which is the same as the expression in the problem. Therefore, the value of the given expression $12x^2 + 18y^2$ is 84.

Hence, Statement 2 alone is sufficient.

Hence, eliminate C/E.

The answer is (b).

30. (d) Let x be the age of John and c be the age of his cousin

$\Rightarrow \quad x = c - 10$

We have to find the value of x + 20.

Considering Statement 1 alone :

This statement implies $2(x - 5) = c - 5$

$2(c - 10 - 5) = c - 5$

$2c - 30 = c - 5$

$c = 25\ \&\ x = 15 \Rightarrow x + 20 = 15 + 20 = 35$

Therefore, Statement 1 alone is sufficient.

Hence, eliminate B/C/E.

Considering Statement 2 alone :

This statement implies that

$c + 5 = 2x = 2(c - 10)$

$c + 5 = 2c - 20$

$c = 25\ \&\ x = 15 \Rightarrow x + 20 = 15 + 20 = 35$

Therefore, Statement 2 alone is also sufficient.

Hence, eliminate C/E.

The answer is (d).

31. (c) **Considering Statement 1 alone:**

On solving the equation $a^2 - a - 6 = 0$

$\Rightarrow (a - 3)\ (a + 2) = 0.$

a = 3 or –2; no unique value.

This statement alone is Insufficient.

Hence, eliminate A/D.

Considering Statement 2 alone :

Given that (a + 5) is a prime number, multiple values of a are possible (a = –3, –2, 0, 2, 4, 6, 8, 12, etc).

This statement alone is Insufficient.

Hence, eliminate B.

Considering statements 1 and 2 together :

Both statements together imply that $a = -2$: the only common value. Sufficient.

The answer is (c).

32. (e) **Considering Statement 1 alone:**

We can replace the value of $3|b|$ from statement 1 with $a + 3|b| = 50 \Rightarrow a + 3|b| = a + a - 20 = 50 \Rightarrow 2a = 70 \Rightarrow a = 35$.

By replacing the value of $a = 35$ in the statement, we get $3|b| = 35 - 20 = 15 \Rightarrow |b| = 5$ or $b = 5$ or -5. We are able to get the unique value of a, but not of b. Hence, Statement 1 alone in insufficient.

Hence, eliminate A/D.

Considering Statement 2 alone:

Upon multiplying by 3 on both sides, statement 2 becomes $3|b| + = 50$, i.e., the same equation given in the question. Therefore, we have only one equation and two variables. Statement 2 alone is insufficient.

Hence, eliminate B.

Considering statements 1 and 2 together:

Since statement 2 does not add any value to solve the question, even after combining both statements, we cannot get the unique value of b.

The answer is (e).

33. (b) **Considering Statement 1 alone :**

$a^2 = 3a + 4 \Rightarrow 2 - 3a - 4 = 0$

$\Rightarrow a^2 - 4a + a - 4 = 0$

$\Rightarrow a(a - 4) + 1(a - 4) \Rightarrow (a - 4)(a + 1) = 0$

$\Rightarrow a = 4$ or -1. Since a does not have a unique value, a^3 cannot have a unique value. This statement is insufficient.

Hence, eliminate A/D.

Considering Statement 2 alone :

$a^3 - 4a^2 = 4 - a \Rightarrow a^3 - 4a^2 + a - 4 = 0$

$\Rightarrow a^2(a - 4) + 1(a - 4) = 0$

$\Rightarrow (a - 4)(a^2 + 1) \Rightarrow a = 4$, or $a^2 = -1$

$\Rightarrow a = \sqrt{-1}$, an imaginary number. Since in the GMAT, variables are real numbers, $a = \sqrt{-1}$ is discarded.

So $a = 4 \Rightarrow a^3 = 4^3 = 64$, a unique value. This statement is sufficient.

The answer is (b).

34. (b) We are given that $f(x) = (c)^{\frac{6}{x}}$, where c is a constant.

We have to find out the value of f(1).

Considering Statement 1 alone :

Given that $f(2) = 125$

Thus, $f(2) = (c)^{\frac{6}{2}} = c^3 = 125$

$\Rightarrow c = (125)^{\frac{1}{3}} = 5$

Thus, $f(1) = (c)^{\frac{6}{1}} = c^6 - 5^6$ – Sufficient

Hence, eliminate B/C/E.

Considering Statement 2 alone :

Given that $f(3) = 25$

Thus $f(3) = (c)^{\frac{6}{3}} = c^2 = 25$

$\Rightarrow c = (25)^{\frac{1}{2}} = \pm 5$

Thus,

$f(1) = (c)^{\frac{6}{1}} = c^6 (\pm 5)^6 = 5^6$ – Sufficient

The answer is (b).

35. (c) **Considering Statement 1 alone :**

Statement 1 states $-x = |-x|$. Since the right-hand side ($|-x|$) is an absolute value, which is always a non-negative number, for the equality to hold true, the left-hand side must also be a non-negative number.

So, since $-x$ is a non-negative number, x must be a non-positive number. But x may be negative or 0. Hence, statement 1 alone is not sufficient.

Hence, eliminate A/D.

Considering Statement 2 alone :

From statement 2, we get $x = 4$ or -4. Since x can be positive or negative, statement 2 alone isn't sufficient.

Hence, eliminate B.

Considering Statements 1 and 2 together :

From both statements, we get that $x = -4$, the answer is yes. Sufficient.

The answer is (c).

36. (c) **Considering Statement 1 alone :**

Let us rewrite $wx > y^3z$ as $wx > yz\,(y^2)$

If $y^2 \le 1$, the answer is YES. However, if $y^2 > 1$, then the answer is YES/NO, depending on the value of y^2. Therefore, Statement 1 alone is insufficient.

Hence, eliminate A/D

Considering Statement 2 alone :

Statement 2 only tells us about y and is therefore insufficient.

Hence, eliminate B.

Considering Statements 1 and 2 together:

Both the statements together give us a fixed value of y. i.e. $y = 1$ implies $wx > yz(y^2)$ $= wx > yz\,(1) = wx > yz$

Therefore, both statements together are sufficient.

The answer is (c).

Chapter 4

Coordinate Geometry

Coordinate geometry is a topic that appears frequently on the GMAT. Questions on this topic can range from simple concepts such as finding the coordinates of a point on a plane, to more complex problems involving slopes, distance, and midpoint formulas.

Coordinate Plane

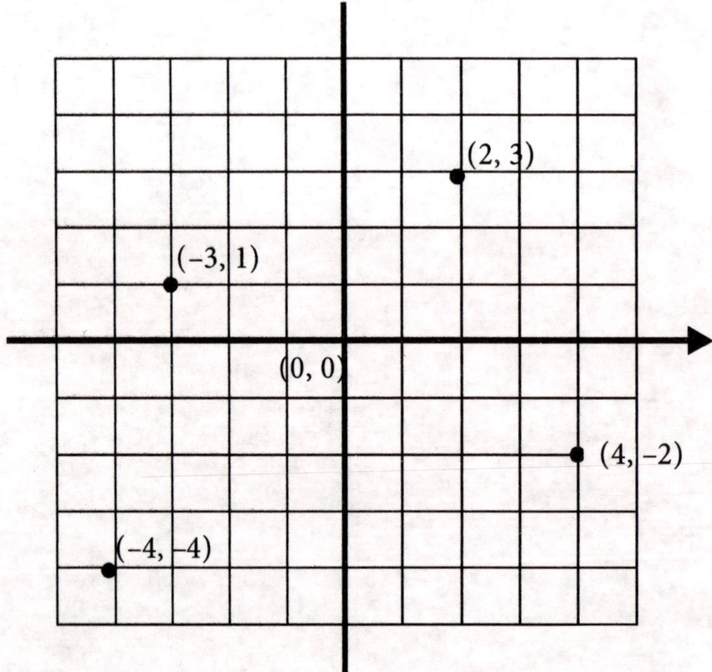

Two real number lines that are perpendicular to each other and that intersect at their respective zero points define a rectangular coordinate system, often called the xy-coordinate system or xy-plane. The horizontal number line is called the x-axis and the vertical number line is called the y-axis. The point where the two axes intersect is called the origin, denoted by O. The positive half of the x-axis is to the right of the origin, and the positive half of the y-axis is above the origin. The two axes divide the plane into four regions called quadrants I, II, III, and IV

Each point P in the xy-plane can be identified with an ordered pair (x, y) of real numbers and is denoted by P(x, y). The first number is called the x-coordinate, and the second number is called the y-coordinate.

Slope

The slope of a line on a coordinate plane tells you how steeply that line goes up or down. If a line gets higher as you move to the right, it has a positive slope. If it goes down as you move to the right, it has a negative slope.

$$m = \frac{(y-b)}{(x-a)}$$

If two lines are parallel, their slopes will be equal

If two lines are perpendicular, their slopes will be negative reciprocal.

Example : What is the slope of the line that contains the points (1, 2) and (4, –5)?

$$\text{Slope} = \frac{(-5-2)}{(4-1)} = -\frac{7}{3}$$

To determine the slope of a line from an equation, put the equation into slope-intercept form: $y = mx + b$, where the slope is m.

The word intercept in "slope-intercept form" is there because b is the value of the y-intercept-the point at which the line crosses the y-axis.

Example : Find the slope of the line passing through the points A(2, 3) and B(5, 7).

Solution : The coordinates of point A are (2, 3) and the coordinates of point B are (5, 7). We can use the slope formula to find the slope of the line passing through the points.

Slope formula : The slope of a line passing through two points with coordinates (x_1, y_1) and (x_2, y_2) is given by:

$$m = \frac{(y_2 - y_1)}{(x_2 - x_1)}$$

Using the slope formula, we have: $m = \frac{(7-3)}{(5-2)} = \frac{4}{3}$

Intercepts

The x-intercept is the point where the line cuts the x-axis. It is found by substituting $y = 0$

The y-intercept is the point where the line cuts the y-axis. It is found by substituting $x = 0$

Distance Formula

To determine the distance between any two points on a coordinate plane, you can use the Pythagorean theorem.

The distance between the points (x, y) and (a, b) is the hypotenuse of a right triangle.

The difference y – b is the measure of the height of the triangle, and the difference x – a is the length of base of the triangle

$$d = \sqrt{\{(x-a)^2 + (y-b)^2\}}$$

Midpoint Formula

The midpoint M between points (x, y) and (a, b) is given by

$$M\left\{\frac{(x+a)}{2}, \frac{(y+b)}{2}\right\}$$

Example : Find the midpoint and distance between the points A(2,3) and B(8,9).

Solution : The coordinates of point A are (2, 3) and the coordinates of point B are (8, 9). We can use the midpoint formula and distance formula to find the midpoint and distance between the points, respectively.

Midpoint formula : The midpoint of a line segment with endpoints (x_1, y_1) and (x_2, y_2) is given by:

$$\left(\frac{(x_1+x_2)}{2}, \frac{(y_1+y_2)}{2}\right)$$

Using the midpoint formula, we have : Midpoint of AB = $\left(\frac{(2+8)}{2}, \frac{(3+9)}{2}\right) = (5,6)$

Therefore, the midpoint of AB is (5,6).

Distance formula : The distance between two points with coordinates (x_1, y_1) and (x_2, y_2) is given by:

$$d = \sqrt{\left[(x_2-x_1)^2 + (y_2-y_1)^2\right]}$$

Using the distance formula, we have: Distance between A and B

$$= \sqrt{\left[(8-2)^2 + (9-3)^2\right]} = \sqrt{[6^2 + 6^2]} = \sqrt{(72)}$$

Problem Solving

1. On the xy-plane, what is the equation of the line that is a reflection the line $y = -2x - 1$ across the x-axis?

   (a) $y = -2x + 1$

   (b) $y = -2x - 1$

   (c) $y = 2x - 1$

   (d) $y = 2x + 1$

   (e) $y = x + 1$

2. The equation of line p is $y = -x + 2$. If the line is the reflection of the line p over the y-axis, what is the slope of line q?

   (a) –2

   (b) $-\frac{1}{2}$

   (c) 0

   (d) $\frac{1}{2}$

   (e) 1

3. If (b, a) lies in Quadrant III of the xy-coordinate plane, in which quadrant does the point (a, b) lie?

   (a) 1 only

   (b) II only

   (c) III only

   (d) IV only

   (e) Any of the four quadrants

4. Which of the following statements is true for the line that passes through (–2, 2) and (2, –2)?

   (a) It crosses the x-axis only

   (b) It crosses the y-axis only

   (c) It has a positive y-intercept.

   (d) It passes through origin (0, 0)

   (e) It has a negative x-intercept and a negative y-intercept.

5. What is the area of the triangular field with the coordinates of the vertices

   (0, 2), (–2, –2) and (2, –2)?

   (a) 2

   (b) 4

   (c) 8

   (d) 12

   (e) 16

Answer Key

1. (d)

2. (e)

3. (c)

4. (d)

5. (c)

Answer Explanations

1. **(d)** A reflection across the x-axis flips all y-coordinates from y to-y and keeps the x-coordinates unchanged Hence, the answer is (d).

2. **(e)** If you reflect a line over the y-axis, the slope of the new line have the opposite sign of the slope of the oldline. The slope of p is –1, so the slope of q is 1.

3. **(c)** If (b, a) is in the third quadrant, then b = –ve and a = –ve.

   Hence, (a, b) is also (–ve, –ve).

   So, it should lie in Quadrant III only.

4. **(d)** The mid-point of (–2, 2) and (2, –2) is

$$\left\{\frac{(+2+2)}{2}, \frac{(2-2)}{2}\right\} = 0,0$$

   So, it passes through origin.

5. **C** You may draw a diagram. The vertices of the triangle are A(0, 2), B(–2, –2), and C(2, 2). Thus, the base of the triangle would be BC = |–1| + 2 = 4, and the height would be 2 + –2| = 4.

$$\text{The area of the triangle} = \frac{1}{2} \times \text{base} \times \text{height}$$

$$= \frac{1}{2} \times 4 \times 4 = 8$$

Data Sufficiency

1. What is the angle between line k and line p?

   1. Equation of line k is $y - 5x = 4$.
   2. Line k and line p do not intersect.

   (a) Statement (1) ALONE is sufficient but statement (2) ALONE is not sufficient.
   (b) Statement (2) ALONE is sufficient but statement (1) ALONE is not sufficient.
   (c) BOTH statements TOGETHER are sufficient, but NEITHER statement ALONE is sufficient.
   (d) EACH statement ALONE is sufficient.
   (e) Statements (1) and (2) TOGETHER are not sufficient.

2. What is the slope of line 1?

   1. Line 1 passes through origin
   2. Line 1 is equidistant from the two points (1, 11) and (7, 7).

   (a) Statement (1) ALONE is sufficient but statement (2) ALONE is not sufficient.
   (b) Statement (2) ALONE is sufficient but statement (1) ALONE is not sufficient.
   (c) BOTH statements TOGETHER are sufficient, but NEITHER statement ALONE is sufficient.
   (d) EACH statement ALONE is sufficient.
   (e) Statements (1) and (2) TOGETHER are not sufficient.

3. What all quadrants in the xy-plane does line k pass through?

   1. Line k is defined by $3x + 4y = 8$
   2. Line k has a negative slope

   (a) Statement (1) ALONE is sufficient but statement (2) ALONE is not sufficient.
   (b) Statement (2) ALONE is sufficient but statement (1) ALONE is not sufficient.
   (c) BOTH statements TOGETHER are sufficient, but NEITHER statement ALONE is sufficient.
   (d) EACH statement ALONE is sufficient.
   (e) Statements (1) and (2) TOGETHER are not sufficient.

4. Does line k pass through the II quadrant in the xy-plane?

   1. Line k is defined by $3x + 4y = 8$
   2. Line k has a negative slope

   (a) Statement (1) ALONE is sufficient but statement (2) ALONE is not sufficient.
   (b) Statement (2) ALONE is sufficient but statement (1) ALONE is not sufficient.
   (c) BOTH statements TOGETHER are sufficient, but NEITHER statement ALONE is sufficient.
   (d) EACH statement ALONE is sufficient.
   (e) Statements (1) and (2) TOGETHER are not sufficient.

5. Does line k pass through (–14, 10)?

   1. Line k passes through (0, 5) and (7, 0)
   2. Line k parallel to line $y = \left(\frac{-5}{7}\right)x + 10$

   (a) Statement (1) ALONE is sufficient but statement (2) ALONE is not sufficient.
   (b) Statement (2) ALONE is sufficient but statement (1) ALONE is not sufficient.
   (c) BOTH statements TOGETHER are sufficient, but NEITHER statement ALONE is sufficient.
   (d) EACH statement ALONE is sufficient.
   (e) Statements (1) and (2) TOGETHER are not sufficient.

6. What is the x-intercept of line k?

1. Equation of line k is $y = 4x + 5$
2. y-intercept of line k is (0, 5)

(a) Statement (1) ALONE is sufficient but statement (2) ALONE is not sufficient.

(b) Statement (2) ALONE is sufficient but statement (1) ALONE is not sufficient.

(c) BOTH statements TOGETHER are sufficient, but NEITHER statement ALONE is sufficient.

(d) EACH statement ALONE is sufficient.

(e) Statements (1) and (2) TOGETHER are not sufficient.

7. Is point Q closer to the point (10, 3) than to the point (3, 10)?

1. Point Q lies on the line $y = x$.
2. Point Q lies on the line $y = -x$.

(a) Statement (1) ALONE is sufficient but statement (2) ALONE is not sufficient.

(b) Statement (2) ALONE is sufficient but statement (1) ALONE is not sufficient.

(c) BOTH statements TOGETHER are sufficient, but NEITHER statement ALONE is sufficient.

(d) EACH statement ALONE is sufficient.

(e) Statements (1) and (2) TOGETHER are not sufficient.

Answer Key

1. (b)	3. (a)	5. (a)	7. (a)
2. (c)	4. (d)	6. (a)	

Answer Explanations

1. (b) Considering statement (1) alone:

Just knowing the equation of one line doesn't help.

INSUFFICIENT

Eliminate AD

Considering statement (2) alone:

If the two lines do not intersect, then the two lines are parallel.

Hence the angle formed by them must be 0, SUFFICIENT

Eliminate CE.

The answer is (b).

2. (c) **Considering statement (1) alone:**

Just knowing one point on a line doesn't help.

INSUFFICIENT

Eliminate AD.

Considering statement (2) alone:

Line 1 passes through the midpoint (1, 11) and (7, 7)i.e (4, 9)

Just knowing one point on a line doesn't help.

INSUFFICIENT

Eliminate B.

Considering both the statements together:

Line I passes through (0, 0) and (4, 9)

Hence, the slope of the line is $\frac{9}{4}$

INSUFFICIENT

Eliminate E.

The answer is (c).

3. (a) **Considering statement (1) alone:**

If we know the equation of a line, then we can plot it and find the quadrants that it passes through.

SUFFICIENT

Eliminate BCE

Considering statement (2) alone:

If the slope is negative, then the line passes through quadrant II and IV for sure. But, it is not enough to determine whether it passes through any other quadrant.

SUFFICIENT

Eliminate D

The answer is (a).

4. (d) If we know the equation of a line, then we can plot it and find the quadrants that it passes through.

SUFFICIENT

Eliminate BCE

Considering statement (2) alone:

If the slope is negative, then the line passes through quadrant II and IV for sure.

SUFFICIENT

Eliminate A

The answer is (d).

5. (a) **Considering statement (1) alone:**

To find whether a line passes through three given points. find the slopes with each of them.

Slope of a line that passes through (0, 5) and (7, 0) = $-\frac{5}{7}$

As the two slopes are not same, the line does not pass through (–14, 10) Sufficient

Eliminate BCE

Considering statement (2) alone:

With this, we just know the slppe of line k. However, that is not helpful to find whether the line passes through (–14, 10) Insufficient.

Eliminate D.

The answer is (a).

6. (a) **Considering statement (1) alone:**

x-intercept means putting y = 0 in the equation.

Hence, x-intercept of line k is $\left(-\frac{5}{4},0\right)$

Sufficient

Elimiante BCE

Considering statement (2) alone:

Knowing the y-intercept does not help find the x-intercept.

Insufficient

Eliminate D

The answer is (a).

7. (a) **Considering statement 1 alone:**

Say the co-coordinates of Point Q on the line y = x is (a, a).

The distance from a point (x_1, y_1) from a point (x_2, y_2) is given by

$$\left|\sqrt{\left[(x_1-x_2)^2+(y_1-y_2)^2\right]}\right|,$$

we can find the distances from both the given points.

Distance of Point Q (a, a) from the point (10, 3)

$$=\left|\sqrt{\left[(10-a)^2+(3-a)^2\right]}\right|;$$

Similarly, the distance of Point Q (a, a) from the point (3, 10),

$$=\left|\sqrt{\left[(13-a)^2+(10-a)^2\right]}\right|.$$

Since both distances are the same, we can conclude that the two points (10, 3) and (3, 10) are equidistant from any point on the line y = x; Statement 1 alone is sufficient.

Hence, eliminate B/C/E.

Considering Statement 2 alone :

Say the co-ordinates of Point Q on the line y = –x is (a, –a).

Distance of Point Q (a, –a) from the point (10, 3)

$$=\left|\sqrt{\left[(10-a)^2+(3-a)^2\right]}\right|$$

$$=\left|\sqrt{100-20a+a^2+9+6a+a^2}\right|$$

$$=\left|\sqrt{[109-14a+2a]}\right|$$

Similarly, the distance of Point Q (a, a) from the point (3, 10)

$$=\left|\sqrt{\left[(13-a)^2+(10-a)^2\right]}\right|$$

$$=\left|\sqrt{9-6a+a^2+100+20a+a^2}\right|$$

$$=\left|\sqrt{109-14a+2a^2}\right|$$

If a = 0, we have

$$=\left|\sqrt{109-14a+2a^2}\right|$$

$$=\left|\sqrt{109+14a+2a^2}\right|,$$

else not. No unique answer.

Statement 2 alone is insufficient.

Hence, eliminate B.

The correct answer is Option (a.)

Chapter 5

Statistics

Statistics topic deals with the collection, analysis, interpretation, presentation, and organization of data. It involves using mathematical and computational tools to gather insights from data and to make informed decisions.

Mean, Median, Mode, Range

Mean

The mean is a measure of central tendency that represents the average value of a set of data. It is calculated by summing all the values in the dataset and dividing by the total number of values.

The formula for calculating the mean is :

$$\text{Mean} = \frac{(\text{sum of all values})}{(\text{number of values})}$$

Example, suppose you have a dataset of test scores : 75, 82, 91, 68, and 88. To calculate the mean, you would add up all the values and divide by the total number of values:

$$\text{Mean} = \frac{(75+80+91+68+88)}{5} \quad \text{Mean} = \frac{404}{5} \quad \text{Mean} = 80.8$$

Therefore, the mean test score for this dataset is 80.8.

Median

The median is a measure of central tendency that represents the middle value of a dataset.

To find the median, you first need to order the values in the dataset from lowest to highest (or highest to lowest). If the dataset has an odd number of values, the median is the middle value. If the dataset has an even number of values, the median is the average of the two middle values.

Example : Suppose you have a dataset of test scores: 75, 82, 91, 68, and 88. To find the median, you would first order the values from lowest to highest:

68, 75, 82, 88, 91

Since the dataset has an odd number of values, the median is the middle value, which is 82. Therefore, the median test score for this dataset is 82.

Now let's take an example where the dataset has an even number of values: 75, 82, 91, 68, 88, and 93. To find the median, you would first order the values:

68, 75, 82, 88, 91, 93

Since the dataset has an even number of values, the median is the average of the two middle values, which are 82 and 88. Therefore, the median test score for this dataset is $\frac{(82+88)}{2} = 85$.

Mode

The mode is a measure of central tendency that represents the most commonly occurring value in a dataset. The mode is the value that appears with the highest frequency in the dataset.

Example, suppose you have a dataset of test scores: 75, 82, 91, 68, 88, 82, 93, 82. The mode of this dataset is 82, because it appears three times and no other value appears more than once.

It's possible for a dataset to have multiple modes if there are two or more values that occur with the same highest frequency. This is called a bimodal or multimodal distribution.

Note that not all datasets have a mode, for example, if all the values in a dataset occur only once, then there is no mode. If two or more values have the same highest frequency, then the dataset is said to have multiple modes.

Range

The range is a measure of dispersion that represents the difference between the maximum and minimum values in a dataset. The range gives an idea of how spread out the values are in the dataset.

The formula for calculating the range is :

$$\text{Range} = \text{maximum value} - \text{minimum value}$$

Example, suppose you have a dataset of test scores: 75, 82, 91, 68, and 88. To calculate the range, first find the maximum and minimum values:

$$\text{Maximum value} = 91 \quad \text{Minimum value} = 68$$

Then subtract the minimum value from the maximum value:

$$\text{Range} = 91 - 68 \quad \text{Range} = 23$$

Therefore, the range of this dataset is 23.

The range can be affected by extreme values or outliers in the dataset.

Standard Deviation

The standard deviation is a measure of dispersion that represents how much the values in a dataset deviate from the mean. The standard deviation is a way of measuring the amount of variability or spread in the dataset.

The steps for calculating the standard deviation is:

1. Find the average (arithmetic mean) of the set.
2. Subtract the average of the set from each term in that set.
3. Square each result.
4. Take the average of those squares.
5. Calculate the positive square root of that average.

Example : suppose you have a dataset of test scores: 75, 82, 91, 68, and 88. To calculate the standard deviation, first find the mean:

$$\text{Mean} = \frac{(75 + 82 + 91 + 68 + 88)}{5} \quad \text{Mean} = \frac{404}{5} \quad \text{Mean} = 80.8$$

Next, calculate the deviation of each value from the mean, square each deviation, and sum the squared deviations:

$$(75 - 80.8)^2 + (82 - 80.8)^2 + (91 - 80.8)^2 + (68 - 80.8)^2 + (88 - 80.8)^2$$

$$= 24.64 + 1.44 + 103.04 + 155.84 + 6.76 = 291.72$$

Then divide the sum of squared deviations by the number of values and take the square root of the result:

$$\text{Standard deviation} = \text{square root of} \left(\frac{291.72}{5}\right)$$

Standard deviation = 7.64

Therefore, the standard deviation of this dataset is 7.64

Example : {1, 2, 3} and {101, 102, 103} have the same standard deviation, since they both have one term on the average and two terms exactly one unit away from the average.

Normal Distribution

The normal distribution is a common topic in the quantitative section of the GMAT. The test may include questions that require you to understand the properties of the normal distribution and use them to solve problems.

A normal distribution (also known as a Gaussian distribution) is a probability distribution that is characterized by a bell-shaped curve. The curve is symmetric around the mean and the spread of the distribution is determined by the standard deviation.

According to the standard deviation about 68% of the values in a normal distribution fall within one standard deviation of the mean, about 95% fall within two standard deviations, and about 99.7% fall within three standard deviations.

Normal Distribution

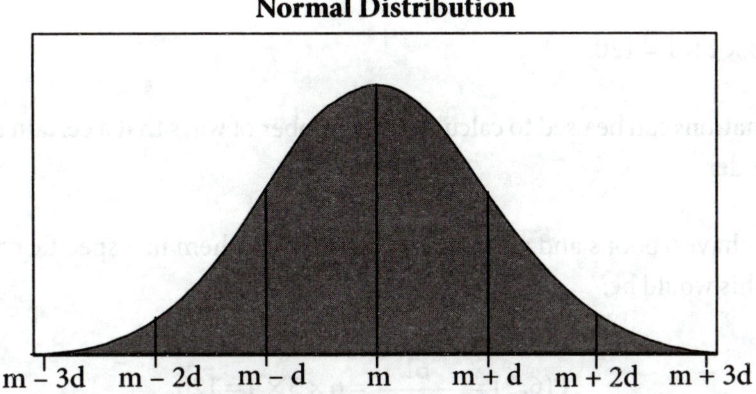

Such data are said to be approximately normally distributed and have the following properties.

- The mean, median, and mode are all nearly equal.
- The data are grouped fairly symmetrically about the mean.
- About two-thirds of the data are within 1 standard deviation of the mean.
- Almost all of the data are within 2 standard deviations of the mean.

Example : Suppose the heights of students in a class are normally distributed with a mean of 68 inches and a standard deviation of 3 inches. What percentage of students in the class are between 62 inches and 74 inches tall?

Solution : To find the percentage of students between 62 inches and 74 inches tall, we need to find the area under the curve between those two points.

Using a standard normal distribution table, we can find that the area under the curve between -2 and 2 is approximately 0.9545. Therefore, approximately 95.45% of students in the class are between 62 inches and 74 inches tall.

Permutation

Some GMAT questions ask you to count the number of possible ways to select a small subgroup from a larger group. If the selection is unordered, then it's a combinations question. But if the selection is ordered, it is a permutations question.

In permutation, order matters.

In permutations, A – B – C and B – A – C are not the same because the ordering is different, though each has the same number of each type of object: A, B, and C as in the base set.

The number of permutations of a set of n distinct objects taken r at a time is denoted by the symbol P(n, r) and can be calculated using the following formula:

$P(n, r) = \frac{n!}{(n-r)!}$, where n! (pronounced "n factorial") represents the product of all positive integers from 1 to n, inclusive.

Example: $5! = 5 \times 4 \times 3 \times 2 \times 1 = 120$.

The formula for permutations can be used to calculate the number of ways that a certain number of objects can be arranged in a specific order.

Example: Suppose you have 6 books and you want to arrange 3 of them in a specific order on a bookshelf. The number of ways to do this would be:

$$P(6,3) = \frac{6!}{(6-3)!} = 6 \times 5 \times 4 = 120$$

Therefore, there are 120 different ways to arrange 3 books out of 6 in a specific order.

Example, if we want to find the number of permutations of 4 objects taken 2 at a time, we have:

$$\frac{4!}{(4-2)!} = \frac{4!}{2!} = 12$$

This means that there are 12 different ways of arranging 2 objects out of a set of 4 objects.

Combination

Combination is a way of selecting a subset of objects from a larger set, where the order of selection does not matter.

Example: if we have a set of three objects {A, B, C}, we can select two objects in different ways:

AB

AC

BC

Note that the order of selection does not matter, so AB and BA are considered the same combination.

The number of combinations of r objects taken from a set of n objects is given by the formula:

$$\frac{b!}{(r!(n-r)!)},$$

where n is the total number of objects in the set, and r is the number of objects being selected in each combination. The exclamation mark represents the factorial operation.

Example, if we want to find the number of combinations of 4 objects taken 2 at a time, we have:

$$\frac{4!}{(2!(4-2)!)} = 6$$

This means that there are 6 different ways of selecting 2 objects out of a set of 4 objects.

In general, if we have n objects and we want to select r objects from them, we have:

$$\frac{n!}{(r!(n-r)!)} \text{ combinations}$$

Example, if we have a set of 5 objects and we want to select 3 objects from it, there are:

$$\frac{5!}{(3!(5-3)!)} = 10 \text{ combinations}$$

Example : Suppose we have a group of 10 people and we want to select a committee of 4 people from this group. How many different committees can we form?

We can use the formula for combinations:

$$\frac{n!}{(r!(n-r)!)},$$

where n is the total number of objects (people in this case) and r is the number of objects being selected (4 people in this case).

Substituting the values, we get :

$$\frac{10!}{(4!(10-4)!)} = 210$$

Probability

Probability is the measure of the likelihood that a particular event will occur. The probability of an event is always a number between 0 and 1, where 0 represents an impossible event and 1 represents a certain event.

The formula for probability is:

P(E) = number of favorable outcomes / total number of outcomes

where P(E) is the probability of event E.

Example : if we roll a fair six-sided die, the probability of getting a 4 is $\frac{1}{6}$, because there is only one favorable outcome (getting a 4) out of six possible outcomes (rolling any number from 1 to 6).

Here are some more examples of probability:

- **Coin toss :** Suppose we toss a fair coin. The probability of getting heads is 1/2, and the probability of getting tails is also 1/2.
- **Dice roll :** Suppose we roll a fair six-sided die. The probability of getting a specific number (e.g., 3) is 1/6, because there is only one favorable outcome out of six possible outcomes.
- **Card draw :** Suppose we draw a card from a standard deck of 52 playing cards. The probability of drawing a spade is 13/52, because there are 13 spades in the deck.

Probability can also be expressed as a percentage or a fraction.

Example : A probability of 0.5 is equivalent to a probability of 50% or a fraction of $\frac{1}{2}$.

The sum of the probabilities of all possible outcomes of an experiment must be equal to 1. This is known as the *law of total probability*.

Example : if we toss a coin, the probability of getting either heads or tails is $\frac{1}{2}+\frac{1}{2}=1$.

Probability is the likelihood that a desired outcome will occur.

Example : If you have 12 shirts in a drawer and 9 of them are white, the probability of picking a white shirt at random is $\frac{9}{12}=\frac{3}{4}$

For events E and F, we have the following rules:

- P(E or F, or both, occur) = P(E) + P(F)– P(both E and F occur), which is the inclusion-exclusion principle applied to probability.
- If E and F are mutually exclusive, then P (both E and F occur) = 0, and therefore, P (E or F, or both, occur) = P(E) + P(F).
- E and F are said to be independent if the occurrence of either event does not affect the occurrence of the other. If two events E and F are independent, then P(both E and F occur) = P(E)P(F).

Set Theory

Set theory is a branch of mathematics that deals with the study of sets, which are collections of objects or elements that share a common property. The objects are called the elements of the set. A set with a finite number of elements may be denoted by listing its elements within a pair of braces. The order in which the elements are listed does not matter.

Example : $\{-5, 0, 1\}$ is the same set as $\{0, 1, -5\}$; that is, $\{-5, 0, 1\} = \{0, 1, -5\}$.

The union of two sets A and B is the set of all elements that are in A or in B or in both.

The union is denoted by $A \cup B$.

Example : $\{3, 4\} \cup \{4, 5, 6\} = \{3, 4, 5, 6\}$

The intersection of two sets A and B is the set of all elements that are both in A and in B. The intersection is denoted by $A \cap B$.

Example : $\{3, 4\} \cap \{4, 5, 6\} = \{4\}$

When counting elements that are in overlapping sets, the total number will equal the number in one group plus the number in the other group minus the number common to both groups.

A Venn Diagram of the Intersection of Two Sets

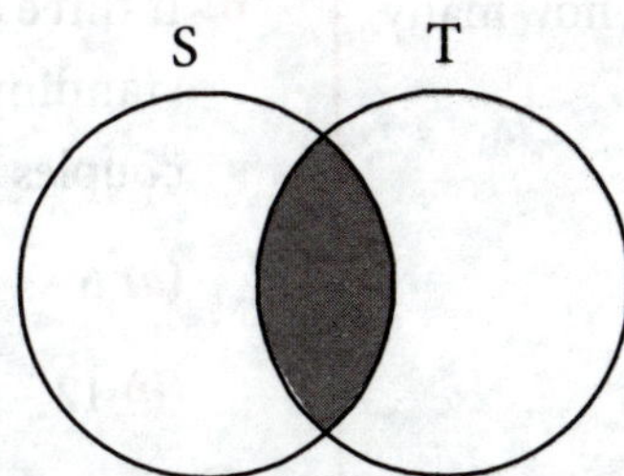

Example, if Set A = $\{1, 2, 6\}$ and Set B = $\{6, 10, 21\}$, then the union of sets A and B would be $\{1, 2, 6, 10, 21\}$ and the intersection would be $\{6\}$

Problem Solving

1. How many 3-digit passwords can be created?

(*a*) ${}^9C_3$

(*b*) ${}^9P_3$

(*c*) 3^9

(*d*) 9^3

(*e*) 10^3

2. Using each digit of the number 12334, how many 5-digit numbers can be formed?

(*a*) 5!

(*b*) $\frac{5!}{2!}$

(*c*) $\frac{{}^5C_5}{2!}$

(*d*) $\frac{{}^5P_5}{2!3!}$

(*e*) $\frac{{}^5C_5}{2!3!}$

3. In an examination, there are 2 sections, and four questions are to be answered. In the first section, there are 3 questions and two must be answered. In the second section, there are four questions and two must be answered. The first section is to be completed before the second section. In how many ways the test can be answered?

(*a*) 12

(*b*) 15

(*c*) 36

(*d*) 72

(*e*) 90

4. In how many ways can the letters of the word MOBILE be rearranged such that the vowels are together?

(*a*) $3! \times 3!$

(*b*) $\frac{6!}{2!}$

(*c*) $\frac{4! \times 3!}{2!}$

(*d*) $4! \times 3!$

(*e*) $\frac{3! \times 3!}{2!}$

5. In how many ways can be letters of the word COLOUR be rearranged such that the vowels are together?

(*a*) $\frac{7!}{2! \times 2!}$

(*b*) $\frac{4! \times 3!}{2! \times 2!}$

(*c*) $\frac{4! \times 3!}{2!}$

(*d*) $\frac{5!}{2! \times 2!}$

(*e*) $\frac{5! \times 3!}{2! \times 2!}$

6. If three couples are standing in a row, how many standing arrangements are possible such that couples are together?

(*a*) 6

(*b*) 12

(*c*) 24

(*d*) 48

(*e*) 96

7. In how many ways 6 people can be seated around a circular table?

(*a*) 6

(*b*) 24

(*c*) 120

(*d*) 720

(*e*) 5040

8. In how many ways three prizes can be distributed among three students such that no one gets more than one prize?

(*a*) 6

(*b*) 24

(*c*) 27

(*d*) 64

(*e*) 128

9. In how many ways three prizes can be distributed among three students such that a student may get any number of prizes?

(*a*) 6

(*b*) 24

(*c*) 27

(*d*) 64

(*e*) 128

10. How many three-digit numbers can be formed with distinct digits?

(*a*) 648

(*b*) 700

(*c*) 720

(*d*) 864

(*e*) 1000

11. In how many ways, a committee of 2 men and 2 women can be formed out of 5 men and 6 women?

(*a*) 6

(*b*) 10

(*c*) 25

(*d*) 128

(*e*) 150

12. In how many ways 5 identical red balls 4 identical balls can be arranged in a now such that no two blue balls are together?

(*a*) 6

(*b*) 10

(*c*) 25

(*d*) 128

(*e*) 150

13. In how many ways 5 men and 5 women can be seated around a circular table such that no two women are together?

(*a*) 24

(*b*) 120

(*c*) 576

(*d*) 2880

(*e*) 3080

14. There is a 10% chance that it won't snow all winter long. There is a 20% chance that schools will not be closed all winter long. What is the greatest possible probability that it will snow and schools will be closed during the winter?

(*a*) 55%

(*b*) 60%

(*c*) 70%

(*d*) 72%

(*e*) 80%

15. There are y different trvelers who each have a choice of vacationing at one of n different destinations. What is the probability that all y travelers will end up vacationing at the same destination?

(a) $\frac{1}{n!}$

(b) $\frac{n}{n!}$

(c) $\frac{1}{n^y}$

(d) $\frac{1}{n^{y-1}}$

(e) $\frac{n}{y^n}$

16. A small, experimental plane has three engines, one which is redundant. That is, as long as two of the engines are working, the plane will stay in the air. Over the course of a typical flight, there is a $\frac{1}{3}$ chance that engine one will fail. There is a 75% probability that engine two will work. The third engine works only half the time. What is the probability that the plane will crash in any given flight?

(a) $\frac{7}{12}$

(b) $\frac{1}{4}$

(c) $\frac{1}{2}$

(d) $\frac{7}{24}$

(e) $\frac{17}{24}$

17. Ms. Barton has four children. You are told correctly that she has at least two girls but you are not told which two of her four children are those girls. What is the probability that she also has two boys? (Assume that the probability of having a boy is the same as the probability of having a girl.)

(a) $\frac{1}{4}$

(b) $\frac{3}{8}$

(c) $\frac{5}{11}$

(d) $\frac{1}{2}$

(e) $\frac{6}{11}$

18. Laura has a deck of standard playing cards with 13 of the 52 cards designated as a "heart". If Laura shuffles the deck thoroughly and then deals 10 cards off the top of the deck, what is the probability that the 10th card dealt is a heart?

(a) $\frac{1}{4}$

(b) $\frac{1}{5}$

(c) $\frac{5}{26}$

(d) $\frac{12}{42}$

(e) $\frac{13}{42}$

19. A license plate in the country Kerrania consists of four digits followed by two letters. The letters A, B, and C are used only by government vehicles while the letters D through Z are used by non-government vehicles. Kerrania's intelligence agency has recently captured a message from the country Gonzalia indicating that an electronic transmitter has been installed in a Kerrania government vehicle with a license plate starting with 79. If it takes the police 10 minutes to inspect each vehicle, what is the probability that the police will find the transmitter within three hours?

(*a*) $\frac{18}{79}$

(*b*) $\frac{1}{6}$

(*c*) $\frac{1}{25}$

(*d*) $\frac{1}{50}$

(*e*) $\frac{1}{900}$

20. A grid of light bulbs measures x bulbs x bulbs, where x > 2. If 4 light bulbs are illuminated at random, what is the probability, in terms of x, that the 4 bulbs form a 2 bulb by 2 square?

(*a*) $\frac{1}{63}$

(*b*) $\frac{2}{63}$

(*c*) $\frac{3}{63}$

(*d*) $\frac{4}{63}$

(*e*) $\frac{5}{63}$

21. Baseball's World Series matches 2 teams against each other in a best-of-seven series. The first team to win four games wins the series and no subsequent games are played. If you have no special information about either of the teams, what is the probability that the World Series will consist of fewer than 7 games?

(*a*) 12.5%

(*b*) 25%

(*c*) 31.25%

(*d*) 68.75%

(*e*) 75%

22. How many diagonals does a polygon with 12 sides have?

(*a*) 54

(*b*) 66

(*c*) 108

(*d*) 132

(*e*) 144

23. There are 5 digit code numbers and each digits of these codes are composed of 0, 1, 2, 3, 4, and 5. The first digit doesn't use "0", and the code doesn't use the same number for different digits. How many such codes are possible?

(*a*) 120

(*b*) 240

(*c*) 360

(*d*) 500

(*e*) 600

24. If you list up 6 letters S, C, H, O, O, and L, how many cases are possible such that at least one letter is in between O and O?

(*a*) 120

(*b*) 180

(*c*) 200

(*d*) 240

(*e*) 280

25. If n is integer between 1 and 30, inclusive, what is the probability that n(n + 1) (n + 2) is divisible 6?

(*a*) 1

(*b*) $\frac{5}{6}$

(*c*) $\frac{4}{5}$

(*d*) $\frac{3}{4}$

(*e*) $\frac{2}{3}$

26. When n is between 1 and 100 inclusive, what is the probability that n(n + 1) is a multiple of 5?

(*a*) $\frac{1}{4}$

(*b*) $\frac{1}{2}$

(*c*) $\frac{3}{4}$

(*d*) $\frac{2}{5}$

(*e*) $\frac{2}{5}$

27. The code numbers consist of 4-digit and 2 digits are different and 2 digits are the same and none of them is zero, for example, 1122, 1212. How many such code numbers are possible?

(*a*) 196

(*b*) 216

(*c*) 236

(*d*) 256

(*e*) 316

28. The club contains 3 female members and 4 male members. If you randomly select 2 members from the club, what is the probability that at least one female will be included?

(*a*) $\frac{3}{4}$

(*b*) $\frac{2}{3}$

(*c*) $\frac{1}{2}$

(*d*) $\frac{5}{7}$

(*e*) $\frac{3}{7}$

29. There are 10 pairs of socks with each pair in different colors. If we select 2 from the 20 socks, what's the probability of selecting the same color socks?

(*a*) $\frac{1}{15}$

(*b*) $\frac{1}{16}$

(*c*) $\frac{1}{17}$

(*d*) $\frac{1}{18}$

(*e*) $\frac{1}{19}$

30. What is the difference between the mean and the median of Set C, a set of the first 100 positive integers?

(*a*) 0

(*b*) 25

(*c*) 50

(*d*) 75

(*e*) Cannot be determined

31. 3, 5, 7, 9

If another number N is added to the list above, which of the following could be the median of the new list of five numbers?

I. 5

II. 6

III. 7

(*a*) None of the above

(*b*) I only

(*c*) II only

(*d*) I and III only

(*e*) I, II and III

32. The "range" of a set of data is defined as the absolute difference between the least value and the greatest value in the set. Four positive integers have an averages (arithmetic mean) of 10. What tis the greatest possible range of the set?

(*a*) 40

(*b*) 36

(*c*) 32

(*d*) 25

(*e*) 10

33. The median of a set of 23 consecutive numbers is 25. What is the largest number in the set?

(*a*) 32

(*b*) 33

(*c*) 34

(*d*) 35

(*e*) 36

34. What is the average of $(x + 4)^2$ and $(x - 4)^2$?

(*a*) x^2

(*b*) $x^2 + 16$

(*c*) $x^2 + 32$

(*d*) $x^2 + 16x$

(*e*) $x^2 + 32x$

35. **Set A :** 4, 7, 9, 20

Set B : x, 4, 7, 9, 20

If the median of Set A is the same as Set B, then what is the value of x?

(*a*) 6

(*b*) 7

(*c*) 8

(*d*) 9

(*e*) 10

36. 4, x, 3, 9, y, 4

The arithmetic mean of the list of numbers above is 5. If x and y are integers and $x \neq y$, what is the median of the list?

(*a*) 2

(*b*) 3

(*c*) 4

(*d*) 5

(*e*) Cannot be determined

37. The average weight of a group of x people is 50 kilograms. If a person weighing 90 kilograms joins the group, the group average increases to 55 kilograms, what is the value of x?

(*a*) 11

(*b*) 10

(*c*) 9

(*d*) 8

(*e*) 7

38. There are ten people in a group. Out of them, 3 people weigh 50kg each, 3 people weigh 55 kg each, and the rest 4 weigh 45 kg each. What is the median weight of the group?

(*a*) 45

(*b*) 47

(*c*) 50

(*d*) 50.5

(*e*) 55

39. What is the difference between range and median of the numbers, x, x + 2, x + 3, x + 5, x + 10?

(*a*) –7

(*b*) –1

(*c*) x – 10

(*d*) x – 7

(*e*) x + 3

40. If the average of 21 consecutive integers is 152, what is the least of these integers?

(*a*) 139

(*b*) 140

(*c*) 141

(*d*) 142

(*e*) 143

41. The average score of seven students in an exam is 81. If score of one student is removed, the average score of the six students is 78. What is the score of the students which is removed.

(*a*) 98

(*b*) 99

(*c*) 100

(*d*) 101

(*e*) 102

42. In list A there are 10 numbers whose average is 70 and in list B there are 30 numbers whose average is 62. What is the average of these 40 numbers when both the lists are combined?

(*a*) 63

(*b*) 64

(*c*) 65

(*d*) 66

(*e*) 67

43. In list A there are 11 numbers whose median is 70 and in list B there are 9 numbers whose median is 62. What is the median of these 20 numbers when both the lists are combined?

(*a*) 62

(*b*) 64

(*c*) 68

(*d*) 70

(*e*) Cannot be determined

44. Set X = {1, 2, 3, 4, 5}

Set Y = {3, 3, 3, 3, 3}

Set Z = {0, 1, 5, 3, 4.5, 6}

Which set has the least standard deviation?

(*a*) Set X

(*b*) Set Y

(*c*) Set Z

(*d*) Set X and Set Y both

(*e*) Set Y and Set Z both

45. Which of the following sets has the smallest standard deviation?

(*a*) {–8, –8, –8, –8, -8}

(*b*) {–2, 0, 0, 0, 2}

(*c*) {1, 2, 3, 4, 5}

(*d*) {–1, –1, –1, –1, 0}

(*e*) {0, 1, 1, 1, 1}

46. If x and y are positive integers and the median of the numbers $3^{x-1}5^y$, 3^x5^{y-1}, and 3^x5^y, not in order, is 6,075, what is the value of xy?

(*a*) 8

(*b*) 9

(*c*) 10

(*d*) 12

(*e*) 15

47. Seven friends have a few candies with them. The numbers of candies with them are 21, 23, 45, 51, 66, 71, and 73.

They redistribute the candies among themselves such that each has at least one candy. The number of candies with them is distinct, and the median number of candies is maximum. What is the range of the number of candies with them?

(*a*) 86

(*b*) 87

(*c*) 88

(*d*) 89

(*e*) 90

48. If two numbers are selected randomly from Set A = {1, 2, 3, 4}, what is the probability that the sum of the numbers is even?

(*a*) $\frac{1}{3}$

(*b*) $\frac{1}{8}$

(*c*) $\frac{2}{3}$

(*d*) $\frac{1}{2}$

(*e*) $\frac{11}{16}$

49. There are five bulbs in a room, and each has its own switch. In how many ways can the room be illuminated if at least one bulb is on?

(*a*) 5

(*b*) 10

(*c*) 25

(*d*) 31

(*e*) 32

50. A committee requires four members. There are six members who are willing to be part of the committee: J, E, M, L, H, and P.E does not want to be in a committee with M, while P wants to be in the committee only if E is part of it. How many committees of four members can be formed?

(*a*) 3

(*b*) 5

(*c*) 6

(*d*) 7

(*e*) 8

51. Drake has 15 clients and wants to identify his clients with either a single character or a pair of two characters. What is the minimum number of characters needed to represent his clients of changing the order of characters does not produce a new pair?

(*a*) 3

(*b*) 4

(*c*) 5

(*d*) 6

(*e*) 7

52. If three single shoes are selected from a group of six pairs of different shoes, what is the probability that no two shoes will make a pair?

(*a*) $\frac{1}{1.320}$

(*b*) $\frac{1}{110}$

(*c*) $\frac{2}{33}$

(*d*) $\frac{13}{33}$

(*e*) $\frac{8}{11}$

53. If Set Q contains the numbers a, b, and c, which of the following set of numbers must have the same standard deviation as Set Q?

(*a*) (a + 1, b, c)

(*b*) (a, b + 1, c)

(*c*) (a, b, c + 1)

(*d*) [(a + bc), b (1 + c), c(b + 1)]

(*e*) (a – 1, b + 1, c)

54. The table below gives the number of victories the tennis player Roger has achieved against opponents. What are the minimum and maximum values of the sum of the median number of victories and the average number of victories for Roger?

Number of victories	Number of opponents
0	5
1	3
2	1
3	4
4	2

(*a*) 0 and 1

(*b*) 1 and 2

(*c*) 2 and 3

(*d*) 3 and 4

(*e*) 4 and 5

55. The mean of a set of eight integers is x. If all the integers in the set are multiplied by 3, then mean is still x. Which of the following statements holds true for the set?

I. x = 0

II. The largest integer in the set = negative of the smallest integer in the set.

III. The set contains both positive and negative integers.

(*a*) I only

(*b*) II only

(*c*) III only

(*d*) I and II only

(*e*) I, II and III

56. The average (arithmetic mean) as well as the median of nine distinct positive integers of a set is 30. If the terms of the set are such that their product is the greatest, what is the difference between the largest and the smallest terms of the set?

(*a*) 10

(*b*) 9

(*c*) 8

(*d*) 5

(*e*) 0

57. Of the 25 students in a class, 10 play football, and 8 play both cricket and football. If 10 students play none of these sports, how many students play cricket but not football?

(*a*) 3

(*b*) 4

(*c*) 5

(*d*) 6

(*e*) 13

Answer Key

1. (e)	16. (d)	31. (e)	46. (d)
2. (b)	17. (e)	32. (b)	47. (d)
3. (d)	18. (a)	33. (e)	48. (d)
4. (d)	19. (d)	34. (b)	49. (d)
5. (c)	20. (b)	35. (c)	50. (b)
6. (c)	21. (d)	36. (c)	51. (c)
7. (c)	22. (b)	37. (e)	52. (e)
8. (a)	23. (e)	38. (c)	53. (d)
9. (c)	24. (d)	39. (d)	54. (c)
10. (a)	25. (a)	40. (d)	55. (a)
11. (e)	26. (d)	41. (b)	56. (c)
12. (e)	27. (b)	42. (b)	57. (c)
13. (d)	28. (d)	43. (e)	
14. (e)	29. (e)	44. (b)	
15. (d)	30. (a)	45. (a)	

Answer Explanations

1. (e) A password can be made using any of the digits from 0 to 9, so there are 10 choices.

A password could be 122 or 221, hence repetition on digits are allowed.

Using slot approach, password can be created with slots, ___ AND ___ AND ___

First slot can be filled in 10 ways

Second slot can be filled in 10 ways

Third slot can be filled in 10 ways

Hence, by the fundamental principle of counting (If an event occurs in p different ways, and another event occurs in q different ways, then the total number of ways the events occur is $p \times q$ ways)

Total number of passwords

$$= 10 \times 10 \times 10 = 10^3.$$

The correct answer is option (e).

2. (b) There are 5 digits given to us 1, 2, 3, 4 out of which 3 coming 2 times

We know, 5 digits can be arranged in 5! Ways

Also, as digit 3 which is 2 times can rearrange within themselves in 2! Ways

Hence, the number of ways the digits can be arranged in $\frac{5!}{2!}$ Ways

The correct answer is option (b).

3. (d) In the first section, there are 3 questions and 2 mut be answered, as answering Q1 then Q2 is different from

Number of ways to answer the first section $= {}^3P_2$

Similarly in the second section, there are 4 questions and 2 must be answered, as answering Q1 and Q2 then Q3 is different from answering Q2, then Q1 then Q3. Hence, order matter, this is permutation question.

Number of ways to answer second section $= {}^4P_2$

Total number of ways of answering the test $= {}^3P_2 \times {}^4P^2 = 6 \times 12 = 72$

The correct answer is option (d).

4. (d) There are 6 different objects M O, B, I, L, E

Since vowels are together consider O, I, E to be one group.

Now, there are 4 object (M, B, L, group of vowels)

These 4 objects can be arranged in 4! ways

Also 3 distinct objects in the group of vowels can be arranged in 3! ways

Hence, by The fundamental principal of counting (If an event occurs in p different ways, and another event occurs in q different ways, then the total number of ways the events occur is $p \times q$ ways)

Therefore, total number of ways = $4! \times 3!$

The correct answer is option (d).

5. (c) There are 6 objects C, O, L, O, U, R

Since vowels are objects (C, L, R, group of vowels), which can be arranged in 4! Ways

Also 3 objects (O, O, U) in the group of vowels can be arranged in $\frac{3!}{2!}$ Ways (as O is coming 2 times)

Hence, by the fundamental principal of counting, total number of ways

$$= \frac{4! \times 3!}{2!}$$

The correct answer is option (c)

6. (c) Let's consider a couple as a group.

So there are three groups, we can arrange three groups of couples in 3! ways = 6 ways

Now, first group of couple can rearrange within themselves in 2! ways

Similarly, second group of couple can rearrange within themselves in 2! Ways

And first third of couple can rearrange within themselves in 2! Ways

Hence, total number of ways in which they can be standing in a row

$= 3! \times 2! \times 2! \times 2!$

$= 6 \times 2 \times 2 \times 2 = 48$ ways

The correct answer is option (d)

7. (c) The number of ways in which n people can be seated around a circular table is (n – 1)! Ways Hence, number of ways 6 people can be seated around a circular table

$= (6 - 1) = 5! = 120$ ways

The correct answer is option (c).

8. (a) The first prize can be given to any of the 3 students, hence there are 3 ways to give first prize.

The second prize can be given to any of the remaining 2 students in 2 ways.

Similarly, third prize can be given to 1 student in 1 way.

Hence, total number of ways are $3 \times 2 \times 1 = 6$

The correct answer is option (a)

9. (c) First prize can be given to any one of the 3 students.

Second prize can be given to any one of the 3 students.

Similarly, third prize can be given to any of the 3 students.

Hence, number of ways in which prizes can be distributed

$= 3 \times 3 \times 3 = 27$

The correct answer is option (c)

10. (a) To fill the hundreds place there are 9 choices, except 0 (as the three-digit number cannot have 0 in the hundreds place)

To fill tens place there are 9 choice (as 0 can come but as repetition is not allowed 1 digit already used in the hundreds place cannot be counted)

To fill one's place there are 8 choices (as repetition is not allowed, 2 digits already used in the hundreds and tens place cannot be counted)

Total number of three-digit numbers

$= 9 \times 9 \times 8 = 648$

The correct answer is option (a)

11. (e) As the order does not matter in the questions, it is combination.

Number of ways in which 2 men can be selected out of 5 men is $^5C_2 = 10$

Number of ways in which 2 women can be selected out of 6 women is $^6C_2 = 15$

A committee is to be formed of 2 men AND 2 women

$= 10 \times 15 = 150$

The correct answer is option (e)

12. (e) 5 red balls can be arranged only in one way as they are identical.

_R_R_R_R_R_

There are 6 places available for arranging 4 balls. So, 4 can be arranged in 6 places in 6C4 ways = 15 ways

Hence, total number of ways in which 5 identical red balls 4 identical blue balls can be arranged = 1 × 15 = 15 ways

The correct answer is option (e)

13. (d) If there are n distinct objects they can be arranged around a circular in (n – 1)! Ways.

Hence, 5 men can be seated at a circular table such that there is a vacant seat between every pair of men in (5 – 1)! = 4! Ways.

Now 5 vacant seats can be occupied by 5 women in 5! Ways.

Hence the required number of seating arrangements

$$= 4! \times 5! = 24 \times 120 = 2880$$

The correct answer is option (d)

14. (e) These is a strong temptation to solve this problem by simply finding probability that it will snow (90%) and the probability that schools will be closed (80%) and multiplying these two probabilities. This approach would the incorrect answer (72%), choice (d).

However, it is only possible to multiply probabilities of separate events if you know that they are independent from each other. This fact is not provided in the problem. In fact, we would assume that school being closed and snow are, at least to some extent, dependent on each other. However, they are not entirely dependent on each other, it is possible for either one to happen without the other. Therefore, there is an unknown degree of dependence; hence there is a range of possible probabilities, depending on to what extent the events are dependent on each other.

Set up a matrix as sown below . Fill in the probability that schools will not be closed and the probability that there will be no snow.

	Schools closed	Schools not closed	Total
Snow			
No snow			10
Total		20	100

Then use subtraction to fill in the probability that schools will be closed and the probability that there will be snow.

	Schools closed	Schools not closed	Total
Snow			90
No snow			10
Total	80	20	100

To find the greatest possible probability that schools will be closed and it will snow, fill in the remaining cells with the largest possible number in the upper left cell.

	Schools closed	Schools not closed	Total
Snow	80	10	90
No snow	0	10	10
Total	80	20	100

The greatest possible probability that schools will be closed and it will snow is 80%.

The correct answer is (e).

15. (d) The easiest way to attack this problem is to pick some real, easy numbers as values for y and n. Let's assume there are 3 travelers (A, B, C) and 2 different destinations (1, 2).

We can chart out the possibilities as follows:

Destination 1	Destination 2
ABC	
AB	C
AC	B
BC	A
	ABC
C	AB
B	AC
A	BC

Thus there are 8 possibilities and in 2 of them all travelers end up at the same destination. Thus the probability is $\frac{2}{8}$ or $\frac{1}{4}$. By plugging in y = 3 and n = 2 into each answer choice, we see that only answer choice D yields a probability of $\frac{1}{4}$.

Alternatively, consider that each traveler can end up at any one of n destinations. Thus, for each traveler there are n possibilities. Therefore, for y travelers, there are n^y possible outcomes.

Additionally, the "winning" outcomes are those where all travelers end up at the same destination.

Since there are n destinations there are n "winning" outcomes.

Thus, the probability

$$= \frac{\text{winning outcomes}}{\text{total outcomes}} = \frac{n}{n^y} = \frac{1}{n^{y-1}}.$$

The answer is (d).

16. (d) There are four scenarios in which the plane will crash. Determine the probability of each of these scenarios individually:

Case one : Engine 1 fails, Engine 2 fails, Engine 3 works

$$= \frac{1}{3} \times \frac{1}{4} \times \frac{1}{2} = \frac{1}{24}$$

Case two : Engine 1 fails, Engine 2 works, Engine 3 fails

$$= \frac{1}{3} \times \frac{3}{4} \times \frac{1}{2} = \frac{3}{24}$$

Case three : Engine 1 works, Engine 2 fails, Engine 3 works

$$= \frac{2}{3} \times \frac{1}{4} \times \frac{1}{2} = \frac{2}{24}$$

Case four : Engine 1 fails, Engine 2 fails, Engine 3 fails

$$= \frac{1}{3} \times \frac{1}{4} \times \frac{1}{2} = \frac{1}{24}$$

To determine the probability that any one of these scenarios will occur, sum four probabilities:

$$\frac{1}{24} + \frac{3}{24} + \frac{2}{24} + \frac{1}{24} = \frac{7}{24}$$

The correct answer is (d).

17. (e) Since each of the 4 children can be either a boy or a girl, there are 2 × 2× 2 × 2 = 2 = 16 possible ways that the children might be born, as listed below:

BBBB (all boys)

BBBG, BBGB, BGBB, GBBBM (3 boys, 1 girl)

BBGG, BGGB, BGBG, GGBB, GBBG, GBGB (2 boys, 2 girls)

GGGB, GGBG, GBGG, BGGG (3 girls, 1 boy)

GGGG (all girls)

Since we are told that there are at least 2 girls, we an eliminate 5 possibilities - the one possibility in which all of the children are boys (the first row) and the four possibilities in which only one of the children is a girl (the second row).

That leaves 11 possibilities (the third, fourth, and fifth row) of which 6 are comprised of two boys and two girls (the third row). Thus, the probability that Ms. Barton also has 2 boys is $\frac{6}{11}$.

The correct answer is option (e).

18. (a) Although this maybe counter-intuitive at first, the probability that any card in the deck will be a heart before any cards are seen in $\frac{13}{52}$ or $\frac{1}{4}$.

One way to understand this is to solve the problem analytically for any card by building a probability "tree" and summing the probability of all of its "branches."

For example, let's find the probability that the 2nd card dealt from the deck is a heart. There are two mutually exclusive ways this can happen: (1) both the first and second cards are hearts or (2) only the second card is a heart.

Case 1 : Using the multiplication rule, the probability that the first card is a heart AND the second card is a heart is equal to the probability of picking a heart on the first card (or $\frac{13}{52}$, which is the number of hearts in a full deck divided by the number of cards) times the probability of picking a heart on the second card (or $\frac{12}{51}$, which is the number of hearts remaining in the deck divided by the number of cards remaining in the deck).

$$\frac{13}{52}\times\frac{12}{51}=\frac{12}{204}$$

Case 2 : Similarly, the probability that the first card is a non-heart AND the second card is a heart is equal to the probability that the first card is NOT a heart (or $\frac{39}{52}$) times the probability of subsequently picking a heart on the 2nd card (or $\frac{13}{51}$).

$$\frac{39}{52}\times\frac{13}{51}=\frac{39}{204}$$

Since these two cases are mutually exclusive, we can add them together to get the total probability f getting a heart as the second card:

$$\frac{12}{204}+\frac{29}{204}=\frac{51}{204}=\frac{1}{4}$$

We can do a similar analysis for any card in the deck, and although the probability tree gets more complicated as the card number gets higher, the total probability that the nth card dealt will be a heart will always end up simplifying to $\frac{1}{4}$.

The correct answer is (a).

19. (d) Since the first two digits of the license plate are known and there are 10 possibilities for each of the remaining two digits (each can be any digit from 0 to 9), the total number of combinations for digits on the license plate will equal $10 \times 10 = 100$.

Because there are only 3 letters that can be used for government license plates (A, B, or C), there are a total of nine two-letter combinations that could be on the license plate (3 possibilities for first letter × 3 possibilities for the second letter).

Given that we have 100 possible digit combinations and 9 possible letter combinations, the total number of vehicles to be inspected will equal $100 \times 9 = 900$.

Since it takes 10 minutes to inspect one vehicle, the police will have time to inspect 18 vehicles in three hours (3 hours = 180 minutes).

Thus, the probability of locating the transmitter within the allotted time is $\frac{18}{900} = \frac{1}{50}$.

The correct answer is (d).

20. (b) Trying to figure this problem out directly is time-consuming and risky. The safest and most efficient way to handle this is to assign a value to x, figure out the probability, and then plug that value into the answer choice until you find one choice that yields the correct probability.

Since x must be greater than 2, let's assign x a value of 3. This produces a 3-by-3 grid as follows (where each letter represents a bulb):

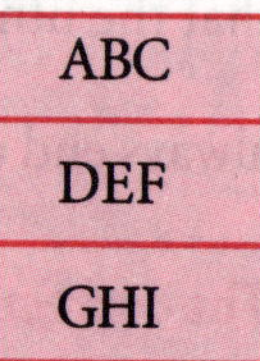

ABC
DEF
GHI

In order to determine the probability, we need to first figure out how many different groups of 4 bulbs could be illuminated. Since we have 9 bulbs, we can represent one way that exactly four bulbs could be illuminated as follows (each letter represents a bulb):

A	B	C	D	E	F	G	H	I
Yes	Yes	Yes	Yes	No	No	No	No	No

There are many other ways this could happen. Using the permutation formula, there are $\frac{9!}{(4!)(5!)} = 126$ different combinations of exactly four illuminated bulbs.

How many of these 126 groups of 4 form a 2-by-2 square? If you analyze the 3-by-3 grid above you'll see there are only 4 groups that form a 2-by-2 square (ABDE, BCEF, DEGH, & EFHI).

Thus the correct probability is $\frac{4}{126}$ or $\frac{2}{63}$.

If we plug in 3 for x in the answer choices, only choice (b) reduces to the same answer.

The correct answer is (b).

21. (d) In order to determine the probability that the World Series will last fewer than 7 games, we can first determine the probability that the World Series Will last exactly 7 games and then subtract this value from 1.

In order for the World Series to last exactly 7 games, the first 6 games of the series must results in 3 wins and 3 losses for each team.

Let's analyze one way this could happen :

Game 1	Game 2	Game 3	Game 4	Game 5	Game 6
T1 Wins	T1 Wins	T1 Wins	T1 Loses	T1 Loses	T1 Loses

There are many other ways this could happen. Using the permutation formula, there are $\frac{6!}{(3!)(3!)} = 20$ ways for the two teams to split the first 6 games (3 wins for each).

There are then 2 possible outcomes to break the tie in Game 7. Thus there are a total of $20 \times 2 = 40$ ways for the World Series at last the full 7 games.

The probability that any one of these 40 ways occurs can be calculated from the fact that the probability of a team winning a game equals the probability of a team losing a game $= \frac{1}{2}$.

Given that 7 distinct events must happen in any 7 game series, and that each of these events has a probability of $\frac{1}{2}$, the probability that any one particular 7 game series occurs is $\left(\frac{1}{2}\right)^7 = \frac{1}{128}$. Since there are 40 possible different 7 game series, the probability that the World Series will last exactly 7 games is:

$$40 \times \frac{1}{128} = \frac{40}{128} = .3125 = 31.25\%$$

Thus the probability that the World Series will last fewer than 7 games is 100% – 31.25% = 68.75%.

The correct answer is (d).

22. **(b)** The number of diagonals in any polygon is $\frac{n(n-3)}{2}$

Here n = 12

$\Rightarrow$ The number of polygons

$$= \frac{12(12-3)}{2} = 12 \times \frac{9}{2} = 54$$

The answer is (a)

23. **(e)** $\Rightarrow$ Since you are forming 5 digit code numbers, from

0, 1, 2, 3, 4, 5

The first digit can't be a 0, so there are 5 ways, and for second digit, since you can't have the same number as the first digit, so there are also 5 ways (since you can have 0 here), and there are 4 ways for third digit. 3 ways for fourth digit, and 2 digit for the fifth digit, so you get (5) (5) (4) (3) (2) = 600.

The correct answer is option (e).

24. **(d)** The number of ways to list the letters S, C, H, O, O, L is $\frac{6!}{2!}$ since there are 6 letters and 2 letters (O, O) of them are the same so you divide it by 2!. In other words, when listing S, C, H, O, O, L, the number of ways that at least one letter is in between O and O is the total number of ways- the number of ways that O and O is next to each other. Thus, from $\frac{6!}{2!}$ (OO)SCHL, you need to subtract the case where OO is next to each other. Then, from $\frac{6!}{2!} - 5! = 360 = 120 = 240$.

The answer is (d).

25. (a) ⇒ Probability $= \frac{\text{Want}}{\text{Total}}$. Then,

Since there is a total of 30 integers, you get Total $= {}_{30}C_1 = 30$.

Since the product of 3 consecutive integers always become the multiple of 6, so it is always divisible by 6 because the 3 consecutive integers always contain 3, and at least 1 is an even number. Then, you get Want $= {}_{30}C_1 = 30$. Thus, when N is a positive integer from 1 to 30, the probability that n(n + 1) (n + 2) is divisible by 6 becomes $\frac{30}{30} = 1$.

The answer is (a).

26. (d) In general, it is best to directly substitute for remainder questions. In other words, the multiple of 5 means that the remainder is 0 when divided by 5, so it becomes a remainder question. If you solve it by direct substitution.

n = 1, (1) (1) ≠ multiple of 5 ...... n = 96, (96) (97) ≠ multiple of 5

n = 2, (2) (3) ≠ multiple of 5 ...... n = 97, (97) (98) ≠ multiple of 5

n = 3, (3) (4) ≠ multiple of 5 ...... n = 98, (98) (99) ≠ multiple of 5

n = 4, (4) (5) = multiple of 5 ...... n = 99, (99) (100) = multiple of 5

n = 5, (5) (6) = multiple of 5 ...... n = 100, (100) (101) = multiple of 5

The correct answer is option (d).

27. (b) First, the number of possible ways of to list 1, 1, 2, 2 is $\frac{4!}{2!2!} = 6$, which are (1, 1, 2, 2), (1, 2, 1, 2), (2, 1, 1, 2), (2, 2, 1, 1), (2, 1, 2, 1), or (1, 2, 1, 2).

Then, from the total 4 digits, each 2 digits are the same, from the 9 numbers 1, 2, 3, 4, 5, , 7, 8, 9, the number of ways to select two numbers is ${}_9C_2 \; \frac{(9)(8)}{2!} = 36$, and the since each of the code numbers can be in 6 ways as shown above, you get (6) (36) = 216.

The answer is (b).

28. (d) It is "at least" question, so from the 7 members, it is the probability of selecting at least 1 female member when randomly selecting 2 members. Thus, you get 1-the probability of not selecting at least one female member=1-the probability of not selecting both male members. Then, the probability of selecting two male members is from $\frac{\text{Want}}{\text{Total}}$, since you are selecting 2 out of 7, you get Total $= {}_7C_2 = \frac{(7)(6)}{2!} = 21$ and since it is the probability of selecting both males, you get Want $= {}_4C_2 = \frac{(4)(3)}{2!} = 6$. Thus, the probability of selecting at least 1 female member when randomly selecting 2 out of 7 members is

$$1 - \frac{6}{21} = 1 - \frac{2}{7} = \frac{5}{7}.$$

Therefore, (d) is the answer.

29. (e) Probability $= \frac{\text{Want}}{\text{Total}}$. Then since there are 20 socks in total, you get Total ${}_{20}C_2 = \frac{(20)(19)}{2!} = 190$, and since you need to select same colored.

socks, from the total 10 pairs, you must select 1 pair, and from the pair, you must select both socks, so you get Want = $({}_{10}C_1)\ ({}_2C_2)$ = (10) (1) = 10. The probability of selecting 2 same colored socks from 20 socks becomes

$$\frac{10}{190} = \frac{1}{19}.$$

The answer is (e).

30. (a) For a set of consecutive integers, the mean

$$= \text{median} = \frac{(1^{st}\ \text{term} + \text{last term})}{2}$$

Hence, the difference between mean and the median is 0.

The answer is (a).

31. (e) Here, we need to take cases

If P < 5, then the new set would be

P, 3, 5, 7, 9 or 3, P, 5, 7, 9

Hence, the median would be 5.

If P = 6, then the new set would be 3, 5, 6, 7, 9

Hence, the median is 6.

If P > 7, then the new set would be

3, 5, 7, P, 9 or 3, 5, 7, 9, P

Hence, the median would be 7.

The answer is (e)

32. (b) $\text{Average} = \frac{\text{Sum}}{\text{Number of terms}}$

$$10 = \frac{\text{Sum}}{4}$$

$\Rightarrow$ Sum = 40

If the four numbers are A, B, C, and D, then

A + B + C + D = 40

For the greatest range, A must be the smallest and D must be the greatest integer.

Smallest positive integer is 1. So, let A, B, and C be 1 each.

Hence 1 + 1 + 1 + D = 40

3 + D = 40

$\Rightarrow$ D = 37

Hence, the range = 37 – 1 = 36

The answer is (b)

33. (e) In a set of 23 consecutive numbers, the 12th numbers is the median.

Hence, the 12th number is 25.

There are 11 numbers greater than 25.

Hence, the largest number in the set is 25 + 11 = 36

The answer is (e)

34. (b) $(x + 4)^2 = x^2 + 16 + 8x$

$(x - 4)^2 = x^2 + 16 - 8x$

$\Rightarrow (x + 4)^2 + (x - 4)^2$

$= (x^2 + 16 + 8x) + (x^2 + 16 - 8x)$

$= 2(x^2 + 16)$

$$\text{Average} = \frac{2(x^2 + 16)}{2} = x^2 + 16$$

The answer is (b)

35. (c) Median of Set A is $\frac{(7+9)}{2} = 8$

For the median of Set B to be 8, x must be 8

The answer is (c)

36. (c) $\frac{(4 + x + 3 + 9 + y + 4)}{6} = 5$

$(20 + x + y) = 30$

$x + y = 10$

As $x \neq y$, there are some possible sets (1, 9), (2, 8), (3, 7), and (4, 6)

If x = 1 and y = 9, then the set is 1, 3, 4, 4, 9, 9 – The median is 4

If x = 2 and y = 8, then the set is 2, 3, 4, 4, 8, 9 – The median is 4

If x = 3 and y = 7, then the set is 3, 3, 4, 4, 7, 9 – The median is 4

If x = 4 and y = 6, then the set is 3, 4, 4, 4, 6, 9 – The median is 4

Hence, the answer is (c)

37. **(e)** We know, Average = sum of readings/ number of readings

50 = sum of weight of x people /x

Sum of weight of x people = 5x

New average = 55

$$= \frac{(\text{sum of weight of x people} + 90)}{(x+1)}$$

$55(x + 1) = 50x + 90$

$55x + 55 = 50x + 90$

$5x = 35$

$x = 7$

The correct answer is option (e)

38. **(c)** Since there are 10 entries, the median weight of the group is the average of the 5th and 6th entries when the weights are arranged in order from least to greatest.

In order from least to greatest, the 5th and 6th entry are:

45, 45, 45, 45, 50, 50

Average of the 5th and 6th entry

$$= \frac{(50 + 50)}{2} = 50$$

The correct answer is option (c)

39. **(d)** x, x + 2, x + 3, x + 5, x + 10

median of the five numbers is the third number, x + 3

Range is the difference between greatest and smallest number

$= x + 10 - x = 10$

Median – Range = x + 3 – 10 = x – 7

The correct answer is option (d)

40. **(d)** Consecutive integers are in arithmetic progression where common difference between any two consecutive numbers is same.

In an AP, average = median = 152 is the middle term

Since there are 21 consecutive integers, the 11th number is the middle term.

Hence, the smallest integer must be 10 less than 152 = 142

The correct answer is option (d)

41. **(b)** Average score of seven students = 81

Then the sum of these seven students

$= 7 \times 81 = 567.$

Since, if one of score is removed, the average of the six-remaining score = 78,

Then the sum of these six scores

$= 6 \times 81 = 567.$

Since, if one of score is removed, the average of the six-remaining score = 78,

Then the sum of these six scores

$= 6 \times 78 = 468.$

Hence, removed score = 567 – 468 = 99

The correct answer is option (b)

42. (b) As average and number of readings in the two given lists is known, we can calculate their respective sums.

Sum of numbers of list A = $10 \times 70 = 700$

Sum of numbers of list B = $30 \times 62 = 1860$

Therefore, sum of 50 numbers

$$= 700 + 1860 = 2560$$

Hence, average of the 50 numbers

$$= \frac{2560}{40} = 64$$

The correct answer is option (b)

43. (e) Median of 11 numbers in list A is 70 means 6th reading is 70

Median of 9 numbers in list B is 62 means 5th reading is 62

When both the lists are combined, there are 20 readings, and median is the average of the 10th and 11th reading.

But, from the given information value of the 10th and 11th reading cannot be determined.

The correct answer is option (e)

44. (b) Standard deviation measures dispersion around the mean. The closer the readings, the lesser is the standard deviation. The more far away the readings, the greater is the standard deviation.

In set X, mean is 3 with two readings below and above the mean, hence there is deviation

In set Y, mean is 3 and all readings are same, hence there is no deviation around the mean.

In set Z, mean is 3 with two readings below and above the mean, hence there is deviation.

The correct answer is option (b)

45. (a) The computation of standard deviation (SD) is not within the scope of the GMAT; however, its analysis is.

Standard deviation is the measure of the spread of values within a set with respect to its mean. The farther the values are on either side of the mean, the greater the standard deviation and vie-versa.

The smallest possible value of SD is 0, and that's when all of the terms in a set are the same. We see that only the set {–8, –8, –8, –8, –8} has all the terms same; thus, its SD = 0, minimum.

Other sets will have SD > 0. We are not asked to choose a set that has the largest SD; had that been the question, the answer would have been option C: {1, 2, 3, 4, 5} because collectively, the spread of the terms in the set w.r.t is mean (=3) would be greater than that in any other set.

The correct answer is option (a).

46. (d) We have the first number, $3^{x-1}\,5^y = \frac{3^x5^y}{3}$

And the second number, $3^x\,5^{y-1} = \frac{3^x5^y}{5}$

Thus, the smallest of the three numbers is $\frac{3^x5^y}{5}$ and the largest is 3^x5^y.

Thus, the three numbers, when arranged in ascending order are $\frac{3^x5^y}{5}$, $\frac{3^x5^y}{3}$ and 3^x5^y.

Thus, the median = the middle-most number $\frac{3^x5^y}{3} = 3^{x-1}5^y$

Thus, we have

$$3^{x-1}5^y = 6{,}075 = 3^5 5^2$$

$\Rightarrow$ $x - 1 = 5, \Rightarrow x = 6$ and $y = 2$

$\Rightarrow$ $xy = 12$

The correct answer is option (d).

47. (d) Thus, total number of candies with the 7 friends

$$= 21 + 23 + 45 + 51 + 66 + 71 + 73 = 360$$

We need to maximize the median value.

$$\text{The median of 7 terms} = \left(\frac{7+1}{2}\right)^{\text{th}} \text{term}$$

$$= 4^{\text{th}} \text{term}$$

Let's arrange the number of candies with the keep terms distinct, the terms following the median, i.e., 6th,6th, and 7th should be 1 greater, 2 greater, and 3 greater than the median, respectively.

We minimize the 1st, 2nd, 7th friends have x, (x + 1), (x + 2), and (x + 3) candies, where x is the median.

Thus, we have

$$x + (x + 1) + (x + 2) + (x + 3) = 354 \Rightarrow x = 87$$

Thus, the numbers of candies are 1, 2, 3, 87, 88, 89, and 90 (the median is maximized).

Thus, the range = 90 – 1 = 89

The correct answer is option (d).

48. (d) Set A contains one even number (2) and three odd numbers (1, 3, and 5).

The sum of two positive integers would be even if both are even or both are odd. Since there's only one even number, we cannot have two even numbers upon selection; thus we must focus on the selection of two odd numbers.

Number of ways of randomly selecting two odd numbers out of three odd numbers from Set A

$$= C_2^3 = C_1^3 = 3; \text{ not that } C_r^n = C_{n-r}^n.$$

Number of ways of randomly selecting two numbers out of four numbers from Set A

$$= C_2^4 = \frac{4.3}{1.2} = 6$$

Thus, the probability that the sum of the two selected numbers is even $\frac{3}{6} = \frac{1}{2}$.

The correct answer is option (d).

49. (d) Each bulb can either be on or off (2 ways). Since there are five bulbs, the number of possibilities are

$$2 \times 2 \times 2 \times 2 \times 2 = 2^5 = 32.$$

From all the above possibilities, we have to subtract the possibility of all the bulbs being switched off, i.e., when the room is not illuminated. Therefore, the answer is 32 – 1 = 31, number of ways the room can have at least one bulb on.

The correct answer is option (d).

50. (b) A committee can be formed either with without E.

Therefore, total number of committees

= Number of committees with E in the committee + Number of committees without E in the committee

Let us find the number of committees with E in the committee.

Since E does not want to be in the committee with M, we can exclude M. P can be in the committee as E is in the committee. Hence the other 3 committee members apart from E can be chosen from J, Luiz, H, and P.

Number of ways of selecting 3 people out of 4 = ${}^3C_4 = 4$.

Number of committees formed without E in the committee.

Paul would not want to be the part of the committee as E is not in the committee.

Hence, the number of ways of forming a 4-member committee out of (J, L, H, and M) is 1.

Total number of committees = 4 + 1 = 5.

The correct answer is option (b).

51. **(c)** Let x be the number of total characters. Then, as per the question,

No. of clients with single character = ${}^xC_1$;

No. of clients with two character = ${}^xC_2$;

As per the question,

$${}^xC_1 + {}^xC_2 \geq 15 \Rightarrow x + {}^xC_2 \geq 15$$

Instead of calculating the value of x, try plugging in 3, 4, 5... etc. for.

It may be time-consuming to solve this question by the traditional approach. The optimum approach is to plug-in the values from the options. But which option should you try first? If start plugging in from options (a), (b), (c) onwards then you may lose more time in case the answer is (d) or (e).

The best way to plug-in is to try option (b), and then (d). It is called (b)/(d) plug in approach for Problem Solving questions.

Under this approach, the values in the options must be arranged in ascending order from options (a) through (e).

Option (b): $x = 4 \Rightarrow 4 + \frac{4.3}{1.2} = 10 \geq 15;$

This is wrong, as 10 cannot be greater than 15. It means that x must be greater than 4. So let us try Option (d).

Option (d): $x = 6 \Rightarrow 6 + \frac{6.5}{1.2} = 21 \geq 15;$

This value qualifies, but we cannot conclude that x = 6 is the minimum possible value, so let's try Option (c).

Option (c): $x = 5 \Rightarrow 5 + \frac{5.4}{1.2} = 15 \geq 15;$

This qualifies and is the minimum possible value of x.

The correct answer is option (c).

52. **(e)** There are 6 pairs or 12 single shoes. Once we select the first shoe, then there is $\frac{10}{11}$ chance that the second shoe selected is NOT its pair. We took 10 shoes for the selection because the paired shoe must be excluded. Similarly, for the third one, there is $\frac{8}{10}$ chance that the third shoe is NOT a pair of the first two.

So, the probability that no two shoes will make a pair

$$= \left(\frac{10}{11}\right) \times \left(\frac{8}{10}\right) = \frac{8}{11}.$$

The correct answer is option (e).

53. (d) Adding or subtracting a constant from each element of a set has no effect on its standard deviation (SD).

For example, the SD of a set {10, 11, 13} is pay p, then the SD for the set {12, 13, 14} will also be p since a constant '2' is added to the original set to get the new set.

Say a = 1, b = 2, and c = 3. Do not calculate the SD now. Let us analyze the options by plugging in the values of a, b, and c. The values would be as follows.

(a) 2, 2, 3

(b) 1, 3, 3

(c) 1, 2, 4

(d) 7, 8, 9 – This is the correct answer as a constant '6' is added to a, b, and c, implying the same SD.

(e) 0, 2, 3

The correct answer is option (d).

54. (c) We write the number of victories against each player: 0, 0, 0, 0,0, 1, 1, 1, 2, 3, 3, 3, 3, 4, 4.

You must do this mentally. The median is the middle term = 1 victory per opponent

The average can be calculated as

$$\frac{\text{Total no. of victories}}{\text{Total no. of apponents}}$$

$$= \frac{0\times5+1\times3+2\times1+3\times4+4\times2}{15}$$

= 1.668 victories per opponent

The sum of the median and the average = 1 + 1.668 = 2.667 victories per opponent

Since 2.667 lies between 2 and 3, option (c) is the answer.

The correct answer is option (c).

55. (a) When all the numbers of a set are multiplied by a number, the mean also gets multiplied by the same number.

After the multiplication by 3, the mean remains same; it can happen only if mean

= 0, hence the statement (I) is true.

Statement (II) is not necessary true as the set {–8, 1, 2, 3, 4, 5, 6, 8} does not satisfy the given condition. We can see that the largest number

= 8 = negative of the smallest number

= –(–8).

Statement (III) is also not necessary true because the set may contain all zeros.

The correct answer is option (a).

56. (c) Let the seven distinct positive integers be a, b, c, d, e, f, g, h and i, such that $a < b < c < d < e < f < g < h < i$.

Since the median is 30, we have:

$$e = 30 \quad ...(i)$$

Since the mean is 30, we have

$$\frac{a+b+c+d+30+f+g+h+i}{9} = 30$$

$$\Rightarrow a+b+c+d+f+g+h+i$$

$$= 270 - 30 = 240 \quad ...(ii)$$

Since the value of e equal to 30 is fixed, and we need to maximize the product of the nine integers, we need to maximize the product of $(a \times b \times c \times d \times f \times g \times h \times i)$.

We know that, for a given value of the sum, the product is maximum if the numbers are equal. (For example, if p, q, r, and s are four numbers and $p + q + r + s = 8$, the maximum value of the product $(p \times q \times r \times s)$ occurs when $p = q = r = s\frac{8}{4} = 2$, and the value of $(p \times q \times r \times s) = 2 \times 2 \times 2 \times 2 = 16$.

Proceeding using the above logic, we should have a

$$= b = c = d = f = h = i = \frac{240}{8} = 30$$

However, we need to keep the numbers distinct as well. Thus, we should assign such values for a, b, c, d, f, g, h, and i that their values are as close as possible to each other and at the same time, they remain distinct.

Thus, the nine distinct integers as close as possible to each other are: 26, 27, 28, 29, 30, 31, 32, 33, and 34.

The difference of the smallest and largest numbers = 34 – 26 = 8

The correct answer is option (c).

57. (c) Let the number of students who play cricket be X.

The total number of students = 25

We know that for two sets A and B, A or B

$$= A + B - A \& B.$$

25 = Number of students who play cricket + number of students who play football + number of students who play none – number of students who play both

$25 = X + 10 + 10 - 8$

$X = 25 - 12 = 13$

Therefore, people who play only cricket = number of people who play cricket – number of people who play both sports

$= 13 - 8 = 5.$

The correct answer is option (c).

Data Sufficiency

1. In an office, there are x employees, how many different committees of 5 employees can be formed?

(I) If the office had x + 2 employees, then 126 different 5 employees committees can be formed.

(II) If the office had x + 1 employees, then 56 different 3 employees committees can be formed.

(*a*) Statement (I) ALONE is sufficient but statement (II) ALONE is not sufficient.

(*b*) Statement (II) ALONE is sufficient but statement (I) ALONE is not sufficient.

(*c*) BOTH statements TOGETHER are sufficient, but NEITHER statement ALONE is sufficient.

(*d*) EACH statement ALONE is sufficient.

(*e*) Statements (I) and (II) TOGETHER are not sufficient.

2. In how many ways k number of students can be selected from 20 students?

(I) There are 1140 ways to select (k + 1) number of students out of 20 students.

(II) There are 20 ways to select (k – 1) number of students out of 20 students.

(*a*) Statement (I) ALONE is sufficient but statement (II) ALONE is not sufficient.

(*b*) Statement (II) ALONE is sufficient but statement (I) ALONE is not sufficient.

(*c*) BOTH statements TOGETHER are sufficient, but NEITHER statement ALONE is sufficient.

(*d*) EACH statement ALONE is sufficient.

(*e*) Statements (I) and (II) TOGETHER are not sufficient.

3. In the game of Funball, each batter can either hit a home run, hit a single, or strikeout, and the likelihood of each outcome is completely determined by the opposing pitcher. A Funball batter scores a point for their team by advancing sequentially through each of four "bases", according to the following rules: Home run: The batter and any players already on a base advance through all four bases.

Single : The batter advances to first base, and any players already on a base advance one base each.

Strikeout : No one advances any bases, and the batter loses his/her turn.

If the batting team has a runner on first base, which pitcher (Roger or Greg) is more likely to allow a point before recording a strikeout?

(I) Greg is twice as likely as Roger to allow a single, and four times as likely as Roger to record a strikeout.

(II) Greg is twice as likely as Roger to allow a single, and one fourth as likely as Roger to allow a home run.

(*a*) Statement (I) ALONE is sufficient but statement (II) ALONE is not sufficient.

(*b*) Statement (II) ALONE is sufficient but statement (I) ALONE is not sufficient.

(*c*) BOTH statements TOGETHER are sufficient, but NEITHER statement ALONE is sufficient.

(*d*) EACH statement ALONE is sufficient.

(*e*) Statements (I) and (II) TOGETHER are not sufficient.

4. Mike recently won a contest in which he will have the opportunity to shoot free throws in order to win $10,000. In order to win the money Mike can either shoot 1 free throw and make it, or shoot 3 free throws and make at lest 2 of them. Mike occasionally makes shots and occasionally misses shots. He knows that his probability of making a single free throw is p, and that this probability doesn't change. Would Mike have a better chance of winning if he chose attempt 3 free throws?

(I) $p < 0.7$

(II) $p > 0.6$

(*a*) Statement (I) ALONE is sufficient but statement (II) ALONE is not sufficient.

(*b*) Statement (II) ALONE is sufficient but statement (I) ALONE is not sufficient.

(*c*) BOTH statements TOGETHER are sufficient, but NEITHER statement ALONE is sufficient.

(*d*) EACH statement ALONE is sufficient.

(*e*) Statements (I) and (II) TOGETHER are not sufficient.

5. There were r red cards and w white cards in bag. If these cards are to be displayed on a wall with 30 possible display boards, in how many ways can they arranged?

(I) $r + 2w = 15$

(II) $2r + 2w = 20$

(*a*) Statement (I) ALONE is sufficient but statement (II) ALONE is not sufficient.

(*b*) Statement (II) ALONE is sufficient but statement (I) ALONE is not sufficient.

(*c*) BOTH statements TOGETHER are sufficient, but NEITHER statement ALONE is sufficient.

(*d*) EACH statement ALONE is sufficient.

(*e*) Statements (I) and (II) TOGETHER are not sufficient.

6. What is the probability of getting 5 on the sixth roll of a dice?

(I) The dice is a regular fair dice with numbers from 1 to 6

(II) The first five rolls had 5 as the result

(*a*) Statement (I) ALONE is sufficient but statement (II) ALONE is not sufficient.

(*b*) Statement (II) ALONE is sufficient but statement (I) ALONE is not sufficient.

(*c*) BOTH statements TOGETHER are sufficient, but NEITHER statement ALONE is sufficient.

(*d*) EACH statement ALONE is sufficient.

(*e*) Statements (I) and (II) TOGETHER are not sufficient.

7. A box is filled with marbles of three colors – red, blue, and green. Is the probability of getting a red marble the same as probability of getting a green marble?

(I) There are a total of 11 marbles in the box.

(II) The number of blue marbles is more than the number of green marbles.

(*a*) Statement (I) ALONE is sufficient but statement (II) ALONE is not sufficient.

(*b*) Statement (II) ALONE is sufficient but statement (I) ALONE is not sufficient.

(*c*) BOTH statements TOGETHER are sufficient, but NEITHER statement ALONE is sufficient.

(*d*) EACH statement ALONE is sufficient.

(*e*) Statements (I) and (II) TOGETHER are not sufficient.

8. What is the probability that either event A or event B will occur but not both?

(I) Probability of event A happening is 0.3

(II) Probability of event B happening is 0.7

(*a*) Statement (I) ALONE is sufficient but statement (II) ALONE is not sufficient.

(*b*) Statement (II) ALONE is sufficient but statement (I) ALONE is not sufficient.

(*c*) BOTH statements TOGETHER are sufficient, but NEITHER statement ALONE is sufficient.

(*d*) EACH statement ALONE is sufficient.

(*e*) Statements (I) and (II) TOGETHER are not sufficient.

9. A box has Physics, Chemistry, and Math books. If a books is randomly selected, what is the probability that it is Math book?

(I) There are 6 Physics books and 4 Chemistry books.

(II) There are 3 times as many Math books as all the other books combined.

(*a*) Statement (I) ALONE is sufficient but statement (II) ALONE is not sufficient.

(*b*) Statement (II) ALONE is sufficient but statement (I) ALONE is not sufficient.

(*c*) BOTH statements TOGETHER are sufficient, but NEITHER statement ALONE is sufficient.

(*d*) EACH statement ALONE is sufficient.

(*e*) Statements (I) and (II) TOGETHER are not sufficient.

10. A box has Physics, Chemistry, and Math books. There are a total of 5 Math books. If two books are randomly selected, what is the probability that both will be Math books?

(I) The probability that the first book picked is Math is $\frac{1}{2}$

(II) If the first selected book is Math, then the probability of selecting the second book as Math book is $\frac{4}{9}$

(*a*) Statement (I) ALONE is sufficient but statement (II) ALONE is not sufficient.

(*b*) Statement (II) ALONE is sufficient but statement (I) ALONE is not sufficient.

(*c*) BOTH statements TOGETHER are sufficient, but NEITHER statement ALONE is sufficient.

(*d*) EACH statement ALONE is sufficient.

(*e*) Statements (I) and (II) TOGETHER are not sufficient.

11. Sam is a newbie football player. Is his probability of hitting the goal with a single free kick lower than the probability of hitting at least two goals with three free kicks?

(I) Probability of hitting a goal in any kick < 0.7

(II) Probability of hitting a goal in any kick > 0.6

(*a*) Statement (I) ALONE is sufficient but statement (II) ALONE is not sufficient.

(*b*) Statement (II) ALONE is sufficient but statement (I) ALONE is not sufficient.

(*c*) BOTH statements TOGETHER are sufficient, but NEITHER statement ALONE is sufficient.

(*d*) EACH statement ALONE is sufficient.

(*e*) Statements (I) and (II) TOGETHER are not sufficient.

12. A box has Physics, Chemistry, and Math books. If a book is randomly selected from the box, what is the probability that it will be Physics or Chemistry book?

(I) The probability that it will a Physics book is $\frac{1}{5}$

(II) The probability that it will be Math book is $\frac{1}{3}$

(*a*) Statement (I) ALONE is sufficient but statement (II) ALONE is not sufficient.

(*b*) Statement (II) ALONE is sufficient but statement (I) ALONE is not sufficient.

(*c*) BOTH statements TOGETHER are sufficient, but NEITHER statement ALONE is sufficient.

(*d*) EACH statement ALONE is sufficient.

(*e*) Statements (I) and (II) TOGETHER are not sufficient.

13. A stationary shop has an inventory of 1,345 different products - all of which it categorizes as "business," "personal," or both. What is the number of products characterized as "personal" only?

(I) 740 products are categorized as "business" only

(II) 520 products are categorized as both

(*a*) Statement (I) ALONE is sufficient but statement (II) ALONE is not sufficient.

(*b*) Statement (II) ALONE is sufficient but statement (I) ALONE is not sufficient.

(*c*) BOTH statements TOGETHER are sufficient, but NEITHER statement ALONE is sufficient.

(*d*) EACH statement ALONE is sufficient.

(*e*) Statements (I) and (II) TOGETHER are not sufficient.

14. If one fruit is randomly selected from a certain box that has only apples and oranges, what is the probability that an apple will be selected?

(I) The total number of fruits that has the box is 20

(II) $\frac{2}{5}$ of all the fruits in the box are the oranges.

(*a*) Statement (I) ALONE is sufficient but statement (II) ALONE is not sufficient.

(*b*) Statement (II) ALONE is sufficient but statement (I) ALONE is not sufficient.

(*c*) BOTH statements TOGETHER are sufficient, but NEITHER statement ALONE is sufficient.

(*d*) EACH statement ALONE is sufficient.

(*e*) Statements (I) and (II) TOGETHER are not sufficient.

15. If the probability of a tossed coin to be tail is not $\frac{1}{2}$, what is the probability of two tossed coins to be both tails?

(I) The probability of two tossed coins to be one head and the other to be tail is $\frac{4}{9}$

(II) The probability of two tossed coins to be both heads is $\frac{1}{9}$

(*a*) Statement (I) ALONE is sufficient but statement (II) ALONE is not sufficient.

(*b*) Statement (II) ALONE is sufficient but statement (I) ALONE is not sufficient.

(*c*) BOTH statements TOGETHER are sufficient, but NEITHER statement ALONE is sufficient.

(*d*) EACH statement ALONE is sufficient.

(*e*) Statements (I) and (II) TOGETHER are not sufficient.

16. In a school X, 40 percent of all the students are females and 50 percent of all the students have Physical major. In school X, what percent of all students are female students who have Physics major?

(I) In school X, 50 percent of the female students have Physics major.

(II) In school X, 30 percent of all students are male students who have Physics major.

(*a*) Statement (I) ALONE is sufficient but statement (II) ALONE is not sufficient.

(*b*) Statement (II) ALONE is sufficient but statement (I) ALONE is not sufficient.

(*c*) BOTH statements TOGETHER are sufficient, but NEITHER statement ALONE is sufficient.

(*d*) EACH statement ALONE is sufficient.

(*e*) Statements (I) and (II) TOGETHER are not sufficient.

17. Set X has only four numbers. Is the average of set X less than 4?

(I) Set X has a mode of 7 and a median of 4

(II) The smallest number in Set X is 0

(*a*) Statement (I) ALONE is sufficient but statement (II) ALONE is not sufficient.

(*b*) Statement (II) ALONE is sufficient but statement (I) ALONE is not sufficient.

(*c*) BOTH statements TOGETHER are sufficient, but NEITHER statement ALONE is sufficient.

(*d*) EACH statement ALONE is sufficient.

(*e*) Statements (I) and (II) TOGETHER are not sufficient.

18. What is the average of x, y, and z?

(I) $x + 2y + 3c = 10$

(II) $3x + 2y + c = 14$

(*a*) Statement (I) ALONE is sufficient but statement (II) ALONE is not sufficient.

(*b*) Statement (II) ALONE is sufficient but statement (I) ALONE is not sufficient.

(*c*) BOTH statements TOGETHER are sufficient, but NEITHER statement ALONE is sufficient.

(*d*) EACH statement ALONE is sufficient.

(*e*) Statements (I) and (II) TOGETHER are not sufficient.

19. Is the range of the given integers 5, 7, x, 6, y, and 9 greater than 5?

(I) $x = 3y$

(II) $x < 2y$

(*a*) Statement (I) ALONE is sufficient but statement (II) ALONE is not sufficient.

(*b*) Statement (II) ALONE is sufficient but statement (I) ALONE is not sufficient.

(*c*) BOTH statements TOGETHER are sufficient, but NEITHER statement ALONE is sufficient.

(*d*) EACH statement ALONE is sufficient.

(*e*) Statements (I) and (II) TOGETHER are not sufficient.

20. What is the median number of hours worked by employees on a particular day at company X, if the number of hours worked is an integer?

(I) 15 percent of employees worked 7 or fewer hours.

(II) 25 percent of the employees sat the company worked 9 or more hours

(*a*) Statement (I) ALONE is sufficient but statement (II) ALONE is not sufficient.

(*b*) Statement (II) ALONE is sufficient but statement (I) ALONE is not sufficient.

(*c*) BOTH statements TOGETHER are sufficient, but NEITHER statement ALONE is sufficient.

(*d*) EACH statement ALONE is sufficient.

(*e*) Statements (I) and (II) TOGETHER are not sufficient.

21. Set X consists of 3 distinct numbers, Is the median of the set equal to the arithmetic mean of set X?

(I) Difference between any two numbers is the same.

(II) Sum of the greatest and smallest is equal to twice the median.

(*a*) Statement (I) ALONE is sufficient but statement (II) ALONE is not sufficient.

(*b*) Statement (II) ALONE is sufficient but statement (I) ALONE is not sufficient.

(*c*) BOTH statements TOGETHER are sufficient, but NEITHER statement ALONE is sufficient.

(*d*) EACH statement ALONE is sufficient.

(*e*) Statements (I) and (II) TOGETHER are not sufficient.

22. Is Jack's average score of his last three tests not greater than 82?

(I) Jack's average score before the last three tests was 86.

(II) Jack's average score after the last three tests was 83.

(*a*) Statement (I) ALONE is sufficient but statement (II) ALONE is not sufficient.

(*b*) Statement (II) ALONE is sufficient but statement (I) ALONE is not sufficient.

(*c*) BOTH statements TOGETHER are sufficient, but NEITHER statement ALONE is sufficient.

(*d*) EACH statement ALONE is sufficient.

(*e*) Statements (I) and (II) TOGETHER are not sufficient.

23. The average (arithmetic mean) of Set L is what percent of the sum of its numbers?

(I) Set L consists of 10 numbers.

(II) The sum of the numbers in Set L is 90.

(*a*) Statement (I) ALONE is sufficient but statement (II) ALONE is not sufficient.

(*b*) Statement (II) ALONE is sufficient but statement (I) ALONE is not sufficient.

(*c*) BOTH statements TOGETHER are sufficient, but NEITHER statement ALONE is sufficient.

(*d*) EACH statement ALONE is sufficient.

(*e*) Statements (I) and (II) TOGETHER are not sufficient.

24. What is the median number of players per team in the Asian Cricket League?

(I) Sixty percent of the teams in the Asian Cricket League have 25 or more players in their teams.

(II) Sixty percent of the teams in the Asian Cricket League have 25 or fewer players in their teams.

(*a*) Statement (I) ALONE is sufficient but statement (II) ALONE is not sufficient.

(*b*) Statement (II) ALONE is sufficient but statement (I) ALONE is not sufficient.

(*c*) BOTH statements TOGETHER are sufficient, but NEITHER statement ALONE is sufficient.

(*d*) EACH statement ALONE is sufficient.

(*e*) Statements (I) and (II) TOGETHER are not sufficient.

25. Does set P have all of its terms smaller than 20?

(I) The smallest term in the set is 5.

(II) The range of set X is 15.

(*a*) Statement (I) ALONE is sufficient but statement (II) ALONE is not sufficient.

(*b*) Statement (II) ALONE is sufficient but statement (I) ALONE is not sufficient.

(*c*) BOTH statements TOGETHER are sufficient, but NEITHER statement ALONE is sufficient.

(*d*) EACH statement ALONE is sufficient.

(*e*) Statements (I) and (II) TOGETHER are not sufficient.

26. Is the median of set M greater than its arithmetic mean?

(I) The set consists of consecutive multiples of 5.

(II) Sum of the elements of the set is 30.

(a) Statement (I) ALONE is sufficient but statement (II) ALONE is not sufficient.

(b) Statement (II) ALONE is sufficient but statement (I) ALONE is not sufficient.

(c) BOTH statements TOGETHER are sufficient, but NEITHER statement ALONE is sufficient.

(d) EACH statement ALONE is sufficient.

(e) Statements (I) and (II) TOGETHER are not sufficient.

27. If p, q, r, s, t, u, and v are seven consecutive odd integers, what is the average (arithmetic mean) of the seven integers?

(I) $p + t = 38$

(II) $r + v = 46$

(a) Statement (I) ALONE is sufficient but statement (II) ALONE is not sufficient.

(b) Statement (II) ALONE is sufficient but statement (I) ALONE is not sufficient.

(c) BOTH statements TOGETHER are sufficient, but NEITHER statement ALONE is sufficient.

(d) EACH statement ALONE is sufficient.

(e) Statements (I) and (II) TOGETHER are not sufficient.

28. The average daily salary of a factory staff consisting of only engineers and supervisors is \$50. If each engineer and each supervisor receive their respective equal salaries, does the staff have a greater number of engineers than supervisors?

(I) The average daily salary of 40% of the engineers and 60% of the supervisors is \$45.

(II) The average daily salary of 60% of the engineers and 40% of the supervisors is \$55.

(a) Statement (I) ALONE is sufficient but statement (II) ALONE is not sufficient.

(b) Statement (II) ALONE is sufficient but statement (I) ALONE is not sufficient.

(c) BOTH statements TOGETHER are sufficient, but NEITHER statement ALONE is sufficient.

(d) EACH statement ALONE is sufficient.

(e) Statements (I) and (II) TOGETHER are not sufficient.

29. If a, b, c and d are distinct positive numbers, can be the average of the four numbers?

(I) The sum of c and d is 3b.

(II) The sum of a, b and c is 3b.

(a) Statement (I) ALONE is sufficient but statement (II) ALONE is not sufficient.

(b) Statement (II) ALONE is sufficient but statement (I) ALONE is not sufficient.

(c) BOTH statements TOGETHER are sufficient, but NEITHER statement ALONE is sufficient.

(d) EACH statement ALONE is sufficient.

(e) Statements (I) and (II) TOGETHER are not sufficient.

30. Does the group have at least 9 people?

(I) The average are of the group is less than 22 years.

(II) If 3 people with an average age of 44 years leave the group, the average age of the group decreases by half of its initial average.

(a) Statement (I) ALONE is sufficient but statement (II) ALONE is not sufficient.

(b) Statement (II) ALONE is sufficient but statement (I) ALONE is not sufficient.

(c) BOTH statements TOGETHER are sufficient, but NEITHER statement ALONE is sufficient.

(d) EACH statement ALONE is sufficient.

(e) Statements (I) and (II) TOGETHER are not sufficient.

31. What was the temperature on Friday?

(I) The average temperature for the consecutive four days, starting Monday was 40°C.

(II) The average temperature for the consecutive four days, starting Tuesday was 35°C.

(a) Statement (I) ALONE is sufficient but statement (II) ALONE is not sufficient.

(b) Statement (II) ALONE is sufficient but statement (I) ALONE is not sufficient.

(c) BOTH statements TOGETHER are sufficient, but NEITHER statement ALONE is sufficient.

(d) EACH statement ALONE is sufficient.

(e) Statements (I) and (II) TOGETHER are not sufficient.

32. Two varieties of tea, a pounds of one, priced at \$x per pounds and b pounds of the other, priced at \$(3x) per pounds are mixed. Is the average price of the mixture greater than $\$\left(\frac{3}{2}x\right)$ pounds?

(I) $a > 2b$

(II) $a = 3b$

(a) Statement (I) ALONE is sufficient but statement (II) ALONE is not sufficient.

(b) Statement (II) ALONE is sufficient but statement (I) ALONE is not sufficient.

(c) BOTH statements TOGETHER are sufficient, but NEITHER statement ALONE is sufficient.

(d) EACH statement ALONE is sufficient.

(e) Statements (I) and (II) TOGETHER are not sufficient.

33. A box contains only red and black balls. If two balls are randomly drawn from the box, what is the probability that both balls are black?

(I) The ratio of block to red balls is 2 : 3.

(II) There are 10 more red balls in the box that black balls.

(a) Statement (I) ALONE is sufficient but statement (II) ALONE is not sufficient.

(b) Statement (II) ALONE is sufficient but statement (I) ALONE is not sufficient.

(c) BOTH statements TOGETHER are sufficient, but NEITHER statement ALONE is sufficient.

(d) EACH statement ALONE is sufficient.

(e) Statements (I) and (II) TOGETHER are not sufficient.

34. The terms of a set are multiples of 3. Is the standard deviation of the set 0?

(I) Each term of the set is positive.

(II) All the terms of the set are equal.

(a) Statement (I) ALONE is sufficient but statement (II) ALONE is not sufficient.

(b) Statement (II) ALONE is sufficient but statement (I) ALONE is not sufficient.

(c) BOTH statements TOGETHER are sufficient, but NEITHER statement ALONE is sufficient.

(d) EACH statement ALONE is sufficient.

(e) Statements (I) and (II) TOGETHER are not sufficient.

35. Are the elements of Set smaller than 10?

(I) The smallest element in Set Q is 1.

(II) The range of Set is 10.

(a) Statement (I) ALONE is sufficient but statement (II) ALONE is not sufficient.

(b) Statement (II) ALONE is sufficient but statement (I) ALONE is not sufficient.

(*c*) BOTH statements TOGETHER are sufficient, but NEITHER statement ALONE is sufficient.

(*d*) EACH statement ALONE is sufficient.

(*e*) Statements (I) and (II) TOGETHER are not sufficient.

36. What is the arithmetic mean of Set Q ?

(I) Set Q is comprised of consecutive even integers.

(II) The range of Set Q is 10.

(*a*) Statement (I) ALONE is sufficient but statement (II) ALONE is not sufficient.

(*b*) Statement (II) ALONE is sufficient but statement (I) ALONE is not sufficient.

(*c*) BOTH statements TOGETHER are sufficient, but NEITHER statement ALONE is sufficient.

(*d*) EACH statement ALONE is sufficient.

(*e*) Statements (I) and (II) TOGETHER are not sufficient.

37. Each of the 40 students in class A is shorter than each of the 40 students in class B. Is the median height of the 80 students less than 160 centimeters?

(I) The shortest student in class A is 150 centimeters in height.

(II) The shortest student in class B is 160 centimeters in height.

(*a*) Statement (I) ALONE is sufficient but statement (II) ALONE is not sufficient.

(*b*) Statement (II) ALONE is sufficient but statement (I) ALONE is not sufficient.

(*c*) BOTH statements TOGETHER are sufficient, but NEITHER statement ALONE is sufficient.

(*d*) EACH statement ALONE is sufficient.

(*e*) Statements (I) and (II) TOGETHER are not sufficient.

38. An auditorium has 40 rows with 20 seats in each row. How many of the seats were occupied for a certain show?

(I) For the front 18 rows, on average (arithmetic mean), there were 5 unoccupied seats per row.

(II) For the back 22 rows, on average (arithmetic mean), there were 15 unoccupied seats per row.

(*a*) Statement (I) ALONE is sufficient but statement (II) ALONE is not sufficient.

(*b*) Statement (II) ALONE is sufficient but statement (I) ALONE is not sufficient.

(*c*) BOTH statements TOGETHER are sufficient, but NEITHER statement ALONE is sufficient.

(*d*) EACH statement ALONE is sufficient.

(*e*) Statements (I) and (II) TOGETHER are not sufficient.

39. Was the average (arithmetic mean) weight of the shipments sent to a certain destination greater than 500 grams?

(I) The total weight of the shipments sent to the destination was greater than 20,000 grams.

(II) Fewer than 40 shipments were shipped to the destination.

(*a*) Statement (I) ALONE is sufficient but statement (II) ALONE is not sufficient.

(*b*) Statement (II) ALONE is sufficient but statement (I) ALONE is not sufficient.

(*c*) BOTH statements TOGETHER are sufficient, but NEITHER statement ALONE is sufficient.

(*d*) EACH statement ALONE is sufficient.

(*e*) Statements (I) and (II) TOGETHER are not sufficient.

Answer Key

1. (d)	11. (b)	21. (d)	31. (e)
2. (c)	12. (b)	22. (c)	32. (b)
3. (d)	13. (c)	23. (a)	33. (c)
4. (b)	14. (b)	24. (c)	34. (b)
5. (b)	15. (b)	25. (c)	35. (c)
6. (a)	16. (d)	26. (a)	36. (e)
7. (e)	17. (a)	27. (d)	37. (b)
8. (c)	18. (c)	28. (c)	38. (c)
9. (b)	19. (a)	29. (a)	39. (c)
10. (d)	20. (c)	30. (c)	

Answer Explanations

1. (d) **Considering statement (I) alone :**

Committee of 5 employees can be formed from (x + 2) employees in ${}^{(x+2)}C_5$

Hence, ${}^{(x+2)}C_5 = 126$.

On simplification this would give

$$\frac{(x+2)!}{5!\times(x-3)!}=126$$

$$\frac{(x+2)(x+1)\times(x-1)(x-2)}{5!}=126$$

$(x + 2)(x + 1) \times (x- 1)(x -2) = 5! \times 126$

Product of 5 consecutive numbers is $5! \times 126$

Now, here only one such of x is possible. We don't need to calculate (x = 7)

Sufficient Eliminate B/C/E.

Considering statement 2 alone :

Committee of 3 employees can be formed from (x + 1) employees in ${}^{(x+1)}C_3$

Hence, ${}^{(x+1)}C_3 = 56$.

Om simplification this would give

$$\frac{(x+1)!}{3!-(x-2)!}=56$$

$$\frac{(x+1)\times(x-1)}{3!}=56$$

Product of 3 consecutive numbers is $3! \times 56$

Now, here only one such of x is possible. We don't need to calculate (x = 7) Sufficient

The correct answer is option (d)

2. (c) Since ${}^nC_r = {}^nC_{(n-r)}$,

for example ${}^6C_2 = {}^6C_4$

Here n = 20 and we need to determine value of k

Considering statement 1 alone :

Value of ${}^{20}C_{(k+1)} = 1140$

From this information we will get two values of k + 1

k + 1 could be 3 or 17, hence k could be 2 or 16

Insufficient Eliminate A/D.

Considering statement 2 alone :

Value of ${}^{20}C_{(k-1)} = 20$

From the information we will get two values of k

k – 1 could be 1 or 19, hence k could be 2 or 20

Insufficient. Eliminate B.

Considering statement (I) and (II) together :

Only one value of k = 2 satisfies both the statements.

Sufficient

The correct answer is option (c)

3. (d) If Roger pitches, let H_R be the probability of a home run, S_R be the probability of a single, and K_R be the probability of a strikeout (all batters face these same probabilities, since the problem states that these probabilities are completely determined by the pitcher).

In Greg pitches, let H_G be the probability of a home run, S_G be the probability of a single, and K_G be the probability of a strikeout.

The following are the only three event sequences in which no points will score before a strikeout occurs:

1. The current batter strikes out. (K)
2. The current batter hits a single, and the next batter strikes out. (SK)

3. The current batter hits a single, the next batter hits a single, and the following batter strikes out. (SSK)

(Note that if three consecutive batters it singles, or if any batter hits a home run, then the batting team will score at least one point.)

If Roger pitches, the probability of any one of the three sequences mentioned above occurring is:

$$R = K_R + S_R K_R + S_R S_R K_R$$

I Greg pitches, the probability of any one of the three sequences occurring is:

$$G = K_G + S_G K_G + S_G S_G K_G$$

We need to be able to determine whether R or G is greater in order to solve the problem.

Statement (I) gives us the following :

$S_G = 2S_R$ and $K_G = 4K_R$ (Note: We also know that S_G, S_R, K_G, and K_R cannot be equal to 0).

We can substitute these equations in the probability expressions for G:

$$R = K_R + S_R K_R + S_R S_R K_R$$

$$G = K_G + S_G K_G + S_G S_G K_G$$

$$= 4K_R + (2S_R)(4K_R) + (2S_R)(2S_R)(4K_R)$$

$$= 4K_R + 8S_R K_R + 16S_R S_R K_R.$$

Since all of the unknowns are positive values, we can see from these equations that G will always be greater than R. This means that Greg is more likely than Roger to record a strikeout before allowing be point (which, in turn, means that Rorger is more likely than Greg to allow a point before recording a strikeout.) Therefore statement (I) is sufficient to solve the problem.

Statement (II) gives us the following :

$S_G = 2S_R$ and $H_G = \dfrac{H_R}{4}$ (Note: We also know that S_G, S_R, H_G, and H_R cannot be equal to 0).

Note that the probabilities G and R are expressed in terms of that S_G, S_R, K_G, and K_R. Whereas statement (I) tells us that and $S_G > S_R$ and $K_G > K_R$ (and therefore that $G > R$, solving the problem), statement (II) lacks information about the size of K_G relative to K_R. (Information about the size of H_G relative to H_R does not help us at all since neither of these variables are part of the probability expressions for G and R.)

As such, the information in statement (II) is insufficient, but statement (II) alone is not sufficient.

The correct answer is option (d).

4. (b) The question require us to determine whether Mike's odds of winning are better if he attempts 3 shots instead of 1. For that to be true, his odds of making 2 out of 3 must be better than his odds of making 1 out of 1.

There are two ways for Mike to at least 2 shots: Either he hits 2 and misses 1, or he hits all 3 :

Odds of hitting 2 and missing 1 $p \times p \times (1 - p)$	# of ways to hit 2 and miss 1 3(HHM, HMH, MHH)	**Total Probability** $3p^2(1 - p)$
Odds of hitting all 3 $p \times p \times p$	**# of ways to hit all 3** 1 (HHH)	p^3
Mike's probability of hitting at least 2 out of 3 free throws =		$3p^2(1\ p) + p^3$

Now, we can rephrase the question as the following inequality :

Is $3p^2(1 - p) + p^3 < p$? (Are Mike's odds of hitting at least 2 of 3 greater than his odds of hitting 1 of 1?)

This can be simplified as follows :

$3p^2(1-p)+p^3>p$

$3p^2-3p^3+p^3<p$

$3p^2-2p^3>p$(we can divide by p since p > 0)

$3p-2p^2>1$

$-2p^2+3p-1<0$

(divide by –2, flipping the inequality)

p3 – 1.5p + .5 < 0

(p – 5) (p – 1) < 0

In order for this inequality to be true, p must be greater than. 5 but less than 1 (since this is the only way to ensure that the left side of the equation is negative). But we already know what p is less than 1 (since Mike occasionally misses some shots). Therefore, we need to know whether p is greater than .5. If it is, then the inequality will be true, which means that Mike will have a better chance of winning if he takes 3 shots.

Statement (I) tells us that p < .7. This does not help us to determine whether p > .5, so statement (I) is not sufficient.

Statement (2) tells us that p > .6. This means that p must be greater than .5. This is sufficient to answer the question.

The correct answer is (b).

5. (b) If he wants the same number on both the dice, then he can get any number on the first dice and the same number on the second dice.

Probability of getting any number of the first dice = $\frac{6}{6}$

Probability of getting the same number on the second dice $\frac{1}{6}$

Hence, the total probability

$$=\left(\frac{6}{6}\right)\times\left(\frac{1}{6}\right)=\frac{1}{6}$$

The answer is (b).

6. (a) **Considering statement (I) alone :**

As it is a regular dice, the chances of getting 5 on any roll of a dice is $\frac{1}{6}$

SUFFICIENT

Eliminate BCE

Considering statement (II) alone :

We don't known if the dice was fair.

INSUFFICIENT

The answer is (a)

7. (e) For the probability of getting a red marble be the same as probability of getting a green marble, the number of red marbles

Considering statement (I) alone :

No information about the number of marbles of each color.

INSUFFICIENT

Eliminate AD

Considering statement (II) alone :

Blue marbles > Green marbles

No information about the relation between number of red marbles and number of green marbles.

INSUFFICIENT

Eliminate B

Considering both the statements together:

No information about the relation between number of red marbles and number of green marbles.

INSUFFICIENT

The answer is (e)

8. (c) Probability (A or B) = P(A) + P(B) – (A and B)

Considering statement (I) alone:

No information about P(B)

INSUFFICIENT

Eliminate AD

Considering statement (II) alone:

No information about P(A)

INSUFFICIENT

Eliminate B

Considering both the statements together:

Probability (A or B) = P(A) + P(B) – (A & B)

$= 0.3 + 0.7 - (0.3 \times 0.7)$

$= 1 - 0.21 = 0.79$

INSUFFICIENT

The answer is (c)

9. (b) **Considering statement (I) alone:**

No information about number of math books.

INSUFFICIENT

Eliminate AD

Considering statement (II) alone:

Let the number of Physics and Chemistry books be x

⇒ The number of Math books is 3x

⇒ Hence, the total number of books is $x + 3x = 4x$

Probability (Math book) $= \frac{3x}{4x} = \frac{3}{4}$

SUFFICIENT

The answer is (b)

10. (d) **Considering statement (I):**

Let the total number of books be x

P(math book) = Number of math books/ Total number of books

P(math boo) $= \frac{5}{x}$

Given that $\frac{5}{x} = \frac{1}{2}$

$\Rightarrow \quad x = 10$

Hence, Probability (Math and Math)

$= \left(\frac{5}{10}\right) \times \left(\frac{4}{9}\right) = \frac{2}{9}$

SUFFICIENT

Eliminate BCE

Considering statement (II) alone:

After a math book is selected, there are 4 more math books

P(Second book as a Math book)

$= \left(\frac{4}{(x-1)}\right) = \frac{4}{9} \Rightarrow \frac{1}{(x-1)} = \frac{1}{9} \Rightarrow x = 10$

SUFFICIENT

The answer is (d).

11. (b) If the probability of hitting a goal in one free kick is p, then

Probability of hitting at least two goals in three free kicks is $3C2 \times (p)(p)\,(! - p) + p^3$

$3(p^2)\,(1 - p) + p^3 = p^2(3 - 2p)$

Question: Is $p^2(3 - 2p) > p$?

Is $p(3 - 2p) > 1$?

Is $3p\ 2p^2 - 1 > 0$?

Is $2p^2 - 3p + 1 < 0$?

Is $\left(\frac{p-1}{2}\right)(p-1) < 0$?

Is $p > \frac{1}{2}$ or $p < 1$?

Is $\frac{1}{2} < p < 1$?

Considering statement (I) alone :

$p < 0.7$

If $p = 0.6$, then we get Yes

If $p = 0.4$, then we get No

INSUFFICIENT

Considering statement (II) alone :

If $p > 0.6$, then $p > 0.5$

SUFFICIENT

The answer is (b).

12. (b) Probability (Physics of Chemistry)

= 1 – Probability (Math)

Considering statement (I) alone :

Probability (Physics) $= \frac{1}{5}$

No information about Math or Chemistry

INSUFFICIENT

Eliminate AD

Considering statement (II) alone :

Probability (Math) $= \frac{1}{3}$

⇒ Probability (Physics or Chemistry = 1 – Probability (Math)

⇒ Probability (Physics or Chemistry $= 1 - \frac{1}{3}$

⇒ Probability (Physics or Chemistry $= \frac{2}{3}$

SUFFICIENT

The answer is (b)

13. (c) Business only + personal only + both = Total

Considering statement (I) alone :

Business only = 740

Still have two more variables.

INSUFFICIENT

Eliminate AD

Considering statement (II) alone :

Both = 520

Still have two more variables.

INSUFFICIENT

Eliminate B

Considering both the statement together :

740 + personal only + 520 = 1345

Personal only = 85

SUFFICIENT

The answer is (c).

14. (b) In the original condition, there are 2 variables (apples' number and oranges' number) and i n order to match the number of variables to the number of equations, there must be 2 equations. Since there is 1 for con 1 and 1 for con 2, C is most likely to be the answer. By solving and con 2 together, there are 20 fruits i n the box, but since $\frac{2}{5}$ are oranges, $20\left(\frac{2}{5}\right) = 8$ are oranges and $20 - 8 = 12$ are apples. Then, the probability that an apple will be randomly selected becomes $\frac{^{12}C_1}{^{20}C_1} = \frac{12}{20} = \frac{3}{5}$, hence it is unique and sufficient.

The answer is (c).

15. (b) If you modify the original condition and the question, when assuming T

(probability of getting a tail) and H (probability of getting a head), you get T + H = 1, and T^2 = ? Then, there are 2 variables (T, H) and 1 equation (T + H = 1), and in order to match the number of variables to the number of equations, there must be 1 more equation. Since there is 1 for con 1 and 1 for con 2, (d) is most likely to be the answer.

For con 1, from TH + HT = $\frac{4}{9}$, if you substitute H = 1 – T, you get T(1 – T) + (1 – T) T = $\frac{4}{9}$, $T - T^2 + T - T^2 = \frac{4}{9}$, $2T - 2T^2 = \frac{4}{9}$, and if you divide both sides by 2, from $T - T^2 = \frac{2}{9}$, $9T^2 - 9T + 2 = 0$, you get (3T – 1) (3T – 2) = 0, T = $\frac{1}{3}, \frac{2}{3}$, hence it is not unique and not sufficient.

For con 2, from $H^2 = \frac{1}{9} = \left(\frac{1}{3}\right)^2$, $H = \frac{1}{3}$, H + T = 1, you get $\frac{1}{3} + T = 1$, in other words, $T = \frac{2}{3}$, hence it is unique and sufficient.

Therefore, the answer is (b).

16. (d) If you modify the original condition and the question, this is a "2 by 2" question that appears most frequently on current GMAT, as shown in the table below.

100%	Physics major (50%)	Not Physics major (50%)
Females (40%)	x%	(40 – x)%
Males (60%)	(50 – x)%	(x + 10)%

As shown above, there is 1 variable (x) and in order to match the number of variables to the number of equations, there must be 1 equation. Since there is 1 for con 1 and 1 for con 2, D is most likely to be the answer.

For con 1, from 40% (50% = 20% = x%, you get x = 20, hence it is unique and sufficient.

For con 2, from (50 – x)% = 30%, you get 50 – x = 3, x = 20, hence it is unique and sufficient.

The answer is also (d).

17. (a) **Considering statement (I) alone:**

Mode is the most repeated number in the set. Hence, there must be at lest 2 numbers equal to 7 in the list.

Also, the median would be the average of the two middle numbers.

As the median is smaller than the mode, the two 7s must be the last two numbers.

So, the list would be x, y, 7, 7.

For the median of the set to be 4, y must be 1.

To make the highest possible average, x must be as high as possible. The highest possible value of x must be 0.

Hence, the maximum possible average of the set is $\frac{(0+1+7+7)}{4} = 3.75$

SUFFICIENT

Eliminate BCE

Considering statement (II) alone :

No information about the other three numbers in the set.

INSUFFICIENT

The answer is (a).

18. (c) Considering statement (I) alone :

No way to find the value of $x + y + z$

INSUFFICIENT

Eliminate AD

Considering statement (II) alone :

Now way to find the value of $x + y + z$

INSUFFICIENT

Eliminate B

Considering the both the statements together:

Adding the two equations, $4x + 4y + 4z = 24$

$\Rightarrow \quad x + y + z = 6$

SUFFICIENT

The answer is (c).

19. (a) The range is the difference between the greatest and the smallest reading.

It is given that, the smallest known integer is 5, and the greatest known integer is 9. x and y are two unknown integers. The question "Is the Range greater than 5?"

Considering statement (I) alone :

From Statement (I) alone, we have $x = 3y$.

Condition 1 : If y is less than 5, lets say $y = 4$, then $x = 12$, range is greater than 6.

Condition 2 : If y is equal to 5, then $x = 15$, range is greater than 5.

Condition 3 : If y is greater than 5, lets say $y = 6$, then $x = 18$, range is greater than 5.

That means with any value of y, range of the integers is greater than 5.

Sufficient

Eliminate A/D.

Considering statement (II) alone :

From Statement (II) alone, we have that $x < 2y$

Condition 1 : If y is less than 5, lets say $y = 4$, then $x < 8$, let $x = 7$, range is not greater than 5.

Condition 2 : If y is equal to 5, then $x < 10$, let $x = 9$, range is not greater than 5.

Condition 3 : If y is greater than 5, lets say $y = 6$, then $x < 12$, let $x = 11$, range is greater than 5.

Insufficient

The answer is (a).

20. (c) Considering statement (I) alone :

We only know that 15 percent of employees worked 7 or fewer hours there is information about the rest 85 percent of the employees. Hence, the median cannot be determined. Insufficient.

Eliminate A/D.

Considering statement (I) alone :

We only know that 25 percent of employees worked 9 or more hours but there is information about rest 75 percent of the employees.

Hence, median cannot be determined, Insufficient.

Eliminate B.

Considering statement (I) & (II) together :

It is known that 15 percent of employees worked 7 of fewer hours and 25 percent of the employees at the company worked 9 or more hours, which means rest 60 percent (100% – 15% – 25%) of the employees must have worked for exactly 8 hours.

As median is the middle term when data is arranged in the ascending or descending order, hence median of the data is 8 hours.

Sufficient

The correct answer is option (c).

21. **(d)** Let three distinct numbers be a, b, and c such that $a < b < c$

Considering statement (I) alone:

If the difference between any two numbers is the same, means that the numbers are in arithmetic progression.

In an AP, median is equal to the average (arithmetic mean)

Sufficient

Eliminate B/C/E

Considering statement (II) alone:

Sum of the greatest and smallest is equal to twice the median

$c + a = 2b$

so, sum of the three numbers

$$= a + b + c = 3b$$

average of the numbers

$$= \frac{3b}{3} = b = \text{median}$$

Sufficient

The correct answer is option (d).

22. **(c)** Let the number of tests taken by Jack before the last three tests = x.

Considering statement (I) alone:

We have no information about the average score after taking the last three tests.

Insufficient Hence, eliminate A/D

Considering statement (II) alone:

We have no information about the average score before taking the last three tests.-

Insufficient

Hence, eliminate B.

Considering statement (I) and (II) together:

Total marks obtained by Jack before taking the last three tests = 86x.

Total marks obtained by Jack after taking the last three tests = 83 (x + 3)

Thus, the total marks scored by Jack in the last three tests

$$= 83(x + 3) - 86x = 249 - 3x$$

Since x (The number of tests taken) is a positive integer, we have $x \geq 1$, or $3x \geq 3$

$\Rightarrow \quad 249 - 3x \leq 246$

Thus, Jack scored at most 246 marks in his last 3 tests.

Thus, Jack's average score in his last 3 tests is at the most $\frac{246}{3} = 82.$

The answer is yes – Sufficient

The correct answer is option (c).

23. **(a)** Let the number of terms in Set L = n

Let the sum of the n numbers = S

Thus, average of the n numbers = $\frac{5}{n}$

Thus, the required percent value

$$\frac{\frac{5}{n}}{S} \times 100\% = \frac{100}{n}\%$$

Considering statement (I) alone:

$$n = 10$$

Thus, the required percent value

$$\frac{100}{10}\% = 10\% - \text{Sufficient}$$

Hence, eliminate B/C/E.

Considering statement (II) alone:

The count of numbers in Set L is not known. The value of the sum is redundant.

Insufficient

Hence, eliminate (d).

24. (c) **Considering Statement (I) alone:**

When the number of players in each team is arranged in ascending order, the median number of players per team for the Asian Cricket League would be the average of the number of players in the team that is ranked 50% and the average of the number of players in the team that is ranked 51%.

Since we do not known the number of players in the teams ranked 50% and 51%, the statement is insufficient.

Hence, eliminate A/D.

Considering statement (II) alone :

With the same reasoning as above, this statement is also insufficient.

Hence, eliminate B.

Considering statement (I) and (II) together :

Followed both the statements, we can deduce that in the band of 40%-60%, where the teams ranked 50% & 51% lie, the average of the number of players per team would be EXACTLY 25, as shown in the image below.

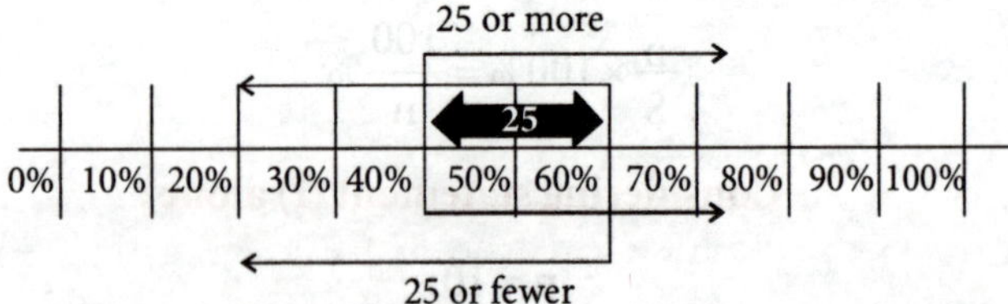

Thus, together, both the statements are sufficient and the median is 25 number of players.

The correct answer is option (c).

25. (c) **Considering statement (I) alone:**

We do not know anything about the remaining terms, so this statement alone is not sufficient.

Hence, eliminate A/D.

Considering statement (II) alone :

Range is 15.

Range = Max. value – Min. value

We do not know anything about the terms of the set, so this statement alone is not sufficient.

Hence, eliminate B.

Considering statements (I) and (II) together :

Smallest element = 5; Range = 15

Range = Max. value – Min. value

$\Rightarrow$ 5 = Largest term –5

$\Rightarrow$ Largest term = 20

Largest term = 20. The answer is no; a unique answer. Hence, statements (I) & (II) together are sufficient.

There is at least one term that is 20. Note that there may be more than one term that is exactly 20.

The correct answer is option (c).

26. (a) **Considering Statement (I) alone :**

It states that the set consists of consecutive multiples of 5.

Note that for any evenly spaced set, Arithmetic mean = Median

For example, for set: {5, 10, 15}: Mean = Median = 10; and

For set: {5, 10, 15, 20};

$$\text{Mean} = \text{Median} = \frac{10+15}{2} = 12.5$$

The answer is no, the median of set M is not greater than its arithmetic mean, a unique answer!

Therefore, statement (I) alone is sufficient.

Hence, eliminate B/C/E.

Considering statement (II) alone :

It states that the sum of the elements in the set is 30, but we don't have any information about the elements of the set. We cannot calculate either mean or median.

Therefore, statement (II) alone is insufficient.

Hence, eliminate D.

The correct answer is option (a).

27. **(d)** Since the numbers are consecutive and there are an odd number of integers, 7, the middlemost integer, s, would be the average (arithmetic mean) of the 7 integers. We have to find the value of s.

Thus, $q = p + 2; r = p + 4; s = p + 6; t = p + 8; u = p + 10; \& v = p + 12$

Considering statement (I) alone :

$p + t = 38$

$\Rightarrow \quad p + p + 8 = 38$

$\Rightarrow \quad 2p = 30$

$\Rightarrow \quad p = 15$

$\Rightarrow \quad s = p + 6 = 15 + 6 = 21$, average. Sufficient.

Hence, eliminate B/C/E.

Considering statement (II) alone :

$r + v = 46$

$\Rightarrow \quad p + 4 + p + 12 = 46$

$\Rightarrow \quad 2p + 16 = 46$

$\Rightarrow \quad p = 30 \Rightarrow p = 15$

$\Rightarrow \quad s = p + 6 = 15 + 6 = 21$, average. Sufficient.

Hence, eliminate A.

The correct answer is option (d).

28. **(c)** **Considering statement (I) alone:**

The average salary of an engineer and the average salary of a supervisor are not known.

We only know that the average salary of all engineers and supervisors is \$50 and that of 40% of the engineers and 60% of the supervisors is \$45.

Thus, we can only conclude that since the proportional share of engineers is reduced (40% against 60%) as compared to supervisors and as a result, the average salary gets reduced (\$45 against \$50), engineers' average salary must be greater than supervisors' average salary.

However, we cannot comment on the number of engineers and the number of supervisors. - Insufficient

Hence, eliminate A/D.

Considering statement (II) alone :

Statement 2 is like statement 1, following the same reasoning. - Insufficient

Hence, eliminate B.

Considering statements (I) and (II) together :

We see that...

For 100% engineers and 100% supervisors, the average salary is \$50.

For 40% engineers and 60% supervisors, the average salary is \$45, i.e., there is a decrease of \$5.

For 60% engineers and 40% supervisors, the average salary is \$55, i.e., there is an increase of \$5.

Thus, we see that when the percentage values of engineers and supervisors are interchanged, the increase and the decrease in the averages are of the same value.

Thus, the effect on the average is the same, only of different signs, implying that the number of engineers and the number of supervisors must be the same, with engineers having a higher salary than the supervisors.

The answer is no. – Sufficient

The correct answer is option (c).

29. (a) We need to determine whether b is the average of the four distinct (unequal) numbers a, b, c and d.

Say b is the average, then

$$\Rightarrow b = \frac{a+b+c+d}{4}$$

$$\Rightarrow \quad 3b = a + c + d \quad \text{...(i)}$$

Let's see each statement one by one.

Considering statement (I) alone :

The sum of c and d is 3b.

$\Rightarrow \quad c + d = 3b$

Thus, equation (i) would be valid only if $a = 0$.

However, it is not possible since a is a positive number.

Thus, was get specific answer that b cannot be the average of the four numbers a, b, c and d. The answer is No - Sufficient.

Hence, eliminate B/C/E.

Considering Statement (II) alone :

The sum of a, b, and c is 3b.

$\Rightarrow \quad a + b + c = 3b$

$\Rightarrow \quad a + = 2b$

Thus, equation (i) would be valid only if $d = b$.

However, it is not possible since the four numbers a, b, c and d are distinct.

Thus, again we get a specific answer than b cannot be the average of the four numbers a, b, c and d.

The answer is No. – Sufficient.

Hence, eliminate C/E.

The correct answer is option (a).

30. (c) Let the number of people in the group be n.

Let the average age of the members of the group be a.

Thus, the sum of the ages of the members in the group = na years.

We have to ascertain whether $n \geq 9$.

Let's see each statement one by one.

Considering statement (I) alone :

We only know that

Thus, nothing can be inferred about the number of people in the group. – Insufficient

Hence, eliminate A/D.

Considering Statement (II) alone :

If 3 people with an average age of 44 years leave the group, the number of members in the group decreases to $(n - 3)$ and the total age decrease to $(na - 3 \times 44) = (na - 132)$ years.

Thus, the new average age of the members in the group

$$= \left(\frac{na - 132}{n - 3}\right) \text{ years}$$

Since the average age becomes half the initial value, we have

$$\frac{na - 132}{n - 3} = \frac{a}{2}$$

$$\Rightarrow \quad 2na - 264 = na - 3a$$

$$\Rightarrow \quad a(n + 3) = 264 \quad \text{...(ii)}$$

Since the value of a is not known, the number of people originally in the group maybe 9, less than 9 or greater than 9. – Insufficient

Hence, eliminate B.

Statements (I) and (II) together :

From (i): $a < 22$

Substituting the above in (ii):

$$n+3 > \frac{264}{22} \Rightarrow n+3 > 11$$

$$\Rightarrow n > 8 \Rightarrow m \geq 9$$

Thus, the answer to the question is Yes. - Sufficient

The correct answer is option (c).

31. (e) We have to find out the temperature on Friday.

Considering Statement (I) alone:

Let the temperatures on Monday, Tuesday, Wednesday, Thursday, and Friday be denoted by m, t, w, r and f, respectively.

Since the average temperature of consecutive four days, starting Monday was 40°C, we have $\frac{m+t+w+r}{4} = 40$

$$\Rightarrow \quad m+t+w+r = 160 \qquad ...(i)$$

Since there is no information about f, its value cannot be determined. – Insufficient

Hence, eliminate A/D.

Considering Statement (II) alone :

Since the average of consecutive four days, starting Tuesday was 35°, we have

$$\frac{t+w+r+f}{4} = 35$$

$$\Rightarrow \quad t+w+r+f = 140 \qquad ...(ii)$$

The value of f cannot be determined from (ii) alone. – Insufficient

Hence, eliminate B.

Considering statement (I) and (II) together :

Subtracting (ii) from (i) :

$$m - f = 20 \qquad ...(iii)$$

The value of f cannot be determined the above equation. – Insufficient

The correct answer is (e).

32. (b) The average price of the mixture formed by mixing the two varieties of tea, a pounds of one, priced at \$x per pounds and b pounds of the other, priced at \$(3x) per pounds is

$$= \$\left(\frac{ax+3bx}{a+b}\right) = \$x\left(\frac{a+3b}{a+b}\right) \quad ...(i)$$

Considering Statement (I) alone :

We have $a > 2b$

We have to ensure whether

$$x\left(\frac{a+3b}{a+b}\right) > \frac{3}{2}x$$

$$\Rightarrow \left(\frac{a+3b}{a+b}\right) > \frac{3}{2}$$

(Cancelling x from both sides)

$$\Rightarrow \quad 2a + 6b = 3a + 3b$$

$$\Rightarrow \quad 3b > a$$

Case 1 : For a = 3 & b = 1, a > 2b, but 3b = a, So, answer is No.

Case 2 : For a = 5 & b = 2, a > 2b, and 3b > a, answer is Yes.

Thus, the answer cannot be uniquely determined. - Insufficient

Hence, eliminate A/D

Considering Statement (II) alone :

We have a = 3b

The average price, from (i)

$= \$\left(\frac{3bx+3bx}{3b+b}\right) = \$\left(\frac{3x}{2}\right)$;

replacing a by 3b

Thus, the above price is $\$\left(\frac{3}{2}x\right)$, not greater than $\$\left(\frac{3}{2}x\right)$.

The answer to the question is 'No'. - Sufficient

Hence, eliminate C/E.

The correct answer is option (b).

33. (c) Considering Statement (I) alone :

Ratio of black (B) to red (R) balls = 2 : 3

Case 1: Let B = 2, R = 4;

Probability of drawing the first black ball

$= \frac{\text{No. of black balls}}{\text{Total no. of balls}} = \frac{2}{5}$,

Probability of drawing the second black ball

$= \frac{\text{No. of remaining black balls}}{\text{Total no. of remaining balls}} = \frac{1}{4}$

Therefore, the required probability $= \left(\frac{2}{5}\right) \times \left(\frac{1}{4}\right) = \frac{1}{10}$

Case 2 : Let B = 4, R = 6;

Probability of drawing the first black ball

$= \frac{\text{No. of black balls}}{\text{Total no. of balls}} = \frac{4}{10} = \frac{2}{5}$,

Probability of drawing the second black ball $\frac{3}{9} = \frac{1}{3}$

Therefore, the required probability $= \left(\frac{2}{5}\right) \times \left(\frac{1}{3}\right) = \frac{2}{15}$

The two answers are different - no unique solution - Insufficient.

Hence, eliminate A/D.

Considering Statement (II) alone :

This statement implies that R = B + 10. Different values of B, we get different values of R, and hence different probabilities. - no unique solution - Insufficient.

Hence, eliminate B.

Considering Statements (I) and (II) together :

If we combine the two statements.

Let B = 2k and R = 3k

R = B + 10

$\Rightarrow$ 3k = 2k + 10, k = 10, B = 20 and R = 30

Therefore, the probability of drawing two black balls $= \left(\frac{20}{30}\right) \times \left(\frac{19}{29}\right)$; there is no need to calculate the answer as it is finite and unique. Hence, both the statements together are sufficient.

The correct answer is option (c).

34. (b) Considering Statement (I) alone :

A set may be like {3, 3, 3} or {9, 9, 9}; in either case, the standard deviation (SD) would be 0 since there is no deviation among the terms. The answer is Yes.

If the set is like {3, 6, 9}, the SD would not be equal to 0 since there are deviations among the terms. The answer is No.

No unique answer; hence, this statement alone is not sufficient.

Hence, eliminate A/D.

Considering Statement (II) alone :

This statement implies that the set consists of only one number with its multiple occurrences.

These sets may be like {3, 3, 3}; {9, 9, 9, 9}; or {12, 12}. In each case, there is no deviation among the terms, therefore SD = 0; answer is Yes.

A unique answer; hence, Statement (II) alone is sufficient.

Hence, eliminate C/E.

The correct answer is option (b).

35. (c) **Considering Statement (I) alone :**

The smallest element is 1. We do not know anything about the remaining elements. The largest element may or may not be smaller than 10.

Hence this statement alone is not sufficient.

Hence, eliminate A/D.

Considering Statement (II) alone :

The Range is 10.

We know that Range (10) Largest element Smallest element

But we do not know anything about the values of the elements. The largest element may or may not be smaller than 10.

Hence this statement alone is not sufficient.

Hence, eliminate B.

Considering statements (I) and (II) together:

Smallest element 1

Range Largest element Smallest element

$\Rightarrow$ Largest element 11. The answer is No; a unique answer.

Hence, statements (I) and (II) together are sufficient.

The correct answer is option (c).

36. (e) **Considering Statement (I) alone :**

Statement 1 is insufficient, as there can be an infinite number of sets that comprise elements of consecutive even integers, thereby have different values of mean.

Hence, eliminate A/D.

Considering Statement (II) alone :

Again, statement 2 is insufficient, as there can be an infinite number of sets that comprise elements that have the range = 10, thereby have different values of mean.

Hence, eliminate B.

Considering statements (I) and (II) together :

Even considering both statements, multiple sets are possible. Set Q could be {2, 4, 6, 8, 10, 12} or {12, 14, 16, 18, 20, 22}. Each set has a different mean with the same Range value = 10. Thus, even both statements are insufficient.

The correct answer is option (e).

37. (b) We are given that each of the 40 students in class A is shorter than each of the 40 students in class B.

(Height of the tallest student in class A) (Height of the shortest student in class B)

You must not assume that the heights of all the 40 students in class A are the same; they could all be of different heights, the same height, or a few of them could be of the same height. The same is true for the students in class B.

We are asked to determine whether the median height of the 80 students is less than 160 centimeters.

We know that to find the median of a dataset, the terms of the dataset must be arranged in either ascending or descending order.

Let's assume that all the 80 students are arranged as per the ascending order of their height. All 40 students of class A would be on the left, arranged as per their increasing heights, and all 40 students of class B would be on the right, arranged as per their increasing heights. Thus, in this ordered arrangement of the 80 students, the tallest student in class A (40th student in order) would be immediately to the left of the shortest student in class B (the 41st in order).

You must know that

(Median value of a dataset) = (Value of the middlemost term)

When the number of terms in the dataset is even, the median is equal to the average of the values of the two middlemost terms.

Thus, (the median height of 80 students)

(Average of the height of the 40th student and the height of the 41st student in the ordered arrangement)

We know that the 41st student is the 1st student of class B.

So, to get the median height of the 80 students, we must know the height of the tallest student in class A and the shortest student in class B.

Note: In the above analysis, we arranged the students into the two groups in ascending order of their heights. If you chose to arrange them in descending order of heights instead, that is fine too. The analysis remains the same.

Considering Statement (I) alone :

The height of the shortest student in class A 150 centimeters

This information is of no use to us as we want the height of the 40th and 41st students to calculate the median height. - Insufficient

Hence, eliminate A/D.

Considering Statement (II) alone :

(Height of the shortest student in class B)

= (Height of the 41st student in ascending order of height)

= 160 centimeters

Though we do not know the height of the 40th student, we can make a deduction about the median. The question does not ask the value of the median; it asks whether the median height of the 80 students is less than 160 centimeters. This is a "Yes/No" type of question.

Since the height of the 41st student = 160 centimeters, and since we're given that even the tallest student in class A is shorter than the shortest student in class B, we can write:

(The height of the 40th student) < 160 centimeters

Say, the height of the 40th student = 159.99 centimeters

Thus, median. The answer is yes. – Sufficient

The correct answer is option (b).

38. (c) Total number of seats = 40 × 20 = 800

Thus, the number of occupied seats

= Total number of seats

– Number of unoccupied seats

Considering Statement (I) alone :

The total number of unoccupied seats in the front 18 rows

= 18 × 5 = 90

However, the total number of unoccupied seats in the back rows (40 – 18 = 22) is not known – Insufficient

Hence, eliminate A/D.

Considering Statement (II) alone :

The total number of unoccupied seats in the back 22 rows

$= 22 \times 15 = 330$

However, the total number of unoccupied seats in the front rows is not known. – Insufficient

Hence, eliminate B.

Considering Statements (I) and (II) together:

The total number of unoccupied seats in the auditorium

$= 90 + 330 = 420$

The total number of occupied seats in the auditorium

$= 800 - 420 = 380$ – Sufficient

The correct answer is option (c).

39. (c) Average weight of the shipments

$$= \frac{\text{Total weight of the shipments}}{\text{Number of shipments}}$$

Considering Statement (I) alone :

The number of shipments is not known. - Insufficient

Hence, eliminate A/D.

Considering Statement (II) alone :

The total weight of the shipments is not known. - Insufficient

Hence, eliminate B.

Considering Statements (I) and (II) together:

Total weight of the shipments is greater than 20,000 grams.

Number of shipments is less than 40.

Let us work with the total weight as 20,000 (least value) and the number of shipments as 39 (greater value):

Average weight of the shipments

$$= \frac{20{,}000}{39} > \left[\frac{20{,}000}{40} = 500\right]$$

When the total weight is greater than 20,000 and the number of shipments is fewer than 39, the average weight would rather increase.

Thus, the average weight of shipments is greater than 500 grams. - Sufficient

The correct answer is option (c).

Chapter 6

Data Sufficiency Practice Questions Set - 1

Multiple Choice Questions

1. The average score in a class of four students is 100. If none of them scored less than 0, how many students scored greater than 90?

   I. The two top scorers each scored 155.

   II. The median score for the class is 90.

   (*a*) Statement (I) ALONE is sufficient but statement (II) ALONE is not sufficient.

   (*b*) Statement (II) ALONE is sufficient but statement (I) ALONE is not sufficient.

   (*c*) BOTH statements TOGETHER are sufficient, but NEITHER statement ALONE is sufficient.

   (*d*) EACH statement ALONE is sufficient.

   (*e*) Statements (I) and (II) TOGETHER are not sufficient.

2. In a co-ordinate plane, if the triangle AXB is right-angled at Point X, what is the value of the x-coordinate of Point X ?

   I. The coordinates of the points A and B are (4, 5) and (6, 3), respectively.

   II. The area of the triangle AXB is 2.

   (*a*) Statement (I) ALONE is sufficient but statement (II) ALONE is not sufficient.

   (*b*) Statement (II) ALONE is sufficient but statement (I) ALONE is not sufficient.

   (*c*) BOTH statements TOGETHER are sufficient, but NEITHER statement ALONE is sufficient.

   (*d*) EACH statement ALONE is sufficient.

   (*e*) Statements (I) and (II) TOGETHER are not sufficient.

3. A merchant purchased three products, P, Q, and R, for $50,000. Did he pay more than $20,000 for R ?

   I. The sum the merchant paid for P and Q combined was 3 times the sum he paid for P.

   II. The merchant paid more for R than for Q.

   (*a*) Statement (I) ALONE is sufficient but statement (II) ALONE is not sufficient.

   (*b*) Statement (II) ALONE is sufficient but statement (I) ALONE is not sufficient.

   (*c*) BOTH statements TOGETHER are sufficient, but NEITHER statement ALONE is sufficient.

   (*d*) EACH statement ALONE is sufficient.

   (*e*) Statements (I) and (II) TOGETHER are not sufficient.

4. If x is a prime number, is $(15x^3 + 30x^2 + 6x + 9)$ divisible by x^2 ?

   I. $4 < x^2 < 30$

   II. $x^2 - 10x + 21 = 0$

   (*a*) Statement (I) ALONE is sufficient but statement (II) ALONE is not sufficient.

   (*b*) Statement (II) ALONE is sufficient but statement (I) ALONE is not sufficient.

   (*c*) BOTH statements TOGETHER are sufficient, but NEITHER statement ALONE is sufficient.

   (*d*) EACH statement ALONE is sufficient.

   (*e*) Statements (I) and (II) TOGETHER are not sufficient.

5. If ab is a two-digit number, where a and b are its tens and units digits, respectively, is the number ab divisible by 21 ?

   I. The sum of the digits is 7.

   II. The product of the digits is 6.

(*a*) Statement (I) ALONE is sufficient but statement (II) ALONE is not sufficient.

(*b*) Statement (II) ALONE is sufficient but statement (I) ALONE is not sufficient.

(*c*) BOTH statements TOGETHER arc sufficient, but NEITHER statement ALONE is sufficient.

(*d*) EACH statement ALONE is sufficient.

(*e*) Statements (I) and (II) TOGETHER are not sufficient.

6. Is x = 4 ?

I. $\sqrt{5x^2 - 64} = x$

II. $\sqrt{x^2 + 5} = x + 2$

(*a*) Statement (I) ALONE is sufficient but statement (II) ALONE is not sufficient.

(*b*) Statement (II) ALONE is sufficient but statement (I) ALONE is not sufficient.

(*c*) BOTH statements TOGETHER are sufficient, but NEITHER statement ALONE is sufficient.

(*d*) EACH statement ALONE is sufficient.

(*e*) Statements (I) and (II) TOGETHER are not sufficient.

7. What is the standard deviation of 1, 2, 3, k, 5, 6 and 7 ?

I. Standard deviation of 2, 3, 4, (k + 1), 6, 7 and 8 is 2.

II. Standard deviation of 0, 1, 2, (k – 1), 4, 5, and 6 is 2.

(*a*) Statement (I) ALONE is sufficient but statement (II) ALONE is not sufficient.

(*b*) Statement (II) ALONE is sufficient but statement (I) ALONE is not sufficient.

(*c*) BOTH statements TOGETHER are sufficient, but NEITHER statement ALONE is sufficient.

(*d*) EACH statement ALONE is sufficient.

(*e*) Statements (I) and (II) TOGETHER are not sufficient.

8. What is the value of $(a^2 - b^2)$?

I. $a - b = 0$

II. $a + b = 0$

(*a*) Statement (I) ALONE is sufficient but statement (II) ALONE is not sufficient.

(*b*) Statement (II) ALONE is sufficient but statement (I) ALONE is not sufficient.

(*c*) BOTH statements TOGETHER are sufficient, but NEITHER statement ALONE is sufficient.

(*d*) EACH statement ALONE is sufficient.

(*e*) Statements (I) and (II) TOGETHER are not sufficient.

9. If x and y are distinct single-digit positive integers, what is the value of x ?

I. The sum of *x* and *y* is 8.

II. Both *x* and *y* are multiples of 2.

(*a*) Statement (I) ALONE is sufficient but statement (II) ALONE is not sufficient.

(*b*) Statement (II) ALONE is sufficient but statement (I) ALONE is not sufficient.

(*c*) BOTH statements TOGETHER are sufficient, but NEITHER statement ALONE is sufficient.

(*d*) EACH statement ALONE is sufficient.

(*e*) Statements (I) and (II) TOGETHER are not sufficient.

10. The population of a country increased by X% after the first year and by Y% after the second year. What is the percentage increase in population after 2 years?

I. $XY = 50$

II. $100X + 100Y + XY = 2,150$

(*a*) Statement (I) ALONE is sufficient but statement (II) ALONE is not sufficient.

(*b*) Statement (II) ALONE is sufficient but statement (I) ALONE is not sufficient.

(*c*) BOTH statements TOGETHER are sufficient, but NEITHER statement ALONE is sufficient.

(*d*) EACH statement ALONE is sufficient.

(*e*) Statements (I) and (II) TOGETHER are not sufficient.

11. A case has at least one white, one pink, and one black marble and no marbles of any other color. If one marble is drawn randomly from the case, is the probability that the marble is white the same as the probability that the marble is black but NOT the same as the probability that the marble is pink?

I. The case contains 5 marbles.

II. The case contains more pink marbles than black marbles.

(*a*) Statement (I) ALONE is sufficient but statement (II) ALONE is not sufficient.

(*b*) Statement (II) ALONE is sufficient but statement (I) ALONE is not sufficient.

(*c*) BOTH statements TOGETHER are sufficient, but NEITHER statement ALONE is sufficient.

(*d*) EACH statement ALONE is sufficient.

(*e*) Statements (I) and (II) TOGETHER are not sufficient.

12. If Amy and Betty together can complete a project in 50 days, is Amy the most efficient of Amy, Betty, and Cherry?

I. Betty and Cherry, together, can complete the same project between 30 to 40 days.

II. Cherry alone can complete the same project in 60 days.

(*a*) Statement (I) ALONE is sufficient but statement (II) ALONE is not sufficient.

(*b*) Statement (II) ALONE is sufficient but statement (I) ALONE is not sufficient.

(*c*) BOTH statements TOGETHER are sufficient, but NEITHER statement ALONE is sufficient.

(*d*) EACH statement ALONE is sufficient.

(*e*) Statements (I) and (II) TOGETHER are not sufficient.

13. Steve rows a certain distance upstream (rowing against the stream) in Boat B in 6 hours. How long would it take him to row the same distance upstream if he used Boat C that runs twice as fast as Boat B?

I. It takes Steve 4 hours to cover the same distance downstream (rowing with the stream) using the slower of the two boats.

II. Rowing upstream, Steve covers 12 miles distance.

(*a*) Statement (I) ALONE is sufficient but statement (II) ALONE is not sufficient.

(*b*) Statement (II) ALONE is sufficient but statement (I) ALONE is not sufficient.

(*c*) BOTH statements TOGETHER are sufficient, but NEITHER statement ALONE is sufficient.

(*d*) EACH statement ALONE is sufficient.

(*e*) Statements (I) and (II) TOGETHER are not sufficient.

Answer Key

1. (*a*)
2. (*e*)
3. (*c*)
4. (*c*)
5. (*d*)
6. (*d*)
7. (*d*)
8. (*d*)
9. (*e*)
10. (*b*)
11. (*e*)
12. (*a*)
13. (*a*)

Answer Explanations

1. (a) **Considering Statement I alone :**

Since there are four students, the total score of the four students = $4 \times 100 = 400$.

Let A, B, C, D be the four students' scores. This statement implies that $C + D = 155 \times 2 = 310 \Rightarrow A + B = 90$. Therefore, given that no student scored less than 0, we can conclude that neither A nor B scored greater than 90. The answer is that two students scored greater than 90.

This statement alone is sufficient.

Hence, eliminate (b)/(c)/(e).

Considering Statement II alone :

Given that that median = 90.

Again, since there are four students, the total score of the four students

$$= 4 \times 100 = 400.$$

Let's take a couple of cases.

Case1: Say the three scores are 90, each; thus, the fourth score $400 - 3 \times 90 = 130$.

Median $= \frac{90 + 90}{2} = 90$. The answer is that only one student scored greater than 90.

Case 2: Say the three scores are 80, 80, 100, and 140; Media n $= \frac{80 + 100}{2} = 90$ and the total score = 400. The answer is that two students scored greater than 90.

No unique answer.

This statement alone is insufficient.

Hence, eliminate (d).

The correct answer is option (a).

2. (e) Let the coordinates of Point X be (m, n).

We need to determine the value of m.

Considering Statement I alone :

It can be seen in the diagram below that there are two possible positions of Point X (X and X') so that triangle AXB is right-angled at Point X.

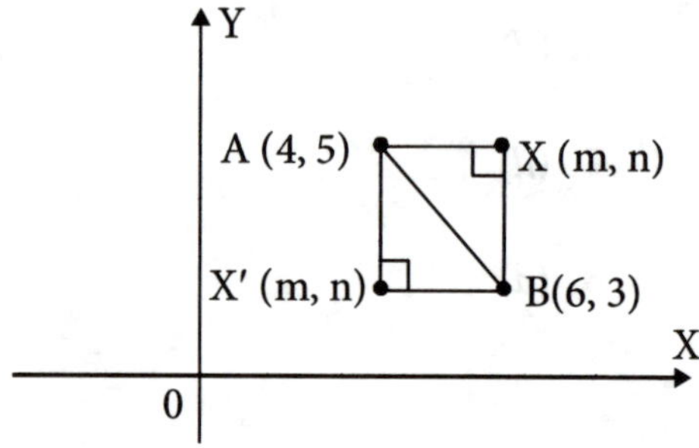

The x-coordinate of X is the same as that of B and the Y coordinate of X is the same as that of A.

Thus, the coordinates of X are (6, 5)

$\Rightarrow \quad m = 6$

The X coordinate of X' is the same as that of A and the Y coordinate of X' is the same as that of B.

Thus, the coordinates of X' are (4, 3)

$\Rightarrow \quad m = 4$

Thus, there is no unique value of m. – Insufficient

Hence, eliminate (a)/(d).

Considering Statement II alone :

We only know that the area of triangle AXB is 2.

We cannot determine the coordinates of X. – Insufficient

Hence, eliminate (b).

Considering statements I and II together:

As in Statement I, for the position X OR X', the area of triangle AXB

$$= \frac{1}{2}(AX)(XB) = \frac{1}{2} \times 2 \times 2 = 2$$

Thus, the coordinates of X are not unique.

Thus, there is no unique value of m. – Insufficient

The correct answer is option (e).

3. (c) We are given that the amount spent on buying P, Q, and R is \$50,000.

Say the amounts spent on buying P, Q, and R are x, y, and z, respectively.

$\Rightarrow x + y + z = 50{,}000$ ... (1)

We have to determine whether $z > 20{,}000$.

Considering Statement I alone:

We are given that the sum the merchant paid for P and Q combined was 3 times the sum he paid for P.

$\Rightarrow x + y = 3x$

$y = 2x$ ... (2)

Substituting equation (2) in equation (1):

$\Rightarrow x + 2x + z = 50{,}000 \Rightarrow 3x + z = 50{,}000$. We have an unknown x. So, we cannot determine whether $z > 20{,}000$. Insufficient!

Hence, eliminate (a)/(d).

Considering Statement II alone:

We are given that the merchant paid more for R than for Q.

$\Rightarrow z > y$ ... (3)

With the help of equation (1): $x + y + z = 50{,}000$ and inequality (2): $z > y$, we cannot determine whether $z > 20{,}000$. Insufficient!

Hence, eliminate (b).

Considering statements I and II together:

Let's put down the two equations (1) and (2) and the inequality (3).

$x + y + z = 50{,}000$ ... (1)

$y = 2x$ ... (2)

$z > y$ ... (3)

Since the inequality (3) has only z and y variables, let's eliminate variable x from equation (1) and (2).

From equation (2), we have $x = \frac{y}{2}$. By plugging in the value x in equation (1), we get

$$\frac{y}{2} + y + z = 50{,}000$$

$$y + 2y + 2z = 100{,}000$$

$3y + 2z = 100{,}000$ ... (4)

$y = \frac{100{,}000 - 2z}{3}$ ... (5)

Substituting (5) in (3):

$$z = \frac{100{,}000 - 2z}{3}$$

$$5z > 100{,}000$$

$$z > 20{,}000$$

So, the answer is 'Yes'. The two statements together are sufficient!

Alternate approach:

Alternate way of solving further after equation (4): $3y + 2z = 100{,}000$

Let's assume that $y = z = n$, and analyze what their values are.

Thus, from equation (4), $3n + 2n = 100{,}000 \Rightarrow 5n = 100{,}000 \Rightarrow n = 20{,}000$

Thus, $y = z = 20{,}000$;

However, this goes against the fact (Statement II) given in inequality (3): $z > y$.

Thus, $y < 20{,}000$ & $z > 20{,}000$. The answer is Yes. Sufficient!

The correct answer is option (c).

4. (c) Since the first two terms of the expression $(15x^3 + 30x^2 + 6x + 9)$ are divisible by $x^2\left[\frac{15x^3+30x^2+6x+9}{x^2} = (15x+30)+\frac{6x+9}{x^2}\right]$, the question becomes whether $(6x + 9)$ is divisible by x^2.

Considering statement I alone :

Since x is a prime number and $4 < x^2 < 30$, the set of x would be {3, 5}.

Case 1: If x = 3, we see that (6x + 9) is divisible by x^2.

$6x + 9 = 6 \times 3 + 9 = 27$ is divisible by $x^2 = 3^2 = 9$. The answer is YES.

Case 2: If x = 5, we see that (6x + 9) is not divisible by x^2.

$6x + 9 = 6 \times 5 + 9 = 39$ is not divisible by $x^2 = 5^2 = 25$. The answer is NO.

No unique answer!

Statement I alone is not sufficient. Hence, eliminate (a)/(d).

Considering statement II alone :

Upon solving $x^2 - 10x + 21 = 0$, we get x = 3 or 7. We already know that for x = 3, the expression (6x + 9) is divisible by x^2 and the answer is YES. However, for x = 7, (6x + 9) is not divisible by x^2

$\Rightarrow (6x + 9 = 6 \times 7 + 9) = 51$, not divisible by $x^2 = 7^2 = 49$. So the answer is NO. Again no unique answer!

Statement II alone is also not sufficient. Hence, eliminate (b).

Considering Statement I and II together :

The only common value of x between statements (1) and (2) is 3, and for x = 3, we know that the expression is divisible, hence the answer is yes; a unique answer.

The correct answer is option (c).

5. (d) A two-digit number is divisible by 21 only if it is divisible by both 3 and 7.

Let's see each statement one by one.

Considering Statement I alone :

Since the sum of digits is 7, we have the following cases:

a	b	ab
1	6	16
2	5	25
3	4	34
4	3	43
5	2	52
6	1	61
7	0	70

Thus, the possible numbers are 16, 25, 34, 43, 52, 61, and 70; none of these are divisible by 21.

Hence, Statement I is sufficient to answer the question, the answer is No – (a) unique answer. Sufficient

Hence, eliminate (b)/(c)/(e).

Considering Statement II alone :

Since the product of the digits is 6, we have the following cases:

a	b	ab
1	6	16
2	3	23
3	2	32
6	1	61

Thus, the possible numbers are 16, 23, 32 and 61; none of these are divisible by 21.

Hence, Statement II is also sufficient to answer the question, the answer being No – (a) unique answer.

Hence, eliminate (a).

The correct answer is option (d).

6. (d) **Considering Statement I alone :**

We have $\sqrt{5x^2 - 64} = x$

Squaring both sides

$(5x^2 - 64) = x^2$

$\Rightarrow 4x^2 = 64$

$\Rightarrow x^2 = 16$

$\Rightarrow x = 4 \text{ or } -4$

Seeing two values of x, you may hurriedly conclude that you cannot get the unique value of x; thus, Statement I is insufficient. However, the left-hand side of the equation: $\sqrt{5x^2 - 64}$ is a square root, which is always non-negative.

Thus, $x \neq -4$.

Thus, we obtain only one value of x = 4.

Thus, Statement I is sufficient to answer the question and the answer is Yes.

Hence, eliminate (b)/(c)/(e).

Considering Statement II alone :

We have $\sqrt{x^2 + 20} = x + 2$

Squaring both sides

$x^2 + 20 = (x + 2)^2$

$\Rightarrow x^2 + 20 = x^2 + 4x + 4$

$\Rightarrow x = 4$

Thus, we obtain only one value of x = 4.

Thus, Statement II is also sufficient to answer the question and the answer is Yes.

Hence, eliminate (a).

The correct answer is option (d).

7. (d) The standard deviation (SD) of a data set is a measure of the deviations of the numbers in the set w.r.t. their average (arithmetic mean). The more deviated (more distant) the numbers are from the mean, the greater their standard deviation, and vice-versa.

Standard deviation doesn't get affected on addition or subtraction of a constant to each term in a given set.

Let's analyze each statement one by one.

Considering Statement I alone :

Note that if each number of a set is decreased by a constant, the standard deviation of the resultant set does not change.

We are given that the standard deviation of 2, 3, 4, (k + 1), 6, 7 and 8 is 2.

This implies that the standard deviation of (2 – 1),(3 – 1),(4 – 1), (k + 1 – 1), (6 – 1), (7 – 1) and (8 – 1) is also 2.

⇒ The standard deviation of 1, 2, 3, k, 5, 6 and 7 is 2. Sufficient.

Hence, eliminate (b)/(c)/(e).

Considering Statement II alone :

Note that if each number of a set is increased by a constant, the standard deviation of the resultant set does not change.

We are given that the standard deviation of 0, 1, 2, (k – 1), 4, 5, and 6 is 2.

This implies that the standard deviation of (0 + 1),(1 + 1),(2 + 1), (k – 1 + 1), (4 + 1), (5 + 1) and (6 + 1) is also 2.

⇒ The standard deviation of 1, 2, 3, k, 5, 6 and 7 is 2. Sufficient.

Hence, eliminate (a).

The correct answer is option (d).

8. (d) We know that $a^2 - b^2 = (a - b)(a + b)$.

Considering Statement I alone :

Substituting $a - b = 0$ in the given equation: $a^2 - b^2 = (a - b)(a + b) = 0 \times (a + b) = 0$; a unique answer. Sufficient.

Hence, eliminate (b)/(c)/(e).

Considering Statement II alone :

Substituting $a + b = 0$ in the given equation:

$a^2 - b^2 = (a - b)(a + b) = 0 \times (a - b) = 0$; a unique answer. Sufficient.

Hence, eliminate (a).

The correct answer is option (d).

9. (e) **Considering Statement I alone :**

Multiple combinations are possible for x and y: (1, 7), (2, 6), (3, 5), etc. Therefore, Statement I alone is insufficient.

Hence, eliminate (a)/(d).

Considering Statement II alone :

Again, multiple values are possible for x and y: 2, 4, 6, and 8. Therefore, Statement II alone is insufficient.

Hence, eliminate (b).

Considering statements I and II together :

Both statements together lead to only one combination for x and y: (2, 6). x and y each cannot be 4 since they are distinct. Moreover, even with only one possible combination for x and y, we cannot fix which of the two values 2 and 6 is the value of x. No unique answer. Insufficient.

The correct answer is option (e).

10. (b) Let the population at start of the first year $= P_0$;

So, the population after first year

$$= P_1 = P_o\left(1 + \frac{X}{100}\right)$$

$$= P_o + P_o x.\left(\text{Assuming } x = \frac{X}{100}\right);$$

So, the population after 2 years

$$= P_2 = P_1\left(1 + \frac{Y}{100}\right)$$

$$= P_1 + P_1 y.\left(\text{Assuming } Y = \frac{X}{100}\right);$$

$= P_o + P_o x + P_o y + P_o xy$; by replacing the value of $P_1 = P_o + P_o x$;

Percentage increase in population

$$= \left[\frac{(P_o + P_o x + P_o y + P_o xy)}{P_o}\right] \times 100\%$$

$$= \frac{(P_o x + P_o y + P_o xy)}{P_o} \times 100\%$$

$= (x + y + xy) \times 100\%$;

taking P_0 common from numerator and denominator and then cancelling it.

So, Percentage increase in population

$= 100(x + y + xy)\%$;

Therefore, we need to find the value of $(x + y + xy)$.

Considering Statement I alone :

Since XY = 50, we get $xy = \frac{50}{10,000}$. But we don't have values for x and y. This statement is not sufficient.

Hence, eliminate (a)/(d).

Considering Statement II alone :

We know that 100X + 100Y + XY = 2,150. Substituting the values of x and y, we get $10,000x + 10,000y + 10,000xy = 2,150$ $\Rightarrow x + y + xy = 0.215$. Therefore, required percentage $= 100 (x + y + xy)\% = 100 \times 0.215\% = 21.5\%$.

This statement is sufficient.

Hence, eliminate (c)/(e).

The correct answer is option (b).

11. (e) We are given that the case has marbles of three different colors–white, pink, and black, and the number of marbles of each color is at least one in count. Thus, the minimum number of marbles in the case = 3.

Let's understand what the question asks.

Say, the probability of drawing a white marble = p(w); the probability of drawing a black marble = p(b); and the probability of drawing a pink marble = p(p).

The question asks: Is $p(w) = p(b) \neq p(p)$?

So, the question boils down to:

"Does the case have white marbles equal to black marbles but NOT equal to pink marbles?"

Considering Statement I alone :

The case contains 5 marbles.

Let's distribute the 5 marbles in three colors such that we have at least one marble of each color.

Case 1 : White: 1 marble; Black: 1 marble; Pink: 3 marbles

We have white marbles equal to black marbles, and NOT equal to pink marbles; the answer is yes.

Case 2 : White: 2 marbles; Black: 1 marble; Pink: 2 marbles

We have white marbles NOT equal to black marbles, but equal to pink marbles; the answer is no.

No unique answer. Insufficient.

Note : Other cases are possible too, but we need not consider them all because, from just two cases, we deduced that Statement I is not sufficient to get a unique answer.

Hence, eliminate (a)/(d).

Considering Statement II alone :

Only with this information, we can deduce that the probability that the marble is pink is NOT equal to the probability that the marble is black; however, we have no clue about the count of white marbles; the count of white marbles may or may not be equal to the count of black marbles. Insufficient.

Hence, eliminate (b).

Considering statements I and II together :

Both the cases discussed in Statement I are applicable here too.

So, this does not add any value. – Insufficient

The correct answer is option (e).

12. (a) We know that Amy and Betty together can complete a project in 50 days ... (i)

Considering Statement I alone :

Betty and Cherry, together, can complete the same project between 30 to 40 days ... (ii)

Thus, from (i) and (ii), we see that if Amy is replaced by Cherry, the time required for the project decreases (30 to 40 days from 50 days).

Thus, the efficiency of Cherry must be greater than that of Amy.

Thus, the efficiency of Amy cannot be the greatest among Amy, Betty and Cherry. – Sufficient

Hence, eliminate (b)/(c)/(e).

Considering Statement II alone :

We only know that the time taken by Cherry to complete the project is 60 days.

Since the individual times taken by Amy and Betty are not known, the efficiency of Amy cannot be compared with that of Betty or Cherry. – Insufficient

Hence, eliminate (d).

The correct answer is option (a).

13. (a) Let the distance Steve covers be d miles.

Given that he uses Boat C that is twice as fast as Boat B, the slower boat is Boat B.

Let the speed of the slower boat (Boat B) in still water be b miles per hour.

Let the speed of the stream be r miles per hour.

Thus, speed while rowing upstream

= (b – r) miles per hour.

Thus, time taken to cover d miles upstream

$= \left(\frac{d}{b-r}\right)$ hours.

Thus, we have

$$\frac{d}{b-r} = 6 \qquad \text{... (i)}$$

If Steve uses Boat C that is twice as fast as Boat B, the speed of Boat C in still water = 2b miles per hour.

Thus, upstream speed = (2b – r) miles per hour.

Thus, time taken to cover d miles upstream

$= \left(\frac{d}{2b-r}\right)$ hours.

Thus, we need to determine the value of $\left(\frac{d}{2b-r}\right)$.

Considering Statement I alone :

Speed while going downstream using the slower boat = (b + r) miles per hour

Thus, time taken to cover d miles downstream $= \left(\frac{d}{b+r}\right)$ hours

Thus, we have

$$\frac{d}{b+r} = 4 \qquad \text{... (ii)}$$

Dividing (i) by (ii):

$$\frac{b+r}{b-r} = \frac{6}{4} \Rightarrow 4b + 4r = 6b - 6r \Rightarrow b = 5r$$

Thus, from (ii):

$$\frac{d}{5r+r} = 4 \Rightarrow d = 24r$$

Thus, we have

$$\frac{d}{2b-r} = \frac{24r}{10r-r} = \frac{8}{3} \text{ hours – Sufficient}$$

Hence, eliminate (b)/(c)/(e).

Considering Statement II alone :

Only knowing the actual value of the distance does not help to establish a relation between b and r. – Insufficient

Hence, eliminate (d).

The correct answer is option (a).

Chapter 7

Data Sufficiency Practice Questions Set - 2

Multiple Choice Questions

1. What is the value of the positive integer x ?

I. The number of trailing zeros in x! is 2.

II. The number of trailing zeros in (x + 1)! is 3.

(a) Statement (I) ALONE is sufficient but statement (II) ALONE is not sufficient.

(b) Statement (II) ALONE is sufficient but statement (I) ALONE is not sufficient.

(c) BOTH statements TOGETHER are sufficient, but NEITHER statement ALONE is sufficient.

(d) EACH statement ALONE is sufficient.

(e) Statements (I) and (II) TOGETHER are not sufficient.

2. Is $|x| < \frac{1}{4}$?

I. $x = \frac{1}{4+y^2}$

II. y is a non-positive integer.

(a) Statement (I) ALONE is sufficient but statement (II) ALONE is not sufficient.

(b) Statement (II) ALONE is sufficient but statement (I) ALONE is not sufficient.

(c) BOTH statements TOGETHER are sufficient, but NEITHER statement ALONE is sufficient.

(d) EACH statement ALONE is sufficient.

(e) Statements (I) and (II) TOGETHER are not sufficient.

3. If the symbol ⊗ represents one of the following operations: addition, subtraction, multiplication, or division, what is the value of 3 ⊗ 5 ?

I. 6 ⊗ 8 <1

II. 4 ⊗ 3 >1

(a) Statement (I) ALONE is sufficient but statement (II) ALONE is not sufficient.

(b) Statement (II) ALONE is sufficient but statement (I) ALONE is not sufficient.

(c) BOTH statements TOGETHER are sufficient, but NEITHER statement ALONE is sufficient.

(d) EACH statement ALONE is sufficient.

(e) Statements (I) and (II) TOGETHER are not sufficient.

4. If $a^2 - 4a = 0$, and $b \neq 0$, is $\frac{a}{b} = 0$?

I. $b^2 - 16 = 0$

II. $a^2 + 8a = 0$

(a) Statement (I) ALONE is sufficient but statement (II) ALONE is not sufficient.

(b) Statement (II) ALONE is sufficient but statement (I) ALONE is not sufficient.

(c) BOTH statements TOGETHER are sufficient, but NEITHER statement ALONE is sufficient.

(d) EACH statement ALONE is sufficient.

(e) Statements (I) and (II) TOGETHER are not sufficient.

5. What is the value of y, if x = 2 ?

I. $|x| = |y|$

II. $y^2 = 4$

(a) Statement (I) ALONE is sufficient but statement (II) ALONE is not sufficient.

(b) Statement (II) ALONE is sufficient but statement (I) ALONE is not sufficient.

(c) BOTH statements TOGETHER are sufficient, but NEITHER statement ALONE is sufficient.

(*d*) EACH statement ALONE is sufficient.

(*e*) Statements (I) and (II) TOGETHER are not sufficient.

6. Is $xyz = 10$?

I. $z = \frac{1}{\sqrt{x}} - \left(\frac{y^2 + 2xy}{\sqrt{x}} + \frac{x^2}{\sqrt{x}}\right)\left(\frac{1}{(x+y^2)}\right)$

II. $x = z$

(*a*) Statement (I) ALONE is sufficient but statement (II) ALONE is not sufficient.

(*b*) Statement (II) ALONE is sufficient but statement (I) ALONE is not sufficient.

(*c*) BOTH statements TOGETHER are sufficient, but NEITHER statement ALONE is sufficient.

(*d*) EACH statement ALONE is sufficient.

(*e*) Statements (I) and (II) TOGETHER are not sufficient.

7. In a certain office, a manager distributed a few food coupons and a few gas coupons to the employees such that each employee got an equal number of food coupons and an equal number of gas coupons. How many employees are there in the office?

I. The manager distributed 200 food coupons and 60 gas coupons.

II. The total number of coupons received by each employee was less than 20.

(*a*) Statement (I) ALONE is sufficient but statement (II) ALONE is not sufficient.

(*b*) Statement (II) ALONE is sufficient but statement (I) ALONE is not sufficient.

(*c*) BOTH statements TOGETHER are sufficient, but NEITHER statement ALONE is sufficient.

(*d*) EACH statement ALONE is sufficient.

(*e*) Statements (I) and (II) TOGETHER are not sufficient.

8. A carpenter distributed nuts, bolts, and screws among the apprentices in his class, such that each apprentice got an equal number of nuts, an equal number of bolts, and an equal number of screws. How many apprentices were in the class?

I. Each apprentice got nuts, bolts, and screws in the ratio 3 : 4 : 5, respectively.

II. The carpenter distributed a total of 27 nuts, 36 bolts, and 45 screws.

(*a*) Statement (I) ALONE is sufficient but statement (II) ALONE is not sufficient.

(*b*) Statement (II) ALONE is sufficient but statement (I) ALONE is not sufficient.

(*c*) BOTH statements TOGETHER are sufficient, but NEITHER statement ALONE is sufficient.

(*d*) EACH statement ALONE is sufficient.

(*e*) Statements (I) and (II) TOGETHER are not sufficient.

9. Did Andrew eat a greater number of toffees than Ricky?

I. Thrice the number of toffees that Andrew ate was greater than 6 less than thrice the number of toffees that Ricky ate.

II. Twice the number of toffees that Andrew ate was greater than 4 less than twice the number of toffees that Ricky ate.

(*a*) Statement (I) ALONE is sufficient but statement (II) ALONE is not sufficient.

(*b*) Statement (II) ALONE is sufficient but statement (I) ALONE is not sufficient.

(*c*) BOTH statements TOGETHER are sufficient, but NEITHER statement ALONE is sufficient.

(*d*) EACH statement ALONE is sufficient.

(*e*) Statements (I) and (II) TOGETHER are not sufficient.

10. While going to the office, Edward drove his car at an average speed of 50 kilometers per hour. While returning home, he drove at a slower speed. What was Edward's average speed for the entire journey?

I. While returning home and taking the same route, Edward drove at a constant speed of 45 kilometers per hour.

II. It takes Edward 1 hour to drive to the office.

(a) Statement (I) ALONE is sufficient but statement (II) ALONE is not sufficient.

(b) Statement (II) ALONE is sufficient but statement (I) ALONE is not sufficient.

(c) BOTH statements TOGETHER are sufficient, but NEITHER statement ALONE is sufficient.

(d) EACH statement ALONE is sufficient.

(e) Statements (I) and (II) TOGETHER are not sufficient.

11. If $z = xy$, is $z = 1$?

I. $x(y - x) = 0$

II. $y(x - y) = 0$

(a) Statement (I) ALONE is sufficient but statement (II) ALONE is not sufficient.

(b) Statement (II) ALONE is sufficient but statement (I) ALONE is not sufficient.

(c) BOTH statements TOGETHER are sufficient, but NEITHER statement ALONE is sufficient.

(d) EACH statement ALONE is sufficient.

(e) Statements (I) and (II) TOGETHER are not sufficient.

12. Is abc an odd integer?

I. ab is an odd integer.

II. bc is an odd integer.

(a) Statement (I) ALONE is sufficient but statement (II) ALONE is not sufficient.

(b) Statement (II) ALONE is sufficient but statement (I) ALONE is not sufficient.

(c) BOTH statements TOGETHER are sufficient, but NEITHER statement ALONE is sufficient.

(d) EACH statement ALONE is sufficient.

(e) Statements (I) and (II) TOGETHER are not sufficient.

Answer Key

1. (c)
2. (e)
3. (c)
4. (b)
5. (e)
6. (a)
7. (c)
8. (e)
9. (e)
10. (a)
11. (e)
12. (c)

Answer Explanations

1. (c) This question deals with the number of trailing 0s in $x! = 1 \times 2 \times 3 \times 4 \times 5 \times 7 \times 6 \ldots x$

Let's discuss how a 0 comes up upon multiplying positive integers.

A trailing 0 comes up when 2 is multiplied by 5. Since 5 > 2, it's sufficient to count the number of 5s in x! to get the number of trailing 0s.

Examples :

- $7! = 1 \times 2 \times 3 \times 4 \times 5 \times 6 \times 7 = 5040$; since 7! has only one 5, it would have only one trailing 0.
- $12! = 1 \times 2 \times 3 \times 4 \times 5 \times 6 \times 7 \times 8 \times 9 \times 10 \times 11 \times 12 = 479001600$; since 12! has two 5s (one in 5 and one in 10), it would have two trailing 0s.

Let's analyze each statement one by one.

Considering statement I alone :

The number of trailing zeros in x! is 2.

The minimum value of x such that the number of trailing zeros in x! is 2 is 10.

At x! = 10!, we already saw that we have two 5s (one in 5 and one in 10).

One more 5, we would get when x! = 15!. Thus, when x = 10 to 14, we have two trailing 0s in x! We do not have a unique value of x. Insufficient

Hence, eliminate A/D.

Considering statement II alone :

The number of trailing zeros in (x + 1)! is 3.

The minimum value of x such that the number of trailing zeros in (x + 1)! is 3 is 14.

At (x + 1)! = 15!, we already saw that we have three 5s (one in 5, one in 10 and one from 15).

One more 5, we would get when (x + 1)!=20! Thus, when x = 14 to 19, we have three trailing 0s in (x + 1)!. We do not have a unique value of x. Insufficient.

Hence, eliminate (b).

Considering statements I and II together :

Only one value of x is common in both the statements, i.e., 14; thus, both the statements together gives us a unique value of x = 14. Sufficient

The correct answer is option (c).

2. (e) We have to ascertain whether $|x| < \frac{1}{4}$.

The minimum value of |x| is 0, thus, we have to determine whether $0 \leq |x| < \frac{1}{4}$.

Let's take each statement one by one.

Considering statement I alone :

$$x = \frac{1}{4 + y^2}$$

Though the value of y is not given, we must not dismiss statement I only because of this reason.

Observe that the minimum value of y^2 is 0 since y^2 is a non-negative number. Whether y is positive or negative, y^2 is positive.

Note that as the value of y^2 increases, the value of $\frac{1}{4+y^2}$ decreases. As y^2 approaches infinity, $\frac{1}{4+y^2}$ approaches 0.

Conversely, as the value of y^2 decreases, the value of $\frac{1}{4+y^2}$ increases. As y^2 approaches 0, $\frac{1}{4+y^2}$ approaches $\frac{1}{4}$.

This implies that $0 \le \frac{1}{4+y^2} \le \frac{1}{4}$.

Case 1 : If $0 \le \frac{1}{4+y^2} < \frac{1}{4}$, the answer is Yes.

Case 2 : If $\frac{1}{4+y^2} = \frac{1}{4}$, the answer is No.

Note that at y = 0, we have $x = \frac{1}{4+y^2} = \frac{1}{4+0^2} = \frac{1}{4} \not< \frac{1}{4}$.

No unique answer. Insufficient.

Hence, eliminate (a)/(d).

Considering statement II alone :

y is a non-positive integer.

We do not have any information on the relationship of y with x.

No unique answer. Insufficient.

Hence, eliminate (b).

Considering statements I and II together :

Both the cases discussed in statement I are applicable here too.

Case 1 : At y = 0 (a non-positive integer), we have $x = \frac{1}{4+y^2} = \frac{1}{4+0^2} = \frac{1}{4} \not< \frac{1}{4}$, the answer is No, $|x| \not< \frac{1}{4}$.

Case 2 : At y = −1 (a non-positive integer), we have

$$x = \frac{1}{4+y^2} = \frac{1}{4+(-1)^2} = \frac{1}{4+1} = \frac{1}{5} < \frac{1}{4},$$

the answer is Yes, $|x| < \frac{1}{4}$.

No unique answer. Insufficient.

The correct answer is option (e).

3. (c) We have to determine the value of $3 \otimes 5$. To get this, we must know which arithmetic operation the symbol $\otimes$ represents. Since there can be four different values of $3 \otimes 5$.

- $3 \otimes 5 = 3 + 5 = 8$
- $3 \otimes 5 = 3 - 5 = -2$
- $3 \otimes 5 = 3 \times 5 = 15$
- $3 \otimes 5 = 3 \div 5 = 0.6$

Question rephrased : What operation does the symbol $\otimes$ represent?

Let's analyze each statement one by one.

Considering statement I alone : $6 \otimes 8 < 1$

- Assuming that $\otimes$ is addition, then $6 \otimes 8 < 1 \Rightarrow 6 + 8 (= 14) \not< 1$. Not correct
- Assuming that $\otimes$ is subtraction, then $6 \otimes 8 < 1 \Rightarrow 6 - 8 (= -2) < 1$. Correct
- Assuming that $\otimes$ is multiplication, then $6 \otimes 8 < 1 \Rightarrow 6 \times 8 (= 48) \not< 1$. Not correct
- Assuming that $\otimes$ is division, then $6 \otimes 8 < 1 \Rightarrow 6 \div 8 (= 0.75) < 1$. Correct

$\otimes$ can be either subtraction or division. No unique answer. Insufficient.

Hence, eliminate (a)/(d).

Considering Statement II alone: $4 \otimes 3 > 1$

- Assuming that $\otimes$ is addition, then $4 \otimes 3 > 1 \Rightarrow 4 + 3 (= 7) > 1$. Correct
- Assuming that $\otimes$ is subtraction, then $4 \otimes 3 > 1 \Rightarrow 4 - 3 (= 1) \not> 1$. Not correct
- Assuming that $\otimes$ is multiplication, then $4 \otimes 3 > 1 \Rightarrow 4 \times 3 (= 12) > 1$. Correct
- Assuming that $\otimes$ is division, then $4 \otimes 3 > 1 \Rightarrow 4 \div 3 (= 1.33) > 1$. Correct

$\otimes$ can be addition, multiplication or division. No unique answer. Insufficient.

Hence, eliminate (b).

Considering statements I and II together:

Statement 1 concludes that $\otimes$ can be either subtraction or division, while statement II concludes that $\otimes$ can be addition, multiplication or division. Only one operation is common in both the statements, i.e., division. Thus, $\otimes$ is subtraction. Sufficient.

There is no need to calculate the value of $3 \otimes 5$ since we know which arithmetic operation the symbol $\otimes$ represents.

For the sake of completeness:

$3 \otimes 5 = 3 \div 5 = 0.6$

The correct answer is option (c).

4. (b) We know that $a^2 - 4a = 0$. we have to determine whether $\frac{a}{b} = 0$.

$\Rightarrow a(a - 4) = 0$

$\Rightarrow a = 0$ or 4

Let's see each statement one by one.

Considering statement I alone:

$b^2 - 16 = 0$

$\Rightarrow b = \pm 4$

Case 1: If $a = 0$ then $\frac{a}{b} = \frac{0}{+4} = 0$

Case 2: If $a = 4$ then $\frac{a}{b} = \frac{4}{+4} = \pm 1$

No unique answer. Insufficient.

Hence, eliminate (a)/(d).

Moreover, since $\frac{a}{b} = 0$ is possible only when $a = 0$ and statement I doesn't give us any information about a.

Considering statement II alone:

$a^2 + 8a = 0$

$\Rightarrow a(a + 8) = 0$

$\Rightarrow a = 0$ or -8

Since from the question ($a^2 - 4a = 0$), we know that $a = 0$ or 4, we can conclude that $a = 0$. We can ignore the values 4 and -8.

At $a = 0$, we have $\frac{a}{b} = \frac{0}{b} = 0$. There is no need to know the value of b.

Unique answer. Sufficient.

Hence, eliminate (c)/(e).

The correct answer is option (b).

5. (e) **Considering statement I alone:**

$|x| = |y| = 2 \Rightarrow y = 2$ or -2. No unique value of y. This statement is insufficient.

Hence, eliminate (a)/(d).

Considering statement II alone:

$y^2 = 4 \Rightarrow y = 2$ or -2. No unique value of y. This statement is insufficient.

Hence, eliminate (b).

Considering statement I and II together:

Since y = 2 or –2 is common in both statements, both statements together are insufficient.

The correct answer is option (e).

6. (a) **Considering statement I alone:**

We can simplify the given equation as shown below:

$$z = \frac{1}{\sqrt{x}} - \left(\frac{y^2 + 2xy}{\sqrt{x}} + \frac{x^2}{\sqrt{x}}\right)\left(\frac{1}{(x+y)^2}\right)$$

$$z = \frac{1}{\sqrt{x}} - \left(\frac{y^2 + 2xy + x^2}{\sqrt{x}}\right)\left(\frac{1}{(x+y)^2}\right)$$

$$z = \frac{1}{\sqrt{x}} - \left(\frac{(x+y)^2}{\sqrt{x}}\right)\left(\frac{1}{(x+y)^2}\right)$$

$$z = \frac{1}{\sqrt{x}} - \left(\frac{(x+y)^2}{(x+y)^2\sqrt{x}}\right)$$

$$z = \frac{1}{\sqrt{x}} - \frac{1}{\sqrt{x}}$$

$$z = 0$$

Thus, $xyz = xy \times 0 = 0$. Sufficient

Hence, eliminate (b)/(c)/(e).

Considering statement II alone:

$x = z$ gives us no idea whether any of x, y or z is 0. Hence, we cannot conclude that xyz is 0.

Thus, this statement is not sufficient.

Hence, eliminate (d).

The correct answer is option (a).

7. (c) Given: Each employee gets an equal number of food coupons and an equal number of gas coupons

Do not assume: Number of food coupons = Number of gas coupons

To find out: The number of employees in the office

Considering statement I alone:

We know that each employee received an equal number of food coupons and an equal number of gas coupons.

Thus, the GCD of the number of food coupons and the number of gas coupons is the largest possible number of employees in the office.

- $200 = 2^3 \times 5^2$
- $60 = 2^2 \times 3 \times 5$

The terms common to both = $2^2 \times 5 = 20$

⇒ GCD of 200 and 60 = 20

Thus, the number of employees could be any number that is a factor of 20 (1, 2, 4, 5, 10, and 20):

- **Case #1**

  Number of employees = 20 (Maximum possible number of employees):

  Number of food coupons received by each employee $= \frac{200}{20} = 10$

  Number of gas coupons received by each employee $= \frac{60}{20} = 3$

- **Case #2**

  Number of employees = 10

  Number of food coupons received by each employee $= \frac{200}{10} = 20$

Number of gas coupons received by each employee $= \frac{60}{10} = 6$

- **Case #3**

Number of employees = 5

Number of food coupons received by each employee $= \frac{200}{5} = 40$

Number of gas coupons received by each employee $= \frac{60}{5} = 12$

There are three more possible cases for the number of employees, i.e., 4 or 2 or 1. Of these, the possibility of the number of employees being 1 can be rejected because the question mentions employees, in plural.

So, the number of employees can be 20, 10, 5, 4, or 2.

Thus, there is no unique answer. – Insufficient

Hence, eliminate (a)/(d).

Considering statement II alone :

There is no information about the number of food coupons and the number of gas coupons distributed. – Insufficient

Hence, eliminate (b).

Considering statements I and II together :

Combining both statements, we find that since the total number of coupons received by each employee is less than 20, the only possible case is case #1, where:

- The number of employees = 20.
- Total number of coupons received by each employee = 10 + 3 =13 < 20.

The total number of coupons received by each employee in other cases is more than 20.

Therefore, we've arrived at a unique answer, the number of employees is 20. Sufficient

The correct answer is option (c).

8. (e) We are given that a carpenter gave an equal number of nuts, an equal number of bolts, and an equal number of screws to each apprentice.

You must NOT assume:

(Number of nuts per apprentice)

= (Numbers of bolts per apprentice)

= (Number of screws per apprentice)

The number of nuts that an apprentice—say apprentice A—got may be different from the number of bolts and from the number of screws he got; however, each apprentice got as many nuts as apprentice A got (and likewise, as many bolts and screws as apprentice A got).

Let the total number of apprentices in the class be n, and each apprentice got x number of nuts, y number of bolts, and z number of screws.

We have to find out n.

Considering statement I alone :

Each apprentice got nuts, bolts, and screws in the ratio 3 : 4 : 5, respectively.

Thus, we have,

$x : y : z = 3 : 4 : 5$

$\Rightarrow x = 3k, y = 4k, z = 5k$, where k is a constant of proportionality.

However, we have no information on n. -- Insufficient!

Hence, eliminate (a)/(d).

Considering statement II alone :

We know that the carpenter distributed a total of 27 nuts, 36 bolts, and 45 screws.

Thus, nx = 27, ny = 36, nz = 45

We have no information about x, y, z.

Hence, we cannot determine the value of n. – Insufficient

Hence, eliminate (b).

Considering statements I and II together :

Substituting the values of x, or y, or z from statement I in the information from statement II, we have

nx = 27 = 3k

$n = \frac{9}{k}$

Since k is unknown, we cannot determine n. The valid values of k can be 1, 3, and 9, which render the values of n = 9, 3, and 1. (k cannot be greater than 9 because n, the number of apprentices, cannot be a fraction. And k cannot be a fraction, for example, $\frac{1}{2}$ etc., because we know that x = 3k, y = 4k, & z = 5k. Since x, y, & z denote the number of items, they cannot be fractions. For x, y, & z to have integer values, k must be an integer.)

No unique value of n. – Insufficient

The correct answer is option (e).

9. (e) We have to find out whether Andrew ate a greater number of toffees than Ricky.

Say Andrew ate x number of toffees, while Ricky ate y number of toffees.

So, we need to determine whether x > y.

Considering statement I alone :

We are given that thrice the number of toffees that Andrew ate was greater than 6 less than thrice the number of toffees that Ricky ate.

$\Rightarrow 3x > 3y - 6$

$\Rightarrow x > y - 2$

We cannot determine whether x > y, since x is greater than a quantity y, which itself is decreased by 2.

Let us take an example.

Say y = 12, thus $x > 12 - 2 \Rightarrow x > 10$.

If x = 11, then $x \not> y$ and the answer is No.

However, if x = 13, then x > y and the answer is Yes. No unique answer. Insufficient!

Hence, eliminate (a)/(d).

Considering statement II alone :

We are given that twice the number of toffees that Andrew ate in the test was greater than 4 less than twice the number of toffees that Ricky ate.

$\Rightarrow 2x > 2y - 4$

$\Rightarrow x > y - 2$

This inequality is the same that we had in statement I. Insufficient!

Hence, eliminate (b).

Considering statements I and II together :

Since each statement gives the same inequality, even combining both statements cannot answer the question! Insufficient.

The correct answer is option (e).

10. (a) The average speed of any travel can be calculated by Total Distance Traveled divided by Total Time Taken.

Let's see each statement one by one.

Considering statement I alone :

The statement gives us the speed of his return journey.

Say the distance between the home and the office is 900 kms. The assumed value of the distance, 900 km, is a convenient number so that it is divisible by both 50 and 45. You can assume any value, say 450 (LCM of 50 and 45). The time taken between home and the office

would be $\frac{900}{50}$ = 18 hrs. Similarly, the time taken between office to home would be $\frac{900}{45}$ = 20 hrs. So, the total time taken for the entire journey would be equal to 18 + 20 = 38 hrs.

Now we know the total time distance traveled = 900 + 900 = 1,800 kms, so the average speed would be $\frac{1,800}{38}$ kmph.

There is no need to calculate the value, as in a DS question, if we are sure of the unique answer, there is no need to get the value.

Statement I is sufficient.

Hence, eliminate (b)/(c)/(e).

Considering statement II alone :

From this information, we know that the distance is 50 kms. However, the statement does not tell us anything about the speed of the return journey and is, therefore, insufficient.

Hence, eliminate (d).

The correct answer is option (a).

11. (e) Since z = xy, we are supposed to find out the value xy.

Considering statement I alone :

x(y – x) = 0 implies that either x = 0 or x = y. If x = 0, we have z = xy = 0 × y = 0: the answer is no; however, if x = y = 1, z = xy = 1: the answer is yes. No unique answer. statement I alone is not sufficient.

Hence, eliminate (a)/(d).

Considering statement II alone :

Same as statement I, we have y(x – y) = 0 implies that either y = 0 or x = y. If y = 0, we have z = xy = x × 0 = 0: the answer is no; however, if = y = 1, z = xy = 1: the answer is yes. No unique answer. statement II alone is not sufficient.

Hence, eliminate (b).

Considering statements I and II together :

Even after combining both statements, we cannot get the unique value of xy.

The correct answer is option (e).

12. (c) Remember that

- Even × Even = Even;
- Even × Odd = Even;
- Odd × Odd = Odd

The products of any two integers would be Odd, only if both the integers are Odd. Similarly, the products of any two integers would be Even if even only one of the two integers is Even; we need not look for the nature of the other integer.

Considering statement I alone :

Statement I states that ab is an odd integer. It means that a and b are odd integers. But we don't have any information regarding c; if c = odd, abc = odd; however, if c = even, abc = even. No unique answer, therefore, statement I alone is insufficient.

Hence, eliminate (a)/(d).

Considering statement II alone :

Statement I states that bc is an odd integer. It means that b and c are odd integers. But we don't have any information regarding a; if a = odd, abc = odd; however, if a = even, abc = even. No unique answer, therefore, statement I alone is insufficient.

Hence, eliminate (b).

Considering statements I and II together :

Both statements together confirm that a, b and c are odd integers, therefore abc must be an odd integer.

The correct answer is option (c).

Chapter 8

Problem Solving Practice Set 1

Multiple Choice Questions

1. If the standard deviation of Set Y = {1, 3, 5, 7} is S, which of the following set(s) have a standard deviation less than S.

   U = {12, 14, 16, 18}

   V = {– 6, – 8, –10, –12}

   W = {2, 4, 6, 8}

   (*a*) Set U

   (*b*) Set V

   (*c*) Set W

   (*d*) Set U and V

   (*e*) None of the sets

2. Which of the following could be the range of a set consisting of odd integers?

   (*a*) –10

   (*b*) 3

   (*c*) 5

   (*d*) 6

   (*e*) 49

3. Two friends, Jack and Jill start walking towards each other's home at a speed of 3 kilometers per hour. The distance between their homes is 36 kilometers. Simultaneously, Francis leaves Jack's home on his bicycle at a speed of 6 kilometers per hour towards Jill's home. When Francis meets Jill, he turns around and starts moving towards Jack. When he meets Jack, he turns around and starts moving towards Jill. He keeps repeating this until Jack and Jill meet and stop at the same point where they all meet. What is the total distance (in kilometers) covered by Francis?

   (*a*) 25

   (*b*) 36

   (*c*) 37.5

   (*d*) 45

   (*e*) 60

4. David and Jack have 12 oranges, each. They toss a coin 6 times; for every head, David receives an orange from Jack, and for every tail, Jack receives an orange from David. After the coin was tossed 6 times, what is the probability that David has more than 12, but fewer than 18 oranges?

   (*a*) $\frac{5}{6}$

   (*b*) $\frac{21}{64}$

   (*c*) $\frac{21}{32}$

   (*d*) $\frac{1}{64}$

   (*e*) $\frac{15}{64}$

5. If $xy = 16$, what is the value of $y(x + x^2 y)$?

   (*a*) 180

   (*b*) 200

   (*c*) 224

   (*d*) 272

   (*e*) Cannot be determined

6. The terms of a series $x_1, x_2, x_3 \ldots x_n$ has the following relation with one other.

   $x_n = x_{n-1} + s$; where s is a constant.

   What is the 5th term of the series if the 4th term is 16 and 7th term is 31 ?

   (*a*) 5

   (*b*) 18

   (*c*) 21

   (*d*) 25

   (*e*) 30

7. How many real roots does the equation $\sqrt{(a^2+3)+(a^2+4)}=2$ have?

(*a*) None

(*b*) One

(*c*) Two

(*d*) Three

(*e*) Four

8. Which of the following expressions has the largest value?

(*a*) 9^{50}

(*b*) 8^{100}

(*c*) 3^{300}

(*d*) 7^{200}

(*e*) 5^{250}

9. How many 2-digit numbers are divisible by 5 ?

(*a*) 10

(*b*) 17

(*c*) 18

(*d*) 19

(*e*) 20

10. If a, b and c are positive integers, how many ordered sets (a, b, c) are possible such that a + b + c = 7?

(*a*) 6

(*b*) 8

(*c*) 9

(*d*) 10

(*e*) 15

11. If $4m + n = 20$, and $|n| \leq 20$

How many ordered pairs (m, n) exist if m and n are integers?

(*a*) Ten

(*b*) Eleven

(*c*) Twenty

(*d*) Twenty-one

(*e*) Forty-one

12. If $x^3 + y^6 > 0$, which of the following must be true?

(*a*) $x > 0$

(*b*) $y > 0$

(*c*) $x^3 < 0$

(*e*) $(x + y^2)$ and $(x^2 + y^4 - xy^2)$ are either both positive or both negative

(*e*) 60

13. What percent of 19 is 30 percent of 361 ?

(*a*) 19

(*b*) 30

(*c*) 57

(*d*) 551

(*e*) 570

14. How many distinct quadrilaterals can be formed using seven distinct points in a plane if no three of them are in a straight line?

(*a*) 5

(*b*) 10

(*c*) 31

(*d*) 35

(*e*) 60

Answer Key

1. (*e*)
2. (*d*)
3. (*b*)
4. (*b*)
5. (*d*)
6. (*c*)
7. (*a*)
8. (*e*)
9. (*c*)
10. (*e*)
11. (*b*)
12. (*d*)
13. (*e*)
14. (*d*)

Answer Explanations

1. **(e)** Adding or subtracting a constant term from all the elements of a set does not change its standard deviation (SD). We see that all the sets: U, V, and W can be obtained by adding or subtracting a constant from the given Set Y, hence all sets have equal standard deviations (SD). The correct answer is option (e).

Remember, if you multiply each element of a set by a constant 'n', then the changed SD would be n times the SD. Say, each element of the set is multiplied by 4, then the revised SD would be 4 times the SD = 4 × SD.

Similarly, if you divide each element of the set by a constant n, then the revised SD would be $\frac{1}{n}$ times the SD.

The correct answer is option (e).

2. **(d)** Range of a set = Maximum value – Minimum value = a nonnegative value

Since the set consists of only odd integers, the range is even as both the maximum, and the minimum values are odd. Odd – odd = even. Therefore, in the case of odd integers, the range should be even.

Since range cannot be negative, option (a), –10 is ruled out.

The only nonnegative even number among the given options is 6. Hence, Option (c) can be the range of a given set.

The correct answer is option (d).

3. **b)** **Concept of Relative speed**

1. If two objects are moving in the same direction at a speed of x and y kilometers per hour, their relative speed is |x – y| kilometers per hour.

2. If two objects are moving in the opposite direction at a speed of x and y kilometers per hour, their relative speed is (x + y) kilometers per hour.

Thus, the relative speed of Jack and Jill = 3 + 3 = 6 kilometers per hour since they are moving in opposite directions.

We know that both Jack and Jill met after covering 36 kilometers, hence the total time spent = $\frac{36}{3+3}$ = 6 hours. Thus, Francis has been riding his bicycle for 6 hours at a speed of 6 kilometers per hour. Therefore, Francis rode his bicycle for 6 × 6 = 36 kilometers

The correct answer is option (b).

4. **(b)** Since David must have more than 12 oranges, it means that he must win at least 4 times out of 6 times; also, since he must have less than 18 oranges, it means he must not win all 6 times. So, he should win 4 or 5 times.

Since he can win 4 or 5 times in any order, the number of ways, he can win

$$= {}^6_4C + {}^6_5C = {}^6_2C + {}^6_1C$$

$$= \left(\frac{6 \times 5}{1 \times 2}\right) + 6 = 15 + 6 = 21$$

ways; ${}^n_rC = {}^n_{n-r}C$

Probability of winning 4 times and losing 2 times in a particular trial

$$= \left(\frac{1}{2}\right)^5 \times \frac{1}{2} = \left(\frac{1}{2}\right)^6 = \frac{1}{64}$$

probability of getting 'Head' = probability of getting 'Tail' = $\frac{1}{2}$.

Similarly, the probability of winning 5 times and losing once in a particular trial

$$= \left(\frac{1}{2}\right)^5 \times \frac{1}{2} = \left(\frac{1}{2}\right)^6 = \frac{1}{64}$$

Since the probability of winning 4 times or 5 times in a particular trial is equal, the probability of winning 4 times or 5 times

$$= 21 \times \left(\frac{1}{64}\right) = \frac{21}{64}$$

The correct answer is option (b).

5. (d) Simplify the expression $y(x + x^2 y)$.

$$= xy + x^2 y^2$$
$$= xy + (xy)^2$$
$$= 16 + 16^2$$
$$= 16 + 256$$
$$= 272$$

The correct answer is option (d).

6. (c) We know that $x_4 = 16$ and $x_7 = 31$.

$x_5 = x_4 + s = 16 + s$

$x_6 = x_5 + s$

and $x_7 = x_6 + s = x_5 + 2s = x_4 + 3s = 16 + 3s$

Hence, $16 + 3s = 31 \Rightarrow s = 5$.

Thus, $x_5 = 16 + s = 21$

7. (a) For the equation

$$\sqrt{(a^2+3)} + \sqrt{(a^2+4)} = 2,$$

the minimum value for $a^2 = 0$ since a^2 is always non-negative.

Substituting a = 0 in the equation $\sqrt{(a^2+3)} + \sqrt{(a^2+4)} = 2$, we get

$$\sqrt{(0+3)} + \sqrt{(0+4)} = \sqrt{(3)} + \sqrt{(4)}$$

$$= \sqrt{(3)} + 2$$

$$= 1.73 + 2 = 3.73,$$

the minimum value of the left-hand side, which, however is greater than the right-hand side: 2; however, this is not possible. Hence, no real value can satisfy the equation. Thus, the equation does not have any real roots.

The correct answer is option (a).

8. (e) We convert each number given in the options to a form such that they have the same exponent. The number with the largest base would be the largest.

(*a*) 9^{50} = Let's keep the exponent 50.

(*b*) $8^{100} = (8^2)^{50} = 64^{50}$

(*c*) $3^{300} = (3^6)v = 729^{50}$

(*d*) $7^{200} = (7^4)^{50} = 2{,}401^{50}$

(e) $5^{250} = (5^5)^{50} = 3{,}125^{50}$

So, we can very easily see that the base of the number 5^{250}: 3,125 is the largest, so 5^{250} is the largest among all.

The correct answer is option (e).

9. (c) The first 2-digit number divisible by 5 is 10.

The last 2-digit number divisible by 5 is 95.

Difference between the two numbers = 85.

The multiples of 5 will come at an interval of 5.

Hence, number of such intervals

$$= \frac{85}{5} = 17.$$

Since the number of intervals is 17, the number of such terms will be one more, i.e., $17 + 1 = 18$.

Alternate approach :

The first 2-digit number divisible by 5 is 10

$= 5 \times 2$

The last 2-digit number divisible by 5 is 95

$= 5 \times 19$

Thus, the number of such multiples is 5×2, $5 \times 3 \ldots 5 \times 18, 5 \times 19$, i.e., counting from 2 to 19 = $(19 - 2) + 1 = 18$ numbers

The correct answer is option (c).

10. (e) The number 7 can be represented as a sum of three positive integers in 4 ways:

(*a*) $1 + 1 + 5 = 7$. It will have $\frac{3!}{2!} = 3$ ordered pairs.

(*b*) $1 + 2 + 4 = 7$. It will have $3! = 6$ ordered pairs.

(*c*) $1 + 3 + 3 = 7$. It will have $\frac{3!}{2!} = 3$ ordered pairs.

(*d*) $2 + 2 + 3 = 7$. It will have $\frac{3!}{2!} = 3$ ordered pairs.

Hence, the total number of possible sets

$= 3 + 6 + 3 + 3 = 15.$

The correct answer is option (e).

11. (b) Given that $|n| \leq 20$, the integer values of n range from –20 to +20. inclusive.

The set of n is (– 20, – 19, – 18, ...0, 1, 2, ...18, 19, 20). We see that there are 41 integer values.

Now let us see how many integer values m can have.

$$4m + n = 20$$

$$\Rightarrow \quad m = \frac{20 - n}{4};$$

$$\Rightarrow \quad m = 5 - \frac{n}{4}$$

We see that for m to be an integer, $\frac{n}{4}$ must be an integer; this follows that n must be a multiple of 4.

Out of the 41 possible values of n above, only 11 values are multiple of '4;' note 0 is also multiple of 4. The set of eligible values of n is (– 20, – 16, – 12, – 8, – 4, 0, 4, 8, 12, 16, 20).

Therefore, there are only 11 ordered (m, n) pairs possible.

The correct answer is option (b).

12. (d) We are given that $x^3 + y^6 > 0$.

Let us discuss each option one by one. Since this is a Must Be True question, our focus will be to find exceptions to the conditions presented in these options. If we can find even one case in which the condition presented in an option is not fulfilled and yet the given expression is positive, then we can reject that option.

(*a*) **$x > 0$:**

If x is positive, then indeed $(x^3 + y^6)$ is positive.

Let's evaluate whether it is possible that if x is NOT positive, but $(x^3 + y^6)$ is positive?

x is NOT positive when either $x = 0$ or $x < 0$.

Case 1 : If $x = 0$, then $x^3 + y^6 = 0 + y^6 = y^6$ is still a positive number. Thus, x need not be positive.

Case 2 : $x < 0$. Say $x = -1$, $y^6 = 8$. For these values, the given expression will be positive.

Thus, we see that for the given expression to be positive, x need not be positive.

(*b*) **$y > 0$:**

Since the exponent of y is 6, an even integer, y^6 must be positive, irrespective of the nature of y: positive or negative. We need not be interested in the nature of y.

For example : $2^6 = (-2)^6 = 32$.

(*c*) **$x3 < 0$:**

Even $x^3 = 0$ or a positive value of x can make $x^3 + y^6 > 0$; this is possible if y^6 is a large value.

Thus, x^3 need not be negative.

(*d*) $(x + y^2)$ and $(x^2 + y^4 - xy^2)$ are either both positive or both negative:

This one is little tricky. At first glance, the expressions $(x + y^2)$ and $(x^2 + y^4 - xy^2)$ seem unrelated to the given expression $(x^3 + y^6)$. However, the phrase 'either both positive or both negative' gives us an idea.

What happens when two numbers are either both positive, or both negative? Then, there product is positive.

So, from this phrase, we get the idea to multiply $(x + y^2)$ and $(x^2 + y^4 - xy^2)$.

$(x + y^2)(x^2 + y^4 - xy^2)$

$= x^3 + xy^4 - x^2y^2 + x^2y^2 + y^6 - xy^4$

$= x^3 + y^6$

Thus, we see that the product of $(x + y^2)$ and $(x^2 + y^4 - xy^2)$ is $(x^3 + y^6)$.

Since we are given that $(x^3 + y^6) > 0$, it follows that $(x + y^2)$ and $(x^2 + y^4 - xy^2)$ must have the same sign: they must either both be positive, or both be negative.

So, option (d) does indeed represent a Must Be True condition.

(*e*) **$|x3| < y6$:**

We can easily think of a case where $|x^3|$ is greater than y^6 and still the given expression is positive.

Say x = 2 and y = 1, then $|2^3| > 1^6$ and $(x^3 + y^6) > 0$. Thus, for $(x^3 + y^6)$ to be positive, it is not necessary that $|x^3| < y^6$.

The correct answer is option (d).

13. (e) Say x% of 19 is 30% of 361.

x% of 19 = 30% of 361

$x\% \times 19 = 30\% \times 361$

$$\frac{x}{100} \times 19 = \frac{30}{100} \times 19^2$$

x = 570; after cancellation

The correct answer is option (e).

14. (d) Instinctively, one is tempted to count the number of possible quadrilaterals out of 7 distinct points. However, this method is time-consuming and error prone. A better way of solving this problem would be to use Combination.

Here, we just need to identify the number of ways of selecting 4 points out of 7 (which is the same as combinations). Using the Combination formula, this can be written as

$$^7C_4 = \left[\frac{7.6.5.4}{1.2.3.4}\right] = 35.$$

Alternatively, memorize the following important properties.

On a plane, if there are n points, of those, no three points are collinear, then

1. The number of straight lines that can be formed by joining them is $^{n}C_{2}$.
2. The number of triangles that can be formed by joining them is $^{n}C_{3}$.
3. The number of polygons with k sides that can be formed by joining them is $^{n}C_{k}$.

On a plane, if there are n points, of those, m points are collinear, then

1. The number of straight lines that can be formed by joining them is $^{n}C_{2} - {^{m}C_{2}} + 1$.
2. The number of triangles that can be formed by joining them is $^{n}C_{3} - {^{m}C_{3}}$.
3. The number of polygons with k sides that can be formed by joining them is $^{n}C_{k} - {^{m}C_{k}}$.

The correct answer is option (d).

Chapter 9

Problem Solving Practice Set 2

Multiple Choice Questions

1. If $(4x - 1)^2 = 81$, which of the following is one of the possible values of x ?

(a) –2

(b) – 1

(c) 1

(d) $\frac{3}{2}$

(e) $\frac{7}{2}$

2. David bought 18 items from a hardware store. The items were of three kinds: nails, hooks, and screws. These items cost 1 cent, 2 cents, and 3 cents per piece, respectively. The total sum that David paid was 32 cents. If David bought twice as many nails as screws, how many hooks did he buy?

(a) 4

(b) 6

(c) 7

(d) 8

(e) 10

3. If the function f(z) is a sum of unique prime factors of z, what is the value of f(f(250))?

(a) 3

(b) 6

(c) 8

(d) 7

(e) 17

4. David took 10 examinations. If range of his scores is zero, what is the standard deviation of his scores?

(a) 0

(b) 0.1

(c) 1

(d) 10

(e) Cannot be determined

5. If X is more than Y by 110%, and Z is less than X by 10%, then Z is what percent of Y ?

(a) 53

(b) 89

(c) 189

(d) 210

(e) 213

6. If A : B : C : D = 2 : 3 : 4 : 5, what is the value of $\frac{A}{B}:\frac{B}{C}:\frac{C}{D}:\frac{D}{A}$?

(a) 5:4:3:2

(b) 40:45:48:150

(c) 20:15:48:120

(d) 3:4:5:2

(e) 8:5:12:10

7. A 20-liter blend of orange juice and water contains juice and water in a ratio of 3 : 2. Ten liters of the blend are removed and refilled with orange juice, and this process is repeated once more. At the end of the two removals and refills, what is the ratio of orange juice to water in the resulting blend?

(a) 2:1

(b) 3:2

(c) 4:1

(d) 5:1

(e) 9:1

8. The probability that a tourist at the market buys a pack of chips is $\frac{1}{4}$. If four tourists come to the market today, what is the probability that exactly two of them will buy packs of chips?

(*a*) $\frac{1}{16}$

(*b*) $\frac{9}{256}$

(*c*) $\frac{27}{128}$

(*d*) $\frac{3}{128}$

(*e*) $\frac{1}{128}$

9. What is the units digit in $2^{18} \times 7^{12} \times 5^{56}$?

(*a*) 0

(*b*) 1

(*c*) 4

(*d*) 5

(*e*) 7

10. Which of the following numbers is a perfect number? A perfect number is one whose sum of factors other than itself is equal to the number itself.

(*a*) 12

(*b*) 2

(*c*) 28

(*d*) 48

(*e*) 60

11. If $\sqrt{12+(a-3)^2} = 4$, what could be the value of a ?

(*a*) −5

(*b*) 1

(*c*) 3

(*d*) 9

(*e*) 19

12. If a right triangle has base a and height b such that $a^2 + b^2 - 4a = 0$; where a and b are integers, which of the following is the set of three corresponding sides of the triangle?

(*a*) (2, 3, 4)

(*b*) (2, 2, 2.82)

(*c*) (3, 3, 4.2)

(*d*) (2, 2.75, 3)

(*e*) (2, 4, 5)

13. Two guards are patrolling a 5-kilometer long road, starting to walk simultaneously, at their respective constant speeds, from the opposite ends of the road. When they reach either end, they turn over. The speeds of the guards are 3 kilometers/hour and 2 kilometers/hour. What total distance, in kilometers, would they have covered when they crossed each other the second time?

(*a*) 6

(*b*) 10

(*c*) 12

(*d*) 15

(*e*) 30

Answer Key

1. (*a*)
2. (*b*)
3. (*d*)
4. (*a*)
5. (*c*)
6. (*b*)
7. (*e*)
8. (*c*)
9. (*a*)
10. (*c*)
11. (*b*)
12. (*b*)
13. (*d*)

Answer Explanations

1. (a) We have $(4x-1)^2 = 81$

$(4x-1)^2 = 9^2$

$(4x-1)^2 = \pm 9$

$4x - 1 = 9$ or -9

$\Rightarrow x = \frac{5}{2}$ or -2

The correct answer is option (a).

2. (b) Let S be the number of screws, N the number of nails, and H the number of hooks bought by David.

We have $N + 2H + 3S = 32$

$\Rightarrow$ Given $N + H + S = 18$;

and $N = 2S$

$\Rightarrow$ $3S + H = 18$ ---(1)

$\Rightarrow$ $N + 2H + 3S = 32$

$\Rightarrow$ $5S + 2H = 32$ ---(2)

Solving the above two equations, we get H = 6.

The correct answer is option (b).

3. (d) The factors of 250 $= 2 \times 5 \times 5 \times 5$

Unique prime factors of 250 = 2 and 5

Sum of unique prime factors = 2 + 5 = 7 = f(250);

Note that the sum of the unique prime factors of 250 is not 2 + 5 + 5 + 5 = 17, since 2 and 5 are the only two unique prime factors.

Thus, f(f(250)) = f(7)

Similarly, unique prime factors of 7 = 7

Sum of unique prime factors = 7

$\Rightarrow$ f(f(250)) = f(7) = 7

The correct answer is option (d).

4. (a) Range refers to the difference between the maximum and minimum values of a set.

Range = Maximum value – Minimum value

The range of David's scores is zero implies that the scores in all the examinations are same–no question of maximum or minimum values.

Standard deviation of a data set comes into picture when there is a variation in data set or there is at least one different value from the others. However, in this case, the standard deviation must be zero for there is no variation at all.

The correct answer is option (a).

5. (c) Say Y = 100, then X = (100 + 110)% of 100

= 210% of 100 = 210

Note that X is not more by 10%; it is more by 110%.

Given: Z = X – 10% of X = 100% of X – 10% of X = 90% of 210 = 189; Z = 189.

Say Z is p% of Y, then $p = \frac{Z}{Y} \times 100\%$

$\Rightarrow p = \frac{189}{100} \times 100\% - 189\%$

The correct answer is option (c).

6. (b) We are given that A : B : C : D = 2 : 3 : 4 : 5, and we have to find out the value of

$$\frac{A}{B}:\frac{B}{C}:\frac{C}{D}:\frac{D}{A}$$

Assume that A = 2x; B = 3x; C = 4x; and D = 5x and plug-in these values in

$$\frac{A}{B}:\frac{B}{A}:\frac{C}{D}:\frac{D}{A}$$

$$\text{So, } \frac{A}{B}:\frac{B}{C}:\frac{C}{D}:\frac{D}{A} = \frac{2x}{3x}:\frac{3x}{4x}:\frac{4x}{5x}:\frac{5x}{2x}$$

$$= \frac{2}{3}:\frac{3}{4}:\frac{4}{5}:\frac{5}{2}.$$

Taking LCM of the denominators (3, 4, 5 and 2) = 60

$$\text{Thus, } \frac{A}{B}:\frac{B}{C}:\frac{C}{D}:\frac{D}{A} = \frac{2}{3}:\frac{3}{4}:\frac{4}{5}:\frac{5}{2}$$

$$= \frac{40}{60}:\frac{45}{60}:\frac{64}{60}:\frac{150}{60}$$

$$= 40 : 45 : 48 : 150.$$

The correct answer is option (b).

7. (e) As per the given ratio of 3 : 2, the initial 20-liter blend contains 12 liters of juice and 8 liters of water. Each time, 10 liters of mixture are removed and refilled with juice, or we can say that each time, 50% of the mixture is removed and refilled with only juice. This means that each time, 50% of the juice and 50% of the water are removed.

After the first removal of 10 liters, the remaining mixture will have 6 liters of juice (12 – 50% of 12) and 4 liters of water (8 – 50% of 8). Adding 10 liters of juice will give us a mixture of 16 liters of juice (6 +10) and 4 liters of water.

Removing 10 liters of this mixture gives us a mixture with 8 liters of juice (16 – 50% of 16) and 2 liters of water (4 – 50% of 4). Adding 10 liters of juice will give us a mixture of 18 liters of juice (8+10) and 2 liters of water. The ratio of juice to water is 18 : 2 or 9 : 1.

The correct answer is option (e).

8. (c) Probability of a tourist to buy a pack of chips $\frac{1}{4}$;

Hence, the probability of a tourist not to buy a pack of chips $= 1-\frac{1}{4}=\frac{3}{4}$;

Probability of two tourists to buy chips and two tourists not to buy chips

$$-\left(\frac{1}{4}\times\frac{1}{4}\right)\times\left(\frac{3}{4}\times\frac{3}{4}\right)=\frac{9}{256};$$

Number of ways two tourists, who buy chips, can be chosen is ${}^{4}_{2}C$ ways

Hence, the probability that exactly two tourists will buy a pack of chips

$$= {}^{4}_{2}C\times\left(\frac{9}{256}\right)$$

$$=\left(\frac{4.3}{1.2}\right)\times\left(\frac{9}{256}\right)=\frac{27}{128}$$

The correct answer is option (c).

9. (a) Product of one 2 and one 5 makes 10. We see that 2 × 5 = 10 appears in the expression $2^{18} \times 7^{12} \times 5^{56}$, hence the units digit of $2^{18} \times 7^{12} \times {}^{556}$ will be 0. The other number 7 doesn't make a difference at the units' place.

The correct answer is option (a).

10. (c) The best approach is to apply the trial-and-error method.

Option (a) : 12 ⇒ Factors, other than $12 = \{1, 2, 3, 4, 6\}$,

Sum of factors $= 1 + 2 + 3 + 4 + 6 = 16 \neq 12$ (Number).

This is not the answer.

Option (b) : 20 ⇒ Factors, other than $20 = \{1, 2, 4, 5, 10\}$,

Sum of factors $= 1 + 2 + 4 + 5 + 10 = 22 \neq 20$ (Number).

This is not the answer.

Option (c) : 28 ⇒ Factors, other than $28 = \{1, 2, 4, 7, 14\}$,

Sum of factors $= 1 + 2 + 4 + 7 + 14 = 28 = 28$ (Number).

This is the answer.

For your ready reference, a few perfect numbers are 6, 28, & 496.

The correct answer is option (c).

11. (b) We are given that $\sqrt{12 + (a-3)^2} = 4$.

Taking the square of both sides, we get, $12 + (a - 3)^2 = 16$

$\Rightarrow \quad (a - 3)^2 = 16 - 12 = 4$

$\Rightarrow \quad (a - 3)^2 = 4;$

Taking the square root of both sides, we get either

$a - 3 = \pm 2 \Rightarrow a = 5$ or 1.

Note this is a "could be" type of a question, not a must be true type of question.

The correct answer is option (b).

12. (b) We know that for a right triangle, the base and the height are always smaller than the hypotenuse. So a and b must be smaller than the third side.

So, if the two smaller integer values satisfy the equation $a^2 + b^2 - 4a = 0$, and the third side matches the third side or hypotenuse, we will consider it the correct answer.

Now have a look at $a^2 + b^2 - 4a = 0$ or $4a - a^2 = b^2$. Since b is a positive integer, and looking at the options, we find that the minimum value of any side is 2, thus, the minimum value of b^2 is 2^2 or 4; thus, $4a - a^2$ ³ 4. Rearranging the inequality, we get

$a^2 - 4a + 4 \leq 0$

$\Rightarrow \quad (a - 2)^2\ 0$

$\Rightarrow \quad 1 \leq a \leq 2$

since a is a positive integer; thus, a can be 1 or 2.

Quickly scanning the options, we find option (a), (c) and (d) cannot be the answers as for options (a) and (e), the popular Pythagorean triplet (2, 3, 5) is refuted; for option D, the two smaller sides are not positive integers (one of them is 2.75), and for option (c), both the smaller sides cannot be 3 since at least one side must be less than 3 $(a \leq 2)$.

Plugging the values from option B satisfy the equation. Let's check.

$a^2 + b^2 - 4a = 0$

$\Rightarrow \quad 2^2 + 2^2 - 4 \times 2 = 0$

$\Rightarrow \quad 0 = 0.$

Let's calculate the hypotenuse.

$c^2 = a^2 + b^2$

$$\Rightarrow \quad c^2 = 2^2 + 2^2 = 8$$

$$\Rightarrow \quad c = 2\sqrt{2}$$

$$= 2 \times 1.414 = 2.82.$$

The correct answer is option (b).

13. (d) Guard A with the speed of 3 kilometers/hr and guard B with the speed of 2 kilometers/hr will cross each other for the first time when A covered 3 kilometers and B covered 2 kilometers, i.e., in 1 hour.

Then guard A will move onwards, cover 2 kilometers, turn over, and cover 1 kilometer in the next 1 hour, while guard B will cover 2 kilometers at the same time.

Now in the 3rd hour, guard A will cover 3 kilometers, and B will cover 1 kilometer, turn over, and cover 1 more kilometer. The guard B will cross guard A at the end of the 3rd hour.

So, the total distance covered by both

= distance covered by guard A + distance covered by guard B

$$= (3 + 2 + 1 + 3) + (2 + 2 + 1 + 1)$$

$$= 15 \text{ kilometers}$$

The correct answer is option (d).

Verbal Aptitude

Chapter 1

Critical Reasoning
Strengthen Weaken Flaw

Introduction

Critical Reasoning (CR) questions in the GMAT assesses the candidate's ability to evaluate arguments, analyze information, and make sound judgments. The section consists of around 12 to 14 multiple-choice questions that test the candidate's ability to think critically and logically in real-world situations. It requires them to apply logic, reason, and analysis to complex problems and situations, and make informed decisions based on the information presented.

The questions in the Critical Reasoning (CR) section are presented as short passages that contain an argument or an assertion. The candidate is required to read the passage carefully and identify the premises, assumptions, and conclusions of the argument. They must then evaluate the logic of the argument and determine whether it is valid or flawed.

Therefore, it is essential for candidates to develop their critical-reasoning skills and practice their ability to analyze and evaluate arguments effectively.

In the section, several types of questions can be asked to test a candidate's ability to analyze and evaluate arguments. Each question type requires a unique approach and strategy to answer correctly, so it is important for test-takers to familiarize themselves with the nuances of each question type. By understanding the different types of questions in GMAT CR, test-takers can prepare themselves better for the exam and increase their chances of success. Let's have a look at the different types of CR questions in GMAT.

Types of Questions

1. Strengthening an argument
2. Weakening an argument/Flawed argument
3. Assumption
4. Inference
5. Paradox
6. Bold Face
7. Evaluate
8. Complete

Critical reasoning questions in the GMAT are typically structured as a brief argument or a set of statements (argument), followed by a question or statement (Q Stem) that requires test-takers to analyze and draw logical conclusions from the given information. Refer to the diagram below to familiarize yourself with a typical GMAT question.

Question Structure

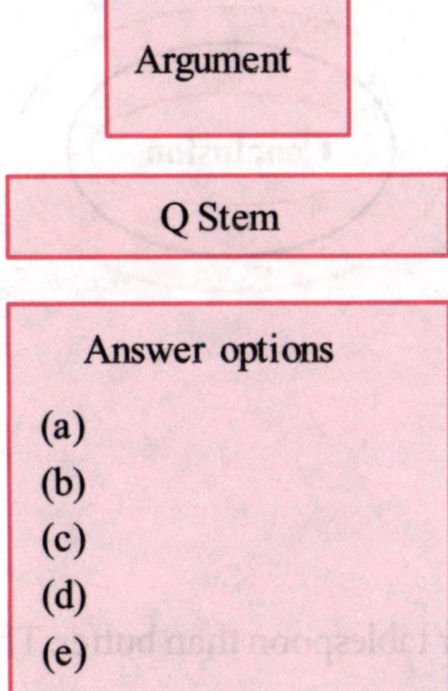

Decoding an Argument

In the context of critical reasoning, an argument is a set of statements that seeks to support or prove a conclusion. The statements that support the conclusion are called premises, and the conclusion is the statement that the argument seeks to establish. Understanding what constitutes an argument and how to evaluate it is essential for success on the test.

To evaluate an argument, it is important to understand the structure and components of an argument. The first step is to identify the conclusion of the argument. The conclusion is typically the most critical statement in the argument, and it is the statement that the premises seek to support.

Once the conclusion is identified, it is essential to identify the premises that support it. The premises are statements that provide evidence or reasons for accepting the conclusion. It is important to assess whether the premises are relevant, reliable, and sufficient to support the conclusion.

Below diagram shows the components of a typical argument.

Premise is the evidence offered by the author in order to support the conclusion.

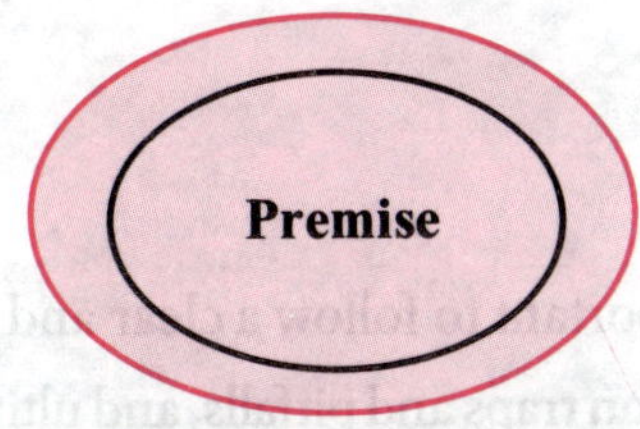

Conclusion is the main point or the central idea of the author.

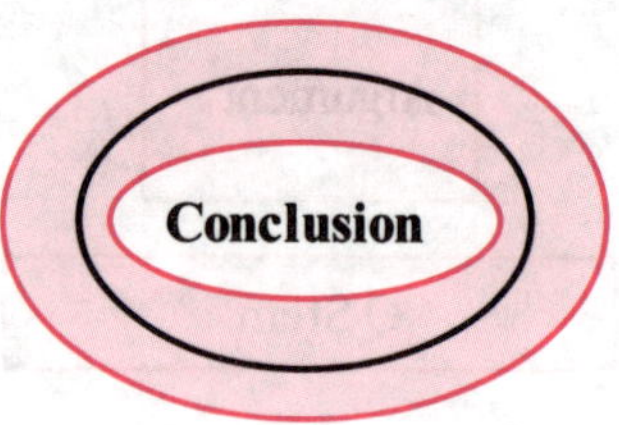

Example

Cream contains 50 percent fewer calories per tablespoon than butter. Therefore, a sandwich with cream is healthier than a sandwich with butter on it.

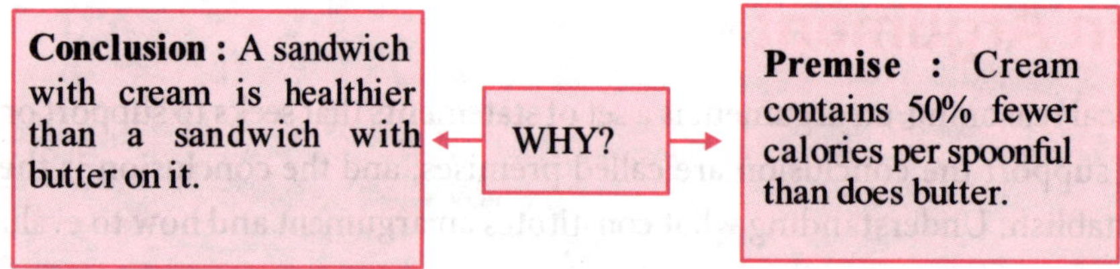

The example above brings us to our strategy to deconstruct any critical reasoning argument. It is a simple four-step approach that allows us to break, even the most complex arguments in no time. The diagram below explains the three steps of the approach.

Strategy

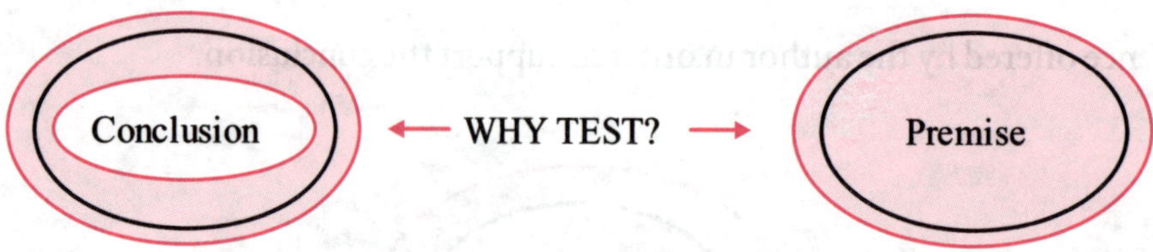

To effectively tackle CR questions, it is important to follow a clear and structured approach. A clear strategy can help test-takers stay organized, avoid common traps and pitfalls, and ultimately improve their chances of answering correctly. By adopting a structured approach, test-takers can confidently navigate even the most-challenging GMAT CR questions.

Basic Approach

- **Step 1 :** Identify the question type–Read question stem.
- **Step 2 :** Read the argument and identify the type of argument
- **Step 3 :** Think of what the right answer will do
- **Step 4 :** Eliminate : Extreme choice

  Out of scope choices

Now, we are going to learn Strengthen, Weaken, and Flaw types of questions. These questions require test-takers to evaluate the argument's logic and identify its strengths, weaknesses, and flaws. Strengthen questions ask test-takers to identify a statement that strengthens the argument's conclusion, while weaken questions ask for the statement that weakens the conclusion. On the other hand, flaw questions require identifying the logical fallacies or errors in reasoning in the argument. Excelling in these types of questions can significantly improve a test-taker's overall GMAT score. So, let's dive deeper.

Strengthen Questions

Strengthen questions ask the candidate to identify the answer option that would make the argument stronger. These questions typically present an argument and then provide a possible answer that supports the argument. The candidate must evaluate the answer options and determine which one makes the argument more convincing.

To approach strengthen questions, it is essential to identify the premises and assumptions in the argument. Once the candidate has a clear understanding of the argument's structure, he/she can evaluate the answer options and determine which one would most effectively support the argument.

Strengthen

- In order to strengthen the argument, we should support the conclusion of the argument.
- Make sure that you don't challenge the fact or evidence given in the argument.

Weaken Questions

Weaken questions ask the candidate to identify the answer option that would make the argument weaker. These questions typically present an argument and then provide a possible answer that undermines the argument. The candidate must evaluate the answer options and determine whether it weakens the argument.

To approach weaken questions, it is essential to identify the premises and assumptions in the argument. Once the candidate has a clear understanding of the argument's structure, he/she can evaluate the answer options and determine which one would most effectively undermine the argument

Weaken

- In order to weaken the argument we should challenge the conclusion of the argument.
- Make sure that you don't challenge the fact or evidence given in the argument.

Flaw Questions

Flaw questions ask the candidate to identify the answer choice that describes a flaw in the argument. These questions typically present an argument and then provide a possible answer that identifies a mistake in the argument's reasoning. The candidate must evaluate the answer choice and determine whether it accurately describes the flaw in the argument.

To approach flaw questions, it is essential to identify the premises and assumptions in the argument. Once the candidate has a clear understanding of the argument's structure, they can evaluate the answer choices and determine which one most accurately describes the flaw in the argument.

Considering how the approach is more or less similar, can consider giving examples to illustrate the strategy.

Multiple Choice Questions

1. **Beverage company representative :** The plastic rings that hold six-packs of beverage cans together, pose a threat to wild animals, which often become entangled in the discarded rings; and suffocate, as a result. Following our lead, all beverage companies will soon use only those rings made of a new plastic that disintegrates after only three days' exposure to sunlight. Once we all complete the switchover from the old to the new plastic rings, therefore, the threat of suffocation that plastic rings pose to wild animals will be eliminated.

   Which one of the following, if true, most seriously weakens the representative's argument?

   (*a*) The switchover to the new plastic rings will take at least two more years to complete.

   (*b*) After the beverage companies have switched over to the new plastic rings, a substantial number of the old plastic rings will persist in most aquatic and woodland environments.

   (*c*) The new plastic rings are slightly less expensive than the old rings.

   (*d*) The new plastic rings rarely disintegrate during shipping of beverage six-packs because most trucks that transport canned beverages protect their cargo from sunlight.

   (*e*) The new plastic rings disintegrate into substances that are harmful to aquatic animals when ingested in substantial quantities by them.

2. Opponents of laws that require automobile drivers and passengers to wear seat belts argue that in a free society people have the right to take risks, as long as they do not harm others, as a result of taking the risks. Thus, they conclude that it should be each person's decision whether or not to wear a seatbelt.

   Which of the following, if true, most seriously weakens the conclusion drawn above?

   (*a*) Many new cars are built with seat belts that automatically fasten when someone sits in the front seat.

   (*b*) Automobile insurance rates for all automobile owners are higher because of the need to pay for the increased injuries or deaths of people not wearing seat belts.

   (*c*) Passengers in airplanes are required to wear seat belts during takeoffs and landings.

   (*d*) The rate of automobile fatalities in states that do not have mandatory seat belt laws is greater than the rate of fatalities in states that do have such laws.

   (*e*) In automobile accidents, a greater number of passengers who do not wear seat belts are injured than are passengers who do wear seat belts.

3. During the Second World War, about 375,000 civilians died in the United States, and about 408,000 members of the United States armed forces died overseas. On the basis of those figures, it can be concluded that it was not more dangerous to be overseas in the armed forces during the Second World War than it was to stay at home as a civilian.

   Which of the following would reveal most clearly the absurdity of the conclusion drawn above?

   (*a*) Counting deaths among members of the armed forces who served in the United States, in addition to deaths among members of the armed forces serving overseas.

   (*b*) Expressing the difference between the numbers of deaths among civilians and members of the armed forces as a percentage of the total number of deaths.

(*c*) Separating deaths caused by accidents during service in the armed forces from deaths caused by combat injuries.

(*d*) Comparing death rates per thousand members of each group, rather than comparing total number of deaths.

(*e*) Comparing deaths caused by accidents in the United States to deaths caused by combat in the armed forces.

4. Recently, in City X, developers have stopped buying land, contractors have found themselves going without work for longer periods, and banks have issued fewer mortgages. There must be fewer new residents moving to City X than there were previously.

Which of the following indicates a flaw in the reasoning above?

(*a*) This year, several housing blocks have gone on the market after being held up for months by legal redtape.

(*b*) The average size of a new home has increased significantly over the past several years.

(*c*) Re-sales of condominiums have increased over the past six months.

(*d*) The cost of materials, such as, lumber and cement has decreased over the past year.

(*e*) Sales of other big-ticket items, such as, automobiles and boats, have remained steady over the past year.

5. Companies that offer "employer-sponsored insurance" (ESI) pay a portion of employees' health care costs. In the manufacturing sector last year, companies that offered ESI had worker absentee rates 22% lower, on average, than those at companies that did not offer ESI.

If, on the basis of the evidence above, it is argued that ESI decreases worker absenteeism, which of the following, if true, would most seriously weaken that argument?

(*a*) Results similar to those cited for the manufacturing sector have been found in other sectors of the economy where ESI is offered.

(*b*) At companies that offer ESI, employees have access to preventative health care, such as, regular check-ups, routine laboratory tests, and nutrition counseling.

(*c*) Because initiating an ESI plan requires a lot of paperwork for the company, employees, and the insurance provider, doing so is complex and time consuming.

(*d*) Many firms in the manufacturing sector have improved workplace safety and decreased the occurrence of on-the-job injuries in the last five years; and most of these companies had introduced ESI at the same time.

(*e*) In manufacturing firms where ESI is offered, the average productivity is 2% higher than it is in those firms where workers are not covered by an ESI plan.

6. The United States government uses only a household's cash income before taxes to determine whether that household falls below the poverty line in a given year; capital gains, non-cash government benefits, and tax credits are not included. However, yearly cash income is not a fool-proof measure of a given household's disposable income. For example, retirees who live off of capital gains from an extensive portfolio could earn hundreds of thousands of dollars, yet be classified by the government as living in "poverty" because this income is not included in the calculation.

Which of the following, if true, validates the contention that the government's calculation methods must be altered in order to provide statistics that measure true poverty?

(*a*) For more than 99% of those classified as living in poverty, yearly cash income comprises the vast majority of each household's disposable income.

(*b*) While the government's calculation method indicated a 12.5% poverty rate in 2003, the same calculation method indicated anywhere from a 9% to a 16% poverty rate during the preceding decade.

(*c*) Most established research studies conducted by the private sector indicate that the number of people truly living in poverty in the U.S. is less than that indicated by the government's calculation method.

(*d*) Several prominent economists endorse an alternative calculation method, which incorporates all income, not just cash income, and adjusts for taxes paid and other core expenses.

(*e*) The government's calculation method also erroneously counts those who do not earn income in a given year but who have substantial assets to live on during that year.

7. Historically, the drug industry has promoted its products to physicians by educating them in their offices or at industry conferences. In the last 10 years, it has become much more commonplace for drug companies to advertise prescription drugs directly to consumers, via television advertising and other media. Some public health advocates have become concerned that patients, encouraged by advertising, might pursue the use of prescription drugs that could be inappropriate for the individual patient or situation. However, since physicians must prescribe these medications, there is no reason for such concern.

Which of the following pieces of information would be most helpful in addressing the concern articulated by the public health advocates?

(*a*) Certain over-the-counter medications are as effective for many common medical conditions as more powerful non-prescription medications.

(*b*) Prescription-medication television advertisements directed at the general public only appear on certain programs; and are not seen by many potential consumers.

(*c*) Physicians are also subject to prescription-drug advertisements that are directed toward consumers.

(*d*) Physicians are not susceptible to pressure from patients in determining appropriate courses of treatment, including prescription drugs.

(*e*) Prescription medicines have been proven to be safe and effective treatments for many patient conditions.

8. Studies in restaurants show that the tips left by customers who pay their bill tend to be larger, when the bill is presented with the server's name hand-written on the bill. Psychologists hypothesize that simply seeing a handwritten name makes many consumers feel more of a personal identification with the server, encouraging larger tips.

Which of the following, if true, most strongly supports the psychologists' interpretation of the studies?

(*a*) The effect noted in the studies applies to patrons paying with either credit card or cash.

(*b*) Nametags for servers have not been shown to have any effect on the size of the bill.

(*c*) Greeting card companies have found that charities, which send holiday cards with handwritten signatures are more likely to receive donations than those which send cards with printed signatures.

(*d*) The studies indicated much larger average tips if the customer ordered alcoholic beverages with his or her meal.

(*e*) Many of the restaurants in which the studies were conducted are located in tourist areas, where people are traveling for leisure activities.

9. **Analyst:** The pace of technological development brings a constant stream of new devices to the market, and many of them enjoy commercial success. But announcing a new technology too soon after the introduction of a successful device can backfire. Once consumers hear about the new device, they might stop buying the one currently on sale. So, if a company wishes to announce the upcoming sale of a new device, it should wait until purchases of the old device have begun to decline.

Which of the following, if true, would best support the analyst's main assertion?

(*a*) New technology often becomes less expensive after an initial surge in sales.

(*b*) Media outlets, such as television programs and magazines, often report on the planned introduction of new devices, while the sales of old devices are still strong.

(*c*) Many consumers are unable to determine whether new technology is superior to current technology.

(*d*) Surveys have shown that some consumers make only one or two technology purchases per year, whereas others make more frequent purchases.

(*e*) Consumers tend to be loyal to technology companies whose products they enjoy using.

10. More and more companies have begun to consume less energy by making themselves more efficient. Over time, these efforts could place the United States at the forefront of an emerging global market for cleaner technologies. Such efforts are also essential to tackling the two big energy-related issues of the age: global warming and the dependence on precarious supplies of oil. The federal government should encourage these efforts by providing the necessary incentives, whether as loans, direct grants, or targeted tax breaks.

Which of the following, if true, provides the most effective support for the argument?

(*a*) On an average, Canadian companies are more energy efficient than those in the United States.

(*b*) Experts believe that energy efficiency could lower the energy use of the United States to the level of 1995.

(*c*) In the past, government incentives have made advances in energy conservation feasible, especially in the auto industry.

(*d*) The dependence on foreign oil is a greater problem in the present than global warming.

(*e*) The market for cleaner technologies is currently relatively small because of the infrastructure requirements.

Answer Key

1. (*b*)
2. (*b*)
3. (*d*)
4. (*a*)
5. (*d*)
6. (*c*)
7. (*d*)
8. (*c*)
9. (*b*)
10. (*c*)

Answer Explanations

1. (b) The conclusion of this argument is the final sentence, which contains the conclusion indicator "therefore," and the conclusion contains a qualification that the threat of suffocation will be eliminated after the switchover is complete. The premises supporting this conclusion are that the new plastic rings will be used by all companies; and that the rings disintegrate after three days' exposure to sunlight.

Personalize this argument and ask yourself: are there any holes in this argument?

Yes, there are several. The most obvious is, "What if an animal becomes entangled in the new rings before they can disintegrate?" Answer option (a): This answer does not hurt the argument because the author qualified the conclusion to account for the date of the switchover, thereby inoculating against this avenue of attack. From a personalizing standpoint, imagine what would happen if you raised this issue to the beverage company representative. He or she would simply say, "Yes, that might be the case, but I noted in my conclusion that the program would be effective once the switchover is complete." This is an attractive answer because it raises a point that would be a difficult public-relations issue to address. Regardless, this does not hurt the argument given by the beverage company representative, and that is the task at hand.

Answer option (b): **This is the correct answer.** Most people select answer option (e), but as you will see, (e) is incorrect. This answer undermines the representative's conclusion by showing that even after the switchover is complete, the threat to animals from plastic rings will persist. Note the carefully-worded nature of the conclusion: the representative does not say the threat from new plastic rings will be eliminated, but rather the threat from plastic rings, which includes both old and new rings.

Answer option (c): This out-of-scope answer addresses an issue that is irrelevant to the representative's argument.

Answer option (d): While this is nice information from a customer-service standpoint (you do not want your six-pack of beer falling apart as you walk out of the store), this answer does not affect the conclusion because it does not address the threat of suffocation to animals.

Answer option (e): **The conclusion is about wild animals, whereas this choice mentions aquatic animals.** The conclusion is specifically **about suffocation,** and answer **option (e) does not address suffocation.**

This is the most commonly chosen answer. In this case, the answer preys upon test-takers who fail to heed the advice: "Read closely and know precisely what the author said. Do not generalize!" Many test-takers read the conclusion and think, "So when they start using these new rings, it will make things better for the animals." When these test-takers get to answer option (e), the answer looks extremely attractive because it indicates that the implementation of the new rings will also have a harmful effect. With this thinking in mind, many test-takers select answer option (e) thinking it undermines the conclusion; and they are certain they have nailed the question. However, the conclusion is specifically **about suffocation**, and answer **option (e) does not address suffocation.**

Instead, answer option (e) attacks a conclusion that is similar to, but different from, the actual conclusion. Remember, one of the rules for weakening arguments is to focus on the conclusion, and knowing the details of the conclusion is part of that focus.

2. **(b)** The principle that people are entitled to risk injury, provided they do not thereby harm others fails to justify the individual's right to decide not to wear seat belts if it can be shown, as (b) shows, that that decision does harm others. Therefore, (b) is the best answer. (a) suggests that the law might be irrelevant in some cases, but it does not address the issue of the law's legitimacy. (c) cites a requirement analogous to the one in hand, but its existence alone does not bear on the legitimacy of issue. The argument implicitly concedes that individuals take risks by not wearing seat belts; therefore, (d) and (e), which simply confirm this concession, do not weaken the conclusion.

3. **(d)** Concluding from the similar numbers of deaths in two groups that the relative danger of death was similar for both groups is absurd if, as here, one group was far smaller. (d) exposes this absurdity by pointing out the need to compare death rates of the two groups, which would reveal the higher death rate for the smaller group. Therefore, (d) is the best answer. Since the conclusion acknowledges the difference between the number of civilian & armed forces deaths, expressing this difference as a percentage, as suggested by (b), is beside the point. (a) is inappropriate because it simply adds a third group to the two being compared. Because cause of death is not at the issue, (c) and (e) are irrelevant.

4. **(a)** The conclusion of the argument is that "there must be fewer new residents moving to City X than there were previously." Why? Because of several observed factors (e.g., developers not buying land, contractors without work, banks issuing fewer mortgages) that the author assumes result from the fewer people trying to buy new homes. We are asked to find a flaw in the reasoning of this argument.

   (a) **Correct.** This suggests that there might be another reason for the decline in home construction: the supply of available housing has been increased through the release of many previously built homes. Therefore, the reasoning in the argument is flawed.

   (b) The size of homes, by itself, does not point to any flaw in the argument.

   (c) The argument centers on new homes, so re-sales of condominiums are not directly related.

   (d) If materials cost less, it seems more likely that any decrease in new home construction could be attributed to the state dcauses.

   (e) Sales of cars and boats are not related to construction of new homes.

5. **(d)** Last year, firms in the manufacturing sector that offered employees employer-sponsored insurance (ESI) plans found that their worker absentee rates were significantly lower than at firms that did not offer ESI. What could have caused the decrease? The argument is made that the existence of the ESI plan caused the decrease in worker absenteeism, but that conclusion would be weakened if another cause were identified.

   (a) Similar findings in other sectors of the economy strengthen, rather than weaken, the argument.

(*b*) If workers have access to preventative health care as a result of the ESI plan, they might be healthier and would miss fewer days of work due to illness. This point supports the argument.

(*c*) The difficulty of initiating an ESI plan is irrelevant to a conclusion about what happens after the plan is established.

(*d*) **Correct.** If there are fewer on-the-job injuries, then workers will miss fewer days of work. This is an alternative explanation for the decrease in absenteeism, and thus weakens the argument that the decrease in absenteeism must have been due to the availability of ESI.

(*e*) The higher productivity of workers covered by ESI plans is consistent with the fact that they miss fewer days of work. This statement does not weaken the argument.

6. (c) The conclusion of the argument is that the government's calculation methods must be altered in order to provide statistics that measure true poverty. To support this position, the author first explains how the government's method works; and then introduces a hypothetical example that would return a "false positive" - that is, a person who has a large income, yet is classified by the government as living in poverty. One example, however, is generally not enough to invalidate an entire method; no method is perfect and there are always a few results that are not consistent with the overall conclusion. In order to validate, or strengthen, the conclusion, we need to show that the government's method is fundamentally inferior to some alternative that would produce more valid results.

(*a*) This option weakens the argument by minimizing the importance of the author's evidence (the hypothetical retiree with capital gains). According to this option, the use of cash income to designate poverty levels is a very sound method because it provides valid results for more than 99% of those classified as living in poverty.

(*b*) This option shows that the government's method provided a wide range of results for the poverty rate over a certain period of time, but it is irrelevant to the argument at hand. It tells us nothing about whether the method provides relevant statistics in any given year.

(*c*) **Correct.** If this statement is true, then the government's calculation method seems to overstate the number of people living in poverty, while the various private-sector studies generally agree with each other that the number of people is lower. Thus, the methods used in the private sector are likely to be more valid than the government's method, lending credence to the author's contention that the government's method should change.

(*d*) Although this option provides an example of people who might agree with the conclusion (several prominent economists), it provides no evidence that the alternative method they endorse would provide more relevant statistics than the government's method.

(*e*) This option adds another hypothetical example of how the current method could include someone in the poverty count, who does not actually live in poverty. It does not, however, address whether there are other calculation methods that are more accurate than the government's method.

7. **(d)** The public health advocates are concerned that patients are subjected to advertisements about prescription drugs, and might use these drugs even though the drugs might not be clinically appropriate. It is argued that, because physicians must prescribe the drugs in question, patient pursuit of these prescription drugs is irrelevant. However, patients who pursue and request particular prescription drugs might be able to encourage or induce a physician to prescribe drugs that he or she might not have, in the absence of such encouragement.

(a) The clinical efficacy of certain over-the-counter medications does not address the public health advocates' concern regarding patient pursuit of inappropriate prescription drugs.

(b) The public health advocates' concern does not rely on every possible consumer to see the advertisements for prescription medications. It is enough that some consumers see the advertisements.

(c) This answer option states the obvious possibility that physicians might also see the advertisements for prescription drugs directed toward consumers. This is irrelevant to the concern expressed by the public health advocates.

(d) **Correct.** This answer option directly addresses the public health advocates' concern by establishing that physicians are not susceptible to patient pressure in prescribing inappropriate drugs. As a result, drugs will be prescribed according to the objective clinical judgment of the prescribing physician, mitigating the danger of inappropriate use.

(e) That certain prescription medications are safe and effective treatments for many conditions does not address the concern of inappropriate use expressed by the public health advocates. Prescription drugs can be safe and effective when used for certain conditions by various individuals; and still be subject to unhealthy use by other patients.

8. **(c)** This argument concerns a potential explanation for larger tips on the part of restaurant patrons. The explanation provided is that customers are more generous toward servers who leave their handwritten name on the bill due to a greater degree of personal identification with the server, which encourages larger tips. The correct answer will either support the fact that a handwritten name strengthens personal identification, or that personal identification encourages larger tips.

(a) The fact that the effect applies equally, regardless of the method of payment, is not relevant to the conclusion.

(b) The argument does not address the size of the bill; rather, it addresses the size of the tip. This option is irrelevant.

(c) **Correct.** This answer option provides further evidence that a handwritten name or signature generates a greater form of personalization and emotional connection among recipients, leading to more donations.

(d) The impact of alcoholic beverages on tipping behavior is irrelevant.

(e) The location of the restaurants and leisure pursuits of the patrons are irrelevant to the argument.

9. **(b)** The conclusion is that a company should wait until purchases of an old device have begun to decline before announcing a new device. The basis for this claim is that consumers stop buying the old device. We are asked to strengthen the argument.

(*a*) The typical drop in the price of new technology does not influence whether a company should wait until sales of an old technology begin to decline before introducing a new one.

(*b*) **Correct.** This option states that media outlets, such as, television and magazines often report on the planned introduction of new devices while sales of old devices are still strong. The argument requires that consumers "hear about the new device"; stories in the media provide a means for consumers to do so.

(*c*) If many consumers are unable to determine the superiority of new technology, then they might be less swayed to wait for a new, recently announced, device than otherwise. As a result, this claim may be seen to weaken the analyst's assertion.

(*d*) The number of technology purchases per year does not directly relate to this argument. The argument is about waiting until the consumer demand declines before announcing a new technology. However frequently consumers typically purchase technology, some will be ready to buy the old device when news of the upcoming device gets out — and according to the argument, this news will cause some of those consumers to wait.

(*e*) The passage makes no mention of whether the technologies belong to the same company or different companies.

10. **(c)** The argument claims that federal incentives should be provided to encourage energy efficiency. The argument also notes that companies are already working in this directions and that this trend will ease the environmental and energy pressures that currently trouble the world. Supporting this argument could involve providing evidence of possible success for these efforts toward their goals.

(*a*) This option is an irrelevant comparison. That Canadian companies are more efficient has no bearing on efforts in the United States or the role of government incentives.

(*b*) This option does not strengthen the claim. Experts' claims are not the same as reality. Furthermore, the option does not state whether reducing energy use to the 1995 level is a significant decrease, nor does it provide any information to strengthen the link between government incentives and reduced energy use.

(*c*) **Correct.** This option provides evidence that government incentives are effective. Thus, it confirms an assumption that the conclusion is feasible.

(*d*) This option is an irrelevant distinction. It does not matter to the argument's conclusion if one of these issues is a greater problem than the other in the present.

(*e*) The passage asserts that the United States should be at the forefront of an emerging market for cleaner technologies; i.e., the market will be significant in the future. The size of the market at present is irrelevant to the argument.

Chapter 2

Critical Reasoning Assumption

Assumption questions are one of the most-common question types in the GMAT Critical Reasoning (CR) section. These questions test a candidate's ability to identify unstated assumptions that are essential to the argument's validity.

Assumptions are unstated premises that must be true for the conclusion to be valid. Therefore, identifying and evaluating assumptions is essential to determine the argument's strength and weaknesses.

Identifying Assumptions

To identify assumptions in an argument, it is essential to understand the structure and components of the argument. The first step is to identify the conclusion and premises of the argument. Once these are identified, it is important to assess whether the premises are relevant, reliable, and sufficient to support the conclusion.

If the premises are insufficient to support the conclusion, there must be an unstated assumption that must be true for the argument to be valid. For example, consider the following argument:

"All politicians are corrupt. Therefore, John must be corrupt."

The conclusion of the argument is that John is corrupt. The premise is that all politicians are corrupt. However, this premise is not sufficient to support the conclusion that John is corrupt. There must be an unstated assumption that must be true for the argument to be valid.

In this case, the unstated assumption is that **John is a politician**. Without this assumption, the argument falls apart. Therefore, the assumption that John is a politician is necessary for the argument's validity.

Key Takeaways

- Assumption of the argument is not stated in the argument but it is there in the logic of the argument. Assumption has to be true for the argument to hold.
- **Negation test :** When reversed, only the right answer option will reverse the argument, as well.
- Words that indicate Assumption questions are : **assumption, depends on, presupposition, and required**

Avoid answer options with **'should'** for assumption questions.

Negation Test

The negation test is a technique used in GMAT Critical Reasoning questions to evaluate the strength of an assumption. It works by negating the statement that is assumed to be true, and then seeing if the argument still holds up.

Here's how you can use the negation test to find the right answer option in GMAT Critical Reasoning Assumption questions:

Identify the conclusion and evidence in the argument.

Identify the assumption that connects the evidence to the conclusion. This is usually an unstated premise.

Negate the assumption by using "not" or "never"; and see if the argument falls apart.

If the argument falls apart, then the assumption is necessary for the argument to hold, and you have found the correct answer option.

For example, let's consider the following argument:

"Studies have shown that people who exercise regularly are healthier. Therefore, everyone should exercise regularly."

The assumption in this argument is that exercising regularly is necessary to be healthy. To use the negation test, we would negate this assumption, and say "Exercising regularly is not necessary to be healthy." If this statement is true, then the argument falls apart, and we would need to find an answer option that assumes that exercising regularly is necessary for good health.

Using the negation test can help you eliminate answer options that are not strong enough to be assumptions, and narrow down the correct answer option. It's important to remember that the negation test is not foolproof, and some arguments might have multiple assumptions. However, it is a useful tool to have in your arsenal when tackling GMAT Critical Reasoning questions.

The GMAT CR questions are designed to evaluate the test-taker's ability to analyze and evaluate arguments. To effectively tackle these questions, it is important to follow a clear and structured approach. Following a clear strategy can help test-takers stay organized, avoid common traps and pitfalls, and ultimately improve their chances of answering correctly. By adopting a structured approach, test-takers can confidently navigate even the most-challenging GMAT CR questions. Below is the basic approach that can make life easier, while answering GMAT Critical Reasoning questions.

Basic Approach

- **Step 1 :** Identify the question type – Read the question stem.
- **Step 2 :** Read the argument and identify the type of argument.
- **Step 3 :** Think of what the right answer will do.
- **Step 4 :** *Eliminate* : Extreme option

  Out of scope options

Multiple Choice Questions

1. The fitness watch Zingar only works with the phone that carries its original code, making it unusable with other phones. Thus, Zingar company claims that their watches would be less likely to be stolen as they are of no use to thieves. Which of the following is an assumption upon which the above argument depends?

(*a*) Severe publishment could also lead to a decline in the number of thefts.

(*b*) Zingar is not significantly more expensive than other watches in a similar category.

(*c*) Zingar's performance and other features are at par with other fitness watches.

(*d*) One of Zingar's main competitors is also planning to launch a watch with the same feature.

(*e*) Thieves are not likely to steal something that is not useful to them.

2. Although censured severely in his previous roles for his abrupt decision-making and poor attitude towards his subordinates, the new manager has gained immense respect from his current team. We know this to be true from the recent group meeting in which the HR Head admired the manager for his attitude.

Which of the following is an assumption upon which the above argument depends?

(*a*) The experience one gains over time helps in learning team management.

(*b*) Some of the reports pertaining to his abrupt decision-making could be fabricated.

(*c*) The view of the HR Head reflects the opinion of the manager's current team.

(*d*) The manager has brought a significant change in his attitude towards his subordinates.

(*e*) The HR Head deals with his subordinates in a respectful manner.

3. In 2002, eighty percent of the population of Desmania read print newspapers. However, only fifty percent of the population reads print newspapers today. The print industry must be suffering major losses, as the number of people has significantly declined over the years.

Which of the following is an assumption upon which the above argument depends?

(*a*) Some people find it increasingly difficult to read news in digital formats.

(*b*) The population of Desmania has remained constant over the years.

(*c*) The population of Desmania has significantly decreased over the years.

(*d*) The population of Desmania has increased over the years.

(*e*) The population of Desmania might have switched to digital newspapers.

4. A company has recently noticed a sharp increase in the cases of malfeasance amongst the management and senior-level managers. Thus, in order to reduce such cases of fraud and misconduct, the stakeholders are planning to appoint an independent body that will report and act upon any wrongdoings.

The stakeholder's plan depends on which of the following assumptions?

(*a*) Hiring an independent body is the only way to control cases of fraud and misconduct (*b*) The independent body would not become a part of the malfeasance.

(*c*) There are no reports of any wrongdoing among mid-level and entry-level managers.

(*d*) Despite the course of action decided by the body as punishment, some people would continue to be involved in misconduct and fraud.

(*e*) The losses incurred due to malfeasance led the company to take action against the management and senior-level managers.

5. Macromen has launched its new car model XMax this year. Anyone who is looking for maximum fuel efficiency should buy this model. The evidence for this claim comes from the fact that, XMax at low speeds, the performance of the XMax is at par with other models in the range. At high speeds, the car provides better fuel efficiency than other models.

Which of the following is an assumption upon which the above argument depends?

(*a*) XMax's fuel efficiency at normal speed is not significantly poor than other models.

(*b*) XMax provides above-average fuel efficiency at normal speed.

(*c*) Like other models, XMax is more fuel efficient than the cars before 20 years.

(*d*) Other car models launched by Macromen are not as popular as XMax.

(*e*) XMax is likely to be the most-preferred choice of buyers for its sleek design.

6. Considering the recent increase in the number of cases of shoplifting in its stores, Maxus Corp has created a permanent power lock for all the digital devices it produces. In case of shoplifting, a device can be permanently locked by the manufacturer making the device lose all its functionality. Thus, Maxus is planning to reduce the cases of shoplifting of expensive devices by adding the power lock function in all its devices.

Maxus's plan assumes that

(*a*) Maxus' competitors are not planning similar features in their devices.

(*b*) People are more likely to shoplift digital devices than any other items.

(*c*) People don't shoplift items that have no functionality.

(*d*) The power lock function will not cost more than a similar feature in a competitor's device.

(*e*) Shoplifting incidents cannot be reduced by imposing any fine or punishment.

7. Studies show that management plays a critical role in a company's profitability. Although there have been numerous complaints about the declining quality of products manufactured by company A, it's the poor management, not the quality of products, that is responsible for the recent losses incurred by company A. Evidence of this comes from the fact that company B, which also manufactures similar-quality products, has consistently increased its profits during the last year.

The above argument assumes that

(*a*) The quality of products manufactured by company A is not significantly different from that of company B.

(*b*) The quality of products manufactured by company A is not inferior to that of manufacturers, other than company B.

(*c*) The target customer base of company A is not significantly different from that of company B.

(*d*) The target customer base of company A could be significantly different from that of company B.

(*e*) Unlike company B, company A might be catering to the demands of the premium customer base that demands higher-quality products.

8. Usually, an activity that requires a fair amount of physical exertion is considered a sport. For this reason, many people argue that golf is not a sport. However, they fail to notice that golf requires skill and practice. Thus, we can conclude that Golf is a sport.

Which of the following, if true, is an assumption of the argument?

(*a*) If an activity does not require physical exertion, it cannot be considered a sport.

(*b*) Some players are more likely to focus on their physical fitness than their skills and practice.

(*c*) If an activity requires skill and practice, it can be considered a sport.

(*d*) Sportsmen should focus on their physical health, as well as, their skill and practice.

(*e*) If an activity is a sport, it must require physical exertion.

9. A company's X Ultra smartwatch model failed to gain any attention from the people last year; and generated huge losses for the company. However, the company's new model Magna smartwatch launched this year is not a failure as the company has already sold over 8000 watches in South Asia, while its competitors have managed to sell only 3000 watches.

Which of the following is assumed in the above argument?

(*a*) If a smartwatch does not sell well in the South Asian market, then it is a complete failure.

(*b*) If a smartwatch sells well in the South Asian market, then it cannot be considered a complete failure.

(*c*) The South Asian market generates a huge demand for watches.

(*d*) The Magna smartwatch is the only watch launched by company X this year.

(*e*) Company X's Magna model offers better design and functionality than the Ultra model.

10. Tourism company, Charism, offers two packages for tourists — an exotic beach package and rejuvenating mountain package. The company has noted that, over the last four years, the exotic package has consistently outsold the rejuvenating mountain package by a large margin, even though the offerings available in both are similar in quality, length of stay, and luxury. This has led the company to conclude that travelers prefer exotic beach destinations to rejuvenating mountain destinations.

Which of the following is assumed in the above argument?

(*a*) Most travelers choose their travel package based on the luxurious offerings than just the destination.

(*b*) Over the last four years, city tour packages have outsold both exotic beach and rejuvenating mountain packages.

(*c*) Exotic beaches are the first preference of people when picking a destination for a vacation.

(*d*) The exotic beach package is not significantly cheaper than the rejuvenating mountain package.

(*e*) The rejuvenating mountain package is significantly more expensive than the exotic beach package.

Answer Key

1. (e)	6. (c)
2. (c)	7. (c)
3. (b)	8. (c)
4. (b)	9. (b)
5. (a)	10. (d)

Answer Explanations

1. **(e)** The argument is based on a language shift. The premise tells us that the watch is "of no use" to thieves. Based on this, the author concludes that the Zingar watch is "less likely to be stolen. " This would be true if people only steal things that they find of any use.

   (a) As per the argument, thefts would likely reduce because thieves won't find the watches of any value.

   (b) Price comparison is out of scope.

   (c) Zingar's performance and other features are irrelevant to the argument.

   (d) This statement gives us information about Zingar's competitor. The argument does not require this.

   (e) **Correct.** This matches our prethinking.

2. **(c)** The argument is based on a sample. The author concludes that admiration from the HR Head shows the team's respect for the new manager. The conclusion will only hold if the HR Head is a true representative of the team.

   (a) This statement presents general information which is not required by the argument to be true.

   (b) The conclusion is not based on any past reports. Thus, this option is irrelevant.

   (c) **Correct.** As discussed, this is necessary for the argument to hold.

   (d) The argument is not based on any change in the manager's attitude. Thus, this option is incorrect.

   (e) The HR Head's conduct with his team is out of scope.

3. **(b)** The argument compares the percentage of the population of Desmania in 2002 and today. However, the argument concludes on the number of readers. Note: Unless we know the total population in both years, we cannot conclude on the absolute number. If the population has significantly increased over the years, 50% of the current population might be more than 90% of the population in 2002.

   (a) Difficult to read news in digital formats is out of scope.

   (b) **Correct.** This matches our prethinking. If the population remained constant, we can be sure that the number of people reading print newspapers has declined from 2002 to today.

   (c) While this statement might support the argument, the "significant decrease" is not required for the conclusion to be true.

   (d) This statement might weaken the argument. As discussed above, in such a case, 50% of the population today might be more than 90% of the population in 2002.

   (e) The reason behind the claimed decline in the number of readers is irrelevant.

4. (b) The argument states a problem, and suggests a solution. The argument assumes that the plan will help in resolving the problem of malfeasance.

(*a*) The argument does not assume that the suggested plan is the "only way" to solve the problem.

(*b*) **Correct.** If the body itself gets involved in malfeasance, the plan would fail. Thus, this statement is necessary for the conclusion to be true.

(*c*) This is out of scope, as the goal and plan are not focused on mid-level and entry-level managers.

(*d*) Continuation of fraud is not in favor of the plan. The assumption must support the plan to achieve the goal.

(*e*) The reason behind the decision to appoint the body is out of scope.

5. (a) The argument mentions that because XMax provides better fuel efficiency than other models at high speeds; and about as well as at low speed, XMax provides the best fuel efficiency. However, we do not know about XMax's fuel efficiency at normal speeds. We must assume that no other model provides better efficiency at normal speeds.

(*a*) **Correct.** This is required for the conclusion to be true.

(*b*) While this statement might support the argument, it is not necessary for the conclusion to hold.

(*c*) This statement highlights a similarity between XMax and other models. This does not support the argument.

(*d*) The popularity of other car models launched by Macromen is irrelevant to the argument.

(*e*) This statement gives no information about the fuel efficiency of XMax.

6. (c) Argument is based on language shift.

(*a*) Maxus's plan is not based on its competitors. Thus, this is not required by the argument.

(*b*) As the plan is only focused on digital devices, the stated comparison with other items is unnecessary for the conclusion to hold.

(*c*) **Correct.** This matches our prethinking. If people shoplift items that have no functionality, the cases of shoplifting may not reduce.

(*d*) This comparison is not required for the conclusion to be true.

(*e*) The argument is not focused on the effectiveness of other measures; and doesn't assume their ineffectiveness.

7. (c) The argument is based on an analogy between company A and company B. The argument assumes that what works in the case of company B, must work in the case of company A. However, if we were to know that the situation of these companies is not entirely similar, the argument might not work. Thus, we need to assume that both companies are comparable.

(*a*) This information is stated in the argument; and thus cannot qualify as an assumption. The assumption is unstated information.

(*b*) The argument is based on the comparison between company A and company B. Thus, the comparison with the product quality of other manufacturers is irrelevant to the argument.

(*c*) **Correct.** This option matches our prethinking.

(*d*) This option weakens the argument by highlighting a difference between company A and company B.

(*e*) Similar to (d), this option weakens the argument by highlighting a difference between company A and company B.

8. **(c)** The argument concludes golf is a sport. The author supports the conclusion by stating that gold requires skill and practice. As per the given logic, if an activity requires skill and practice, it can be considered a sport. This argument is based on the language shift. Be careful not to consider the conclusion of the people as the conclusion of the argument.

(*a*) This expresses the reasoning of the people, not of the author. Thus, this can't be the assumption of the argument.

(*b*) As the argument is based on skill and practice and not on fitness level, the given comparison is not relevant.

(*c*) **Correct.** This option matches our prethinking.

(*d*) This option states a piece of advice. ***Note:*** Advices are not assumptions.

(*e*) The author's argument is not based on physical exertion; and thus this is not necessary for the argument to hold.

9. **(b)** The argument is based on sales of a particular model launched by company X this year. The author concludes that the model cannot be considered a failure, as it has sold more pieces than any of its competitors. The argument is based on a language shift.

(*a*) This is not required by the argument. Even if the smartwatch doesn't sell in the South Asian market, it can sell elsewhere. In such a case, it cannot be considered a failure.

(*b*) **Correct.** This option must be true for the argument to hold.

(*c*) As this option talks about watches in general, and doesn't provide any necessary support to the conclusion, this is not the correct assumption.

(*d*) This information is not required by the argument. Even if the company has other models this year, the argument can still hold.

(*e*) The given comparison is irrelevant to the argument, as the conclusion is not based on any specific feature of the smartwatches.

10. (d) The argument concludes that just because exotic beach packages sell more than rejuvenating mountain packages, travelers prefer beach destinations to the mountain destination. We are told that the offering included in both packages are the same. But if we were to know that there are other differences because of which tourists prefer the exotic package, then the argument will get weakened.

(*a*) As both packages provide a similar offering, this option is not relevant.

(*b*) This argument is only concerned with exotic beach packages and rejuvenating mountain packages; city packages are out of scope.

(*c*) While this option supports the argument, this is not necessary for the argument to be true.

(*d*) **Correct.** This option must be true for the argument to hold. If the exotic beach package is significantly cheaper than the rejuvenating mountain package, the price could be the differentiating factor; and the reason behind choosing the exotic package.

(*e*) This option weakens the argument by introducing price as an alternative factor behind tourists choosing exotic beach packages over mountain packages.

Chapter 3

Critical Reasoning Paradox & Bold Face

Paradox

Paradox questions are a common type of question in the GMAT Critical Reasoning section. These questions present a situation, or a set of facts, that appears to be contradictory or paradoxical and require the candidate to resolve the contradiction.

Identifying a Paradox

A paradox is a statement or situation that contradicts itself or appears to be contradictory. To identify a paradox in an argument, it is essential to look for statements or situations that one not expected to co-exist.

For example, consider the following argument:

"Studies have shown that people who watch less television are more informed about current events. However, people who watch more television tend to be more knowledgeable about the world."

This argument presents a paradox because the first sentence suggests that watching less television leads to greater knowledge about current events, while the second sentence suggests that watching more television leads to greater knowledge about the world. These statements seem to contradict each other.

Resolving the Paradox

To resolve a paradox, it is essential to look for underlying assumptions that can explain the apparent contradiction. These assumptions can help reconcile the seemingly contradictory statements and provide a logical explanation.

- In these arguments two contradictory facts will be given; and the right answer option will explain how both facts can be true at the same time.
- Words that indicate paradox questions are: explain, resolve, justify, paradox, discrepancy, best accounts for, and reconcile.
- Do not pick one-sided answer options or the ones which make the conflict worse. Remember, we have to select the best-possible explanation among the given answer options. So, rely on elimination.

The GMAT Critical Reasoning (CR) questions are designed to evaluate the test-taker's ability to analyze and evaluate arguments. To effectively tackle these questions, it is important to follow a clear and structured approach. Following a clear strategy can help test-takers stay organized, avoid common traps and pitfalls, and ultimately improve their chances of answering correctly. By adopting a structured approach, test-takers can confidently navigate even the most-challenging GMAT CR questions. Below is the basic approach that can make life easier while answering GMAT critical reasoning questions.

Basic Approach

- **Step 1 :** Identify the question type– Read question stem.
- **Step 2 :** Read the argument and identify the type of argument
- **Step 3 :** Think of what the right answer will do.
- **Step 4 :** *Eliminate* : Extreme choice,

Bold Face

Bold face questions are a challenging type of question in the GMAT Critical Reasoning section. These questions require the candidate to identify the role of different parts of the argument and determine the overall structure of the argument.

Identifying the Bold Face Parts

A bold face question consists of an argument with two bold face parts, followed by a prompt that asks the candidate to identify the role of these parts in the argument. The candidate must identify the main conclusion, premise, and any intermediate steps in the argument; and determine how the bold face parts contribute to the overall structure of the argument.

For example, consider the following argument:

"**Companies should prioritize social responsibility over profits.** (I) While it may seem counterintuitive, companies that focus on social responsibility tend to perform better financially in the long run. (II) Additionally, companies that prioritize social responsibility are viewed more favorably by the public, leading to better brand reputation and customer loyalty."

In this argument, (I) presents a premise that supports the main conclusion that companies should prioritize social responsibility over profits, while (II) presents an additional reason to prioritize social responsibility.

To identify the role of the bold face parts, it is essential to understand the overall structure of the argument and how the different parts contribute to the argument's main point.

For example, in the above argument, (I) presents a premise that supports the main conclusion, while (II) presents an additional reason to prioritize social responsibility. Therefore, (I) is a premise that supports the conclusion, while (II) presents additional evidence to support the conclusion.

Here is a step-by-step strategy to tackle these types of questions:

Read the passage carefully: Before you can identify the role played by the bold-faced phrases, you need to understand the passage as a whole. Read the passage carefully, and identify the main conclusion and any supporting evidence presented.

Identify the bold-faced phrases: Once you have read the passage, identify the two bold-faced phrases or sentences that the question is asking you about.

Determine the role of each bold-faced phrase: To answer the question, you need to determine the role played by each bold-faced phrase. The GMAT uses specific terminology to describe the different roles that bold-faced phrases can play in an argument. Here are some key terms to know:

Conclusion : The main point that the argument is trying to prove.

Premise : A piece of evidence used to support the conclusion.

Assumption : An unstated premise that must be true for the argument to be valid.

Counter-premise : A piece of evidence that contradicts a premise or conclusion.

Explanation : A statement that clarifies why something is the case.

Hypothesis : A proposed explanation for a phenomenon.

Evaluate the answer options : Once you have determined the role played by each bold-faced phrase, evaluate the answer options to identify the one that accurately describes the role played by both the bold-faced phrases.

Verify your answer : After you have selected an answer option, read the passage again to verify that your answer accurately describes the role played by both the bold-faced phrases.

In summary, to tackle bold face questions in GMAT CR, you need to carefully read the passage, identify the bold-faced phrases, determine their roles, evaluate the answer options, and verify your answer. Knowing the specific terminology used to describe the different roles played by bold-faced phrases can also be helpful in cracking these questions.

Multiple Choice Questions

Paradox

1. When Bob's Bistro opened in the town of Montrose last year, the proprietors of Andrew's Eatery, the only other restaurant in town, feared that their business would suffer. Surprisingly though, in the past year, the average number of meals per day served at Andrew's Eatery has actually increased significantly.

   Which of the following, if true, provides the best explanation for this occurrence?

   (*a*) The meals at Andrew's Eatery are substantially lower in price than those offered at Bob's Bistro.

   (*b*) Bob's Bistro is closed on Sundays, and so, for Sunday brunch, residents of Montrose would either go to Andrew's Eatery or venture to a neighboring town.

   (*c*) The profit per meal is higher, on an average, at Bob's Bistro than it is at Andrew's Eatery.

   (*d*) Bob's Bistro attracts a large number of patrons that had never dined in Montrose before, and on many days Bob's Bistro attracts more customers than it can seat.

   (*e*) Andrew's Eatery serves considerably more meals on weekends than it does on weekdays, which is not the case at Bob's Bistro.

2. On an average, residents of City X devote a greater percentage of their yearly incomes to housing costs than do residents of City Y, though the costs of insurance and fuel generally are exorbitant in both the commuter-heavy cities. Yet, in Wealth Magazine's annual list of the country's least-affordable cities, City Y is deemed less affordable than City X.

   Which of the following, if true, best explains the contrast described above?

   (*a*) A greater percentage of residents of City Y sends their children to private schools than is the case in City X.

   (*b*) Unlike City Y, City X has an efficient and inexpensive public transportation system.

   (*c*) The average price of a new house is higher in City X than in City Y.

   (*d*) A number of high-priced restaurants and boutiques have recently opened in City Y.

   (*e*) Several large businesses have recently relocated from City Y to City X.

3. Certain oil companies have been called poor corporate citizens because they have opposed government action to limit global warming by undermining scientific research that characterizes the issue as severe. However, these same oil companies have also invested millions of dollars in scientific research to address the long-term effects of climate change.

   Which of the following best explains the apparent discrepancy in the situation described above?

   (*a*) The oil companies only recently began investing in scientific research to address climate-change issues.

   (*b*) The research dollars invested by the oil companies are specifically earmarked for developing practical technologies that might be used to combat global warming.

   (*c*) The government action opposed by the oil companies would negatively impact their profits.

(*d*) The scientific research that characterizes global warming as a severe problem has not been definitively proven.

(*e*) The oil companies don't believe that any scientific research related to climate change will ultimately serve their interests.

4. Country X contains many rivers that flow down from its high mountains. These rivers have been dammed to harness the hydroelectric power that can be derived from this resource. More than enough power is generated from these dams to meet the country's energy needs. Yet, citizens of Country X often experience power shortages or even outages.

Which of the following, if true, best explains the situation described above?

(*a*) The flow of the rivers is heavier in spring than at other times of the year.

(*b*) Citizens of Country X rely heavily on electronic appliances in their homes.

(*c*) Country X has not invested in alternative sources of energy.

(*d*) Most of the electricity generated in Country X is sold to other countries.

(*e*) Some of the most-powerful rivers in Country X one yet to be dammed.

5. As a result of consumers' increased awareness of the health risks associated with heavy consumption of red meat, the meat of the ostrich has become increasingly popular as a low-fat, low-cholesterol alternative to beef. Accordingly, the number of ostrich farms in the United States has nearly quadrupled since 1980, flooding markets with ostrich products. However, the price-per-pound of ostrich meat, adjusted for inflation, has not decreased at all over the past several years.

Which of the following, if true, would best explain the steady price-per-pound of ostrich meat?

(*a*) The demand for ostrich products has outpaced the supply.

(*b*) Ostriches are especially difficult to breed in captivity.

(*c*) Other types of meat, such as pork and poultry, have decreased in price over the past several years.

(*d*) Purveyors of beef have not attempted to counter beef's poor public image.

(*e*) The number of supermarkets that carry ostrich meat has increased steadily since 1980.

Bold Face

6. Musical composers have generally made their most-significant contributions to the musical canon before they reached the age of thirty. It is commonly believed that **this is the case because aging brings about a loss of cognitive ability and creative capacity.** However, a study has pointed out that a disproportionately large number of those composers, who have made their most-significant contributions to the canon after the age of thirty, became musicians at an older age than is generally the case. Since, **by the age of thirty, many composers have been engaged as musicians for a decade or more,** these findings suggest that the real reason musicians over thirty rarely make significant contributions to the musical canon is not that they have aged but rather that they have spent too much time as musicians.

In the argument above, the two portions in bold face play which of the following roles?

(*a*) The first is an explanation that is challenged by the argument; the second is a finding used to support that explanation.

(*b*) The first is an explanation that the argument opposes; the second is an objection raised against the alternative explanation advocated by the argument.

(*c*) The first is a claim advanced in support of a position; the second is a finding that clarifies that position.

(*d*) The first is an explanation advocated by the argument; the second is a finding used to challenge that explanation.

(*e*) The first is an explanation that the argument challenges; the second is a finding on which that challenge is based.

7. The city government should invest surplus funds in improving the city's transportation network. **Most of the network was put in place at a time when the city was much smaller, in both area and population.** The subway system is outdated and understaffed. The buses rarely run on schedule; and their routes are inconvenient. **If the city does not make changes soon to the network, it will see many of its prized industries relocate to more convenient cities, and, as a result, the city's financial health will be jeopardized.**

In the argument above, the two portions in bold face play which of the following roles?

(*a*) The first is an explanation of a current state of affairs; the second is a prediction based on that state of affairs.

(*b*) The first is a statement of fact in opposition to the author's conclusion; the second is that conclusion.

(*c*) The first emphasizes an existing problem; the second offers a proposal to solve that problem.

(d) The first is information the author suggests has been overlooked in the situation at hand; the second describes that situation.

(*e*) The first is a justification of an impending problem; the second describes the consequences of that problem.

8. **Chief Economist :** Usually, **the release of economic data about higher-than expected growth in the Gross Domestic Product (GDP) results in an increase in stock prices.** However, this quarter, the release of data about strong GDP growth is most likely to result in a decrease – rather than an increase – in stock prices. **Robust GDP growth will lead to higher interest rates, increasing the attractiveness of bonds, and causing a shift of capital from equity to debt securities.**

In the above argument, the statements in bold face play which of the following roles?

(*a*) The first acknowledges a consideration against the main conclusion of the chief economist; the second is that conclusion.

(*b*) The first is a pattern of cause and effect that the chief economist predicts will not hold in the case at issue; the second offers a consideration in support of that prediction.

(*c*) The first is a generalization that the chief economist accepts as true; the second is a consequence that follows from that generalization.

(*d*) The first is evidence that the chief economist provides in support of a certain prediction; the second is that prediction.

(*e*) The first is a pattern of cause and effect that the chief economist predicts will be repeated in the case at issue; the second acknowledges a circumstance in which that pattern would not hold.

9. **Political Analyst :** After the Soviet Union collapsed, some hoped that freedom would encourage Russians to multiply, but as a result of dislocation and insecurity, the Russian population continues to dwindle at the rate of 700,000 a year. The government proposes to address the problem with a wide range of financial incentives, along with investments in improved health care, road safety, and the like. These are positive measures, but **they have been tried before, to little avail.** A better plan to reverse the population decline is to improve the country's governance in both the public and the private spheres. **If a greater part of the population participated in important decisions, and shared in the country's wealth, then larger families would result.** In addition, if corruption and greed among the elite were curbed, public health would improve; and the average life expectancy would increase.

The two bold faced statements serve what function in the argument above?

(*a*) The first is the main point of the analyst's argument; the second is a premise that supports the first.

(*b*) The first is a premise that undermines an alternative to the analyst's proposal; the second is a premise that supports the analyst's main claim.

(*c*) The first is a premise that contradicts the main point made by the analyst; the second is the main point of the argument.

(*d*) The first is a premise that supports a proposal; the second is that proposal.

(*e*) The first is a conclusion that the argument endorses; the second is a premise that opposes that conclusion.

10. United Energy recently invested in a series of large windmills, which are able to produce renewable energy with minimal negative effect to the environment. The company has not drilled oil wells in the same area, even though **greater revenues and profits could be generated from oil wells.** Because any drilling would disrupt the native habitat of certain marine species in the area, some environmentalists assert that, by foregoing this drilling, **United Energy has established that it places environmental impact over financial returns.** However, United Energy could be acting in a manner consistent with its financial goals. Recent patterns of increasing annual hurricane activity have some experts questioning the long-term viability and profitability of oil wells in the area.

The two bold faced portions play which of the following roles?

(*a*) The first supports the conclusion of the argument; the second calls that conclusion into question.

(*b*) The first states the conclusion of the argument; the second supports that conclusion.

(*c*) The first supports the environmentalists' conclusion; the second states that conclusion.

(*d*) The first states the environmentalists' conclusion; the second provides a consideration in support of that conclusion.

(*e*) The first supports the conclusion of the argument; the second also supports the conclusion of the argument.

Answer Key

Paradox

1. (*d*)
2. (*b*)
3. (*b*)
4. (*d*)
5. (*a*)

Bold Face

6. (*e*)
7. (*a*)
8. (*b*)
9. (*b*)
10. (*c*)

Answer Explanations

Paradox

1. **(d)** This question asks us to explain a counterintuitive result - why is it the case that the arrival of a new restaurant, Bob's Bistro, somehow increased the number of meals served per day at the only other restaurant in town, Andrew's Eatery? If the number of meals served in the town of Montrose were to stay constant, then the business at Andrew's Eatery would certainly be reduced by the opening of Bob's Bistro. In order to provide an explanation for the surprising increase, we must find a reason that either more people are coming to Montrose to eat than was the case last year or that the people in Montrose are eating out more frequently.

   (*a*) The fact that Andrew's Eatery is less expensive than Bob's Bistro would not explain an increase in the number of meals served; it would only explain that perhaps some price-sensitive consumers in Montrose would continue to eat at Andrew's Eatery.

   (*b*) That Bob's Bistro is closed on Sundays does not explain an increase in the number of meals served at Andrew's Eatery on an everyday basis.

   (*c*) Higher profit margins at Bob's Bistro do not explain an increase in business at Andrew's Eatery; they simply suggest that Andrew's Eatery might be providing a slightly better value for certain price-sensitive consumers.

   (*d*) **Correct.** This statement explains that the number of diners in the town of Montrose as a whole has increased due to the opening of Bob's Bistro, and also explains why the patronage at Andrew's Eatery has increased. Bob's Bistro has apparently brought in many out-of-towners to eat at Montrose; and many of these first-time diners, when turned away from Bob's Bistro, arrive at Andrew's Eatery as the only alternative in town.

   (*e*) The fact that Andrew's Eatery serves more meals on weekends than on weekdays relative to Bob's Bistro does not explain the increase in business.

2. **(b)** The question asks us to find an option that contributes most towards explaining why City Y is considered less affordable than City X. This situation is surprising because the percentage of yearly income devoted to housing costs is higher in City X than in City Y, implying that it is more expensive to live in City X. We do know, however, that insurance and fuel costs are generally exorbitant in both cities, and that both cities are home to many commuters.

   (*a*) This does not explain why City Y is less affordable than City X. Private school is a choice. Public schools remain a free option for parents in both cities.

   (*b*) **Correct.** If City Y has no effective public transportation system, its residents will need to provide their own means of transportation. Since insurance and fuel costs are exorbitant in both cities, we know that residents of City Y will likely be forced to spend significant amounts on car insurance and gasoline. Because City X has an inexpensive public transportation system, its residents might be able to avoid these specific expenses.

(*c*) If new houses are more expensive in City X than in City Y, one would expect City X to be considered less affordable than City Y. This does not explain why City Y is considered less affordable than City X.

(*d*) The presence of expensive restaurants and boutiques in City Y is not relevant, since these represent only one end of the retail spectrum; and do not preclude the presence of inexpensive alternatives. Moreover, we know nothing about the retail establishments in City X; they could be even more expensive.

(*e*) We do not know whether the relocations have affected the ability of residents of City Y to cover their living expenses.

3. **(b)** The passage describes an apparent discrepancy. On the one hand, oil companies undermine scientific research that portrays global warming as a severe problem, presumably because this research will lead to government action that might harm the companies' profits. On the other hand, these same companies invest millions of dollars in climate-change research. The correct answer must provide a motive for the companies to invest in certain research related to global warming.

(*a*) This option establishes a time frame for when the oil companies began investing research dollars. However, it does not provide a reason to make this investment.

(*b*) **Correct.** This option provides a motive for companies to invest in global-warming research. If the research is specifically geared towards developing technologies used to combat global warming, this research represents a long-term strategy for finding new ways for the companies to profit. This is in contrast to the research that the oil companies oppose — research focused on the severity and immediacy of the issue, which might lead to government action that could have a negative impact on the profitability of the oil companies in the short term.

(*c*) The fact that the government action would negatively affect the oil companies explains why they would oppose this scientific research. It does not provide a reason they would also invest in scientific research related to global warming.

(*d*) The fact that the scientific data related to the severity of global warming is not definitive does not provide a reason for oil companies investing millions of dollars in research that accepts that global warming will have long-term effects.

(e) If oil companies didn't believe that any scientific research related to climate change will serve their interests, there would be no reason for them to invest any money in such research.

4. (d) The hydroelectric dams in Country X generate "more than enough power... to meet the country's energy needs." Yet, Country X still experiences power shortages and outages. This could result from several causes: perhaps, the system breaks down frequently, or the energy generated in Country X is not actually used by the citizens of Country X.

(a) If the flow is heavier, that would provide even more energy during spring. This does not address a potential cause of shortages or outages.

(b) The argument states that the dams provide "more than enough power... to meet the country's energy needs" - including a reliance on electric appliances.

(c) This option is irrelevant; the topic is why the country experiences shortages even though the current energy system provides "more than enough" energy.

(d) **Correct.** If the electricity produced is sold to other countries, then there might not be enough left unsold to accommodate the needs of Country X's citizens.

(e) This would just mean that the country has the potential to produce even more power than it already does; it does not address a potential cause of shortages or outages.

5. (a) The passage states that the price-per-pound of ostrich meat has not decreased even though the supply of the meat has been abundant. We are asked to find an explanation for this seeming contradiction.

(a) **Correct.** If the demand has outpaced the supply, even if the supply is abundant, it is likely that the price will remain steady, at the very least.

(b) The difficulty of breeding ostriches is not relevant to the market price, given that the supply of the meat is abundant.

(c) If other types of meat have decreased in price, one might expect that ostrich meat would decrease as well, to remain competitive.

(d) The lack of effort on the part of the beef industry to counter beef's poor image does not address the issue of why the price of ostrich meat has remained steady despite an abundant supply.

Bold Face

6. (e) This question is an Analyze the Argument Structure question; the best approach is to identify the conclusion, and then check each bold-face portion of the question for how it relates to the conclusion; and eliminate the incorrect answer options on that basis. Here, the conclusion of the argument appears in the last sentence, that

"these findings suggest that the real reason musicians over thirty rarely make significant contributions to the musical canon is not that they have aged but rather that they have spent too much time as musicians." This conclusion is drawn in contrast to the conventional explanation that age erodes creative ability, which appears in the first bold face. The second bold face is a description of the findings that are used to support the argument's conclusion.

(*a*) The description of the first bold face is accurate, as it does present an explanation that is challenged by the argument. However, the second bold face is not a finding that supports the challenged explanation. Rather, the second bold face is a finding that supports a different explanation altogether, and is the primary evidence for the challenge, as opposed to the explanation itself.

(*b*) The description of the first bold face is accurate, as it does present an explanation that is opposed by the argument. However, the second bold face is not an objection raised against the alternative explanation advocated by the argument, but the primary evidence in support of the alternative explanation.

(*c*) The first bold face is not a claim advanced in support of a position, but is itself a position or explanation. Additionally, the second bold face does not serve to clarify the position proposed by the first bold face.

(*d*) The first bold face is not an explanation advocated by the argument, as the argument advocates an alternative explanation. The description of the second bold face is accurate.

(*e*) **Correct.** The first bold face does present an explanation that the argument challenges. The second is a finding that provides the basis for the challenge to the conventional explanation.

7. **(a)** The conclusion of the argument is that the city will witness many of its prized industries relocate to more convenient cities; and that the city's financial health will be jeopardized if the city does not make changes soon to its transportation network. This is also the second bolded sentence. The first bolded sentence states that most of the network was put in place at a time when the city was much smaller in both area and population. We need to find an option that correctly describes both of these bolded statements.

(*a*) **Correct.** This option states that the first statement is an explanation of a current state of affairs. It is consistent with the passage. The answer option goes on to describe the second bolded statement as a prediction based on that state of affairs. This is also consistent with the passage: the second bolded statement predicts what will happen as a result of the inadequacy of the current transportation network.

(*b*) The first statement is indeed a statement of fact, but the author cites it in order to bolster his or her claim; thus the statement is not in opposition to the conclusion. The second statement is the conclusion of the argument.

(*c*) The first statement does not "emphasize an existing problem" but rather explains that existing problem (of an overtaxed subway). Moreover, the second statement does not "offer a proposal to solve that problem" but rather warns of what will happen if the problem is not solved.

(*d*) The first statement arguably presents information that "the author suggests has been overlooked in the situation at hand"; however, the second statement does not describe that situation, but rather proposes a hypothetical outcome in the future.

(*e*) The first statement is not really a "justification" (a term that implies approval on the part of the author) but rather an "explanation"; nor does it refer to an "impending problem" but rather an existing problem. Also, the second statement does not exactly describe "consequences" but rather "potential consequences" if the problem is left unchecked.

8. **(b)** The chief economist begins his/her argument by describing the usual relationship of cause and effect. Thus, the first statement in bold face represents a generalization that the chief economist accepts as accurate. He/she then goes on to conclude that this time, however, the usual cause-and-effect relationship will not hold; and strong figures of the GDP will cause a decrease, rather than an increase, in stock prices. To support this conclusion, the economist offers evidence explaining how strong GDP figures can lead to lower stock prices. Therefore, the second statement in bold face represents evidence that supports the main conclusion of the economist.

(*a*) This answer option correctly describes the role of the first statement but incorrectly states that the second statement in bold face represents the conclusion of the economist rather than the evidence that supports that conclusion. Remember, the conclusion of the economist is that, strong GDP figures will result in a decrease, rather than an increase, in stock prices.

(*b*) **Correct.** This answer option correctly identifies the role of each of the two parts in bold face. The first part represents a generalization that is typically accurate but will not be repeated in the case at issue. The second portion presents evidence in support of the economist's prediction.

(*c*) This answer option correctly describes the role of the first portion but mistakenly states that the second part in bold face follows from this generalization. The second statement in bold face presents evidence that supports the opposite effect from that described in the first portion. Namely, the economist claims that this time, stock prices will decrease rather than increase, as would be usual.

(*d*) This answer option incorrectly states that the first portion supports, rather than weighs against, the economist's prediction. In addition, this answer option incorrectly states that the second portion in bold face represents the economist's prediction, rather than evidence supporting it.

(*e*) This answer option incorrectly states that the first statement will be repeated in the case at issue. Remember, the economist argues that the usual pattern will not hold this time. The second statement is correctly described as acknowledging a circumstance in which the usual pattern will not hold.

9. **(b)** The analyst recounts a proposal by the Russian government to increase the Russian population. The analyst then dismisses that proposal and makes a counterproposal that he or she then supports with hypothetical scenarios. The claim that the counterproposal (to try good governance) is preferable is the conclusion of the argument.

(*a*) This option is incorrect. The first bold face is a fact that indicates the government plan has failed before; it is not the conclusion of the argument. However, the second is a premise in support of the argument's proposal.

(*b*) **Correct.** The first is the fact that the government plan has "been tried before, to no avail," a fact that undermines the alternative proposal made by the government. The author's proposal is to improve the country's governance, and the second bold face supports that plan by showing one way in which better governance might lead to a population increase.

(*c*) The first does not contradict the argument's conclusion that improved governance will reverse the decline in population. Rather, it undermines the other proposal presented by the government, which is a claim that the argument does not support. The second is not the argument's main point, but an assertion that supports the conclusion of the argument by showing one way in which better governance might lead to a population increase.

(*d*) The first is a premise that the government plan has "been tried before, to no avail," which weighs against the preceding proposal. The second is not the proposal that the first directly supports, but an assertion that supports the conclusion of the argument by showing one way in which better governance might lead to a population increase.

(*e*) The first is not a conclusion at all, rather a factual premise that these measures "have been tried before, to little avail." The second bold face does not oppose the first, rather it is an assertion that supports the conclusion of the argument by showing one way in which better governance might lead to a population increase.

10. (c) The argument concludes that United Energy might be acting in a manner consistent with reaching its financial goals. However, this conclusion must be distinguished from the assertion of the environmentalists described in the question – that the actions taken by United Energy indicate that the company is putting environmental concerns ahead of financial returns. The answer options might consider either the author's conclusion (which is considered the overall conclusion) or the conclusion asserted by the environmentalists (which is considered the opposing opinion).

This is an Analyze the Argument Structure question. The best approach is to consider each bold face in turn.

(*a*) The first bold face does not support the author's conclusion that United Energy could be acting in a manner consistent with its financial goals; the second does not call the conclusion into question as much as state its opposite.

(*b*) The first bold face does not state the conclusion of the argument; the second bold face does not support the conclusion of the main argument, which is that United Energy might be acting in a manner consistent with its financial goals.

(*c*) **Correct.** The first bold face supports the environmentalists' conclusion that United Energy is acting in a manner that places environmental impact ahead of financial returns. The second boldface states thisconclusion.

(*d*) The first boldface is a relationship that does support the environmentalists' conclusion; however, the second states this conclusion, and does not undermine it.

(*e*) The first bold face does not support the author's conclusion, which is that United Energy might be acting in its financial interest; the second bold face also does not support this conclusion.

Chapter 4

Critical Reasoning Inference & Evaluate

Inference

Inference questions are a common type of question in the GMAT Critical Reasoning section. These questions require the test-taker to draw a logical conclusion that can be inferred from the given information in the argument. Understanding how to approach inference questions can help you improve your Critical Reasoning skills and score higher in the GMAT.

Understanding Inference Questions

An inference question in the GMAT Critical Reasoning section typically consists of an argument, followed by a prompt asking the test-taker to identify the inference that can be drawn from the argument.

For example, consider the following argument:

"Studies have shown that people who eat a balanced diet and exercise regularly tend to have lower rates of heart disease. John eats a balanced diet and exercises for at least 30 minutes every day."

In this argument, the test-taker must infer **that John is at a lower risk for heart disease based on the information provided**. The inference can be drawn by combining the information about the benefits of a balanced diet and exercise with the fact that John engages in these activities.

Identifying the Correct Inference

To identify the correct inference, the test-taker must carefully analyze the argument and use the information provided to draw a logical conclusion. It is essential to consider both the explicit and implicit information in the argument; and identify any assumptions or logical gaps in the argument.

Evaluating Answer Options

In the GMAT critical reasoning section, each inference question will have several answer options, and the test-taker must choose the option that best represents the correct inference, based on the argument's information.

To evaluate the answer options, the test-taker must consider each option carefully and determine whether it accurately represents the inference that can be drawn from the argument. It is essential to eliminate answer options that are not supported by the information in the argument or that do not logically follow from the given information.

For example, in the above argument, an incorrect inference might be "John will never get heart disease." This option is not supported by the information in the argument, which only suggests that John is at a lower risk for heart disease.

Key Takeaways:

- In these questions, we have to find the conclusion based on the information given to us in the paragraph.
- **You must be thinking :** "What can you logically conclude based on the information without adding any external information?"
- Eliminate answer options that bring external information

Basic Approach

- **Step 1 :** Identify the question type– Read question stem.
- **Step 2 :** Read the argument and identify the type of argument
- **Step 3 :** Think of what the right answer will do.
- **Step 4 :** *Eliminate* : Extreme choice,

  Out of scope choicesStrengthen questions

Evaluate

In GMAT Critical Reasoning (CR) questions, an "evaluate" question asks you to determine which answer option would be most helpful in evaluating the argument presented in the passage.

In other words, the goal of an "evaluate" question is to assess the strength (or weakness) of the argument; and to identify the missing information (or assumptions) that would be necessary to come to a conclusion.

To answer an evaluate question, you will need to carefully analyze the argument and the answer options provided, and consider how each option would impact the reasoning presented in the passage. You should look for answer options that either strengthen or weaken the argument or provide information that is relevant to drawing a conclusion.

It is important to note that the correct answer to an evaluate question is not necessarily the one that proves the argument to be true or false. Rather, the correct answer is the one that most effectively assists you in evaluating the reasoning presented.

Example of an "Evaluate" question :

Argument : Studies have shown that taking multivitamins can improve overall health. Therefore, everyone should take a multivitamin daily.

Which of the following would be most useful to evaluate the argument above?

(a) How many people in the studies took a multivitamin versus a placebo?

(b) How many different brands of multivitamins were used in the studies?

(c) What was the average age of the participants in the studies?

(d) What were the specific health benefits reported by the participants in the studies?

(e) What is the cost of a daily multivitamin?

To answer this question, you need to identify which answer option would be most useful in determining whether the argument is valid or not. In this case, the argument is that everyone should take a multivitamin daily because studies have shown that they improve overall health. To evaluate the argument, you need to determine whether the studies are reliable; and whether the conclusion logically follows from the evidence presented.

Option (a) is the correct answer. By knowing how many people in the studies took a multivitamin versus a placebo, we can determine whether the results are statistically significant, and whether the conclusion that everyone should take a multivitamin is justified.

Option (b) is not relevant to the argument because the specific brands of multivitamins used in the studies are not important.

Option (c) is not useful in evaluating the argument because the average age of the participants is not relevant to the validity of the conclusion.

Option (d) might be useful in determining the specific health benefits of taking a multivitamin, but it does not address the question of whether everyone should take a multivitamin daily.

Option (e) is not relevant to the argument because the cost of a daily multivitamin is not related to the validity of the conclusion.

To solve "Evaluate" questions, you need to carefully analyze the argument presented in the passage, and identify the key premises and conclusions. Then, you need to consider each answer option and determine whether it would be helpful in evaluating the validity of the argument. In general, the correct answer will be the one that directly addresses the question of whether the evidence supports the conclusion.

Multiple Choice Questions

1. According to a recent study on financial roles, one-third of high-school seniors say that they have "significant financial responsibilities." These responsibilities include, but are not limited to, contributing to food, shelter, or clothing for themselves or their families. At the same time, a second study demonstrates that a crisis in money management exists for high-school students. According to this study, 80% of high-school seniors have never taken a personal finance class, even though the same percentage of seniors has opened bank accounts; and one-third of these account holders have bounced a check.

   Which of the following conclusions can be properly drawn from the statements above?

   (*a*) High schools would be wise to incorporate personal finance classes into their core curricula.

   (*b*) At least one-third of high-school seniors work part-time jobs after school.

   (*c*) The number of high-school seniors with significant financial responsibilities is greater than the number of seniors who have had a check bounced.

   (*d*) Any high-school senior who contributes to food, shelter, or clothing for themselves or their families has significant financial responsibilities.

   (*e*) The majority of high-school students have no financial responsibilities towards their families.

2. **Analyst :** Creative professionals, such as fashion designers, graphic designers, and decorators, often have very poor managerial skills; and do not succeed when they try to run their own businesses. In fact, most of these creative types are less-skilled in business than is the average white-collar professional, who does not work in a creative field. Generally, creative talent and business acumen rarely go hand in hand.

   If the analyst's argument is taken as true, which of the following statements can properly be concluded?

   (*a*) No successful business people is creative.

   (*b*) Some creative types are not less-skilled at business than the average white-collar worker, who is not creative.

   (*c*) Creativity precludes success in business.

   (*d*) Any white-collar worker who is not creative is more successful in business than any creative professional.

   (*e*) Business is not a creative endeavor.

3. Advocates insist that health-savings accounts are an efficient method to reduce medical expenses. However, widespread adoption of these accounts will soon undermine the public's health. One reason for this is that most people will be reluctant to deplete their accounts to pay for regular preventive examinations; so that, in many cases, a serious illness will go undetected until it is far advanced. Another reason is that poor people, who will not be able to afford health-savings accounts, will no longer be administered vaccinations against infectious diseases.

   The statements above, if true, support which of the following the most?

   (*a*) Wealthy individuals will not be affected negatively by health-savings accounts.

   (*b*) Private health insurance will no longer be available.

(c) Most diseases are detected during regular preventive examinations.

(d) Some people without health-savings accounts are likely to contract infectious diseases.

(e) The causal relationship between an individual's health and that person's medical care has been adequately documented.

4. Albinism is a rare genetic condition that inhibits the production of melanin, or pigmentation, in the skin and hair. People born with albinism are unusually susceptible to sunburn, melanoma, and a range of other health issues that are generally connected to excessive exposure to the sun.

The statements above, if true, support which of the following conclusions the most?

(a) People born with albinism develop different types of biological protections against melanoma and other sun-related health issues.

(b) Humans with a high production of melanin can easily ignore health issues related to exposure to the sun.

(c) When a non-albino person gets sunburn, the amount of melanin produced by that person decreases.

(d) In humans, melanin plays a role in protecting the skin from developing sunburn and other sun-related ailments.

(e) It is not possible for a person born with albinism to adopt other artificial protective measures against excessive exposure to thesun.

5. Celiac disease results from an inability of the digestive tract, specifically the small intestine, to absorb gluten, a protein found in wheat, barley, and certain other grains. The body's immune system attacks the gluten, as if the protein were a harmful pathogen, often resulting in serious damage to the intestinal lining. People who suffer from celiac disease must eliminate gluten from their diets. Symptoms of the disease include abdominal cramps, bloating, and anemia.

If the statements above are true, which of the following assertions can be made on the basis of them?

(a) Anyone who suffers from celiac disease will experience anemia.

(b) Eliminating gluten from one's diet will cure celiac disease.

(c) People experiencing abdominal cramps, bloating, and anemia have celiac disease.

(d) Gluten is found only in grains.

(e) The human body cannot always recognize harmless substances.

6. The director of programming at NNN, the National News Network, proclaimed that, despite charges to the contrary, the Network does not have a conservative bias. The director acknowledged that, when a liberal news personality was recently added to the Network, an additional conservative news program was also established. However, the director argued that far from demonstrating any bias, these actions reflect a commitment to presenting a balanced perspective in interpreting current events. Which of the following pieces of information would be most useful in evaluating the validity of the programming director's argument?

(a) The Network has established an additional liberal news program whenever an additional conservative news personality has been added.

(*b*) The Network airs a program focused largely on the opinions of its viewers on contemporary issues.

(*c*) The newly added liberal news personality came from a rival network with an acknowledged liberal bias.

(*d*) The newly added liberal news personality has indicated that he has not felt any editorial pressure in his new environment.

(*e*) The viewer ratings of the Network have been lower this past year than in previous years.

7. Child-development specialists have observed that adolescents, who receive large weekly allowances tend to spend money on items considered frivolous by their parents; whereas, adolescents who receive small weekly allowances, do not. Thus, in order to ensure that their children do not spend money on frivolous items, parents should not give their children large weekly allowances. Which of the following pieces of information would be most useful in evaluating the validity of the conclusion above?

(*a*) The average amount of money received by adolescents who receive large weekly allowances.

(*b*) Any differences among parents in the standard used to judge an item as frivolous.

(*c*) The educational background of the child-development specialists, who made this observation.

(*d*) The difference between the average annual income of families in which the parents give their children large weekly allowances and that of families in which the parents give their children small weekly allowances.

(*e*) The percentage of adolescents who receives no weekly allowance.

8. The downturn in the economy last year has prompted many companies to make widely publicized layoffs, resulting in thousands of lost jobs. Economists predicted that these layoffs would cause people generally to cut back on their discretionary spending, even if their jobs were secure, in anticipation of the coming hard times. However, this prediction has not come to pass, since there has been no increase in the amount of money set aside by the general public in savings accounts. The answer to which of the following questions would be most useful in evaluating the significance of the savings patterns described above?

(*a*) Which business sectors were most affected by the layoffs?

(*b*) How much of their savings, on an average, do laid-off employees deplete before finding new employment?

(*c*) What has been the increase (%) in the cost of necessities, such as, food, housing, and utilities during the period since the layoffs?

(*d*) What percentage of people laid off have savings accounts?

(*e*) What has been the average salary during the period since the layoffs?

9. Because of a rare type of fungus that killed off many cacao trees in Brazil, there was an unusually meager harvest of cocoa beans this year. The wholesale price of cocoa solids and cocoa butter has increased significantly, and does not look likely to fall in the foreseeable future. As a result, the retail price of chocolate is certain to increase within six months. The answer to which of the following questions would provide information relevant to evaluating the claims made in the argument above?

(*a*) Has the price of cocoa remained steady during other periods of poor harvest?

(*b*) Are consumers willing to spend more on chocolate?

(*c*) Have the prices of other ingredients in chocolate decreased recently?

(*d*) What percentage of cacao trees in Brazil were affected by the fungus?

(*e*) Can the fungus be eliminated within the next six months?

10. Scientists have determined that an effective way to lower cholesterol is to eat three servings of whole grains every day. Studies have shown that the cholesterol levels of people who did so were significantly lower after six months than were those of people who did not, even though the cholesterol levels of the two groups were the same before the studies began. Clearly, eating whole grains can have an appreciable effect on cholesterol levels. The answer to which of the following questions, if true, would be most useful in evaluating the claim above about whole grains?

(*a*) Is it realistic to expect people to eat three servings of whole grains per day?

(*b*) Were the two groups of people in the study involved in the same exercise program?

(*c*) Can the same drop in cholesterol be achieved through medication?

(*d*) Did the study continue to track the subjects beyond six months?

(*e*) Are most consumers aware of the difference between whole grains and processed grains?

Answer Key

1. (*c*)
2. (*b*)
3. (*d*)
4. (*d*)
5. (*e*)
6. (*a*)
7. (*b*)
8. (*c*)
9. (*c*)
10. (*b*)

Answer Explanations

1. **(c)** This passage relates information from two studies concerning high-school seniors: the first discusses the financial responsibilities of high-school seniors, while the second explains the coursework in finance taken by typical high-school seniors. In the GMAT, a proper response to a draw-a-conclusion question must be directly supported by evidence from the passage.

   (*a*) Although, it might be true that schools would be wise to educate students in finance, this is an opinion; it doesn't necessarily need to follow from the given evidence. A conclusion must be directly supported by evidence from the passage without any additional information or assumptions.

   (*b*) The fact that one-third of high-school seniors claim "significant financial responsibilities" towards their families does not necessarily mean that these same students work "part-time jobs after school." There are many possible ways that these students might be earning money for their families. If they do work, they might work on weekends or over the summer, for example.

   (*c*) **Correct.** The first study states that one-third of all high-school seniors have significant financial responsibilities towards their families. The second study states that 80% of seniors have opened a bank account, and of this 80%, one-third has had a check bounced. The number of seniors that has bounced a check (one-third of 80%) is fewer than the number of seniors with significant financial responsibilities towards their families (one-third of 100%).

   (*d*) The passage states that certain-high school seniors who contribute to the food, shelter, or clothing for themselves or their families rate themselves as having significant financial responsibilities. This does not mean that any high-school senior, who contributes to these categories has significant financial responsibilities.

   (*e*) The passage states that one-third of high-school seniors say that they have "significant financial responsibilities." This, in no way, indicates that the other two- thirds have "no" responsibilities. Because no information is given about the other two-thirds of the students, a reasoned conclusion cannot be drawn about them.

2. **(b)** The analyst presents several points about the business talents of creative professionals. In drawing a conclusion from the analyst's argument, we must be careful to choose a provable claim, whether or not this claim pulls together all the premises. We also must avoid extending the analyst's argument, or selecting statements that are too extreme. Finally, we must not allow this process to be clouded by reactions to the content of the argument; whether or not we agree with the premises, we have to find a provable conclusion.

   (*a*) This option takes the passage's claim that creativity and business acumen rarely go hand in hand to an extreme. The analyst does not assert that absolutely no successful people are creative.

(*b*) **Correct.** The passage states that most creative types are less skilled in business than the average white-collar worker who does not work in a creative field. This implies that some creative types are not less skilled than the average white-collar worker who is not creative.

(*c*) This option again takes the passage's claim that creativity and business acumen rarely go hand in hand to an extreme. Creativity and business acumen are not mutually exclusive.

(*d*) The passage does not say that all white-collar workers are successful, nor does it say that no creative professionals are successful.

(*e*) The passage makes a distinction between creative talent and business acumen. This does not mean that there are no aspects of business that fall under the realm of creativity.

3. **(d)** The passage states that health-savings accounts will undermine the health of the public because people will not use them for preventive care. Furthermore, people who cannot afford them will not be able to receive even basic care, such as, vaccinations. The correct answer will be a conclusion that can be supported solely by the facts stated in the argument, without relying on external information or additional assumptions.

(*a*) The argument does not provide enough information to conclude that wealthy individuals will not be affected negatively by health-savings accounts. The argument never specifically mentions wealthy individuals, just people in general.

(*b*) The argument does not provide enough information to conclude that private health insurance will no longer be available. In fact, private health insurance is never mentioned.

(*c*) The author argues that people will not get regular preventive examinations, and will therefore not receive medical attention until diseases are advanced. This logic, even if true, does not allow us to conclude that most diseases are detected during regular preventive examinations.

(*d*) **Correct.** The argument states that "poor people, who will not be able to afford health savings accounts, will no longer receive vaccinations". Based on this statement, it is reasonable to conclude that some people without health savings are likely to contract infectious diseases.

(*e*) The argument does not provide enough information to conclude that the causal relationship between an individual's health and that person's medical care has been adequately documented. In fact, neither the link between medical care and health nor documentation of such a link is directly discussed.

4. **(d)** This argument provides that albinos, or people whose bodies do not produce melanin, are unusually susceptible to solar exposure. This suggests a connection between the production of melanin in humans and protection from sunburn and other sun-related ailments. We should look for a conclusion that draws this connection.

(*a*) The argument does not indicate that people born with albinism somehow develop other natural defenses against sun-related health issues.

(*b*) This conclusion is too extreme to be supported by the argument; nothing in the argument suggests that humans whose bodies produce high levels of melanin can "easily ignore" sunburn or other sun-related health issues.

(*c*) There is no indication in the argument that sunburn reduces melanin production.

(*d*) **Correct.** The argument does strongly suggest that melanin plays some role in protecting the skin from developing sunburn and other sun-related ailments, since albinos do not produce melanin and are unusually susceptible to sun-related ailments.

(*e*) It is not suggested in the argument that an albino person could not protect him or herself from solar exposure through artificial means, e.g., wearing protective clothing or powerful sunblock.

5. (e) The text tells us that celiac disease results when the body mistakes gluten for a harmful pathogen, causing damage to the intestine. We are also told that gluten is a protein found in certain grains, and that people suffering from celiac disease must eliminate it from their diets. Finally, we are told that symptoms of the disease include cramps, bloating, and anemia. We need to find an answer option that is inferable from these facts alone.

(*a*) Anemia is just one of several symptoms of the disease. We do not know whether everyone who has the disease will also develop anemia.

(*b*) We do not know whether eliminating gluten will cure the disease; only that people with the disease must not eat gluten. Perhaps, the disease will exist anyway in a latent form.

(*c*) We do not know whether the symptoms mentioned are also symptoms of other conditions.

(*d*) We do not know whether gluten is found only in grains. It may exist in other foods as well.

(*e*) **Correct.** If the body mistakes gluten for a harmful pathogen, then it must be true that the body cannot always recognize harmless substances.

6. (a) The director of programming argues that the addition of a conservative news program in response to the hiring of a liberal news personality represents an institutional attempt at balancing different perspectives, rather than any conservative bias. The evidence provided by the director is outside of the context of any past actions on the part of the Network; it would be useful to have more information about actions the Network has taken in response to the hiring of conservative (or liberal) news personalities in the past to determine a pattern of behavior.

(*a*) **Correct.** If the Network responds to the addition of a liberal news personality in the same way that it does the addition of a conservative news personality, then the argument presented by the director is valid. An identical response to the hiring of a personality from either side of the political spectrum suggests that the Network does act in a fair and balanced manner, at least in this regard.

(*b*) Whether the Network presents a program airing the opinions of its viewers on contemporary issues does not indicate either a balanced approach or a conservative bias. This statement is irrelevant.

(*c*) The nature of the former employer of the newly-hired liberal news personality is not relevant in determining whether or not there is a systematic conservative bias regarding the overall programming of the Network.

(*d*) Whether the new liberal news personality has indicated that he has felt any editorial pressure is not relevant; he might not want to admit to such pressure, even if it did exist. Moreover, the experience of one employee does not address the overall programming of the Network.

(*e*) That the Network has suffered from lower ratings in the past year is not relevant to determining the bias, or lack thereof, of the Network; though it might explain why new personalities and programming are being added.

7. **(b)** The conclusion of the passage is that parents can ensure that their children will not spend money on frivolous items by limiting their children's allowances. This claim is based on the observed difference between the spending habits of children who receive large allowances and those of children who receive small allowances. The argument assumes that the high dollar amount of the allowance – as opposed to some other unobserved factor – is directly linked to the fact that children spend the money on items their parents consider frivolous. Information that provides data about any other factor that might be the cause of the children's spending behavior would help to evaluate the validity of the conclusion.

(*a*) The actual dollar amount received by adolescents who receive large weekly allowances is not related to the conclusion of the passage. Whether this amount is $40 or $10, the key is that it is considered by the child-development specialists to be a "large" weekly allowance.

(*b*) **Correct.** One alternative to the conclusion of the passage is that the standard used to judge an item as frivolous was much lower for parents who gave their children large weekly allowances than for parents who gave their children small weekly allowances. If for example, the former group of parents considered all movie tickets to be frivolous, while the latter did not, then this fact (and not the difference in allowance money) might explain the difference observed by the child-development specialists. Thus, information about any differences among parents in the standard used to judge an item as frivolous would be extremely relevant in evaluating the validity of the conclusion of the passage.

(*c*) The background of the child-development specialists who made the observation has no bearing on the conclusion. The conclusion is based on the observation, not on the credentials of those making the observation.

(*d*) Family-income differences have no clear relevance to the link posited between high allowances and spending on frivolous items.

(*e*) Adolescents who receive no weekly allowance play no role in the argument. Thus, information about this group of adolescents has no relationship to the conclusion of the passage.

8. (c) The conclusion of the argument is that the prediction of decreased consumer spending has not come to pass. The evidence for this is that there has been no corresponding increase in the amount of money set aside in savings accounts by the general public.

This question asks us to choose a question whose answer will provide information relevant to evaluating the significance of the fact that the amount of money placed in savings accounts has not increased. The author mentions this savings pattern to support the claim that people have not been curtailing their discretionary spending. So we need to find a question whose answer will relate to savings and spending patterns.

(*a*) Information about which business sectors were most affected by the layoffs will not help us establish the relevance of the savings pattern to the claim.

(*b*) The savings used by those who are laid off has no bearing on the savings patterns of those who are not laid off, which is the group this argument addresses ("even if their jobs were secure").

(*c*) **Correct.** This question asks about the prices of necessities, such, as food and utilities. If people have not been saving their money, perhaps they have been spending it on necessities (as opposed to spending it on discretionary items). If these items have become more expensive, then, perhaps, people have not been able to save money despite curtailing their discretionary spending.

(*d*) The percentage of people with savings accounts is not related to the question of whether people have curtailed their discretionary spending or increased the amount they save.

(*e*) Knowing the statistics for average salaries during the period since the layoffs will not help us evaluate the significance of the spending and savings patterns during that time. It might help to be able to compare the statistics for the periods before and after the layoffs, but knowing just one of those statistics tells us nothing about the trends.

9. (c) The correct answer is (c). The conclusion of the argument is that the price of chocolate will increase within six months. The basis for that claim is that the wholesale price of cocoa has increased. However, if the price of other ingredients in the chocolate has dropped, the decrease could offset the higher price of cocoa and render the argument invalid. The only option to address this is (c).

10. (b) The correct answer is (b). The conclusion of the argument is that "eating whole grains can have an appreciable effect on cholesterol levels." This assertion is based on the fact that some people who ate three servings of whole grains every day for six months had lower cholesterol than people who did not, even though their cholesterol levels were the same before the study began. The argument does not take into account, however, other factors, such as exercise, that could have contributed to the difference in cholesterol levels. Option (b) asks whether there is indeed another factor — exercise — that should be taken into account.

Chapter 5

Reading Comprehension Introduction & Basic Approach

The Format

Since GMAT is a Computer-Based Test (CBT), the passage appears on the left side of the screen and the questions appear on the right, one question at a time. Only after you answer the first question, the next question appears in its place, since the Verbal section is a Computer Adaptive one (just like the Quantitative section). The passage remains on the screen, so you can always refer to it when answering a particular question.

The Pattern (RC)

Reading comprehension questions constitute roughly one-third of the questions in the Verbal section. The passages cover a variety of topics, but will generally come from the fields of business, natural science, humanities, and social science. It is worth noting that neither the passages nor the questions assume knowledge of the topics discussed. Generally, you can expect to see four reading comprehension passages in the Verbal section, and each passage will have three or four questions. The general pattern is: two medium-sized passages (50-70 lines), one long passage (75+ lines), and one short passage (30 lines). The passages can appear in a random order, but all the questions related to the passage will come together.

The Approach

The passages that appear in the GMAT are more often than not dense, wordy, and sometimes convoluted. So, if you start out by reading the whole passage with the aim of understanding all the details, you might end up 'zoning out', becoming confused, or even forgetting what you've read. What is worse, you will lose precious time.

Hence, it follows that you simply skim through the passage to get a sense of the main idea or the big picture. Skip any complicated phrase or a new word in the initial process of skimming. You can also benefit by focusing on the first sentence of each paragraph and the last sentence of the whole passage.

As you are skimming, look for trigger words to help you get a sense of the structure and tone of the passage. Some trigger words may indicate that the author's ideas are changing; and some indicate that there will be no change in the author's ideas. Following are some trigger words that you will usually encounter:

Same Direction	Change Direction
In addition	But
Likewise	Yet
Therefore	Although
Consequently	However
Similarly	Despite
Thus, Hence, Indeed	Nonetheless, Whereas, Notwithstanding
For instance	Nevertheless

Mapping the Passage

Taking notes of the passage, in the right way, does help you improve your accuracy and speed, when attempting to solve a reading comprehension passage. The idea behind creating a map is to quickly know where to look for particular information in the passage, if you feel the need to go back to the passage. A good map also helps you in answering the ***main idea*** questions. When taking notes, keep the following points in mind:-

- Don't re-write the passage; and refrain from writing complete sentences. Try to use abbreviations, symbols, and arrows on the scratch paper to map your thoughts.
- Focus on main messages, important examples, and shifts in tone (trigger words).

Over time, you might find yourself creating seamless mental maps with increased efficiency.

Answering the Question

It is quite normal, if, at first, all the answer options to a particular question seem indistinguishable. Make sure you understand **exactly** what the question is asking and what the answer options are. Answer the questions on the basis of what is stated or implied in the passage itself. If you need to, refer back to the passage for clarification.

A note of caution : Don't select an answer choice before carefully reading all the answer options. Instead, try to eliminate the INCORRECT options.

Other Strategies

Become an Active Reader : The first step towards active reading is to be engaged with the passage. It is harder to be engaged when the passage talks about an obscure tribe or some inconsequential microorganism but you need to acknowledge that you find the passage uninteresting and that you need to read for the 'Big Picture'. Another method is to link the characters or situations given in the passage to what you already know. This technique helps you visualize information but you always run the risk of introducing outside information. So, proceed with caution!

Try practicing these techniques on non-GMAT material, especially major journals and newspapers, such, as *The Economist, The New York Times,* etc. to improve your efficiency.

Importance of Vocabulary in GMAT

The GMAT doesn't explicitly emphasize on testing students on difficult vocabulary. It is very rare that a single arcane word in the passage hampers your understanding of the passage as a whole or proves to be a serious deterrent when answering the questions. However, knowledge of certain words can help you understand the answer options better, such as, *aggravate, commonplace, exempt, lobby, marginal, reconcile, undermine, etc.* The list might not necessarily be long but a suggestion is that you take a note of these words when you encounter them in the answer options, as the GMAT tends to be fairly repetitive with these words.

Multiple Choice Questions

Directions (Q. 1 – 3) :

After the race in 2019-20 to find a suitable vaccine to contain the pathogen, it is now the scarcity of Covid-19 vaccines in many countries around the globe which continues to put everyone in the world in peril. That's because as long as large populations around the world remain unvaccinated, variants of the virus will continue to emerge, including some that might be able to evade existing vaccines. Therefore, one of the most probable solutions to end the pandemic is global vaccination. However, economic models of vaccine manufacturing indicate many countries won't be likely to achieve widespread immunization until the end of 2022.

We must do more than wring our hands. We can take actions now to add order to the vaccine market, mitigate bottlenecks, and increase the global supply of – and access to – the portfolio of Covid-19 vaccines. The horrific situation in India underscores the need to expand investment and coordination of the worldwide supply chain and the infrastructure for responding to future pandemics.

The manufacturing of Covid-19 vaccines and auxiliary supplies have emerged as a daunting global challenge. The early competitive procurement of vaccines by the United States and other high-income countries has fed a widespread assumption that each country will be solely responsible for its population, a stance that has sparked protests outside Moderna's headquarters in Cambridge, Massachusetts. It is clear that this vaccine nationalism was short-sighted.

We should prepare for an equitable global deployment of a portfolio of Covid-19 vaccines by making investments in available technology and infrastructure. Unfortunately, many of those actions aren't happening, which partly explains the current supply-demand mismatch around the world.

The events of 2021 reinforce the need for governments to conduct **'scenario planning'** to procure, negotiate and distribute the vaccine doses. While having more capacity may ease the situation, it is not necessarily sufficient to achieve high vaccination coverage equitably. (Sourced from HBJ).

1. The primary purpose of the passage is to

(*a*) question the claim that more vaccines mean the world being safe from coronavirus.

(*b*) examine the relationship between vaccination and pandemic cure.

(*c*) argue that the supply-demand mismatch of vaccines around the world will continue.

(*d*) discuss the need for more and equitable distribution of vaccines.

(*e*) challenge the theory that more vaccines do not lead to more safety from Covid-19.

2. In the context of the passage as a whole, the third paragraph serves primarily to

(*a*) provide an example to support the discussion presented in the first paragraph.

(*b*) demonstrate the likely fallout of competitive vaccine procurement.

(*c*) support the conclusion regarding vaccination coverage.

(*d*) reinforce the need to embrace vaccine nationalism.

(*e*) remind about the importance of equitable vaccine distribution.

3. 'Scenario planning', as mentioned in the last paragraph, is best defined as planning that

(*a*) determines the vaccination rights of people of a particular area.

(*b*) includes the production and distribution of vaccines as per current and prospective needs.

(*c*) gives the companies freedom to produce vaccines as per the requirements.

(*d*) results in doing away with the current supply-demand mismatch around the world.

(*e*) dictates which region gets how much of the vaccine supply.

Directions (Q. 4 – 4) :

The constitution makers in the US had the property rights of married women in mind when they gave the Senate the authority to grant Marital Asset License (MAL) to women entering into a wedlock. They were of the opinion that protecting property rights of women would accelerate the socio-economic growth of the nation. Since then, this License System has become a trail blazer for other nations too. Of late, there have been skepticism among the **scholars** about the American system achieving the goals which the constitution makers had in mind when MAL was born. The scholars contending the success of the License here cite the period between 1798 and 1840, when the American married women could not enforce their property rights because **arbitrators were 'anti-license', invalidating licenses for flimsy reasons**. This argument stems from examination of court proceedings where women license holders (licensees) filed suits alleging infringement of their MAL rights. In the 1830s, for instance, only 20% of the verdicts went in favour of married women. This proportion began to increase in the 1840s, giving indications to these **scholars** about a change in judicial attitudes towards MAL rights.

At the same time, not all license disputes went for litigation. At the same time, litigated cases were not drawn randomly from overall disputes. So, the proportion of verdicts in favour of licensees cannot be the sole measure to make one believe that there have been changes in the attitude of the arbitrators or the enforceability of license rights. If it is supposed that earlier verdicts had a hostile attitude against licensees, it is natural to expect subsequent courts to reject the former legal precedents. However, this has not been the case. Judgments prior to 1840s continue to be cited as liberally as later decisions. It suggests that the earlier decisions, many favouring married women's property rights, provided a strong foundation for licensee law. The number of verdicts favouring licensees started climbing up in the 1840s because of a change in the process of filing of cases standing trial. A revision was introduced to the License here in 1844 which entailed careful scrutiny of each application vis-a-vis its adherence to the license law. This system continues till date, replacing the automatic grant of license on receipt of a nominal fee of $20.

4. The passage implies which of the following was a reason that the proportion of verdicts in favour of the licensees began to increase in the 1840s?

(*a*) License applications approved after 1844 were more likely to adhere closely to license law.

(*b*) License laws enacted during the 1840s better defined license rights better.

(*c*) Arbitrators became less prejudiced against licensees during the 1840s.

(*d*) After 1844, litigated cases became less representative of the proportion of license disputes.

(*e*) The proportion of license disputes brought to trial began to increase after 1844.

5. The passage implies that the scholars mentioned in the first paragraph would agree with which of the following criticisms of the American License System before 1840?

(*a*) Its definition of property rights relating to marriage was too vague to be useful.

(*b*) Its criteria for the granting of licenses were not clear.

(*c*) It made it excessively difficult for married women to receive licenses.

(*d*) It led to excessive numbers of license-infringement suits.

(*e*) It failed to encourage socio-economic growth.

6. It can be inferred from the passage that the frequency with which pre-1840 cases have been cited in court decisions is an indicator that

(*a*) judicial support for license rights was strongest in the period before 1840.

(*b*) judicial support for license rights did not increase after 1840.

(*c*) courts have returned to judicial standards that prevailed before 1840.

(*d*) verdicts favouring licensees in license-infringement suits did not increase after 1840.

(*e*) judicial bias against licensees persisted after 1840.

7. It can be inferred from the passage that the author and the scholars referred to at the end of the first paragraph disagree about which of the following aspects of the licenses defended in license-infringement suits before 1840?

(*a*) Whether the licenses were granted for marriages that were redundant.

(*b*) Whether the licenses were actually relevant to the socio-economic growth of the country.

(*c*) Whether the licenses were particularly likely to be annulled by the arbitrators.

(*d*) Whether the licenses were routinely invalidated for arbitrary reasons.

(*e*) Whether the licenses were vindicated at a significantly lower rate than the licenses in later suits.

8. The author of the passage cites which of the following as evidence challenging the argument referred to in "arbitrators were 'anti-license', invalidating licenses for flimsy reasons" in the first paragraph?

(*a*) The very low proportion of cases that were decided in favour of the licensees in the 1830s.

(*b*) The total number of license disputes that were litigated from 1798 to 1840.

(*c*) The fact that later courts drew upon the legal precedents set in pre-1840 cases.

(*d*) The fact that the proportion of judicial cases in favour of the licensees began to increase during the 1840s.

(*e*) The constitutional rationale for the 1844 revision of the license system.

Answer Key

1. (*d*)
2. (*a*)
3. (*b*)
4. (*a*)
5. (*e*)
6. (*b*)
7. (*d*)
8. (*c*)

Answer Explanations

1. **(d)** (*a*) There is no claim mentioned as such in the passage. While it says that 'one of the most probable solutions to end the pandemic is global vaccination', it can't be inferred that more vaccines can lead to such a situation.

(*b*) Vaccination is the only eventual cure from the pandemic, but the passage does not delve into the relationship between the two.

(*c*) The passage unequivocally mentions that there is 'supply-demand' mismatch in the world currently. Whether, the same will continue, the passage is silent on it.

(*d*) **Correct.** There is a need for large-scale manufacturing of Covid-19 vaccines. However, the passage also makes it clear that, this in itself, is not enough. A fair distribution of vaccines throughout the world is equally important.

(*e*) The passage does not challenge such a viewpoint. In fact, it categorically states that more vaccines need not necessarily mean more safety.

2. **(a)** (*a*) **Correct.** The first paragraph mentions that global vaccination is the need of the hour to end the pandemic. Parochial attitude like that of the US, as seen in the third paragraph, will hinder this end.

(*b*) The paragraph clearly mentions the result of such a strategy, but that is not the aim of the paragraph.

(*c*) It is not vaccination coverage which the third paragraph brings up for discussion, but equality in vaccination distribution.

(*d*) The paragraph does just the opposite. It does not want vaccine nationalism to happen.

(*e*) While equitable vaccine distribution is important, the paragraph does not go into the reasons for it.

3. **(b)** (*a*) The passage does not mention vaccination rights of any region or people.

(*b*) **Correct.** The passage discusses the importance of mass production as well as equitable distribution of vaccines.

(*c*) There is no mention of companies in the passage.

(*d*) That there is supply-demand mismatch in the world is stated in the passage. Scenario planning might have an impact on it, but can't be limited to just this one factor.

(*e*) There are no regions mentioned in the passage.

4. **(a)** (*a*) **Correct.** The passage implies that licenses granted after the 1844 law went into effect were more likely to adhere to license law.

(*b*) The passage does not indicate that any law mentioned made changes to the definition of license rights, rather it indicates that the license system was revised to require that license applications be reviewed for adherence to existing law.

(*c*) The passage rejects the explanation that arbitrators' attitudes towards license rights became more favourable.

(*d*) The passage indicates that the population of disputes that were litigated changed after 1844, but it does not suggest that the population of litigated disputes differed from that of license disputes as a whole.

(*e*) The passage does not indicate any change in the proportion of license disputes brought to trial.

5. **(e)** (*a*) The scholars contend that arbitrators rejected licenses for arbitrary reasons, not because the definition of property right relating to marriage was vague.

(*b*) The passage does not indicate that the scholars were too critical of the idea for granting licenses.

(*c*) The scholars are concerned with married women's attempts to protect their licenses, not the difficulty in acquiring the licenses.

(*d*) The passage does not imply that the scholars in question believed that too many license-infringement suits were brought to court, but rather that too few succeeded.

(*e*) **Correct.** The scholars doubt that the license law helped to accelerate socio-economic growth.

6. **(b)** (*a*) The passage argues that judicial support for license rights did not change in the 1840s.

(*b*) **Correct.** Pre-1840s court decisions have been cited as frequently as later decisions, suggesting no change in judges' attitudes.

(*c*) The passage does not indicate that judicial standards changed from, and then returned to, those that prevailed before 1840.

(*d*) Although, actual numbers of favourable verdicts are not mentioned, the passage indicates that the proportion of verdicts decided in favour of licensees did, in fact, increase, beginning in the 1840s.

(*e*) The passage rejects the notion that judges were biased against licensees either before or after 1840.

7. **(d)** (*a*) The author and the scholars are both focused on protecting married women's property rights, not their being 'genuinely real'.

(*b*) Though the passage suggests that the scholars thought America's License System did not help accelerate socio-economic growth, there is no suggestion that either of them believes that licenses were irrelevant to socio-economic growth.

(*c*) Both the scholars and the author believe that licenses defended in courts prior to 1840 were more likely to be invalidated than licenses in later legal disputes.

(*d*) **Correct.** The scholars claim that judges before 1840 decided against licenses for arbitrary reasons, but the passage suggests that the licenses might have been invalidated because they failed to adhere to license law.

(*e*) Both the scholars and the author accept that licenses were upheld in court less often before 1840 than after.

8. (c) (*a*) The proportion of cases decided against licensees in the 1830s is cited as evidence that supports the scholars' argument in the first paragraph, not as evidence challenging their views.

(*b*) The total number of disputes litigated is not mentioned in the passage.

(*c*) **Correct.** The fact that judges after 1840 cited earlier cases as precedents is used as evidence to challenge scholars' claims that the judges' attitudes shifted around 1840.

(*d*) The change in the proportion of decisions in favour of licensees is a fact that both the scholars and the author of the passage attempt to explain.

(*e*) No constitutional rationale for the 1844 law is mentioned in the passage.

Chapter 6

Reading Comprehension Identifying Common Traps

GMAT reading comprehension passages can be quite challenging, not only because of their complexity but also because of the variety of answer options that are designed to trap test-takers. These trap answer options are intended to deceive test-takers into choosing an incorrect response; and can be difficult to identify. In this chapter, we will discuss some common trap answer options in GMAT reading comprehension; and how to identify them.

1. Extreme Language Trap

One of the most-common types of trap answer options in GMAT reading comprehension is the extreme language trap. These answers use language that is overly strong or absolute, such as "always," "never," or "completely," to make a statement seem more significant than it is. Test-takers should be wary of these options and be sure that the answer they choose is supported by the text.

Example :

Passage : "Some people believe that exercise is essential to maintain good health."

Trap Answer : "Exercise is the only way to maintain good health."

2. Out of Scope Trap

Another common trap answer option is the out of scope trap. These answers are designed to distract test-takers by presenting information that is related to the passage but is not directly relevant to the question being asked. Test-takers should be careful not to choose an answer that is too broad or too narrow and should focus on information that is directly related to the question.

Example :

Passage : "The study found that students who read for pleasure have higher academic achievement."

Trap Answer : "Students who participate in sports have lower academic achievement."

3. Opposite Choice Trap

The opposite choice trap is another common type of trap answer option in GMAT reading comprehension. These answers are designed to trick test-takers by presenting the opposite of what is stated in the passage. Test-takers should be careful to read the question and passage carefully to ensure that they are not choosing an answer that contradicts the information presented in the text.

Example :

Passage : "Research suggests that a plant-based diet can reduce the risk of heart disease."

Trap Answer : "A vegan diet is not an effective way to reduce the risk of heart disease."

4. Partially Correct Trap

The partially correct trap is a trap answer option that is partially correct but ultimately incorrect. These answers are designed to deceive test-takers by presenting information that is true but does not fully answer the question being asked. Test-takers should be careful to choose an answer that fully addresses the question and is supported by the text.

Example :

Passage : "The new law will increase taxes on businesses to fund education."

Trap Answer : "The new law will increase taxes."

Point to note is that this answer option could refer to any 'tax'.

5. True but Irrelevant :

Such answer options are difficult to identify. Usually, these include facts or ideas stated in the wrong part of the passage but do not address the point of the question. These answer options act as easy traps since they look *familiar* because they look like something you have just read.

Multiple Choice Questions

Directions (Q. 1 – 5) :

During the 19th century, information about land use that was provided by the United States Land Record Census, a survey conducted each decade, became more detailed and precise in response to environmental changes.

Through 1840, enumeration by agencies was **simple**. It was most basic of land use pattern which was mirrored: the land area was specified by category, government or private, whereas sustainable land use was only indicated by total area under forest cover, including grasslands. For pastures, land use was determined by the number of acres designated for grazing rather than the type of vegetation.

In the 1850 census, partly responding to Green Movement and Animals' Rights Movements, the collection of specific information about specific vegetation and biodiversity in an area was started so as to maintain sustainable ecosystems.

Not until 1870, was information about land analysed by sustainability: the Census Officer reported 1.8 million acres of forest land. In addition, he arbitrarily attributed to each area a dominant vegetation essential for sustainable land use.

Overlap between land use and sustainable land use was not calculated until 1890. It was then that the rapid speed of deforestation and urbanization made **environmentalists and land record statisticians** to press for more thorough and accurate accounting of the vegetative characteristics and man-made use of the land's surface, so that a better idea of sustainable land use can be arrived at.

1. The primary purpose of the passage is to

(*a*) explain and criticize the methods used by early land record surveyors.

(*b*) compare and contrast a historical situation with a current-day one.

(*c*) describe and explain a historical change.

(*d*) discuss historical opposition to an established institution.

(*e*) trace the origin of a contemporary controversy.

2. Each of the following aspects of nineteenth century United States censuses is mentioned in the passage EXCEPT the

(*a*) year in which data on land use began to be analyzed by sustainable land use.

(*b*) year in which specific information began to be collected on vegetation in addition to the land use.

(*c*) year in which overlap between land use and sustainable land use was first calculated.

(*d*) way in which 1890 census measured vegetative cover and its role in sustainability.

(*e*) way in which land use was determined in the 1840 census.

3. It can be inferred from the passage that the 1840 United States land record census provided a count of which of the following?

(*a*) land use for construction

(*b*) most basic of land use pattern

(*c*) land use in farming

(*d*) land use for providing pastures to animals

(e) land use for cultivation

4. The author uses the adjective 'simple' in line 5 to most probably emphasize that the

(*a*) collection of land records became progressively more difficult throughout the nineteenth century.

(*b*) technology for tabulating land records was rudimentary during the first half of the nineteenth century.

(*c*) human activity on land of the early nineteenth century was easier to analyze than the later human activity on land.

(*d*) land use was better defined in the early nineteenth century than in the late nineteenth century.

(*e*) information collected by early nineteenth century census was limited in its amount of detail.

5. The passage suggests which of the following about the environmentalists and land record statisticians mentioned in line 23?

(*a*) They wanted to call attention to the limited government land.

(*b*) They believed that previous land record information was inadequate and did not reflect sustainable land use in the United States.

(*c*) They had begun to press for changes in land record methods as part of their participation in the Green Movement.

(*d*) They thought that statistics about land use would be more accurate if more land owners were employed as census officials.

(*e*) They had conducted independent studies that disputed the official statistics provided by previous United States census.

Directions (Q. 6 – 8) :

For quite some years there has been a talk to 'monetize' domestic chores which a homemaker does selflessly. It is being felt that the time to put a monetary value to the otherwise thankless job of running the house has come. Concerns about her 'taken for granted' status in the family have been widespread for long. However, in the absence of an economic argument for her status as a housewife and mother, these concerns have not translated into significant progress for her.

Some critics blame this irony on **gender activists**, they believe fail to address the economic issues pertaining to household work, which is bound to appear of no value when compared with the economic returns derived from converting the skills required in running the house into explicitly commercial ones like housekeeping. But, according to Freddy Hustler, that 'illusion' stems from the fact that 'services' rendered by a housewife can never undergo a price tag and thus are bereft of any real quantifiable value. To remedy this, he says, one has to show that all services have economic value — indeed that all household services are economic services. Saving on money to be spent on domestic helps is the same like generating income for the family. In Barber's view, 'monetization' while not so popular with gender activists, reflects the dominant role that economic considerations play in human behavior. When social issues are expressed in an economic form taking the shape of a common currency, it facilitates gender equality.

6. Information in the passage suggests that Freddy Hustler would most readily endorse which of the following statements concerning monetization?

(*a*) Monetization represents a strategy that is attractive to both gender activists and their critics.

(*b*) Monetization is an untested strategy but it is increasingly being embraced by gender activists.

(*c*) Monetization should be restricted first to domestic chores and then gradually be extended.

(*d*) Monetization can serve as a means of representing persuasively the value of household jobs.

(*e*) Monetization should facilitate gender equality only if it is accepted by gender activists.

7. According to the passage, Barber sees monetization as an indication of which of the following?

(*a*) The centrality of economic interests to people's actions.

(*b*) The reluctance of the critics of gender activists to acknowledge the importance of household chores.

(*c*) The inability of financial interests and social interests to reach a common ideological ground.

(*d*) The inevitability of gender inequality.

(*e*) The inevitability of the growth of household services as economic services in the future.

8. Which of the following can be inferred from the passage concerning 'gender activists' mentioned in line 8?

(*a*) They are organized in opposition to the generation of income produced by monetizing domestic chores.

(*b*) They are fewer in number but better organized and better connected to the media than their critics.

(*c*) They have sometimes been charged with failing to use a particular strategy in their pursuit of gender goals.

(*d*) They have been in the forefront of politicizing gender issues.

(*e*) They define gender equality differently and more conservatively than do other organized groups of activists.

Answer Key

1. (*c*)
2. (*d*)
3. (*b*)
4. (*e*)
5. (*b*)
6. (*d*)
7. (*a*)
8. (*c*)

Answer Explanations

1. (c) (*a*) Although the first paragraph mentions how land surveyors would collect land information, there is no criticism.

   (*b*) The purpose of the passage is not to make any comparison.

   (*c*) **Correct.** The passage mentions how a change has occurred over the years in maintenance of land records.

   (*d*) No established institution has been mentioned in the passage.

   (*e*) There is no contemporary controversy mentioned in the passage.

2. (d) (*a*) It is mentioned that in 1870 land was analyzed on the basis of sustainability.

   (*b*) In the same year, dominant vegetation was also mentioned.

   (*c*) It is mentioned that this overlap was calculated in 1890.

   (*d*) **Correct.** Vegetative cover and its role in sustainability were not measured, but demands were made for the same.

   (*e*) How land use was determined is mentioned in the passage.

3. (b) (*a*) Land use for construction isn't mentioned.

   (*b*) **Correct.** It is mentioned that through 1840, simple enumeration by agencies mirrored land use and the most basic of land use pattern.

   (*c*) The 1840 census did not provide any information on farm land.

   (*d*) No such count is provided in the passage.

   (*e*) It was just category of land which was mentioned.

4. (e) (*a*) Collection of land records became progressively more elaborate, and not difficult, with time.

   (*b*) The passage does not mention any technology used.

   (*c*) The author talks of enumeration of land records, not human activity on land.

   (*d*) Land use was better defined later than in the early nineteenth century.

   (*e*) **Correct.** The passage mentions that the information collected was most basic.

5. (b) (*a*) The environmentalists and land record statisticians do not discuss the area of land either under government or private use.

   (*b*) **Correct.** They wanted thorough and accurate accounting; meaning that they definitely did not believe that previous land record information was adequate.

   (*c*) The environmentalists and land record statisticians pressed for change in the enumeration of land records, but it was not as a result of the Green Movement.

(*d*) No such suggestion is made by them.

(*e*) The passage makes no such claims.

6. (d) (*a*) The passage attributes to Barber the view that monetization is unpopular with gender activists. The passage gives no indication that Freddy Hustler would endorse the idea that gender activists currently find monetization attractive.

(*b*) The passage gives no indication that monetization is increasingly being embraced by gender activists, even if Freddy Hustler thinks it should be.

(*c*) The passage indicates Freddy Hustler's belief that all services have economic value.

(*d*) **Correct.** Freddy Hustler believes that services rendered by a housewife are quantifiable; and so, monetization can serve as a means of representing persuasively the value of household jobs.

(*e*) Freddy Hustler is arguing, against some gender activists, that monetization should facilitate gender equality.

7. (a) (*a*) **Correct.** According to Barber, economic interests are central to people's actions. The passage states that "monetization reflects the dominant role that economic considerations play in human behavior."

(*b*) Monetization, as Barber sees it, is a way of assigning value to household chores; and thus acknowledging their importance.

(*c*) For Barber, monetization represents a way for financial interests and social interests to reach a common ideological ground with the use of a common currency.

(*d*) Monetization, according to Barber, would facilitate gender equality.

(*e*) Barber does not view monetization as inevitably spurring the growth of domestic services, but leading to some sort of gender equality.

8. (c) (*a*) They are not opposed to the generation of income produced by monetizing domestic chores, although they did not bring it into as much focus as expected of them.

(*b*) The passage does not speak of numbers or compare activists and their critics.

(*c*) **Correct.** The passage indicates that critics of gender activists believe that they failed "to address the economic issues pertaining to household work."

(*d*) The passage does not provide grounds to infer that they have been in the forefront of politicizing gender issues.

(*e*) The passage does not distinguish between gender groups.

Chapter 7

Reading Comprehension Mastering Question Types

Most reading comprehension questions can be broadly categorized into six types. An ability to quickly identify the question type helps in understanding the aim of the question, which, in turn, improves accuracy when selecting the right answer and/or eliminating the incorrect ones.

1. Main Idea

These questions require you to determine the central point from the overall organization or development of the passage. 'Passage Map' serves as a valuable tool when answering questions of this type.

Main Idea Question Stems

- Which of the following most accurately states the main idea of the passage?
- The primary purpose of the passage is to
- The passage is primarily concerned with which of the following?
- The author of this passage is primarily concerned with
- The main point made by the passage is that

2. Supporting Idea

These questions test your ability to find a specific piece of information, often contained in a particular paragraph in the passage. Sometimes these questions can ask why the author has mentioned a specific piece of information.

Supporting Idea Question Stems

- According to the passage, which of the following is a factor that affects X?
- The author mentions X in order to
- According to the passage, which of the following is true of X?
- The passage mentions each of the following EXCEPT

3. Inference

Although these questions might seem as though they ask you to go beyond what the passage says, the correct answer will always require you to stay as close to the facts in the passage as possible. Sometimes, the questions would also want you to draw conclusions. But make sure that you don't make far-fetched conclusions. Instead draw conclusions that are obvious logical consequences of the information stated in the passage.

Inference Question Stems

- Which of the following does the passage imply about X?
- Which of the following can be inferred about X from the passage?
- The passage suggests all of the following about X EXCEPT

4. Applying Information to a Context Outside the Passage Itself

These questions test your ability to understand the relationships between situations or ideas presented in the passage; and then extrapolate them to similar relationships. The information given in the answer options will not be a part of the passage but the correct answer option will be like/parallel to the situation cited in the passage.

Application Question Stems

- Identify a hypothetical situation that is comparable to a situation presented in the passage.
- Select an example that is similar to an example provided in the passage.
- Which of the following would the author probably agree or disagree with on the basis of statements made in the passage?

5. Logical Structure

These questions test your ability to appreciate and evaluate the organization of different parts in the passage. These not only require you to comprehend the passage but also critically analyze how the author has connected various details in the passage.

Logical Structure Question Stems

- One function of the first paragraph of this passage is to
- The author uses the phrase "X" in the second paragraph to emphasize that
- Which of the following best describes the relation of the last paragraph to the passage as a whole?
- The author refers to X primarily to

6. Style & Tone

These questions test your ability to understand the meaning expressed by the author through her choice of words. A common mistake is to deduce the tone of the author by just a single word that she has used. One needs to consider the language of the passage as a whole; and sometimes go beyond the literal meanings of words or phrases.

Tone Question Stems

- The tone of the author is best described as
- The attitude of the author of the passage toward X is best described as one of

Multiple Choice Questions

Directions (Q. 1 – 8) :

Indonesia, once a sports powerhouse, now trails many nations in games. The problem is not the country's players, who are talented, but Indonesia's sports policy. Going by the current scenario, Indonesia faces the prospect of dismal performances in sports events, until the country's sports bodies and government recognize the fundamental differences between Indonesian sports practices and the sports system abroad. Today the key issue is not protection versus exposure, but diminishing returns in sports versus improved performances of other nations.

Indonesia is in a time warp. Its sports policy is stuck in the mid-1960s when Indonesia and Malaysia dominated world sports. A protectionist attitude of these countries was the principal obstacle to exposure in sports for the other nations. Indonesian supremacy was unchallenged across all the main sports. However, in the intervening period, the sports scenario has changed worldwide, but the Indonesian sports policy hasn't.

Today, Indonesian sports policy is seeing an unending conflict between proponents of 'home grown' and 'professional' coaches. Those supporting the 'home grown' coaches argue that they are better suited to the system than someone from outside. Those in favor of the 'professional' coaches assert that the system demands keeping up with changing times and changing international standards. In a way both are correct. The 'home grown coaches' require professional knowledge of the game, but at the same time 'professional coaches' also have to know the system from the 'home grown' coaches.

But both sides base their positions on two outdated premises. Firstly, that world sport is conducted under the terms of the 'General Agreement on Sports and Sports Practices' (GASSP) and dominated by Indonesia and similar sports systems abroad. Secondly, multilateral mutual exchanges in sports are the most effective way to enhance sports performances.

However, both the assumptions are wrong. The 60-year-old GASSP covers less than 10% of world sports, which is no longer dominated by the 'home grown' theory. Nearly 80% of world sports follows sports practices which are at odds with those of Indonesia. Multilateral mutual exchanges in sports across so many disciplines and so many countries are virtually impossible. And while talks on multilateral mutual exchanges drag on, Indonesia misses opportunities to recover lost ground.

1. Which of the following best states the difference between 'home grown' and 'professional' coaches, as explained in the passage

   (*a*) 'Home grown' coaches require protection, whereas 'professional' coaches look for multilateral mutual exchanges in sports.

   (*b*) 'Home grown' coaches are better suited to the system, whereas 'professional' coaches, though they bring international standards, are dependent on them.

   (*c*) The sports policies of countries like Indonesia are based on the theory of 'home grown' coaches, whereas the sports policies of other nations are based on 'professional' coaches.

   (*e*) Nations, following 'home grown' coaches' theory, enter into individual sports agreements with each other, whereas nations following 'professional' coaches' theory conduct multilateral mutual exchanges.

   (*e*) 'Home grown' coaches assume a constant level of world sports, whereas 'professional' coaches assume a steady expansion of world sports.

2. It can be inferred from the passage that the author would most likely agree with which of the following statements about 'multilateral mutual exchanges'?

(*a*) 'Multilateral mutual exchanges' are the most effective way to enhance sports performances.

(*b*) They are most effective in dealing with issues pertaining to professional coaches between nations.

(*c*) They have only recently begun to make an impact on global sports.

(*d*) Indonesian reliance on 'multilateral mutual exchanges,' is inadequate in today's sports scenario.

(*e*) The principles of 'multilateral mutual exchanges' are incompatible with current Indonesian sports policy.

3. Which of the following statements best summarizes the author's opinion of 'home grown' coaches and 'professional' coaches?

(*a*) The 'home grown' and 'professional' coaches debate provides a healthy and effective forum for examining Indonesian sports policy.

(*b*) The proponents of 'professional' coaches are essentially correct, while those who advocate 'home grown' coaches are not.

(*c*) The proponents of 'home grown' coaches are better able to deal with current sports problems than are the 'professional' coaches.

(*d*) Neither the 'home grown' nor 'professional' coaches can come up with a workable sports policy because neither takes 'multilateral mutual exchanges' into account.

(*e*) The proponents of both 'home grown' and 'professional' coaches have based their positions on out-of-date premises that do not reflect current sports scenario.

4. The author mentions all of the following as characteristic of sports in the mid-1960s except

(*a*) Indonesia played a major role in world sports.

(*b*) Malaysia played a major role in world sports.

(*c*) Protectionism was the principal obstacle to exposure in sports for the other nations.

(*d*) 'Professional' coaches dominated world sports.

(*e*) Indonesian players were unsurpassed in most disciplines.

5. In presenting the argument in the passage, the author uses all of the following except

(*a*) statistical information about world sports.

(*b*) definitions of terms concerning world sports.

(*c*) generalizations about Indonesia's sports system.

(*d*) historical background of Indonesia's sports policy.

(*e*) an example of a sports system whose sports practices differ from those of Indonesia.

6. The author asserts which of the following about Indonesia's sports policy?

(*a*) A revision of Indonesia's sports policy is necessary unless Indonesian players improve their performance.

(*b*) The most crucial issue facing Indonesian sports policy makers is that of exposure versus protection.

(c) Indonesia's current sports policy was developed during the 1960s; and has changed little since that time.

(d) Indonesia's sports policy is widely emulated throughout the world.

(e) Indonesia's sports policy has gradually evolved over the past sixty years.

7. The passage is primarily concerned with

(a) illustrating the erosion of Indonesian position in world sports.

(b) examining the differences between 'home grown' and 'professional' coaches.

(c) advocating a reassessment of Indonesia's sports policy.

(d) criticizing the terms of the 'General Agreement on Sports and Sports Practices' (GASSP).

(e) comparing the different sports practices of countries.

8. The author implies that the main obstacle to a truly effective sports policy in Indonesia is

(a) weak position that Indonesia currently holds in world sports.

(b) inability of the Indonesian government in recognizing the fundamental differences between Indonesian sports practices and the sports system abroad.

(c) dominance of the supporters of 'home grown' coaches in the debate between 'home grown' and 'professional' coaches.

(d) the inability to perform on the part of Indonesian sports players.

(e) 'protection' that characterizes Indonesia's sports policy.

Answer Key

1. (*b*)
2. (*d*)
3. (*e*)
4. (*d*)
5. (*e*)
6. (*c*)
7. (*c*)
8. (*b*)

Answer Explanations

1. **(b)** (*a*) The distinction between 'home grown' coaches and 'professional' coaches may have, by inference, something to do with protection and exposure but in the context of Indonesia it is not a valid difference.

(*b*) **Correct.** The passage states that 'home grown' coaches know the system better. 'Professional' coaches are dependent on them.

(*c*) It does not provide anything resembling a definition of 'home grown' and 'professional' coaches and their difference.

(*d*) The passage does not distinguish between the two.

(*e*) The expansion of world sports has no direct bearing on 'home grown' and 'professional' coaches.

2. **(d)** (*a*) The author calls 'multilateral mutual exchanges' nearly impossible; so, the question of their efficacy does not arise.

(*b*) The passage does not mention if they are most effective or not. No such comparison is made in the passage.

(*c*) The passage does not mention any impact of 'multilateral mutual exchanges' on global sports.

(*d*) **Correct.** Indonesian reliance on 'multilateral mutual exchanges' is inadequate. Not only is it virtually impossible, but also nearly 80% of global sports is conducted by principles which are at odds with those of Indonesia.

(*e*) The passage does not say whether 'multilateral mutual exchanges' are incompatible with Indonesian sports policy.

3. **(e)** (*a*) The passage implies that the debate between the 'home grown' and 'professional' coaches is unlikely to make any progress because of two outdated assumptions that both sides make.

(*b*) The passage states that both are correct in a way.

(*c*) Both are incompatible with current sports problems.

(*d*) Both wrongly assume that the best way to enhance sports performance is through 'multilateral mutual exchanges.'

(*e*) **Correct.** The passage is clear that the assumptions on which both the proponents of 'home grown' and 'professional' coaches base their arguments are outdated.

4. **(d)** (*a*) The passage states that this was so in the mid-1960s.

(*b*) This is stated in the passage.

(*c*) The passage states that "a protectionist attitude of these countries was the principal obstacle to exposure in sports for the other nations".

(*d*) **Correct.** The passage does not mention this that in the mid-1960s 'professional' coaches dominated world sports.

(*e*) The passage states that "Indonesian supremacy was unchallenged across all the main sports".

5. (e) (*a*) The passage gives some statistical information about world sports, like, nearly 80% of world sports is conducted by principles which are at odds with those of Indonesia.

(*b*) The passage defines 'home grown' and 'professional' coaches.

(*c*) The passage states that the Indonesian supremacy was unchallenged across all the main sports.

(*d*) The passage indicates that Indonesian sports policy is stuck in the mid-1960s – the time when it dominated world sports.

(*e*) **Correct.** No sports system has been cited except that of Malaysia; and that it has adopted the same sports practices as Indonesia.

6. (c) (*a*) The passage states that the problem is not Indonesia's players.

(*b*) The passage clearly mentions that the key issue today is not exposure versus protection.

(*c*) **Correct.** Indonesia is in a time warp; and its sports policy is stuck in the mid-1960s.

(*d*) Much of world sports follows sports practices which are at odds with those of Indonesia. Hence the question of emulation does not arise.

(*e*) The passage emphasizes the lack of change in Indonesia's sports policy.

7. (c) (*a*) The passage gives no examples to show how the erosion happened.

(*b*) The passage is not primarily concerned with this difference. Moreover, it states that both rely on the same assumptions.

(*c*) **Correct.** The passage advocates the need for a reassessment of Indonesia's sports policy.

(*d*) It is not criticism, but the irrelevance of GASSP which the passage touches on.

(*e*) No such comparison is made.

8. (b) (*a*) That Indonesia is lagging behind in world sports is true but it is not an obstacle to a truly effective sports policy. On the other hand, it is a cause for it.

(*b*) **Correct.** The passage clearly states that Indonesia faces the prospect of dismal performances in sports events, until the country's sports bodies and government recognize the fundamental differences between Indonesian sports practices and the sports system abroad.

(*c*) The passage does not talk of any such dominance.

(*d*) The passage says that the problem is not the country's players. It also mentions that they are talented.

(*e*) Though Indonesia's sports policy continues to be in a protection mode, the passage mentions that it is no longer a key issue.

Chapter 8

Common Argument Types

Critical reasoning questions in the GMAT typically involve a set of facts, a conclusion drawn from those facts, and an argument that supports or undermines the conclusion. The argument can take different forms, but some common argument patterns include:

- **Cause and Effect :** This argument pattern involves establishing a causal relationship between two events or phenomena. For example, "Because the temperature is rising, the ice caps are melting."
- **Generalization (Sample) :** It involves making a broad statement about a group, based on a limited number of examples. For example, "All cats hate water because my neighbor's cat doesn't like to be bathed."
- **Analogy :** This argument pattern involves comparing two things that are not identical, but share some similarities. For example, "The human brain is like a computer because both process information."
- **Planning :** It typically involves evaluating a proposal or plan of action to determine its feasibility or effectiveness. The proposal relies on certain assumptions about the feasibility, cost-effectiveness, or efficacy of the plan. For example, "A company proposes to reduce employee turnover by offering more flexible work arrangements, such as, telecommuting and flexible work hours."
- **Statistics :** These arguments typically involve the interpretation of data or the use of statistical methods to draw conclusions. Here's an example of a statistical argument:
- **Argument :** A study found that 80% of people who drink coffee experience some level of increased heart rate. Therefore, coffee is bad for your heart health.

  This argument uses statistical data to make a claim about the health effects of coffee. However, there are several problems with this argument. For one, it doesn't take into account other factors that might contribute to heart health, such as exercise, diet, and genetics. Additionally, the study only found an association between coffee consumption and increased heart rate; it doesn't prove causation.

  Understanding these common argument patterns can be helpful in solving critical reasoning questions accurately because it allows test takers to identify the structure of the argument and the assumptions made. By understanding the argument's structure, test takers can determine whether the conclusion follows logically from the given facts; and whether there are any logical fallacies present. Additionally, by identifying the assumptions made, test takers can evaluate the argument's validity; and consider alternative explanations for the given facts.

1. Causal Argument

- In this type of argument there is a causal relationship between the conclusion and the premise.

  X → Y (when you have x causes y scenario)

- **Assumption:**

  (a) X is the only cause

  (b) It's not a coincidence

  (c) Effect follows cause

Example :

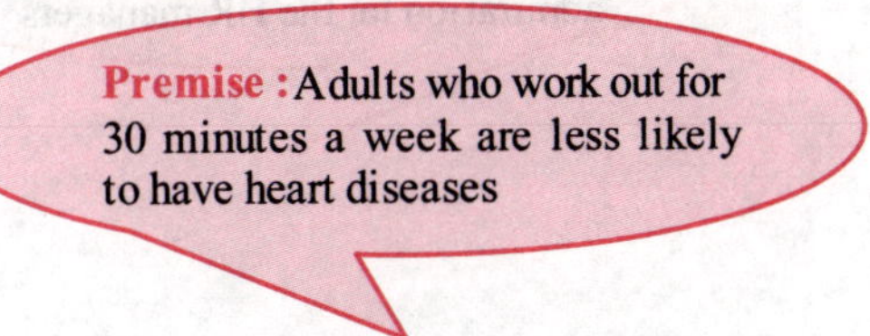

A study indicated that adults who work out for 30 minutes a week are less likely to have heart diseases. Clearly, regular exercise helps improve cardiovascular health.

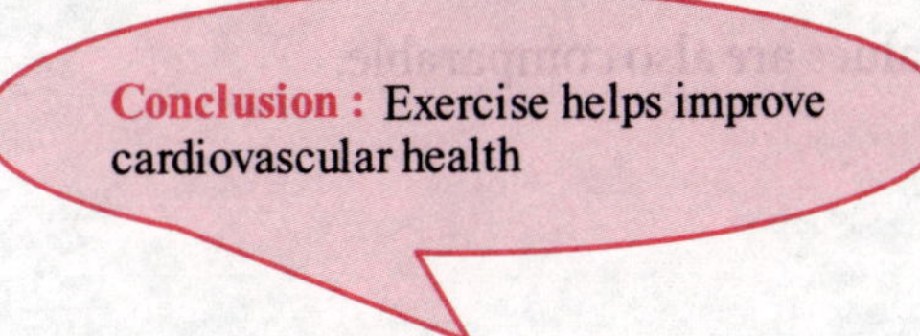

2. Sample & Survey

When the author picks a subset and generalizes the subset.

- **Assumption :**

  (a) Subset is a general representative.

  (b) Data is valid

- Indicators: Sample, survey, volunteers, group of people, etc....

Example :

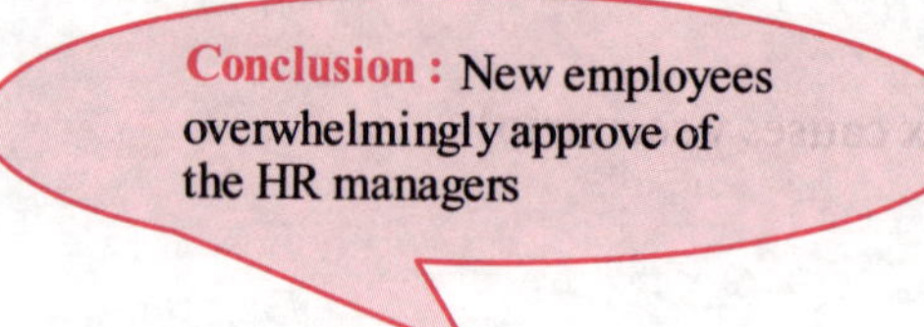

Contrary to popular belief, new employees overwhelmingly approve of the HR managers. We know this to be true because the new employee representative committee expressed admiration for the HR managers in the committee's quarterly feedback for the senior management.

Premise : The new employee representative committee expressed admiration for the HR managers

3. Data & Statistics

- When the author uses percentages, averages, or ratio as evidence; and compare them with numbers.
- **Assumption :** Actual values are also comparable.

Example :

Premise : 90% in rural areas in 1800, now only 20%

Ninety percent of the population of Wakanda lived in rural areas in 1800. Today, only 20 percent of the population lives in rural areas. Clearly, more people lived in the countryside two centuries ago.

Conclusion : More people lived in the countryside two centuries ago.

4. Planning

- The author presents a problem; and offers a plan to solve the problem.

Assumption : Plan will work /plan will solve the problem /plan will achieve the goal.

Break the argument into problem, goal, and plan.

Strengthen : Support the plan.

Weaken : Challenge the plan.

Indicators : Plan, proposal, goal, aim, recommend, strategy, policy etc…

Example :

Premise : Success in the field of medicine requires understanding the minds of patients.

Psychology expert : Few medical colleges require that students who are specializing in medicine take a course in human psychology. The reason being, success in the medicine field requires understanding of the minds of patients. Thus, to help medical students succeed in their careers, medical colleges should increase the duration of the course in human psychology.

Conclusion/Plan : Increase the duration of Human Psychology in medicine dourse.

5. Comparisons

When the author draws a comparison between two things, it is referred to as a comparison argument.

Assumption : X and Y are similar

Strengthen : Show that X and Y are similar.

Weaken : Show that X and Y are different.

Example :

Premise : Best-selling toffee flavor is strawberry

Surveys consistently show that the best-selling toffee flavor is strawberry, although those who prefer chocolate rarely order strawberry. Strawberry-flavored cake, then, probably sells better than chocolate-flavored cake.

Conclusion/Comparison : Strawberry-flavored cake will probably sell better than chocolate-flavored cake.

Chapter 9

Critical Reasoning Practice Questions

Multiple Choice Questions

Q. 1 - Q. 80 Also available in aspiration.ai under post-class assignments.

1. **Historiographer :** Slavery, unquestionably, foreshadowed racial discrimination in the United States. As Africans began to be imported to the English colonies, the colonial administrations began to slacken the terms of service and the preferences for freedom for the then-indentured white servants to encourage more English servants to habilitate the colonies. However, the African laborers were not the beneficiary of such conciliatory legislation, and could be enslaved, that is, indentured for a life devoid of liberty; therefore, they became the preferred choice of their masters for the lowest social status, and the least-desirable works. Due to this continuing association with lowly work, they progressively came to be seen as innately low-grade people.

   Which of the following, if true, most strengthens the inference that racial discrimination in the United States was fostered because of slavery?

   (*a*) In the early 1600s, African laborers were considered more desirable than English laborers.

   (*b*) By the late 1600s, the American colonies witnessed a mass influx of Africans.

   (*c*) In the initial years of the Africans being imported to the English colonies, the masters treated their white and African servants impartially.

   (*d*) The English colonists displayed bias against every other race in the colonies they ruled.

   (*e*) Indentured white servants continued to inhabit the English colonies for about 150 years after the Africans were first imported there.

2. Which of the following best completes the argument?

   Whenever a supermarket outlet increases the price of fruits by 5 to 10%, sales fall by 10 to 15%. However, when the price of grapes was increased by 7%, the quantity of grapes sold did not change. This exception is because________

   (*a*) the rule of demand and supply is not absolute.

   (*b*) the price rise must follow the sale drop.

   (*c*) grapes are, on an average, more expensive than other fruits.

   (*d*) other supermarket outlets in the neighborhood also did not report sales drops of grapes.

   (*e*) the sale of grapes is dependent not only on the price but also on other factors.

3. Which of the following best completes the argument?

   Zenith Systems is one of the most-flourishing Information Technology (IT) consulting corporations. It predominantly deals in cloud computing. David is an IT consultant who specializes in IT cyber security services. Thus, David certainly cannot be employed at Zenith Systems because

   (*a*) David does not have expertise in cloud computing.

   (*b*) cyber security domain is not an area of interest of Zenith Systems.

   (*c*) there is no commonality between the domains that Zenith Systems deals in and David's skillset.

   (*d*) the market size of the cyber security consulting business is insignificant.

   (*e*) a cyber security specialist cannot be a cloud computing specialist.

4. The Kentucky Tennis Board plans to convert the 8 grass tennis courts in the city to floodlit asphalt courts. The floodlit asphalt courts can be used in all weathers and in the evenings, whereas grass courts can only be used during daylight and in summers. Therefore, adding 8 floodlit asphalt courts through this overhaul to the list of existing 12 such courts would significantly increase the year-round availability of quality tennis courts to the public, a benefit that the tennis board asserts will more than offset, in the long term, for the high one-time expenditure of overhaul and an increase, if at all, in yearly outlays for court maintenance.

Which of the following would it be most worthwhile to determine to evaluate the argument?

(*a*) Whether the cost of converting the grass tennis courts to floodlit asphalt courts would be less than the cost of building new floodlit asphalt courts

(*b*) Whether the yearly outlay for maintaining a grass tennis court is less than that for a floodlit asphalt court

(*c*) Whether or not the existing floodlit asphalt courts in the city are able to meet the demand for tennis courts in winters or evenings

(*d*) Whether the grass courts in the city are fully utilized on weekends and in the summer evenings

(*e*) Whether the tennis board can afford to provide free coaching to tennis aspirants at the floodlit asphalt courts

5. The column space given in business periodicals to the success story of a businessman is proportional to the net worth of the businessman. These periodicals are read predominantly by proprietors of small and medium businesses. Therefore, most readers of business periodicals never get to read success stories about businessmen like them in these periodicals.

Which of the following is a valid criticism of the claim made by the author?

(*a*) It is unjustified to club the proprietors of small and medium businesses into one category, as they portray different behaviors.

(*b*) It is wrong to presume that stories about proprietors of small and medium businesses do not get any column space in business periodicals.

(*c*) Many businessmen, who later appear in business periodical stories, start as proprietors of small or medium businesses.

(*d*) The proprietors of small and medium businesses buy business periodicals only to motivate themselves to enhance their net worth.

(*e*) Not all businessmen who have high net worth get appeared in business periodical stories.

6. All over the world, lower socioeconomic status is observed to be closely related to worse population health and higher mortality rates. In the United States, the average household income, education, and standard of health services of Latin American immigrants are much lower than those of American whites. However, the mortality rate for the elderly population of the Latin American immigrants in the United States was observed to be 20 percent lower than that of the American whites.

Which of the following, if true, would help resolve the apparent paradox revealed above?

(*a*) The mortality rate for the young population was observed to be 20 percent higher for the Latin American immigrants in the United States than the American whites.

(*b*) The health of Latin American immigrants who had recently migrated to the United States was observed to be better than the health of second- and third-generation Latin Americans born and raised in the United States.

(*c*) The Latin Americans who migrate to the United States tend to be healthier than both the average population of their home country and the average native American whites, thus requiring occasional medical attention.

(*d*) When immigrants first migrate, they have to pick more physically demanding jobs; but over the period, as they pick better jobs, they develop a sedentary lifestyle similar to that of most white Americans.

(*e*) Upon growing old, many Latin American immigrants return to their home countries; and, when they die, their deaths are not registered by the United States.

7. Which of the following most logically completes the passage?

Tomato, an indigenous Central Mexican plant, was identified by the Spanish colonists when they raided the territory in the sixteenth century. In Nahuatl, the native language of the territory, the name of the tomato plant was 'tomatl' and was amended to 'tomate' in Spanish. After the Spanish colonists took the plant to Spain, it became prevalent through trade in some parts of Europe, including the United Kingdom. The English word 'tomato' is undoubtedly originated from the Spanish 'tomate' and not directly from the Nahuatl 'tomatl' because ________.

(*a*) the English language originated later than Nahuatl

(*b*) before, during, or soon after the Spanish raid in Central Mexico, the English did not have any access to Mexico

(*c*) Nahuatl is now a nonexistent language

(*d*) the English language contains many words of Spanish origin but contains only a few directly from Nahuatl

(*e*) the name 'tomato' in most European languages is derived from the Spanish 'tomate'

8. Medics face an ethical dilemma with glaucoma patients over choosing between prescribing a legal drug with some harmful side effects or advising an illegal drug, cannabis, which works better despite causing hallucination effects. The European Medical Association (EMA) has officially warned medical practitioners that recommending patients an illicit drug is prohibited under federal law, and punishment can include sentencing. So far, no medic has been detained, but it is certain that medics will not be able to avert punitive action against them for long.

Which of the following, if true, would undermine the conclusion derived from the argument?

(*a*) Glaucoma patients do not experience any side effects from cannabis use.

(*b*) Medics respect the European Medical Association's (EMA) directives above their ethics.

(*c*) Medical use of cannabis is not illegal in many non-European countries.

(*d*) Many patients have been booked for consuming illegal drugs following medics' advice.

(*e*) Some drugs now commonly used for medical purposes, such as marijuana, were once illegal to use.

9. The Golden Era company cheats artifact collectors by selling some artifacts labelled as "antique." Furthermore, these artifacts are common and available in the local market at significantly cheaper rates.

Which of the following can be inferred from the above argument?

(*a*) Not all of the Golden Era company's artifacts are non-antique.

(*b*) Some artifacts with the Golden Era are duplicates of the original artifacts.

(*c*) The prices of some artifacts in the local market must be nearly the same as those of similar artifacts with the Golden Era company.

(*d*) Non-antique artifacts with the Golden Era company must be of lower quality.

(*e*) The state-run The Archaeological Department should be the only approval agency that can tag any artifact as "antique."

10. To simplify the tax computation and collection system in the country, the trade and commerce minister recommended a single rate of tax of 8 percent for all goods and services that are currently taxed.

Which of the following must be evaluated before taking the decision to simplify the tax system?

(*a*) Whether the traders, who deal in goods and services on which the current tax rate is higher than the recommended rate, would oppose it

(*b*) Whether the bill recommending a single tax rate on all currently taxable goods and services would pass the assembly unanimously

(*c*) Whether the tax revenue after the implementation of the recommended single tax rate would at least be equal to the current tax revenue

(*d*) Whether nation-wide preparation to implement the recommended single tax rate plan is complete

(*e*) Whether the government's prior reforms resulted in the desired outcome

11. The economic slump in the country is over, and the recovery is underway now, although some critics remain skeptical. The employment commission's predictions for employment trends between 1990 and 2000 clearly suggest that **the greatest increase in the number of people employed will be in the low-paying hospitality sector. Though low-paying hospitality jobs will not increase their percentage share of overall employment, high-paying hospitality jobs will**; proving critics wrong.

In the argument given, the two portions in boldface play which of the following roles?

(*a*) The first is a premise that has been used against the author; the second supports the main conclusion.

(*b*) The first is a statement accepted by the author; the second is a consequence of the critics' skepticism.

(*c*) The first is a consideration that the author offers in support of his/her conclusion; the second is a fact that the author believes does not contradict his/her conclusion.

(*d*) The first is evidence advanced by the critics to build their position; the second is evidence offered advanced by the author to explain his/her position.

(*e*) The first is evidence that undermines the author's position; the second is a statement that follows from that position.

12. All popular movie stars are great voice actors. All popular politicians are acclaimed orators, which requires great voice acting. Thus, no popular movie star-turned-politician is a popular politician.

The argument above assumes which of the following?

(*a*) Not all acclaimed orators become popular politicians.

(*b*) No popular movie stars become popular politicians.

(*c*) Most of the popular movie stars focus less on voice acting than their oratorship skill.

(*d*) All popular movie stars are poor orators.

(*e*) Oratorship requires one to speak at length extempore, while popular movie stars depend solely on written scripts.

13. People consider cars an investment, whereas, in reality, they are depreciating assets. Even if a buyer consistently follows the periodic service schedule of the car, within just three years, noticeable changes unavoidably accrue. Such a car appears as good as new to the owner, who thinks that the car's value would only have depreciated marginally. However, any resale car dealer will tell the owner that he/she will be lucky to get even half of the car's purchase price.

Which of the following, if true, supports the resale car dealer's claim the most?

(*a*) A car depreciates by 30% the moment it is driven out of the showroom, and double-digit depreciation is unavoidable for the next year onward.

(*b*) Many people purchase cars to use casually, only to pass them off to their kids or someone close to them later.

(*c*) For those people who purchase a car for the first time, the car has more sentimental value attached to it than its current value.

(*d*) Some drivers follow the habit of reckless driving and intermittent servicing of their cars.

(*e*) In most cases, car rental companies are always willing to buy used cars of foreign models off the market.

14. Although Dalton International School provided skilled teachers and a refurbished curriculum, moral science and history scores for grade X students failed to reach the desired level. Therefore, the parents suggested to the headmaster that moral science and history be taught in their native language, instead of in English.

The parents' suggestion presupposes which of the following?

(*a*) Unlike subjects, such as, math and natural science, moral science and history can be better understood by teachers in their native language.

(*b*) Subjects, such as, math and natural science can be better explained by teachers and comprehended by students in the English language than in their native language.

(*c*) The average scores for grade X students in subjects other than moral science and history must be significantly above the desired level of parents.

(*d*) There are a sizable number of English-medium schools in town in which a few subjects are taught in the native language.

(*e*) Comprehension of the content in subjects, such as, moral science and history would be greatly enhanced if they are taught in the native language.

15. Which of the following best completes the argument?

Recent research conducted by the National Military Forces' tropical disease branch indicates that the malaria parasite has an incubation period of no more than 95 days. Surprisingly, examinations of over 85 military service members revealed that 22 of them had contracted malaria even after more than 100 days of their return to the United States from a malaria-bearing zone. The longest period was 122 days for a pilot who contracted malaria after returning to the United States. This is a reasonable exception since

(*a*) insecticide-resistant mosquitos have become commonplace in the United States

(*b*) mosquitoes getting trapped inside aircraft is a common complaint among pilots while returning from malaria-bearing zones

(*c*) the malaria parasite's incubation time is considered a maximum of 95 days, with the exception of 1%

(*d*) the incubation period of malaria parasites varies depending on the breed of mosquito

(*e*) the effectiveness of anti-malaria vaccines has weakened in the last two decades

16. Forty percent of car mechanics who own garages and pursued a qualifying course from the Industrial Training Institute earn more than $70,000 per year, whereas only 20% of those who own garages but did not pursue the qualifying course from the Industrial Training Institute earn more than $70,000 per year. These figures indicate a positive correlation between the importance of technical qualification and higher earnings.

Which of the following must be considered before concluding that technical qualifications help in earning more?

(*a*) Whether the fee for the qualifying course is affordable for the members of the second group

(*b*) Whether the average earning of the first group is significantly more than that of the second group

(*c*) Whether the members of the first group are more professional in their approach

(*d*) Whether the members of the first group are less proficient than those of the second group

(*e*) Whether the minimum earnings of a member of each of the groups are nearly the same

17. In cases of cardiac arrest, rapid response is vital to enhance the chances of recovery for the victims. However, especially in thinly populated rural areas, a consistently rapid response is impossible to attain, chiefly because of long distances. For this reason, prior to the dispatch of mobile treatment teams, to ascertain the severity of the cardiac arrest, emergency attendants have been issued a list of diagnostic questions to go through with those reporting cardiac arrest. It is clear that victims will suffer because of this additional procedure, and that few will benefit from it.

In making the conclusion, the author has necessarily assumed which of the following?

(*a*) A mobile treatment team is unlikely to be dispatched if there is no severity to cardiac arrest.

(*b*) Those who report cardiac arrests are ill-equipped to handle a diagnostic questioning procedure at that time.

(*c*) There are other ways of ensuring chances of recovery other than a quick response in the case of cardiac arrest.

(*d*) Ascertaining the severity of cardiac arrests is not possible through a list of diagnostic questions asked over the telephone.

(*e*) No patient suffering from cardiac arrest in rural areas can benefit from this additional procedure of diagnostic questioning.

18. A couple of months after the completion of the national elections, Mega Poll claimed to measure the popularity of politicians and **placed the prime minister of the country 35 points below the leader of a small party and 20 points below the leader of the opposition**. Subsequently, another poll carried out by a leading magazine confirmed the findings of the poll but suggested that the figures were only an accurate reflection of voters' opinions within a 5 percent range. Clearly, however, **the electorate is more influenced by the policies of political parties than their leaders**.

In the argument given, the two portions in boldface play which of the following roles?

(*a*) The first is a claim that the argument disputes; the second is a conclusion that is based on that claim.

(*b*) The first is a claim whose implication supports a conclusion that the argument rejects; the second is that conclusion.

(*c*) The first is evidence that is presented to call the main conclusion into question; the second is the main conclusion of the argument.

(*d*) The first is a claim that is consistent with the second; the second is a claim derived from understanding the implication of the first.

(*e*) The first is a finding whose accuracy is evaluated in the argument; the second is evidence presented to establish that the finding is accurate.

19. TMZ Corporation has had a bad business quarter. Rather than laying off workers to cut costs, it plans to defer their salaries by 30 days; and invest the accrued money in a debt fund to earn interest to cover the operational expenses. By implementing this, TMZ and its workers will avoid the undesirable consequences often linked with earning deficits.

Which of the following can be properly inferred from the argument above?

(*a*) The workers have consented to invest their salaries in the debt fund for 30 days.

(*b*) Investing in a debt fund is the only option left for TMZ to avoid the undesirable consequences.

(*c*) Some workers will have to borrow money for 30 days to meet their monthly expenses.

(*d*) The debt fund under consideration has the potential to earn interest to cover operational expenses.

(*e*) TMZ has adequate sales orders for the upcoming quarter.

20. The Georgian government has decided to limit the import of confectionery items from the neighboring countries that export the greatest amount of confectionery to Georgia. A business consultant hired by the government opines that this move will soon increase the sales of Made-In-Georgia confectionery items.

The consultant assumes which of the following?

(*a*) The quality of Georgian-made confectionery items is below that of international brands.

(*b*) The unavailability of foreign-made confectionery items will boost the sales of Made-In-Georgia confectionery items.

(c) Made-In-Georgia confectionery items are relatively more expensive than similar foreign-made confectionery items.

(d) Made-In-Georgia confectionery items are mostly in short supply.

(e) Import duties on foreign-made confectionery items are significantly lower in Georgia.

21. If you study for three hours daily, your problem-solving skills will improve. If your problem-solving skills improve, you are assured of a good score. So, if you study for three hours daily, you are assured of a good score.

Which one of the following most closely parallels the reasoning in the argument above?

(a) If you solve quantitative reasoning questions daily for an hour, your reasoning will improve. If your reasoning improves, you can crack data-sufficiency questions with ease. So, if you solve quantitative reasoning questions daily for an hour, you can crack problem-solving questions with ease.

(b) If you do not consume excess carbonated beverages, you will feel energetic. If you consume excess carbonated beverages, you will not feel light. So, if you do not consume excess carbonated beverages, you will feel light.

(c) If a country's currency depreciates, imports rise. If imports rise, inflation rises. So, when a country's currency appreciates, inflation does not rise.

(d) If you sleep for less than six hours a day, you will feel dissatisfied and sluggish. If you feel dissatisfied and sluggish, your efficiency will drop. So, if you sleep for less than six hours a day, your efficiency will drop.

(e) If a chef cooks your favorite dish, you will love it. If you are a connoisseur of food, you must love cooking. So, if you are a connoisseur of food, you are a chef.

22. Recently, during the rice-growing season, Kyushu, Japan encountered a huge flood. This will lead to the doubling of the rice price this season, and eventually to the rise in the cost of making rice-cakes. Ultimately, rice-cake consumers in Kyushu will now have to pay more.

Which of the following best describes the flaw in the reasoning of the argument?

(a) Considering that the outcome of an event is dependent on other events

(b) Considering that many causes are capable of affecting one event

(c) Considering that the cause is capable of affecting many events

(d) Considering that the outcome of an event is solely dependent on one event

(e) Considering that the law of supply and demand is not applicable in this case

23. A recent study on brand preferences showed that brand X is considered the best among all cheese brands. It is ahead of the next two preferred brands : brands Y and Z, by big margins. Yet country-wide sales figures disclosed that brands Y and Z each sold many more packs of cheese than did brand X.

Which of the following would most help to resolve the apparent discrepancy depicted in the argument?

(a) Brand Z sold more packs than brands Y and X combined.

(b) The average per kilogram price of brand Y cheese is lower than that of brand Z cheese.

(*c*) The study was carried out only in selected cities, where the distribution network of brand X is strong, but not country-wide.

(*d*) The average per kilogram price of brand X cheese is not considerably higher than that of brand Z and brand Y.

(*e*) A few stores do not stock brand X cheese because its wholesalers demand that brand X be stocked exclusively.

24. The depreciation of Europe's currency, the Euro is giving mixed feelings. **The German economy, in particular, is prospering with increasing exports of almost everything, from heavy industries to hospitality and services.** The French economy is echoing the same, with a special weightage on defense equipment. However, the European Central Bank has issued its most stern warning yet that the Euro will depreciate by at least 4 percent over the next five-to-seven months, implying that its intervention to stop the Euro's depreciation is critical.

In the given argument, the boldface portion plays which of the following roles?

(*a*) A fact that strengthens the main conclusion

(*b*) A fact that weakens the main conclusion

(*c*) A supposition whose accuracy is tested in the argument

(*d*) An assumption that is upheld as incorrect

(*e*) A conclusion that is called into question by the argument

25. The government of Maldova must not let mafia-run opium companies deduct shipping costs from their revenues when calculating payments that go to the government. These opium companies must pay a larger sum of money. Consequently, they will have to increase the opium price, thereby discouraging buyers on the global market from buying Maldovan opium.

Which of the following, if true, would weaken the claim that Maldovan opium companies would have to increase the opium price?

(*a*) The shipping costs are now considerably lower than before.

(*b*) Opium companies will need government approval before they increase the opium price.

(*c*) The closest competitor to the Maldovan opium companies prices its opium higher than the Maldovan opium companies do.

(*d*) The sum of money Moldovan government would earn because of increased payments would be used to eradicate the drug menace.

(*e*) A study conducted by the International Pharmaceutical Federation endorses the therapeutic use of opium.

26. Typically, the average per-quintal price of Basmati rice ranges from $50 to $80; however, due to ill-timed rain wreaking havoc on paddy farms in the western part of the country, which supplies over 75 percent of Basmati rice, the average per-quintal price was expected to skyrocket to $110 per quintal. Unexpectedly, it has remained in the range of $60 to $90.

Which of the following, if true, would best explain the unexpected scenario above?

(*a*) There was no ill-timed rain in other parts of the country that also harvest Basmati rice.

(*b*) The average Basmati rice harvest from other parts of the country was not significantly impacted.

(*c*) "Jasmine rice," another popular variety of rice, is relatively cheaper than Basmati rice and tastes similar to Basmati rice; it witnessed record production in the eastern part of the country.

(*d*) Per-capita consumption of Basmati rice in the eastern part of the country decreased.

(*e*) Four leading food-processing companies in the country invested heavily in the packaged rice business that excluded Basmati rice.

27. Synocare asserts that its computerized scrutiny system will be able to simplify the registration of new claimants throughout the US. The system will decrease the likelihood of fraudulent claims by cross-checking the names of claimants against past employment records and birth certificates. The government spokesperson claims that, once the system is on the roll, it will be able to save around $750 million every year, which is currently paid for miscellaneous prescriptions that are then sold to people unqualified to receive Synocare assistance.

Which of the following, if true, most weakens the claim of the government spokesperson?

(*a*) The Synocare system has a great reputation for reliability.

(*b*) The experts claim that the annual maintenance of the Synocare system would be as high as 25 percent of the system's cost.

(*c*) The Synocare system will not be able to prevent all fraudulent claims.

(*d*) Many healthcare professionals have expressed concern that the support staff cannot be fully trained to handle the Synocare system.

(*e*) Critics claim that the Synocare system will discourage some of the most underprivileged patients from getting critical medication.

28. **In a breakthrough decision, a Nepalese judge recently rejected a NPR 20 million claim for earthquake damage by the Kathmandu Metropolitan City against the Nepal Insurance Company.** The judge said that, as geological technology has advanced to the point where environmental calamities can almost be forecasted, it is the responsibility of the Kathmandu Metropolitan City to seek expert technical advice on probable threats and take safeguards accordingly. Seismic scientists have charted the specific regions of the earth that, within the next two years, will possibly experience seismic activity of sufficient strength to cause structural damage, loss of life, and casualties.

Which of the following best explains the role played by the portion in boldface in the above argument?

(*a*) It states the position that the argument opposes.

(*b*) It presents evidence against the position that the argument supports.

(*c*) It is a fact that is first contested and then supported with an example.

(*d*) It asserts the position that the argument approves.

(*e*) It asserts a position that is refuted by the argument.

29. At Milton Utility Products Limited, the year-on-year increase in the salaries of the executives who head product lines depends only on the extent of revenue growth shown by their respective product lines during the year. The product line headed by Manager X showed a year-on-year revenue growth of 10 percent, while the product line headed by Manager Y showed a year-on-year revenue growth of 50 percent. However, Manager X, received a 40%

year-on-year salary increase, while Manager Y received a 5% year-on-year salary increase.

Which one of the following, if true, most helps to explain the apparent discrepancy in the information given above?

(*a*) The product line headed by Manager X accounts for 50 percent of the total annual costs of the company, while the product line headed by Manager Y accounts for only 10 percent.

(*b*) For the past five years, Manager X has consistently achieved a higher year-on-year salary increase than Manager Y.

(*c*) Manager X is better connected than Manager Y with the senior executives who approve each year-on-year increase in the salaries of the executives who head product lines.

(*d*) The product line headed by Manager X operates in a shrinking market whose total revenue, across all companies, had a year- on-year decrease of 30 percent, while the product line headed by Manager Y operates in a booming market whose total revenue, across all companies, had a year-on-year increase of 1,000 percent.

(*e*) The number of units sold by the product line headed by Manager X during the year was eight times that of the product line headed by Manager Y.

30. A premium tea brand is advertised as healthy tea since the brand contains ginger flakes, dried basil leaves, and ginseng extract. It is ironic that the tea brand overlooks the fact that it contains caffeine, too. If you add caffeine to milk, the milk will no longer be healthy.

Which of the following most accurately depicts the method of reasoning applied in the argument?

(*a*) Quoting a claim to establish a point

(*b*) Quoting an example to ascertain a theory

(*c*) Quoting a claim to refute a theory

(*d*) Quoting a new fact to challenge a claim

(*e*) Asserting a questionable claim to challenge a claim

31. The price of lemons has been rising for over a couple of months. Thus, it is inevitable that the price of the Supreme dishwashing bar that contains lemon extract will rise soon.

Which one of the following states an assumption upon which the argument depends?

(*a*) One of the ingredients used in the Supreme dishwashing bar is lemon extract.

(*b*) Prices of other ingredients used in the Supreme dishwashing bar are also rising.

(*c*) The Supreme dishwashing bar contains a significant proportion of lemon extract.

(*d*) Prices of popular soap bars that also contain lemon extracts are also rising.

(*e*) The increased price of Supreme dishwashing bar can be borne by customers.

32. The digital magazine, Crompton Business Review, has earned a reputation for publishing cutting-edge, incisive, and insightful blogs. However, many blogs written by editors fall far beyond the defined scope. Such blogs do not succeed in being published in the digital magazine.

Which one of the following can be properly inferred from the statements above?

(*a*) A few blogs written by editors are too technical.

(*b*) The blogs that do not succeed in being published in the digital magazine are imperfect.

(*c*) The digital magazine does not publish blogs that are intriguing.

(*d*) If a blog is not published in the digital magazine but is within the defined scope, it is not written by the magazine's editor.

(*e*) A few blogs that go far beyond the defined scope do not qualify to be published in the digital magazine.

33. An acclaimed media mogul is always looking for ways to improve his portfolio of media channels, but he has a reputation for aggressively pursuing his dwindling newspapers. When the mogul ran a campaign to secure control of a waning, but respectable, political magazine in the country where he already maintains a satellite television station and numerous national dailies, the media indicted him of trying to influence public opinion; and filed a plea in court for the sale to be ceased. The attorneys for the mogul refute this allegation, pointing out that the mogul has assured them that he will not influence the editorial policies of the target magazine, and demanded that the acquisition of the magazine be allowed by the court.

Which of the following, if true, would most weaken the media mogul's case?

(*a*) He has a reputation for building declining companies into sustainable ones.

(*b*) He has a reputation for dismissing young journalists from declining newspapers he has acquired.

(*c*) Usually, newspaper owners do not meddle in editorial policies.

(*d*) To save costs, editorial content from the news bank serving his other media channels will be used for the magazine.

(*e*) He runs several charitable trusts.

34. Consultant to the Excel Entertainment executive: In a survey, the leading entertainment magazine Showbiz indicates that as many as two-thirds of its readers want more movie shows per day on smaller multiplex screens than fewer of those per day on bigger multiplex screens. Therefore, in your new multiplex, you must plan more smaller screens than bigger ones.

Which of the following, if true, supports the argument above?

(*a*) An increasing number of people have been preferring to watch movies on television.

(*b*) Compared to single-screen theaters, a significantly greater number of multiplex theaters are coming up in the country.

(*c*) The proportion of smaller multiplex screens to bigger multiplex screens in the most under-construction multiplexes is greater than that in the existing multiplexes.

(*d*) The ratio of space needed for a standard smaller multiplex screen to that for a standard bigger multiplex screen is 9 : 16.

(*e*) Most movies in regional languages are shown on smaller screens.

35. There is a growing population of elderly people; however, **despite a prolonged shortage of skilled workers throughout the US, companies are still averse to inducting elderly workers**. Senior Pro, an elderly people's rights organization, works for the employment of retired workers. **Senior Pro mentions several examples of successful enterprises that have been employing senior citizens** and, therefore, claims that employing elderly workers is beneficial for business.

Which one of the following best describes the roles played by the two boldfaced portions in the argument?

(*a*) The first is a fact that challenges the second; the second is the conclusion.

(*b*) The first is a fact that is consistent with the conclusion; the second is a claim that works against the conclusion.

(*c*) The first is a consideration that goes against the second; the second is a consideration that forms the basis for the conclusion.

(*d*) The first is the conclusion that goes against the second; the second is a fact.

(*e*) The first is a concern that the argument denies; the second is a conclusion that could be drawn if that concern were allowed to stand.

36. Which of the following best completes the argument?

A study shows that children, who are usually beaten, grow up believing that it is not inappropriate to occasionally beat their children, as well. This cycle is just one instance of beatings perpetuating child abuse. Certain societies opine, however, that beating children is a method of disciplining them, not child abuse; and that disciplining children is necessary to develop good habits in them because.

(*a*) young children often, for no reasonable reason, succumb to tears or laughter, thereby exhibiting mixed emotions at times

(*b*) if beaten adequately, they become mentally tough to endure the adversities of the world

(*c*) they are capable of differentiating between right and wrong; and understanding what to do and what not to do

(*d*) those who are more intelligent are beaten for different reasons than those who are less intelligent

(*e*) child beating is a customary social norm

37. This year, the Arzania government's steep tax hike on tobacco and alcohol was severely criticized by one and all. However, the government has defended this steep hike, claiming that it is the only effective measure against tobacco and alcohol abuse. However, critics claim that such a policy is flawed, as the huge sum collected from taxes finances many governmental welfare schemes, and if the government truly wanted to deter tobacco and alcohol consumption, the government would collapse.

Which of the following can properly be inferred based on the information given above?

(*a*) Taxes collected from tobacco and alcohol fund a few emergency services in Arzania.

(*b*) Arzania charges the highest amount of tax on tobacco and alcohol in the world.

(*c*) Extreme tobacco and alcohol consumption is a menace in many countries.

(*d*) Gradual tax rises result in a gradual decrease in tobacco and alcohol consumption.

(*e*) The Arzania government collects a significant amount of tax money from the sale of tobacco and alcoholic products.

38. The salaries of professors at Dalton University change proportionally with changes in the revenue earned by the university from student tuition. **The government has passed a law this year that forbids universities from increasing tuition fees for the next five years**. At the same time, there are credible reports that the number of student enrolments at Dalton University will be lower next year than it was this year. Therefore, **the professors at Dalton University should expect their salaries next year to be less than they are this year.**

In the argument given, the two portions in boldface play which of the following roles?

(*a*) The first is the only premise that supports the explicit conclusion of the argument; the second is that explicit conclusion.

(*b*) The first is a conclusion that is supported by the argument, but it is not the argument's main conclusion; the second is the main conclusion of the argument.

(*c*) The first is a premise supporting the argument's main conclusion; the second is a conclusion, for which, support is provided but is not the argument's main conclusion.

(*d*) The first is a statement that provides background information to provide the context of the argument; the second is the only explicit conclusion of the argument.

(*e*) The first is a premise supporting a conclusion that is implied by the argument; the second is the only explicit conclusion of the argument.

39. Workers whose jobs are monotonous have poorer mental health than those whose jobs are interesting. Machine-driven jobs involve recurring tasks, and are monotonous for workers. Therefore, replacing workers with mechanical robots to execute machine-driven jobs will improve their mental health, since they can now take up more interesting jobs.

Which of the following would be most helpful to evaluate the argument?

(*a*) Whether the workers who execute machine-driven jobs are competent to execute more interesting jobs

(*b*) Whether the more interesting jobs pay workers at least as much as the mechanical jobs do

(*c*) Whether mechanical robots will soon replace workers in the more interesting jobs too

(*d*) Whether mechanical robots will execute the machine-driven jobs at least as well as workers do

(*e*) Whether there are enough mechanical robots to replace all the workers who execute machine-driven jobs

40. No married woman can lack cooking skills, but girls are not married women. Therefore, the argument that girls can lack cooking skills is not justified.

The flawed reasoning in the argument above is most closely paralleled in which of the following arguments?

(*a*) Many creatures are agile, but ants are not creatures. Therefore, it is right to state that ants are agile.

(*b*) All enterprises must pay taxes, but non-governmental organizations are not enterprises. So, it is sensible to tax non-governmental organizations.

(*c*) No enterprise can avoid filing a tax return. Therefore, the argument that Joe and Jack Inc., which operates in a tax-free region, must file its tax return is befitting.

(*d*) When a fishpond is full of water, fish eat creatures, but when the fishpond is empty, creatures eat fish. Therefore, it is incorrect to state that small organisms cannot overpower big organisms.

(*e*) A pen is mightier than a sword, but the media is mightier than a pen. Therefore, it is right to state that both the pen and the media are mightier than a sword.

41. A survey conducted by the Fish More blog shows that as many as 60 percent of the blog's readers wish to buy fishing boats. However, fishing boat manufacturers can only produce enough boats to satisfy 25% of potential buyers.

Which of the following, if true, would help explain the inconsistent data cited above?

(*a*) The fishing boat industry is a labor-intensive business.

(*b*) The demand for fishing boats is not even across the country.

(*c*) The number of fishermen who buy fishing boats has been increasing every year for the past five years.

(*d*) The number of readers of the Fish More blog is far less than that of potential buyers.

(*e*) A greater number of Fish More blog readers wants to buy fishing boats for investment purposes.

42. Instead of attributing an automobile accident to driver error, insurance companies should first try to figure out why the error was made by analyzing flaws in road design, automobile design, and the criteria used to determine eligibility for a driver's license. Only then will the insurance companies be able to effectively issue guidelines to prevent future accidents, instead of merely punishing the concerned driver.

Which of the following states the assumption the argument makes?

(*a*) Driving errors are an insignificant factor in most automobile accidents.

(*b*) The insurance companies, not the road transportation division, should be the ones to investigate automobile accidents.

(*c*) Issuance of effective guidelines will help drivers avoid being penalized.

(*d*) Investigation of accidents should contribute to the prevention of future accidents.

(*e*) If flaws in road design, automobile design, or the criteria used to determine eligibility for a driver's license are addressed, the number of accidents committed by drivers would come down to negligible.

43. Which one of the following most logically completes the argument?

Although technological advances are essential to making things more affordable and efficient at a lower cost, they also make workers feel subordinate. Due to this, workers do not feel content because they do not face challenges in their work, realizing that their skills are not crucial to creation. Therefore, we can conclude that technological advances .

(*a*) are solely accountable for the proficiency in production

(*b*) help increase the compensation of white-collar workers

(*c*) are more welcomed by managers than by workers

(*d*) have made workers' skills less important to their jobs

(*e*) indirectly lay off many workers

44. Carleton has invented a central heating mechanism that industry experts predict will soon be adopted by traditional heating equipment makers. Prior to this innovation, gas-burning heating systems employed a mechanism similar to the carburetors in vehicles : the mixture of air and gas is then fed to the heating burner. However, the Carleton researchers have developed a gas

injection mechanism that heats air before it mixes with gas, raising volatility. Carleton claims that this mechanism will reduce fuel consumption by nearly 30%.

Which of the following represents a necessary assumption for the argument?

(*a*) The gas injection mechanism takes more time to ignite than a traditional mechanism.

(*b*) A 30% reduction in fuel consumption will motivate traditional heating equipment makers to adopt the Carleton mechanism.

(*c*) Central heating systems using traditional mechanisms must be cheaper than those using the Carleton mechanism.

(*d*) The Carleton mechanism creates a less humid environment than traditional mechanisms do.

(*e*) Preheating air before it mixes with gas consumes significantly less energy.

45. The standard bottle sizes of body lotion are 50 ml., 100 ml., 300 ml., 500 ml., and 1,000 ml. Compared with the per milliliter price of body lotion for a 50 ml. bottle, that for a 100 ml. bottle decreases by 10%, that for the 300 ml. bottle decreases by 20%, that for the 500 ml. bottle decreases by 30%, and that for the 1,000 ml. bottle decreases by 40%. Thus, it makes sense to buy a larger bottle of body lotion.

Which of the following must be considered before deciding to buy a larger bottle size EXCEPT:

(*a*) Is the bottle's "best before date" too short?

(*b*) Will a larger than 1,000 ml. bottle become available in the near future?

(*c*) Is the brand of body lotion preferable?

(*d*) Is the brand of body lotion being considered, advertised?

(*e*) Is the per milliliter price of body lotion for a sachet less than the per milliliter price of body lotion for a 1,000 ml. bottle?

46. When the economy is thriving, people are more motivated to learn new skills rather than earn a formal degree. However, when the economy is declining, people prefer to earn a formal degree rather than learn new skills. Thus, when people anticipate that the economy is going to be slow, they become less excited about learning new skills and want to get a degree.

Which of the following can be inferred from the argument above?

(*a*) Those who learn new skills earn more than those who earn only degrees.

(*b*) The foreshadowing of an economic slowdown has intensified over the years.

(*c*) The likelihood of people preferring to learn new skills depends on the extent to which the economy is booming.

(*d*) There are a greater number of professional courses available when the economy is thriving.

(*e*) People's premonition that the economy will slow down determines how many are keen on earning a formal degree.

47. T&T Motors claims that even though it entered the bike market five years after the market leader, about half of the most fuel-efficient bikes on the market are its 100-cc bikes.

Which of the following, if true, most strongly supports T&T's claims?

(*a*) T&T Motors licensed cutting-edge engine technology from Tsuyu Motors, the global leader in the 2-wheeler market.

(*b*) 80-cc bikes are less fuel efficient than 100-cc bikes.

(*c*) Any bike of any make other than T&T's 100-cc bike is less fuel efficient than T&T's 100-cc bike.

(*d*) T&T Motors has approximately 60% of the bike market.

(*e*) Of all the bikes, T&T's 100-cc bike is the most fuel efficient, and all of T&T's competitors together sell less than 50% of all 100-cc bikes.

48. Some analysts in the Kerbian republic believe that the sanction imposed by Turkmenistan on a certain petroleum byproduct would increase the price of that byproduct in Kerbia by 10 times. They also point out that a few countries trade that byproduct; however, Kerbia will have to rely on unproven fuel technologies to procure it.

Which of the following, if true, most seriously supports the expert's apprehension?

(*a*) Turkmenistan's economy relies on earnings derived from the export of the petroleum byproduct to other countries.

(*b*) The embargo on the supply of the byproduct by Turkmenistan would drive up its cost exorbitantly in Kerbia.

(*c*) Petroleum analysts believe the byproduct might possibly exist in yet-unexplored regions of Kerbia.

(*d*) No new sources of the petroleum byproduct has been discovered in the last decade.

(*e*) Procuring the byproduct from countries that do not have proven fuel technologies will not drive up its cost disproportionately in Kerbia.

49. Since less-than 15 brake horsepower (bhp) bikes do not provide an adrenaline rush, to decrease the number of accidents caused by youngsters, the Road Transport Sergeant plans to restrict them to driving less-than 15 bhp bikes.

The Road Transport Sergeant (RTS) assumes that

(*a*) some automobile experts opine that less-than 15 bhp bikes are not less prone to causing accidents than more-than 15 bhp bikes

(*b*) youngsters drive only more-than 15 bhp bikes

(*c*) all more-than 15 bhp bikes have disk-brakes as standard fitment, inducing youngsters to drive fast

(*d*) imposing penalty will decrease the number of accidents youngsters commit

(*e*) many youngsters do not drive bikes that do not provide an adrenaline rush

50. In a certain communist country, on an average a ruling party affiliate earns twice as much as a non-ruling party affiliate. Party affiliates work in sectors that offer higher wages. Many non-party affiliates, who also work in those sectors, get nearly the same wages as party affiliates. Therefore, higher wages do not inevitably result from affiliation with the party.

Which of the following, if true, most seriously weakens the argument above?

(*a*) Besides wages, party affiliates also receive other benefits.

(*b*) Some of the high-earning businesspeople in that country are not party affiliates.

(*c*) Wages in many sectors vary from one part of the country to the other.

(*d*) Due to the lobbying by party affiliates, non-party affiliates often receive higher wages.

(*e*) Becoming an affiliate of the party often motivates others to follow suit.

51. Three months after Goreville city launched a traffic discipline experimental program to decrease the number of signal jumpers at its main junction by mounting cameras to catch signal violators, the program was withdrawn. The traffic commissioner claimed that the system led to an increase in the number of signal jumpers.

Which of the following, if true, would most effectively help explain why the system reported an increase, rather than a decrease, in the number of signal jumpers?

(*a*) The junction chosen for the experiment had a higher occurrence of traffic violators than other junctions.

(*b*) The rate of increase in traffic violations was higher in the junction with the system than at other junctions.

(*c*) The count of signal jumpers at the main junction reported an increase as a result of the capability of the system to catch traffic violators who might otherwise have gone unreported.

(*d*) The three-month period during which the camera was in place was representative of normal traffic violation data.

(*e*) Such a system installed on a highway has also been helpful in catching drivers who drive beyond the permissible speed limit.

52. The proposal to shift the monetary commitment to provide public services away from the central government to the local communities is appreciated by its advocates as a leap forward on the path to real democracy. They assert that by making communities accountable to fund everything from education, health, welfare, to emergency services, and housing, it will not only upgrade these services but also promote a greater sense of community. However, such a proposal would imply that thickly populated regions, having a larger tax base, would do well; and thinly populated, rural regions would still be dependent on complementary subsidies from the central government.

Which of the following, if true, would weaken the argument that rural regions would still be reliant on complementary subsidies from the central government?

(*a*) Services for rural regions require relatively less funding than those for metropolitan regions.

(*b*) The central government funds many public services nationwide.

(*c*) The central government has conventionally funded higher educational services.

(*d*) Most communities in the rural regions are employed in the agriculture business; and the agriculture business is taxable in the country.

(*e*) Many private health and educational services are currently privately run and funded.

53. **Granted by the US Constitution, a clause protecting the right of its citizens to keep and bear arms** is the most compelling argument used by the US gun lobby to oppose the ban on the possession of guns. However, the proponents of the ban quote the most-recent United Nations statistics that show unequivocally that **worldwide there is a correlation between accidental shooting incidents and the leniency of gun control regulations**. Thus, guns must be banned.

Which of the following best describes the roles played by the two boldfaced portions in the argument?

(*a*) The first is a fact whose implication is at issue in the argument; the second is a claim advanced to argue for that implication.

(*b*) The first is a consideration that supports the main conclusion; the second is a claim that counters the main conclusion.

(*c*) The first is the evidence that supports a position; the second is the evidence that supports the counter-position.

(*d*) The first is the consideration that counters the conclusion; the second is the conclusion.

(*e*) The first is the consideration that forms the basis for the conclusion; the second is the conclusion.

54. Which of the following best completes the argument?

Springville City imposed an Odd-Even car plying policy on commuters. Cars with registration numbers ending in odd numbers will be allowed on the roads on odd days, and cars with registration numbers ending in even numbers will be allowed on the roads on even days. It was a part of the mayor's pollution control plan to tackle the city's hazardous air after the Air Quality Index (AQI) breached 500. However, AQI did not decrease significantly because, on specific days, _______.

(*a*) those whose cars were ineligible to ply the roads commuted by buses

(*b*) many of those whose cars were ineligible to ply the roads commuted with their cars

(*c*) some of those whose cars were ineligible to ply the roads commuted with their other cars that were eligible to ply

(*d*) many of those whose cars were ineligible to ply the roads commuted by carpools

(*e*) some of those whose cars were ineligible to ply the roads commuted by cabs

55. President of a retail chain: Although our stores deal in over fifty cell phone brands, we limited ourselves to stocking only cell phones from the eleven top-selling brands. However, to increase profits, the company plans to stock cell phones from three others popular brands.

Which of the following, if true, points out a major weakness in the plan to include three more popular brands to increase profits?

(*a*) The four top-selling brands account for approximately two-thirds of the company's revenue.

(*b*) The ten top-selling brands account for almost all of the company's revenue.

(*c*) As cell phone users are becoming more cost-conscious, they are willing to buy less-popular models and brands.

(*d*) Less-popular cell phone brands often yield less profit to a retailer because they are discounted to appeal to customers.

(*e*) The leading cell phone brand has been losing market position to less-popular brands.

56. When a big fire breaks out in Goreville, the number of television media reports about the fire surges, triggering fear-factor responses that often last a few days after the incident. Emergency response administrators in Goreville claim that the fear fostered by the television anchors is responsible for the increased number of fire reports rather, than a surge in the number of real fires causing the fire reports.

Which of the following, if true, would seriously weaken the claim of the emergency response administrators?

(*a*) The hype surrounding fires is mostly restricted to the city in which the incident occurred. Fire breaks out more often during summers when the climate is dry and hot.

(*b*) Television media are mandated to give a code name to a fire incident and run a scroll, updating viewers on whether the incident has been reported.

(*c*) The media do not have any benchmark to help them decide how big a fire must be for it to receive reportage.

(*d*) Fire breakouts are covered only when the media find reporting them advantageous.

(*e*) Data show that the number of fire incidents in Goreville is nearly the same every month.

57. Garrison Motors had a big surge in cargo truck sales after it hired a design team to give its cargo trucks a more upmarket look to appeal to more aspiring clients. Garrison Motors is now planning to launch a compact sports utility vehicle (compact-SUV) using a similar concept.

Garrison Motors' plan assumes that

(*a*) a compact-SUV with an upmarket look does not yet exist in the market

(*b*) at least Garrison Motor's aspiring clients would be interested in buying a compact-SUV

(*c*) the design concept that was employed for the cargo truck project would be employed for the compact-SUV project

(*d*) a design team is needed to give an upmarket look to the compact-SUV

(*e*) Garrison Motors itself will not design the compact-SUV

58. As per industry reports, by 2030, fossil-fueled cars are likely to lose approximately 10 percentage points of their worldwide market share, expressed in annual revenues, to solar-powered cars. Since ongoing developments in technology are expected to significantly decrease the manufacturing cost of solar-powered cars, the profits of their manufacturers are expected to surge by more than 10 percent by 2030.

Which of the following is an assumption that the author makes to forecast the profits of the manufacturers of solar-powered cars?

(*a*) By 2030, the worldwide market for cars will not decrease significantly.

(*b*) By 2030, selling prices of solar-powered cars will have decreased significantly.

(*c*) By 2030, the manufacturing cost of fossil-fueled cars will not decrease as much as that of solar-powered cars.

(*d*) In 2030, the average selling price of solar-powered cars will be less than that of fossil-fueled cars.

(*e*) In 2030, a greater number of solar-powered cars will be sold than fossil-fueled cars.

59. **CEO :** The shrinking of purchasing power has not been the major reason for the current decline in the real estate sector in this region.

President : In recent years, low interest among prospective property, buyers has been caused largely by buyers' not experiencing any improvements in infrastructure services in the region; and, subordinately, by the non-provision of the amenities promised to them for their apartments.

Which of the following, if true, would most support the president's claim?

(*a*) Many buyers emphasize on the good infrastructure services and amenities in their apartments.

(*b*) Many property buyers would not have purchased their apartments amid the current economic slump.

(*c*) Some potential buyers have cited the shrinking of purchasing power as the reason for the current decline in the real estate sector in the region.

(*d*) Many potential buyers are interested in buying properties in other regions.

(*e*) Many buyers have cited inadequate commuter facilities and internal security as reasons for selling their homes.

60. Which of the following most logically completes the argument?

In Aberdeen, schools that are affiliated with the central education board charge significantly higher fees than schools that are affiliated with the state education boards. Therefore, it follows that, students studying in schools that are affiliated with the central education board are more scholarly than students studying in schools that are affiliated with the state education boards because _____.

(*a*) the average salary of a teacher in schools that are affiliated with the central education board is significantly more than that of schools that are affiliated with the state education boards

(*b*) the efficacy of teaching resources employed in schools that are affiliated with the central education board is significantly higher than that in schools that are affiliated with the state education boards

(*c*) expenditure on infrastructure in schools that are affiliated with the central education board is significantly higher than that in schools that are affiliated with the state education boards

(*d*) schools that are affiliated with the central education board are driven by a profit motive, whereas schools that are affiliated with the state education boards are non-profit organizations

(*e*) teachers at schools that are affiliated with the central education board are known to teach students privately, too

61. A recent report on higher education in the United States revealed that twenty universities with the highest tuition fees also hand out the largest amounts of financial aid to inbound students with exceptional academic performance. Because these universities believe in the virtue of equal opportunity, they are able to reallocate resources from those who can afford them to those who cannot afford them.

If the statements above are true, which of the following must be true?

(*a*) Following a belief in the virtue of equal opportunity is a clever way to disguise charging higher tuition fees.

(*b*) It is feasible for universities that believe in equal opportunity to lay different financial obligations on students.

(*c*) Universities that award the largest amounts of financial aid must do so because they believe in the virtue of equal opportunity.

(*d*) Universities that do not charge high tuition fees often hand out little financial aid.

(*e*) Universities that do not believe in equal opportunity do not award financial aid.

62. Statistical evidence suggests that the number of metastatic prostate cancer patients in the US has increased by approximately 10% over the last two years. Surprisingly, Chicago reported a sharp decrease in the number of such patients visiting public clinics during the same period.

Which of the following, if true, would best explain the anomaly expressed in the argument?

(*a*) The statistics for the US represent those for Chicago, too.

(*b*) A significantly greater number of patients in cities, such as, San Jose, Seattle, and Los Angeles are not more likely to get themselves treated in private clinics than in public clinics.

(*c*) A significantly greater number of patients in Chicago get themselves treated in private clinics.

(*d*) The rate of increase in the number of metastatic prostate cancer patients in Chicago is marginally less than that for the US.

(*e*) The awareness of metastatic prostate cancer across the US is greatly varied.

63. A biologist claims that **microorganisms have a considerably greater influence on the entire ecosystem than is often recognized by scientists**. Now, a team of scientists has compiled and preserved the data of hundreds of studies on animal-bacterial interactions, proving conclusively that the biologist was correct. The combined study implies that the evidence supporting his hypothesis has reached a critical point, requiring scientists to reexamine the fundamental aspects of life through the prism of the intricate, intertwined interactions among microorganisms and other extremely diverse organisms. **The findings will significantly alter how future scholars pursue their own areas of interest**.

In the argument given, the two boldfaced portions play which of the following roles?

(*a*) The first identifies the content of the intermediate conclusion of the argument; the second is the main conclusion of the argument.

(*b*) The first provides support for the main conclusion of the argument; the second identifies the content of that conclusion.

(*c*) The first states the main conclusion of the argument; the second calls that conclusion into question.

(*d*) The first provides support for the main conclusion of the argument; the second calls that conclusion into question.

(*e*) Each boldface provides support for the main conclusion of the argument.

64. Alpha City residents desire a cleaner environment and a better quality of life. This requires the development of more parks and green spaces in the urban hub. Housing prices will increase in the long run, if they develop more parks and designate some regions as "green parks," as less land will be left for human occupancy. The rise in housing prices will negatively impact their quality of life as they will have to spend more for the same amount of area.

The answer to which of the following questions would be LEAST relevant to evaluating whether the residents' lives would be negatively impacted because of the proposed development of more parks and green spaces in the urban hub?

(*a*) Can the development of parks and green spaces take place with an alternative plan without affecting the cost of living?

(*b*) Would the development of parks and green spaces benefit the residents of neighboring cities?

(*c*) Would the jobs created to develop the parks and green spaces be given to Alpha City residents?

(*d*) Is Alpha City's environment unhealthy?

(*e*) Will the housing prices remain the same if the development of parks and green spaces does not take place?

65. Which of the following most logically completes the argument below?

Airline companies have been demanding the central government to assure them of heightened security against terrorist attacks. They anticipate that the heightened security will bring in an additional revenue of $30 million a year, mostly from those who ________.

(*a*) are afraid of traveling by air because of the fear of terrorist attacks

(*b*) are accustomed to travelling by luxurious trains

(*c*) have been spending more money on traveling

(*d*) travel by air because such travel is a status symbol

(*e*) travel by air because it saves time

66. In an enterprise, the number of cell phones assembled by technicians per month ranges from 140 to 160 phones in the fifth month of joining the enterprise. Therefore, if the output of a technician is less than 140 phones in the fifth month of joining the enterprise, he is an unskilled technician.

Which of the following best denotes a flaw in the reasoning above?

(*a*) The number of cell phones assembled is the only measure of the enterprise's productivity.

(*b*) The number of cell phones assembled by a few technicians might be less than 140 in the fifth month of joining the enterprise.

(*c*) The number of cell phones assembled by a few technicians might be greater than 160 in the fifth month of joining the enterprise

(*d*) The quality parameters in the assembling process are ignored.

(*e*) A technician might have unfavorable working conditions in the fifth month of joining the enterprise.

67. PayLess buys free-holiday coupons from those who earned them from Fairy-tale Holidays by vacationing frequently at their destinations. PayLess sells these coupons at half the price that buyers would have to pay had they bought them from Fairy-tale Holidays. This buying and reselling of coupons results in a loss of revenue for Fairy-tale Holidays.

Which of the following would be the best strategy for Fairy-tale Holidays to discourage the buying and reselling of free coupons?

(*a*) Limit the use of free coupons to those who earned them and their family members.

(*b*) Limit the number of free coupons that a person can earn in a particular season.

(*c*) Limit the number of holiday seasons in which the free coupons can be used.

(*d*) Limit the period within which the free coupons can be used after their issuance.

(*e*) Limit the number of holiday destinations for which a person can use the free coupons.

68. Dalton University plans to buy new digital whiteboards that satisfy the "value for money" criterion. Both the Alpha and Beta brands of digital whiteboards qualify for the selection. However, the Beta brand of digital whiteboards is costlier than the Alpha brand of digital whiteboards.

If the statements above are true, which of the following must be true?

(*a*) The Alpha brand of digital whiteboards does not satisfy the "value for money" criterion.

(*b*) The Alpha brand of digital whiteboards is the cheapest of all the digital whiteboards that the university considered.

(*c*) The university is looking for digital whiteboards that are neither too cheap nor too costly.

(*d*) The "value for money" imparted by the Alpha brand of digital whiteboards is greater than that by the Beta brand of digital whiteboards.

(*e*) On at least one aspect, the Beta brand of digital whiteboards is better than the Alpha brand of digital whiteboards.

69. This year, pollution levels, mainly in suburban areas, reached such alarming levels that city municipal corporations in many states erected provisional exhaust regulator points on the highways connecting inner city roads. This move led to an instant drop in the number of people suffering from asthma. Because of this, many cities have decided to make the exhaust regulator points permanent.

The decision to make the exhaust regulator points permanent on highways is based on which of the following assumptions?

(*a*) All highways pass through the peripheries of suburban-uninhabitable areas.

(*b*) Persistent exposure to high levels of pollution causes asthma.

(*c*) The move will make pollution reach a safer level.

(*d*) Other measures to control pollution affecting people had failed.

(*e*) Asthma is the most chronic health issue people in suburban areas are facing.

70. The Liberal Democratic Party's manifesto states that its top decision-making body must include a few women from lower-caste backgrounds; however, no women from lower economic classes are members of the body. It, therefore, follows that the party is not complying with its manifesto.

The conclusion of the argument follows logically if which one of the following is assumed?

(*a*) No woman who belongs to a lower economic class is a member of the party.

(*b*) The only way to comply with the party's manifesto is to select a few women from lower economic classes to represent them in the top decision-making body.

(*c*) Women with lower-caste backgrounds belong to the lower economic classes.

(*d*) There is at least one man who belongs to the lower economic class in the top decision-making body.

(*e*) Women from middle or upper economic classes do not belong to lower-caste backgrounds.

71. Toddlers often succumb due to collisions because they are not properly secured in their car seats that conform to their flexible bodies. Love-a-Tod, a manufacturer of safety seats for bikes and cars, has recently designed an innovative safety seat that is able to conform more closely to the curves in the backs and necks of toddlers. This safety seat also cushions the head even better. According to Love-a-Tod, these safety seats will reduce toddler mortality rates in fatal car collisions by up to 70%.

Which of the following, if true, presents the greatest challenge to Love-a-Tod's claim?

(*a*) The safety seats are very light in weight.

(*b*) The plastic compound that is used to make the safety seats catches fungus if left moist.

(*c*) Parents are wary of new products that are meant for toddlers' use.

(*d*) The leading safety-seat brand commands over two-thirds of the market share.

(*e*) The plastic compound that is used to make the safety seats is not banned for toddlers' use.

72. **President :** Some board members assert that the company's recent market devaluation is attributed to my policies and that I am personally liable for it. Although I acknowledge that **the company has faced market devaluation during my tenure**, I do not concur that I am accountable for it. The business policies of the former president spurred the recent devaluation, and if **my business policies were not adhered to, the devaluation could have been worse**.

In the president's argument, the two boldface portions play which of the following roles?

(*a*) The first is a fact that goes against the president; the second is a hypothesis that supports the board members.

(*b*) The first is a fact accepted by the president as true; the second supports the board members' claim.

(*c*) The first is a fact that the president supposes does not oppose his claim; the second offers support for the claim.

(*d*) The first as well as the second support the president's claim.

(*e*) The first is evidence that weakens the president's position; the second is a claim that follows from that position.

73. Approximately 500 third-stage cancer patients at a Middlesex hospital underwent an experiment to ascertain the power of prayers. Half of them were randomly chosen to receive remote, healing prayers for 30 days from intercessors who were given only the first names of the selected patients. All patients' progress or decline was tracked on a daily basis; and at recovery or death, each received a summed numerical score. It was seen that the patients who had intercessions done for them got a 12% higher score. Believers point to this as proof that God exists.

Which of the following, if true, best supports the claim of the believers?

(*a*) Third-stage cancer disease is frequently fatal.

(*b*) The intercessors reciting healing prayers are noble souls.

(*c*) Sixty percent of all the patients were over seventy.

(*d*) Apex medical bodies accept that the results of the experiment are statistically significant.

(*e*) The healing prayers were supervised by people from three different faiths.

74. Cheetahs, the fastest animal on land, use their remarkable maneuvering and acceleration capabilities when they run to hunt. In a study of approximately 400 hunting chases, ethologists found that in most chases, cheetahs achieved 50 to 60 kilometers per hour, speeds close to half of their maximum possible speed. Therefore, while hunting, cheetahs rely more on maneuvering than on speed.

Which of the following, if true, would most support the conclusion?

(*a*) For cheetahs, speed has never been an issue, and some special physical characteristics empower them to succeed as predators.

(*b*) A veterinarian followed six cheetahs for six months and found that they accelerated and changed direction rapidly, rarely running at their peak speed.

(*c*) A study found that cheetahs can accelerate their speed by nearly 10 kilometers per hour in one stride.

(*d*) Cheetahs form a strong grip and can even break the ground as they run.

(*e*) Cheetahs' claws enable them to accelerate and decelerate swiftly.

75. Contrary to expectations, the privatization of utility services has increased prices. The restructuring of workforces and other resources may well have reduced operational costs, but the savings have been passed as dividends to shareholders instead of to customers. The capital investment made has been recovered, particularly for water supplies. Upon the claim of consumer interest groups that water companies are overcharging consumers, the companies assert that the higher charges are due to the persistent need for repairs and maintenance.

Which of the following must be looked into to validate the assertion made by the water companies?

(*a*) Is "repairs and maintenance" the only cost that water companies have to bear?

(*b*) Have many regions faced a severe water shortage?

(*c*) Is the number of paying customers far higher than the number of non-paying customers?

(*d*) Do "repairs and maintenance costs" form a significant proportion of the cost of water supply and management?

(*e*) Are shareholders of the companies satisfied with the dividends?

76. Recently, a significantly higher number of residents of a certain district have stopped buying new apartments, largely because high taxes have been announced by the district municipal corporation and because the unemployment rate is high. However, the average price of new apartments has risen by more than 20 percent in the last year.

Which of the following, if true, best explains the rise in the average price of new apartments?

(*a*) The average price of apartments that are not new has also risen by more than 20 percent in the last year.

(*b*) Beginning next year, the district municipal corporation is expected to cut tax rates.

(c) Beginning next year, the district municipal corporation is expected to cut tax rates.

(d) It is expected that starting next year, the number of jobs will go up by more than 10 percent.

(e) Anticipating that there will be low demand for new apartments, the rate of new apartment construction has significantly slowed.

77. An automobile company, severely hit by the recession, split into two business units: a private-vehicle unit and a commercial-vehicle unit. It proved to be a rewarding decision. In five years, the private-vehicle unit, primarily due to increased sales of luxury cars, accounted for approximately 40 percent of the company's sales and 20 percent of profit. The commercial-vehicle unit contributed the rest.

Which of the following can be inferred about the company's performance in the last five years?

(a) On an average, a commercial vehicle was more profitable than a luxury car.

(b) The private-vehicle unit realized a lower profit per dollar sale than the commercial-vehicle unit.

(c) The commercial-vehicle unit had to face tougher competition than the private-vehicle unit.

(d) On an average, a luxury car made the company more money than a commercial vehicle.

(e) The number of units sold by the commercial-vehicle unit is more than that by the private-vehicle unit.

78. Which of the following best completes the argument below?

The foremost demerit of the old promotion system is that it places greater emphasis on an employee's seniority than on competence. However, not wishing to disgrace the work records of certain employees who have faithfully served the company for many years, .

(a) more qualified employees have been promoted ahead of them

(b) they undoubtedly should be in positions of greater responsibilities

(c) it's high time that they seek voluntary retirement

(d) they must ask themselves whether they deserve automatic promotions

(e) they might consider such automatic promotions, demotions

79. The degree of financial assistance given by rich nations to poorer nations to increase the latter's industrial capabilities is directly influenced by the degree to which the contributors fear competition and the threat of curtailed exports. The amount of financial assistance approved by the Congress is truncated by the select committee evaluating aid packages solely from the US business perspective. Consequently, many poorer nations must find areas of industrial capability that pose no threat to US business.

If the above statements are true, which one of the following must also be true?

(a) The neediest nations are those that have the lowest industrial output.

(*b*) The amount of financial assistance for industrial projects received by poorer nations is governed by the extent to which they develop new industrial capabilities that do not compete with those of rich nations.

(*c*) The poorer nations solely depend on external financial assistance to advance their industrial capability.

(*d*) By offering financial assistance to poorer nations, rich nations can expand their industrial capabilities around the world because they can influence poorer nations' industrial capabilities.

(*e*) No poorer nation can have the industrial capability that the rich nations have.

80. Which of the following best completes the argument below?

Dalton Motor Company has been undergoing dramatic changes. Most of its mechanical engineers have received in-house training, although none of the mechanical engineers specializing in hydraulics has won the esteemed Engineering Heritage Award. So far, engineers who have won the Engineering Heritage Award have gone on to become department heads.

Therefore,________.

(*a*) all the department heads have won the Engineering Heritage Award

(*b*) all the winners of the Engineering Heritage Award have received in-house training

(*c*) none of the department heads, who specialized in hydraulics, received in-house training

(*d*) all the department heads are Engineering Heritage Award-winning engineers

(*e*) all the department heads are engineers, who have won the Engineering Heritage Award

Answer Key

1. (*c*)	**22.** (*d*)	**43.** (*d*)	**64.** (*b*)
2. (*e*)	**23.** (*c*)	**44.** (*e*)	**65.** (*a*)
3. (*c*)	**24.** (*b*)	**45.** (*d*)	**66.** (*e*)
4. (*c*)	**25.** (*a*)	**46.** (*c*)	**67.** (*a*)
5. (*b*)	**26.** (*c*)	**47.** (*e*)	**68.** (*e*)
6. (*e*)	**27.** (*d*)	**48.** (*d*)	**69.** (*b*)
7. (*b*)	**28.** (*d*)	**49.** (*e*)	**70.** (*c*)
8. (*b*)	**29.** (*d*)	**50.** (*d*)	**71.** (*b*)
9. (*a*)	**30.** (*d*)	**51.** (*c*)	**72.** (*c*)
10. (*c*)	**31.** (*c*)	**52.** (*d*)	**73.** (*d*)
11. (*c*)	**32.** (*e*)	**53.** (*c*)	**74.** (*b*)
12. (*d*)	**33.** (*d*)	**54.** (*b*)	**75.** (*d*)
13. (*a*)	**34.** (*c*)	**55.** (*b*)	**76.** (*e*)
14. (*e*)	**35.** (*c*)	**56.** (*b*)	**77.** (*b*)
15. (*b*)	**36.** (*b*)	**57.** (*b*)	**78.** (*d*)
16. (*b*)	**37.** (*e*)	**58.** (*a*)	**79.** (*b*)
17. (*a*)	**38.** (*e*)	**59.** (*e*)	**80.** (*c*)
18. (*d*)	**39.** (*a*)	**60.** (*b*)	
19. (*d*)	**40.** (*b*)	**61.** (*b*)	
20. (*b*)	**41.** (*d*)	**62.** (*c*)	
21. (*d*)	**42.** (*d*)	**63.** (*a*)	

Answer Explanations

1. (c) Argument construction

A historiographer claims that slavery existed before racial discrimination in the United States. He/she then explains the basis of this claim. When Africans began to be imported to the English colonies:

- White English servants used to be indentured (forced to work by some contract). As the number of Africans increased,
  - the English colony administrations began to loosen the terms of service for the then-indentured white servants
- **Reason :** to encourage more English servants to settle in the colonies.
- This was conciliatory legislation (meant to appease English servants)
- These eased rules did not apply to Africans after slavery was legitimized:
- Africans could be indentured for life devoid of liberty, i.e., they could be enslaved
- As a result, masters preferred Africans over English servants.
- So, a greater number of English servants gat replaced by Africans.
- The lowest social status in the society was accorded to the servants doing lowly works.
- As Africans replaced English servants in this lowest section of the society, with no hope of freedom, they were tagged as innately low- grade people; and thus racial discrimination was born.

So, this timeline presented by the historiographer demonstrates how slavery – permanently indentured – foreshadowed racial discrimination.

To strengthen the argument, we would need evidence that supports this proposition. For example, something that demonstrates that before the advent of slavery, racial discrimination did not exist in the United States.

Let's analyze each option one by one.

Answer options explanations

(*a*) This is **incorrect**. Although the argument does not specify the timeline (whether early 1600s or some other period), it, in fact, already stated that African laborers were considered more desirable than English laborers. So, this option is merely a restatement.

(*b*) This is **incorrect**. This information is not relevant, for it does not relate to racial discrimination.

(*c*) This is **correct**. In the initial years of the Africans being imported to the English colonies, the rules for indentured white servants were still being slackened. Therefore, at this time, the masters had not wholly started to prefer Africans over English servants. Slavery had not yet been established. If, in these years, the masters treated their white and African servants impartially, it does certainly strengthen the argument that racial discrimination in the United States was fostered because of slavery.

(*d*) This is **incorrect**. The argument is not about whether the English colonists demonstrated bias against the other race (the Africans) but only about whether such bias came before or after slavery was instituted. This option does not help to strengthen the timeline backed by the passage.

(*e*) This is **incorrect**. Like option (b), this information is also not relevant, for it does not relate to racial discrimination.

The correct answer is option (c).

2. (e) **Argument construction**

The argument is simple to understand. For a supermarket, the price increase of fruits always follows a sales drop. However, grapes did not follow this rule. This exception is because _____.

So, this is essentially a resolve the paradox question under the 'complete the argument' question category.

The paradox : Despite the increase in the price of grapes, the quantity of grapes sold did not decrease.

Predictive resolutor : The price of grapes was significantly lower than normal; thus, the increase in price made no difference to the customers.

Answer options explanations:

(*a*) This is **incorrect**. The aspect of demand and supply is out of scope for the question. Though, in the real world, demand and supply follows an inverse relationship, in this question, we are looking for the reason for the inverse relationship between price and sale.

(*b*) This is **incorrect**. This, in fact, is a restatement of the natural outcome. However, we are searching for a reason for the exception.

(*c*) This is **incorrect**. The premise, "*Whenever a supermarket outlet increases the price of fruits by 5 to 10%, sales fall by 10 to 15%.*" does not exclude expensive fruits. The rule would apply to grapes, a relatively expensive fruit, too.

(*d*) This is **incorrect**. The scenarios in other supermarket outlets are out of scope. The argument focuses on one specific supermarket outlet.

(*e*) This is **correct**. Since the sale of grapes is dependent not only on price but also on other factors, the rise in price will not necessarily impact the quantity sold.

The correct answer is option (e).

3. (c) **Argument construction:** Let us understand the argument. An IT company Zenith Systems mainly deals in cloud computing. David is an IT consultant, who specializes in cyber security. The conclusion is that David cannot be working in Zenith Systems. We have to find out the missing reasoning that leads to such a conclusion.

Conclusion : David surely cannot be employed at Zenith Systems.

Thus, though this is one of the 'complete the argument' questions, it is actually a 'find the assumption' question.

(*a*) This is **incorrect**. This option answers partially. However, if Zenith Systems also does business in the cyber security domain (albeit in smaller proportion), David is qualified to work at Zenith.

(*b*) This is **incorrect**. Like option (a), this option also answers partially. If David has skill in cloud computing too (albeit not primary), David is qualified to work at Zenith.

(*c*) This is **correct**. It is aligned with our predictive assumption.

(*d*) This is **incorrect**. There is no reason to suppose that a flourishing IT company, Zenith Systems would not be interested in a small-size business such as cyber security. The argument does not suggest that.

(*e*) This is **incorrect**. Like option (d), there is no reason to suppose that a cyber security expert cannot qualify to be a cloud computing expert. The argument does not suggest that.

The correct answer is option (c).

Predict an Assumption

Since the conclusion states that David certainly cannot be employed at Zenith Systems, it implies that there is no overlap between David's skill set and the area of interest of Zenith.

Predictive Assumption : There is no overlap of David's skill set and area of interest of Zenith.

4. (c) Argument Construction

The Kentucky Tennis Board plans to convert the 8 grass tennis courts in the city to floodlit asphalt courts.

The pros cited of floodlit asphalt courts over grass courts: the former can be used in all weathers and evenings, whereas grass courts can only be used in the summers and in daylight.

The city currently has 8 grass courts and 12 floodlit asphalt courts. After the conversion, the city will have 20 floodlit asphalt courts.

This move, the argument claims, would offer an attractive benefit: greatly enhanced all-time availability of quality tennis courts to the public.

The Tennis Board asserts that this benefit will more than offset, in the long term, for the high one-time expense of overhaul and an increase, if at all, in yearly outlays of court maintenance.

To evaluate whether the decision taken by the Tennis Board is correct, the following questions: we need to answer.

- Whether the proposed conversion plan will succeed in meeting its stated goal

  Example of a scenario, in which it might not : Most people deem grass courts to be of higher quality than asphalt courts. Therefore, this massive exercise would, to them, seem like a lowering of the quality of tennis courts.

- Whether the stated goal is desirable at all

  For example, if most tennis games in the city are played in the daylight and in summers, and only a few play in winters, bad weather or in evenings, there is not much benefit derived from increasing the number of asphalt courts. The existing 12 floodlit asphalt courts might already be adequate to meet such needs.

Let's analyze each option one by one.

Answer options explanation

(*a*) This is **incorrect**. The argument seems to imply that the Tennis Board is ready to bear the high one-time conversion cost; the high cost is worth the increased year-round accessibility of courts to the public. Therefore, a comparison of the costs is not relevant to evaluate the worth of the argument.

(*b*) This is **incorrect**. Like option (a), the comparison of the costs is not relevant to evaluate the argument.

(*c*) This is **correct**. If the existing floodlit asphalt courts in the city can meet the demand in winters or in evenings, there is no need for a greater number of floodlit asphalt courts; this means, there is no justified reason for the Board to go ahead with this massive exercise.

(*d*) This is **incorrect**. Even if the grass courts are fully used on weekends and in summer evenings, the Board's argument is that year-round, all-weather accessibility is better than full utilization on only a few days. Therefore, this option fails to affect the Board's argument.

(*e*) This is **incorrect**. The argument is only concerned with year-round, 365-day accessibility of the courts to the public, not with the skill level of tennis aspirants or provision of means to improve their skill level.

The correct answer is option (c).

5. (b) Argument Construction

In business periodicals :

(Column space given to narrate success story of a businessman) ? (Net-Worth of the businessman)

That is, the column space given to a businessman whose net-worth is, say, $1B will be about ten times that to a businessman whose net-worth is $100M.

Most readers of these periodicals are :

Proprietors of small and medium businesses

Questions:

How does one decide whether a business is small, medium, or large? What is the net-worth of these proprietor-readers likely to be?

Is the proprietor of a small business likely to be worth a few hundred thousand dollars, a million dollars, or a few hundred million dollars?

- Can such a simplification of the net-worth of the proprietor from the size of the business even be made?
- What about medium-sized businesses?
- The argument does not answer or hint at the answers to these questions.

Conclusion : Most readers of business periodicals never get to read success stories about businessmen like them in these periodicals.

Finding the flaw :

Note that the conclusion contains the absolute word 'never.' It doesn't say that most readers seldom read success stories about businessmen like them in these periodicals; the conclusion utterly declares that they never read such success stories. So, it claims that no column space is provided.

Since the column space is proportional to the net-worth, it can be nil only if the net-worth of the proprietors of small and medium businesses is zero. The argument offers nothing to infer that their net-worth is zero.

Therefore, the conclusion is unsubstantiated and flawed. Let's analyze each option one by one.

Answer options explanations

(*a*) This is **incorrect**. The argument does not suggest that the general behavior of small and medium business proprietors is the same.

(*b*) This is **correct**. This option is in line with the analysis done above.

(*c*) This is **incorrect**. This option suggests that the businessmen who appeared in business periodical stories were, previously, like the readers of these periodicals. However, the conclusion is that readers never get to read success stories about people who are presently like them. Since the rest of the argument too is based on the present, this option that talks of the past of the published businessmen is irrelevant to it.

(*d*) This is **incorrect**. The argument makes no claim about why the readers of business periodicals purchase them. Therefore, this option is irrelevant in our attempt to find criticism.

(*e*) This is **incorrect**. This option is irrelevant to the argument assessment because the argument makes no claim that all businessmen with a high net worth get published in business periodical success stories. It only claims that proprietors of small and medium businesses never get published in these periodicals.

The correct answer is option (b).

6. (e) Argument Construction

All over the world :

- (Lower socioeconomic status) is related to:
- (Worse population health) and
- (Higher mortality rates)

An exception to this rule : The Latin American immigrants in the United States

- Their average household income, education, and standard of health services — meaning, their socioeconomic status — is MUCH LOWER than that of American whites. [So, one would expect:
- (Worse population health) and
- (Higher mortality rates.)]
- BUT, in reality,
- The mortality rate for their elderly population was 20 percent LOWER (NOT HIGHER). We need an explanation that helps to answer why, despite lower socioeconomic status, the mortality rate for elderly Latin American immigrants is lower than that for elderly American whites.

Let's analyze each option one by one.

Answer options explanations

(*a*) This is **incorrect**. This option deliberates on the mortality rate of the young population. However, we are concerned about the mortality rate anomaly for the elderly population.

(*b*) This is **incorrect**. The option does not compare the health statistics of Latin American immigrants and American whites – where the paradox lies. This option is irrelevant.

(*c*) This is **incorrect**. This option talks about Latin American immigrants as a whole — across all age-groups — and not precisely about elderly Latin American immigrants (the actual subjects of the paradox). To explain the paradox, this option requires the assumption that those Latin American immigrants who are children, or young adults, today would remain healthy for many decades to come, in spite of their lower income and lack of access to health services; and would age into elderly people who are healthier than the elderly population of the American whites. This is a big assumption to make without any basis, and therefore, ought to be discarded.

(*d*) This is **incorrect**. If immigrants (note that this option talks about immigrants in general, not about Latin American immigrants in particular) tend to develop a lifestyle similar to that of most white Americans, their mortality rates should be similar, too. This option does not help to resolve the paradox.

(*e*) This is **correct**. This option suggests that the 20 percent difference in the mortality rates of the two groups is only in recording, not in actual deaths. The actual mortality rate for the Latin American elderly immigrants might be the same as, or even higher than, that of elderly American whites, but the system does not identify this, since many of these elderly immigrants die without being recorded.

The correct answer is option (e).

7. (b) Argument Construction

- Tomato is an indigenous plant of Central Mexico
- The native language of Central Mexico is Nahuatl
- In Nahuatl, tomato plant was called 'tomatl'
- Spanish colonists raided Central Mexico in the sixteenth century
- They identified this plant
- The name of tomato plant was 'tomatl' and was amended to 'tomate' in Spanish
- So, 'tomate' name was given by the Spanish.
- The Spanish colonists took 'tomate' plant back to Spain
- Through trade, 'tomate' plant became prevalent in some parts of Europe, including the United Kingdom
- The English named the plant 'tomato'

Conclusion: The English word 'tomato' is undoubtedly originated from the Spanish 'tomate' and not directly from the Nahuatl 'tomatl.' So, the etymology of the English word 'tomato' as per the conclusion is:

Nahuatl 'tomatl' → Spanish 'tomate' → English 'tomato'; and not

Nahuatl 'tomatl' → English 'tomato'

We need to provide a reason for this conclusion such that there can be no doubt left of the Spanish ancestry of the English word 'tomato.'

So, to show that the Spanish origin of the English word 'tomato' is indisputable, we need to rule out the likelihood of independent contact between the English and Nahuatl-speaking Central Mexicans.

Let's analyze each option one by one.

Answer options explanations

(*a*) This is **incorrect**. How does this information explain (that too, unquestionably) that a word from Nahuatl did not make its way into English? The exchange of words between languages depends on the interaction between the languages and not on their relative ages.

(*b*) This is **correct**. It is per the analysis we have done above.

(*c*) This is **incorrect**. Nahuatl might be a nonexistent language now but the period in question is around the sixteenth century when Nahuatl was very much existing.

(*d*) This is **incorrect**. If English has even one word borrowed directly from Nahuatl and that word happens to be 'tomatl,' the conclusion drawn by the argument is shaken. In fact, since this option acknowledges that English have a few words directly from Nahuatl, it actually casts doubt (rather than proving unquestionably) on the contested conclusion that the English word 'tomato' was derived from the Spanish word 'tomate.'

(*e*) This is **incorrect**. 'Most' does not mean 'all.' English could well be an exception; English could be one of the few European languages in which the name of the tomato plant was not derived from the Spanish 'tomate.'

The correct answer is option (b).

8. (b) Argument Construction

Medics have two options for glaucoma patients: prescribing a legal drug but with some harmful side effects, or recommending cannabis, which is illegal but works better. The EMA can detain medics for advising illegal drugs. The argument concludes that the medics will get detained sooner or later, implying that many medics do advise cannabis.

Conclusion : Medics cannot evade punitive actions against them for long. We have to weaken the argument.

(*a*) This is **incorrect**. Just because glaucoma patients do not experience any side effects from cannabis use does not mean that medics will not be punished for advising an illegal drug. A drug with no side-effects does not make it legal.

(*b*) This is **correct**. If medics regard EMA's directives above their ethics, they are likely to respect the EMA warning and comply, implying that they will not advise an illicit drug. This weakens the conclusion by showing that the medics will not invite any punitive action against them.

(*c*) This option is **incorrect**. The argument is concerned with Europe and not with non-European countries. This option is out of scope.

(*d*) This option is **incorrect**. This is also out of scope since the conclusion deals with likely punitive action against medics.

(*e*) This option is **incorrect**. EMA directives are binding on medics, and any argument behind a now legal drug is unjustified.

The correct answer is option (b).

9. (a) Argument construction

This is a question about finding the inference.

The argument is simple to understand. The Golden Era company cheats artifact collectors by selling some artifacts, labelling them "antique." The author reasons that these artifacts, in fact, are common and available in the local market at significantly cheaper rates.

Let's analyze each option one by one.

(*a*) This option is **correct**. Since the author blames the company of selling some artifacts as "antique," it implies that some artifacts with the Golden Era company are antique. Or, in other words, not all Golden Era company's artifacts are non-antique.

(*b*) This option is **incorrect**. This is a tricky option. We cannot label non-antique artifacts duplicates or fake. They could be genuine but not antique.

(*c*) This option is **incorrect**. We cannot infer anything about the pricing of the two markets. It is more likely that the prices of artifacts available in the local market are significantly lower than those with the Golden Era company.

(*d*) This option is **incorrect**. This is also a tricky option. We cannot tag non-antique artifacts with low-quality. They may be quality artifacts but are not antique.

(*e*) This option is **incorrect**. There is no reason to infer that the state-run The Archaeological Department should be the only approval agency that can tag artifacts as "antique."

The correct answer is option (a).

10. (c) Argument construction

This is a question about evaluating the argument.

The argument is simple to understand. The minister recommended a single tax rate for all goods and services to simplify the tax system. We have to select an option statement that must be evaluated before taking such a sweeping decision.

Let's analyze each option one by one.

(*a*) This option is **incorrect**. On the contrary, the traders who deal in goods and services on which the current tax rate is higher than the recommended rate would be happy with this plan.

(*b*) This option is **incorrect**. This is a tricky option. It is not necessary for the plan to get executed ONLY if the assembly approves it UNANIMOUSLY. Even if the plan is passed with a majority (not unanimously), it is acceptable.

(*c*) This is **correct**. It is important to know beforehand whether the tax revenue after the implementation of the recommended single tax rate would at least be equal to the current tax revenue after applying the multiple rates of taxes on goods and services. If, as per the recommended plan, there is a significant revenue loss, the plan will not serve its purpose.

(*d*) This is **incorrect**; it is out of scope. Since the minister has so far only recommended a single tax rate, the implementation aspect as of now is out of scope.

(*e*) This option is **incorrect**; it is not relevant. It is not necessary to know whether the government's prior reforms had realized the desired outcome. It has no bearing on the recommended plan.

The correct answer is option (c).

11. (c) Argument construction

Let us break down the argument and analyze.

Conclusion : The economic slump in the country is over, and the recovery is underway now.

Statement 1 : (The economic slump ... underway now): It is the main conclusion of the author.

Statement 2 + BF 1: (The employment commission's ... low-paying hospitality sector): The author uses this report as proof that the economic slump is over and the recovery is underway.

Statement 3 + BF 2 : (Though, the low-paying hospitality ... critics wrong): In this statement the author presents a fact that could be the reason the critics are being skeptical, but the author counters it later and proves the critics wrong.

So, BF1 is the author's evidence/fact. BF2 is a fact that the author concedes might be construed wrongly, but something he/she believes does not weaken his conclusion/position and is consistent with BF1.

Let's analyze each option one by one.

(*a*) This is **incorrect**. BF1 is a premise/fact but not used against the author; BF1 supports the author's position. BF2 can be taken as supporting the main conclusion.

(*b*) This is **incorrect**. BF1 is accepted and presented as proof by the author, but BF2 is not a consequence of critics' skepticism. It's probable proof of critics' claims that the author believes does not weaken his/her conclusion.

(*c*) This is **correct**. BF1 is a consideration/fact presented by the author in support of his/her position. BF2 is probable proof of critics' claims that the author believes does not weaken/contradict his/her conclusion.

(*d*) This is **incorrect**. BF1 is not advanced by the critics but by the author. BF2 is not the evidence offered by the author to explain his/her position but acknowledged/explained by the author as the one that does not weaken his/her conclusion.

(*e*) This is **incorrect**. BF1 is not a fact/evidence used against the author. BF2 is not a position; it's a fact that the author believes does not weaken his/her conclusion.

The correct answer is option (c).

12. (d) Argument construction

The argument is simple to understand.

ALL movie stars are great voice actors. ALL popular politicians are acclaimed orators, which requires great voice acting. This implies that ALL popular politicians are great voice actors, too.

Conclusion : No popular movie star who becomes a politician is popular.

We see that all popular politicians, as well as all popular movie stars, are great voice actors; however, when the popular movie stars become politicians, NONE of them is popular.

We must focus on what qualities the popular politicians possess that the popular movie stars do not. Both groups are popular and possess the skill of voice acting. The quality that differentiates the two groups is oratorship.

Predictive assumption: All popular movie stars do not possess the quality of oratorship. Let's analyze each option one by one.

(*a*) This option is **incorrect**. This does not address why popular movie stars do not become popular. We are not concerned about acclaimed orators.

(*b*) This option is **incorrect**. This statement is against the conclusion. The conclusion states that NO (zero) popular movie star-turned- politician is a popular politician.

(*c*) This option is **incorrect**. This statement is, in fact, the opposite. Had the popular movie stars focused less on their voice acting than on their oratorship, at least a few could have been popular politicians.

(*d*) This is **correct**. It is aligned with the predictive assumption derived above.

(*e*) This is **incorrect** because it is irrelevant. This is not a required assumption. This does explicitly state that popular movie stars do not possess oratorship.

The correct answer is option (d).

13. (a) Argument construction

The purpose of this question is to strengthen the conclusion that car values go down by at least half in three years, irrespective of how consistently a buyer follows the periodic service schedule of the car.

Let's analyze each option one by one.

(*a*) This is **correct**. If the value of a car depreciates by 30% on the day it is bought; and, thereafter, it depreciates by at least 10% per annum, we can conclude that the car will depreciate by at least 50% in 3 years. It is a strengthener.

(*b*) This option is **incorrect** because it is irrelevant. The argument discusses the value of the car three years after the purchase. It does not discuss the scenario of when an owner passes on the car.

(*c*) This option is **incorrect** because it is irrelevant, as well. The argument discusses the value of the car three years after the purchase. Sentimental value attached to cars is irrelevant to the argument.

(*d*) This is **incorrect** because it is inconclusive. Reckless driving and intermittent (not regular) car servicing cannot necessarily be taken to mean that those cars will depreciate by 50% in 3 years.

(*e*) This is **incorrect** because even though rental companies might buy foreign models of cars, it does not say that they buy them at less than 50% of the original car price. Moreover, this option focuses only on foreign models of cars.

The correct answer is option (a).

14. (e) Argument construction

This is a question about finding the assumption.

Dalton International School employs skilled teachers; and uses a refurbished course curriculum. Still, the moral science and history scores for grade X students are not satisfactory.

Conclusion : Moral science and history subjects should be taught in the native language. Let's analyze each option one by one.

(*a*) This option is **incorrect** because it focuses on Dalton's teachers rather than students. The parents won't be concerned about the comprehension of the teachers; rather, they will be concerned about the explanations from the teachers and the comprehension of the students. Hence, this option is incorrect.

(*b*) This option is **incorrect** because it focuses on subjects, such as math and natural science, rather than on moral science and history. Although parents can assume that math and natural science can be satisfactorily explained by teachers and comprehended by students in the English language, they might not necessarily assume that these subjects can be BETTER explained by teachers and comprehended by students in the English language than in their native language.

(*c*) This option is **incorrect** because parents cannot necessarily assume that the average scores for grade X students in subjects other than moral science and history must be significantly above the desired level; they can at least assume that the average scores for those subjects are at a satisfactory level. This is an extreme option.

(*d*) This option is **incorrect**. The aspect of other schools is out of scope.

(*e*) This option is **correct**. It is a necessary assumption. Parents must assume that teaching in the native language will enhance the comprehension of the students enough to recommend that subjects, such as, moral science and history be taught in the native language.

The correct answer is option (e).

15. (b) Argument construction

According to the research, the malaria parasite has an incubation period of no more than 95 days. But when 85 military personnel who returned to the US from a malaria-bearing zone after spending more than 100 days in the US were tested for malaria, 22 of them contracted malaria. This is a reasonable exception since ______.

So, this is essentially a resolve the paradox question under the 'complete the argument question' category.

The paradox : Since the malaria parasite does not last for more than 95 days, someone who is bitten by a malaria-bearing mosquito (in a zone where it is populated) will be tested positive for malaria within 95 days. If that person is not found infected within 95 days, he can be considered safe. But a few military personnel who returned to the US from a malaria-bearing zone contracted malaria even after 95 days.

It is likely that malaria-bearing mosquitoes bit those 22 military personnel after they returned to the U.S.

Predictive resolutor 1 : Malaria-bearing mosquitoes bit those 22 military personnel after they returned to the U.S.

It is possible that the top medical research body refutes the findings presented by the National Military Forces' tropical disease branch, suggesting that the malaria parasite's incubation period could go well beyond 100 days.

Predictive resolutor 2 : The apex medical research body suggested that the malaria parasite's incubation period could go well beyond 100 days.

Let's analyze each option one by one.

(*a*) This is **incorrect**. This statement is inconclusive. Though this alludes to the fact that mosquitoes are widespread in the US too, are they malaria-bearing mosquitoes? This option does not answer this.

(*b*) This is **correct**. Given that while returning from the malaria-bearing zone, pilots complain of mosquitoes getting trapped inside aircraft, those mosquitoes are malaria-bearing. They could have made their home there and could have bit those 22 personnel in the US. This resolves the paradox.

(*c*) This is **incorrect**. Even if we consider the upper limit, 1% of 95 days is 0.95 = ~1 day, so the maximum incubation period is 96 days, which is less than 100 days. This option does not help resolve the paradox.

(*d*) This is **incorrect**. This option can be eliminated because the argument states that the maximum incubation period is 95 days; so, any variations in incubation among the breeds must be below this limit.

(*e*) This is **incorrect**. The argument is concerned with the contraction of malaria after the incubation period of the parasite is over, and not about the effectiveness of anti-malaria vaccines.

The correct answer is option (b).

16. (b) Argument construction

The argument is simple to understand. As many as 40% of car mechanics who own garages and are technically qualified earn more than $70,000, while only 20% of car mechanics who own garages but are not technically qualified earn more than $70,000. The claim is that the higher proportion of car mechanics earning more than $70,000 is due to the first group of mechanics having completed a qualifying course.

We have to evaluate the argument.

Conclusion : Pursuing a qualifying course helps in earning more. Let's analyze each option one by one.

(*a*) This is **incorrect**. Even if the fee is unaffordable, the moot question of whether pursuing a qualifying course helps in earning more stands unchallenged.

(*b*) This is **correct**. What if the remaining (100% – 20%) = 80% of the second group members, who earn less than $70,000, earn significantly more than the remaining (100% – 40%) = 60% of first group members, who earn less than $70,000? [Most of the remaining 80% of the second group members, say, for example, can make as much as $69,000, while most of the remaining 60% of the first group members could possibly make less than, say, $20,000, making the whole comparison shaky.] This example will make the average earning of the second group higher than that of the first group; and the conclusion will be shattered, revealing the flaw. So, we cannot conclude that technical education helps mechanics earn more. Thus, for the conclusion to be valid, it is necessary to confirm that the average earning of the second group is significantly less than that of the first group.

(*c*) This is **incorrect**. Even if we assume that the first group is more professional in their approach, can we assume that they are professional because they are technically qualified? There is no evidence to support this.

(*d*) This is **incorrect**. Proficiency is out of scope. The argument is concerned with the correlation between technical education and earnings.

(*e*) This is **incorrect**. Comparable minimum earnings of both groups do not address the question of whether the technical education helps earn more. It is possible that the minimum salary of a group is less than that of the other, while its average earning is significantly more than that of the other. The minimum earning considers the earning of only one member, while the average earning considers the earnings of all. Minimum and maximum earning cases are exceptions and; must be ignored.

The correct answer is option (b).

17. (a) Argument construction

The question asks us to find the assumption in the given argument. Let's first derive the conclusion.

Conclusion : The cardiac arrest victims will suffer because of this additional procedure (diagnostic questioning), and very few will benefit from it.

Let's analyze each option one by one.

(*a*) This is the correct **answer**. The purpose of following the procedure of diagnostic questioning is to assess which of the reported cases of cardiac arrest are severe and need urgent attention, requiring mobile treatment teams. Since the argument states that in thinly populated rural areas, a consistently rapid response is impossible to achieve, mainly because of the long distances, it is unlikely that with the implemen-tation of the new procedure, mobile treatment teams would be dispatched if there was no severity of cardiac arrest. This is a necessary assumption for the conclusion to hold true.

(*b*) This is **incorrect** because the author does not imply that those who would report cardiac arrest are incompetent to handle the new diagnostic questioning procedure.

(*c*) This is **incorrect** because if the author assumed that there were other ways to treat cardiac arrest, he would not imply that the extra procedure would cost some victims dearly. This weakens the conclusion.

(*d*) This is **incorrect** because the author does not imply that the diagnostic questioning will not help determine the severity of the cardiac arrest. He implies that more time will be wasted by way of asking diagnostic questions over the phone.

(*e*) This is **incorrect** because it is too extreme to be the author's assumption. He/she says more will suffer and only few will benefit. So, some will still benefit.

The correct answer is Option (a).

18. (d) Argument construction

In the above argument, Mega Poll conducted a poll after the election, and found the prime minister of the country less popular than thc opposition leader and the leader of a small party. Another poll also confirmed the above findings with some margin of error. However, the argument concluded that electorates voted according to the policies of political parties and not just the popularity of their leaders.

We have to find the role of the boldface portions in the argument.

Main conclusion : The electorate is more influenced by the policies of parties than by their leaders.

Statement 1 : Placed the prime minister of the country 35 points below the leader of a small party and 20 points below the leader of the opposition : This statement includes the facts about how the prime minister is less popular than other politicians. It can also be called a claim.

Statement 2 : (Subsequently, percent range): This is another set of facts that affirms the fact/claim stated in BF1.

Statement 3 : The electorate is more influenced by the policies of political parties than their leaders : This is a claim that the author makes, saying that despite the above facts/claim, the not-the-first choice prime minister was elected because the citizens voted for the party and not the leader. It is the main conclusion of the argument.

It is important to note that the poll was conducted a couple of months after the election. Though the incumbent prime minister was less popular, he was elected because he belonged to the party that citizens ranked higher than other parties.

Let us analyze each option one by one.

(*a*) This is **incorrect**. Though BF1 can be called a claim, the argument does not dispute it. BF2 is indeed the conclusion and can be taken as based on BF1.

(*b*) This is **incorrect**. Though BF1 can be called a claim whose implication supports the main conclusion, the argument does not reject it; BF1 and BF2 are consistent with each other. BF2 is the main conclusion of the argument.

(*c*) This is **incorrect**. While BF1 can be called evidence, it does not call the main conclusion into question. BF1 and BF2 are consistent with each other. BF2 is the main conclusion of the argument.

(*d*) This is the **correct** answer. BF1 is a claim that suggests that the leader of a ruling party is less popular than the leaders of other parties. Since the party of the least-popular leader won the election, it implies that the party's popularity scored over its leader's popularity. BF2 also states the same. So, BF1 and BF2 are consistent with each other.

(*e*) This is **incorrect**. While BF1 can be called a finding, its accuracy is not evaluated in the argument. BF2 is not evidence but a claim/conclusion; moreover, it is not presented to establish that finding as accurate.

The correct answer is option (d).

19. (d) Argument construction

This is a question about finding the inference.

TMZ Corporation had bad business in the last quarter. Instead of laying off workers to cut costs, it plans to invest their 30-day salaries in a debt fund to earn interest to cover the operational expenses. By doing this, TMZ and its workers will avoid the undesirable consequences.

Let's analyze each option one by one.

(*a*) This is **incorrect** because it is inconclusive. From the argument, we cannot infer whether the workers agreed to the plan. They may or may not have given their consent.

(*b*) This is **incorrect** because we cannot infer whether investing in a debt fund is the only option left with TMZ. It may have had a few workable options, but it chose the option of investing money in a debt fund.

(*c*) This is **incorrect** because we cannot necessarily infer whether some workers will have to borrow money to meet their monthly expenses. It is possible they have enough savings to meet their monthly expenses.

(*d*) This is the **correct** answer. TMZ chose to invest in a debt fund with the hope that the fund has the potential to earn interest to cover operational expenses.

(*e*) This is **incorrect** because it is out of scope. We cannot infer that TMZ has adequate sales orders for the upcoming quarter. At best, we can infer that the corporation has some orders for the next few days.

The correct answer is option (d).

20. (b) Argument construction

This is a question about finding the assumption.

The argument is simple to understand. The goal of the Georgian government is to increase the sales of Made-in-Georgia confectionery items by decreasing competition from imports that are hurting the domestic confectionery industry.

Conclusion : Limiting the import of confectionery items into Georgia will result in an increase in the sales of Made-In-Georgia confectionery items soon.

Let's analyze each option one by one.

(*a*) This option is **incorrect**. We cannot necessarily assume that the quality of Made-In-Georgia confectionery items is below that of international brands. It is possible that though the quality of Made-In-Georgia confectionery items is at par with international brands, they are not competitive vis-a-vis foreign-made confectionery items; for example, they are relatively expensive or poorly marketed.

(*b*) This is the **correct** answer. The consultant assumes that if buyers do not find foreign-made confectionery items in stores, they will have no option but to buy Made-In-Georgia confectionery items.

(*c*) This option is **incorrect**. We cannot necessarily assume that Made-In-Georgia confectionery items are more expensive than similar foreign-made confectionery items. It is possible that, despite being competitively priced, Made-In-Georgia confectionery items are not perceived to be on par with foreign-made confectionery items.

(*d*) This option is **incorrect**. The consultant cannot assume that Made-In-Georgia confectionery items are mostly in short supply since this would endanger his/her plan to boost their sale.

(*e*) This option is **incorrect**. This cannot be an assumption but rather an inference. However, we cannot necessarily infer that because import duties on the foreign-made confectionery items is significantly lower in Georgia; they are competitive in comparison to Georgian-made confectionery items. It could be that the foreign-made confectionery items are preferred over Georgian-made confectionery items because of their quality or some other aspect.

The correct answer is option (b).

21. (d) Argument construction

Let us understand the argument. The argument is simple to follow. The structure is : If X then Y. If Y then Z. So if X, then Z.

Where X, Y, and Z are:

X : You study for three hours daily.

Y : Your problem-solving skills will improve.

Z : You are assured of a good score.

Let's analyze each option one by one.

(*a*) This is **incorrect**. The structure is: If X then Y. If Y then Z. So, if X then ?. 'Data-sufficiency question' (Z) is replaced with 'Problem-solving question (?).' They are not identical to that of the argument.

(*b*) This is **incorrect**. The structure is: If (Not X) then Y. If X then (Not Z). So, if (Not X) then Z. They are not identical to that of the argument.

(*c*) This is **incorrect**. The structure is: If X then Y. If Y then Z. So, if (Not X) then (Not Z). They are not identical to that of the argument.

(*d*) This is the **correct** answer. The structure is: If X then Y. If Y then Z. If X then Z. They are identical to that of the argument.

(*e*) This is **incorrect**. The structure is: If X then Y. If Z then ?. So if Z then X. They are not identical to that of the argument.

The correct answer is option (d).

22. (d) Argument construction

Due to a massive flood in Kyushu during the rice-growing season, the price of rice will double. This price rise for rice will make rice-cakes expensive.

Conclusion : The doubling of the price of rice will make consumers in Kyushu pay more for rice-cakes.

We have to find the flaw in the reasoning that rice-cakes will become expensive. The author concludes that the massive flood in Kyushu will double the price of rice.

The author seems to assume that rice used for rice-cakes in Kyushu is mostly supplied by Kyushu rice farmers. What if Kyushu is not the only source of rice in Japan? Kyushu could import rice from other parts of Japan, at what would be an almost normal price.

We can consider the given situation as cause and effect. The effect is "rice-cakes will be expensive," and the cause is "the price of rice will double."

The flaw in the reasoning is that the effect is produced by ONLY one cause. Let's analyze each option one by one.

(*a*) This is **incorrect**. Only two aspects are discussed; one, the effect : rice-cakes will be expensive, and two, the cause : the price of rice will double. No other events are discussed.

(*b*) This is **incorrect**. Only one event and one cause are discussed.

(*c*) This is **incorrect**. Like option (b), only one event and one cause are discussed.

(*d*) This is the **correct** answer. It is aligned with our analysis done above. The flaw is that the argument considers that the outcome rice-cakes will be expensive is solely dependent on one event : the expensive rice from Kyushu. As discussed, what if Kyushu procures rice from other parts of the country? In that case, the conclusion is shattered.

(*e*) This is **incorrect**. The author does consider the law of supply and demand; based on which he/she assumes that due to expensive rice, rice-cake prices will rise.

The correct answer is option (d).

23. (c) Argument construction

The argument is simple to understand. Brand X is the most-preferred cheese brand, yet its rival brands, brands Y and Z, sell more.

Let's analyze each option one by one.

(*a*) This is **incorrect**. This information rather worsens the paradox. We already know that brand Z sells more packs than brand X.

(*b*) This is **incorrect**. It compares the prices of brands Y and Z with no reference to the price of brand X. This information does not serve any purpose.

(*c*) This is the **correct** answer. Since the study was carried out only in select cities where the distribution network of brand X is strong, it is likely that cheese buyers in those cities preferred brand X to other brands; however, the sales figures are country-wide, so it is likely that brands Y and Z are preferred in other parts/cities. This resolves the discrepancy.

(*d*) This is **incorrect**. This option is tricky. Though the price of brand X cheese is higher than that of brands Z and Y, it is not higher to the extent that it is understandable why brand X sells far fewer packs than brands Y and Z.

(*e*) This is **incorrect**. This option is tricky. "A few" stores refusing to stock brand X does not make a significant impact. Had the option been "Far too many stores do not stock brand X cheese because its wholesalers demand that brand X be stocked exclusively," it would have been the correct answer.

The correct answer is option (c).

24. (b) Argument construction

The Euro is depreciating; this depreciation is advantageous to some sectors and countries but disadvantageous to others. The German economy and the French economy are performing well. Despite these positives, the European Central Bank (ECB) has cautioned that the Euro will depreciate by at least 4% over the next 5-to-7 months; thus, the ECB must take action to halt the depreciation of the Euro.

Let's examine the argument.

Conclusion : The Euro will depreciate by at least 4% over the next five-to-seven months.

Statement 1 : (The depreciation ... mixed feelings): This is a claim. It implies that due to the depreciation of the Euro, some sectors and countries are gaining, while others are losing.

Statement 2 : (Boldface/BF) (The German economy ... services): Clearly, the German economy is performing well; thus, this phenomenon helps the Euro to not continue its downfall.

Thus, BF weakens the ECB's decision to take any measure.

Statement 3 : (The French economy... defense equipment): As with the German economy, the French economy is also performing well; thus, this phenomenon also aids the Euro in avoiding further decline. Thus, it also weakens the ECB's decision to take any measures.

Statement 4 : (However, the ... is critical): As stated earlier, it is the main conclusion, and it goes against the BF.

Let's analyze each option one by one.

(*a*) This option is **incorrect**. As discussed above, the BF weakens the conclusion.

(*b*) This is the **correct** answer. It is aligned with the analysis done above.

(*c*) This option is **incorrect**. Though it can be called a supposition, its accuracy is not tested in the argument. The BF is a fact that goes against the main conclusion.

(*d*) This option is **incorrect**. Neither is it an assumption nor is it upheld as incorrect. The BF is a fact that weakens the main conclusion.

(*e*) This option is **incorrect**. Neither is it a conclusion nor is it called into question by the argument.

The correct answer is option (b).

25. (a) Argument construction

The argument is simple to understand. Currently, the mafia-run opium companies deduct shipping charges from their revenue to calculate the payments that go to the Maldovan government. The argument is that they must not be allowed to do so; this way, they will have to increase their opium prices, making their opium expensive. This price increase will discourage buyers in the world market.

This is a question on weakening the argument. Let us find out the conclusion of the argument.

Conclusion : Maldovan opium companies will have to increase their opium prices; and this price rise would discourage buyers in the world market from buying Maldovan opium.

As per the question stem, we have to weaken the conclusion that the mafia-run companies would have to increase their opium prices, making them less competitive in the world market.

Let's analyze each option one by one.

(*a*) This is the correct answer. Since the shipping costs are now considerably lower than before, it is likely that the opium companies might not increase their opium prices, making them still competitive in the global market. This is certainly a weakener.

(*b*) This is incorrect. It is out of scope. This statement relates to seeking approval to do something; however, it does not impact our goal – why the opium price might not necessarily increase. This option does not provide an acceptable reason for not increasing the opium price.

(*c*) This is incorrect. Since the competitor charges higher, there is at least some scope for Maldovan companies to increase their prices. This is certainly not a weakener.

(*d*) This is incorrect. It is out of scope. It focuses on the use of money received by the government. It is not our goal.

(*e*) This is incorrect. It is inconclusive. It focuses on the use of opium. Endorsing the therapeutic use of opium does not mean that the global market for opium will increase with immediate effect and, in turn, benefit Maldovan opium companies.

The correct answer is option (a).

26. (c) Argument construction

Let us understand the argument. The per-quintal price of Basmati rice ranges from $50 to $80. Basmati rice crop has been affected due to heavy rains in the western part of the country, from where more than three-fourth of Basmati rice comes. Despite this distress, the price of Basmati rice remained fairly stable, though it was anticipated that it might go as high as $110 per quintal. The unexpected scenario is why the price remained fairly stable.

Let's analyze each option one by one.

(*a*) This is incorrect. This suggests that at the maximum, 25% of Basmati rice crop is unaffected. However, this would not be sufficient to let the price increase significantly across the country; 75% of the crop is still affected.

(*b*) This is incorrect. The explanation of option (b) is the same as that of option (a).

(*c*) This is the correct answer. Since "Jasmine rice," another popular variety of rice, similar in taste to Basmati yet cheaper than it, had a record production, it is explainable that consumers might have chosen Jasmine rice over Basmati, and so, the price of Basmati rice did not skyrocket.

(*d*) This is incorrect. It is focused only on the eastern part (one of the parts) of the country. Had the option stated this for the entire country, it would have been the correct answer.

(*e*) This is incorrect. Since Basmati rice is included in the discussion, this option is irrelevant.

The correct answer is option (c).

27. (d) **Argument construction**

The argument is simple to understand. The Synocare computerized system will ease the registration process for new claimants. The new system claims to detect any fraudulent claims by cross-checking claimants' credentials. The government claims that the new system will save around $750M per annum, which it claims goes to miscellaneous prescriptions for unverified people.

Conclusion : Once the system is on the roll, it will be able to save around $750 million every year.

The claim that needs to be weakened is that the Synocare system will save money by decreasing fraudulent claims.

Let's analyze each option one by one.

(*a*) This is **incorrect**. It vouches for the reliability of the system, supporting the conclusion. This option is rather a strengthener.

(*b*) This is **incorrect**. First, we do not know how much 25% of the cost of the Synocare system amounts to. Second, we have no idea whether the computation of saving $750M took the cost of annual maintenance into account. This option is inconclusive.

(*c*) This is **incorrect**. This is an extreme statement. Neither the system nor the government spokesperson claimed that the system would stop all fraudulent claims. Even if most fraudulent claims are checked, the system is a success.

(*d*) This is the **correct** answer. If the support staff cannot be fully trained to handle the Synocare system, the goal of commissioning the system will be lost. This is a weakener.

(*e*) This is **incorrect**. Does it affect the conclusion? Not at all. So, this aspect is out of scope.

The correct answer is option (d).

28. (d) **Argument construction**

We are asked to identify the role of the boldfaced portion in the argument.

Statement 1 : BF (In a breakthrough... Nepal Insurance Company.): This statement narrates an incident that happened in Nepal, in which a judge rejected an insurance claim for Kathmandu Metropolitan City (KMC) because the judge ordered that it was the responsibility of KMC to ensure that adequate measures were taken against the earthquake.

Statements 2 & 3 : (The judge said... Seismic scientists... casualties.): These statements justify the claim rejection. The judge made KMC liable for not taking adequate measures against the earthquake when scientists have charted earthquake regions.

Thus, BF is a discomforting judgment/fact, which the argument justifies by providing opinion and facts.

Let's analyze each option one by one.

(*a*) This is **incorrect** because BF is not opposed by the argument. The argument is aligned with BF; it rather defends BF.

(*b*) This is **incorrect** because BF does not offer any evidence against the argument. The BF and the argument are in sync. The position of the argument is that if a structure does not employ anti-earthquake technology, it might not have the right to receive a claim from an insurance company in case the structure gets damaged because of an earthquake. The BF forms the basis for that position.

(*c*) This is **incorrect** because BF is neither contested nor supported with any examples. It is supported by providing opinion and facts.

(*d*) This is the **correct** answer. This is in sync with the discussion above.

(*e*) This is **incorrect** because BF is not refuted by the argument; it is rather supported.

The correct answer is option (d).

29. (d) At Milton Utility Products Limited, the year-on-year increase in the salary of the executives who head product lines depends only on the extent of revenue growth shown by their respective product lines during the year.

This is Premise 1.

The product line headed by Manager X showed a year-on-year revenue growth of 10 percent, while the product line headed by Manager Y showed a year-on-year revenue growth of 50 percent.

This is Premise 2.

From this statement, it looks like the product line headed by Manager Y did much better than the one headed by Manager X. By combining these two premises, therefore, one would expect that: Manager Y would get a higher year-on-year salary increase than Manager X. However, what actually happened was just the opposite!

Manager X, on the other hand, received a 40% year-on-year salary increase, while Manager Y received a 5% year-on-year salary increase.

This, then, is the discrepancy (between what we expected to happen and what actually happened) that we need to explain. Let us try to think of the kind of explanations that might work.

Premise 1 and premise 2 are both facts, they cannot be challenged. It is a fact that an executive's y-o-y salary increase depends on the extent of revenue growth of the executive's product line. And, it is a fact that X's product line had a y-o-y revenue growth of 10% while the figure for Y was 50%.

Further, it is a fact that X got a higher y-o-y salary increase than Y. This fact, when put in conjunction with premise 1, suggests that: Manager X's product line had a higher "extent of revenue growth" than Manager Y's product line.

Now, when we compare this inference with premise 2, we get the idea that "the extent of revenue growth" is not the same as "y-o-y revenue growth."

So, the answer option that we are looking for will probably explain why, though Manager X's product line had a lower "y-o-y revenue growth" than Manager Y's product line, it had the higher "extent of revenue growth."

Let's analyze each option one by one.

(*a*) This option is **incorrect**. The share of a product line in the total costs of the company does not impact the y-o-y salary increase of the executive who heads that product line.

(*b*) This option is **incorrect**. The past y-o-y salary increases of managers X and Y are irrelevant to the apparent discrepancy observed this year.

(*c*) This option is **incorrect**. Premise 1 clearly states that the year-on-year increase in the salary of the executives who head product lines depends only on the extent of revenue growth shown by their respective product lines during the year. Therefore, one executive's better connections with his seniors than another will not get him a higher y-o-y salary increase.

(*d*) This option is **correct**. If the market for product line headed by Manager X is shrinking, then it is a tremendous achievement of Manager X that he still managed to grow the revenue of his product by 10%. On the other hand, the market for the product line headed by Manager Y has had an y-o-y revenue increase of a whopping 1,000%. So, this is the amount of growth potential that Manager Y's product line had! In the light of this, we realize that a revenue growth of only 50% is actually an underachievement. Manager Y failed to grow the revenue of his product line to the full extent (1,000%) of which it was capable. Therefore, his performance is not as credible as Manager X's.

(*e*) This option is **incorrect**. The y-o-y salary increase of an executive depends on the extent of revenue growth of his product line, and not on the number of units sold.

The correct answer is option (d).

30. (d) Argument construction

Let us understand the argument. The argument is simple to follow. The claim made by the tea brand that tea is healthy is challenged by providing an undisputable fact: milk with caffeine will not be healthy anymore.

Let's analyze each option one by one.

(*a*) This is **incorrect**. Although the counterpoint made by providing the fact (caffeine added to milk) can be called a claim to prove a point, the indisputable fact is more specific than a claim. If none of the other options fit well, this is the correct answer.

(*b*) This is **incorrect**. The fact (caffeine added to milk) is not used to ascertain a theory. It is used to counter an arguable and tall claim made by the brand.

(*c*) This is **incorrect**. Like option (b), the fact (caffeine added to milk) is not used to refute a theory. It is used to counter an arguable and tall claim made by the brand.

(*d*) This is the **correct** answer. The fact (caffeine added to milk) is indisputable. The new fact counters an arguable and tall claim made by the brand.

(*e*) This is **incorrect**. The claim (fact) (caffeine added to milk) is unquestionable, not questionable.

The correct answer is option (d).

31. (c) Argument construction

The argument is simple to comprehend. The price of lemons has been rising. Thus, the price of the Supreme dishwashing bar that contains lemon extract will also rise.

Conclusion : The price of the Supreme dishwashing bar will also rise.

Let's look at each option one by one.

(*a*) This is **incorrect**. This is not an assumption but a fact; the argument states that the bar contains lemon extract.

(*b*) This is **incorrect**. The prices of other ingredients are out of scope.

(*c*) This is **correct**. This is the assumption on which the conclusion rests, or else the conclusion will shatter. If the bar does not contain a significant proportion of lemon extract, the impact of the price rise of lemon would be insignificant, so it could happen that the bar's price does not rise. This option is a necessary assumption.

(*d*) This is **incorrect**. The prices of soap bars are out of scope.

(*e*) This is **incorrect**. Whether or not the increased price of the bar can be borne by customers does not impact the conclusion.

The correct answer is option (c).

32. (e) Argument construction

Let us understand the argument. Many blogs written by editors fall far beyond the stated scope; these blogs are not published in the digital magazine.

Let's analyze each option one by one.

(*a*) This is **incorrect**. All that we know is that blogs falling outside the defined scope are not eligible for publishing in the digital magazine. We cannot infer that some of the blogs written by editors are too technical. The blogs being outside the defined scope does not mean that the blogs are too technical; they could all be conventional, but the digital magazine does not want them to be published since they do not fall within the defined scope.

(*b*) This is **incorrect** for the same reason as stated in option (a). We cannot infer that some of the blogs written by editors are imperfect. They might all be perfect, but the digital magazine does not want them to be published since they do not fall within the defined scope.

(*c*) This is **incorrect**. Applying the same reasoning as we did in options (a) & (b), we cannot infer that the digital magazine does not publish blogs that are intriguing.

(*d*) This is **incorrect**. There is no strong basis to infer this. The two-sentence argument does not state enough to infer such.

(*e*) This is **correct**. Given that many blogs written by editors are far beyond the defined scope, and such blogs do not succeed in being published in the digital magazine, we can properly infer that there are at least a few blogs that fall far beyond the defined scope and do not qualify to be published in the digital magazine.

The correct answer is option (e).

33. (d) Argument construction

We have to weaken the conclusion.

Conclusion : The acquisition of the magazine is allowed by the court.

Support : The media mogul will not influence the editorial policies of the acquired magazine. Let's analyze each option one by one.

(*a*) This option is **incorrect**. It is irrelevant to the conclusion. We cannot conclude that the mogul would influence the editorial content. Turning failing companies profitable by no means implies that the mogul would influence content.

(*b*) This option is **incorrect**. Though this is against the mogul, we cannot conclude that the mogul would influence the editorial content. It could be arguably justified to sack young journalists (not very influential in editorial content) of declining newspapers, as it is the mogul's obligation to run sustainable businesses. Had the option stated that the mogul has a reputation for dismissing senior journalists of the declining newspapers he acquired, the conclusion could be weakened.

(*c*) This option is **incorrect**. It is rather a strengthener. This works in favor of the mogul : he would also not influence the editorial policies.

(*d*) This is **correct**. That editorial content will be acquired from the news bank serving his media channels, not only hints that he will be meddling with editorial content, but also hints that he will be in a position to influence public opinion by using all his media channels to propagate anything he desires.

(*e*) This option is irrelevant. It has no bearing on the conclusion.

The correct answer is option (d).

34. (c) Argument construction

This is a question on strengthening the argument.

The survey from a leading magazine shows that most of its readers want more movie shows per day on smaller multiplex screens than fewer shows per day on bigger multiplex screens.

We have to support the consultant's recommendation that Excel Entertainment must plan more smaller screens than bigger ones in its new multiplex venture.

Let's analyze each option one by one.

(*a*) This option is **incorrect**. Does the increasing number of people preferring to watch movies at home do so because they don't get more movie shows per day on multiplexes? We cannot draw such an inference from this information.

(*b*) This option is **incorrect**. It compares single-screen theatres and multiplexes, whereas we want to compare the number of smaller multiplex screens and the number of bigger multiplex screens. This option is out of scope.

(*c*) This option is **correct**. Since the proportion of smaller screens to bigger screens in most under-construction multiplexes is greater than that in the existing multiplexes, the consultant's recommendation gains weight. This option certainly strengthens the recommendation.

(*d*) This option is **incorrect**. It simply suggests that a smaller multiplex screen needs less space than a bigger multiplex screen. We can infer this; this is not additional information.

(*e*) This option is **incorrect**. We cannot infer that since most movies in regional languages are screened on smaller multiplex screens, people want more shows per day on smaller multiplex screens.

The correct answer is option (c).

35. (c) Argument construction

The argument is simple to understand. The population of the elderly is growing, but despite the shortage of skilled workers, companies are reluctant to hire elderly workers. Senior Pro states that a few companies that induct elderly workers are successful. Thus, employing elderly workers is beneficial for business.

This is a question on role play.

Let us analyze the argument and understand the role of the boldfaced portions.

Main conclusion: Employing elderly workers is beneficial for business.

Statement 1 : (There is... people) : It is a fact that states that the elderly population is growing.

BF1 : (despite... workers) : It is a claim/ fact. The argument seeks to contradict it. It is on the opposite side of the conclusion.

Statement 2 : (Senior Pro... workers) : It is background information.

BF2 : (Senior Pro... senior citizens) : It is a counterexample or a fact that goes against BF1 and forms the basis for the main conclusion that follows.

Let's analyze each option one by one.

(*a*) This is **incorrect**. While the first part is correct, the second part is incorrectly described. BF2 is not a conclusion; it is a counterexample or a fact that goes against BF1 and forms the basis for the conclusion.

(*b*) This is **incorrect**. The description of both portions is wrong. The correct description should be, "The first is a fact that is inconsistent with the conclusion; the second is a claim that supports the conclusion."

(*c*) This is the **correct** answer. It is aligned with our analysis above.

(*d*) This is **incorrect**. BF1 is not a conclusion; it is correct to describe BF2 as a fact.

(*e*) This is **incorrect**. BF1 can be seen as a concern that the argument denies. However, BF2 is not the conclusion; it is a fact/counterexample.

The correct answer is option (c).

36. (b) Argument construction

Children who are beaten usually grow up believing that it is not inappropriate to beat their children, as well. This practice is child abuse.

But some societies' view is that beating children inculcates discipline in them and is not child abuse, and that discipline develops in them good habits because.

From the context, we can infer that the correct option must directly support the assertion that child-beating is not a bad act.

Let us discuss each option one by one.

(*a*) This is **incorrect**. From the society's point of view, it does not logically follow that they would justify beating children to normalize their emotions.

(*b*) This is **correct**. People beat their children for their own good, believing that by disciplining through beating, children will grow strong and capable of facing the world.

(*c*) This is **incorrect**. The option rather advises that children need not be beaten. This is the opposite answer.

(*d*) This is **incorrect**. It is improbable that societies would justify the reason for beating children based on their intelligence.

(*e*) This is **incorrect**. From the argument, it follows that people beat their children for their own betterment and not just to follow a social norm. "Child beating is a customary social norm" does not state a reason but merely points out a norm.

The correct answer is option (b).

37. (e) Argument construction

Arzanian government defended the steep tax hike on tobacco and alcoholic products; it claims that such a hike is the only effective measure to control tobacco and alcohol abuse. However, critics argue that such a policy is a sham because the massive sum collected from taxes funds many governmental welfare schemes, and if the government truly wanted to discourage tobacco and alcohol consumption, the government would go bankrupt.

Let's analyze each option one by one.

(*a*) This is **incorrect**. We can only infer from the argument that high taxes fund some welfare schemes, but we cannot necessarily infer that one of those services would be emergency services.

(*b*) This is **incorrect**. There is nothing in the argument to infer such a wild claim.

(*c*) This is **incorrect**. This is a real-world trap option. In the real world, it is reasonable to suppose that extreme tobacco and alcohol consumption is a nuisance, but we cannot infer such an inference from the given argument.

(*d*) This is **incorrect**. Again, this is a real-world trap option. While this could be true in the real world, does the argument even indirectly support this? The answer is no.

(*e*) This is the **correct** answer. The critics claim that the huge sum collected from taxes finances many governmental welfare schemes, and if the government didn't collect such a huge sum of money, it would fall. This implies that the Arzania government collects a significant amount of tax money from the sale of tobacco and alcoholic products.

The correct answer is option (e).

38. (e) Argument construction

The salaries of professors at Dalton University change proportionally with changes in the revenue earned by the university from student tuition.

So, an increase in the university's tuition revenue would lead to a proportional increase in the professors' salaries. And, a decrease in the university's tuition revenue would lead to a proportional decrease in the professors' salaries.

Now, the government has passed a law this year that forbids universities from increasing tuition fees for the next five years. This means, the tuition fees are not going to increase next year (over the fees this year).

Further, there are credible reports that the number of student enrolments at Dalton University will be lower next year than it was this year.

So, the number of students enrolled at the university next year will be lower than the number this year. (University's Revenue from Student Tuition) = (Tuition Fees) × (Number of Students)

So, it can be inferred that the university's revenue from student tuition next year is going to be lower than what is this year. This will be an implicit subsidiary conclusion.

When the above conclusion is combined with the first statement of the argument, we can infer that the professors at Dalton University should expect their salaries next year to be less than they are this year.

Let's analyze each option one by one.

(*a*) This option is **incorrect**. While the second is indeed an explicit conclusion, the first is one of TWO premises that support an implicit conclusion.

(*b*) This option is **incorrect**. While the second is the main conclusion of the argument, the first is not a conclusion but a premise.

(*c*) This option is **incorrect**. The first is a premise that (indirectly) supports the argument's main conclusion by supporting an implicit subsidiary conclusion that, in turn, supports the main conclusion. However, the second is the main conclusion.

(*d*) This option is **incorrect**. While the second is indeed the only explicit conclusion of the argument, the first is a premise and not a context-setting statement that merely provides background information.

(*e*) This option is **correct**. It is exactly in line with the argument structure drawn in the 'Argument Construction' section.

The correct answer is option (e).

39. (a) Argument construction

Workers whose jobs are monotonous have poorer mental health than those whose jobs are interesting.

This is Premise 1.

Machine-driven jobs involve recurring tasks and are monotonous for workers.

This is Premise 2.

Combining these two premises, we can draw a subsidiary conclusion:

Workers who execute machine-driven jobs have poorer mental health than those whose jobs are interesting.

Replacing workers with mechanical robots to execute machine-driven jobs will induce these workers to take up more interesting jobs.

This is Premise 3.

The author of the argument combines premise 3 with the subsidiary conclusion to draw the main conclusion of the argument: Replacing workers with mechanical robots to execute machine-driven jobs will improve the mental health of these workers.

We note that the author's conclusion depends on the assumption that the workers, who earlier performed machine-driven jobs, will be able to find more interesting jobs. If this happens, then indeed, these workers will go from a state of 'poorer mental health' to a state of 'better mental health,' and so, will show improved mental health.

Therefore, to evaluate the assumption, we need to determine if this assumption is plausible. If it is, then the argument is strengthened. If it is not, then the argument is considerably weakened.

Let's analyze each option one by one.

(*a*) This option is **correct**. As discussed in the 'Argument Construction' section, this statement will adequately test the assumption that the author makes for his/her conclusion.

(*b*) This option is **incorrect**. The argument is based on a premise that the workers who do interesting jobs have better mental health than those who do machine-driven jobs. Accordingly, the conclusion drawn is also about how the mental health of workers who did machine-driven jobs would change when a particular event happens. A comparison of the salaries offered by each type of jobs is irrelevant to this conclusion.

(*c*) This option is **incorrect**. The conclusion is about one specific impact of replacing workers with mechanical robots in machine-driven jobs. The question of whether workers will be replaced with mechanical robots in more interesting jobs is not relevant to evaluating the conclusion.

(*d*) This option is **incorrect**. How well the mechanical robots execute the machine-driven jobs in comparison to workers will determine how beneficial the replacement of workers with mechanical robots proves to be for the companies that employed these workers. This consideration is irrelevant to the conclusion of the argument.

(*e*) This option is **incorrect**. The answer to this question will determine the extent to which workers who execute machine-driven jobs are replaced with mechanical robots. It will not help evaluate the claim that the workers who do get replaced with mechanical robots will have improved mental health.

The correct answer is option (a).

40. (b) Argument construction

Let us understand the argument. There are two premises: "No married woman can lack cooking skills," and "but girls are not married women." Based on these premises, there follows a valid conclusion: "girls can lack cooking skills."

However, the flawed conclusion is: "That girls can lack cooking skills is not justified." We must look for an option that has two premises, and a flawed conclusion based on them.

Let's analyze each option one by one.

(*a*) This is **incorrect**. If many creatures are agile, but ants are not creatures, then it logically follows that ants are NOT agile. However, to make the argument parallel to the flawed conclusion drawn in the argument, the conclusion of the option should have been: Therefore, it is not right to conclude that ants are not agile.

(*b*) This is the **correct** answer. Since all enterprises must pay taxes, but non-governmental organizations (NGOs) are not enterprises, then it logically follows that NGOs should not pay tax. So, the flawed conclusion should be: therefore, it is sensible to tax NGOs, which is the same as given in the option. Thus, the option argument is parallel to the flawed argument.

(*c*) This is **incorrect**. There is only one premise and the conclusion. The correct argument must have two premises and the conclusion. So, this argument is not parallel to the flawed argument.

(*d*) This is **incorrect**. Only one premise and the conclusion are not parallel. Moreover, the conclusion brings in new elements: small and big organisms.

(*e*) This is **incorrect**. The conclusion drawn is a valid conclusion, not a flawed one. This option argument is not parallel.

The correct answer is option (b).

41. (d) Argument construction

A survey shows that 60 percent of a blog's readers want to buy fishing boats. However, fishing boat manufacturers can only produce enough boats to satisfy 25 percent of potential buyers.

This is a question on resolving the paradox.

The paradox : While 60% of the readers of the blog want to buy fishing boats, fishing boat manufacturers can make boats to satisfy only 25% of total potential buyers.

This question deals with different reference points.

How can the figure of 60% of the readers of the blog relate to 25% of the potential buyers?

This inequality can hold true if 'the number of potential buyers' is significantly greater than 'the blog's readers.' Say, the number of potential buyers = 10,000, and the number of the blog's readers = 1,000, then 60% of 1,000 = 600, and 25% of 10,000 = 2,500; it is quite evident that 600 < 2,500. Option (d) correctly states it.

Let's analyze each option one by one.

(*a*) This is **incorrect** because it is not relevant to the discrepancy.

(*b*) This is **incorrect**. Like option (a), it is not relevant.

(*c*) This is **incorrect** because it does not explain the noticeable discrepancies exhibited by the two figures: 60% and 25%.

(*d*) This is the **correct** answer. It is aligned with the discussion above.

(*e*) This is **incorrect** because whether buyers want boats for self-use or to loan them, does not explain the inconsistent data.

The correct answer is option (d).

42. (d) Argument construction

Usually, insurance companies blame drivers for accidents. However, they must analyze the details of accidents by studying flaws in road design, vehicle design, and the criteria to determine eligibility for a driver's license. Only then will the insurance companies be able to successfully issue guidelines to prevent accidents.

Conclusion : By studying flaws in road design, automobile design, and the criteria used to determine eligibility for a driver's license, insurance companies can help prevent accidents.

We have to find out the assumption the argument takes. Let us analyze each option one by one.

(*a*) This is **incorrect**. This option is extreme. The argument implies that driving errors are neither an insignificant factor nor a significant factor in most automobile accidents.

(*b*) This is **incorrect**. This option is out of scope. It talks about the agency that should investigate accidents rather than the causes of accidents.

(*c*) This is **incorrect**. Issuance of effective guidelines is the by-product of the analysis. Moreover, the penalization of drivers is not the core issue. The primary issue is the analysis of accidents.

(*d*) This is the **correct** answer. It is the unstated, necessary premise of the argument.

(*e*) This is **incorrect**. This option is extreme because of the word "negligible." Had it been "reasonable," the option would have been correct.

The correct answer is option (d).

43. (d) Argument construction

The argument is simple to understand. The argument underscores two positive aspects of technological advances in the workplace: making things more affordable and efficient at a lower cost.

However, workers are discontented because they feel that their particular skills are no longer essential.

We have to complete the phrase that starts with "Therefore, we can conclude that technological advances ______."

Let's analyze each option one by one.

(*a*) This is **incorrect**. The argument is about technological advances and their impact on workers. The aspect of proficiency in production does not logically follow as a conclusion.

(*b*) This is **incorrect**. The remuneration aspect is out of scope. It's the lower sense of accomplishment in their work that disappoints workers.

(*c*) This is **incorrect**. This is factually wrong. As is clear from the argument, workers do not welcome technological advances in their work. Managers' viewpoints are out of scope.

(*d*) This is the **correct** answer. Indeed, technological advances have made workers' skills less important to their jobs; this option logically follows.

(*e*) This is **incorrect**. This option is unsubstantiated and extreme. Laying off workers cannot be inferred from the argument.

The correct answer is option (d).

44. (e) Argument construction

Carleton has invented a central heating mechanism that industry experts predict will soon be adopted by traditional heating equipment makers.

Traditional mechanism : similar to the carburetors in vehicles – the mixture of air and gas is then fed to the heating burner.

Carleton mechanism (Gas injection mechanism): Heating air before it mixes with gas, raising volatility.

Conclusion : Carleton mechanism will reduce fuel consumption by nearly 30%.

Why does Carleton claim that this mechanism will reduce fuel consumption by nearly 30%?

Based on the information, we can conclude that heating of air before it mixes with gas would save fuel consumption. The traditional mechanism does not preheat air, and the mixture of air and gas reaches the heating furnace at a normal temperature.

Predictive assumption : Heating the air before it mixes with gas, raising volatility, will reduce fuel consumption by nearly 30%. Let us analyze each option one by one.

(*a*) This is **incorrect**. This option is out of scope. How much time preheating takes is immaterial, as long as the mechanism claims to save 30% fuel consumption.

(*b*) This is **incorrect**. Whether traditional heating equipment makers adopt the Carleton mechanism is not the focus. The focus is on the claim that the new mechanism will reduce fuel consumption by nearly 30%.

(*c*) This is **incorrect**. The cost aspect is out of scope.

(*d*) This is **incorrect**. This option is irrelevant. The humidity aspect is not under contemplation.

(*e*) This is the **correct** answer. If heating air before it mixes with gas does not consume significantly less energy, fuel consumption by both mechanisms will have no difference; thus, it is necessary to assume that heating air before it mixes with gas consumes significantly less energy.

The correct answer is option (e).

45. (d) Argument construction

This is a question on evaluating the argument.

This is a relatable real-life scenario. Though smaller containers of products cost less, their per-unit cost is greater than the per-unit cost of a larger-sized container. For example, a 50 ml. bottle may cost $2 [0.04/ml.], but a 1,000 ml. bottle might cost only $24 [0.024/ml.] instead of $40; this is because the argument states that viz.-a-viz. 50 ml. bottle, there is a 40% reduction in the price for a 1,000 ml. bottle.

Conclusion : Larger packs offer more value for money, and, therefore, should be preferred over the smaller packs. When deciding to buy a large bottle of body lotion, we have to choose an option that DOESN'T need consideration.

Let's analyze each option one by one.

(*a*) This is **incorrect**. This aspect needs consideration. If "Best before date" is short, it makes sense to buy a smaller bottle. However, if it is not, buying a larger bottle offered at the lowest per milliliter price is a good decision.

(*b*) This is **incorrect**. This aspect needs consideration. If a larger than 1,000 ml. bottle becomes available in the near future, one might wait to reap the price advantage, as that bottle's per ml. price could be less than that of a 1,000 ml. bottle.

(*c*) This is **incorrect**. This aspect needs consideration. Just because a brand's offering is cheaper than a trusted brand's, one need not fall for it.

(*d*) This is the **correct** answer. This aspect doesn't need consideration. It doesn't matter whether the brand of body lotion being considered is advertised or not. The important aspect is whether the brand offers consistent quality and fulfills needs.

(*e*) This is incorrect. This aspect needs consideration. The explanation for this option is the same as that for option (b). One must consider before buying, whether a sachet or a larger bottle offers the minimum per ml. cost.

The correct answer is option (d).

46. (c) Argument construction

This is a question on finding the inference.

When the economy is thriving, people are more inclined to learn new skills, but when it slows down, they prefer to earn a formal degree. Thus, when the economy declines, people's keenness to learn new skills goes down, and they prefer to earn a formal degree.

Let's analyze each option one by one.

(*a*) This is **incorrect**. There is nothing to support this out-of-scope claim.

(*b*) This is **incorrect**. Nothing of this sort can be inferred considering the premises.

(*c*) This is the **correct** answer. This option statement is a derivative/paraphrase of the premise, "When the economy is thriving, people are more motivated to learn new skills rather than earn a formal degree."

(*d*) This is **incorrect**. It might be true in real life. But if we only look at the argument, we can't infer this.

(*e*) This is **incorrect**. All is fine with this option except the phrase "how many." The number of people who want to get a formal degree is not in the scope of this argument.

The correct answer is option (c).

47. (e) Argument construction

This is a question on strengthening the argument. T&T Motors claims two things:

1. About half of the most fuel-efficient bikes on the market are its 100-cc bikes.

2. Its 100-cc bike is one of the most fuel-efficient bikes.

We have to strengthen the two claims. Let's analyze each option one by one.

(*a*) This is **incorrect**. Licensing cutting-edge engine technology from the global leader does not mean that a bike is the most fuel-efficient and commands more than 50% of the market share.

(*b*) This is **incorrect**. This statement can be discarded at first glance because it does not state that the 100-cc bike mentioned is a T&T Motors bike. Moreover, even if it were from T&T, it does not mean that it is the most fuel efficient. What if a 125-cc bike is the most fuel efficient?

(*c*) This is **incorrect**. "Any bike of any make" refers to all bikes from all competitors and of any capacity: 80-cc, 100-cc, 125-cc, etc. The option statement means that T&T's 100-cc bike is the most fuel efficient. It strengthens T&T's 2nd claim. If we get an option that does not strengthen both claims, this is the correct answer.

(*d*) This is **incorrect**. At first sight, this option seems to strengthen T&T's first claim; however, upon close analysis, we find that though T&T Motors has approximately 60% of the bike market, it could happen that T&T has more than 60% market share of its non-100-cc bikes and less than 50% market share of its 100-cc bikes. So, this option is inconclusive.

(*e*) This is the **correct** answer. This option strengthens both the claims. (1) T&T's 100-cc bike is the most fuel-efficient bike. (2) Given that all of T&T's competitors together sell less than 50% of all 100-cc bikes, T&T must sell more than 50% of all 100-cc bikes.

The correct answer is option (e).

48. (d) Argument construction

Some analysts in the Kerbian republic believe that if Turkmenistan imposed a sanction on the export of a particular kind of petroleum byproduct, it would increase its price by 10 times. A few countries sell that byproduct. Dealing with the embargo, Kerbia might have to turn to these countries for this byproduct; however, they do not process it with proven fuel technologies.

Conclusion/Apprehension : Kerbia will have to rely on unproven synthetic fuel technologies to procure the byproduct. We have to strengthen/support the conclusion.

Let's analyze each option one by one.

(*a*) This is **incorrect**. Going deeper into the statement, we can infer that since Turkmenistan's economy relies on earnings from the export of the byproduct, it might not impose the sanction on Kerbia. If Turkmenistan does so, Kerbia need not depend on other countries. This option is rather a weakener.

(*b*) This is **incorrect**. We already know this. This is not additional information.

(*c*) This is **incorrect**. This is a wishful thinking statement. It does not affect the analyst's apprehension. This is irrelevant.

(*d*) This is the **correct** answer. Given that no new sources of the petroleum byproduct has been discovered in the last decade, Kerbia has no choice but to procure the byproduct from other countries and be ready to face the consequences of unproven fuel technologies.

(*e*) This is **incorrect**. This is an assumption, not a strengthener.

The correct answer is option (d).

49. (e) Argument construction

Based on the premise, less-than 15 bhp bikes do not provide an adrenaline rush to youngsters, the RTS plans to restrict youngsters to driving less-than 15 bhp bikes, so that the number of accidents caused by them will decrease. It implies that the RTS assumes that many youngsters find more-than 15 bhp bikes worth-providing adrenaline rush.

Let us analyze each option one by one.

(*a*) This is **incorrect**. The option statement implies that, as per some automobile experts, it's wrong to conclude that more-than 15 bhp bikes commit a greater number of accidents. This rather goes against the RTS's decision; thus, the RTS would not assume this.

(*b*) This is **incorrect**. Because of the word "only," this option is extreme. Indeed, as per the argument, youngsters find an adrenaline rush in more-than 15 bhp bikes. However, we cannot infer that RTS would assume that youngsters drive ONLY more-than 15 bhp bikes.

(*c*) This is **incorrect**. This option is irrelevant. Why youngsters drive fast is not relevant.

(*d*) This is **incorrect**. This option is out of scope. The penalty aspect is out of scope.

(*e*) This is the **correct** answer. It is aligned with the discussion above. With the usage of non-extreme quantifier "many," and not "all," this option wins over option (b).

The correct answer is option (e).

50. (d) Argument construction

In a certain communist country, on an average ruling party affiliates earn twice as much as non-ruling party affiliates. Party affiliates work in sectors that offer higher wages, but many non-party affiliates who also work in those sectors get nearly the same wages as party affiliates do. This means that higher wages don't always result from being an affiliate of the party.

Conclusion : Higher wages do not inevitably result from affiliation with the party. We have to weaken the argument.

Let's analyze each option one by one.

(*a*) This option is **incorrect**. The argument is concerned with wages; we cannot consider other benefits similar to wages. If 'other benefits' were expressed in financial terms, in relation to wages, this could be the answer. It would have corroborated that, due to affiliation with the party, party affiliates earn more compared to non-party affiliates. However, this option is inconclusive.

(*b*) This option is **incorrect**. "Some" is a tricky word; it ranges from "too few" to "many." If few high-earning businesspeople in that country are not party affiliates, the conclusion is weakened; however, if many high-earning businesspeople in that country are non-party affiliates, the conclusion is strengthened.

(*c*) This option is **incorrect** because it is out of scope. It does not address any difference between party affiliates and non- party affiliates.

(*d*) This is the**correct** answer. This option proves conclusively that due to affiliation with party affiliates, non-party affiliates often receive higher wages.

(*e*) This option is **incorrect**. This option is tricky. Just because one becomes an affiliate of the party does not prove that higher wages are guaranteed and are due to the affiliation with the party.

The correct answer is option (d).

51. (c) Argument construction

This is a question on resolving the paradox.

The argument is simple to understand. Despite expecting that after the mounting of cameras to deter signal jumpers, the number of signal jumpers would decrease, it rather increased.

We have to select an option that explains why such a contradiction occurred. Let's analyze each option one by one.

(*a*) This is**incorrect**. This option does not help explain the discrepancy. It compares the circumstances at two junctions; we have to comprehend why the increase, instead of a decrease, in the number of signal jumpers took place at the main junction.

(*b*) This is **incorrect**. With the same reasoning as in option (a), this option does not help explain the discrepancy.

(*c*) This is the **correct** answer. Since the capability of the system to catch signal jumpers is more than that of the previous system, more reports of signal jumpers occurred. Earlier, they were unreported due to the absence of a capable system. This option helps to explain the paradox.

(*d*) This is **incorrect**. If the 3-month period was not representative, the findings would be vulnerable to criticism. However, this option endorses that the experiment cannot be doubted; it rather worsens the contradiction to some extent.

(*e*) This is**incorrect**. This option does not add any value; it does not help to explain the paradox.

The correct answer is option (c).

52. **(d)** Argument construction

Instead of the central government providing economic support to local communities, they themselves will have the power to generate revenue and expend it on community services. The supporters of this proposal appreciate this move as a leap forward on the road to real democracy.

They assert that by making the communities accountable for funding their services, the quality of services will improve, and it will also foster a greater sense of belonging. However, as per the author, although such a proposal would mean that high-population regions would generate more funds because of a greater tax base; on the other hand, low-population regions, rural communities would still look for subsidies from the government to fund their services.

Conclusion : Rural regions would still be dependent on complementary subsidies from the central government. This is a question on weakening the conclusion.

Let's analyze each option one by one.

(*a*) This option is **incorrect**. It only suggests that compared to metropolitan regions, rural regions require relatively fewer funds. However, this option does not focus on how to generate even that funding.

(*b*) This option is **incorrect** . The concern is about generating funds for local-level services. This option is irrelevant.

(*c*) This option is **incorrect**. The explanation for this is the same as that for option (b).

(*d*) This is the **correct** answer. This option shows that rural communities can collect taxes, which will make them autonomous; thus, they need not look for centrally supported subsidies.

(*e*) This option is **incorrect** . This implies that many services are not to be supported, but the option does not address how to finance other local-level services.

The correct answer is option (d).

53. (c) Argument construction

The argument of the gun lobby : The US Constitution grants every citizen the right to possess a gun. Their position: Do not ban gun possession.

The argument of the proponents of the ban : Statistics show that there is a correlation between accidental shooting incidents and the leniency of gun control regulations.

Their position: Ban gun possession.

Main Conclusion : Ban gun possession. Let us analyze the argument and understand the roles the boldfaced portions play.

BF1 : (Granted ... arms) - It is a claim/fact/ evidence/consideration. It supports the "Do not ban gun possession" position. But the argument seeks to counter BF1. It contradicts the main conclusion - Ban gun possession.

Second portion of Statement 1 : (is the ... guns.) - This portion reinforces the position of the gun lobby. It should be read with BF1 to understand its role.

First portion of statement 2 : (However, ... that) - It presents the reference of evidence used by the proponents of the ban. It should be read with BF2 to understand its role.

BF2 : (worldwide... regulations.) - It is a counterevidence or a counterclaim that goes against BF1 and forms the basis for the main conclusion - ban gun possession.

Statement 3 : (Thus, ... banned) - As stated earlier, it is the main conclusion.

Let's analyze each option one by one.

(*a*) This is **incorrect**. BF1 is a fact whose implication is at issue in the argument, but BF2 is not advanced to argue for that implication; it is the other way around. BF1 and BF2 have counter positions.

(*b*) This is **incorrect**. BF1 does not support the main conclusion; it is against the main conclusion - Ban gun possession. BF2 does not counter the conclusion; it is a counterclaim that supports the conclusion.

(*c*) This is the **correct** answer. BF1 is the evidence that supports a position - Do not ban gun possession. BF2 is the evidence that supports the counter position - Ban gun possession.

(*d*) This is **incorrect**. BF1 is the consideration that counters the conclusion, but BF2 is not the conclusion; it forms the basis for the conclusion.

(*e*) This is **incorrect**. BF1 does not form the basis for the conclusion; rather, it counters the conclusion. Also, BF2 is not the conclusion.

The correct answer is option (c).

54. (b) Argument construction

This is a question on completing the argument.

Springville imposed an Odd-Even car plying policy on commuters. Cars with registration numbers ending in odd numbers (1, 3, 5, 7, and 9) will be allowed on the roads on odd days, and cars with registration numbers ending in even numbers (0, 2, 4, 6, and 8) will be allowed on the roads on even days. Since the city's Air Quality Index (AQI) breached 500, a hazardous level, the mayor, by implementing the Odd-Even car plying policy, attempted to bring down polluting exhaust gases discharged by cars.

The assumption that the mayor carries is that most car owners have one car: either odd-numbered or even-numbered, and that this policy will ensure that far fewer cars play the roads, leading to improved Air Quality Index (AQI).

However, contrary to expectations, AQI did not decrease significantly. We have to find out the reason for the unexpected outcome.

Let's analyze each option one by one.

(*a*) This is **incorrect**. Since many did not commute by their cars (single passenger) but by bus (carries many passengers), AQI should have decreased significantly.

(*b*) This is the **correct** answer. The option implies that "many" flouted the rule. The success of the Odd-Even policy hinges on citizens' allegiance to the rule. Since they did not obey the rule, AQI did not decrease significantly.

(*c*) This is **incorrect**. This could be the correct answer if "many" replaced "some." In the GMAT CR, "some" can be "few" or "many." So, this cannot be the correct answer if "few" replaces "some." This option is inconclusive.

(*d*) This is **incorrect**. The explanation is the same as that of option (a). A carpool can have three-to-four passengers, ensuring that two-to-three cars are not plying on the roads.

(*e*) This is **incorrect**. Using "cab" (single passenger) instead of "car" (single passenger) will not decrease AQI. However, like option (c), this could be the correct answer if "many" replaced "some."

The correct answer is option (b).

55. (b) Argument construction

This is a question on weakening the argument.

The argument is simple to understand. Though a retail chain trades in over 50 cell phone brands, it stocks only the top 11 top-selling models. It plans to stock another three popular brands to increase its profits.

Conclusion : Stocking another three popular brands will yield additional profit.

We have to weaken the decision that, by stocking another three popular brands, the retail chain will increase its profit. Let's analyze each option one by one.

(*a*) This option is **incorrect**. Given that four top-selling brands account for approximately two-thirds of the company's revenue, we do not have any information about how the remaining revenue comes. If there's a scope to increase profit by stocking another three popular brands, there's no harm in it. This option does not weaken the decision.

(*b*) This is the **correct** answer. Since the top 10 brands out of 11 bring in all the revenue, another three popular brands will not make any difference. This certainly weakens the decision.

(*c*) This option is **incorrect**. This rather strengthens the decision. It talks in favor of stocking less popular brands, or more brands.

(*d*) This option is **incorrect**. This option is tricky. It does have the undercurrent of weakening the decision, as it does not support stocking less popular brands. However, it does not mean that another three popular brands will not also increase profits.

(*e*) This option is **incorrect**. This option is inconclusive. What we get from this option is that the #1 brand is no longer #1; at least a couple of brands have toppled it. However, we cannot conclude anything from this.

The correct answer is option (b).

56. (b) Argument construction

This is a question on weakening the argument. Emergency response administrators claim that a significantly greater number of fire incidents are not occurring; it's just that non-stop reporting of the same incidents triggers people to report a significantly greater number of fire incidents. A fact that weakens the claim will be something that exhibits that a significantly greater number of fire incidents are occurring, or that non-stop media reports have no connection to the reporting of the number of fire incidents.

Let's analyze each option one by one.

(a) This is **incorrect**. Even if the hype surrounding fires is mostly restricted to the city in which the incident occurred, are there sufficiently fewer/greater numbers of fire incidences? We cannot get the answer to this question.

(b) This is the **correct** answer. Given that the television media are mandated to give a code name to a fire incident and run a scroll updating viewers on whether the incident has been reported, the media are conducting themselves responsibly. While giving a code name to an incident avoids multiple reports of the same fire, updating on scroll about the status of reporting avoids multiple reports by many people. This fact certainly weakens the emergency response administrators' claim.

(c) This is **incorrect**. If the media do not have any benchmark to help them decide how big a fire must be for it to receive reportage, they will report even those incidents that are not severe, and, hence, the claims of emergency response administrators would rather be reasonable. It is a strengthener.

(d) This is **incorrect**. We cannot draw any inference from this statement. The media might report severe or non-severe incidents if such reporting is beneficial to them. This does not suggest that the media report those fires that don't occur. It is inconclusive.

(e) This is **incorrect**. Since the number of fire incidents in Goreville is nearly the same every month, excessive coverage for a few months means that the media do create hype. With this, the claims of emergency response administrators would rather be reasonable. It is a strengthener.

The correct answer is option (b).

57. (b) Argument construction

The argument is easy to comprehend. Garrison Motors had great success in cargo truck sales after a design team gave its cargo trucks a more upmarket look to appeal to more aspiring clients. Leveraging on the trucks' success, Garrison Motors is now planning to launch a compact sports utility vehicle (compact-SUV) using a similar concept.

Though the conclusion is missing from the argument, we can infer it.

Implied conclusion: By applying a similar concept that Garrison Motors did for its trucks, it plans to launch a compact-SUV and hopes to make good sales.

Let us analyze each option one by one.

(*a*) This is **incorrect**. It is not a necessary assumption. Even if there are compact-SUVs in the market, Garrison Motors can plan to manufacture its own compact-SUV. It does not impact the conclusion.

(*b*) This is the **correct** answer. Since Garrison Motors already has a loyal base of aspiring and upmarket clients, it assumes that at least Garrison Motors' aspiring clients would be interested in the compact-SUV to be manufactured by it, given that its cargo trucks have been making great sales.

(*c*) This is **incorrect**. This is not necessary. The argument states that Garrison Motors plans to make a compact-SUV using a similar, but not the same, concept.

(*d*) This is **incorrect**. This is not necessary. Banking on the experience of the cargo trucks, Garrison Motors itself can design the compact-SUV.

(*e*) This is **incorrect**. The explanation is same as that of option (d).

The correct answer is option (b).

58. (a) Argument construction

By 2030, fossil-fueled cars (petrol, diesel, etc.) are likely to lose approximately 10°A of their market share, measured in revenues, to solar-powered cars. By 2030, the manufacturing cost of solar-powered cars will significantly decrease; thus, their manufacturers expect profits to increase by more than 10%.

Let's first understand the difference between percentage and percentage point.

Say, last month, the inflation rate of a country was 10°A, and by the end of the month, it reached 1196. Thus, the inflation increased by

p × 100°A = 10°% or 10 percent.

However, we can also say that inflation increased by 11% - 10% = 1% or 10 percentage, Coming to the question.

Say, currently, the market is $100 million, and solar-powered cars have a 10% market share; thus, fossil-fueled cars will have a 90°6 market share. The author forecasts that by 2030, solar-powered cars will have a 20% market share; thus, fossil-fueled cars will have an 80°A market share. This does not mean that the business of fossil-fueled cars will decrease. It might increase desp'ite the decrease in market share by 10 percentage points.

Let's understand this Say, by 2030, the market is 5200 million; thus, market for fossil-fueled cars = 80% of 5200 = S160M, which is greater than the current market = 90°% of 5100 = $90M.

Given that by 2030, the manufacturing cost of solar-powered cars will significantly decrease, and the manufacturers can expect profits to increase by 10°A, it is necessary that the worldwide market does not decrease considerably. If it does, the forecast will shatter.

Let's see how.

Say currently, the market is $100 million, solar-powered cars have 10°A of the market share, and solar cars make a 2096 profit. Thus, 20% profit of1096 of$100-$2 million.

Say, by 2030, the market is $20 million, solar-powered cars then have a 20% market share, and solar cars make 25% profit (profit percent increased due to the decrease in cost). Thus, 25% profit of 20% of 510 = S1 million.

With this data, we see that profits decrease by 50% (= 2 × 100% = 50%). However, this contradicts the forecast that manufacturers can expect profits to increase by 10° profit. With this example, the profits should be $2 million + 10% of $2 million = $2.2 million, and not $51 million.

Thus, the necessary assumption is that by 2030, the worldwide market for cars will not decrease significantly.

Lets analyze each option one by one.

(*a*) This option is **correct**. It is in line with the analysis done above.

(*b*) This option is **incorrect**. Even if selling prices of solar-powered cars decrease significantly, by selling a significantly greater volume of cars, profits can be accrued.

59. (e) Argument construction

The question makes two claims.

1. **CEO's claim :** The shrinking of purchasing power has not been the major reason for the current decline in the real estate sector in this region.

2. **President's claim :** Unsatisfactory infrastructure services and the non-provision of amenities in buyers' apartments are the reasons for the current decline in the real estate sector in this region.

We have to strengthen the president's claim. Let's analyze each option one by one.

(*a*) This option is **incorrect**. It is tricky. Though many buyers emphasize on good infrastructure and amenities in their apartments, does this mean that they are deprived of these? We cannot draw such an unsubstantiated inference.

(*b*) This option is **incorrect**. If many buyers would not have purchased the apartments in the current economic scenario, it supports the CEO's, rather than the president's, claim.

(*c*) This option is **incorrect**. While option (b) talks about the buyers who bought apartments, option (c) talks about the potential buyers. Both rather weaken the claim and support the CEO's claim that shrinking purchasing power has been the major reason for the current decline in the real estate sector in the region.

(*d*) This option is **incorrect**. It is also a tricky option. Though it endorses the CEO's claim that shrinking of purchasing power has not been the major reason for the current decline in the real estate sector in this region, it does not support the president's claim that below-par infrastructure services and non-provision of amenities are the reasons of not buying properties in the region. There could be other reasons behind buying properties in other regions.

(*e*) This is the **correct** answer. "inadequate commuter facilities" is a subset of infrastructure services, and "internal security" is a subset of amenities. This information strengthens the president's claim.

The correct answer is option (e).

60. (b) Argument construction

This is a question on completing the argument.

We have to determine the reason students studying in schools that are affiliated with the central education board are more scholarly (knowledgeable) than those studying in schools that are affiliated with the state education boards.

Let's analyze each option one by one.

(*a*) This is **incorrect**. A greater average salary is not necessarily a benchmark of imparting more knowledge. This option does not state the reason.

(*b*) This is the **correct** answer. This option correctly fills the logical gap. Teaching resources comprise competent teachers, books, teaching methodology, school infrastructure, and other related resources; this option states that resources that make students scholarly are more effective in schools that are affiliated with the central education board than in schools that are affiliated with the state education boards.

(*c*) This is **incorrect**. Expenditure on infrastructure and students' competence to gain knowledge are not necessarily related.

(*d*) This is **incorrect**. Motives for running schools and students' competence to gain knowledge are unrelated.

(*e*) This is **incorrect**. Teaching students privately does not imply that the teachers can make students more scholarly, too. Moreover, we do not know whether teachers at schools that are affiliated with the state education boards also teach students privately.

The correct answer is option (b).

61. (b) Argument construction

The 20 universities that charge the highest tuition fees also hand out the largest amounts of financial aid to those students who exhibit exceptional academic performance. These universities believe in the virtue of equal opportunity, and thus are able to charge more fees from those who can afford to pay, and charge less from those who cannot afford to pay.

Since the quantum of financial aid is based on academic performance, the fees for students vary. A few would pay $100, a few $80, a few $60, or a few $40.

Let us analyze each option one by one.

(*a*) This is **incorrect**. We cannot infer that the belief in the virtue of equal opportunity is followed to mask charging higher tuition fees. This option is hypercritical and does not align with the tone of the passage.

(*b*) This is the **correct** answer. Yes, it is feasible for universities that believe in equal opportunity to charge different fees from students. It is aligned with what we discussed above.

(*c*) This is **incorrect**. This is an extreme option. The issue with the option is the compulsion due to the usage of "must do." Had "do" replaced "must do," it would have been correct.

(*d*) This is **incorrect**. This is the classic mix-up option. All we can infer is that universities that do not charge HIGHEST tuition fees DO NOT hand out the LARGEST financial aid. The words "high" and "little" are too vague to decipher.

(*e*) This is **incorrect**. The argument does not offer any support for inferring such an extreme claim.

The correct answer is option (b).

62. (c) Argument construction

The number of metastatic prostate cancer patients in the US has increased by around 10% during the last two years. However, Chicago reported a sharp decrease in the number of such patients visiting public clinics during the same 2-year period.

What is the paradox? The paradox is that while the pertinent figure for the US is 10%, that for Chicago, a prominent city in the US, is way too low.

What could resolve the paradox?

1. In terms of metastatic prostate cancer, Chicago is unrepresentative of the US.
2. A considerably greater number of cancer patients go to private clinics.
3. A considerably greater number of cancer patients undergo alternative therapies that are not accounted for.

Let us analyze each option one by one.

(*a*) This is **incorrect**. This information rather reinforces the paradox; it is the opposite of the #1 resolution, we discussed above.

(*b*) This is **incorrect**. This option is irrelevant. Had it talked about Chicago, it would have been the correct answer.

(*c*) This is the **correct** answer. This is aligned with the #2 resolution, which we discussed above.

(*d*) This is **incorrect**. This is tricky but an incorrect option. The argument states that Chicago reported a SHARP DECREASE in the number of such patients visiting public clinics during the same period, and this option states that the rate of increase in the number of such patients in Chicago is MARGINALLY LESS than that for the US. It does not resolve the paradox.

(*e*) This is **incorrect**. This option is tempting but inconclusive. Even if we assume that the awareness of metastatic prostate cancer in Chicago is greater than that in the US, does this mean that the rate of increase in the number of metastatic prostate cancer patients would be significantly less? This cannot be inferred.

The correct answer is option (c).

63. (a) Argument construction

A biologist claimed that the role of microorganisms is far greater than scientists currently comprehend. The studies have found this hypothesis correct. These findings will bring about renewed perspective in many areas of study.

Let's analyze each statement and boldface portions.

Statement 1 (BF 1) : (microorganisms... scientists): This is the claim made by the biologist. Hence, BF1 is a claim. The boldfaced portion is the claim that is found correct in the argument and supports the argument's intermediate conclusion that the biologist was correct.

Statement 2 : (Now, a team... the biologist was correct): This statement is clearly the evidence that the author uses to support that the biologist was correct. However, the part "the biologist was correct" is an intermediate conclusion of the author.

Statement 3 : (The combined... very diverse organisms.): This statement consists of a hypothesis or proclamation that supports the biologist's and the author's claims; it contains forecasts of what the claim will result in.

Statement 4 (BF 2) : (The findings... of interest): It is a claim that will happen because the biologist was correct. Thus, BF2 is the main conclusion of the argument.

Let us analyze each option one by one.

(*a*) This is the **correct** answer. As discussed, BF1 is a claim that is found correct and supports the argument's intermediate conclusion: the biologist was correct. We can consider BF1 as the "content of the intermediate conclusion;" as discussed above, BF2 is the main conclusion.

(*b*) This is **incorrect**. While BF1 can be considered support for the main conclusion of the argument, BF2 is not the content of the conclusion; BF2 itself is the conclusion. We discussed above that BF1 is the claim, and BF2 is the main conclusion.

There's a subtle difference between options (a) and (b); option (a) is unambiguous, while option (b) is vague.

(*c*) This is **incorrect**. BF1 is the claim of the biologist, not the main conclusion of the argument/author. BF2 does not question the conclusion; BF2 itself is the conclusion.

(*d*) This is **incorrect**. While BF1 can be considered support for the main conclusion of the argument, BF2 does not call the conclusion into question; BF2 itself is the conclusion.

(*e*) This is **incorrect**. While BF1 can be considered support for the conclusion of the argument, BF2 is not support for the conclusion. As discussed, BF2 itself is the conclusion.

The correct answer is option (a).

64. (b) Argument construction

The argument is easy to understand. Alpha City citizens want better life and cleaner environment. This requires the development of more parks and green spaces in the urban hub. However, doing so will raise housing prices.

Conclusion: Allocating lands for parks and green spaces will negatively impact residents' lives.

The question is to find the LEAST relevant option that needs evaluation whether the residents' lives would be negatively impacted because of the proposed development of more parks and green spaces in the urban hub. So, four options would qualify as evaluators; the option that does not qualify as an evaluator is the correct answer.

Let us analyze each option one by one.

(*a*) This is **incorrect**. This option qualifies to be an evaluator. It talks about the impact on the cost of living — a matter of concern to the residents.

(*b*) This is the **correct** answer. This option does not qualify to be an evaluator. It talks about benefit for residents of neighboring cities — a matter of no interest to Alpha City residents.

(*c*) This is **incorrect**. This option qualifies to be an evaluator. It talks about job creation — a matter of interest to Alpha City residents. If jobs are given to them, the positive impact could offset the negative impacts.

(*d*) This is **incorrect**. This option qualifies to be an evaluator. It talks about the health of Alpha City residents — a matter of concern to the residents.

(*e*) This is **incorrect**. This option qualifies to be an evaluator. It talks about the rise in housing prices — a matter of concern to Alpha City residents. If the development of parks and green spaces does not take place and the housing prices remain the same, the residents will not want the housing prices to go up if the proposed plan takes place.

The correct answer is option (b).

65. (a) Argument construction

The argument is simple to understand.

This is a question on inference. If it is true that the heightened security will bring in an additional revenue of $30 million a year, what kind of people will bring in the increased revenue?

Certainly, those who are scared of inadequate security will feel more confident and will start traveling by air more often if security is enhanced.

Predictive Inference: are scared of inadequate security.

Let us analyze each option one by one.

As discussed, the answer is option (a). It is aligned with our predictive inference.

The correct answer is option (a).

66. (e) Argument construction

The standard number of cell phones assembled per month per technician = 140 — 160 phones in the fifth month of joining the enterprise.

Conclusion: If the number of cell phones assembled by a technician is less than 140 in the fifth month, he is an unskilled technician. There can be many flaws in the reasoning; one such is:

The number of defective cell phones an average technician assembles in the fifth month of joining is ignored.

Let us analyze each option one by one.

(a) This is **incorrect**. This is out of scope. The argument does not suggest that the number of cell phones assembled is the only measure of the enterprise's productivity.

(b) This is **incorrect**. This does not reveal a flaw; given that a technician can assemble between 140 and 160 phones, the minimum quantity, 140, is taken care of. The option fails to consider why less than 140 phones in the fifth month must be taken into account.

(c) This is **incorrect**. This is irrelevant. It talks about greater than the higher range.

(d) This is **incorrect**. The quality aspect is outside the scope of the argument.

(e) This is the **correct** answer. If a competent technician had unfavorable working conditions in the fifth month of joining, resulting in fewer than 140 assembled phones, it would be unfair on him to be adjudged unskilled. Thus, the argument has this flaw.

The correct answer is option (e).

67. (a) Argument construction

PayLess buys free-holiday coupons from frequent holidaymakers who earn them from Fairy-tale Holidays for vacationing at Fairy-tale Holidays destinations. PayLess sells these coupons at a cheaper price of their value. This sale of free coupons is the loss of the potential revenue for Fairy-tale Holidays.

Conclusion : This buying and reselling of free coupons results in a loss of revenue for Fairy-tale Holidays.

We have to discourage the buying and reselling of free-holiday coupons issued by Fairy-tale Holidays to its customers for their use.

Predictive solution : Limit the benefit of the free coupons to those who earned them.

Let us analyze each option one by one.

(a) This is the **correct** answer. It is aligned with the predictive solution. By limiting the usage of the coupons to

the clients and their family members, the buying and reselling of free coupons will cease to exist, as those coupons would be worthless to buyers.

(*b*) This is **incorrect**. The move to limit the number of free coupons that a person can earn in a particular season will not solve the problem. Even those limited number of free coupons can still be sold.

(*c*) This is **incorrect**. Like option (b), the move to limit the number of seasons in which the free coupons can be used will not solve the problem. Even those limited number of free coupons can still be sold.

(*d*) This is **incorrect**. The explanation of this option is the same as that of options (a) and (b).

(*e*) This is **incorrect**. This option is irrelevant. While the free coupons can still be traded, this move would be disadvantageous to clients of Fairy-tale Holidays.

The correct answer is option (a).

68. (e) Argument construction

Let us understand the argument.

The selection criterion for digital boards is "value for money."

Given that both the Alpha and Beta brands of digital whiteboards qualify for the selection, we can infer that both brands qualify for the "value for money" criterion.

What is the "value for money" criterion? In short, it is the optimum combination of whole-life cost and quality (or fitness for purpose) to meet the user's requirements.

A cheaper brand, if it does not serve the purpose well, can score lower on the "value for money" criterion than a costly brand, if it serves the purpose well.

Given that the Beta brand of digital whiteboards is costlier than the Alpha brand of digital whiteboards, and both qualify for the "value for money" criterion, we can infer that on at least one criterion, the Beta brand scores over the Alpha brand.

Let's analyze each option one by one.

(*a*) This is **incorrect**. Both brands of digital whiteboards qualify for the "value for money" criterion.

(*b*) This is **incorrect**. It is not necessarily true; it is certainly not the costliest, but we cannot infer that it is the cheapest of all the digital whiteboards.

(*c*) This is **incorrect**. It is not necessarily true. The only criterion is "value for money;" cost criterion is not stated.

(*d*) This is **incorrect**. Based on the information available, we cannot compare the "value for money" scores of the two brands. We can only infer that both brands of digital whiteboards qualify for the "value for money" criterion.

(*e*) This is the **correct** answer. This option is in line with our analysis.

The correct answer is option (e).

69. (b) Argument construction

Because of pollution reaching alarming levels, mainly in suburban areas, city municipal corporations in many states erected provisional exhaust regulator points on the highways connecting inner city roads. This move led to an instant drop in the number of people affected by asthma in suburban areas.

Conclusion : By making the exhaust regulator points permanent on highways, asthma can be controlled considerably in suburban areas.

Let us analyze each option one by one.

(*a*) This is **incorrect**. This option attempts to establish that people do not live near highways; hence, there are no ill-effects due to exhaust in those areas. However, this is a weakener; it can't be an assumption.

(*b*) This is the **correct** answer. This is a necessary assumption. The erection of exhaust regular points and the instant drop in the number of asthma cases are correlated.

(*c*) This is **incorrect**. This option is extreme. Had the option been "the move will NOT make pollution reach alarming levels," it would have been correct. Note that, as per the premise, "this move led to an instant drop in the number of people suffering from asthma," we cannot deduce that no one would be affected by asthma.

(*d*) This is **incorrect**. Like option (c), this option is also extreme. At most, we can conclude that the other measures to control pollution are not as effective as the erection of exhaust regulator points.

(*e*) This is **incorrect**. No substantiative, available information supports this.

The correct answer is option (b).

70. (c) Argument construction

This is a question about finding the assumption.

The argument is simple to understand. The party must select few women from lower-caste backgrounds to its top decision-making body. But no women from lower economic classes are in the top decision-making body. So, the party is not abiding by its manifesto.

Conclusion : The party is not complying with its manifesto.

How do "lower-caste backgrounds" and "lower economic classes" relate? The underlying assumption is that women from "lower-caste backgrounds" come from "lower economic classes."

Let's analyze each option one by one.

(*a*) This option is **incorrect**. This option talks about the party membership, but the argument is about the membership of the top decision-making body.

(*b*) This option is **incorrect**. Reading the word "only," we can infer that this is an extreme option. There can be many stipulations in the manifesto: the selection of few women from lower-caste backgrounds in the top decision-making body is one of them.

(*c*) This is the **correct** answer. This is in line with the analysis done above.

(*d*) This option is **incorrect**. The aspect of men is out of scope.

(*e*) This option is **incorrect**. There is nothing in the argument to support such an unsubstantiated claim.

The correct answer is option (c).

71. (b) Argument construction

This is a question on weakening the argument.

What is Love-a-Tod's claim? It is that the new safety seats for toddlers are much safer. They will reduce toddler mortality rates in fatal collisions by up to 70%.

We have to weaken the claim.

Let's analyze each option one by one.

(*a*) This option is **incorrect**. What to make of this information? This is inconclusive. If "light in weight" is a positive attribute, then this option is a strengthener; however, if "light in weight" implies brittleness, then this option is a weakener.

(*b*) This is the **correct** answer. This option articulates the greatest challenge. If a toddler leaves water or food on the seat, and it is not cleaned properly, it might get moist and, in turn, catch fungus, which can be injurious to the toddler's health.

(*c*) This option is **incorrect**. That parents are wary of new products that are meant for toddlers' use does not mean that the new safety seat is rejected by the parents.

(*d*) This option is **incorrect**. That the leading safety-seat brand commands over two-thirds of the market share does not mean that people will not try a new product if it is promising.

(*e*) This option is **incorrect**. This is rather a strengthener.

The correct answer is option (b).

72. (c) Argument construction

Let us understand the argument.

Some board members believe that the serving president's business policies are the reason for the company's market devaluation. However, the president does not think so. The president's position: I am not accountable for it. While he acknowledges that the company's market devaluation took place during his tenure, he reasons that it is because of the former president's policies. Further, he bolsters his position by stating that had his policies not been in place, the situation would have been even worse.

Board members' claim : The president is liable for the company's market devaluation.

The president's claim : I am not at fault for the company's market devaluation.

Let us understand the roles the boldfaces play.

Boldface 1 : It is a fact that the board members hold the president accountable for the disaster.

Boldface 2 : It is a hypothesis used by the president (counterevidence) to strengthen his position that he's not at fault.

Let us analyze each option one by one.

(*a*) This is **incorrect**. While the first part is correct, the second boldface does not support the board members; it, in fact, counters them.

(*b*) This is **incorrect**. The first part is correct; the president acknowledges that the market devaluation did occur during his tenure. The second boldface, however, is the president's counterevidence to strengthen his position.

(*c*) This is the **correct** answer. The first boldface is a fact that the president believes does not contradict his position or oppose his claim. The second boldface undoubtedly supports the president's claim.

(*d*) This is **incorrect**. While the second supports the president's claim, the first opposes it.

(*e*) This is **incorrect**. While the first part of the statement is correct, the second boldface does not follow from the president's position. In fact, the opposite is true; the president's position (I'm not at fault) follows from the second (counterevidence).

The correct answer is option (c).

73. (d) Argument construction

Nearly 500 third-stage cancer patients were subjected to an experiment to evaluate the power of prayers. Nearly 250 were selected to receive remote healing prayers for 30 days from intercessors. Progress or decline of all the patients was recorded daily and, at recovery or death, each patient was given a numerical score. It was observed that the patients for whom prayers were performed had a 12% higher score than those for whom prayers were not performed. Based on this, believers now claim that God exists.

Conclusion : God exists.

We have to strengthen the conclusion.

Let us analyze each option one by one.

(*a*) This is **incorrect**. This option is irrelevant. It does not distinguish between the two groups of randomly selected 250 patients.

(*b*) This is **incorrect**. This option is inconclusive. "Noble soul" is a vague qualification. We cannot conclude anything from this. All we can interpret from this is that thc hcaling prayers performed by them would reach God. But the moot question is whether God exists, at all.

(*c*) This is **incorrect**. This option is irrelevant. It does not distinguish between the two groups of randomly selected 250 patients.

(*d*) This option is the **correct** answer. It could be that the 12% higher score is insignificant and cannot be used as a basis to form any conclusion. It could just be a chance. However, given that the Apex medical bodies acknowledge the 12% figure as statistically significant, it strengthens the claim that God exists.

(*e*) This is **incorrect**. This option is irrelevant. How prayers are performed does not matter. The moot question is whether God exists, at all.

The correct answer is option (d).

74. (b) Argument construction

The argument is about the cheetah's capability to maneuver and accelerate while hunting. Though cheetahs are the fastest land animals in the world, in most of the hunting chases, cheetahs attained speeds of 50 to 60 kilometers per hour and did not reach their peak speed.

Conclusion: While hunting, cheetahs rely more on maneuvering than on speed. We have to strengthen the conclusion.

Let us analyze each option one by one.

(*a*) This is **incorrect**. Though for cheetahs, the option dismisses speed as the most significant factor for hunting, it mentions another factor, not necessarily maneuvering, as the most significant factor. This option is inconclusive.

(*b*) This is the **correct** answer. This option is evidence that states that cheetahs accelerated and changed direction rapidly and ran fast very rarely.

If cheetahs succeeded at hunting without utilizing their capability of speed to the fullest, they must have maneuvered effectively. In other words, while hunting, cheetahs relied more on maneuvering than on speed.

(*c*) This is **incorrect**. This option is irrelevant. The question is not how swiftly cheetahs can increase their speed — this is the acceleration. The conclusion would be strengthened if there was supporting evidence that cheetahs seldom run at their peak speeds.

(*d*) This is **incorrect**. This option focuses on the speed aspect, which is not the issue.

(*e*) This is **incorrect**. Like options (c) and (d), this option also focuses on the speed aspect and not on maneuvering capability.

The correct answer is option (b).

75. (d) Argument construction

Against expectations, the water companies increased the water supply charges. But the water companies assert that the higher prices are because of how often repairs and maintenance need to be done.

The consumer interest groups' outrage stems from the fact that they had anticipated a drop in utility bills due to the privatization of services.

Conclusion: Higher water bills are due to the persistent need for repairs and maintenance.

We must evaluate the conclusion by asking a question: the valid question is one that, if answered yes, supports the conclusion and, if answered no, breaks it.

Let us analyze each option one by one.

(*a*) This is **incorrect**. Even if "repairs and maintenance" is NOT the only cost that water companies have to bear, is it justified for water companies to overcharge? This option does not relate to the companies' assertion.

(*b*) This is **incorrect**. Like option (a), even if many regions faced a severe water shortage, is it justified for water companies to overcharge? This option does not relate to the companies' assertion.

(*c*) This is **incorrect**. It has no relevance to the assertion. We are evaluating whether the companies' overcharging is justified, and not what proportion of customers are paying bills.

(*d*) This option is the **correct** answer. If "repairs and maintenance costs" account for a significant proportion of the cost of water supply and management, the assertion is valid; however, if it is not so, the assertion is invalid.

(*e*) This is **incorrect**. This option is irrelevant. It does not relate to the assertion, which is the subject of the dispute.

The correct answer is option (d).

76. (e) Argument construction

Recently many residents in a certain district have stopped buying new apartments. There are two reasons behind this: (1) high taxes imposed on buying new apartments, and (2) the high unemployment rate. Surprisingly, the average price of new apartments has risen by more than 20 percent in the last year.

The paradox: The paradox is that despite many residents deferring their decision to buy new apartments (low demand), and a high unemployment rate, the average price of new apartments has risen significantly.

We need a factor that explains why new apartment prices have gone up, despite their low demand. The option that explains what made the prices rise is the correct answer.

Let us analyze each option one by one.

(*a*) This is **incorrect**. This option is irrelevant since it talks about not-new apartments. The argument is concerned only with new apartments. Even if we take this fact into account, this option rather worsens the paradox.

(*b*) This is **incorrect**. Given that beginning next year, the district municipal corporation is expected to cut tax rates, residents have a reason to put off buying new apartments; they might wait till next year. Why the average price of new apartments has risen significantly is not answered.

(*c*) This is **incorrect**. This information is in sync with the rise in the average price of new apartments. At best, what this option does is bolster the claim that the average price of new apartments has risen significantly.

(*d*) This is **incorrect**. Given that starting next year, the number of jobs will go up by more than 10 percent, will people start buying new apartments now in anticipation? This option does not provide sound reasoning.

(*e*) This is the **correct** answer. The rule of demand and supply works here. Low demand led to low supply, resulting in a rise in the average price of new apartments. This additional information resolves the paradox.

The correct answer is option (e).

77. (b) Argument construction

The private vehicle unit, primarily due to increased sales of luxury cars, accounted for 40% of the company's sales and 20% of profit. The commercial vehicle unit accounted for the rest.

According to the passage, the private vehicle unit contributed 40% of dollar sales and 20% of profit, so the commercial vehicle unit contributed 60% of dollar sales and 80% of profit.

- The private vehicle unit contributed 20% /40% = \$0.50 profit per dollar sale, and
- The commercial vehicle unit contributed 80% /60%= \$1.33 profit per dollar sale

Thus, the profit per dollar sale for the commercial vehicle unit is more than double that of the private vehicle unit.

Let us analyze each option one by one.

(*a*) This is **incorrect**. We cannot compare the profitability of individual units. It might happen that a commercial vehicle was less profitable than a luxury car; however, we can infer that the commercial-vehicle unit was more profitable than the private-vehicle unit.

(*b*) This is the **correct** answer. It is aligned with our predictive inference. The private vehicle unit realized a lower profit per dollar (0.50) than the commercial vehicle unit (1.33).

(*c*) This is **incorrect**. We cannot infer that the commercial-vehicle unit had to face tougher competition than the private-vehicle unit. The argument does not support this.

(*d*) This is **incorrect**. This is the converse of option (a). We can neither infer that a luxury car made the company more money than a commercial vehicle nor infer that a luxury car made the company less money than a commercial vehicle. Just because a car is a luxury car does not imply that it must be more expensive than a commercial vehicle. We have no information about what kinds of commercial vehicles the company makes.

(*e*) This is **incorrect**. The argument does not provide any data to support this. Greater sales by the commercial-vehicle unit does not imply that it sold a greater number of units than the private vehicle unit.

The correct answer is option (b).

78. (d) Argument construction

The author criticizes the old promotion system. He reasons that it places greater weightage on seniority than on proficiency. Although, he/she acknowledges the work records of certain senior personnel,_____.

With the understanding of the argument, we can infer that the author is critical of the old promotion system, which weighs length of service more than competence. Though the author respects certain senior employees' contributions, he/she has.

From the context, we get the author's certain opinion would be negative or critical.

Let us analyze each option one by one.

(*a*) This is **incorrect**. This option is against the author's view; the author would not think this way. We know that, as per the argument, irrespective of the competence/qualification, personnel with greater length of service are promoted.

(*b*) This is **incorrect**. Well, they (seniors) are already in positions of more responsibilities since they have been promoted.

(*c*) This is **incorrect**. This is an extreme option. Given that the author respects certain senior employees' contributions, his/her views cannot be that it's high time that they (seniors) seek voluntary retirement.

(*d*) This is the **correct** answer. "They must ask themselves whether they deserve automatic promotions" is critical of the seniors and is a justified inferable view of the author. This is a balanced critical view.

(*e*) This is **incorrect**. There's no reason to think that (seniors) might think of these automatic promotions as demotions.

The correct answer is option (d).

79. (b) Argument construction

How much financial assistance rich nations offer to poorer nations to raise the latter's industrial capabilities depends on the degree to which rich nations fear competition from the would be-competing poorer nations, thereby looming the threat of curtailed exports. The amount of financial assistance approved by the Congress is reduced by the select committee evaluating assistance packages solely from the US business viewpoint. As a consequence, many poorer nations have to find areas of industrial capability that offer no threat to the industrial capability of the US.

From the argument, we can infer that the amount of financial assistance to poorer nations will be proportionately skewed if the industrial capability of the receiving nations affects the US's business interest.

Let us analyze each option one by one.

(*a*) This is **incorrect**. The argument does not define "neediest nations" and "industrial output." It only talks about "rich nations," "poorer nations," and "industrial capability;" thus, we cannot infer this statement.

(*b*) This is the **correct** answer. It is aligned with our predictive inference, discussed above.

(*c*) This is **incorrect**. We cannot conclude that poorer nations solely depend on external financial assistance to advance their industrial capability. The argument implies that the poorer nations get curtailed financial assistance to develop their industrial capabilities in areas other than the ones in which the US excels.

(*d*) This is **incorrect**. This is an extreme option. It is correct to claim that by offering financial assistance to poorer nations, rich nations can expand their industrial capabilities around the world; however, we cannot infer that it is because they (rich nations) can influence poorer nations' industrial capabilities. Rich nations can expand their industrial capabilities around the world because of multiple factors, and one such factor is that they (rich nations) can influence poorer nations' industrial capabilities. There's a subtle meaning change due to the usage of the extreme language.

(*e*) This is **incorrect**. This is also an extreme option. If a poorer nation chooses not to seek aid from rich nations, it will not be bound by those nations' directives.

The correct answer is option (b).

80. (c) Argument construction

At a motor company, most of the mechanical engineers received in-house training, but no mechanical engineer specializing in hydraulics has yet won the Engineering Heritage Award. Till now, engineers who have won the award have become department heads. Therefore____.

We can further simplify the facts for better understanding.

- Most of the mechanical engineers received in-house training.
- No engineer specializing in hydraulics (a branch of mechanical engineering) won the award.
- Only award-winning engineers have become department heads.

Let us infer from the given information. Since engineers who have won the award have so far become department heads, and none from hydraulics has won the award so far, we can infer that the hydraulics department head would not be an in-house-trained mechanical engineer who specialized in hydraulics.

Let us analyze each option one by one.

(*a*) This is **incorrect**. This option is not necessarily true inference since non-engineers who might not necessarily have won the award could be department heads.

(*b*) This is **incorrect**. This option is not necessarily true since non-mechanical engineers who might not necessarily have won the award could be department heads.

(*c*) This is the **correct** answer. We already deduced that no engineer specializing in hydraulics (a branch of mechanical engineering) won the award, and since engineers who have won the award have gone on to become department heads, we can infer that none of the department heads who specialized in hydraulics received in-house training.

(*d*) This is **incorrect**. Its explanation is the same as that of option (a). Even non-engineers could be department heads.

(*e*) This is **incorrect**. Its explanation is the same as that of option (d).

The correct answer is option (c).

Chapter 10

Reading Comprehension Practice Questions

Multiple Choice Questions

Q. 1 - Q. 78 Also available in aspiration.ai under post-class assignments.

Direction for the following six questions :

Passage

It is often observed that organizations' chief executive officers are frequently motivated by their own short-range self-gains rather than the long-range goal of their organization. As a result, it is the boards' vital role to establish that CEO remuneration is tied to such performance targets that cannot be easily manipulated by the CEO; and can thus be attained only if the CEO creates real and sustained value for the firm. Only such performance targets may be considered acceptable. Furthermore, because they are harder to influence, CEOs are statistically as likely to meet these targets as they are not; it is improbable that, if no trickery occurs, CEOs will simply outperform more often. A recent study, however, has demonstrated that, in fact, CEOs meet their targets more often than they do not.

CEOs' performance goals are frequently focused only on one metric, such as, semi-annual profits or earnings per share. CEOs can readily exploit such a metric, for instance, by reducing crucial research and development investment for the company's future. Conversely, when their remuneration is dependent on many performance targets depending on unrelated variables, the chance that CEOs fail to meet a specific target is the same as if they meet it.

Boards frequently set their CEO's performance objectives based on business and industry growth estimates offered by external experts and the CEO himself. CEOs frequently understate predictions in order to achieve readily achievable goals. However, the low performance objectives that arise hinder their firm from developing to its full potential. Another aspect of the CEO remuneration system worsens the problem. Most boards set a minimum performance level for their CEOs, below which no incentive is paid. Then, his incentives gradually increase until he meets the target. Incentives after exceeding this target rise much more slowly and finally die down. As a result, a CEO receives little direct gain from attaining outstanding outcomes and, as a result, seldom pushes for them. As a consequence, the CEO is satisfied, but the firm's growth is crippled.

1. Due to which of the following consequences, CEOs meet their targets more often than they miss, as suggested by the research finding mentioned in Paragraph 1?

   (*a*) Most board members act in their self-interest even if doing so is detrimental for their organization.

   (*b*) Most boards are unable to set such performance targets that cannot be gamed by CEOs.

   (*c*) Most boards exercise correlated performance metrics to assess CEO performance.

   (*d*) Most boards accept without deliberation the organization and industry-specific growth estimates presented to them by CEOs.

   (*e*) Most boards pay hefty remuneration to their CEO upon the accomplishment of the targets.

2. If a CEO is entrusted to meet three performance targets, P, Q, and R and the CEO is more likely to meet them, which of the following is most likely implied?

   (*a*) The board that set the performance targets P, Q, and R did not heed external analysts before setting the targets.

(*b*) The performance targets P, Q, and R must be quantitative metrics; thus, they are easier to monitor.

(*c*) The performance targets P, Q, and R must comprise a broader range of organizational activities.

(*d*) Achieving any of the three targets P, Q, and R automatically results in the achievement of the other two.

(*e*) The performance targets P, Q, and R must be the popular metrics.

3. According to the author, which of the following is NOT a characteristic of befitting performance targets set for a CEO by its board?

(*a*) They must comprise multiple metrics.

(*b*) They must be challenging to accomplish.

(*c*) They must not be vulnerable to being manipulated by the CEO.

(*d*) They must be designed to reward the CEO for excellent performance.

(*e*) They must be aligned with the long-term goal of the enterprise.

4. Which of the following justification that CEO compensations beyond the set performance targets must die down can be inferred from the passage?

(*a*) CEO payouts should seem rational to the shareholders.

(*b*) It is improbable that CEOs will go beyond their targets.

(*c*) CEOs are usually keener to earn their compensation than to progress beyond the set targets.

(*d*) If the compensations are not pegged around the targets, CEOs are urged to manipulate their performance metrics.

(*e*) If CEO compensations surge at a constant rate relative to performance, CEOs are urged to take undue risks to achieve greater compensations.

5. The passage supports each of the following statements EXCEPT

(*a*) Most boards fail to set performance targets for their CEOs that are in sync with their company's mission and values.

(*b*) If a greater proportion of CEO compensations depends on the earnings per share of their company, CEOs are urged to make strategic decisions that increase earnings per share, even though such decisions hurt their company's revenue growth.

(*c*) Most CEOs go all out to meet their performance targets that are connected to their compensation.

(*d*) Most boards are unable to set many performance targets for their CEOs.

(*e*) In most companies, relative to performance targets, CEO compensations do not rise at a steady rate.

6. The author is primarily concerned with

(*a*) evaluating the consequences of an entity's conduct

(*b*) deliberating the shortcomings in the way an entity performs its duty

(*c*) presenting counter-examples against a claim made about an entity

(*d*) detailing the responsibilities of an entity

(*e*) advocating for an improved way to perform a particular job

Direction for the following three questions:

Passage

Earlier generations of European feminists understood well that "remembrance of things past" is important for plotting the future. "Study, study our history, Spanish ladies and gentlemen, before accusing a feminist of being foreign," advised Maria Lejarraga Martinez Sierra in 1917, under the cover of her celebrated dramatist husband's name. Indeed, in the twentieth century, the act of recording and remembering feminism's history and passing it along on behalf of the future have become an increasingly compelling concern to feminists throughout Europe.

There is some truth in the sarcastic, yet extravagant, observation made recently by a Czech historian, in response to a tiny glimmer of interest in Czech women's history, "The future is not enough for the feminists; they want to get hold of the past as well and reinterpret it from a women's point of view." When women ask questions, the past assumes new shapes. And not only from a women's point of view, but from a feminist point of view, which encompasses more than efforts to write and teach the history of feminism and also to get women included in "standard accounts".

Feminist scholars are also formulating a critique of how and why history has been written and taught by academic professionals, both in Europe and in North America. For feminists, history has important implications, and setting the record straight is only one part of the task. In the early 1930s, the Polish historian Lucie Charewiczowa argued the case for writing women's history before the International Congress of Historical Sciences, noting that "the feminist movement... grows from day to day" and that knowledge of women's and feminist history could serve to overturn "every prejudice and antifeminist superstition that is still rooted in public opinion."

7. The author's primary purpose to write the passage is to

(*a*) narrate a skewed historical perspective of feminist movements in Europe and North America to enlighten future generations

(*b*) present the European feminists' urge to rewrite and teach history from the feminism point of view to form a new future

(*c*) evaluate the pro-feminism views of three European feminists and historians urging to rewrite history from women's and feminists' perspectives

(*d*) educate about antifeminist European history, call for it to be vetted to inculcate a holistic perspective, and advocate that it be taught by feminists

(*e*) discern the extreme perspectives of several European feminists, acknowledge the rational perspective, and subtly advocate it

8. The author of the passage will NOT necessarily agree with which of the following assertions?

(*a*) There is a compelling case that European history should be reinterpreted from a feminist's perspective.

(*b*) Instead of academic professionals, feminists should teach rewritten history in academic institutions.

(*c*) Revisiting the past is critical to paving the way for a bright future.

(*d*) Posing pertinent questions helps remodel history.

(*e*) History must be reinterpreted from not only women's points of view but also feminists' points of view.

9. In relation to the second sentence of paragraph 3, "For feminists, … only one part of the task," which of the following could be the other part of the task?

(*a*) Educate society about feminism.

(*b*) Rewrite history from a feminist's perspective.

(*c*) Fight for equality with men.

(*d*) Participate in active politics.

(*e*) Spread the feminist movement in other parts of the world.

Passage

Compared to other supermassive black holes scattered throughout the universe, the one at the core of our galaxy is mysteriously dormant. And now NASA thinks it knows why. A powerful magnetic field at the center of the Milky Way is oriented just right to keep our galaxy's black hole, Sagittarius A*, from spewing high-energy radiation out into the cosmos or churning out the raw materials for new stars, according to NASA scientists. Other black holes' magnetic fields funnel nearby gas straight into them, fueling the black holes and turning them into volatile cosmic furnaces.

NASA scientists used a new instrument called the "High-resolution Airborne Wideband Camera-Plus," in SOFIA, an airborne observatory housed inside a Boeing 747. The instrument gave NASA a look at 100,000 years' worth of the magnetic field's activity, per the NASA researchers. "The spiral shape of the magnetic field channels the gas into an orbit around the black hole," Darren Dowell, the NASA scientist who leads the new research, said. "This could explain why our black hole is quiet while others are active." Until NASA gathered this data, scientists weren't sure why Sagittarius A* was so tranquil compared to others in surrounding galaxies. Now it seems like our galaxy's bizarre magnetic field may deserve credit.

10. The main point of the passage is to

(*a*) explain why our galaxy's magnetic field is unusual

(*b*) explain why, compared to other galaxies, our galaxy is bafflingly quiet

(*c*) explain how a strong magnetic field keeps a black hole inactive in a galaxy

(*d*) explain why a black hole at the core of our galaxy is quiet

(*e*) explain how NASA unearthed the mystery behind the inactivity of the black hole in our galaxy

11. According to the passage, which of the following can be inferred from the passage?

(*a*) If our galaxy's magnetic field were not powerful, Sagittarius A* might be discharging high-intensity radiation or producing new stars.

(*b*) Our galaxy's weird magnetic field is dues to the inactive black hole at the core of our galaxy.

(*c*) All galaxies, except ours, discharge high-energy radiation out into the cosmos or churn out the raw materials for new stars.

(*d*) The spiral shape of the magnetic field channels the gas into an orbit around black holes of other galaxies.

(*e*) Had our galaxy had a weaker magnetic field at the center of the Milky Way, the black hole in our galaxy would have been active.

12. According to the passage, which of the following CANNOT be inferred?

(*a*) The High-resolution Airborne Wideband Camera-Plus helped resolve the mystery of why Sagittarius A* is inactive.

(*b*) The shape, as well as the orientation, of the magnetic field of our galaxy determines the degree of activity of Sagittarius A*.

(*c*) All new stars in the universe are formed by the raw materials discharged by volatile black holes.

(*d*) Other black holes' magnetic fields funnel nearby gas straight into them, while Sagittarius A*'s magnetic field channels the gas into an orbit around Sagittarius A*.

(*e*) There are innumerable black holes dispersed throughout the universe.

Direction for the following four questions:

(From a text published in 1999) The U.S. Senate is making efforts to establish criteria for psychotherapy, requiring that it be effective, safe, and appropriate to complement Congressional mandates that health maintenance organizations and health insurance companies provide more funding for psychotherapy. This has focused attention on evidence that some psychotherapy practices at best get approximately the same results as placebos and, at worst, are harmful. The possibility of imposing standards for psychotherapy, comparable to the standards the FDA has established for drugs and drug therapy, raises major issues about psychotherapy, including the possibility that some psychotherapy could be banned. An important hidden issue is that the social and legal systems have created a situation in which every person can be diagnosed as having symptoms of mental illness.

Psychotherapists attempting to gain authorization from Congress for third-party payments for psychotherapy have stirred up problems for themselves. By drawing attention to their practices, some psychotherapists could be banned from doing psychotherapy and, along with psychiatrists, could be prohibited from attempting to treat people believed to have schizophrenia.

Psychotherapists have tried for many years to get the U.S. Congress to revise the Medicare Act so that people qualified for Medicare could go to psychotherapists in private practice and have the government pay the expenses. While sympathetic to the needs of people on Medicare, the 97th Congress rejected automatic third-party reimbursement for psychotherapeutic services, but by specifying the essential criteria for psychotherapy, the door has been left ajar.

13. Why is the Senate trying to establish psychotherapy criteria?

(*a*) To draw attention to the inadequacy of psychotherapy

(*b*) As a result of Congressional mandates

(*c*) As a result of lobbying from health maintenance organizations and health insurance companies

(*d*) To regulate psychotherapy

(*e*) To avoid having to fund psychiatric treatment

14. Why is the question of Medicare for psychiatric treatment pressing to Congress?

(*a*) Because it could lead to the sacking of many psychiatrists

(*b*) Because some psychiatric therapies could be banned

(*c*) Because of its potential to overwhelm the public healthcare system

(*d*) Because of effective lobbying by the psychotherapy profession

(*e*) Because of the opposing stands of the Congress and the Senate

15. What dilemma will the psychotherapy profession face if the criteria for psychotherapy are proposed by Congress?

(*a*) That Congress might propose criteria that are less stringent than those required for psychotherapy.

(*b*) That imposing criteria could restrain many psychotherapy practices.

(*c*) That psychotherapy professionals who rely on private practices are unable to handle Medicare patients.

(*d*) That if the criteria were imposed, psychotherapists would lose many private patients.

(*e*) That the nature of psychotherapy defies adherence to the criteria.

16. According to the passage, what would be the consequences if the psychotherapy criteria were to be imposed?

(*a*) Some schizophrenics would be left without treatment.

(*b*) Many psychotherapists would ignore the criteria.

(*c*) Psychotherapies that are not efficacious would be practiced illegally.

(*d*) Psychotherapists that are unable to meet the criteria will be denied Medicare funding.

(*e*) Psychotherapists that are unable to meet the criteria would be required to pay damages.

Direction for the following four questions:

Black communities have undergone much academic research, more often than not, from the University of Chicago's (UC) Sociology Department graduates. A devoted inheritor of this tradition, William Wilson is one of the keenest analysts of the problems of racism and poverty. The new urban poor that Wilson describes populate segregated areas where 97 percent of adults are outside of the workforce. He is one of our foremost authorities on race and poverty, challenges decades of liberal and conservative hypocrisies to look squarely at the devastating effects that joblessness has had on our urban ghettos.

Racism, Wilson argues, plays increasingly less of a role in urban problems. He traces this not simply to a 'culture of poverty,' but to a more complicated, interacting set of social, cultural, and psychological facets. He does not ignore the behavioral problems of the ghetto, illegitimate children, crime, and drugs, but, unlike many conservatives, Wilson does not focus on an irredeemable culture of poverty but rather stresses the structural obstacles to mainstream behavior and social mobility. Wilson claims the only way out is a display of race-neutral government interventions. However, even though Wilson accepts that the problem has a moral behavioral component, he is strangely silent on the question of how to deal with it.

17. According to the passage, what can be inferred about Wilson?

(*a*) He did not establish University of Chicago's Sociology Department.

(*b*) He considers race to be the prime factor behind urban poverty.

(*c*) He believes that the culture of poverty can be transformed.

(*d*) He supports governmental positive discrimination to fight urban poverty.

(*e*) He discounts race as having any relevance to the problem of urban poverty.

18. Which of the following would the author be least likely to agree with?

(*a*) The University of Chicago's Sociology Department has a fine academic record.

(*b*) Wilson over-focuses on the moral behavior of the urban poor.

(*c*) Unemployment is at the core of the plight of the urban poor.

(*d*) No single course of action will resolve the problem of the urban poor.

(*e*) Wilson doesn't discount the culture of poverty as a cause of urban deprivation.

19. What does Wilson recommend as a solution to urban poverty?

(*a*) Ignoring the moral behavior element of the problem.

(*b*) Positive discrimination when implementing government policies.

(*c*) A wide range of racially unbiased government-backed projects.

(*d*) Interacting with a set of social, structural, cultural, and psychological pathologies.

(*e*) Focusing on the structural obstacles to mainstream behavior and social mobility.

20. The main point of the passage is to

(*a*) describe Wilson's analysis of the problems of racism, poverty, and unemployment

(*b*) analyze Wilson's work on racism, poverty, and unemployment

(*c*) evaluate the problems of racism, poverty, and unemployment from Wilson's perspective

(*d*) establish Wilson as one of the foremost authorities on racism, poverty, and unemployment

(*e*) reinforce Wilson's viewpoint that racism plays increasingly less of a role in urban problems

Direction for the following three questions:

The Women's Liberation Movement (WLM) was a political alignment of women and feminist intellectualism that emerged in the late 1960s and continued into the 1980s, primarily in the industrialized nations of the Western world, which affected great change (political, intellectual, and cultural) throughout the world. The WLM branch of radical feminism, based on contemporary philosophy, comprised women of racially and culturally diverse backgrounds who proposed that economic, psychological, and social freedom were necessary for women to progress from being second-class citizens in their societies.

Towards achieving women's equality, the WLM questioned the cultural and legal validity of patriarchy and the practical validity of the social and patriarchal hierarchies used to control and limit the legal and physical independence of women in society. Women's liberationists proposed that gender-based discrimination — legalized formal and informal discrimination predicated on the existence of the social construction of gender — was the principal political problem with the power dynamics of their societies.

In general, the WLM proposed socio-economic change from the political party, rejected the idea that piecemeal equality, within and according to social class, would eliminate discrimination against women, and fostered the tenets of humanism, especially respect for the human rights of all people. In the decades during which the women's liberation movement flourished, liberationists successfully changed how women were perceived in their cultures, redefined the socio-economic and political roles of women in society, and transformed mainstream society.

21. The main point of the passage is to

(*a*) analyze the factors that helped the Women's Liberation Movement (WLM) achieve its objective

(*b*) highlight the journey of the Women's Liberation Movement (WLM)

(*c*) underscore the stiff challenges the Women's Liberation Movement (WLM) faced during the late 1960s and 1980s

(*d*) assert the subdued success the Women's Liberation Movement (WLM) had during the late 1960s and 1980s

(*e*) deliberate how gender-based discrimination against women led to the rise of the Women's Liberation Movement (WLM)

22. According to the passage, which of the following can be inferred from the passage?

(*a*) The Women's Liberation Movement (WLM) emerged in the late 1960s and continued into the 1980s, primarily in the developed nations of the Western world.

(*b*) That women are second-class citizens in societies fostered gender-based discrimination against them.

(*c*) The Women's Liberation Movement (WLM) disputed male supremacy in society.

(*d*) By rejecting the idea of piecemeal equality, the Women's Liberation Movement (WLM) proposed equal male-to-female representation in the political process.

(*e*) Being socially weak harmed women's interests more than being economically weak.

23. According to the passage, with which of the following statements would the author be least likely to agree?

(*a*) The Women's Liberation Movement (WLM) must be credited for changing the political discourse globally, to some extent.

(*b*) The Women's Liberation Movement (WLM) must be credited with changing the perceptions society has of women.

(*c*) Since women had already progressed from being second-class citizens in their societies by 1960, the WLM branch of radical feminism proposed economic, psychological, and social freedom for women.

(*d*) The Women's Liberation Movement (WLM) did not accept the idea of incremental equality.

(*e*) Before the Women's Liberation Movement (WLM), women had restricted personal liberty.

Direction for the following three questions:

The World Trade Organization (WTO) is run by its member governments. All major decisions are made by the membership as a whole, either by ministers, who meet at least once every two years, or by their ambassadors or delegates, who meet regularly at the WTO headquarters in Geneva. Decisions are normally taken by consensus. In this respect, the WTO is different from some other international organizations such as the World Bank and International Monetary Fund. In the WTO, power is not delegated to a board of directors or the organization's head.

When WTO rules impose disciplines on countries' policies, that is the outcome of negotiations among WTO members. The rules are enforced by the members themselves under agreed procedures that they negotiated, including the possibility of trade sanctions. But those sanctions are imposed by member countries and authorized by the membership as a whole. This is quite different from other agencies whose bureaucracies can, for example, influence a country's policy by threatening to withhold credit.

Reaching decisions by consensus among some 150 members can be difficult. Its main advantage is that decisions made this way are more acceptable to all members. And despite the difficulty, some remarkable agreements have been reached. Nevertheless, proposals for the creation of a smaller executive body — perhaps like a board of directors each representing different groups of countries — are heard periodically. But for now, the WTO is a member-driven, consensus-based organization.

24. According to the passage, each of the following is true about the WTO EXCEPT:

(*a*) Despite the large number of members it contains, a few extraordinary decisions have been made by the WTO.

(*b*) The WTO does not have an executive branch, despite suggestions for the same.

(*c*) Because of the manner in which decisions are made at the WTO, they are agreed upon by most members.

(*d*) The head office of the WTO is in Geneva.

(*e*) The WTO will never seek to have an executive council, such as, a board of directors.

25. The major difference between the WTO and other international organizations is that

(*a*) the members of the WTO meet at least once every two years, whereas the members of the other organizations do not

(*b*) as opposed to other international organizations, at the WTO, the power to make decisions does not rest with a few people

(*c*) while the WTO consists of around 150 members, other international organizations have fewer members

(*d*) unlike other international organizations, the WTO does not have an individual heading it

(*e*) the WTO, unlike other international organizations, has never been able to reach a consensus on its decisions

26. The primary purpose of the passage is to

(*a*) establish that despite being a consensus-driven organization, the WTO has made some remarkable decisions

(*b*) compare the functioning of the WTO with that of other international organizations

(*c*) describe the structure, functioning, and achievements of the WTO

(*d*) reinforce that consensus-driven organizations face difficulties in making remarkable agreements

(*e*) evaluate the pros and cons of a consensus-driven organization

Direction for the following three questions:

Members of the dolphin family — which comprise dozens of species, including the familiar bottlenose dolphins and killer whales — have the second-largest brain size relative to body size, after humans. And, big brains are more expensive energetically than their smaller counterparts — because larger brains cost a lot, they have to be doing something important.

For instance, only a few animals recognize their own images — researchers test them by marking their bodies in a place they can't see without a mirror. Species that pay attention to the mark or try to touch it are thought to be aware that they're looking at themselves. A recent study described an experiment showing that young dolphins got interested in their reflections as young as seven months. This is earlier than human babies, who typically pass the milestone around 12 months. Interestingly, the dolphins also tried to get a better look at the mark on their bodies at two years old.

But what do these results really mean? The trouble with the mirror test in dolphins is that they do not have hands to touch or wipe off markings on their face like chimps do, and so, the test might not be particularly useful. Because of this, there is no evidence that the test demarcates a key cognitive boundary like 'self-awareness,' and it has no relevance to their lives in the wild.

27. Which of the following can be inferred based on the information in the passage?

(*a*) Of the brains of all the living species in the world, the human brain is the biggest.

(*b*) The size of a living creature's brain is directly proportional to the amount of energy it consumes.

(*c*) Animals with small brains are more evolved than those with larger brains.

(*d*) The size of the brain in living creatures changes and develops with time.

(*e*) The bigger the brain size of living creatures, the more they are able to recognize themselves.

28. The "milestone" mentioned in line 12 (paragraph 2/sentence 4) refers to

(*a*) the ability of a dolphin to recognize itself and others in the mirror

(*b*) the ability of a dolphin to observe its reflections

(*c*) the ability of a dolphin to get a better look at the mark on its body

(*d*) the ability of a dolphin to touch and feel the markings on its body

(*e*) the ability of a dolphin to wipe off markings on its body

29. Which of the following information does the author offer as evidence to prove that the mirror test might not be useful in dolphins?

(*a*) The dolphins might not be able to clean the markings because they do not have hands.

(*b*) The test does not demonstrate self-awareness in dolphins.

(*c*) The dolphins become aware of the mark on their bodies much later than when humans do.

(*d*) The mirror test does not accurately describe the circumstances that dolphins encounter in the wild.

(*e*) The dolphins might not be the only mammals that recognize themselves in a mirror.

Direction for the following three questions:

Customers have long considered buying enterprise software packages a time-consuming and complex exercise. Notably, during the last decade, both the number of competing brands and the amount of information available for each brand have increased dramatically. It is well known that increased availability of both options and information increases the time it takes for customers to decide, as they carefully analyze the benefits and disadvantages of various options. Such deep knowledge of the benefits of the abandoned options and the drawbacks of the chosen option decreases customer satisfaction with the purchase decision; and leads to buying regret.

Most enterprise software package sellers are ignorant of the issues that potential customers face. In an effort to be customer-centric, they urge their sales professionals to let the consumer define his/her requirements and to only reply to specific queries made by the customer, rather than preemptively recommending solutions to him. They think that by presenting all available options and giving a variety of information, such as, data, use cases, research papers, and testimonials for each option, they are educating their clients. Nonetheless, according to a study, this responsive selling strategy reduces customers' purchase ease by 20% and raises purchase regret by 50%, when compared to the comparable scores for these measures in the baseline scenario in which the seller did not influence the client's purchase choice. In comparison to the baseline situation, preemptively recommending one specific solution from a suite of many alternatives with a clear justification based on a detailed understanding of the customer's requirements was found to increase purchase ease by 90% and decrease purchase regret by 40%.

30. The passage provides support for which of the following assertions?

(*a*) An abundance of choice is likely to lead most people to depression and feelings of loneliness.

(*b*) A greater number of options is likely to help most customers make better purchase decisions.

(*c*) The quality of a decision is directly proportional to the number of alternative options considered.

(*d*) Severely limiting the options that are presented to customers can greatly reduce their likelihood of being dissatisfied with purchase decisions.

(*e*) Decreasing the number of options available to customers can greatly enhance product sales.

31. If the findings of the study are correct, which of the following assertions about the purchase process of enterprise software packages will also be true?

(*a*) The purchase ease reported by customers to whom sales professionals proactively recommended a suitable solution was greater than the purchase ease reported by customers subjected to a responsive selling strategy (RSS).

(*b*) The purchase ease reported by customers to whom sales professionals proactively recommended a suitable solution was less than the purchase ease reported by customers subjected to a responsive selling strategy.

(*c*) The purchase ease reported by customers to whom sales professionals proactively recommended a suitable solution was equal to the purchase ease reported by customers subjected to a responsive selling strategy.

(*d*) The purchase regret reported by customers to whom sales professionals proactively recommended a suitable solution was equal to the purchase regret reported by customers subjected to a responsive selling strategy.

(*e*) The purchase regret reported by customers to whom sales professionals proactively recommended a suitable solution was greater than the purchase regret reported by customers subjected to a responsive selling strategy.

32. The author is most likely to agree with the suggestion that suppliers of enterprise software packages should urge their sales professionals to

(*a*) be more customer-centric

(*b*) proactively recommend one option to customers based on their business requirements

(*c*) provide less information to the customers about the disadvantages of different options

(*d*) offer use cases and testimonials, instead of research papers, about the different options to customers

(*e*) not offer unsolicited advice to the customer and, instead, wait till the customer makes an explicit request for help

Direction for the following six questions:

The early legislative successes of the women's movement in the United States were in eliminating "coverture" and thus securing the rights of married women to own property, to control their earnings, and to enter into contracts. In most states, the property laws preceded, or were enacted in conjunction with, laws granting married women control over their earnings and laws allowing women to engage in contracts or business without their husband's consent, often referred to as "sole trader" laws.

Changes to property rights altered the relationship between men and women within marriage. Therefore, these changes must be discussed in terms of how the allocation of property rights within marriage affects household decisions. One theoretical approach asserts that women place a higher value on children's welfare than men, and men recognize that giving women more economic power will increase investments in children's education. When the returns to human capital are low, as they were in the preindustrial, mostly agricultural, economy in the early nineteenth century, the benefits to men of being able to control their wives' property outweigh any benefits from investing more in children's education. As the returns to human capital increase, the scale tips toward more education for children, and men are more likely to grant women greater economic power in terms of owning property.

An alternative, yet complementary, approach emphasizes how coverture reduces married women's incentives to pursue economic opportunities, and hence, reduces household earnings and wealth. The costs to households of these disincentives grow as the economy develops and women have more opportunities in the formal labor market. Eventually, these costs lead men to grant women property rights. An empirical examination of the timing of the enactment of married women's property laws across states finds that the early movers were states with larger urban populations, higher female school enrollment, and higher wealth per capita: results that are consistent with both approaches. Women's economic opportunities and the returns to human capital would have been greater in urban than rural areas, and the higher rates of female school enrollment indicate increased investments in expectation of these returns. Further supporting these approaches, the enactment of married women's property laws led to increases in women's patenting of inventions: once women had the legal right to control their property and earnings in marriage, they were more willing to engage in commercial activities.

33. The primary purpose of the passage is to

(*a*) analyze the impact and consequences of property rights on women in the United States

(*b*) discuss two theories that explain the reasons that led to the elimination of coverture in the United States

(c) evaluate the advancement of economic rights for women in the United States

(d) assess the advantages and disadvantages of "sole trader" laws in the United States

(e) reconcile the differences in expert opinions about why women were granted economic rights in the United States

34. By saying that the women's movements were successful in "eliminating coverture" (line 2), the author most likely means that

(a) a married woman was freed from the status of being considered under her husband's protection and authority

(b) a married woman was given the liberty to choose whether she wanted to be economically independent or not

(c) a married woman was given the privilege of filing a patent

(d) a married woman was given the right to make decisions on issues concerning her children's education

(e) a married woman was entrusted with the condition of being under the care and influence of her spouse

35. A sole trader law would enable a married woman to do each of the following EXCEPT:

(a) give her the right to use her salary or business profits as she wishes

(b) give her the right to own property that she has inherited

(c) give her the right to start her own business without seeking the permission of her husband

(d) give her the right to sign a business contract with a third party without seeking the consent of her husband

(e) give her the right to work in a professional setup

36. The second paragraph is primarily concerned with

(a) offering a theory to explain why married women were granted the right to own property

(b) discussing a hypothesis that demonstrates the impact of human capital on the relationship between men and women within a marriage

(c) describing an approach to elaborate on how married women are more capable of making prudent decisions with regard to their children's welfare

(d) contrasting the economic conditions of families in preindustrial times to the later times

(e) presenting a hypothetical scenario to discuss how coverture was eliminated in the United States

37. Which of the following most accurately describes the relationship between the two approaches discussed in the passage?

(a) The two approaches are interchangeable and state the same reasons for the elimination of coverture.

(b) The second approach contradicts the first and renders the first weak.

(c) The second approach brings out the exceptional cases that the first does not.

(d) The second approach enhances or completes the first to bring about the same conclusion.

(e) The two approaches are diametrically opposite, with one weakening the other.

38. According to the passage, why did more women patent their inventions?

(*a*) The authority over their earnings made them more inclined to be associated with businesses.

(*b*) The economic opportunities for women increased dramatically, making women more inclined towards working professionally.

(*c*) The returns on human capital increased, tipping the scale towards women patenting their inventions.

(*d*) The sole trader laws gave women the liberty and the ease of patenting inventions.

(*e*) The states with large urban populations promoted higher female school enrollment, which, in turn, resulted in more women filing patents.

Direction for the following three questions:

Historically, feminism is often divided into three main traditions, usually called liberal, reformist or mainstream feminism, radical feminism, and socialist/Marxist feminism, sometimes known as the "Big Three" schools of feminist thought. Since the late 20th century, a variety of newer forms of feminism have also emerged, some of which are viewed as branches of the three main traditions.

Judith Lorber distinguishes among the three broad kinds of feminist discourses: gender-reform feminism, gender-resistant feminism, and gender-revolution feminism. In her typology, gender-reform feminism is rooted in the political philosophy of liberalism with its emphasis on individual rights. Gender-resistant feminism focuses on specific behaviors and group dynamics through which women are kept in subordinate positions, even in subcultures that claim to support gender equality. Gender-revolution feminism seeks to disrupt the social order through deconstructing its concepts and categories and analyzing the cultural reproduction of inequalities.

Some argue that every feminist has an altered standpoint on the movement due to the varying hurdles women of different backgrounds come across. Depending on their class, some women will have different experiences of patriarchy and oppression than others. Issues have also arisen over how 'masculine' and 'feminine' have been defined, and whether previously gendered values are natural or nurtured.

Some movements consider men primarily the causative agents of gender bias. Mary Daly wrote, "The courage to be logical — the courage to name — would require that we admit to ourselves that males and males only are the originators, planners, controllers, and legitimators of patriarchy. Patriarchy is the homeland of males; it is the Father Land, and men are its agents." The Redstockings declared that men, especially a few leading men, oppress women and that "all men receive economic, physical, and psychological benefits from male supremacy."

Other movements differ on whether discrimination against women adversely affects men. Movements represented by writers Betty Friedan and Gloria Steinem consider men to be oppressed by gender roles. Friedan argued that feminism would benefit both genders and was part of the human rights movement. Steinem suggested that liberation was for both genders, as men's burdens would be shared. Susan Faludi states that men, while not currently rebelling, can rebel on a scale with women and liberate both genders toward a more humane world. Ellen Willis, weighing economics and feminism, considered an alliance with men necessary for women's liberation. Florynce Kennedy wrote, "Men are outraged, turned off, and mentally disconnected by threats that women might withdraw consent to oppression because they — men-subconsciously (and often consciously) know that they — men-are oppressed." According to Kristin Kaisem, a common interest in the upward mobilization of women as a whole has prompted a desire for a more inclusive and universal feminist movement.

39. The main point of the passage is to

(*a*) educate about three key feminist traditions and their ideologies

(*b*) educate about several feminist theories and their ideologies

(*c*) argue that until males are included in the feminist movement, a true universal feminist movement cannot be fostered

(*d*) argue that males, as well as females, play the role of oppressor, jeopardizing the true universal feminist movement

(*e*) present many feminist theories and thinkers' perspectives on feminism

40. According to the passage, which of the following can be inferred?

(*a*) Gender-resistant feminism advocates securing the individual rights of women.

(*b*) Gender-reform feminism advocates conduct in societies that fosters male-female equality.

(*c*) Gender-revolution feminism advocates redefining the social structure of societies within the purview of gender discrimination.

(*d*) Liberal, reformist, or mainstream feminism is the most progressive of the "Big Three" schools of thought.

(*e*) How 'masculine' and 'feminine' have been defined depends on to what degree women assert themselves in their societies .

41. How does paragraph 5 relate to paragraph 4?

(*a*) While paragraph 4 considers men the perpetrators of gender discrimination, paragraph 5 considers men oppressed by gender discrimination.

(*b*) While paragraph 4 considers men the causative agents of gender bias, paragraph 5 considers females.

(*c*) While paragraph 4 considers patriarchy the homeland of males, paragraph 5 considers matriarchy.

(*d*) While paragraph 4 considers male supremacy the root cause of oppression against women, paragraph 5 considers the distorted differentiation between 'masculine' and 'feminine.'

(*e*) While paragraph 4 considers, all but a few, men the causative agents of gender bias, paragraph 5 considers hyper feminism.

Direction for the following six questions:

Why do organizations have so much trouble enabling employee creativity? The answer lies in subtle and deeply ingrained behaviors that prevent companies from creating a creative culture. We will discuss the "productivity illusion," a misconception that managers must overcome to effectively build creative cultures.

A few months ago, articles critical of Google CEO Sundar Pichai argued that Pichai's slow decision-making process stifled innovation. The articles incorrectly equated decision-making speed with innovation. The misconception that slow decision-making stifles innovation often leads to the illusion that productivity requires speed. Coupled with other measures that Pichai has taken, notably distributed decision-making and cutting down on vanity projects, it is just as likely that Pichai is taking a disciplined approach to innovation and productivity.

You have likely come across a person like the fictional employee "Dave." Dave is known for his quick thinking and decisiveness, and most people regard him as someone who gets things done. On a typical day, he spends most of his time in group meetings. He listens carefully to the issues his team addresses. He weighs in and helps them resolve the challenges. He prides himself on not leaving the office until he has executed his to-do list. With every item that he ticks off his list, he feels good about his impact. As he leaves the office, he is happy to have had such a productive day. Given Dave's ability to address issues and help teams make progress, most people would consider him a great leader. Not so quickly (and we mean that literally).

Trying to resolve things too quickly, especially for complex problems, is detrimental to innovation because you fall prey to premature closure. Resistance to premature closure — a key aspect of creativity — is our ability to keep an open mind when we already have a potential solution. Some of the best solutions do not emerge during the first meeting or two, but rather after a long period of incubation period. While mantras like "move fast and break things" can help push people towards action, they can backfire when the underlying problem is complex. In such situations, resisting the temptation to find a solution quickly (and often less creatively) and instead urging the team (much to their frustration) to keep searching for more ideas can lead to more innovative and far-reaching solutions.

To avoid premature closure, teams should arrive at an "almost final" decision and then intentionally delay action in favor of additional incubation time. During this time, everyone should commit to thinking about the problem and sharing their ideas. If the team cannot find a better approach during the incubation period, it should proceed with its original solution.

42. According to the passage, the author of the passage would certainly agree with which of the following?

(*a*) Fast decision-making hampers innovation.

(*b*) Productivity requires speed.

(*c*) Because company cultures are not conducive to fostering creativity, managers prefer being efficient rather than being innovators.

(*d*) Dave, a fictional employee, is a slow decision-maker, but he can deal with urgent problems and come up with innovative solutions.

(*e*) If a team cannot discover a better solution during the incubation period, it should proceed with the "almost final" solution.

43. Which of the following best describes the main point of paragraph 4?

(*a*) Resistance to premature closure is one of the biggest challenges innovative organizations face.

(*b*) The search for a creative and innovative solution must not be compromised with an efficient solution.

(*c*) Doctrines like "move fast and break things" can work well if the underlying problem is not complex.

(*d*) To be innovative and creative, organizations must follow a slow decision-making policy while dealing with all kinds of problems.

(*e*) To build a culture of resistance to premature closure in practice, teams should make an "almost final" decision and then deliberately delay its implementation, taking more time to think about it.

44. Which of the following fictional cases does not reflect resistance to premature closure?

(*a*) To address the engine oil leakage issue, TMZ Auto appointed a team of engine experts to contemplate redesigning the engine.

(*b*) To address the conflict between Suzy of the sales department and David of the distribution department, the human resource department recommends transferring and promoting Suzy to the planning department.

(*c*) To address the low sales of robotic vacuum cleaners, the much-deliberated solution— reducing their sale prices — is locked in as an "almost final" decision, while deliberately delaying its implementation.

(*d*) To address the high employee attrition rate, recruiters are advised not to demonstrate their efficiency.

(*e*) To address the rising customer complaints, SMB Mart keeps rejecting solutions for want of a better one.

45. According to the passage, which of the following is true about the productivity illusion misconception?

(*a*) Fast decision-making is the hallmark of productivity.

(*b*) A productive employee cannot produce innovative solutions.

(*c*) If an innovative and creative solution is brought up by an employee, he might not be a productive employee.

(*d*) An unproductive employee produces creative solutions.

(*e*) Slow decision-making, delivering innovative solutions, are the assurances of productivity.

46. The primary purpose of the passage is to

(*a*) dispel the misconception about productivity illusion

(*b*) advocate slow decision-making

(*c*) emphasize creativity in problem solving

(*d*) discuss multiple factors that affect creativity

(*e*) dismiss the misconception that slow decision-making stifles innovation

47. According to the passage, which of the following CANNOT be inferred from the passage?

(*a*) For complex problems, slow and disciplined decision-making is better than fast and decisive decision-making.

(*b*) The fictional employee, Dave, is a fast decision-maker.

(*c*) Intentionally delaying the implemention of an "almost final" solution in favor of additional incubation time invariably leads to a better solution.

(*d*) The right mindset for dealing with complex problems necessitates not implementing a probable solution at first sight.

(*e*) That a slow decision-making process curbs innovation is a misconception.

Direction for the following four questions:

Many ethnic groups are more likely to be obese than whites. The storage of fat for people in these groups is more likely to be in the trunk and upper limbs, both places that are associated with increased chances of health problems when associated with excess fat. While there are some differences in the skeletal structure of ethnic groups, this alone does not account for differences in obesity prevalence. There is a hypothesized reason for the high rate of obesity among American Indians; it is proposed that, because of natural selection, those individuals who were obese survived during the time when America was being settled. Similarly, there is a hypothesis that Pacific Islanders have "thrifty genes" that allows for the storage of excess fat during times when there is plenty of food to allow for food shortages and migration. Since there are differences between ethnic groups and their rates of obesity, it has been proposed that different ethnic groups need alternative weight loss plans to maintain healthy levels of fat.

Obesity is not considered a psychiatric diagnosis, yet there is a correlation between obesity and psychotic symptoms. A study of patients undergoing weight loss treatment found that they had significantly higher rates of depression and psychosocial disabilities. When these things are better understood, clinics will be able to make weight loss programs that are best for each person.

48. According to the passage, all of the following are true of American ethnic groups, EXCEPT:

(*a*) They have different skeletal structures.

(*b*) They might suffer from health problems associated with obesity.

(*c*) They have a genetic tendency to be obese.

(*d*) They have a genetic tendency to contract psychiatric disorders.

(*e*) They have different rates of obesity.

49. The primary purpose of the passage is to

(*a*) describe the relationship between psychiatric disorders and genetic obesity in American ethnic groups

(*b*) provide an overview of obesity, assisting in the identification of various causes and the development of an obesity treatment plan

(*c*) relate American ethnic groups to the prevalence of obesity in the US

(*d*) outline methods for achieving weight loss among the obese American ethnic groups

(*e*) identify various causes of obesity in American ethnic groups, thereby assisting in the development of obesity treatment

50. The passage supplies information for answering which of the following questions?

(*a*) Why are those suffering from depression and psychosocial disabilities obese?

(*b*) What is considered to be a healthy level of fat?

(*c*) How are weight loss programs designed?

(*d*) What similarities in lifestyle exist among some ethnic groups?

(*e*) What is the possible cause of obesity among certain ethnic groups?

51. According to the passage, what do the ethnic groups have in common?

(*a*) They exhibit significantly higher rates of psychosocial disabilities.

(*b*) They suffer from excessive weight, tending to accumulate fat from the waist up.

(*c*) They eat similar foods.

(*d*) They have similar skeletal structures.

(*e*) They all possess 'thrifty genes.'

Direction for the following three questions:

In the 19th century, bicycles became emblematic of women's bid for freedom and self-determination. Riding a bicycle gave women new confidence and mobility, and challenged Victorian restrictions on female behavior. A woman on a bicycle no longer needed to depend on a man for transportation. She could come and go as she pleased. Enthusiasm for biking and women's rights became so entwined that famed women rights leader Susan Anthony once said that the bicycle had done more to emancipate women than anything else in the world.

All kinds of claims were made to discourage women from taking to the bike. Some critics warned that the bicycle would harm women's health. The sensitivity and fragility of women were a common theme. Women's magazines often featured doctors' warnings of the dangers the bike posed to women's health. Others said the bicycle would get young women into trouble by allowing them to stray further from watching eyes during courtship. A woman on a bike was a threat to the social order.

But the freedom that many women found on the bike took many forms, not the least of which was clothing. The restrictive corsets and long skirts that women wore were not exactly conducive to pedaling. Cycling required a more comfortable and practical form of clothing. Those women who did adopt a new outfit, often loose-fitting trousers known as bloomers, earned the scorn and mockery of cartoonists and critics who viewed a woman in pants as unfeminine and scandalous. However, this controversy seemed only to spur women's interest in the bicycle. And once women started riding, they never stopped.

52. According to the passage, the bicycle helped women achieve each of these EXCEPT:

(*a*) Better overall health and fitness

(*b*) More comfortable form of clothing

(*c*) More independence in terms of movement

(*d*) Less reliance on men

(*e*) More self-belief

53. The author mentions Susan Anthony in paragraph 1/sentence 5 most likely in order to

(*a*) emphasize that women's rights leaders were in approval of the use of the bicycle for women

(*b*) reinforce the importance of the bicycle in the movement for women's rights

(*c*) demonstrate that the lack of dependence on men was the primary advantage of the bicycle

(*d*) show that Susan Anthony was a prominent figure in the women's rights campaign

(*e*) justify women riding bicycles

54. Which of the following would NOT be an example of the critics of women bicycling?

(*a*) A doctor who endorses that bicycling could make a woman's already-feeble body weaker

(*b*) An editor of a magazine who writes articles discouraging women from riding bicycles, stating that it would be inappropriate for women to do so

(*c*) A teacher who teaches her students that riding a bicycle will make them independent and free

(*d*) An activist who promotes that the overexertion caused by even moderate bicycle riding would not be conducive to women's health

(*e*) A lawyer who argues that women would become masculine in their behavior and appearance if they rode bicycles

Direction for the following six questions:

From 1851 until the turn-of-the-century, American men and women expressed a variety of opinions regarding the dresses that white middle- and upper-class women typically wore. Advocates of "dress reform" suggested that women abandon traditional fashions and adopt more comfortable, healthful clothing, although the dress-reform advocates did not agree on one alternative to fashion. Activists of the dress-reform movement were manifold, pooling their energies into small task forces with varying agendas. Dress reformers included regular doctors, health reformers, spiritualists, and women's-rights activists. Obviously, this was a diverse crowd, and predictably, regular licensed doctors addressed dress reform in radically different ways than spiritualists. For fifty years, these individuals shared an interest in improving the health of American middle- and upper-class women; however, their motivations and convictions were so varied, it is easy to forget they were advocating one cause: the transformation of American women's fashions to improve health and comfort.

Dress reformers in the period of 1850-1870 usually promoted shortened skirts worn over pantaloons, commonly referred to as "bloomers" by their contemporaries. These reformers included women's-rights advocates, health reformers, farmers, and factory women. Their chief priorities differed, yet all of these reformers shared an interest in women's health. They saw dress reform as an opportunity to advance women into positions of economic, social, and political equality with men; they believed dress reform could advertise a woman's usefulness and worth. This first generation of dress reformers often used dress to attack gender norms, suggesting that women should not rely solely on societal notions of beauty for their self-worth.

Clubwomen, doctors, health reformers, a small number of women's rights advocates, and aesthetes led dress reform between 1870 and 1900. These reformers rarely proposed that women adopt shortened skirts, although a few did. During this second stage of dress reform, reformers concentrated their efforts on removing or loosening the corset and cutting off skirts that trailed on the ground. They shared their predecessors' interest in women's health. However, they did not attempt to use dress reform to campaign for women's equality or challenge the gender norms of the late-nineteenth century. Instead, they reinforced these gender norms, campaigning for dress reform on maternalistic and aesthetic grounds. While earlier reformers challenged gender norms that expected women to remain in the home as mothers and archetypes of fashion, the second generation of reformers supported these roles for women. They were careful to design alternatives to fashion that did not differ too starkly from traditional styles, informing middle- and upper-class women that it was a woman's duty to be beautiful. And, unlike their predecessors of the 1850s, female dress reformers rarely wore their reformed clothing in public, preferring to educate women on the need for change before adopting an unusual dress themselves.

55. The primary purpose of the passage is to

(*a*) review and approve the work of dress reformers from 1850 to 1900

(*b*) provide a prelude to the dress reforms that occurred in the late nineteenth century

(*c*) evaluate the success of dress reformers of the second half of the nineteenth century

(*d*) discuss the perspectives of dress reformers from 1850 to 1870

(*e*) reconcile the discrepancy between the views of dress reformers from 1850 to 1900

56. The author lists the professions of dress reformers in paragraph 1/sentence 4 most likely in order to

(*a*) show that these groups had small task forces

(*b*) underscore that the perspectives and actions towards dress reform could be varied

(c) demonstrate that the aim of bringing healthier and more comfortable clothing for women could never be achieved due to the presence of so many diverse groups

(d) explain that people of other groups and professions were not interested in bringing about dress reforms for women

(e) justify the inclusion of these groups in the broader community of dress reformers

57. Why does the author mention that it was easy to forget that the dress reformers were advocating for the same cause?

(a) Because each reformer had his/her own ulterior motive behind supporting the cause of dress reform

(b) Because all the reformers did not take decisions with consensus

(c) Because the reformers had varied notions about the beauty of women

(d) Because no two reformers came from the same professional background

(e) Because all reformers had their own beliefs and perspectives regarding dress reforms

58. Which of these could NOT be an example of a dress reformer from the period of 1850-70?

(a) A health reformer who campaigns for the idea that women should wear clothing that improves their health

(b) A suffragist who believes that dress reform could help women gain an equal footing with men in the field of politics

(c) A man who emphasizes that women should break away from the stereotypical opinions of beauty and carve their own ideas of what constitutes beauty

(d) A teacher who teaches her female students that the true value of women can be unlocked by dress reforms

(e) A woman who believes that her motherly duties might be hindered because of dress reforms

59. According to the passage, dress reformers from the periods of 1850-1870 and 1870-1900 disagreed on each of the following, EXCEPT:

(a) An interest in the health of women

(b) Challenging the social principles that governed the behavior of women

(c) The role of women in the workforce

(d) Their ideas of beauty for women

(e) Wearing reformed clothing in public

60. The passage states that the second group of dress reformers were campaigning for dress reforms for which of these reasons?

(a) The equality of women

(b) The perception of beauty in women

(c) The financial independence of women

(d) The happiness of women

(e) The education of women

Direction for the following five questions:

Net Promoter Score (NPS) is a measure used to gauge customer loyalty and experience with a company. It is calculated by asking customers one question: "On a scale of 0 to 10, how likely are you to recommend this product/company to a friend or colleague?" Aggregate NPS scores help businesses improve upon factors such as service, customer support, and delivery, resulting in increased customer loyalty.

NPS is a valuable metric on a strategic level, but by itself, the score is not enough to be useful or paint a complete picture. The overall NPS system is important because it allows businesses to ask follow-up questions as part of the standard NPS survey — by asking customers why they have given a specific score, organizations of any size can understand what they are doing well and where they could improve; track and quantify a score over time, creating internal benchmarks; and rally all employees around one mission-critical objective: earning more enthusiastic customers.

On the other hand, Customer Satisfaction (CSAT) is measured by one or more variations of this question that usually appears at the end of a customer feedback survey: "How would you rate your overall satisfaction with the goods/service you received?" Respondents use a 1 to 5 scale with options that include very unsatisfied, unsatisfied, neutral, satisfied, and very satisfied. The results can be averaged out to give a Composite Customer Satisfaction Score, although CSAT scores are more usually expressed as a percentage scale: 100% being total customer satisfaction, 0% total customer dissatisfaction.

In terms of measuring customer experience, CSAT targets a "here and now" reaction to a specific interaction, product, or event, but it is limited when it comes to measuring a customer's ongoing relationship with a company. However, the NPS system asks customers to take a much wider view of the brand or product and focuses on their intention, rather than their overall feeling of satisfaction, making it, perhaps, more efficacious than CSAT.

61. The primary purpose of the passage is to

(*a*) describe the features of two metrics of customer satisfaction

(*b*) demonstrate why NPS is better than CSAT as a measure of customer experience

(*c*) discuss and assess two indices of measuring customer experience

(*d*) recommend that all organizations use either NPS or CSAT

(*e*) list the merits and demerits of two metrics to measure customer experience

62. From the passage, it can be inferred that which of the following would be an example of an NPS follow-up question for a retail store?

(*a*) Can you please let us know the reason for your score?

(b) How often would you like to shop with us in the future?

(*c*) How would you rate our products/services on a scale of 5?

(*d*) How did you hear about us?

(*e*) Can you let us know how easy it was to shop at our store?

63. Which of the following most accurately describes the organization of the passage?

(*a*) Two conventional metrics for measuring a particular phenomenon are introduced. The pros and cons of each phenomenon are discussed.

(*b*) Two metrics and their features are introduced. Finally, an evaluation of the two metrics is undertaken.

(*c*) An index is introduced, and its attributes are listed. Subsequently, a contrary index and its features are introduced.

(*d*) Two competing indices and their pros and cons are discussed. One of them is rejected as ineffective.

(*e*) Two methods for analyzing a phenomenon are compared. Further study of the methods is recommended.

64. The last paragraph of the passage serves primarily to

(*a*) outline the difference between NPS and CSAT to determine which is the better metric

(*b*) give multiple reasons to reinforce CSAT is as more effective metric than NPS

(*c*) discuss the advantages and disadvantages of both NPS and CSAT

(*d*) evaluate the reasons for the adoption of NPS and CSAT by businesses

(*e*) underscore the importance of both the metrics for businesses

65. According to the information in the passage, each of the following is true about NPS EXCEPT:

(*a*) It can be used by businesses of all proportions.

(*b*) It gives a more holistic picture of an organization's relationship with its customers.

(*c*) It could be expressed as a percentage.

(*d*) The NPS system can help employees of an organization become more customer-centric.

(*e*) One of the outcomes of a good NPS score is greater customer loyalty.

Direction for the following five questions:

When faced with an intertemporal selection, a decision involving a tradeoff between costs and benefits at different periods in time, regarding events in the far future, most individuals tend to make the sensible decision — the one that yields a greater reward. For example, virtually everyone would prefer a $1,000 in 10 years over a $800 in 9 years. However, when one or both of the time-points involved approaches the present, individuals begin to favor smaller but sooner rewards over larger but later rewards. Many would rather have $1,000 today than $1,200 in a year. To these individuals, the perceived value of $1,000 obtained today appears to be larger than the worth of $1,200 gained a year later. Behavioral economists refer to this general propensity to discount benefits as they move away from "now" and toward a temporal horizon in the future as present-bias or temporal discounting.

The discount rate for deferred future events of a person is a measure of his/her impatience and impulse. A person who considers $1,000 now to be as appealing as $10,000 in one year has a far greater discount rate — and is more impulsive and lacks self-control — than a person who considers $1,000 today to be as appealing as $10,100 in one year. Individuals with greater discount rates are less likely to save enough for retirement and have considerably higher credit card debt; while they may wish the rewards that come from exercising fiscal discipline, those rewards would come in the long term and thus heavily discounted and seems less appealing than the gratification derived by spending cash now.

Marketers employ temporal discounting strategy to drive impulsive purchases with "buy now, pay later" or "free trial" offers. Such programs lure customers by emphasizing the immediate pleasures (the joy of owning a new product), while the costs move further away into the future and hence discounted by the customers, become less significant to the purchase decisions. Marketers also try to persuade customers that purchasing a product would enhance their public image; believing in such an image-enhancing effect gives the buyer an instant reward upon purchasing a merchandise.

The discounting rate for future rewards or costs vary inversely with age and more approving community comparisons, and directly with the abundance of enticing distractions. The discounting rate can be reduced by intensely visualizing the significant future rewards that would result from rejecting the little rewards now, or the grave future repercussions of succumbing to the current temptations. Such visualization brings future rewards and costs forward to the here and now, allowing a person to make a more accurate evaluation of the intertemporal costs and rewards that would emerge from his/her decision.

66. The primary purpose of the passage is to

(*a*) converse disparate elements that influence a phenomenon explored by behavioral economists

(*b*) deliberate on the impact of a phenomenon explored by behavioral economists on individuals and recommend a way to control it

(*c*) discuss certain marketing strategy with a phenomenon explored by behavioral economists

(*d*) discuss a phenomenon explored by behavioral economists; and forecast its short-term and long-term repercussions

(*e*) ascertain the causes of a phenomenon explored by behavioral economists; and suggest ways to address it

67. If phenomenon A is the opposite of temporal discounting in the context of intertemporal selection, it can be inferred from the passage that phenomenon A is the propensity to

(*a*) refuse smaller but sooner rewards in want of larger but later rewards

(*b*) refuse smaller but sooner rewards in want of larger but sooner rewards

(*c*) accept smaller rewards over larger rewards

(*d*) take rational decisions about the future rewards but impulsive ones about the present rewards

(*e*) defer costs into the future and grab the rewards at the present

68. If person A is more impulsive than person B and prefers $20 today over $40 two months later, according to the intertemporal selection concept, all of the following are unlikely to be person B's preference EXCEPT

(*a*) less than $20 today over $40 two months later

(*b*) $20 today over more than $40 two months later

(*c*) $20 today over $40 less than two months later

(*d*) a less than $20 now over less than $40 two months later

(*e*) less than $40 two months later over $20 today

69. According to the passage, to increase its product sales as much as possible, a marketer can do which of the following?

(*a*) Not hide from potential customers the likely long-term adverse effects of using its product.

(*b*) Avail easy credits for potential customers.

(*c*) Highlight to potential customers the long-term benefits of purchasing its product.

(*d*) Increase both the product price and the time gap between a customer's purchase of the product and its delivery to him.

(*e*) Promote its higher-priced and useful products more to its potential customers than its lower-priced and unsafe products.

70. Which of the following best describes the purpose of paragraph 3 of the passage?

(a) To explain the reason for a phenomenon made in paragraph 2

(b) To describe an exception to a general observation described in paragraph 2

(c) To provide an example of a phenomenon described in paragraph 1

(d) To present an application of a phenomenon elaborated in paragraph 1

(e) To discuss some repercussions of a phenomenon described in paragraph 1

Direction for the following five questions:

When faced with an intertemporal selection, a decision involving a tradeoff between costs and benefits at different periods in time, regarding events in the far future, most individuals tend to make the sensible decision-the one that yields greater reward. For example, virtually everyone would prefer a $1,000 in 10 years over a $800 in 9 years. However, when one or both of the time-points involved approaches the present, individuals begin to favor smaller but sooner rewards over larger but later rewards. Many would rather have $1,000 today than $1,200 in a year. To these individuals, the perceived value of $1,000 obtained today appears to be larger than the worth of $1,200 gained a year later. Behavioral economists refer to this general propensity to discount benefits as they move away from "now" and toward a temporal horizon in the future as present-bias or temporal discounting.

The discount rate for deferred future events of a person is a measure of his impatience and impulse. A person who considers $1,000 now to be as appealing as $10,000 in one year has a far greater discount rate-and is more impulsive and lacks self-control-than a person who considers $1,000 today to be as appealing as $10,100 in one year. Individuals with greater discount rates are less likely to save enough for retirement and have considerably higher credit card debt; while they may wish the rewards that come from exercising fiscal discipline, those rewards would come in the long term and thus heavily discounted and seems less appealing than the gratification derived by spending cash now.

Marketers employ temporal discounting strategy to drive impulsive purchases with "buy now, pay later" or "free trial" offers. Such programs lure customers by emphasizing the immediate pleasures (the joy of owning a new product), while the costs move further away into the future and hence discounted by the customers, become less significant to the purchase decisions. Marketers also try to persuade customers that purchasing a product would enhance their public image; believing in such an image-enhancing effect gives the buyer an instant reward upon purchasing a merchandise.

The discounting rate for future rewards or costs vary inversely with age and more approving community comparisons, and directly with the abundance of enticing distractions. The discounting rate can be reduced by intensely visualizing the significant future rewards that would result from rejecting the little rewards now, or the grave future repercussions of succumbing to the current temptations. Such visualization brings future rewards and costs forward to the here and now, allowing a person to make a more accurate evaluation of the intertemporal costs and rewards that would emerge from his decision.

71. According to the passage, which of the following persons prefers a high discounting rate for future rewards?

(a) A vendor imposing severe financial penalties on the buyers who attempt to alter or withdraw from a planned transaction

(b) An employee preferring a 15% increase in salary later to a 10% increase in salary today

(c) A person with tickets to both a low-quality restaurant and a high-quality restaurant, preferring to first go to the low-quality restaurant

(d) An indebted person staying on a strict budget and working two jobs to clear his/her debts

(e) A person preferring to eat 250 grams of his/her favorite ice cream now than to eat 100 grams each day for five consecutive days

72. The passage cites each of the following as a factor that affects an individual's discounting rate of future rewards EXCEPT

(a) An individual's age

(b) Temporal distance of the future rewards

(c) The quality of the future rewards

(d) Availability of temptations

(e) The degree to which an individual imagines future rewards or costs

73. According to the passage, an individual who is aware of his/her poor self-control should take which of the following measures to increase his/her small retirement savings?

(a) He/she should enable the automatic debit facility in his check-in bank account towards his/her retirement savings to be made from his/her paychecks with a high penalty for flouting this auto-debit mandate.

(b) He/she should search for retirement funds that offer attractive rates of return.

(c) He/she should clear all outstanding credit card debt and then resolve to improve his/her retirement savings.

(d) He/she should refrain from impulse-buying and should limit his/her shopping expenditure till he/she reaches the desired level of retirement savings.

(e) He/she should make a rational assessment of the short-term costs and long-term benefits of saving for his/her retirement.

74. The passage provides information in support of which of the following assertions?

(a) People with a high present-bias are often unaware of their self-control problems.

(b) People with a high discounting rate for future rewards are less likely to make intertemporal choices.

(c) Marketers selectively offer "buy now, pay later" programs to consumers with high credit-card debt.

(d) People with high credit-card debt are also likely to be the ones who rarely make a conscious effort to visualize the repercussions of fiscal imprudence.

(e) The lower the discount rate of a person, the less likely he/she is to assess the long-term costs and benefits of a product he/she plans to buy.

75. Which of the following, if true, would most seriously weaken the assertion that people's preference for smaller but sooner rewards over larger but later rewards is a result of their increasingly discounting rewards as they move away from the present?

(*a*) People need to visualize future rewards vividly to make them as salient as the sooner rewards.

(*b*) People have a natural tendency to avoid uncertainty, and in general, the further a reward is, the more uncertain its realization is.

(*c*) People tend to favor bigger rewards over smaller rewards.

(*d*) An individual's tendency to make decisions that would fetch him/her immediate social approval is inversely proportional to his/her self- confidence.

(*e*) The presence of distracting temptations depletes a person's willpower and impairs his/her decision-making capabilities.

Direction for the following three questions:

Music is good for the health. And drumming could be the best of all. As well as being physically demanding, it requires people to synchronize their limbs and to react to outside stimuli, such as what the rest of the band is up to. It is particularly helpful for children who have emotional and behavioral difficulties. Researchers at the Clem Burke Drumming Project have shown that teaching such children to drum helps them to control their reactions more generally, to focus more effectively on tasks they are given, and to communicate better with people.

The project's latest work goes a step further: it looks at the neurological changes that accompany these shifts. Researchers recruited 36 autistic teenagers and split them into two groups. One lot had drum lessons twice a week for eight weeks. The other did not. At the beginning and end of the project, everyone was asked to stay still for 45 minutes in a functional magnetic-resonance imaging (FMRI) machine, to see how the activity of their brains had changed. Their behavior, as reported by their guardians, was also recorded. As expected, most of the drumming group showed positive behavioral changes. And these were indeed reflected in their brains. The FMRI scans showed that several clusters of connectivity among parts of those brains had strengthened during the experiment. In particular, two regions involved in attention control, the right dorsolateral prefrontal cortex and the right inferior frontal gyrus, formed strong links, respectively, with places associated with introspection and with areas involved in deciphering facial expressions. These changes in the brain's "wetware" thus nicely match the changes in behavior that learning to drum induces. Not a surprise, perhaps. But a gratifying confirmation of drumming's power to heal.

76. The primary purpose of the passage is to

(*a*) emphasize the importance of music for good health in children

(*b*) discuss how drumming can bring positive behavior changes in children with behavioral difficulties

(*c*) evaluate whether playing the drums can bring any behavioral changes in children

(*d*) recommend that all children must learn to drum to change the brain's "wetware"

(*e*) describe the changes in the brains of autistic children that occur as a result of drumming

77. Which of the following would most likely strengthen the fact that positive neurological changes were observed in children who were involved in drumming (lines 15-20)?

(*a*) Before the start of the experiment, the FMRI brain scans of children belonging to both groups were similar.

(*b*) The group of children who drummed regularly during the time the experiment was conducted was also involved in other activities that strengthened their brain connections.

(*c*) One group of children was more interested in playing the drums than the second group.

(*d*) The guardians of children involved in the experiment observed their wards very keenly.

(*e*) The right dorsolateral prefrontal cortex and the right inferior frontal gyrus are the only two areas of the brain involved in attention control.

78. According to the passage, drumming helps children with behavioral problems in each of these areas EXCEPT

(*a*) Self-evaluation and self-examination

(*b*) Communication

(*c*) Recognition of facial expressions

(*d*) Focus and attention on tasks

(*e*) Empathy

Answer Key

1. (*b*)
2. (*d*)
3. (*d*)
4. (*e*)
5. (*a*)
6. (*b*)
7. (*b*)
8. (*b*)
9. (*a*)
10. (*d*)
11. (*a*)
12. (*c*)
13. (*d*)
14. (*c*)
15. (*b*)
16. (*d*)
17. (*a*)
18. (*b*)
19. (*c*)
20. (*a*)
21. (*b*)
22. (*c*)
23. (*c*)
24. (*e*)
25. (*b*)
26. (*c*)
27. (*b*)
28. (*b*)
29. (*a*)
30. (*d*)
31. (*a*)
32. (*b*)
33. (*b*)
34. (*a*)
35. (*b*)
36. (*a*)
37. (*d*)
38. (*a*)
39. (*e*)
40. (*c*)
41. (*e*)
42. (*e*)
43. (*b*)
44. (*b*)
45. (*a*)
46. (*c*)
47. (*c*)
48. (*d*)
49. (*e*)
50. (*e*)
51. (*b*)
52. (*a*)
53. (*b*)
54. (*c*)
55. (*d*)
56. (*b*)
57. (*e*)
58. (*e*)
59. (*a*)
60. (*b*)
61. (*c*)
62. (*a*)
63. (*b*)
64. (*a*)
65. (*c*)
66. (*b*)
67. (*a*)
68. (*e*)
69. (*b*)
70. (*d*)
71. (*e*)
72. (*c*)
73. (*a*)
74. (*d*)
75. (*b*)
76. (*b*)
77. (*a*)
78. (*e*)

Answer Explanations

1. **(b)** The 'research finding' mentioned in Paragraph I is this :

"... in fact, CEOs meet their targets more often than they do not."

From the previous reference, we know that CEO remuneration is tied to such performance targets that cannot be easily manipulated by the CEO.

So, we need to decipher how the author is most likely to complete this following sentence. "In fact, most CEOs manipulate their targets, and this occurs because_____."

Now, the author clearly mentions that it is the board's vital role to set such targets for CEOs that cannot be manipulated. "In fact, most CEOs manipulate their targets, and this occurs because most boards do not religiously play their vital role."

Let us analyze the options one by one.

(*a*) This option is **incorrect**. The author mentions that CEOs are motivated by their self-gains (even at the expense of their organization's long-range goal). The author states nothing about the self-interest of the board members.

(*b*) This option is **correct**. It agrees with the analysis done above.

(*c*) This option is **incorrect**. The option mentions (multiple) 'correlated' performance metrics, whereas Paragraph 2 states that most boards, in fact, exercise a single performance metric.

(*d*) This option is **incorrect**. The question of whether the boards accept 'without deliberation' or 'after deliberation' the estimates presented to them by CEOs is outside the scope of the passage. Also, the boards accepting CEOs' feedback when setting the performance targets is only one of the two ways mentioned in the passage about how CEOs game the targets. The other way is that the boards set only one performance metric for their CEOs instead of multiple — not correlated — metrics. So, the author is likely to explain the research finding by stating that the boards stumble by using only one metric and by using the CEO's estimates in setting the performance targets. Both these errors are responsible for CEOs manipulating the metrics. It would be wrong to attribute the phenomenon of manipulation of metrics to only one of these errors [which is what you would do if you selected option (d) as an answer].

(*e*) This option is **incorrect**. While it explains why CEOs would work hard to accomplish the set performance targets, it fails to explain why most CEOs manipulate their targets.

The correct answer is (b).

2. **(d)** This question involves three performance targets P, Q, and R.

'Many performance targets' is mentioned in Paragraph 2. Quoting the relevant, simplified sentence would be:

"(many performance targets that are not correlated) cannot be manipulated by a CEO."

So, if P, Q, and R were not closely correlated, they could not be manipulated by a CEO.

Now, the question states that a CEO who is given P, Q, and R as the performance targets is more likely to meet their targets than to miss them. That is, the CEO can manipulate the performance targets. It follows that P, Q, and R are in fact, correlated. That is, a change in one metric automatically leads to an analogous change in the other two metrics.

Let us analyze the options one by one.

(*a*) This option is **incorrect**. The passage provides no reason to understand that 'performance targets that get manipulated' are those in whose setting, the service of external analysts was not taken. The relation of external analysts and the vulnerability of performance targets getting manipulated is not discussed or implicit in the passage.

(*b*) This option is **incorrect**. The ease of monitoring or quantitative nature of metrics is outside the scope of the passage.

(*c*) This option is **incorrect**. Metrics that represent a 'broad range' of organizational activities could be 'uncorrelated' or 'correlated.' It would be impossible to make any inference about the extent of their correlation till we know exactly what organizational activities they comprise.

(*d*) This option is **correct**. It is aligned with the analysis done above.

(*e*) This option is **incorrect**. The vulnerability of performance targets getting manipulated suggests their close correlation and not their popularity.

The correct answer is (d).

3. **(d)** According to the passage, befitting performance targets are those that

- cannot be manipulated
- can only be achieved by the CEO by actually adding long-term (viable) value for the corporation.

For our answer, we are looking for the option that is NOT a characteristic of befitting performance targets. Let us analyze the options one by one.

(*a*) This option is **incorrect**. Targets that comprise multiple metrics are befitting because they will be difficult to manipulate.

(*b*) This option is **incorrect**. Paragraph 3 mentions that targets that can be easily accomplished are not in the long-term interest of a corporation. Therefore, targets that are challenging (not easy) to accomplish are befitting.

(*c*) This option is **incorrect**. Targets that cannot be easily gamed by the CEO are, in fact, good.

(*d*) This option is **correct**. 'Targets' do not reward a CEO for excellent performance; 'Compensation/Incentive structure' does.

(*e*) This option is **incorrect**. Targets that are aligned with the long-term goal of the enterprise are befitting targets.

The correct answer is (d).

4. (e) In Paragraph 3, the author suggests that dying down executive incentives for performance beyond the set targets is incorrect practice because it provides little motivation to CEOs to excel beyond the set targets, and so it is damaging to the interests of the company.

This question, however, asks for the correct option that

- provides a redundant dying down the incentives in such a manner is fine, and
- is supported by the passage.

Let us analyze the options one by one.

(*a*) This option is **incorrect**. That boards want executive payouts to seem rational to the shareholders does not explain why it is fine to die down the incentives for performing better than the targets. Also, since the passage does not cite this concern of the boards at all, this option is not supported by the passage.

(*b*) This option is **incorrect**. The implausibility of an event does not explain why it is fine to not reward that event if it takes place. Also, the passage mentions only that CEOs usually have little motivation to strive beyond their set targets. But if an executive did work hard to go beyond his set targets, would he succeed or not? The passage gives us no clue about the odds. So, the phrase 'it is improbable' is not supported by the passage.

(*c*) This option is **incorrect**. That CEOs are keener to do A than B does not explain why not rewarding them with A for B is fine.

(*d*) This option is **incorrect**. The passage clearly states that good performance targets are those that cannot be manipulated by CEOs. So, if not pegging the rewards around the set targets leads to manipulation of the performance, it is fine to peg the compensations. So, this option does explain why it is fine to die down the compensations beyond the set targets. However, this explanation is not supported by the passage.

(*e*) This option is **correct**. If compensations increase at a constant rate relative to performance, there would be no dying down of rewards for performance beyond the set targets. So, the higher the performance, the more the rewards (and hence, more the personal gains of CEOs). The first sentence of the passage states that executives are likely to act in their self-gain even at the expense of their business. Therefore, the passage does support the explanation that the overlook of higher compensations is likely to make CEOs take greater risks. Such excessive risk-taking might hurt the long-term goals of the corporation. So, to avoid such a possibility, it is fine to die down executive compensations for performance beyond the set standards. Thus, this option explains why the dying down of compensations is fine; and is supported by the passage.

The correct answer is (e).

5. (a) We are looking for the one statement that is NOT supported by the passage. Let us analyze the options one by one.

(*a*) This option is **correct**. It is NOT supported by the passage. The passage only suggests that the performance targets for most CEOs are such that the targets can be gamed by them. This, the passage suggests, might not be in the goals of a corporation. However, the passage does not suggest that these targets are not in sync with the company's mission and values.

(*b*) This option is **incorrect**. It is supported by the passage. The first sentence of Paragraph 1 states that a CEO is likely to act for his self-gain even if it harms the interests of his organization. So, if his dividend depends on earnings per share, he will strive to maximize earnings per share even if this harms other key metrics of the organization (such as, income).

(*c*) This option is **incorrect**. It is supported by the passage. This aspect is already discussed a few times.

(*d*) This option is **incorrect**. It is supported by the passage. Paragraph 2 states that the performance targets of CEOs are frequently based on only one metric.

(*e*) This option is **incorrect**. It is supported by the passage. Paragraph 3 explains how the executive compensations are nil below the minimum performance level, increase speedily till the set target, and then die down above the set target. So, the compensations do not increase at a steady rate with the performance.

The correct answer is (a).

6. (b) Let's see the organization of the passage.

- **Paragraph 1 :** Explains why it is essential for the boards to tie CEO compensation with befitting performance targets. Mentions research finding suggests the boards are not setting befitting targets.
- **Paragraph 2 :** Lists a drawback in most performance targets.
- **Paragraph 3 :** Lists a problem in the procedure boards follow to set performance targets. Then, lists a drawback in the way CEO rewards are tied to performance targets.

Since the answer options use abstract words, let us make a generic version of the above organization summary:

- **Paragraph 1 :** Explains why a particular duty of an entity is essential. The research finding suggests that this entity is not performing its duty well.
- **Paragraph 2 :** Lists a problem in the way the entity performs its duty.
- **Paragraph 3 :** Lists two more problems in the way the entity performs its duty. Let us analyze the options one by one.

(*a*) This option is **incorrect**. The entity whose conduct is discussed is the CEO. But, as the above summary demonstrates, the author is not primarily concerned with evaluating the consequences of the self-centered conduct of CEOs. Had the author done so, the passage would probably have been organized as:

a. **Paragraph 1 :** Introduce and explain the self-centered conduct of CEOs

b. **Paragraph 2 :** Consequence 1 of this self-centered conduct

c. **Paragraph 3 :** Consequence 2 of this self-centered conduct

(*b*) This option is **correct**. It is in line with the discussion above.

(*c*) This option is **incorrect**. The author claims about the self-centered conduct of CEOs. Then, he/she presents examples for, and not counter-examples against, such self-centered conduct.

(*d*) This option is **incorrect**. Only two entities are mentioned in the passage: CEOs and the boards. The author details the responsibilities of neither.

(*e*) This option is **incorrect**. The author lists ways in which an entity (the boards) fails to perform a particular job (setting performance targets) well. From this discussion, improved ways to perform this job can certainly be inferred but that is not the primary purpose of the author.

The correct answer is (b).

7. **(b)** This is a main-point question. Let's jot down the key points of each paragraph and derive the main point of the passage.

Paragraph 1:

- "remembrance of things past" is important for plotting the future
- Study history from a feminist's point of view
- Record history

Paragraph 2 :

- Not only the future but get hold of the past
- Not only rewrite but also teach history from a feminist's point of view

Paragraph 3 :

- Why history has been written and taught by academic professionals
- Reinterpreting history is only one part of the task
- The feminist movement…grows from day to day
- Feminist history could overturn prejudice and antifeminist superstition in society.

Encapsulating the four paragraphs, a succinct main point can be derived.

Main Point: Make a compelling case for reinterpreting history not only from a woman's perspective, but also from a feminist's perspective; rewriting and teaching history to create an unbiased future.

Let us look at each option one by one.

(*a*) This is **incorrect**. There is no issue with the use of the verb "narrate." The author does narrate the feminist movements in Europe. However, there are a couple of issues with this option. First, this option is myopic in scope: the author not only narrates the skewed (biased) historical perspective of feminist movements in

Europe but also presents the quest of feminists to rewrite and teach history to create a better future. Second, the passage is limited to the feminism movement in Europe and not in North America. The reference to North America was brought up as additional information.

(*b*) This is **correct**. As discussed in option (a), this option best articulates the main point of the passage.

(*c*) This is **incorrect**. The author does not evaluate the pro-feminism views of three European feminists and historians. "Evaluating" means to assess, weigh one opinion over the other, and view one perspective better than the other.

(*d*) This is **incorrect**. There are three parts to it: (1) educate about antifeminist European history. This part is correct; the author does educate (inform) about antifeminist European history. (2) call for it to be vetted to inculcate a holistic perspective. This part is incorrect; the author does not do so. It's the feminists who call for history be vetted (assessed) to inculcate a holistic perspective. (3) advocate that it be taught by feminists. This part is also incorrect; again, the author does not do so. It's the feminists who do so.

(*e*) This is **incorrect**. There are three parts to it, and none of them is correct. The author neither identifies any perspective as extreme nor recognizes/advocates any perspective.

The correct answer is option (b).

8. (b) Note that we have an option that the author is not likely to agree with; the other options he/she might agree with. Let us look at each option one by one.

(*a*) This is **incorrect**. As discussed in the main point question, there is a compelling case for reinterpreting history not only from a woman's perspective but also from a feminist's perspective, rewriting and teaching history to create an unbiased future. So, the author will agree with this.

(*b*) This is **correct**. The author will not NECESSARILY agree to this. The feminists will, but given the information in the passage, we cannot infer that the author would also agree to it.

(*c*) This is **incorrect**. Refer to the first sentence of the passage: "remembrance of things past" is "important for plotting the future." Thus, the author will agree to this.

(*d*) This is **incorrect**. Refer to the second sentence of paragraph 2, "When women ask questions, the past assumes new shapes." This option statement is its paraphrase, so the author would agree to it.

(*e*) This is **incorrect**. Refer to the third sentence of paragraph 2, "And not only from a women's point of view, but from a feminist point of view." Like option (d), this option statement is its paraphrase, so the author would agree to it.

The correct answer is option (b).

9. (a) **Let us bring out the referred sentence :**

"For feminists, history has important implications, and setting the record straight is only one part of the task." To infer about the other part(s) of the task, we must look at at the sentences before and after this one.

(Paragraph 2) "And not only from a women's point of view, but from a feminist point of view, which encompasses more than efforts to write and teach the history of feminism and also to get women included in "standard accounts".

(Paragraph 3) "Feminist scholars are also formulating a critique of how and why history has been written and taught by academic professionals, both in Europe and in North America. For feminists, history has important implications, and setting the record straight is only part of the task."

The highlighted phrases, "write and teach," and "written and taught" suggest that "setting the record straight" implies write history; thus, it is only one part of the task. Thus, teach history must be other part of the task.

Let's see each option one by one.

(*a*) This is **correct**. "Educate society about feminism" is a paraphrase of the phrase: "teach history about feminism."

(*b*) This is **incorrect**. "Rewrite history..." is already mentioned as ONE part of the task.

(*c*) This is **incorrect**. No such inference we can draw from the passage.

(*d*) This is **incorrect**. Like option (c), no such inference can be drawn from the passage.

(*e*) This is **incorrect**. Like option (c) and (d), no such inference can be drawn from the passage.

The correct answer is option (a).

10. (d) **This is a main point question :**

Let's jot down the key points of both paragraphs and then derive the main point.

Paragraph 1:

- Acknowledgement of the fact that compared to other black holes of other galaxies, the black hole at the core of our galaxy is mysteriously dormant.
- NASA explains the reason the black hole at the core of our galaxy is bafflingly quiet.

  The reason: a powerful magnetic field keeps our galaxy's black hole from spewing high-energy radiation or churning out the raw materials for new stars. Other black holes' magnetic fields are not able to do so.

Paragraph 2:

- A description of NASA's equipment and process to study the magnetic field's activity
- Technical details of the magnetic field
- Summarizing why our black hole is quiet, while others are active
- Our galaxy's bizarre magnetic field keeps its black hole, Sagittarius A* quiet.

Main point : NASA solves the mystery of why, while black holes in other galaxies are active, our galaxy's black hole is not. Let's look at each option one by one.

(*a*) This is **incorrect**. The stated fact is partly correct, but why our galaxy's magnetic field is unusual is not the main point of the passage.

(*b*) This is **incorrect**. This is incorrect and distorted information.

(*c*) This is **incorrect**. This is a tricky option. How a strong magnetic field keeps a black hole inactive in a galaxy is certainly discussed in the passage in detail, but is it the main point of the passage? We may choose this if we do not get a better option.

(*d*) This is **correct**. This correctly captures the main point we derived above; moreover, it is better than option (c).

(*e*) This is **incorrect**. The stated fact is correct, but this is not the main point. This could compete with option (c) but not with option (d).

The correct answer is option (d).

11. (a) This is a question on inference.

We have to infer the statement that is supported by the passage. Let's look at each option one by one.

(*a*) This is **correct**. This is supported by paragraph 1/sentence 2, "A powerful magnetic field at the center of the Milky Way is oriented just right to keep our galaxy's black hole, Sagittarius A*, from spewing high-energy radiation out into the cosmos or churning out the raw materials for new stars."

Since the option statement used the possibility word "might," we can reasonably infer that if our galaxy's magnetic field were not powerful, Sagittarius A* might be discharging high-intensity radiation or producing new stars.

(*b*) This is **incorrect**. This is a classic mix up. The other way round is correct: the inactivity of the black hole at the core of our galaxy is due to our galaxy's weird magnetic field.

(*c*) This is **incorrect**. This option could have been correct had "All" been replaced with "Many." As per the given information, we cannot infer about all galaxies' black holes.

(*d*) This is **incorrect**. This fact is correct for "our galaxy" and not for "other galaxies."

(*e*) This is **incorrect**. The problem with this option is the omission of reference to "black hole." The passage is not about why our galaxy is mysteriously dormant, but about why the black hole at the core of the galaxy is mysteriously dormant (inactive).

The correct answer is option (a).

12. (c) This is a question on inference.

However, we have to infer a statement that is NOT supported by the passage; in other words, four statements are supported by the passage.

Let's look at each option one by one.

(*a*) This is **incorrect**. This can be inferred. It is supported by paragraph 2/ sentence 1.

(*b*) This is **incorrect**. This can be inferred. It is supported by paragraph 1/ sentence 3, "A powerful magnetic field at the center of the Milky Way is oriented just right .... and paragraph 2/sentence 3, "The spiral shape of the magnetic field channels ..."

(*c*) This is **correct**. This cannot be inferred. The problem with the statement is the word "All." Though it is correct that new stars in the universe are formed by raw materials discharged by volatile black holes, stars can also be formed by other activities, which are beyond the scope of the passage.

(*d*) This is **incorrect**. This can be inferred. It is supported by paragraph 1/ sentence 4, "Other black holes' magnetic fields funnel nearby gas straight into them ..." and paragraph 2/sentence 3, "The spiral shape of the magnetic field channels the gas into an orbit around the black hole."

(*e*) This is **incorrect**. This can be inferred. It is supported by paragraph 1/ sentence 1, "Compared to other supermassive black holes scattered throughout the universe, ..."

The correct answer is option (c).

13. (d) This is a purpose question.

The answer can be inferred from the first sentence, "Efforts are being made by the U.S. Senate to establish criteria for psychotherapy" and the last sentence, "by specifying the essential criteria for psychotherapy, the door has been left ajar" of the passage. However, it also concerns the central issue of the passage, namely that as much as those involved in psychotherapy desire Medicare funding, the imposition of criteria makes them aware of the constraints this would imply.

Let us analyze the options one by one.

(*a*) This option is **incorrect**. It has a negative undertone, and this is not the central idea of the passage or the Senate's purpose.

(*b*) This option is **incorrect**. The criterion for psychotherapy must conform to complement Congressional mandates and not otherwise.

(*c*) This option is **incorrect**. Nothing of this sort can be inferred from the passage.

(*d*) This option is **correct**. As stated above, it is in line with the discussion.

(*e*) This option is **incorrect**. Nothing of this sort can be inferred from the passage; there is no intent to not fund psychiatric treatment at all. From the last sentence, "Congress rejected automatic third-party reimbursement for psychotherapeutic services, by specifying the essential criteria for psychotherapy, the door has been left ajar" of the passage, we get that the door is open for funding.

The correct answer is option (d).

14. (c) This is a function question.

We have to find out why the issue of Medicare for psychiatric treatment is so important to Congress.

Let's look at the options one by one.

(*a*) This option is **incorrect**. Though the passage mentions that some psychotherapists..., along with psychiatrists, could be prohibited from attempting to treat people believed to have schizophrenia, this is rather an after-effect of gaining authorization from Congress.

(*b*) This option is **incorrect**. Though this is true, it is unlikely to be a pressing question for Congress.

(*c*) This option is **correct**. The answer can be found in paragraph 1/last sentence: "An important hidden issue is that the social and legal systems have created a situation in which every person can be diagnosed as having symptoms of mental illness." The consequences for the health care system would be devastating if everybody in the US could be described as in need of mental care.

(*d*) This option is **incorrect** because nothing of this sort can be inferred.

(*e*) This option is **incorrect** because nothing of this sort can be inferred.

The correct answer is (c).

15. (b) This is a detail question.

We have to find an option that articulates the dilemma (catch/problem) that the psychotherapy profession is facing if the criteria for psychotherapy are proposed by Congress.

Let's look at the options one by one.

(*a*) This option is **incorrect**. In fact, it is otherwise; the psychotherapists would be jittery with stricter criteria than with weaker ones because, if stricter criteria were imposed, some psychotherapists, along with psychiatrists, could be banned from practicing psychotherapy.

(*b*) This option is **correct**. That imposing criteria could restrain many psychotherapy practices is the central idea of the passage and underlines the dilemma the profession faces in trying to obtain Medicare funding.

(*c*) This option is **incorrect**/. This can be a good problem to deal with. The real dilemma with psychotherapists is that they would come under stricter watch, losing some privileges.

(*d*) This option is **incorrect**. This could be the correct option, but option (b) is stronger than this. Option (b) talks about banning certain psychotherapy practices, while option (d) talks about certain patients.

(*e*) This option is **incorrect**. There is no such inference that we can draw from the passage.

The correct answer is option (b).

16. (d) This is a question on inference.

We have to find an option that is supported by the passage.

Let's look at the options one by one.

(*a*) This option is **incorrect**. Refer to paragraph 2/sentence 2, "... along with psychiatrists, could be prohibited from attempting to treat people believed to have schizophrenia." This does not mean that psychiatrists could be prohibited from treating schizophrenics.

(*b*) This option is **incorrect**. We cannot draw such an unsubstantiated inference.

(*c*) This option is **incorrect**. There is not even an indirect reference to infer such an extreme claim.

(*d*) This option is **correct**. Refer to paragraph 2/sentences 2 and 3, "This has focused attention on evidence that...that some psychotherapy could be banned." This implies that some psychotherapies are often ineffective; and therefore couldn't satisfy the stringent criteria that Medicare funding would require.

(*e*) This option is **incorrect**. As with option (c), there is not even an indirect reference to infer such an extreme claim.

The correct answer is (d).

17. (a) This is an inference question.

Let us look at the options one by one.

(*a*) This option is **correct**. Refer to paragraph 1/sentences 1 & 2, "Black communities have undergone much academic research, more often than not, from the University of Chicago's (UC) Sociology Department graduates. A devoted inheritor of this tradition, William Wilson is one of the keenest analysts of the problems of racism and poverty."

The crux of the sentences is that UC's Sociology Department graduates have a keen interest in analyzing the problems of racism and poverty. From the phrase, "A devoted inheritor of this tradition," we can infer that Wilson was (1) a UC alumnus and (2) he inherited (carried on) the tradition of analyzing the problems of racism and poverty in the black community.

This implies that he did not establish UC's Sociology Department.

(*b*) This option is **incorrect**. Refer to paragraph 2/sentence 1, "Racism, Wilson argues, plays increasingly less of a role in urban problems." In fact, as per Wilson, the opposite is true.

(*c*) This option is **incorrect**. Refer to paragraph 2/sentence 3, "Wilson does not focus on an irredeemable culture of poverty." Thus, as per Wilson, the culture of poverty cannot be redeemed (transformed).

(*d*) This option is **incorrect**. Refer to paragraph 2/sentence 4, "Wilson claims the only way out is a display of race-neutral government interventions." In fact, as per Wilson, the opposite is true.

(*e*) This option is **incorrect**. This is a little tricky. Refer to paragraph 2/sentence 1, "Racism, Wilson argues, plays increasingly less of a role in urban problems." As per Wilson, race does have some relevance to the problem of urban poverty, but its role is increasingly diminishing.

The correct answer is option (a).

18. (b) This is an inference question. We have to find an option statement with which the author would either disagree or least likely agree with.

Let us look at the options one by one.

(*a*) This option is **incorrect**. From the first two sentences of the passage, we can infer that the University of Chicago's Sociology Department, of which Wilson is an alumnus, has been doing some great work in analyzing the problems of racism and poverty. So the author would not like to disagree with it.

(*b*) This option is **correct**. Refer to paragraph 2/sentence 5, "However, even though Wilson accepts that the problem has a moral behavioral component, he is strangely silent on the question of how to deal with it." This sentence can be summed up as a criticism by the author of Wilson's failure to give enough attention to the moral element of the problem. So, the author would like to disagree with it.

(*c*) This option is **incorrect**. Refer to paragraph 1/sentence 3, "The new urban poor that Wilson describes populate segregated areas where 97 percent of adults are outside of the workforce." Given that 97% of adults are unemployed, the author would likely agree that unemployment is at the core of the plight of the urban poor.

(*d*) This option is **incorrect**. From the passage, we understand that racism, unemployment, drugs, crime, and moral behavior are among the many issues that add to the plight of the urban poor. Thus, the author would likely agree with this statement.

(*e*) This option is **incorrect**. Refer to paragraph 2/sentence 4, "Wilson does not focus on an irredeemable culture of poverty." Thus, as per Wilson, the culture of poverty cannot be redeemed (transformed). Or, in other words, the culture of poverty has deep roots. So, the author would agree with this statement.

The correct answer is option (b).

19. (c) This is an inference question.

Let us look at the options one by one.

(*a*) This option is **incorrect**. Refer to paragraph 2/sentence 5, "... Wilson accepts that the problem has a moral behavioral component," Thus, the option statement is factually incorrect.

(*b*) This option is **incorrect**. Refer to paragraph 2/sentence 4, "Wilson claims the only way out is a display of race-neutral government interventions." The term "positive discrimination" implies that Wilson is biased in favor of Blacks; however, according to the quoted statement, he advocates a race-neutral approach.

(*c*) This option is **correct**. The explanation for option (b) is the same as that for this option.

(*d*) This option is **incorrect**. Though this reflects Wilson's thoughts, he does not recommend it as a solution.

(*e*) This option is **incorrect**. Like option (d), though this reflects Wilson's thoughts, he does not recommend it as a solution.

The correct answer is option (c).

20. (a) **This is a main point question.**

The passage is about Wilson's work, analysis, and ideologies. Both paragraphs talk about Wilson's analysis of the problems of racism, poverty, and unemployment in the Black community. The author presents him as a scholar whose work is described by the author. The author is not opinionated in tone, except in the last sentence of the passage, "However, even though Wilson accepts that the problem has a moral behavioral component, he is strangely silent on the question of how to deal with it."

Let us look at the options one by one.

(*a*) This option is **correct**. This is aligned with the discussion above.

(*b*) This option is **incorrect**. The author does not analyze Wilson's work; he/she rather presents Wilson's analysis of the problems of racism, poverty, and unemployment in the Black community.

(*c*) This option is **incorrect**. Evaluation means to assessment/appraisal. Like in option (b), the author does not evaluate Wilson's work from Wilson's perspective. In the last sentence of the passage, we do find the author expressing his/her opinion; however, that too was not an evaluation.

(*d*) This option is **incorrect**. The author did state that Wilson is one of the foremost authorities on racism and poverty, but the intent was not to establish him as one.

(*e*) This option is **incorrect**. As explained in the previous options, the author does not express his/her viewpoint; he/she only presents Wilson's work.

The correct answer is option (a).

21. (b) **This is a main point question.**

Let's jot down the key points of each paragraph and then derive the main point.

Paragraph 1 :

- What is the Women's Liberation Movement (WLM)?
- WLM's emergence in the late 1960s and continuation till then 1980s
- Ideology of the WLM branch of radical feminism

Paragraph 2 :

- WLM questioned the cultural and legal validity of patriarchy
- WLM proposed that gender-based discrimination is the key political problem

Paragraph 3 :

- Various proposals of WLM towards achieving women's equality
- Success of WLM in achieving its objectives.

Let's derive the main point.

Main point : The passage educates about what is WLM, its emergence, and ideology. How WLM questioned the status quo, proposed changes, and attained success.

Let's look at each option one by one.

(*a*) This is **incorrect**. No factors that helped WLM achieve success were discussed.

(*b*) This is **correct**. It broadly captures the main point. Though it is broad in scope, it cannot be ruled out as the correct answer. If no better option than this is available, it is the best answer.

(*c*) This is **incorrect**. Though the challenges the Women's Liberation Movement (WLM) faced were indirectly stated, the passage does not highlight them as stiff challenges.

(*d*) This is **incorrect**. This is incorrect for two reasons: 1. The success of WLM is discussed only in paragraph 3, so it does not cover the whole passage. 2. We cannot infer that WLM had a subdued (lukewarm) success.

(*e*) This is **incorrect**. Though the issue of gender-based discrimination was discussed in paragraph 2, the passage does not imply that gender-based discrimination against women led to the rise of the WLM.

The correct answer is option (b).

22. (c) This is a question about finding inference.

Let's look at each option one by one.

(*a*) This is **incorrect**. The statement is correct except for the word "developed." The correct inference is, "The Women's Liberation Movement (WLM) emerged in the late 1960s and continued into the 1980s, primarily in the industrialized nations of the Western world."

(*b*) This is **incorrect**. At the end of paragraph 1, we find a reference to "second-class citizens in their societies," and in the middle of paragraph 2, we find a reference to "gender-based discrimination." However, we cannot establish any relationship between them.

(*c*) This is **correct**. Refer to paragraph 2/sentence 1, "... the WLM questioned the cultural and legal validity of patriarchy..." Male supremacy is another name for patriarchy, so we can infer this.

(*d*) This is **incorrect**. This is a half-right/half-wrong statement. Indeed, WLM rejected the idea of piecemeal equality, but it did not demand equal male-to-female representation in the political process.

(*e*) This is **incorrect**. As per the limited information in the passage, we cannot compare which of the two aspects weighs more than the other.

The correct answer is option (c).

23. (c) This is a question about finding inference.

Since this is a question on finding the option with which the author would be least likely agree, we must find four options that the author would agree to.

Let's look at each option one by one.

(*a*) This is **incorrect**. Refer to paragraph 1/sentence 1, "The Women's Liberation Movement ... which effected great change (political, intellectual, and cultural) throughout the world." Since it is supported by the passage, the author would agree with it.

(*b*) This is **incorrect**. Refer to paragraph 3/sentence 2, "In the decades ... liberationists successfully changed how women were perceived in their cultures," Since it is supported by the passage, the author would agree with it.

(*c*) This is **correct**. Refer to paragraph 1/sentence 2, "The WLM branch of radical feminism ... social freedom were necessary for women to progress from being second-class citizens in their societies." From the passage, we get that between 1960 and 1980, women fought to be recognized as first-class citizens in their societies. Since the option statement is factually incorrect, the author would disagree with it.

(*d*) This is **incorrect**. Refer to paragraph 3/sentence 1, "In general, the WLM ... rejected the idea that piecemeal equality ... would eliminate discrimination against women." The contextual meaning of piecemeal is gradual/in parts/incremental. Thus, the author would agree with it.

(*e*) This is **incorrect**. Refer to paragraph 2/sentence 1, "Towards achieving women's equality, the WLM questioned ... physical independence of women in society." Physical independence is synonymous with personal liberty. Thus, before WLM, women had restricted personal liberty. Thus, the author would agree with it.

The correct answer is option (c).

24. (e) This is a detail question.

Because there is no specific location where you can find your answer, it is best to solve this question by eliminating answer options.

(*a*) This option is **incorrect**. Refer to paragraph 3/sentence 2, "And despite the difficulty, some remarkable agreements have been reached." This means that the WTO has made some extraordinary decisions.

(*b*) This option is **incorrect**. Refer to paragraph 3/sentence 4-5, "Nevertheless, proposals for the creation of a smaller executive body — perhaps like a board of directors each representing different groups of countries — are heard periodically. But for now, the WTO is a member-driven, consensus-based organization." This indicates that the WTO, until now, does not have an executive branch.

(*c*) This option is **incorrect**. Refer to paragraph 3/sentence 2, "Its main advantage is that decisions made this way are more acceptable to all members." This indicates that the decisions reached by consensus among members are acceptable to all members.

(*d*) This option is **incorrect**. Refer to paragraph 1/sentence 2, "All major decisions are made by the membership as a whole, either by ministers, who meet at least once every two years, or by their ambassadors or delegates, who meet regularly at the WTO headquarters in Geneva." This clearly shows that the WTO has its head office in Geneva.

(*e*) This option is **correct**. While the WTO does not have an executive body at this point, the passage does not indicate that it will "never seek" to do so.

The correct answer is option (e).

25. (b) This is an inference question.

Because there is no specific location where you can find your answer, it is best to solve this question by eliminating answer options.

(*a*) This option is **incorrect**. While we know that members at the WTO meet once every two years, the passage does not state how frequently members of other organizations meet.

(*b*) This option is **correct**. Refer to paragraph 1/sentence 4-5, "In this respect, the WTO is different from some other international organizations such as the World Bank and International Monetary Fund. In the WTO, power is not delegated to a board of directors or the organization's head." From this, it is fair to infer that the power to make decisions at the WTO is not vested in a few people.

(*c*) This option is **incorrect**. The number of members of the WTO is stated, but the number of members of other international organizations is not.

(*d*) This option is **incorrect**. Refer to paragraph 1/last sentence, "In the WTO, power is not delegated to a board of directors or the organization's head." The power to make decisions at the WTO does not rest with the organization's head. However, it is not fair to say that the WTO does not have a head.

(*e*) This option is **incorrect**. Refer to paragraph 3/sentence 3, "And despite the difficulty, some remarkable agreements have been reached." From this information, it can be inferred that agreements at the WTO have been reached.

The correct answer is option (b).

26. (c) This is a main point question.

The correct answer must encapsulate the information stated in the passage as a whole.

Let us look at each of the paragraphs to understand their purpose.

The first paragraph introduces the structure of the WTO and the fact that decisions at the WTO are generally taken by consensus of its members. This differentiates it from other international organizations.

The second paragraph describes how the WTO functions. The third paragraph shows the achievements of the WTO despite it being a consensus-driven organization.

So, the overall purpose is to discuss the structure, functioning, and achievements of the WTO. Let us look at the options.

(*a*) This option is **incorrect**. It is only a part of the passage and cannot be characterized as the primary purpose of the passage.

(*b*) This option is **incorrect**. This information encapsulates only a part of the passage and cannot be characterized as the primary purpose of the passage.

(*c*) This option is **correct**. It describes the overall purpose of the passage appropriately.

(*d*) This option is **incorrect**. It is not the purpose of the passage as a whole.

(*e*) This option is **incorrect**. The passage does not seek to evaluate the pros and cons of a consensus-driven organization.

The correct answer is option (c).

27. (b) This is an inference question.

Because there is no single location that you can go back to, the best way to solve this question is by eliminating the answer options.

Let us look at the options.

(*a*) This option is **incorrect**. Refer to paragraph 1/sentence 1, "Members of the dolphin family — which comprise dozens of species, including the familiar bottlenose dolphins and killer whales — have the second-largest brain size relative to body size, after humans."

This clearly states that humans have the largest brain size relative to body size. However, this does not mean that humans have the biggest brain. A whale or an elephant can have the biggest brain, but relative to their body size, their brains are smaller than those of humans.

(*b*) This option is **correct**. Refer to paragraph 1/sentence 2, "And, big brains are more expensive energetically than their smaller counterparts; because larger brains cost a lot, they have to be doing something important." This sentence clearly states that big brains are more expensive energetically than small ones. From this statement, it is fair to infer that the size of the brain is directly proportional to the energy it consumes.

(*c*) This option is **incorrect**. It is, perhaps, the opposite of the information stated in the passage. Refer to paragraph 1/sentence 2, "And, big brains are more expensive energetically than their smaller counterparts; because larger brains cost a lot, they have to be doing something important." This sentence implies that big brains do something important.

(*d*) This option is **incorrect**. It is not mentioned in the passage.

(*e*) This option is **incorrect**. The passage does not establish a correlation between the size of the brain and the ability of living creatures to recognize themselves in the mirror.

The correct answer is option (b).

28. (b) This is a detail question.

Often, to answer such questions, you are required to reread specific locations in the passage and pick the answer that best matches with the information given.

Refer to paragraph 2/sentences 3-4, "A recent study described an experiment showing that young dolphins got interested in their reflections as young as seven months. This is earlier than human babies, who typically pass the milestone around 12 months."

According to the context, the word 'milestone' would refer to the idea discussed in the previous sentence, which is that of young dolphins getting interested in their reflections.

Let us look at the options.

(*a*) This option is **incorrect**. The passage does not discuss the ability of dolphins to recognize "others."

(*b*) This option is **correct**. It rightly refers to the milestone.

(*c*) This option is **incorrect**. As discussed earlier, the milestone is not that of looking at the markings on its body.

(*d*) This option is **incorrect**. As discussed earlier, the milestone is not that of touching and feeling the markings on its body.

(*e*) This option is **incorrect**. As discussed earlier, the milestone is not that of wiping off the markings on its body.

The correct answer is option (b).

29. (a) This is a detail question.

These questions often require you to reread certain specific locations in the passage. Refer to paragraph 3/sentence 2, "The trouble with the mirror test in dolphins is that they do not have hands to touch or wipe off markings on their face like chimps do, and so, the test might not be particularly useful."

So, the author believes that the mirror test might not be useful in dolphins because they cannot touch or wipe off markings on their faces.

Let us look at the options.

(*a*) This option is **correct**. This is exactly what the information in the passage states.

(*b*) This option is **incorrect**. This is a result of the test not being useful in dolphins; it is not a reason for the test not being useful.

(*c*) This option is **incorrect**. The comparison between humans and dolphins in terms of recognizing marks on their bodies is not stated in the passage.

(*d*) This option is **incorrect**. Like option (b), this option is a result of the test not being useful.

(*e*) This option is **incorrect**. It is irrelevant to the information stated in the passage.

The correct answer is option (a).

30. (d) Let us analyze the options one by one.

(*a*) This option is **incorrect**. 'Depression' and 'feelings of loneliness' are out of scope of the passage.

(*b*) This option is **incorrect**. The passage does not suggest the metrics that decide the quality of a purchase decision (whether a purchase decision was bad, good, better, or best). For example, does this quality depend on purchase ease, purchase satisfaction, the quality of a purchased product, the longevity of a purchased product, the amount of discount received, or some other factor, or all of these factors? The passage cites evidence that greater number of options for a particular product (ESP) lead to decreased purchase ease and increased purchase regret. While this may have some bearing on the quality of the purchase decision, we cannot be sure of the exact effect. Therefore, this statement is not supported by the passage.

(*c*) This option is **incorrect**. The reason for rejecting this option is similar to that for option (b) above.

(*d*) This option is **correct**. From the last sentence of paragraph 1, we know that purchase regret arises out of customer dissatisfaction with the purchase decision. This is premise 1. Paragraph 2 cites a study that shows that recommending only one option (hence, "severely limiting the options that are presented") to the customers of a particular product greatly reduces their purchase regret. This is premise 2. Putting these premises together, we can conclude that presenting severely limited options to the customers of a particular product greatly reduces customer dissatisfaction with the purchase decision. Note that this conclusion is specific to a particular type of customers - the customers of ESP - while the options statement talks about customers in general. The case of ESP customers, as described in this passage, serves as a specific example of the general point made by this option statement.

(*e*) This option is **incorrect**. The passage talks about the impact of decreasing the number of options available to customers of a particular product on their "purchase ease" and "purchase regret." The impact of this action on "product sales" is out of the passage's scope.

The correct answer is option (d).

31. (a) Looking at the answer options, we see that they are based on the findings of the study mentioned in paragraph 2 and that all of them deal with:

- Either the relationship between 'Purchase Ease' for PRSS and 'Purchase Ease' for RSS.
- Or the relationship between 'Purchase Regret' for PRSS and 'Purchase Regret' for RSS

Let's tabulate these metrics (their relative values with respect to the baseline scenario):

	RSS	PRSS
Purchase Ease of buyers	20% less than baseline	90% more than baseline
Purchase Regret of buyers	50% more than baseline	40% less than baseline

Let's assign a value of '100' each to 'Purchase Ease' and 'Purchase Regret' for the baseline scenario. Then, the above table may be simplified as:

	RSS	PRSS
Purchase Ease of buyers	80	190
Purchase Regret of buyers	150	60

Let us analyze the options one by one.

(*a*) This option is **correct**. The statement is supported by the simplified table above.

(*b*) This option is **incorrect**. It contradicts the simplified table above.

(*c*) This option is **incorrect**. It contradicts the simplified table above.

(*d*) This option is **incorrect**. It contradicts the simplified table above.

(*e*) This option is **incorrect**. It contradicts the simplified table above.

The correct answer is option (a).

32. (b) The author would be likely to agree with a recommendation that is well-supported by the passage. Since the passage describes how the current selling strategy used by most suppliers (RSS) ends up inadvertently aggravating the customers' difficulties in the buying process and how PRSS eases these difficulties, the author is likely to agree with a measure that increases purchase ease and decreases purchase regret for the customers. The passage suggests that this would be a measure that goes against RSS and in favor of PRSS.

Let us analyze the options one by one.

(*a*) This option is **incorrect**. The suppliers are already customer-centric, and presumably so are their sales professionals (since these professionals do the activities that their suppliers urge them to do in the belief that these activities are customer-centric). The problem discussed in the passage is that their customer-centricity is mistaken — what the suppliers and sales professionals think to be a customer-centric activity actually ends up overwhelming the customer. Merely encouraging the sales professionals to be more customer-centric will not solve this problem.

(*b*) This option is **correct**. It accords with PRSS and therefore the author is likely to agree with this suggestion.

(*c*) This option is **incorrect**. The passage does not suggest the impact of providing less information, specifically about the disadvantages of different options (while presumably providing as much information as before about the advantages of these options) on the difficulties faced by customers in the process of purchasing ESPs. Therefore, we cannot infer whether the author would agree with this suggestion or not.

(*d*) This option is **incorrect**. Paragraph 2 mentions 'use cases', 'testimonials' and 'research papers' as the types of information provided by sales professionals to customers about the available options. The relative effectiveness or impact of these three types of information is not discussed. Therefore, we cannot infer whether the author would agree with this suggestion or not.

(*e*) This option is **incorrect**. Such a suggestion accords with the RSS and therefore is one that the author would be likely to disagree with.

The correct answer is option (b).

33. (b) This is a main point question.

To get to the answer, let us understand the key points of each paragraph.

The introductory paragraph sets the context for the information to follow. It introduces the idea of the success of women's movements in eliminating coverture and giving married women the right to own property.

The second paragraph introduces an approach to explain why women were given the right to own property. The third presents a complementary approach to explain the same phenomenon of women given the right to own property. The latter half of the third paragraph discusses data to support the two theories.

(*a*) This option is **incorrect**. The passage does not primarily discuss the results of property rights; rather, it discusses the reasons for the property rights being awarded to married women.

(*b*) This option is **correct**. The passage does discuss two approaches to the elimination of coverture in the United States.

(*c*) This option is **incorrect** for multiple reasons. Firstly, it is too broad — the passage primarily discusses property laws and not the overall economic condition of married women. Further, the passage is not an 'evaluation' as the author does not present his opinion — it is a mere discussion of facts.

(*d*) This option is **incorrect**. It is too specific — the sole trader laws in the United States have only been discussed in the first paragraph and cannot be characterized as the primary purpose.

(*e*) This option is **incorrect**. The author does not present his/her opinion — hence, he/she does not aim to reconcile any expert opinion.

The correct answer is option (b).

34. **(a)** This is an inference question with a specific location provided. The best way to answer this question is to read the information in the location provided. Refer to paragraph 1/sentence 1, "The early legislative successes of the women's movement in the United States were in eliminating coverture and thus securing the rights of married women to own property, to control their earnings, and to enter into contracts."

The use of the transition word 'thus' shows a result. So, it can be inferred that the result of the elimination of coverture was that married women were able to own property, control their money, and enter into a contractual agreement. From this, it can also be inferred that before coverture was eliminated, married women did not have these rights and were dependent on their husbands.

Let us look at the answer options.

(*a*) This option is **correct**. This can be inferred from the information stated in the passage.

(*b*) This option is **incorrect**. According to the information in the passage, eliminating coverture is giving women the right to control their earnings and enter into contracts. It is not associated with women not wanting to become economically independent. Hence, the use of the words "choose whether she wanted to be economically independent" is incorrect.

(*c*) This option is **incorrect**. Coverture is a broad term that gave women freedom to "own property, to control their earnings, and to enter into contracts." Filing a patent is a very specific case and is not the best answer.

(*d*) This option is **incorrect**. According to the information in the passage, coverture is unrelated to child welfare.

(*e*) This option is **incorrect**. It is, perhaps, the opposite of the correct answer. "Eliminating coverture" indicates eliminating the status of women as a dependent on her husband, not otherwise.

The correct answer is option (a).

35. **(b)** **This is a detail question.**

Because information about sole trader laws is provided in the first paragraph, let us read the specific location.

Refer to paragraph 1/sentence 2, "In most states, the property laws preceded, or were enacted in conjunction with, laws granting married women control over their earnings and laws allowing women to engage in contracts or business without their husbands' consent, often referred to as "sole trader" laws."

The context says that the property laws were enacted together with sole trader laws, which

1. granted married women control over their earnings
2. allowed women to engage in contracts or business without their husbands' consent

Also, because this is an EXCEPT question, you must pick the answer that is either not stated or cannot be inferred from the information stated in the passage.

Let us look at the options.

(*a*) This option is **incorrect**. It is directly stated in the passage.

(*b*) This option is **correct**. This is a property law and is not related to the sole trader laws.

(*c*) This option is **incorrect**. It is stated in the passage.

(*d*) This option is **incorrect**. It is stated in the passage.

(*e*) This option is **incorrect**. It is stated in the passage.

The correct answer is option (b).

36. (a) This is a purpose question.

It asks for the purpose of the entire second paragraph. The best way to answer the question would be to reread the entire paragraph.

This paragraph discusses one theoretical approach to explaining why women were granted the right to property.

(*a*) This option is **correct**. It accurately describes the main idea of the paragraph.

(*b*) This option is **incorrect**. While the passage does discuss the impact of human capital on the welfare of children and the relationship between a man and a woman in a marriage, this cannot be characterized as the main idea of the paragraph. Rather, this is part of the bigger idea of stating the theoretical approach to explain property ownership by women.

(*c*) This option is **incorrect**. Like option (b), this is only part of the passage and cannot be characterized as the main idea of the paragraph.

(*d*) This option is **incorrect**. It is out of context and is not stated in the paragraph.

(*e*) This option is **incorrect**. The paragraph does not present a hypothetical scenario — it rather discusses a hypothesis.

The correct answer is option (a).

37. (d) This is an inference question.

It asks for the relationship between the two approaches discussed in the passage. Refer to paragraph 3/sentence 1, "An alternative, yet complementary, approach emphasizes how coverture reduces married women's incentives..."

Now, this tells us that while the second is an alternative to the first, it is also complementary. Let us look at the answer options.

(*a*) This option is **incorrect**. The two approaches are certainly not interchangeable — the author mentions that the second is an 'alternative'.

(*b*) This option is **incorrect**. The two approaches are complementary; the second does not weaken the first.

(*c*) This option is **incorrect**. The second does not bring out any exceptions.

(*d*) This option is **correct**. As the two approaches are complementary, it is fair to infer that the first completes the second.

(*e*) This option is **incorrect**. The two approaches are not opposite nor do they weaken each other.

The correct answer is option (d).

38. (a) This is a detail question.

To answer this correctly, you must reread certain specific locations in the passage. Refer to paragraph 3/last 2 sentences, "Further supporting these approaches, the enactment of married women's property laws led to increases in women's patenting of inventions: once women had the legal right to control their property and earnings in marriage, they were more willing to engage in commercial activities."

This information indicates that married women were more willing to engage in businesses and commercial activities knowing that they had control over their property and salary. This, perhaps, resulted in more patents being filed by women.

(*a*) This option is **correct**. It rightly discusses why more women patented their inventions.

(*b*) This option is **incorrect**. While the economic opportunities did increase, this option is unrelated to more women patenting their inventions.

(*c*) This option is **incorrect**. It is not related to the context.

(*d*) This option is **incorrect**. It is not related to the context.

(*e*) This option is **incorrect**. It is not related to the context.

The correct answer is option (a).

39. (e) This is a main point question.

Let's jot down the key points of each paragraph and then derive the main point.

Paragraph 1 :

- The "Big Three" schools of feminist thought: liberal, reformist, or mainstream feminism; radical feminism; and socialist/Marxist feminism
- A variety of newer forms of feminism has also emerged, some of which are viewed as branches of the three main traditions.

Paragraph 2 :

- Differences among gender-reform feminism, gender-resistant feminism, and gender-revolution feminism: their focus area

Paragraph 3 :

- Every feminist has an altered standpoint on the movement due to the varying hurdles women of different backgrounds come across
- Different experiences of patriarchy and oppression
- How 'masculine' and 'feminine' have been defined: gender values are natural or fostered?

Paragraph 4 :

- Men, primarily the causative agents of gender bias: men, the culprit
- Patriarchy is the homeland of males
- All men receive economic, physical, and psychological benefits from male supremacy

Paragraph 5 :

- A couple of feminists consider men to be oppressed by gender roles
- A feminist argued that feminism would benefit both genders and was part of the human rights movement
- A feminist argued that liberation was for both genders, as men's burdens would be shared
- A feminist argued that including men in the movement is the true universal feminist movement

Main point : Introduction to various feminist schools of thought; altered viewpoint on feminism by feminists; males are the culprits in women's oppression; the inclusion of men in the universal feminist and human rights movements

Let's look at each option one by one.

(*a*) This is **incorrect**. This is myopic in scope. It can be the central idea of paragraph 1 but not the passage.

(*b*) This is **incorrect**. Though this is too broad, it cannot be denied for not covering the scope of the passages. We see that many feminists' ideas and theories have been stated. The first two paragraphs talk about several feminist theories and their ideologies. The other three paragraphs talk about many feminists' perspectives on the movement. Although this option is not the best, if we do not find a better option, we can freeze on this.

(*c*) This is **incorrect**. This is myopic in scope. It can be the central idea of paragraph 5 but not the passage.

(*d*) This is **incorrect**. We cannot infer anything of the sort; this is factually incorrect information.

(*e*) This is **correct**. Again, this is broad in scope but covers all the five paragraphs. Given the choice between options (a) and (e), we must choose option (e) because feminist theories and their ideologies have been discussed only in the first two paragraphs, while many feminist thinkers' perspectives have been discussed in all five. This option covers option (b).

The correct answer is option (e).

40. **(c)** This is a question about finding inference. Let's look at each option one by one.

(*a*) This is **incorrect**. Refer to paragraph 2/sentence 2, "... gender-reform feminism is rooted in the political philosophy of liberalism with its emphasis on individual rights." In fact, gender-reform feminism advocates securing the individual rights of women.

(*b*) This is **incorrect**. No such advocacy of male-female equality is discussed in the passage.

(*c*) This is **correct**. Refer to paragraph 2/ sentence 4, "Gender-revolution feminism seeks to disrupt the social order through deconstructing its concepts and categories and analyzing the cultural reproduction of inequalities." From this sentence, we can surely infer that gender-revolution feminism advocates redefining the social structure of societies from the purview of gender discrimination.

(*d*) This is **incorrect**. No such comparison is made among the "Big Three" schools of feminist thought as is made in the first paragraph.

(*e*) This is **incorrect**. Refer to paragraph 3/sentence 3, "Issues have also arisen over how 'masculine' and 'feminine' have been defined, and whether previously gendered values are natural or nurtured." Given the reference, we cannot infer such an unsubstantiated statement.

The correct answer is option (c).

41. (e) This is a detail question.

Let's look at each option one by one.

(*a*) This is **incorrect**. While the first part of the sentence, "paragraph 4 considers men the perpetrators of gender discrimination," is correct, the second part, "paragraph 5 considers men oppressed by gender discrimination." is incorrect. Paragraph 5 talks about including men in the larger goal of the human rights movement and the universal feminist movement.

(*b*) This is **incorrect**. Again, while the first part of the sentence is correct, the second part is incorrect.

(*c*) This is **incorrect**. Again, like option (b), while the first part of the sentence is correct, the second part is not.

(*d*) This is **incorrect**. Again, like options (b) and (c), while the first part of the sentence is correct, the second part is not.

(*e*) This is **correct**. There is no contention about whether the first part is correct. Let's verbalize the second part, "paragraph 5 considers hyper feminism the causative agent of gender bias." Note that paragraph 5 advocates that women, as well as men, can be victims of the distorted view of feminism. When a lopsided view of feminism (hyper feminism) is considered, friction between the two genders is bound to surface.

The correct answer is option (e).

42. (e) This is a mix of detailed and inference questions. We have to dig out information from the passage and cross-check with the option statements, validating the correct option.

Let's analyze each statement one by one.

(*a*) This is **incorrect**. Referring to a phrase from paragraph 2, "...The misconception that slow decision-making stifles innovation, ..." This implies that the author opines that slow decision-making does not necessarily stifle innovation. However, extrapolating the author's opinion to fast decision-making hampers innovation is unsubstantiated.

(*b*) This is **incorrect**. Again, refer to a phrase from paragraph 2, "... the illusion that productivity requires speed." The author opines that the notion that productivity requires speed is an illusion (misconception); the author would rather disagree with this.

(*c*) This is **incorrect**. Refer to paragraph 1, "Why do organizations have so much trouble enabling employee creativity? The answer lies in subtle and deeply ingrained behaviors that prevent companies from creating a creative culture." It is not that company cultures are not conducive to fostering creativity; it is employees' deeply rooted behaviors that prevent companies from creating a creative culture. It's the opposite.

(*d*) This is **incorrect**. Refer to paragraph 3. The passage rather describes Dave as an efficient manager or a fast decision-maker. It can be inferred that he can formulate workable solutions but not innovative ones.

(*e*) This is **correct**. This is the gist of paragraph 5.

The correct answer is option (e).

43. (b) The main point of paragraph 4 lies in the last sentence:

"In such situations, resisting the temptation to find a solution quickly (and often less creatively), and instead urging the team (much to their frustration) to keep searching for more ideas can lead to more innovative and far-reaching solutions."

In other words, the sentence means that while dealing with complex problems, one must not strive for fast, but less creative, solutions; one must, instead, motivate the team to search for creative and far-reaching solutions.

Let's analyze each statement one by one.

(*a*) This is **incorrect**. First things first, the opposite of that is true. Refer to the phrase, "Resistance to premature closure — a key aspect of creativity." Secondly, the aspect of resistance to premature closure does not wholly encompass the main point of paragraph 4.

(*b*) This is **correct**. Although this is not verbatim of what we derived above, it is the closest in implication and wholly encompasses the main point of paragraph 4.

(*c*) This is **incorrect**. This is a classic mix-up. Refer to the sentence from paragraph 4, "While mantras like "move fast and break things" can help push people towards action, they can backfire when the underlying problem is complex." In other words, the "move fast and break things" policy can go wrong if the underlying problem is complex; however, we cannot infer that the "move fast and break things" policy can work well if the underlying problem is NOT complex. Moreover, this option is myopic; it does not talk about the aspect of creative/innovation solutions.

(*d*) This is **incorrect**. The problem with this option is the usage of the extreme word "all." It would be rational to state that to be innovative and creative, organizations must follow a slow decision-making policy while dealing with problems that are not complex.

(*e*) This is **incorrect**. This is rather the main point of paragraph 5, not paragraph 4.

The correct answer is option (b).

44. **(b)** The concept of resistance to premature closure is discussed in paragraph 4/ sentence 2, "Resistance to premature closure — a key aspect of creativity — is our ability to keep an open mind when we already have a potential solution."

The author opines that resistance to premature closure is a key aspect of creativity. Moreover, earlier in the passage, the author states that slow decision-making in complex problems is desirable and leads to innovative solutions. Later in the paragraph, the mantra "move fast and break things" is rejected because it does not lead to more ideas or more innovative and far-reaching solutions. Also, in paragraph 5, the author states that "To avoid premature closure, teams should arrive at an "almost final" decision and then intentionally delay action in favor of additional incubation time."

Coming back to the question, we have to pick an option that does NOT reflect resistance to premature closure. Thus, four out of five options would reflect resistance to premature closure.

Let us analyze each option one by one.

(*a*) This is **incorrect**. Appointing a team of experts to contemplate redesigning the engine implies that TMZ is not exercising fast decision-making but slow decision-making and that it wants a far-reaching solution to the leakage issue; thus, TMZ reflects resistance to premature closure attribute.

(*b*) This is **correct**. We see that, without deep diving into the issue, the HR department hurriedly recommends separating Suzy and David. This reflects fast decision-making. There is no reflection on creativity, innovation, or far-reaching consequences. What if one or both of Suzy and David have some issues? If so, the new set of colleagues might also have issues with them. What if none of them has any issues? It could be that the system itself is designed in such a way that it creates a rift between them. So, this option reflects a propensity for premature closure, or in other words, it does NOT reflect resistance to premature closure.

(*c*) This is **incorrect**. This is the crux of paragraph 5, as discussed above. This option reflects resistance to premature closure.

(*d*) This is **incorrect**. This option reflects effectiveness over efficiency, or it discourages fast decision-making. So, this option reflects resistance to premature closure.

(*e*) This is **incorrect**. This is also the crux of paragraph 5, as discussed above. This option reflects resistance to premature closure.

The correct answer is option (b).

45. **(a)** The misconception "productivity illusion" is discussed in paragraphs 1 and 2. Paragraph 2/sentence 3 defines it. It states the misconception: that slow decision-making stifles innovation often leads to the illusion that productivity requires speed.

So, the misconception is that productivity requires speed. Or, productivity requires fast decision-making.

With this understanding in mind, let us discuss the options. Except for option (a), we cannot infer any of the statements. The passage does not support any of these unsubstantiated statements.

The correct answer is option (a).

46. (c) This is a primary purpose/main point question. Let's write down the main points of each paragraph and then derive the main point of the passage.

Paragraph 1 : Subtle and deeply-ingrained employee behaviors prevent companies from creating a creative culture. The productivity illusion is a misconception that managers must overcome to effectively build creative cultures.

Paragraph 2 : Example of Pichai's slow decision-making. Misconceptions such as "slow decision-making stifles innovation" and "productivity requires speed" are dispelled. Pichai's slow decision-making should be viewed as a disciplined approach to innovation and productivity.

Paragraph 3 : Example of an efficient, productive, fast decision-maker; and a respected employee, Dave, is discussed. The author reserved the right to call Dave a great leader.

Paragraph 4 : Emphasis on the concept of resistance to premature closure, a key aspect of creativity. Resist less-creative solutions. The author advocates to keep searching for more ideas, more innovative & far-reaching solutions.

Paragraph 5 : Arrive at an "almost final" decision and then intentionally delay action in favor of additional incubation time to think of a better solution.

Taking all five paragraphs into account, we can draw the main point.

Main point : To come up with more innovative and far-reaching solutions, employees must foster creativity in decision-making. Let's analyze each option one by one.

(a) This is **incorrect**. Dispelling the productivity illusion misconception is certainly one of the key points of the passage, but it is not the primary purpose of the passage. The productivity illusion misconception is discussed only in paragraphs 1, 2, and 3.

(b) This is **incorrect**. Slow decision-making (in complex problems) is certainly one of the key points of the passage, but it is not the primary purpose of the passage. This aspect is discussed only in paragraphs 2, 4 and 5.

(c) This is **correct**. As discussed above and in the main point, the primary purpose of the passage is to emphasize creativity in decision-making or problem-solving. Furthermore, creativity, directly or indirectly, is reflected throughout the passage.

(d) This is **incorrect**. In paragraph 1, only one factor (not multiple factors) is discussed. It prevents companies from creating a creative culture due to employees' subtle and deeply ingrained behaviors. This option is not only incorrect but also narrow in scope.

(e) This is **incorrect**. Indeed, one of the purposes of the passage is to dismiss the misconception that slow

decision-making stifles innovation, but that is not the main purpose of the passage. Moreover, this aspect is discussed only in paragraphs 2 and 4.

The correct answer is option (c).

47. **(c)** This is a question about inference, but we have to find the option that cannot be inferred. In other words, four of the five options can be inferred or supported by the passage.

Let's look at each option one by one.

(*a*) This is **incorrect**. It is supported by the passage. Refer to paragraph 4/ sentence 1, "Trying to resolve things too quickly, especially for complex problems, is detrimental to innovation..." This implies that for complex problems, fast decision-making is detrimental, or slow decision-making is preferred. In paragraph 2 (the Pichai example), a disciplined approach to innovation and productivity is discussed. Here, the author implies that "disciplined approach" means "slow decision-making."

(*b*) This is **incorrect**. It is supported by the passage. The example of Dave, discussed in paragraph 3, is taken to illustrate the qualities of a productive and fast decision-maker.

(*c*) This is **correct**. This option takes us to paragraph 5. All is fine with this option except the extreme word "invariably." The author does not mean that intentionally delaying action in favor of additional incubation time ALWAYS leads to better solutions. In fact, in the last sentence, he/she even writes, "If the team cannot find a better approach during the incubation period, it should proceed with its original solution."

(*d*) This is **incorrect**. It is supported by the passage. This statement is, in fact, the rephrased version of the main point of paragraph 5, "... teams should arrive at an "almost final" decision and then intentionally delay action in favor of additional incubation time [to find a better solution]."

(*e*) This is **incorrect**. It is supported by the passage. Refer to paragraph 2 (the Pichai example). Taking two phrases, "...articles critical of Google CEO Sundar Pichai argued that Pichai's slow decision-making process stifled innovation." and "...it is just as likely that Pichai is taking a disciplined approach to innovation and productivity." The author advocates that for complex problems, slow decision-making is desirable for innovation.

The correct answer is option (c).

48. **(d)** **This is a detail question.**

Let us look at the options one by one.

(*a*) This option is **incorrect**. Refer to paragraph 1/sentence 3, "... there are some differences in the skeletal structure of ethnic groups." So, this is true.

(*b*) This option is **incorrect**. Refer to paragraph 1/sentence 2, "The storage of fat for people in these groups is more likely to be in the trunk and upper limbs, both places that are associated **with increased chances of health problems** when associated with excess fat." So, this is true.

(*c*) This option is **incorrect**. This fact has to be inferred from the passage; it is not directly stated. For American Indians, the author blames "natural selection" and for Pacific Islanders, the author blames "thrifty genes" as the causes, or genetic tenancy, of obesity. So, this is true.

(*d*) This option is **correct**. This is not true; it is extreme. Though the author states that there is a correlation between obesity and psychotic symptoms, that American ethnic groups have a **genetic tendency** to contract psychiatric disorders is not implied.

(*e*) This option is **incorrect**. Refer to paragraph 1/sentence 6, "... Since there are differences between ethnic groups and their rates of obesity." So, this is true.

The correct answer is option (d).

49. (e) This is a main point question.

Reading the passage, we find that the passage talks about the obesity problem in many ethnic groups in the US, especially American Indians and Pacific Islanders. Genetic causes of obesity are discussed. The author stresses that both groups have different reasons for obesity, and thus, each group has a different weight loss program.

In the second paragraph, the author discusses psychiatric issues with the obese. It states that though obesity is not considered a psychiatric diagnosis, there is a correlation between obesity and psychotic symptoms. It further adds that there is significantly higher rates of depression and psychosocial disabilities among the obese.

Main point : Understand the causes of obesity in American ethnic groups, design different weight loss programs for American Indians and Pacific Islander groups, and address the issue of psychotic symptoms.

The only option that best covers the scope is option (e); though it does not address the issue of psychotic symptoms, it is the best of all. Option (b) is incorrect because the passage does not provide an overview of obesity but rather specific concerns about obesity among American ethnic groups.

Other options are either too vague or irrelevant.

The correct answer is option (e).

50. (e) This is a detail question.

3. Let us look at the questions one by one.

(*a*) This option is **incorrect**. This is factually incorrect. The opposite might be true: obese people can suffer from depression and psychosocial disabilities.

(*b*) This option is **incorrect**. No such information is available in the passage.

(*c*) This option is **incorrect**. The passage states that different weight loss programs must be designed for different ethnic groups; however, there is no reference to "how" those must be designed.

(*d*) This option is **incorrect**. No such information is available in the passage. This can be an unsubstantiated inference.

(*e*) This option is **correct**. The passage discusses the reasons for obesity among American Indians. It proposed that, because of natural selection, those individuals that were obese survived during the time when America was being settled. So, natural selection is the possible cause of obesity for American Indians. Similarly, there is a hypothesis that Pacific Islanders have "thrifty genes" that allow for the storage of excess fat during times when there is plenty of food to allow for food shortages and migration.

The correct answer is option (e).

51. (b) This is a detail question.

Let us look at the options one by one.

(*a*) This option is **incorrect**. This is not supported; no information to support this claim is given in the passage. Though the author states that there is a correlation between obesity and psychotic symptoms, that American ethnic groups exhibit significantly higher rates of psychosocial disabilities is not implied.

(*b*) This option is **correct**. Refer to paragraph 1/sentence 2, "The storage of fat for people in these groups is more likely to be in the trunk and upper limbs." So, this is supported.

(*c*) This option is **incorrect**. No such information is available in the passage. This can be an unsubstantiated inference.

(*d*) This option is **incorrect**. This is not supported. Refer to paragraph 1/ sentence 3, "While there are some differences in the skeletal structure of ethnic groups, this alone does not account for differences in obesity prevalence." Though the sentence means that the ethnic groups have some differences in skeletal structures, as compared to whites,' we cannot infer that the ethnic groups have similarities in their skeletal structures.

(*e*) This option is **incorrect**. This is true only for Pacific Islanders, not for all ethnic groups.

The correct answer is option (b).

52. (a) This is a detail question.

To answer this question, you must reread specific locations in the passage and eliminate answer options. However, because this is an EXCEPT question, you are required to choose an answer that is not stated in the passage or cannot be implied from the given information.

The benefits of cycling for women are stated in the first and third paragraphs. So, it would help to read those locations. Let us look at the options one by one.

(*a*) This option is **correct**. The passage does not show the link between bicycling and fitness for women.

(*b*) This option is **incorrect**. It is stated in the passage. Refer to paragraph 3/ sentence 1-4, "But, the freedom that many women found on the bike took many forms, not the least of which was clothing. The restrictive corsets and long skirts that women wore were not exactly conducive to pedaling. Cycling required a more comfortable and practical form of clothing. Those women who did adopt a new outfit, often loose-fitting trousers known as bloomers..."

(*c*) This option is **incorrect**. It is clearly stated in the passage. Refer to paragraph 1/sentence 3-4, "A woman on a bicycle no longer needed to depend on a man for transportation. She could come and go as she pleased."

(*d*) This option is **incorrect**. It can be inferred from the information given in the passage. Refer to paragraph 1/ sentence 3-4, "A woman on a bicycle no longer needed to depend on a man for transportation. She could come and go as she pleased."

(*e*) This option is **incorrect**. Refer to paragraph 1/sentence 2, "Riding a bicycle gave women new confidence and mobility, and challenged Victorian restrictions on female behavior."

The correct answer is option (a).

53. (b) This is a purpose question.

To answer purpose questions, you must read the context in which a given idea is stated. So, reading one line above and one line below the idea in question is always recommended.

The question asks why the author mentions Susan Anthony in the passage. The context (paragraph 1/last sentence) says, "Enthusiasm for biking and women's rights became so entwined that famed women rights leader Susan Anthony once said that the bicycle had done more to emancipate women than anything else in the world."

This sentence indicates that two entities — women biking and women's rights — became very closely connected. It brings up Susan Anthony in the same context, referring to her as a "famed women rights leader."

So, the purpose of bringing in Susan Anthony is to show how closely connected bicycling and the women's rights movement were. Let us look at the options one by one.

(*a*) This option is **incorrect**. The context does not discuss any women's rights leaders other than Susan Anthony. So, an inference about other women's rights leaders' views on women's cycling cannot be made.

(*b*) This option is **correct**. This option correctly links the bicycle and women's rights campaign.

(*c*) This option is **incorrect**. While it can be partially true (we cannot infer that the lack of dependence on men was the "primary" advantage of cycling), it is irrelevant to Susan Anthony.

(*d*) This option is **incorrect**. Susan Anthony is not brought up merely to show that she was a prominent figure in the women's rights campaign. She is discussed to show the relationship between the women's rights campaign and the bicycle.

(*e*) This option is **incorrect**. It is vague and is irrelevant to Susan Anthony.

The correct answer is option (b).

54. (c) This is an application question.

You are asked to pick an answer that would not be an example of a critic of women's cycling.

Refer to paragraph 2, "Some critics warned that the bicycle would harm women's health. The sensitivity and fragility of women were a common theme. Women's magazines often featured doctors' warnings of the dangers the bike posed to women's health. Others said the bicycle would get young women into trouble by allowing them to stray further from watching eyes during courtship. A woman on a bike was a threat to the social order."

Also, refer to paragraph 3, sentence 4, "Those women who did adopt a new outfit, often loose-fitting trousers known as bloomers, earned the scorn and mockery of cartoonists and critics who viewed a woman in pants as unfeminine and scandalous."

By reading these locations, we get a fair idea of the beliefs of the critics. Let us look at the options one by one.

(a) This option is **incorrect**. It directly points to a doctor who spreads the idea that cycling is not conducive to women's health.

(b) This option is **incorrect**. The editor discourages women from riding bicycles and calls it "inappropriate." This clearly points to him/her being a critic of women riding bicycles.

(c) This option is **correct**. The teacher endorses cycling by women, referring to it as a phenomenon that will make women independent and free.

(d) This option is **incorrect**. This activist believes that even moderate bicycling is harmful to women's health, making him/her a critic of women's cycling.

(e) This option is **incorrect**. The lawyer is clearly a critic of women bicycling: he/she says that women could become masculine in their behavior and appearance if they rode cycles.

The correct answer is option (c).

55. (d) This is a main point question.

To answer this question appropriately, you must choose an answer that encapsulates the essence of the entire passage. So, let us look at the purpose of each paragraph.

The first paragraph introduces the concept of dress reform and the activists behind it. The author provides his/her opinion at the end of paragraph one, stating that the group of dress reformists was so varied that it was "easy to forget they were advocating one cause: the transformation of American women's fashions to improve health and comfort." From here, we can infer that the dress reformers had varied perspectives on dress reform.

The second paragraph focuses on the group of dress reformists from 1850-1870 and elaborates on their ideas and beliefs. The third paragraph, on the other hand, discusses the dress reformers of 1870 to 1900, discussing their values and beliefs.

So, on the whole, the passage discusses the dress reformers of 1850 to 1900 and elaborates on their belief system. Let us look at the options one by one.

(a) This option is **incorrect**. While the author does, perhaps, review the work of dress reformists, he/she does not "approve" of their work. Rather, he/she does convey that because of the diversity of the reformists, it was not easy to remember that they were all supporting the same cause.

(*b*) This option is **incorrect**. Firstly, the author does not provide a prelude to the dress reforms; rather, he/she discusses the reforms of the period of 1850-1900. This is also why the second part of the option is incorrect - the dress reforms of only the "late nineteenth century" are not discussed. Rather, the reforms from mid- to the end of the nineteenth century are discussed.

(*c*) This option is **incorrect**. The author certainly discusses the perspectives of the dress reformists of the second half of the nineteenth century. However, their "success" is not discussed - whether they were successful or not in bringing about the dress reforms is uncertain.

(*d*) This option is **correct**. The author discusses the perspectives of dress reformers from 1850 to 1870.

(*e*) This option is **incorrect**. While the author shows the differences in opinion between the reformers of the two periods, he/she does not reconcile the differences between them.

The correct answer is option (d).

56. (b) This is a purpose question.

To answer it correctly, you must understand the context in which the sentence is used. Read paragraph 1/ sentence 3-5, "Activists of the dress-reform movement were manifold, pooling their energies into small task forces with varying agendas. Dress reformers included regular doctors, health reformers, spiritualists, and women's-rights activists. Obviously, this was a diverse crowd, and predictably, regular licensed doctors addressed dress reform in radically different ways than spiritualists."

We must understand why the author has listed the professions of these dress reformers. The use of the word "manifold" tells us that the group of dress reformers was varied. Also, the subsequent sentence reveals that this diverse set of reformers had "radically different" approaches to dress reform. So, it can be inferred that the author lists the professions of all the dress reformers to reinforce that they had different views from each other.

Let us look at the options one by one.

(*a*) This option is **incorrect**. The broader idea of mentioning the professions of the reformers is not to show that they had small taskforces but to demonstrate that their approaches to dress reform were different.

(*b*) This option is **correct**. It rightly describes the purpose of the author in mentioning the list of professions of dress reformers.

(*c*) This option is **incorrect**. Firstly, the option is very strongly worded; the use of the words "never be achieved" conveys this. Furthermore, at this point, the author does not bring up the idea of dress reforms not being successful; he/she merely mentions that the approach of each of these groups towards dress reforms was different.

(*d*) This option is **incorrect**. All professional groups, other than the ones mentioned, are out of context.

(*e*) This option is **incorrect**. The author does not provide his/her opinion on whether the inclusion of these groups is justified or not.

The correct answer is option (b).

57. (e) **This is a detail question.**

Refer to paragraph 1/last sentence, "For fifty years, these individuals shared an interest in improving the health of American middle- and upper-class women; however, their motivations and convictions were so varied, it is easy to forget they were advocating one cause: the transformation of American women's fashions to improve health and comfort."

This indicates that the "motivations and convictions" of the dress reformers were varied; hence, it was easy to forget that they were supporting the same cause.

Let us look at the options one by one.

(a) This option is **incorrect**. The passage does not indicate that the reformers had "ulterior motives" behind supporting the dress reform movement.

(b) This option is **incorrect**. The idea of taking decisions is not stated in the passage, let alone taking decisions with consensus.

(c) This option is **incorrect**. The idea of the beauty of women is only a minute part of the reason the two groups disagreed. In totality, they disagreed on many other points, such as how dress reform could advance women in society, how it could showcase their worth, and how women should not believe the societal conventions of beauty.

(d) This option is **incorrect**. While the author does mention that the dress reformers came from varied backgrounds, we cannot infer that no two reformers came from the same background.

(e) This option is **correct**. It closely matches with the words, motivations and convictions, as stated in the passage.

The correct answer is option (e).

58. (e) This is an application question that asks for an example that does NOT demonstrate the dress reformers of 1850 to 1870.

The characteristics of dress reformers of this period are stated in paragraph 2. Refer to paragraph 2/sentence 3-5, "Their chief priorities differed, yet all of these reformers shared an interest in women's health. They saw dress reform as an opportunity to advance women into positions of economic, social, and political equality with men; they believed dress reform could advertise a woman's usefulness and worth. This first generation of dress reformers often used dress to attack gender norms, suggesting that women should not rely solely on societal notions of beauty for their self-worth."

Let us look at the options one by one.

(a) This option is **incorrect**. Because these dress reformers focused on women's health, this is an example of a dress reformer from this period.

(b) This option is **incorrect**. Because these reformers saw "dress reform as an opportunity to advance women into positions of economic, social, and political equality with men," this is an example of the dress reformers of this period.

(c) This option is **incorrect**. Because this group believed that "women should not rely solely on societal notions of beauty for their self- worth," this is an example of the dress reformers of this period.

(*d*) This option is **incorrect**. If this teacher believes that dress reforms could result in women's potential being unlocked, she certainly belongs to the first group.

(*e*) This option is **correct**. Refer to paragraph 3/sentence 7, "While earlier reformers challenged gender norms that expected women to remain in the home as mothers and archetypes of fashion, the second generation of reformers supported these roles for women." So, if a woman believes that dress reform could interfere with her maternal duties, she belongs to the second group of dress reformers, rather than the first.

The correct answer is option (e).

59. (a) This is a detail question.

Ideally, to solve such questions, you must read specific locations in the passage and reach the answer using elimination. However, because there is no specific location you can refer to, the best way to solve this question is by elimination. However, because this is an EXCEPT question, you are required to pick an answer that is an agreement between the reformers of both periods.

There are a few clues in the passage that show what the two groups of dress reformers agreed upon. Refer to paragraph 1/sentence 2, "Advocates of "dress reform" suggested that women abandon traditional fashions and adopt more comfortable, healthful clothing, although the dress-reform advocates did not agree on one alternative to fashion." This indicates that both the reformers agreed on comfortable, healthful clothing for women.

Refer to paragraph 3/sentence 4, "They shared their predecessors' interest in women's health." This indicates that both the groups agreed that dress reforms must be conducive to women's health.

Let us look at the options one by one.

(*a*) This is **correct**. The idea of women's health was an agreement between the two groups.

(*b*) This is **incorrect**. While the first group was interested in challenging social norms, the second was not.

(*c*) This is **incorrect**. While the first group advocated for the role of women in the workforce, the second did not.

(*d*) This is **incorrect**. While the first group challenged the societal notions of beauty and encouraged women to not rely on them, the second did not.

(*e*) This is **incorrect**. Refer to paragraph 3/last sentence, "And, unlike their predecessors of the 1850s, female dress reformers rarely wore their reformed clothing in public, preferring to educate women on the need for change before adopting an unusual dress themselves." This indicates that while the earlier reformers wore reformed clothing in public, the latter did not.

The correct answer is option (a).

60. (b) This is a detail question.

Ideally, to solve such questions, you must read specific locations in the passage and reach the answer using elimination. Refer to paragraph 3/sentence 5-6, "However, they did not attempt to use dress reform to campaign for women's equality or challenge the gender norms of the late-nineteenth century. Instead, they reinforced these gender norms, campaigning for dress reform on maternalistic and aesthetic grounds."

This indicates that this group was campaigning for dress reform for "maternalistic and aesthetic" reasons.

Of the given options, the only one that is appropriate is option (b) - the perception of beauty in women, which refers to aesthetics. The other four options are irrelevant.

The correct answer is option (b).

61. (c) This is a main point question.

The correct answer must accurately describe the overall purpose of the passage. To answer this question, let us look at the information provided in each paragraph.

The first paragraph gives an introduction to the concept of the Net Promoter Score (NPS), while the second gives more details about the same. The third paragraph discusses the Customer Satisfaction (CSAT) metric. The fourth paragraph discusses the differences between the two. It ends with the author's opinion, with the author stating that the NPS is, perhaps, a more efficacious metric than CSAT.

So, the primary purpose of the passage is to give more details about the two metrics and to assess their efficaciousness.

Let us look at the answer options.

(a) This option is **incorrect**. First, the author does not merely describe the two metrics. He/She also evaluates them by giving his opinion. Secondly, NPS is not merely a measure of "customer satisfaction." Hence, it cannot be called a metric of customer satisfaction; rather, it is a metric of customer loyalty and experience.

(b) This option is **incorrect**. The main purpose of the author is not merely to state that NPS is better than CSAT - this idea is just one part of the passage.

(c) This option is **correct**. Initially, the author discusses the two indices. Later, he/she evaluates the features of both to give his/her opinion on which might be a better indicator of customer experience.

(d) This option is **incorrect**. The author does not seek to recommend that all organizations must use NPS or CSAT.

(e) This option is **incorrect**. It is incomplete. The author is not merely listing the pros and cons of the two metrics - he/she is also evaluating them.

The correct answer is option (c).

62. (a) This is an inference question.

It is asking for an example of the follow-up question. Refer to paragraph 2/sentence 2, "The overall NPS system is important because it allows businesses to ask follow-up questions as part of the standard NPS survey – by asking customers why they have given a specific score, organizations of any size can understand what they are doing well..."

From this information, it is safe to infer that the follow-up question asks customers why they have given a specific score. Let us look at the answer options.

(*a*) This option is **correct**. It appropriately asks customers the reason for the score they have given.

(*b*) This option is **incorrect**. Whether the customer would use the products or services in the future is unrelated to the NPS follow-up question.

(*c*) This option is **incorrect**. It is redundant — asking for a rating on a 1 to 5 scale is not the purpose of the NPS follow-up question; it is rather the purpose of CSAT.

(*d*) This option is **incorrect**. From where the customer got information about this retail store is unrelated to the NPS follow-up question.

(*e*) This option is **incorrect**. The ease of shopping is unrelated to the NPS follow-up question.

The correct answer is option (a).

63. (b) This is a question testing your understanding of the organization of the content in the passage. To answer this question, you must understand the flow of the content.

The first paragraph of the passage gives an introduction to the concept of the Net Promoter Score (NPS). The second adds more details to the first, discussing the various attributes of NPS. The third paragraph discusses the Customer Satisfaction (CSAT) metric and its various features. The fourth paragraph discusses the difference between the two. The passage concludes with the author's opinion, stating that the NPS is, perhaps, a more efficacious metric than CSAT.

In sum, the author introduces and discusses the features of two metrics. Finally, he/she assesses the two and provides his/her opinion. Let us look at the answer options.

(*a*) This option is **incorrect**. The first half of the option is correct: the author does discuss two conventional metrics for measuring a phenomenon — customer experience. However, the second half is incorrect. The author does not discuss the pros and cons of customer experience.

(*b*) This option is **correct**. It accurately describes the organization of the text in the passage.

(*c*) This option is **incorrect**. The first part of the option is certainly correct — the passage does discuss a measure and its attributes. However, the word "contrary" is incorrect and vague — the two indices are competing but not contrary.

(*d*) This option is **incorrect**. Firstly, the cons of NPS have not been discussed in the passage. Secondly, the author does not reject CSAT; he/she merely states that NPS is the more effective of the two.

(*e*) This option is **incorrect**. The author does not recommend any further study in the passage.

The correct answer is option (b).

64. (a) This is a purpose question.

It asks for the purpose of the last paragraph only. To answer this question, it is important to read the paragraph again.

This paragraph compares and evaluates the two metrics. The author clearly states his/her opinion by saying that the NPS is, perhaps, a more efficacious option than CSAT.

Let us look at the answer options.

(*a*) This option is **correct**. In stating the differences between the two options, the author is determining which is the better metric.

(*b*) This option is **incorrect**. It is, perhaps, the opposite of the correct choice. In this passage, the author is seeking to reinforce why NPS might be a more effective metric than CSAT, not otherwise.

(*c*) This option is **incorrect**. This paragraph does not merely seek to discuss the pros and cons of both the metrics; it seeks to provide an answer to which metric is better. Further, the disadvantage of NPS is not discussed.

(*d*) This option is **incorrect**. Essentially, the paragraph outlines the difference between the two metrics. It discusses one drawback of CSAT and the positives of NPS. So, to say that this paragraph discusses a reason for the "adoption" of CSAT by business is incorrect as the flaw of CSAT is discussed in the paragraph.

(*e*) This option is **incorrect**. In this paragraph, the author does not seek to emphasize why each of the two metrics is important. Rather, he/she seeks to emphasize why the NPS is better and more effective than CSAT.

The correct answer is option (a).

65. (c) This is a detail question.

For detail questions, ideally, you are required to reread specific locations in the passage and eliminate options to arrive at the right answer. However, because there is no specific location that is given in this question, the better approach is to eliminate answer options.

Also, because this is an EXCEPT question, the one option that cannot be determined from the passage or is irrelevant to the information provided, is the right answer.

Let us look at the answer options.

(*a*) This option is **incorrect**. Refer to paragraph 2/sentence 2, "The overall NPS system is important because it allows businesses to ask follow-up questions as part of the standard NPS survey — by asking customers why they have given a specific score, organizations of any size can understand what they are doing well and where they could improve..." So, businesses of all sizes can use NPS to improve their customer experience.

(*b*) This option is **incorrect**. Refer to paragraph 4/sentence 2, "However, the NPS system asks customers to take a much wider view of the brand or product, and focuses on their intention, rather than their overall feeling of satisfaction..." So, the NPS does give a wider, or more holistic, view of organizations and their customers.

(*c*) This option is **correct**. The author mentions that NPS, not CSAT, can be expressed as a percentage.

(*d*) This option is **incorrect**. It can be inferred from the passage. Refer to paragraph 2/sentence 2, "The overall NPS system is important because it allows businesses to ask follow-up questions as part of the standard NPS survey — by asking customers why they have given a specific score, organizations of any size can understand what they are doing well and where they could improve; track and quantify a score over time, creating internal benchmarks; and rally all employees around one mission-critical objective: earning more enthusiastic customers." So, NPS can help employees become more aligned with the goal of earning more enthusiastic customers.

(*e*) This option is incorrect. Refer to paragraph 1/sentence 1, "Net Promoter Score (NPS) is a measure used to gauge customer loyalty and experience with a company." From this information, it is fair to infer that a good NPS score correlates with higher customer loyalty.

The correct answer is option (c).

66. (b) The passage starts with presenting the concept of temporal discounting (paragraph 1), then discusses some traits of an individual with a high discounting rate (paragraph 2), then goes on to describe how marketers exploit this concept (paragraph 3), and finally lists the aspects that affect an individual's discounting rate and a measure to control it (paragraph 4).

With this outline in mind, let us analyze the options one by one.

(*a*) This option is **incorrect**. The 'phenomenon explored by behavioral economists' is, of course, temporal discounting. However, the disparate elements that affect temporal discounting (or the discounting rate) are only cited in paragraph 4. Therefore, this option does not summarize the all-inclusive scope of the passage.

(*b*) This option is **correct**. Paragraph 1 presents the 'phenomenon explored by behavioral economists', paragraphs 2 and 3 deliberate on the impact of this phenomenon on individuals, and paragraph 4 recommends a way to control this phenomenon.

(*c*) This option is **incorrect**. Only paragraph 3 talks about a marketing strategy. Therefore, this option does not summarize the all-inclusive scope of the passage.

(*d*) This option is **incorrect**. The long-term repercussion of (high) temporal discounting is briefly cited at the end of paragraph 2. Short-term repercussion is not detailed in the passage.

(*e*) This option is **incorrect**. The passage only states temporal discounting as a normal trait; it never probes into why this trait exists in individuals. Therefore, the first half of this option statement is outside the scope of the passage; regarding the second half, while the passage does suggest a way to address (control) temporal discounting, this option statement wrongly uses the plural word 'ways.'

The correct answer is option (b).

67. (a) Temporal discounting is the propensity to favor smaller, but sooner, rewards over larger, but later, rewards in intertemporal selection.

Since phenomenon A is the opposite of temporal discounting, it follows that phenomenon A is the propensity to favor larger, but later, rewards over smaller, but sooner, rewards (in intertemporal selection).

Let us analyze the options one by one.

(*a*) This option is **correct**. It aligns with the analysis done above.

(*b*) This option is **incorrect**. Temporal discounting is a phenomenon that applies to intertemporal selection (two different time frames); however, this option only talks about a single point in time (the present time — sooner).

(*c*) This option is **incorrect**. The question statement tells us that phenomenon A applies to intertemporal selection; however, this option does not state two different time frames.

(*d*) This option is **incorrect**. The option-statement in fact describes the phenomenon of the passage and not the opposite of it, i.e., phenomenon A.

(*e*) This option is **incorrect**. Like option (d), to defer costs into the future and grab sooner rewards is the crux of the phenomenon of the passage and not the opposite of it, i.e., phenomenon A.

The correct answer is option (a).

68. (e) Person A is more impulsive than person (b).

As per paragraph 2, for future rewards

(Discounting factor of person A)>(Discounting factor of person B)

Person A is so impatient that he/she cannot wait 2 months even when the offer is to **double** his/her money; he/she would rather have $20 today. Person B is relatively patient. He/She can wait longer than person A.

We need to find the one option that person B will **not reject** outright. Let us analyze the options one by one.

(a) This option is **incorrect**. To process this option easily, let's say that 'less than $20' means $18. This person's money would more than double in two months and if he/she still goes for $18 today, he/she is even more impulsive than person A. Person B, who is less impulsive than person A, would not make such a choice.

(b) This option is **incorrect**. Let's say that 'more than $40' means $42. This person's money would more than double in two months and if he/she still goes for $20 today, he/she is even more impulsive than person A. Person B would not make such a choice.

(c) This option is **incorrect**. To process this option easily, let's say that 'less than two months later' means 1 month. This person's money would double in only one month and if he/she still goes for $20 today, he/she is even more impulsive than person A. Person B would not make such a choice.

(d) This option is **incorrect**. We cannot comment on it. Let's take two scenarios: (1) Say, person B gets $18 now and $22 two months later. Person B will surely accept this offer, as he/she will not get more than double the money in two months that he/she gets now. (2) Say, person B gets $1 now and $38 two months later. Person B will surely reject this offer as he/she will not get more than double (in fact 38 times) the money in two months that he gets now. This option is inconclusive.

(e) This option is **correct**. Person B, being less impulsive than person A, would have a lower discounting rate than person A. So, the perceived value of $40 two months later could seem bigger to him/her than $20 today and therefore, he/she might choose this option. (We cannot be sure that he/she would choose it because we do not know his discounting rate — just how less impulsive than person A, he/she is.)

The correct answer is option (e).

69. **(b)** The passage mentions marketers in paragraph 3, which mentions the following ways in which they apply temporal discounting to increase their product sales:

- "Buy now, pay later" strategy
- Promote free trials
- Convince a customer that buying => instant reward of enhanced public image

Let us analyze the options one by one.

(*a*) This option is **incorrect**. The marketer's uprightness about future costs of using its product is not argued as a strategy in the passage.

(*b*) This option is **correct**. Easy credits facilitate the "buy now, pay later" strategy, which, as the passage mentions, marketers do offer to increase their sales.

(*c*) This option is **incorrect**. The passage suggests that long-term benefits get discounted in the customers' minds, and, therefore, are not very effective. Instead, the marketers highlight the short-term, or immediate, benefits to influence potential customers.

(*d*) This option is **incorrect**. This is an outright flawed strategy, bound to fail as both aspects are negative.

(*e*) This option is **incorrect**. The passage does not mention marketers' relative preferences between their higher-priced and lower-priced products or between their beneficial and unsafe products.

The correct answer is option (b).

70. **(d)** Paragraph 3, in a nutshell, discusses how marketers apply the concept of temporal discounting. Let us analyze the options one by one.

(*a*) This option is **incorrect**. This is not a paragraph that explains the reason for the phenomenon.

(*b*) This option is **incorrect**. Paragraph 3 offers no exception to any general observation made in paragraph 2.

(*c*) This option is **incorrect**. Paragraph 1 describes the phenomenon of temporal discounting. An example of temporal discounting ($1,000 now or $1,200 in one year) is provided in paragraph 1 itself. Paragraph 3 provides no example.

(*d*) This option is **correct**. As noted above, paragraph 3 discusses how marketers apply temporal discounting, which is elaborated in paragraph 1.

(*e*) This option is **incorrect**. Paragraph 3 discusses application (marketing strategy), and not repercussions of a phenomenon, temporal discounting.

The correct answer is option (d).

71. **(e)** Persons with high discounting rates are, as mentioned in paragraph 2, impulsive, impatient, and have poor self- control.

Let us analyze the options one by one.

(*a*) This option is **incorrect**. Such a vendor is acting in his/her own best interest. His/Her act does not demonstrate his/her impulsiveness, impatience, or poor self-control.

(*b*) This option is **incorrect**. Such an employee could resist the temptation of having a 10% higher salary today, preferring instead to have a 15% (15% > 10%) much higher salary in the future. Therefore, this employee shows self-control and must have a low discounting rate.

(*c*) This option is **incorrect**. Such a person is saving his/her better reward (the high-quality restaurant) for later. So, he/she is preferring 'larger, but later, rewards' over 'smaller, but sooner, rewards.' This shows, he/she is a sensible decision-maker, possesses good self-control, and thus, has a low discounting rate.

(*d*) This option is **incorrect**. Such a person is sacrificing present desires for a financially better future. He/She prefers 'larger, but later, rewards' over 'smaller, but sooner, rewards.' So, he/she has a low discounting rate.

(*e*) This option is **correct**. So, the person has two options: (1) Each 250 grams of ice cream NOW or (2) 500 grams, double the quality, in parts. His/Her decision to choose option (1) suggests that he/she succumbs to temptation. So, he/she is likely to be someone with poor self-control and a high discounting rate.

The correct answer is option (e).

72. **(c)** We need to look for the option that does not impact the discounting rate. Let us analyze the options one by one.

(*a*) This option is **incorrect**. Paragraph 5 line 1 "The discounting rate for future rewards or costs vary inversely with age…)" mentions this as a factor that impacts discounting rate.

(*b*) This option is **incorrect**. Paragraph 1 mentions this as a factor that impacts discounting rate.

(*c*) This option is **correct**. The impact, if any, of the quality of the future rewards on the discounting rate is not mentioned in the passage.

(*d*) This option is **incorrect**. Paragraph 5 line 1 "The discounting rate for future rewards or costs vary … directly with the abundance of enticing distractions" mentions this as a factor that impacts discounting rate.

(*e*) This option is **incorrect**. Paragraph 5 line 2 "The discounting rate can be reduced by intensely visualizing the significant future rewards…" mentions this as a factor that impacts discounting rate.

The correct answer is option (c).

73. **(a)** Let us analyze the options one by one.

(*a*) This option is **correct**. This individual has poor self-control and often succumbs to the temptation to spend, instead of contributing to his/her retirement. So, he/she cannot be trusted to make a judicious decision in the present. However, as the passage mentions in paragraph 1, we are all capable of making rational choices about the distant future. Therefore, this individual should enter into a difficult-to-break commitment to save for his/her future.

(*b*) This option is **incorrect**. The question does not suggest that the reason for this individual's poor savings is that he/she is not convinced of his/her investment attractiveness. Rather, the individual's vulnerability is his/her poor self-control.

(*c*) This option is **incorrect**. For an individual with poor self-control, resolving to improve his/her retirement savings cannot be trusted; he/she can always break such resolve. The individual must take some concrete action to improve his/her retirement savings.

(*d*) This option is **incorrect**. Like option (c), this is also a kind of advisory statement that can be broken. The individual must take some concrete action to improve his/her retirement savings.

(*e*) This option is **incorrect**. This individual may already be aware of and aspire to — the long-term benefits of saving for his/her retirement. His/her weakness is that he/she discounts these benefits at a higher rate, and so the short-term costs of such savings appear quite large to him/her, and he/she ends up saving little.

The correct answer is option (a).

74. **(d)** Let us analyze the options one by one.

(*a*) This option is **incorrect**. The passage does not talk about the self-awareness, or lack thereof, of people with a high present-bias. They could be aware of their self-control problems, but they do not have self-control.

(*b*) This option is **incorrect**. The passage is all about intertemporal selections only; it talks about the kinds of intertemporal selections ("smaller, but sooner, rewards" > "larger, but later, rewards") that people with a high discounting rate for future rewards might make. The passage does not mention any relation between an individual's discounting rate and his/her tendency to make intertemporal choices.

(*c*) This option is **incorrect**. The passage does not mention that marketers selectively offer "buy now, pay later" programs to consumers with high credit-card debt.

(*d*) This option is **correct**. The passage mentions that people with high credit-card debt are those who have high discounting rate. The last paragraph suggests that visualizing the future repercussions might decrease the discounting rate. Keeping these two propositions together, we can infer that people with high credit-card debt are also likely to be the ones who rarely make a conscious effort to visualize the future consequences of fiscal imprudence.

(*e*) This option is **incorrect**. The lower the discount rate of an individual, the less impatient he/she is and the more self-control he/she has. Therefore, he/she is, in fact, more likely to assess the long-term costs and benefits of a product he/she plans to buy.

The correct answer is option (d).

75. (b) Observation : "Smaller, but sooner, rewards" > "Larger, but later, rewards" for most people

Passage's assertion : The above happens because people increasingly discount rewards, as the rewards move away from the present.

To answer this question, we need to find the statement that would weaken this assertion. This statement could be one that provides an alternative explanation for the observation, or it could cast doubt on the validity of this assertion.

Let us analyze the options one by one.

(*a*) This option is **incorrect**. This statement neither provides an alternative explanation for the observation nor does it discredit the passage's assertion.

(*b*) This option is **correct**. This statement provides an alternative explanation for the observation. If people have a natural tendency to avoid uncertainty — and the further a reward is, the more uncertain its realization is — then it stands to reason that people would prefer sooner (and therefore, less uncertain) rewards over future (and therefore, more uncertain) rewards, even if the sooner rewards are smaller than the future rewards.

(*c*) This option is **incorrect**. People tending to favor bigger rewards over smaller rewards makes it even more surprising that in intertemporal choice, they should prefer "smaller, but sooner, rewards" over "larger, but later, rewards". This option does not provide an alternative explanation for the observation.

(*d*) This option is **incorrect**. The passage does not mention any relationship between an individual's discounting rate for future rewards and his/her self-confidence. This option does not provide any alternative explanation for the observation, nor does it discredit the passage's assertion.

(*e*) This option is **incorrect**. The passage does not mention that the observation (for most people, "smaller, but sooner, rewards" > "larger, but later, rewards") holds only in the presence of distracting temptations. Therefore, this option does not provide an alternative explanation.

The correct answer is option (b).

76. (b) This is a main point question.

The correct answer to this question will capture the message of the passage as a whole.

Let us look at the purpose of each of the paragraphs.

The first paragraph introduces how drumming could be beneficial to children with emotional and behavioral difficulties, stating three major benefits: better control over reactions, better focus on tasks, and better communication skills.

The second paragraph discusses an experiment involving autistic children and the positive neurological changes that occur in such children as a result of drumming. In the third paragraph, the author concludes by stating how these changes are a "gratifying confirmation" of the power of drumming to heal. So, overall, the passage discusses how drumming can help improve the behavior of children with emotional and behavioral difficulties. Let us look at the options one by one.

(*a*) This option is **incorrect**. This passage does not pertain to "music" in general; rather, it focuses on drumming. Also, the term "good health" is a little vague.

(*b*) This option is **correct**. It rightly states that drumming has a positive impact on children with emotional and behavioral difficulties.

(*c*) This option is **incorrect**. The passage does not "evaluate" whether playing drums is beneficial; rather, it asserts that it is.

(*d*) This option is **incorrect**. The author does not give any recommendations in the passage.

(*e*) This option is **incorrect**. The description of the changes in the brains of autistic children is only one part of the passage and cannot be described as its primary purpose.

The correct answer is option (b).

77. **(a)** This is a critical-reasoning question based on the concept of strengthening the stated information.

If there is a reason X that causes result Y, to strengthen the argument, you must prove that

a. Only X causes Y.

b. No reason other than X can cause Y.

Lines 24-26 of the passage state the neurological changes that occur in children as a result of drumming. Any information that would confirm that these changes were, indeed, due to drumming and due to no other factor would strengthen the argument.

Because inferring an answer would be difficult, it is recommended that you eliminate the answer options.

Lines 24-26 of the passage state the neurological changes that occurred in children as a result of drumming. Any information that would confirm that these changes were, indeed, due to drumming and due to no other factor would strengthen the argument.

(*a*) This option is **correct**. If the FMRI brain scans of children belonging to both the groups were similar before the experiment started, it is, indeed, drumming that caused the positive neurological changes in one group.

(*b*) This option is **incorrect**. It is a weakener, rather than, a strengthener. If the children who drummed were also involved in other activities that strengthened their brain connections, then the neurological changes could have been due to the other activities, and not necessarily through drumming.

(*c*) This option is **incorrect**. Interest in drumming has no bearing on — and is irrelevant to — the stated information.

(*d*) This option is **incorrect**. It is irrelevant to the information stated in the passage.

(*e*) This option is **incorrect**. Even if the right dorsolateral prefrontal cortex and the right inferior frontal gyrus are the only two areas of the brain involved in attention control, this information does not strengthen the stated information.

The correct answer is option (a).

78. (e) This is a detail question.

You are merely required to read specific locations in the given passage and pick the options that most closely match the given options. However, because this is an EXCEPT question, you are required to pick that option which is either not stated in the passage or cannot be inferred from the passage.

Refer to paragraph 1/last sentence, "Researchers at the Clem Burke Drumming Project have shown that teaching such children to drum helps them to control their reactions more generally, **to focus more effectively on tasks** they are given, and to **communicate better** with people."

Refer to paragraph 2/sentence 10, "In particular, two regions involved in attention control, the right dorsolateral prefrontal cortex and the right inferior frontal gyrus, formed strong links, respectively, with places associated with **introspection** and with **areas involved in deciphering facial expressions**."

From these two areas, it can be inferred that drumming helps with introspection (self-evaluation and self-examination), communication, recognition of facial expressions, and focus on tasks.

The only option not stated in the passage is empathy.

The correct answer is option (e).

Data Insight

Chapter 1

Multi Source Reasoning

PASSAGE-1

Software Company Government Response

A bill before Parliament would require all of government to use only open-source software, i.e., software that is nonproprietary, based on code the user is allowed to redistribute and alter in any way. The bill appears to assume that open-source software is free. However, research has shown that the purchase cost of open source software is about 8% of the total cost associated with the use of the software, and that the cost of utilization– the sum of all non-purchase costs including installation, maintenance, administration, and downtime–is much higher than it is in the case of proprietary software.

The bill would require government to undergo an intensive program of software migration, at considerable immediate cost and risk. And because multiple versions of open-source software exist, the bill's measures are likely to increase compatibility problems between the information-technology systems of government agencies, as well as between government systems and private-sector systems.

Software Company Government Response

We are aware that open-source software is not always offered free of charge. And although savings are indeed mentioned in the bill, its primary aim is to protect citizen's free access to information. Because the bill requires that encoding of data not be tied to a single software provider, it is able to guarantee this free access.

The bill would indeed require government to begin an intensive process of software migration that would not otherwise be undertaken. However, the high cost of software migration in general is an argument in favor of the bill. The longer a particular information technology system is used, the more expensive migration to a different system becomes. Because open-source software allows the encoding of data in standard and adaptable formats, software migration becomes much easier and less expensive once open-source software is installed. And of course, migration from proprietary to open-source software would entail no greater cost than would migration between two different proprietary software systems.

For each of the following statements, select Undermines if it would, if true, undermine the arguments made in one or the other of the two passages. Otherwise, select Does not undermine.

Undermines	Does not undermine	
		Migration from proprietary software to open-source software would be significantly more expensive for the government thant would migration from proprietary software to other proprietary software.
		The measures included in the bill will, if complied with, ensure compatibility among software systems used by all the various relevant stakeholders.
		As a software package is used for a longer period of time, it becomes less expensive to migrate from that package to another.

PASSAGE 2

T1

The Sterling Plant utilizes a assembly line setup comprising of three conveyor belts. Furthermore, there are three inspection stations, each positioned at the end of a conveyor belt. In the tenth year of operation (Y10), the plant employed a total of 15 workers directly involved in the assembly line, with three workers assigned to man the inspection stations, one per station. During Y10, the assembly line at Sterling Plant produced 250,000 units, resulting in a profit of $15,000,000.

T2

For Year 11 (Y11), the Sterling Plant assembly line was modernized as follows:

Conveyor-belt speeds were increased by a fixed percentage.

The assembly line's administrative unit was restructured to maximize efficiency.

Each inspection post was automated, and the 3workers who formerly staffed the posts were laid off and were not replaced.

There were no other personnel changes on the assembly line for Y11.

T3

Year 10 > Year 11 > Table

Sterling Plant Assembly Line Modemization, Y11

Element of modermization project	Resulting increase in output for Y11, as % of Y10 output	Resulting increase in profit for Y11, as % of Y10 profit	Total cost of implement
Inspection-post automation	2%	5%	$100,000
Conveyor-belt speed increase	3%	4%	$45,000
Administrative unit restructuring	—	1%	$15,000
Total	5%	10%	$160,000

1. Which one of the following statements is supported by the information provided about the assembly line and the assembly-line modernization plan at the Sterling Plant?

A. On the assembly line, conveyor-beit speed is directly proportional to total annual output of assembled units.

B. Administrative unit restructuring accounted for the greatest increase in the dollar amount of profit from Y10 to Y11.

C. Conveyor-belt speed increase accounted for the greatest increase in the dollar amount of profit from Y10 to Y11.

D. Conveyor-belt speed increase accounted for the greatest increase in annual output of assembled units from Y10 to Y11.

E. Inspection-post automation accounted for the greatest increase in annual output of assembled units from Y10 to Y11.

2. For a given production year, let Q denote the total output, in assembled units, from the Sterling Plant assembly line, and let N denote the number of workers employed directly on the line. For each of the following statements about the quotient Q/N, select Yes if it is true based on the information provided. Otherwise, select No.

Yes	No	
		Q/N was less than 10,000 for Y10.
		Q/N was unchanged from Y10 to Y11.
		Q/N remained below 30,000 in Yi0 and Y11.

PASSAGE 3

T1: Discussion

Star Research is in the process of relocating to a new office space, which is laid out according to the provided Floor Plan. The office space consists of eight individual offices (numbered 111, 112, 114, 115, 116, 117, 120, and 121) and four cubicles (numbered 119A through 119D). Each employee will be assigned a single workspace, either an office or a cubicle, and there will be no more than one employee per office or cubicle. It should be noted that supervisors will not be assigned to work in cubicles. In cases where an employee has an immediate supervisor, the employee's workspace, whether an office or cubicle, must be located adjacent to their supervisor's office.

T2 : Table

The table lists the ten employees at Star Research and shows each employee's immediate supervisor, if any. The supervisors are also employees, so each supervisor's name appears in both columns.

Employee	Supervisor
Saina	Claire
Regal	Stuart
Stuart	
Joey	Lara
Lara	
Amold	Jerad
Emma	Claire
Jerad	
Mary	Jerad
Claire	Lara

T3 : Floor Plan

Discussion | **Table** | **Floor Plan**

The floor plan shows the office space that Star Research will occupy, in the northeast corner of one floor of a building. Two offices are adjacent to each other if and only if they are separated by a common wall. A different definition of adjacent applies to cubicles : cubicles 119A and 119B are adjacent only to office 121, while 119C and 119D are adjacent only to office 120.

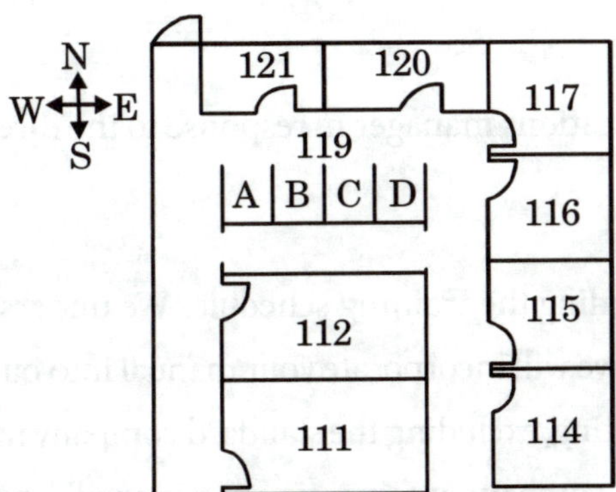

Based on the information and workspace assignment rules provided, how many employees are there, each of whom could be assigned to office 112?

A. 1 B. 2 C. 3 D. 4 E. 5

For each of the following situations, select Yes if, based on the information and workspace assignment rules provided, it would PREVENT some employees from being assigned workspace using the current rules. Otherwise, select No.

Yes	No	
○	○	Mary, Joey and Saina need offices because the projects they work on require the highest levels of security.
○	○	Two additional employees are hired and will be supervised by Jerad.
○	○	Regal resigns his position at Star Research.

PASSAGE 4

T1

E-mail from the director of the training department to the technical publications manager

September 12, 8:03 A.M.

We are in the process of finalizing the schedule for the training session of new clients for our EXM software, which is planned to take place on November 1st. As of now, we have received 23 reservations, and we anticipate that the class will reach its maximum capacity of 35 students, which is the capacity of our training room. The training manuals are currently being produced and will be available for content review on September 15th. Assuming a two-week turnaround for the developer's review, we expect to have a three-week timeframe for your department to handle the necessary formatting, inclusion of standard company information, and printing of the manuals. It would be helpful if you could provide us with a specific delivery date for 35 manuals before October 21st. Please note that we will require an additional week to 10 days to allow our trainers enough time to prepare their computer-based exercises.

T2

E-mail from the technical publications manager in response to the director of the training department

September 12, 9:12 A.M.

Thank you for the update regarding the training schedule. We understand the importance of meeting the heavy schedule in October, and we will incorporate your manual into our calendar accordingly. To provide an estimate, the manual we are creating, excluding the standard company information, is expected to be a certain number of pages. The standard company information section will be fixed at 3 pages. Please note that our department will be charged on a per-page basis, along with the fixed costs of collating and preparation, which are currently $2.00 per manual. Additionally, if the manual includes color graphics, an extra cost of $0.50 per page will be incurred, in addition to the standard rate of $0.25 per page for black and white text. If the total number of pages in the manual is less than 100, we should be able to deliver it by your deadline.

T3

E-mail from the director of the training department in response to the technical publications manager

September 12, 9:46 A.M.

The manual for this three-day training will exceed 100 pages and may run as long as 115 pages, with 5 pages of color graphics. I will know the exact number once the review is completed on October 1.

1. If the information contained in all three e-mails is correct, the total cost of the requested manuals will be closest to __________.

A. $1,060

B. $1,080

C. $1,100

D. $1,120

E. $1,190

2. Consider each of the following statements. Does the information in the three sources support the inference as stated?

Yes	No	
		The director of the training department believes that the software training class will be filled to capacity.
		The director of the training department expects that printing of the training manual will exceed the department's printing budget.
		The technical publications department will most likely be able to deliver 35 copies of the training manual by October 21st.

PASSAGE 5

Tab 1 : Memo

Following is a memo between Riley Green, head of the Admissions office for Syrandon College for 20 years, and Vice President Larry Show, who was brought in to Syrandon after short administrative tenures at two state universities.

To : Larry Shaw, Vice President; Syrandon College

From : Riley Green, Head of Admissions; Syrandon College

I have some concerning news to share. After analyzing the data, it appears that our in-state undergraduate admissions have declined by 25% since 2010. It's worth noting that many of our in-state freshmen are legacies, meaning they have family members who attended Sarandon before them. On the other hand, out-of-state undergraduate admissions tend to consist of transfer students who come to Sarandon. Our strongest connections and relationships are with our in-state undergraduate students, and a majority of our alumni were once in-state undergraduates themselves. Unfortunately, this decrease in the percentage of in-state admissions may have a noticeable impact on future alumni sponsorship, which is crucial for our small private college. We heavily rely on our alumni to fund special projects that are not covered by tuition.

Given this situation, I highly recommend implementing a more aggressive recruiting program. The goal is to hopefully compensate for the decline in in-state admissions and achieve higher numbers of in-state graduates next year. I have attached a graphic that provides a visual breakdown of our admissions for 2011, which might help illustrate the situation more clearly.

Tab 2 : Graph

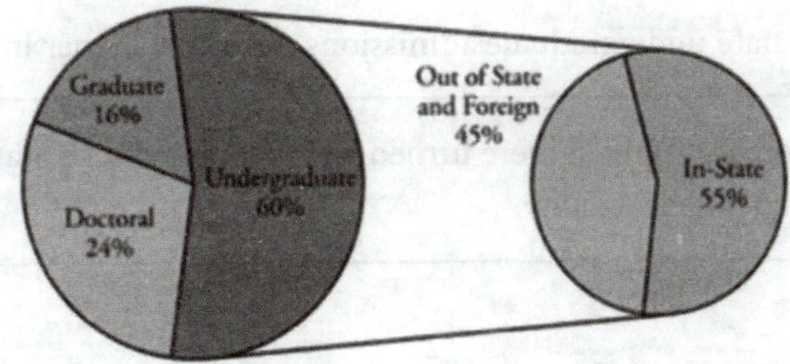

Tab 3 : Response

The below is an excerpt of Vice President response.

To : Riley Green, Head of Admissions; Syrandon College

From : Larry Shaw, Vice President; Syrandon College

While there has been a decline in the percentage of in-state graduate students this year, it is important to note that our overall student population is not significantly different from last year. We do not have an excess of empty spaces at the moment. Based on my experience at other educational institutions, when there is a decrease in a specific student demographic, other demographics tend to fill those vacancies. This is particularly true for international students. To provide an example, at Western State University, we were forced to reject 50% of qualified foreign applicants due to limited capacity. These are students who would be eager to enroll in a reputable institution like Sarandon.

Therefore, considering the situation, there is potential for us to attract a greater number of foreign students who can contribute to our student body. It may be beneficial to explore opportunities to enhance our recruitment efforts and attract qualified international applicants who are seeking admission to a respected institution like Sarandon.

1. **For 2011, if foreign students comprise exactly 1/8 of the number of out-of-state undergraduates, indicate which could be the number of in-state undergraduates.**

Yes	No	Statements
		200
		330
		1320

2. **Indicate which statements could properly be inferred based on the text and the graph. Select Yes if the statement can be inferred. Otherwise, select No.**

Yes	No	Statements
		In-state undergraduates comprise the largest proportion of all the admitted students for 2011.
		The in-state undergraduate admissions were 25% higher in 2010 than in 2011.
		Some foreign students were turned away from Western State for reasons other than academic suitability.

3. Which of the following is an assumption underlying Vice President Shaw assertion in the excerpt of her response to Relay Green?

A. The number of admitted students has not increased since last year.

B. Foreign students are just as likely to attend a private college as a state university.

C. Universities in the United States offer courses that would otherwise not be available to foreign students.

D. The number of foreign students attending Syrandon is steadily rising.

E. The amount of financial support offered by the alumni will remain constant.

PASSAGE 6

The features of five mobile communication devices are compared in the table. Each feature is rated from 0 to 5, with greater ratings indicating greater quality. A device (P) is said to be ratings-dominant over another device (Q) if P matches or exceeds the ratings of Q for every single feature in the table but Q does not match all of the ratings of P.

Feature Quality Ratings

	Device				
Feature	**X1**	**X2**	**XS**	**XL**	**XZ**
A	5	0	1	0	0
B	2	0	2	5	1
C	0	3	3	4	2
D	0	3	5	0	2
E	0	0	4	4	0
F	0	0	0	0	1
G	0	0	0	3	0
H	0	2	2	1	0

For each of the following devices, select Yes if the device is ratings-dominant over any of the other devices in the table. Otherwise, select No.

Yes	No	
		Device X1
		Device XS
		Device XZ

PASSAGE 7

FINANCES

Stephen University offers seven spring break destinations for tourists. The provided table presents information such as the price of plane tickets, discounted prices (if applicable), the spring break operator, rates for waterfront beach houses in the block area, and the lowest rate available for a waterfront beach house. It's important to note that the rates for beach houses are listed per night and per group, and each group will require four nights of lodging. All plane ticket prices are also per group, accommodating up to six passengers, as each beach house has six beds. If waterfront options are not available, the lowest rate for a beach house outside of the waterfront is $70.

ARTICLE

The waterfront beach houses are arranged in three rows. The spring break company has allocated a block of beach houses, specifically the first row along the waterfront, for its clients. These beach houses in the block area have higher rates compared to the normal waterfront beach houses.

Although many spring breakers prefer staying in beach houses along the waterfront, they often adopt alternative strategies to avoid the additional cost of reserving a house in the block area. Some attendees opt for reserving beach houses outside the waterfront area, following the ROWFA strategy. Others choose to reserve beach houses outside the allocated block, known as the ROB strategy, and instead secure beach houses in row 2 or row 3 along the waterfront.

Spring break operators have effectively reduced the frequency of these alternative strategies by increasing the plane ticket price by a fixed amount. However, they offer an equivalent discount on the plane ticket price to spring breakers who book beach houses within the front waterfront block. Research has demonstrated that if this plane ticket discount is equal to at least half of the potential savings associated with a spring breaker's chosen cost-saving strategy, they are significantly more likely to reserve a beach house within the first row of the waterfront block.

Destination	Ticket Price	Discounted Ticket Price	Tour Guide	Block Rate	Lowest Rate for Waterfront
Miami	$210	$150	Contiki	$100	$70
Hawaii	$525	$450	World Springs	$140	$115
Jamaica	$220	$200	Spring Breakers	$160	$135
Cancun	$480	$350	Cancuna Breakers	$150	$120
Daytona	$200	$170	Spring Bling	$135	$100
Bahamas	$240	$210	Sun Fun	$115	$90
Puerto Rico	$425	$400	Beach Burn	$200	$150

1. **Jill and her friends are planning a 5-day/4-night spring break trip to Cancun. Their group has 10 people and they want to stay in the first block of the waterfront area. What is the total cost for Jill and her friends traveling from Stephen University?**

A. $500

B. $950

C. $1000

D. $1900

E. $5000

2. **For each of the following destinations, select Yes if a spring break traveler group would spend more money by employing the ROB strategy -- paying the lowest possible waterfront beach house rate in the waterfront area and paying the nondiscounted plane ticket price -- than by reserving a beach house in the first row of the waterfront block. Otherwise, select No.**

Yes	No	Statements
		Cancun
		Jamaica
		Miami

Assume that all beach houses at the waterfront are available for the 4 days indicated and all beach houses in the city are available at their lowest rates during these 4 days.

3. **Which one of the following destinations is most likely to have spring break travelers favoring the ROB strategy over the ROWFA strategy?**

A. Hawaii

B. Jamaica

C. Daytona

D. Miami

E. Bahamas

Assume that spring break operators receive a reimbursement from the waterfront beach housing organization (which owns the waterfront beach houses) for 25% of the front row block rate for each unoccupied beach house in the front row block of the waterfront area.

4. For each of the following spring break operators, select Yes if the spring break operator would lose beach house revenue if a room in the block is vacant because a traveler group employed the ROB strategy. Otherwise, select No.

Yes	No	Statements
		Contiki
		WorldSprings
		SunFun

5. Select Yes if the percentage discount on the plane ticket (compared to the original price) exceeds the percentage discount for reserving the lowest rate beach house in the waterfront area (compared to the block rate in the waterfront area). Otherwise, select No.

Yes	No	Statements
		Miami
		Hawaii
		Cancun

6. For each of the following spring break destinations, select Yes if a spring break traveler going for the 4-night package would spend less money by employing the ROWFA strategy -- paying the lowest possible beach house rate outside the waterfront area and paying the non-discounted plane ticket price -- than by reserving a front row beach house in the block. Otherwise, select No.

Yes	No	Statements
		Cancun
		Daytona
		Puerto Rico

7. Many individuals stand to benefit financially from spring breakers coming out for their vacations. For each of the following individuals, choose Gain if the individual would likely earn more money if beach houses in the front row block are vacant because of attendees using ROWFA strategies. Otherwise select No Gain.

Yes........	No........	Statements
		Rap artist hired to throw a concert alongside the waterfront beach houses.
		Morning breakfast delivery by a delivery waitress at the beach house whose earnings are primarily from gratuities.
		Taxi cab driver bringing guests from outside of the waterfront area to the waterfront area where vacationers tend to hangout.

Assume that for the four nights that spring break travelers stay, beach houses outside the waterfront area are available at their lowest rate.

8. For the following cities, select Yes if spring break traveler groups would be more likely to reserve a beach house in the front row of the waterfront block than getting a beach house outside the waterfront area. Otherwise, select No.

Yes	No	Statements
		Miami
		Jamaica
		Cancun

PASSAGE 8

Promotions

Quantity (packs)	Diapers	Toys	Baby Food
20–49	5% off	10% off	None
50+	10% off	10% off	20% off

Product

Product	Package	Price
HuggyD's Diapers	6 diapers per pack	$ 15
Barney's Action Toys	2 toys per pack	$ 20
Mighty Avenger Toys	3 toys per pack	$ 12
Baby Food	5 cans per pack	$ 25

Babycare

BabyCare, a daycare center catering to babies aged 0-5, is in the process of purchasing supplies for the month. In February, BabyCare will be responsible for taking care of 30 babies, operating 5 days a week for the duration of 4 weeks. Each day, each baby will require two diaper changes and consume 3 cans of baby food. Additionally, every baby will be provided with one toy. It's worth noting that the daycare center regularly refreshes the toys in the playpens, introducing new toys every 2 weeks and disposing of the old ones.

1. Assess the following statements as either True or False based on the information provided.

True.......	False.......	Statements
		The cost of supplying baby food for the month for BabyCare is more than $7,500.
		The pre-discount cost of getting all Mighty Avenger Toys for the month is cheaper than getting all Barney's Action Toys for the month.
		BabyCare can supply enough toys for the month with a budget of less than $220.

2. Baby Care is placing this month's order for 400 cans of baby food. How much will BabyCare have to pay for the 400 cans of baby food?

A. $1,500

B. $1,600

C. $2,000

D. $5,000

E. $10,000

While BabyCare is currently accomodating 30 babies per month, it is contemplating improving its quality of service or increasing the number of babies it cares for in order to increase profit. Currently, management is trying to determine whether to run its business at a 20-baby maximum or at a 50-baby maximum.

3. Which of the following pieces of information would increase the total cost per baby of running a 50-baby maximum day care center versus a 20-baby maximum day care center. Assume the business runs at full capacity and it is not eligible for any bulk discounts for the month of February.

Yes	No	Statements
		At a 20-baby maximum, each baby gets his own toy; at a 50-baby maximum each baby must share his toy with one other baby.
		At a 20-baby maximum, BabyCare plans to allot 1 baby food package per baby per day and supply 1 diaper package per baby per week.
		At a 20-baby maximum, BabyCare will supply 1 package of diapers each week to the babies but no toys. At a 50-baby maximum, the babies' parents will have to supply their own diapers; BabyCare will not supply diapers. BabyCare will, however, supply a Barney's Action toy package to each baby each week.

PASSAGE 9

Stainless Steel

Stainless steels are iron and carbon alloys that also include a minimum of 10.5% chromium and various other alloying elements, such as molybdenum, manganese, and nickel. These steels are identified with three-digit SAE numbers typically ranging from the 200s to the 600s, sometimes followed by a single letter. The three primary categories of stainless steel are explained below, and tables following the descriptions list seven specific varieties within each category.

Ferritic steels consist of 12.5%-17% chromium, less than 0.1% carbon, and up to 1% nickel. They exhibit magnetic properties and can be strengthened through cold working but are not suitable for heat treatment. Ferritic steels find application in automotive exhaust systems, agricultural equipment, and high-temperature environments like furnaces and boilers.

Austenitic steels contain 16%-26% chromium, up to 0.8% carbon, and 6%-15% nickel. They are nonmagnetic and cannot be heat treated. Austenitic steels are the most commonly used stainless steels worldwide, finding application in food-processing equipment, piping systems, and kitchen utensils.

Martensitic steels consist of 10.5%-17% chromium, up to 1.2% carbon, and not more than 0.4% nickel. They are magnetic and can undergo heat treatment. Martensitic steels are frequently employed in the manufacturing of knives, cutting tools, and dental and surgical equipment.

Partial Composition of Various Stainless Steels

SAE number	Chromium %	Carbon %	Nickel %
304	18.0-20.0	0.08	8.0-10.5
309S	22.0-24.0	0.08	12.0-15.0
316	16.0-18.0	0.08	10.0-14.0
321	17.0-19.0	0.08	9.0-12.0
409	10.5-11.75	0.08	0.50
410	11.5-13.5	0.15	0.75
430	16.0-18.0	0.20	0.75

Select Physical Properties of Various Stainless Steels

SAE number	Density (Kg/M³)	Rockwell hardness	Heat treatable	Magnetic
304	7,900	90	No	No
309S	7,950	85	No	No
316	8,000	95	No	No
321	7,900	95	No	No
409	7,800	75	No	Yes
410	7,850	80	Yes	Yes
430	7,800	89	No	Yes

1. Consider each of the following statements. Indicate Yes if the given information supports the statement. Otherwise, indicate No.

Yes	No	
		All of the listed stainless steels with a carbon content of 0.08% are Austenitic.
		A stainless steel among those listed with a Rockwell hardness of at least 85 must be either Austenitic or Ferritic.
		Of the steels listed, the average density of Austenitic steels is greater than the average density of Ferritic steels.

2. Based on the information in the passage and tables, the stainless steel with the highest ratio of carbon to nickel has which of the following hardness ratings?

A. 80

B. 85

C. 89

D. 90

E. 95

PASSAGE 10

Table 1: Expectancy Value model

Marketers propose that consumers' purchase decisions are influenced by their perception of value. This perception is often shaped by conducting a cost-benefit analysis, where adding more features or reducing the price can manipulate the perception of value. This concept is known as the expectancy-value model. Let's consider an example to understand this better.

Steve is in the market to buy a laptop and has narrowed down his options to four different laptop brands (A, B, C, D). He is interested in evaluating these brands based on five attributes: Processor Performance (PP),

Graphics Capability (GC), Size & Weight (SW), Battery Life (BL), and Marked Price (MP). Steve assigns different priorities to these attributes, with 30% weightage given to Processor Performance, 10% to Graphics Capability, and equal importance to Size & Weight, Battery Life, and Price. To assess the offerings of each brand, Steve calculates a value called Composite Attribute Value, which represents the weighted average of how well each brand performs in relation to his priorities.

Brands	Attributes				
	Processor Performance (PP)	Graphic Capability (GC)	Size & Weight (SW)	Battery Life (BL)	Marked Price (MP)
A	8	6	4	4	8
B	6	9	6	4	6
C	5	4	9	7	4
D	7	8	4	6	7

Table 2 : Customer Cost and Benefit

Cost Heads ($)	A	B	C	D
Marked Price (MP)	120	100	80	75
Acquisition Cost	17	20	20	15
Usage Cost	3	8	11	15
Maintenance Cost	2	2	3	4
Ownership Cost	3	4	4	5
Disposal Cost	5	5	9	8
Customer Cost	**150**	**139**	**127**	**122**

Customer Value is the difference between Customer Benefit and Customer Cost, where Customer Benefit is calculated by multiplying Customer cost with Customer Composite Attribute Value and dividing the product by 5.

1. Consider each of the information given in tabs. Does the information in three tabs support the inference as stated below?

Yes	No	
		Composite Attribute Value for Steve is greatest for brand A
		Steve purchase brand A based on customer value
		Brand C scores lowest both in terms of customer value and Customer benefit

2. Let X denote Customer Value, Y denote Customer Cost, and let Z denote Composite Attribute Value. Which of the following algebraic expressions represents relationship among X, Y & Z?

A. $X = \frac{Y(Z-5)}{5}$ B. $X = \frac{4}{5*Y*Z}$ C. $X = \frac{Y(5-Z)}{5}$

D. $X = \frac{Y}{5(5-Z)}$ E. $X = \frac{YZ-5Z}{5}$

3. If Steve will decide buying laptop based on Customer Value, which of the possible strategies should company C implement so that it becomes Jack's preferred choice?

Yes	No	
		Reduce the marked price to \$60
		Add a faster processor to increases its Processor Performance rating to 9
		Improve its graphics capability to the highest possible ranking

PASSAGE 11

Table 1 : Flow Chart

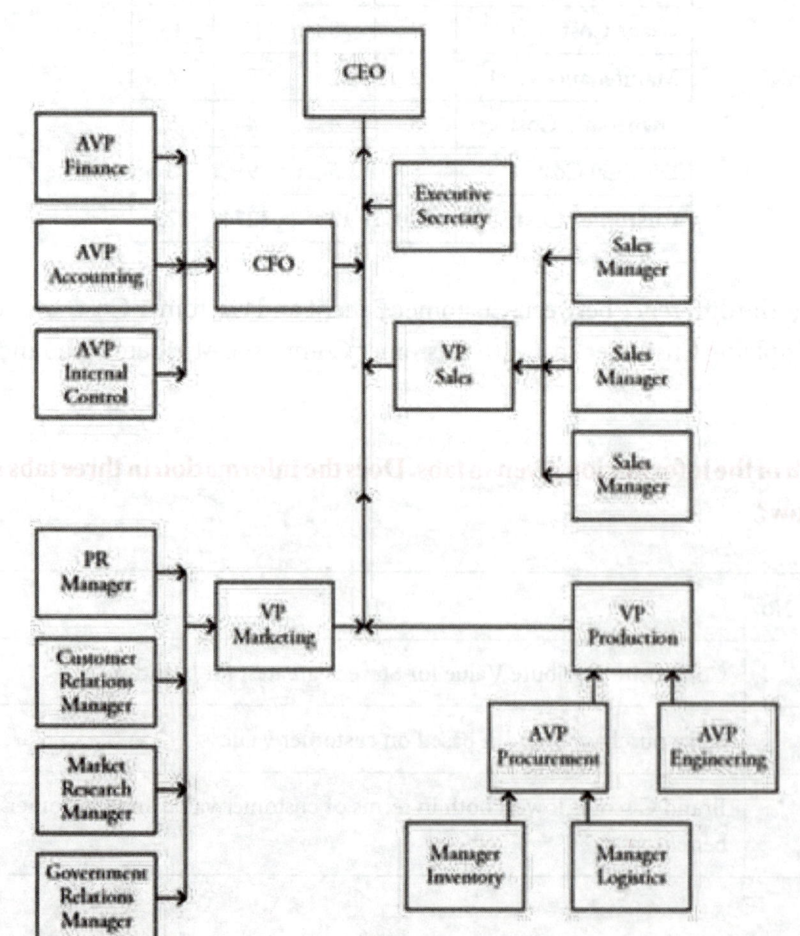

Tab 2: Memo

Please find attached the organizational chart for Articulus Partners in Spring 2010. In response to recent growth in the past few quarters, the company has made some structural changes by introducing two new VP-level positions: AVP Accounting and AVP Procurement. Additionally, a Chief Financial Officer (CFO) has been added to the organization. As per the revised hierarchy, the CFO will report directly to the CEO. The AVP of Accounting will report directly to the CFO, while the AVP of Procurement will report to the VP of Production.

In terms of salary levels within the organization, all employees reporting directly to the CEO are classified as salary level A. Subsequent reporting levels are classified as salary level B, and employees below the B-level employees are classified as salary level C.

1. Based on the flow chart and the text in the Memo tab, indicate whether each of the following statements is true or false.

True	False	
		Sales managers are B-level employees.
		The new AVP of Procurement is a C-level employee.
		The AVP of Engineering is under the new AVP of Procurement.

2. Based on the flow chart and the text in the Memo tab, indicate whether each of the following statements is true or false.

True	False	
		The ratio of B-level employees to C-level employees is 6:1.
		The ratio of B-level employees to A-level employees is 5:1.
		Each A-level employee has at least 3 employees below him or her.

3. If employees at each level of the organizational chart earn close to 1.2 times what employees one level below earn, then the CEO earns approximately how many times what the AVP of Accounting earns?

A. 1.2

B. 1.4

C. 2.2

D. 2.4

E. 3.2

PASSAGE 12

TAB 1: Price List

Chocolate Cost :		
	$3.58/lb	Dark Chocolate
	$3.24/lb	Milk Chocolate
	$2.94/lb	White Chocolate/Vanilla
	$3.78/lb	Specialty Colors Colors Available Include : Pink, Light Green, Dark Green, Yellow, Orange Purple, Light Blue, Dark Blue and Red
	$5.85/lb	Sugar-Free Chocolates Flavors Available Include : Dark Chocolate, Vanilla, and Milk Chocolate
	$2.95/lb	Coconut Shavings
	$5.20/lb	Caramel
	$1.40/oz	High-Quality Flavorings for Chocolate

TAB 2: Email Order

Hi Candy Man,

I would like to make a request to order chocolate mints for a retirement celebration scheduled on April 14th. We will need 6 pounds of small mints, preferably in the midsize range. It would be appreciated if the presentation of the mints includes at least three colors, with a preference for including blue and green, as they are the primary colors in our company logo. The shape of the mints is not a significant factor as long as they maintain a professional appearance. Basic round mints or flower-shaped mints would both be acceptable options.

Thanks,

Betsy Carver

Tab 3 : Invoice

Invoice :# 200515 — Customer : Betsay Carver, Bandercom Inc.

Order: April 1, 2015 — Delivery Date : April 14, 2015

Order # 1

	2 pounds white mint discs	$7.89	$15.78
	2 pounds blue floral mints	$8.99	$17.98
	2 pounds green leaf mints	$8.99	$17.98
Delivery Charge (not taxed)		$10.00	
	Subtotal	$61.74	
	Tax (7.85%)	$4.06	
	Total	**$65.80**	

Consider each of the following statements. Does the information in the three sources support the inference as stated?

Yes	No	
		The average price per pound of the mints including tax and delivery is $10.29.
		Sugar-free chocolates cost about 80% more, on average, than regular varieties of chocolate.
		The Candy Man charged $0.75 per pound for delivery services.

PASSAGE 13

The following emails came from Public Relations Division of a large non-profit organization

EMAIL 1

Hello Diana!

We are currently in the process of selecting a caterer for our upcoming gala event. There are two caterers that we are considering: DoxySource and BrightRight. While DoxySource has provided satisfactory service in the past, we anticipate that our First Annual Sponsors Gala will be our largest event to date. BrightRight is reputed for their expertise in planning and executing large-scale events. However, before making a decision to switch from a trusted contractor, I would like to gather more information. Additionally, I want to explore how to justify any potential additional costs if we choose BrightRight and exceed our budget. It is important to note that we can only engage the services of one provider.

To assist with the evaluation, I would like to request a comparison of the costs of services and rentals for both BrightRight and DoxySource. Specifically, we require information on tables, audio equipment, food services, and the availability of a punch fountain or fountains (with the possibility of a dessert fountain as well). Our allocated budget for the event is $6,000.00, and we anticipate a maximum attendance of 400 people.

Thanks!

Arren Smith

Gala Coordinator

Email 2

Hello Arren

I've broken out the data in the following chart :

	Doxy Source		Bright Right	
	Description	**Price**	**Description**	**Price**
AUDIO	200 Watt P.A. System (up to 40 people)	$65.00	Party Sound System	$650.00
	500 Watt P.A. System (up to 120 people)	$90.00	Marquee Sound System	$850.00
CATERING	Choice of appetizers (shrimp or spring roll)	$2.00 per piece	The Classic Western BBO	$14.00 per person
	Choice of entrée (chicken or beef w/rice)	$6.25 per piece	The Greek Feast	$17.50 per person
	Choice of dessert (cupcakes or lemon bars)	$3.40 per piece	The Far East Extravaganza	$19.50 per person
TABLES	Trestle Table (seats 8)	$15.50 each	Classroom (seats 8)	$20.00 each
	Circular Table (seats 7)	$17.00 each	Bistro/Hightop (seats 6)	$22.00 each
FOUNTAINS	Chocolate Fountain (supplies not included)	$105.00	Chocolate Fountain (supplies included)	$500.00
	Punch Fountain (7 gallons, provided, serves approx. 70)	$47.00	Punch Fountain, waterfall tier (40 gallons, provided)	$350.00

Bright Right provides more upscale and comprehensive packages, albeit at a higher cost, offering options like "The Greek Feast" for the entire gala. Choosing DoxySource, on the other hand, may be more cost-effective and flexible, but it requires more hands-on involvement from our side.

The most significant price difference lies in the audio systems. BrightRight, accustomed to hosting large-scale events, offers complex setups that include lighting, sound effects, and high-definition audio reproduction. In contrast, DoxySource offers two standard public address systems. While I'm uncertain if the Gala necessitates the flashy features of a high-end sound system, the projected attendance exceeds the recommended capacity for DoxySource's P.A. systems. However, we should note that due to electrical limitations, we can only accommodate one P.A. system at the gala.

Diana Ross

Administrative Assistant, Public Relations

1. **If the maximum number of guests attend the gala, determine if each of the statements is true or false based on the information in the two emails.**

True	False	Values
		If the coordinator uses DoxySource and orders one appetizer, one entrée, and one dessert per person, then the least amount that can be spent on tables to seat all guests is approximately 16.6% of the cost of food.
		If the large punch fountain from BrightRight is sufficient for 400 guests, then using smaller fountains from DoxySource to serve the same number of guests would cost at least 20% less per gallon.
		If BrightRight is used, the project will go over its present budget by at least 15%.

2. Suppose the Gala Coordinator uses DoxySource for the maximum number of guests. If she wants to use at least one of each type of table, what is the least possible cost for the tables?

A. $775.00

B. $787.00

C. $792.00

D. $873.21

E. $971.43

3. Based on the information in the messages between the Gala Coordinator and the Administrative Assistant, select Yes if the statement can be inferred. Otherwise, select No.

Yes	No	Values
		The Gala Coordinator is willing to ask for a budgetary increase, if necessary.
		According to the Administrative Assistant, audio costs are not the only determining factor in choosing one event planning service over another.
		Fountains are an optional element of the gala.

PASSAGE 14

TAB 1: Residents Association

Statement by Medical Residency Association president :

Medical residents play a crucial role in delivering medical care to the community, providing round-the-clock coverage and support to both physicians and nursing staff as they strive to obtain their medical licenses. Residents handle various tasks performed by licensed physicians, including patient intake, ordering tests and labs, making diagnoses, and administering treatments, including surgeries. However, residents often face significant challenges and unfair treatment within hospitals.

Residents are frequently subjected to exploitative practices, such as being assigned to 24-hour shifts and experiencing undermining or mistreatment from senior doctors, sometimes in the presence of patients. Additionally, they are compensated well below minimum wage, receiving a fixed salary based on the assumption that they only work one-third of the hours during their assigned shifts. Technically, they are considered to be "on call" during these shifts, although they are required to be present on the hospital grounds at all times and end up working far more hours than the assumed amount. In the past month alone, each resident has averaged 17.5 active working hours during a 24-hour shift, with only 3.5 hours of sleep at a time. Such working conditions pose significant risks to both patients and residents, leading to serious errors that have been caught by senior staff at the last minute.

It is crucial to address these unsafe working conditions to ensure the well-being of both patients and medical residents.

TAB 2 : Hospital Board

Response to Medical Residency Association president by Hospital Board Spokesperson :

We firmly believe that medical residents are essential members of the medical care delivery team within our network of hospitals. It is important to recognize that medical residencies are a vital part of the process for individuals to become licensed physicians. Until residents complete their residency, they cannot reasonably be considered fully licensed physicians. Residencies operate in a similar manner to traditional apprenticeships, providing hands-on training under the supervision and guidance of experienced mentors.

Contrary to the misconception, residents are not expected to work for the entire 24-hour duration of their shifts or even close to that. The purpose of assigning them 24-hour shifts is to ensure their presence on-site when beneficial learning opportunities arise. It is up to each resident to decide their level of involvement in routine activities that could be adequately managed by nursing or medical staff. The entire residency system is structured to provide both training and oversight. Whenever a resident is called upon to make a diagnosis or perform a minor procedure, there is always an experienced physician present to verify the diagnosis, take over the procedure if necessary, or rectify any potential errors.

The residency program is designed to strike a balance between training and supervision, ensuring the highest standard of patient care while providing residents with valuable learning experiences under the guidance of experienced physicians.

1. **For each of the following statements, select Yes if it can be inferred that the Medical Residency Association president and the Hospital Board spokesperson both agree with the statement. Otherwise, select No.**

Yes	No	
		The degree to which medical residents' errors pose a danger of lasting patient harm.
		Whether it is possible for medical residents to work more than 8 hours during a 24-hour shift.
		The degree to which a resident is as qualified as a licensed physician.

2. **For each of the following statements, select Yes if, based on the information provided, both the Residency Association and the Hospital Board would likely accept that the statement is true. Otherwise, select No to indicate that it cannot be inferred that both individuals would likely accept the statement as true.**

Yes	No	
		Medical residents should not be allowed to work for more than 8 hours during a 24-hour shift.
		A hospital should ensure that medical resident errors are minimized or prevented entirely.
		Medical residents should not be undermined or treated poorly by licensed physicians when patients are present.

3. If residents are paid $105 per 24-hour shift, what is the difference, rounded to the nearest hundredth of a dollar, between the hourly wage based upon the assumed number of hours worked per 24-hour shift and the hourly wage based upon the actual average number of hours worked per 24-hour shift?

A. $6.00

B. $6.49

C. $6.79

D. $7.00

E. $7.13

PASSAGE 15

TAB 1 : Chieftain

Among the three phones we evaluated, the Chieftain stands out with its significantly faster processor and superior search interface. This phone is particularly well-suited for individuals who intend to download and utilize a wide range of applications. However, it's worth noting that the baseline phone's internal memory may fill up rapidly. As a result, we strongly advise against purchasing this phone without also acquiring an additional memory card.

Display	3.50 inches diagonal
CPU speed	1.5 gigahertz
Camera	Back : 8 megapixel; Front : none
Memory	0.5 gigabytes
Average critical rating	4.3 of 5 stars
Average customer rating	3.8 of 5 stars
Price	$450.00
Price with 2-year contract	$150.00

TAB 2 : Estrella

If visual quality is a top priority, the Estrella LS is the ideal phone to consider. It features a generously-sized screen that not only stands out as the largest among the three phones reviewed but also excels at displaying vibrant and true-to-life colors. This makes it perfect for photography enthusiasts and web browsing. However, it is important to note that the Estrella's overall performance is hindered by its unusually slow processor. As a result, it may struggle to run high-definition games that would otherwise showcase its exceptional display capabilities.

Display	4.00 inches diagonal
CPU speed	0.9 gigahertz
Camera	Back : 10 megapixel; Front : 1.5 megapixel
Memory	2.0 gigabytes
Average critical rating	3.9 of 5 stars
Average customer rating	4.0 of 5 stars
Price	$500.00
Price with 2-year contract	$150.00

TAB 3 : Radical

Contrary to its name, Cortana's latest phone model, the Radical, does not bring anything particularly new to the table. In fact, it closely resembles a previous model with minimal changes. As a result, the Radical falls into the middle range among the three phones reviewed and fails to stand out in any significant manner, except for its weight, as it happens to be the heaviest among them. However, the Radical still performs adequately across all aspects. While it may not excel in any specific area, it is also free from any major drawbacks. Therefore, for customers who prioritize affordability, the Radical can serve as a suitable option without any notable shortcomings.

Display	3.75 inches diagonal
CPU speed	1.1 gigahertz
Camera	Back : 8 megapixel; Front : 1.5 megapixel
Memory	1.5 gigabytes
Average critical rating	3.7 of 5 stars
Average customer rating	4.1 of 5 stars
Price	$250.00
Price with 2-year contract	$0.00

1. For each of the following statements, indicate yes if the statement can be reasonably inferred from the tabbed reviews. Otherwise, indicate no.

Yes	No	
		The phone with the largest discount (in dollars) for purchasing a contract has the most memory.
		No front camera has more than 25 percent of the resolution, measured in megapixels, of a back camera.
		The reviewers considered factors other than those in the tables when writing their reviews.

2. For each of the following statements, select would help explain if the statement would, if true, help explain some of the information in the tabbed reviews. Otherwise select would not help explain.

Would help explain	Would not help explain	
		The Chieftain was more heavily advertised than the other two phones.
		Critics, unlike customers, don't pay for the products they review and are therefore less likely to let low prices influence their reviews of budget electronics.
		Using lighter parts to make a phone significantly increases manufacturing costs.

3. If the phone with the smallest screen has received 40 critical ratings, how many additional 5-star critical ratings must it receive to improve its average critical rating to 4.5?

A. 4

B. 8

C. 12

D. 16

E. 20

PASSAGE 16

TAB 1 : Special Education

Pandora County boasts one of the largest school districts in its state, but it also faces the challenge of having one of the highest proportions of students with special needs across the nation.

In Pandora County, many students receive accommodations known as "504s," which are named after section 504 of the Rehabilitation Act of 1973. These accommodations are provided to students with physical disabilities, as well as those with cognitive or learning impairments that do not significantly hinder their ability to learn in a standard classroom setting. Students with 504s follow the same curriculum and grading standards as their peers but are offered various forms of assistance, such as text readers for those with visual impairments or preferential seating for students with attention-deficit disorders.

For students who have learning, cognitive, or emotional impairments that significantly impact their ability to learn, Individualized Education Plans (IEPs) are developed. These IEPs involve tailored curricula and grading standards. Whenever feasible, Pandora County strives for inclusive IEPs, where students receive accommodations within a regular classroom environment. However, students with the most severe needs are "mainstreamed," participating in select subjects within general education classes while spending the majority of their day in separate special-needs classrooms.

TAB 2 : Budget

In Pandora County, the expenses directly related to providing accommodations are covered by a county-wide fund. However, the individual schools within Pandora County bear the responsibility of managing the administrative costs associated with designing, certifying, and monitoring the 504s and IEPs of their students. Each school in Pandora County's budget includes provisions for administering an unlimited number of 504s. Additionally, they allocate resources for the administration of 12 inclusive IEPs and 4 mainstreamed IEPs for every 100 students enrolled.

TAB 3 : Employees

There are no educational requirements to work as an assistant to a student on a 504 plan in the Pandora County School District. Many assistants to students with mobility restrictions do not have high school diplomas.

All aides who provide assistance to students with must have college degrees. Additionally, these aides must complete a special six-month certification, unless they majored in education.

Pandora County teachers must have a master's degree. Teachers are occasionally allowed to begin working for the district while still enrolled in their master's programs, but this exception does not apply to teachers of children with special needs; these teachers must complete additional education and observation requirements after earning their degrees but before teaching.

1. **For each of the following scenarios, select Yes if the administrative costs of the accommodation described are within the school's budget, on the basis of the given information. Otherwise, select No.**

Yes	No	
		A 250-student middle school requires 32 sign-language interpreters for students with hearing impairments.
		A 1,000-student high school has 120 students who receive an exemption from the oral presentations that are normally part of final grading.
		A 500-student school has 30 students who spend most of the day in a special-needs classroom.

2. **For each of the following scenarios, select Possible if the described scenario is possible in the Pandora County School District, on the basis of the given information. Otherwise, select Not possible.**

Possible	Not Possible	
		A school with $50,000 remaining in its budget orders $100,000 of textbooks in Braille to meet the needs of its students with visual impairments.
		A student's need for alternative homework assignments requires the school to seek additional funding, as the certification of the student's accommodation would exceed the school's budget.
		A student with a severe learning disability spends most of the school day learning from a teacher with only a bachelor's degree.

3. **Suppose in an Pandora County school with a total student population of 316, there are 12 students with IEPs who are mainstreamed. Based on the information provided, select the answer that must be true about this group of 12 students.**

   A. At least some of these students spend all of their class time in special needs classes.

   B. The school's budget does not cover the administration of the IEP of at least one of these students.

   C. Some of these students are taught the same curriculum and graded by the same standards as are students without IEPs.

   D. All of the aides who assist these students have completed a special six month certification.

   E. These students spend a minority of their time, if any, in general education classes.

Answer Explanations

PASSAGE 1

Solution

All the statements Undermine the point put forth

Explanation :

Undermines	Does not undermine	Statement
✓		Migration from proprietary software to open-source software would be significantly more expensive for the government than would migration from proprietary software to other proprietary software
	✓	The measures included in the bill will, if compiled with, ensure compatibility among software systems used by all the carious relevant stakeholders
✓		As a software package is used for a longer period of time, it becomes less expensive to migrate from that package to other

Statement 1 : Migration from proprietary software to open-source software would be significantly more expensive for the government than would migration from proprietary software to other proprietary software.

Undermines the government's argument. The government argues that the bill would make software migration easier and less expensive in the long run. However, if statement 1 is true, then the opposite would be the case. Migration from proprietary software to open-source software would be significantly more expensive than migration from proprietary software to other proprietary software, which would make the bill more expensive in the long run.

Statement 2 : The measures included in the bill will, if complied with, ensure compatibility among software systems used by all the various relevant stakeholders.

Does not undermine either argument. The company's argument is that the bill would increase compatibility problems, while the government's argument is that the bill would decrease compatibility problems. Statement 2 does not address either of these arguments directly, so it does not undermine either one.

Statement 3 : As a software package is used for a longer period of time, it becomes less expensive to migrate from that package to another.

Undermines the company's argument. The company argues that the cost of open-source software is much higher than the cost of proprietary software, and that this would make migration to open-source software more expensive. However, if statement 3 is true, then the opposite would be the case. As software packages are used for longer periods of time, they become more complex and interconnected, which would make migration from them more difficult and expensive.

PASSAGE 2

Solution

1. D. Conveyor-belt speed increase accounted for the greatest increase in annual output of assembled units from Y10 to Y11.

2.

Yes	No	Statement
	✓	Q/N was less than 10,000 for Y10.
	✓	Q/N was unchanged from Y10 to Y11.
✓		Q/N remained below 30,000 in Yi0 and Y11.

Explanation

1. As given in the first tab-

   Yr 10 : Output = 250,000 and Profit = 15,000,000

   For Yr 11- check third tab to find the changes in output and profit after Automation

   1. Inspection Post Automation- Increased output by 2% and Profit by 5% i.e Output = 255,000 and Profit = 15,750,000

   2. Conveyor Belt speed increase -Increased output by 3% and Profit by 4% i.e Output = 257500 & Profit = 15,600,000

   3. Administrative cost- Increased profit by 1% i.e Profit = 15,150,000

   Now lets check each given choices

   A. On the assembly line, conveyor-belt speed is directly proportional to total annual output of assembled units.

      - We do not know what was the speed of conveyor belt, we only know output. So Eliminate

   B. Administrative unit restructuring accounted for the greatest increase in the dollar amount of profit from Y10 to Y11.

      - As cal above , administrative unit restructuring is not the greatest increase in dollar amt of profit. It is lowest among all three elements. So Eliminate

   C. Conveyor-belt speed increase accounted for the greatest increase in the dollar amount of profit from Y10 to Y11.

      - Clearly no , conveyor belt speed accounted less than automation so eliminate.

   D. Conveyor-belt speed increase accounted for the greatest increase in annual output of assembled units from Y10 to Y11.

      - CORRECT-- Yes as can been seen from cal done above . Conveyor belt increase accounted for greatest increase in output.

E. Inspection-post automation accounted for the greatest increase in annual output of assembled units from Y10 to Y11.

- No it is incorrect based on cal above. So Eliminate.

2. Part 1: No.

output in year 10 was 250,000 (Q) and the number of direct line workers (N) was 15.

250,000/15 = 16,666.67 which is > than 10,000 and therefore not less than 10,000

Part 2: No.

Q/N in year 10 is 16,666,67 as calculated in part 1.

If we know N decreased, and we know Q increased, then we know the number increased overall. When the numerator increases the number as a whole increases, when the denominator decreases the whole number increases. This means between the two years, Q/N did NOT remain unchanged.

Part 3: Yes.

Q/N is 16,666.67 from part 1, which is less than 30,000

Now we need to check year 11.

In year 11, they laid off 3 people, meaning they now only have 12 workers (N).

Between year 10 and 11, output increased by 5%, so output went from 250,000 ⇒ 262,500

(1.05)(250,000) = 262,500

Q/N = 262,500/12 = 21,875, which is also less than 30,000.

PASSAGE 3

Solution

1. 2

2.

Yes	No	Statement
✓		Mary, Joey, and Saina need offices because the projects they work on require the highest levels of security
✓		Two additional employees are hired and will be supervised by Jerad
	✓	Regal resigns his position at Star Research

Explanation

1. The question asks for which people only have a single relationship. Lets go through the table one by one:

   1. Saina - If Saina is in 112, Ciaran can only be in 111 which leaves no place for Emma or Lara. Not qualified.
   2. Regal - If Regal is in 112, Stuard can be in 111. No other conditions need to be satisfied. Qualified.
   3. Stuard - Same reason as 2. Qualified.

4. Joey - If Joey is in 112, Lara can only be in 111 which leaves no place for Ciaran. Not qualified.
5. Lara - Same reason as 1. Not qualified.
6. Arnold - If Arnold is in 112, Jerad can only be in 111 which leaves no place for Mary. Not qualified.
7. Emma - Same reason as 1. Not qualified.
8. Jerad - Same reason as 6. Not qualified.
9. Mary - Same reason as 6. Not qualified.
10. Ciaran - Same reason as 1. Not qualified.

So, only Stuard and Regal are qualified

PASSAGE 4

Solution

1. E. $1,190

2.

Yes	No	
✓		The director of the training department believes that the software training class will be filled to capacity.
	✓	The director of the training department expects that printing of the training manual will exceed the department's printing budget.
	✓	The technical publications department will most likely be able to deliver 35 copies of the training manual by October 21st.

Explanation

1. Costs of collating and preparation, which is currently $2.00/manual

   total cost will be 2 × 35 : $70

   printing cost will be for 118 pages of which 110 pages are b/w , 5 pages are color and 3 pages are of company information

   Color graphics charges are $.75/page

   normal b&w $.25/page

   total charge per manual : (.75 × 5) + (113 × .25) = $32

   total for manual 35 ; 35 × $32 ; $1120

   net cost will be $70+$1120 ; $1190

2. The director of the training department believes that the software training class will be filled to capacity.

   Yes, the director expects class to be filled to 35 which is the the capacity training room

   The director of the training department expects that printing of the training manual will exceed the department's printing budget.

NO there is no information about budget of department

The technical publications department will most likely be able to deliver 35 copies of the training manual by October 21st.

NO since manual is more than 100 pages so it will not be possible to meet deadline

PASSAGE 5

Solution

1.

Yes	No	Statements
	✓	200
	✓	330
✓		1320

2.

Yes	No	Statements
✓		In-state undergraduates comprise the largest proportion of all the admitted students for 2011.
	✓	The in-state undergraduate admissions were 25% higher in 2010 than in 2011.
✓		Some foreign students were turned away from Western State for reasons other than academic suitability.

3. B. Foreign students are just as likely to attend a private college as a state university

Explanation

1. This question asks you to indicate which answers could be the number of in-state undergraduates, so you need to reference the graph on Tab 2. If foreign students comprise exactly 1/8 of the number of out-of-state undergraduates, then the number of in-state undergraduates would have to be a value that yields an integer value for the number of foreign students. In-state undergraduates are 55% of 60% of the total, or (.55)(.6) = (.33) of the total. Plug In the Answers to discover which values will work.

   If 200 is the number of in-state undergraduates, which comprise 33% of the total, then you can calculate the total number of admitted students:

   (0.33) (total) = 200 so total = 200/0.33 = 606.06

   Since this value does not return an integer for number of students, this answer is incorrect. So the answer for 200 is No.

PASSAGE 6

Solution

1.

Yes	No	Statements
	✓	Device X1
✓		Device XS
	✓	Device XS

Explanation

RO1

To be ratings-dominant over one of the other devices, Device X1 must match or exceed all the ratings of the other device in every other category. In other words, it could not have a lower rating than the other device in any category. By sorting the table on X1, it is clear that Device X1 has a zero rating for every feature except A and B, and no other device has zero ratings in all those categories. Thus, Device X1 cannot be ratings-dominant over any of the other devices in the table.

The correct answer is No.

RO2

Sorting the table by XS shows that every rating for Device XS matches or exceeds the rating for Device X2. Moreover, the ratings for Features A, B, D, and E for Device XS exceed those of Device X2. Therefore, Device XS is ratings-dominant over Device X2.

The correct answer is Yes.

RO3

Sorting the table by XZ shows that Device XZ's ratings for both Features C and D exceed those of Device X1, but of no other device. However, Device X1 has higher ratings than Device XZ for Features A and B. Thus, Device XZ cannot be ratings-dominant over any of the other devices.

The correct answer is No.

PASSAGE 7

Solution

1. A. $500

2.

Yes	No	Statements
✓		Cancun
	✓	Jamaica
	✓	Miami

3. A. Haweli

4.

Yes	No	Statements
✓		Contiki
	✓	World Springs
	✓	Sun Fun

5.

Yes	No	Statements
	✓	Miami
	✓	Hawaii
✓		Cancun

6.

Yes	No	Statements
✓		Cancun
✓		Daytona
✓		Puerta Rico

7.

Yes	No	Statements
✓		Rap artist hired to throw a concert alongside the waterfront beach houses
✓		Morning breakfast delivery by a delivery waitress at the beach house whose earnings are primarily from gratuities
	✓	Taxi cab driver bringing guests from outside of the waterfront area to the waterfront area where vacationers tend to hangout

8.

Yes	No	Statements
✓		Miami
	✓	Jamaica
	✓	Cancun

Explanation

1. D,since the total flight price would be 350×2(since there are 10 people so two groups would be formed)+ $150 \times 4 \times 2$ (2 groups and 4 nights=1900
2. (a) Yes, In Cancun without ROB the price of 1 group for 1 night would be $350+150 \times 4$ (4 days) = 950

   While with ROB : $120 \times 4 + 480 = 960$

   (b) No, In Jamaica without ROB the price of 1 group for 1 night would be $200 + 160 \times 4 = 840$

   While with ROB : $220 + 135 \times 4 = 760$

   (c) No, In Miami without ROB the price of 1 group for 1 night would be $100 \times 4 + 150 = 550$

   While with ROB : $210 + 4 \times 70 = 490$
3. D, I think the answer should be Miami since the lowest cost for beach house is 70$ and outside is also 70$ so a person would prefer ROB
4. (a) In Contiki loss would be there since occupying 2nd row house will cost 70 while for the first row room which is not occupied the owner will get a discount of 25% so final price to him would be $100\text{-}100 \times .25 = 75$,so a loss of 5$ is there

   (b) In Worldsprings no loss would be there since occupying 2nd row house will cost 115 while for the first row room which is not occupied the owner will get a discount of 25% so final price to him would be $140\text{-}140 \times .25 = 105$, so no loss is there

   (c) In Sunfun no loss would be there since occupying 2nd row house will cost 90 while for the first row room which is not occupied the owner will get a discount of 25% so final price to him would be $115\text{-}115 \times .25 = 86.25$,so no loss is there

5. (a) No, In Miami the % discount on plane is (210 – 150)/210 = 28.57

while discount on room in 1st block vs other rows = 100 –70/100 = 30

(b) No,In Hawai the % discount on plane is (525 – 450)/525 = 14

while discount on room in 1st block vs other rows = 140 – 115/140 = 17.8

(c) Yes,In Cancun the % discount on plane is (480 – 350)/480 = 27

while discount on room in 1st block vs other rows = 150 – 120/150 = 20

6. (a) Yes, In Cancun Total for 4 nights with RoWFA=480+70 × 4=760

while occupying first block = 350 + 150 × 4 = 950

(b) Yes, In Daytona Total for 4 nights with RoWFA = 200 + 70 × 4 = 480

while occupying first block = 170 + 135 × 4 = 710

(c) Yes, In Puerto Rico Total for 4 nights with RoWFA = 425 + 70 × 4 = 705

while occupying first block = 400 + 200 × 4 = 1200

7. Here only cab driver will not suffer since he is bringing people from outside to inside the beach area in waterfront and if people are not staying inside then the rapper and waiter will not get a chance to perform or serve anyone and thus will have lossess

8. So here in this question only people in Miami they will try to book house in first block beacuse the price difference is lowest among the three choices given in the question as the difference between inside and outside is lowest for Miami = 100-70=30$,so the likelihood is also high here that people will book houses inside the first row here

PASSAGE 8

Solution

1.

False	True	Statements
✓		The cost of supplying baby food for the month for Baby Care is more than $7,500
	✓	The pre-discount cost of getting all Mighty Avenger Toys for the month is cheaper than getting all Barney's Action Toys for the month.
	✓	Baby Care can supply enough toys for the month with a budget of less than $220.

2. B. $1600

3.

Yes	No	Statements
	✓	At a 20-baby maximum, each baby gets his own toy; at a 50-baby maximum each baby must share his toy with one other baby.
	✓	At a 20-baby maximum, Baby Care plans to allot 1 baby food package per baby per day and supply 1 diaper package per baby per week.
✓		At a 20-baby maximum, Baby Care will supply 1 package of diapers each week to the babies but no toys. At a 50-baby maximum, the babies' parents will have to supply their own diapers; Baby Care will not supply diapers. Baby Care will, however, supply a Barney's Action toy package to each baby each week.

Explanation

1. (a) False, since the baby food requires:

   $30 \times 3 = 90$ cans ,now for 20 days it is

   $90 \times 20 = 1800$ cans, now each can is of 5$, so total amount is $1800 \times 5 = 9000$, but on 50 + cans it is giving 20% off so final price would be $9000 \times .8 = 7200$, which is less than 7500

   (b) True, For babies each baby requires $30 \times 1 = 30$ toys and each one requires $30 \times 2 = 60$ toys,since after 2 weeks new toys are required, so for Barneys toys price per toy is 10$, so total is 600,while for Mighty avenger per toy price is 4$, so total is 240, hence mighty is cheaper than Barneys

   (c) True,yes after discount we can Mighty avenger toys with a budget < 220$

2. B, So here for 400 cans the per can amount is 5$,so total is $400 \times 5 = 2000$\$, now with a 20% discount final price is $2000 \times .8 = 1600$\$

3. (a) If sharing of toys is there then problem for 50 baby vs 20 baby wouldn't be there.

   (b) In this case the cost wouldn't increase.

   (c) If diapers are not supplied at 50 baby then the cost would increase and it will not be offset by giving toys

PASSAGE 9

Solution

1.

Yes	No	
	✓	All of the listed stainless steels with a carbon content of 0.08% are Austenitic.
✓		A stainless steel among those listed with a Rockwell hardness of at least 85 must be either Austenitic or Ferritic.
✓		Of the steels listed, the average density of Austenitic steels is greater than the average density of Ferritic steels.

2. C. 89

Explanation

1. Consider each of the following statements. Indicate Yes if the given information supports the statement. Otherwise, indicate No.

All of the listed stainless steels with a carbon content of 0.08% are Austenitic.

The text in Tab 1 indicates that Austenitic steels contain 16%-26% chromium, not more than 0.8% carbon, and 6%-15% nickel. These steels are also neither magnetic nor heat treatable. The question restricts itself to steels that are 0.08% carbon, so find those steels in Tab 2. They are SAE 304 through SAE 409. Of these, all have allowable chromium percentages, but SAE 409 has only 0.5% nickel. Therefore, it is not Austenitic. Alternatively, you could check Tab 3 for the magnetic and heattreatable characteristics. Here, you'll see that SAE 409 is magnetic and therefore not Austenitic.

The answer is No.

A stainless steel among those listed with a Rockwell hardness of at least 85 must be either Austenitic or Ferritic.

Because this specifies a hardness of 85 or above, begin by examining the table in Tab 3; all of the SAE 300-series steels and SAE 430 have a hardness of 85 or higher. Next, return to the text in Tab 1 to determine what constitutes Ferritic steel: it is magnetic but not heat treatable. You've already determined from the previous question that an Austenitic steel is neither. Put another way, any steel in the table that is not heat treatable is either Austenitic or Ferritic. According to the table in Tab 3, none of the SAE 300-series steels is heat treatable and neither is SAE 430, so

The answer is Yes.

Of the steels listed, the average density of Austenitic steels is greater than the average density of Ferritic steels.

From the first two questions in this set, you've determined from the information in the text and the table in Tab 3 that all of the SAE 300-series steels are Austenitic. You've also determined that SAE 409 and SAE 430 are Ferritic. A glance at Tab 3 will confirm that SAE 410, being both magnetic and heat treatable, is neither Austenitic nor Ferritic. Rather than doing complex calculations, notice that the two Ferritic steels, SAE 409 and SAE 430, each have a density of 7,800, while all of the Austenitic steels are above 7,850. Thus, you can conclude that the Austenitic steels have a higher average density, so

The answer is Yes.

2. Based on the information in the passage and tables, the stainless steel with the highest ratio of carbon to nickel has which of the following hardness ratings?

Because this question asks for a ratio of carbon to nickel, think of carbon as the numerator of a fraction and nickel as the denominator. The highest ratio will be the fraction with the largest numerator relative to the denominator. Therefore, you can quickly eliminate all of the SAE 300-series steels, since their denominators are many times greater than any of the SAE 400-series steels while their numerators are less than or equal to those of the 400 series. Now use estimation to compare SAE 409 to SAE 410: 0.08 over 0.50 is less than 0.15 over 0.75, since 0.15 is nearly twice 0.08 but 0.75 is considerably less than twice 0.50. What about SAE 430? Since it has a bigger numerator than SAE 410 but the same denominator, it must have the highest ratio. Now find its hardness rating in the table in Tab 3: 89.

Therefore, (C) is correct.

PASSAGE 10

Solution

1.

Yes	No	
	✓	Composite Attribute Value for Steve is greatest for brand A
✓		Steve purchase brand A based on customer value
✓		Brand C scores lowest both in terms of customer value and Customer benefit

2. A. $X = \frac{Y(Z-5)}{5}$

3.

Yes	No	
	✓	Reduce the marked price to $60
✓		Add a faster processor to increases its Processor Performance rating to 9
✓		Improve its graphics capability to the highest possible ranking

PASSAGE 11

Solution

1.

True	False	
✓		Sales managers are B-level employees.
	✓	The new AVP of Procurement is a C-level employee.
	✓	The AVP of Engineering is under the new AVP of Procurement.

2.

True	False	
✓		The ratio of B-level employees to C- level employees is 6:1
	✓	The ratio of B-level employees to A-level employees is 5:1
	✓	Each A-level employee has at least 3 employees below him or her

3. B. 1.4

PASSAGE 12

Solution

1.

Yes	No	
	✓	The average price per pound of the mints including tax and delivery is $10.29.
✓		Sugar-free chocolates cost about 80% more, on average, than regular varieties of chocolate.
	✓	The Candy Man charged $0.75 per pound for delivery services.

Explanation

A. The average price per pound of the mints including tax and delivery is \$10.29.

We just divide the final bill by 6 since that includes the (sum of 6 pounds) + (tax) + (delivery)

Hence, $65.8 / 6 = 10.96$ which is not 10.29

B. Sugar-free chocolates cost about 80% more, on average, than regular varieties of chocolate.

Here we average price of regular varieties (dark, milk and white)

We get $(3.58+3.24+2.94)/3 = 3.25$

Now increase 3.25 by 80% to see if it costs similar to Sugar free (which is 5.85)

Hence, $3.25 \times 1.8 = 5.85$ (Hence YES)

C. The Candy Man charged \$0.75 per pound for delivery services.

Delivery was 10\$ for 6 pounds hence it was more than 1\$ for a pound and NOT 0.75\$.

Hence NO

PASSAGE 13

Solution

1.

True	False	Values
✓		If the coordinator uses DoxySource and orders one appetizer, one entrée, and one dessert per person, then the least amount that can be spent on tables to seat all guests is approximately 16.6% of the cost of food.
✓		If the large punch fountain from BrightRight is sufficient for 400 guests, then using smaller fountains from DoxySource to serve the same number of guests would cost at least 20% less per gallon.
✓		If BrightRight is used, the project will go over its present budget by at least 15%.

2. C. \$ 792.00

3.

Yes	No	Values
✓		The Gala Coordinator is willing to ask for a budgetary increase, if necessary.
✓		According to the Administrative Assistant, audio costs are not the only determining factor in choosing one event planning service over another.
	✓	Fountains are an optional element of the gala.

Explanation

1. (a) True, since 16.67% of food is = .1667 × 11.65 = 1.93 and cost of tables = (1/8) × 15.50 (Per the least priced plan)

   (b) True, since the per gallon cost for Bright right is 350/40 = 8.75 while for DoxySource it is (47 × (400/70))/40 gallons = 7 which is at least 20% less than Bright right's value.

   (c) True, since if we choose Bright right with the least possible options it is providing the budget will go up by more than 15% (budget will be more than 6900)

2. Total cost is 17 × 1 + 50 × 15.50 = 792

3. (a) Yes,since they are preferring Bright right for which more budget is required

   (b) Yes,since food also plays an important role here

   (c) No,it is required

PASSAGE 14

Solution

1.

Yes	No	
	✓	The degree to which medical residents' errors pose a danger of lasting patient harm.
✓		Whether it is possible for medical residents to work more than 8 hours during a 24-hour shift.
	✓	The degree to which a resident is as qualified as a licensed physician.

2.

Yes	No	
	✓	Medical residents should not be allowed to work for more than 8 hours during a 24-hour shift.
✓		A hospital should ensure that medical resident errors are minimized or prevented entirely.
	✓	Medical residents should not be undermined or treated poorly by licensed physicians when patients are present.

3. E. $7.13

Explanation

1. **Statement 1: No.** In the last sentence of the Residency Association statement, the president says:

   "Such working conditions are dangerous for both patients and residents; some serious mistakes have already been made and were caught only at the last minute by senior staff."

   The residency president, then, believes that the situation is dangerous and that there is at least the possibility of serious consequences from mistakes made by residents.

In the last sentence of the Hospital Board statement, the spokesperson says

"...there is always an experienced physician on hand to verify the diagnosis, take over the procedure, or otherwise correct any potential errors [made by residents]."

The spokesperson, then, believes that there is an oversight system in place that will correct any potential errors-in other words, that there is no danger of lasting harm due to a resident's mistake. Thus, the spokesperson and the president disagree.

Statement 2: Yes. The Residency Association president explicitly states that residents have averaged 17.5 hours during the past month, so the president does believe that residents are working more than 8 hours during a 24-hour shift. The Hospital Board spokesperson says that residents are not expected to work 24 hours in a 24-hour shift, nor anywhere close to that but also that if a resident chooses to participate in many routine activities that can ably be handled by the nursing or medical staff, that is the resident's choice. In other words, the spokesperson is acknowledging that it is possible for a resident to work more than 8 hours in a shift-if he or she chooses to do so. The two parties, then, both agree that it is possible for residents to work longer than 8 hours during a 24-hour shift.

Statement 3: No. The Hospital Board spokesperson states clearly that until someone has finished the residency, he or she is not, and cannot reasonably be considered, a licensed physician. The spokesperson, then, believes that residents are not as qualified as licensed physicians.

The Residency Association president states that residents are responsible for all of the licensed physician tasks, including intake, the ordering of tests and labs, diagnosis and treatment, including surgery (emphasis added). This could be taken as evidence that the residency president believes residents are as qualified as licensed physicians. Alternatively, it may be interpreted as not providing any opinion as to whether residents are as qualified. Either way, this is not the same as the spokesperson's opinion that residents are not as qualified as licensed physicians.

2. **Statement 1: No.** The Residency Association president indicates that the residents are assumed to work 1/3 of the 24-hour shift, or 8 hours, but the president does not claim that residents should not work more than that amount. They claim only that they work too much. It can be inferred that they think they should work less than 17.5 hours, but it is unclear what they think of an 8-hour cutoff. Likewise, the Hospital Board never indicates a specific time beyond which residents should not be able to work.

   Statement 2: Yes. As part of their argument, the residents complain that their working conditions are dangerous and that, as a result, serious mistakes have been made. It can be inferred, then, that the residents believe that the hospital is responsible for setting reasonable working hours in order to minimize or prevent errors made by residents (among other goals). The Hospital Board indicates that

   "...when a resident is called upon to make a diagnosis or perform a minor procedure, there is always an experienced physician on hand to verify the diagnosis, take over the procedure, or otherwise correct any potential errors."

   The board, then, also believes that the hospital is responsible for minimizing or preventing errors made by medical residents.

Statement 3: No. The residents state that they are taken advantage of terribly and complain that they are undermined or treated poorly by senior doctors-sometimes when patients are present. The residents, then, agree with this statement.

You might surmise that any ethical hospital board also would not want doctors to treat medical residents poorly when patients are present (or at any time!), but the Hospital Board's statement never addresses this aspect of the resident's complaint. Therefore, nothing can be inferred regarding the board's position on this issue.

3. According to the first tab, the association president states that residents are assumed to work one-third of the hours in our assigned shifts. If the shift is 24 hours long, then, a resident is assumed to work for one-third of that time, or 8 hours. In that case, the hourly wage would be $105 / 8 hours = $13.125. Rounded to the hundredths digit, this is $13.13.

The resident indicates that the average time worked over the past month was actually 17.5 hours in a 24-hour shift. The hourly wage in this case would be $105 / 17.5 hours = $6.00.

The difference between the two is $13.13 – $6.00 = $7.13.

The correct answer is (E).

PASSAGE 15

Solution

1.

Yes	No	
✓		The phone with the largest discount (in dollars) for purchasing a contract has the most memory.
✓		No front camera has more than 25 percent of the resolution, measured in megapixels, of a back camera.
✓		The reviewers considered factors other than those in the tables when writing their reviews.

2.

Would help explain	Would not help explain	
	✓	The Chieftain was more heavily advertised than the other two phones.
✓		Critics, unlike customers, don't pay for the products they review and are therefore less likely to let low prices influence their reviews of budget electronics.
✓		Using lighter parts to make a phone significantly increases manufacturing costs.

3. D. 16

PASSAGE 16

1.

Yes	No	
✓		A 250-student middle school requires 32 sign-language interpreters for students with hearing impairments.
✓		A 1,000-student high school has 120 students who receive an exemption from the oral presentations that are normally part of final grading.
	✓	A 500-student school has 30 students who spend most of the day in a special-needs classroom.

2.

Possible	Not Possible	
✓		A school with $50,000 remaining in its budget orders $100,000 of textbooks in Braille to meet the needs of its students with visual impairments.
✓		A student's need for alternative homework assignments requires the school to seek additional funding, as the certification of the student's accommodation would exceed the school's budget.
	✓	A student with a severe learning disability spends most of the school day learning from a teacher with only a bachelor's degree.

3. E. These students spend a minority of their time, if any, in general education classes

Chapter 2

Table Analysis

PASSAGE 1

The table below shows the number of deaths (in thousands) due to car accidents and the total number of deaths due to all causes (in thousands) in Country Y over a period of 6 years.

Year	Total deaths	Deaths due to car accidents
2000	20	0.9
2001	22	1.12
2002	24.2	1.55
2003	26.62	2.02
2004	29.28	1.91
2005	32.21	2.42

1. Assuming that the trend of deaths have been consistent since 1990, what would be the estimate number of deaths in country Y in the year 1998

(A) 19800

(B) 19605

(C) 18180

(D) 16530

(E) 16200

2. During which two consecutive years did Country Y witness the greatest percentage change in the ratio of deaths caused by car accidents to the total number of deaths?

(A) 2000 - 2001

(B) 2001 - 2002

(C) 2002 - 2003

(D) 2003 - 2004

(E) 2004 - 2005

3. If the percentage of deaths caused by natural disasters in the year 2000 is equivalent to the percentage of deaths caused by car accidents in the year 2001 in Country Y, what is the approximate number of deaths resulting from natural disasters in 2000?

(A) 495

(B) 990

(C) 1020

(D) 1230

(E) 1410

4. If the number of deaths caused by heart disease doubles every year from 2001 to 2004, and the number of deaths attributed to heart disease in 2000 was 10,000, what would be the estimated number of deaths due to heart disease in 2004?

(A) 625

(B) 2,000

(C) 40,000

(D) 160,000

(E) It cannot be determined from the information given

PASSAGE 2

This table displays data on coffee sold by a Guatemalan producer in 2015.

VARIETY	SALES, National Share (%)	SALES, National Rank	EXPORTS, National Share (%)	EXPORTS, National Rank
Coarse ground	18	4	7	5
Dark roast	31	1	60	1
Espresso roast	12	4	87	1
Fine ground	20	5	15	4
French roast	53	2	49	2
Light roast	21	2	32	2
Medium ground	36	1	58	1
Medium roast	71	1	58	1
Whole bean	50	3	22	4

For each of the following statements, select Yes if the statement can be shown to be true based on information in the table. Otherwise, select No.

Yes	No	
		This producer is responsible for a majority of the nation's exports of French roast coffee.
		This producer exports more fine-ground than coarse-ground coffee.
		The top two exporters of light-roast coffee combined export a majority of the nation's light-roast coffee.

PASSAGE 3

Coastline region	State	Country	Number of hurricanes	Percent change in population, 1960–2008
Gulf of Mexico	Florida	Monroe County	15	50.8
Gulf of Mexico	Louisiana	Lafourche Parish	14	67.2
Atlantic	North Carolina	Carteret County	14	104.3
Atlantic	North Carolina	Dare County	13	465.9
Atlantic	North Carolina	Hyde County	13	10.1
Gulf of Mexico	Louisiana	Jefferson Parish	12	108.9
Atlantic	Florida	Palm Beach County	12	454.7
Atlantic	Florida	Miami-Dade County	11	156.5
Gulf of Mexico	Louisiana	St. Bernard Parish	11	17.2
Gulf of Mexico	Louisiana	Cameron Parish	11	4.8
Gulf of Mexico	Louisiana	Terrebonne Parish	11	78.7

The table provides information on the 11 coastal counties in the United States that experienced the highest number of hurricanes between 1960 and 2008. Additionally, it includes the percentage change in population for each county during the same time period. Positive percentages indicate population growth.

Consider the following statements. For each statement, evaluate whether that statement is True or False, according to the information in the table.

True	False	
		The median number of hurricanes in the Florida counties was higher than the median number of hurricanes in each of the other states' counties.
		The counties listed in the table that experienced the three greatest percent changes in population during the period are all part of the coastline region whose listed counties had the greater range in number of hurricanes during the same period.
		The Gulf of Mexico coastline region experienced fewer hurricanes per county listed in the table, on average, than did the Atlantic coastline region.

PASSAGE 4

Course	Certification			
	A	B	C	D
1	*	*	*	*
2	*	*		
3			*	
4		*		
5	*		*	
6		*		*
7	*			*
8			*	
9	*			

There are four technical certifications available (Certifications A, B, C, and D), each with its own set of required courses selected from Courses 1 through 9. To obtain a certification, candidates must complete all the courses specified for that particular certification. Notably, if a course is already completed for one certification, it does not need to be retaken for other certifications that also include it. The table displays the specific courses needed for each certification. For instance, Certification A mandates the completion of Courses 1, 2, 5, 7, and 9.

Meredith, who has not yet taken any of the courses, intends to acquire all four certifications. She has devised a strategic plan: she will initially focus on taking exclusively the courses required for the certification that has the fewest number of courses. Subsequently, she will proceed to the certification that requires the least number of additional courses compared to what she has already completed. Meredith will continue this approach until she has successfully completed all the required courses for all four certifications.

For each of the following statements about these certifications, select Yes if the statement is accurate based on the information provided. Otherwise, select No.

Yes	No	
		Meredith will receive Certification A first.
		Meredith will receive Certification B second.
		Meredith will receive Certification C third.

PASSAGE 5

Country	# of Pan-Global Games (Judge)	Average Score (Judge)	Highest Score given	Lowest Score Given	# of Pan-Global Games (Competitor)	Average Score (Competitor)
Albania	1	6.7	9.2	5.4	1	8.6
Estonia	2	8.4	9	6.9	3	7.7
Finland	3	6.2	8.9	4.2	2	8.5
Germany	3	8.2	9.4	7.6	2	8.3
Japan	1	7.3	9.7	6.4	3	8.8
Norway	2	7.9	8.4	5.2	4	6.5
Russia	5	6.8	9.6	5.4	3	7
South Korea	3	7.9	9.3	6.3	2	8.3
United States	4	8.1	9.2	7.1	2	7.1

The provided table presents information regarding a group of judges participating in the 2012 Pan-Global Games. It includes details such as the country represented by each judge, the number of previous Pan-Global Games they had participated in as a judge, their average score given as a judge, the highest score given, the lowest score given, the number of Pan-Global Games they had participated in as a competitor, and their average score received as a competitor. The scores are rated on a scale of 1 to 10, with increments of one-tenth of a point.

Consider each of the following statements about the Pan-Global Games judge's scores. For each statement indicate whether the statement is supported based on the information provided in the table.

Yes	No	
		On average, the lowest score given for judges who had judged in 3 Pan-Global Games was higher than that for judges who had competed in 3 Pan-Global Games.
		The judge with the greatest absolute difference between the highest score given and lowest score given also had the greatest percent difference between the lowest score given and highest score given.
		The average (arithmetic mean) number of Pan-Global Games that judges participated in as judges was higher than the average number of Pan-Global Games that judges participated in as competitors.
		The probability that a given judge competed in more Pan-Global Games than she judged is the same as the probability that a judge gave a higher average score as a judge than she received as a competitor.

PASSAGE 6

A research bureau conducted a survey among the residents of Catalonia to gather information about their attendance at entertainment and cultural events in the year 2015. The provided chart presents the percentages of citizens in different age groups who spent money to attend specific cultural events during that year.

Age	Galleries or museums	Sporting Events	Performing Arts Events	Movies or films
0 - 25	70	75	64	82
25 - 34	65	68	67	85
35 – 44	64	62	68	83
45 - 54	58	55	45	88
55 – 64	62	57	56	78
65 and older	68	45	64	62

1. For each of the following statements, choose "would help explain" if it would, if true, help explain the information given in the chart. Otherwise, choose "would not help explain".

Would help explain	Would not help explain	Statement
		Per capita spending on the performing arts is the highest among communities that invest heavily in the arts and that best advertise the performing arts.
		Most major sporting events take place in urban areas, where the average age of residents is significantly lower than that of rural or suburban areas.
		A greater percentage of towns contain at least one movie theater than contain at least one performing arts venue.

2. Which of the following can be reasonably inferred from the information provided in the table?

Can be reasonably inferred	Cannot be reasonably inferred	
		In Catalonia, per capita spending on sporting events tends to decrease as individuals age.
		The average age of Catalonia citizens who attended performing arts events in 2015 was under the age of 45.
		At least 45% of Catalonia citizens under the age of 25 attended both a sporting event and a gallery or museum in 2015.

PASSAGE 7

The table summarizes information in several categories about the 9 stores in a small grocery chain. The table also includes chain-wide averages where appropriate.

Store	Self-check express lanes	Self-check unlimited lanes	Pharmacy	Fuel	Restaurant	Average Customer Age
A	8	4	Yes	No	No	34.5
B	8	6	No	No	No	28.4
C	6	4	Yes	No	Yes	32
D	8	0	Yes	No	No	50.5
E	12	4	Yes	Yes	No	42.5
F	8	6	No	No	Yes	34.6
G	8	0	No	Yes	No	38.8
H	4	8	Yes	No	Yes	29.9
I	0	0	Yes	Yes	Yes	56.7
Averages	6.89	3.56	–	–	–	38.73

For each of the following statements, select True if the statement can be verified to be true based on the information provided. Otherwise, select False.

True	False	Statements
		In each store whose average customer age falls between 34 and 36, the number of self-check express lanes is above average.
		There is a negative correlation between the number of self-check unlimited lanes and the average customer age.
		Stores in this table that have fewer self-check express lanes than the chain-wide average are less likely to have restaurants than stores that have more self-check express lanes than the chain-wide average.

PASSAGE 8

Serial #	Weight, Ounces	Radius, inches	Shape	Magnetic?
K01	4.2	0.94	Cylinder	No
K02	2.3	0.16	Cone	Yes
K03	4.1	0.32	Sphere	Yes
K04	6.2	0.71	Cylinder	Yes
K05	4.3	0.76	Cylinder	No
K06	5.5	0.54	Cylinder	No
K07	4.4	0.84	Cone	Yes
K08	4.7	0.37	Sphere	No
K09	1	0.42	Sphere	No
K10	2.7	0.63	Cylinder	No
K11	6.3	0.67	Cone	No
K12	1.1	0.76	Sphere	No

Students measured a group of metallic solids of various alloys and represented their findings in the table above. In addition to weight and radius, information about shape and magnetism is depicted.

True	False	Statements
		The median weight is closer to the greatest weight than to the least weight.
		Ranking from greatest to least values, K05 has a higher rank according to weight than it does according to radius.
		The ratio of magnetic cones to magnetic spheres is equal to the percentage of solids that are either heavier than 5 ounces or magnetic.

PASSAGE 9

Country	Coastal	Water Polo	Rugby	Rowing	Cricket
Australia	Yes	25	23	26	26
China	No	18	56	18	8
France	No	13	48	14	25
India	No	9	21	5	65
New Zealand	Yes	44	8	35	13
South Africa	Yes	17	20	18	45
Spain	No	7	65	10	18

The table shows percentage of youngsters who train for specific sport in select few countries.

For each of the following statements select Would help explain if it would, if true, help explain some of the information in the table. Otherwise, select Would not help explain.

Would help explain	Would not help explain	Statements
		The proportion of the population of New Zealand that lives close to the ocean is larger than that of South Africa. Note that each youngster plays only one sport.
		Relative to other sports in South Africa, professional cricket players earn more money than any other professional sport players do.
		People in coastal countries have a greater interest in water sports than those in inland countries

PASSAGE 10

Manager	Employee satisfaction rating (%)	Yearly sales (thousands of dollars)	Percent change in sales over previous year	Underground parking	Free shipping	Size of sales force
L. Jenkins	32.3	58.4	5.3	no	no	5
P. Parsons	44.4	92	−7.8	yes	yes	11
A. Yangzhou	65.7	105.2	−1.2	no	yes	10
D. Xin	55.7	85.1	10.8	yes	yes	15
M. Stover	18	116.9	15.5	no	yes	12
Z. Szymes	50.1	64.7	4.8	no	no	8
T. Emerald	64.2	77.4	0.3	yes	no	11
O. McDonough	75.5	79.6	31.2	no	yes	8
K. Eriksson	46.9	58.9	−20.0	no	no	13
B. Stripley	48.7	101.7	−9.4	yes	yes	16

A small furniture store chain conducted performance reviews of its 10 branch managers. The managers' performance in several metrics over the last year has been compiled in the table. The table also lists some relevant features of each manager's branch.

For each of the following statements, select True if the statement can be verified to be true based on the given information. Otherwise, select False.

True	False	
		A majority of the managers who oversaw an increase in sales over the previous year have an employee satisfaction rating higher than the median.
		There is a positive correlation between the size of a branch's sales force and that branch's change in year-over-year sales.
		The branch that had the highest sales in the previous year has underground parking.

PASSAGE 11

The following table displays the recorded maximum and minimum temperatures, as well as humidity levels, observed over a span of 5 days in two coastal regions located in western India.

Date	Region	Maximum Temperature	Minimum Temperature	Humidity (%)
6/1/2012	Colaba	35.5	28.4	63
6/1/2012	Santacruz	34.5	28.6	60
6/2/2012	Colaba	35.5	28.6	68
6/2/2012	Santacruz	34.2	28.8	61
6/3/2012	Colaba	34.6	29	61
6/3/2012	Santacruz	35.2	28.2	70
6/4/2012	Colaba	34.6	29	61
6/4/2012	Santacruz	34.6	28	69
6/5/2012	Colaba	35.6	29	74
6/5/2012	Santacruz	34.3	27.9	66

For each of the following statements, select 'Yes' if statement is true based solely on the information provided in the table; otherwise select 'No'.

Yes	No	Statements
		If range is taken into consideration, then humidity in Sanatcruz is more consistent than humidity in Colaba.
		Median of temperature difference between maximum and minimum temperature in Santacruz is more than that in Colaba.
		Mean maximum temperature of 1st June is lower than that of 2nd & 4th June.

PASSAGE 12

The table contains data on 11 subway systems from around the world. For each subway system, the city and continent in which it is located is provided, along with the total number of lines and stations it contains. The length, measured in kilometers, of the average line in each system is also provided.

City	Continent	Lines	Average Line Length (km)	Stations
Buenos Aires, Argentina	South America	6	8.98	86
Toronto, Canada	North America	4	17.73	75
Santiago, Chile	South America	6	19.62	118
Beijing, China	Asia	20	28.6	306
Paris, France	Europe	16	13.74	302
Mexico City, Mexico	North America	12	16.76	163
Madrid, Spain	Europe	13	22.54	301
London, England	Europe	11	36.55	270
Chicago, USA	North America	8	20.75	145
New York, USA	North America	25	14.08	424
Singapore	Asia	5	39.84	119

Yes	No	
		The average (arithmetic mean) number of stations in the European subway systems is more than double the average (arithmetic mean) number of stations in the South American subway systems.
		The number of lines in the New York subway system exceeds the median number of lines by more than 13.
		The London subway system has the greatest total length as measured by kilometers of lines.

PASSAGE 13

Following table shows the percentage of population visiting Selected Cultural Institutions in one year

Country/political union	Public Library	Zoo/ Aquarium	Natural History Museum	Science/ technology museum
Russia	15	8	5	2
Brazil	25	28	7	4
European Union	35	27	20	18
South Korea	35	37	30	10
China	41	51	13	19
Japan	48	45	20	12
US	65	48	27	26

For each of the following statements select Would help explain if it would, if true, help explain some of the information in the table. Otherwise select Would not help explain.

Would help explain	Would not help explain	Statements
		The proportion of the population of Brazil that lives within close proximity to at least one museum is larger than that of Russia.
		Of the countries/political unions in the table, Russia has the fewest natural history museums per capita.
		Of the countries/political unions in the table, the three that spend the most money to promote their natural history museums are also those in which science is most highly valued.

PASSAGE 14

The table displays the performance scores of five computer models (Models V through Z) across three different tests (Tests A, B, and C). When sorted by a specific test, the models are arranged in ascending order based on their performance on that particular test, with the highest scores appearing at the top

Model	Test		
	A	B	C
X	10068	87	68
W	9675	104	82
Y	8369	121	103
Z	7667	130	93
V	6970	119	87

Sorted by Test B :

Model	Test		
	A	B	C
X	10068	87	68
W	9675	104	82
V	6970	119	87
Y	8369	121	103
Z	7667	130	93

Sorted by Test C :

Model	Test		
	A	B	C
X	10068	87	68
W	9675	104	82
V	6970	119	87
Z	7667	130	93
Y	8369	121	103

For each of the following performance tests, select Greater scores are better if greater numerical scores on that performance test indicate better performance. Otherwise, select Greater scores are worse.

Greater scores are better	Greater scores are worse	
		Test A
		Test B
		Test C

PASSAGE 15

Interstate Number	Length (Miles)	States Served	Westernmost State Served	Easternmost State Served
1-10	2460	8	California	Florida
1-20	1539	6	Texas	South Carolina
1-40	2554	8	California	North Carolina
1-70	2153	10	Utah	Maryland
1-80	2900	11	California	New Jersey
1-90	3021	13	Washington	Massachusetts
1-94	1585	7	Montana	Michigan

The provided table presents data on the seven longest east-to-west Primary Interstate Highways in the United States. Along with the length of each Interstate in miles, the table includes the number of states that the Interstate serves and the western and eastern endpoints of the respective Interstate.

Consider each of the following statements about the Interstates. For each statement indicate whether the statement is true or false, based on the information provided in the table.

True	False	
		The ratio of the number of states served by the interstate with median length to the number of states served by the shortest interstate is equal to 4 to 3.
		The ratio of the length of the Interstate that serves the fewest states to the length of the Interstate that serves the most states is approximately 1 to 5.
		The Interstate with the median Interstate Number has a number of states served equal to the mode of the number of states served.

Answer Explanations

PASSAGE 1

1. D. 16530

For this question we need to know what is the % age is going on year over year.

From 32 to 29 to 26.6 to 24 to 22 to 20 it is approx. 10% each year.

The question required us to calculate the approximate total deaths in 1998

Let number of deaths in 1998 be x

$X \times 1.1 \times 1.1 = 20000$

$X = 16528.92$ which is approximately equal to 16530

The nearest answer is D

2. B. 2001 - 2002

percentage change in the ratio of number of deaths due to car accidents to total number of deaths year to year is equal to:

Year 2000 $\Rightarrow \frac{0.9}{20} \times 100 = 4.5\%$

Year 2001 $\Rightarrow \frac{1.12}{22} \times 100 = 5.09\%$

Year 2002 $\Rightarrow \frac{1.55}{24.2} \times 100 = 6.41\%$

Year 2003 $\Rightarrow \frac{2.02}{26.62} \times 100 = 7.59\%$

Year 2004 $\Rightarrow \frac{1.91}{29.28} \times 100 = 6.52\%$

Year 2005 $\Rightarrow \frac{2.42}{32.21} \times 100 = 7.51\%$

The question is the biggest difference between two years:

5,09 % (2001) to 6,41 % (2002) is the biggest difference of 1,32 %. So from 2001 to 2002 is the biggest difference in %, hence "B".

3. C. 1020

The percentage of deaths due to natural disasters in 2000 is the same as the percentage of deaths due to car accidents in 2001 = 5.09%

Approximately how many people died in 2000 due to natural disasters = 5.09/100 × 20 × 1000 = 1018

The nearest is C

4. E. It cannot be determined from the information given

We dont know the % difference of the numbers from 2000 to 2001, it can be everything. Wihtout the % or total 2001 number it cannot be determined from the information given.

PASSAGE 2

True	False	
✓		The median number of hurricanes in the Florida counties was higher than the median number of hurricanes in each of the other states' counties.
✓		The counties listed in the table that experienced the three greatest percent changes in population during the period are all part of the coastline region whose listed counties had the greater range in number of hurricanes during the same period.
	✓	The Gulf of Mexico coastline region experienced fewer hurricanes per county listed in the table, on average, than did the Atlantic coastline region.

(a) **No.** From the table we can clearly see that this exporter is only responsible for 49% of the nation's exports of French Roast Coffee. The majority needs to be more than 50%.

(b) **No.** There is no information in the table that would lead us to this conclusion. The table only shows the percentage of national share of exports, not the actual export quantities.

(c) **Yes.** The given producer is responsible for 32% of the nation's exports for light-roast coffee and is ranked in the 2nd place for exports in this category. Therefore, the producer who exports the most light-roast coffee will be greater than 32%. Therefore the top two exporters combined export a majority of the nation's light roast coffee.

PASSAGE 3

True	False	
✓		The median number of hurricanes in the Florida counties was higher than the median number of hurricanes in each of the other states' counties.
✓		The counties listed in the table that experienced the three greatest percent changes in population during the period are all part of the coastline region whose listed counties had the greater range in number of hurricanes during the same period.
	✓	The Gulf of Mexico coastline region experienced fewer hurricanes per county listed in the table, on average, than did the Atlantic coastline region.

(a) The median number of hurricanes in the Florida counties was higher than the median number of hurricanes in each of the other states' counties.

No. of hurricanes in Florida counties - 11,12,15

Median ⇒ 12

No. of hurricanes in Louisiana counties - 11,11,11,12,14

Median ⇒ 11

No. of hurricanes in North Carolina counties - 13,13,14

Median ⇒ 14

Clearly, the median number of hurricanes in the Florida counties was NOT higher than the median number of hurricanes in each of the other states' counties.

False

(b) The counties listed in the table that experienced the three greatest percent changes in population during the period are all part of the coastline region whose listed counties had the greater range in number of hurricanes during the same period.

Counties that experienced the three greatest percent changes in population during the period - Dare County, Palm Beach County, Miami-Dade County. All these 3 counties belong to the Atlantic coastline region.

Basically, the question stem is whether counties belonging to the Atlantic coastline had a greater range in the number of hurricanes than counties belonging to the Gulf of Mexico coastline?

Coastline region and its Range

Atlantic ⇒ 14 – 11 = 3

Gulf of Mexico ⇒ 15 – 11 = 4

False

(c) The Gulf of Mexico coastline region experienced fewer hurricanes per county listed in the table, on average, than did the Atlantic coastline region.

Total number of hurricanes experienced by the Gulf of Mexico coastline region – 73

The average number of hurricanes per county - 74/6 ⇒ 12.3

Total number of hurricanes experienced by the Atlantic coastline region – 63

The average number of hurricanes per county - 63/5 ⇒ 12.5

True

PASSAGE 4

Yes	No	
	✓	Marina will receive Certification A first.
✓		Marina will receive Certification B second.
	✓	Marina will receive Certification C third.

Sequence for Courses (based on the recommended sequence in the Stimulus)

D (Courses 1,6,7) → least number of courses

B (Courses 2,4) → least number of additional courses

A (Courses 5,9) → least number of additional courses

A (Courses 3,8) → least number of additional courses

Based on the above sequence, we get the answers as

Q.1. Marina will receive Certification A first. → NO

Q.2. Marina will receive Certification B second. → YES

Q.3. Marina will receive Certification C third. → NO

PASSAGE 5

Yes	No	
	✓	On average, the lowest score given for judges who had judged in 3 Pan-Global Games was higher than that for judges who had competed in 3 Pan-Global Games.
✓		The judge with the greatest absolute difference between the highest score given and lowest score given also had the greatest percent difference between the lowest score given and highest score given.
✓		The average (arithmetic mean) number of Pan-Global Games that judges participated in as judges was higher than the average number of Pan-Global Games that judges participated in as competitors.
✓		The probability that a given judge competed in more Pan-Global Games than she judged is the same as the probability that a judge gave a higher average score as a judge than she received as a competitor.

(1) No,since the lowest score given for judges who had judged in 3 Pan-Global Games (6.03) was lower than that for judges who had competed in 3 Pan-Global Games(7).

(2) Yes,Finland has the highest difference between the highest score and lowest score given (4.7) and even the % is greatest since here only the numerator(difference between the two values is greater than the denominator,when taking the lowest given as denominator

(3) Yes since the Avg for participation as a judge is 24/9 while as a competitor is 22/9

(4) Yes, since the probability that a given judge competed in more Pan-Global Games than she judged is= 3/9 and the probability that a judge gave a higher average score as a judge than she received as a competitor is 3/9, so both are same

PASSAGE 6

1.

Would help explain	Would not help explain	Statement
	✓	Per capita spending on the performing arts is the highest among communities that invest heavily in the arts and that best advertise the performing arts.
✓		Most major sporting events take place in urban areas, where the average age of residents is significantly lower than that of rural or suburban areas.
✓		A greater percentage of towns contain at least one movie theater than contain at least one performing arts venue.

2.

Can be reasonably inferred	Cannot be reasonably inferred	
	✓	In Federland, per capita spending on sporting events tends to decrease as individuals age.
	✓	The average age of Federland citizens who attended performing arts events in 2015 was under the age of 45.
✓		At least 45% of Federland citizens under the age of 25 attended both a sporting event and a gallery or museum in 2015.

PASSAGE 7

True	False	Statements
✓		In each store whose average customer age falls between 34 and 36, the number of self-check express lanes is above average.
✓		There is a negative correlation between the number of self-check unlimited lanes and the average customer age.
	✓	Stores in this table that have fewer self-check express lanes than the chain-wide average are less likely to have restaurants than stores that have more self-check express lanes than the chain-wide average.

The last row in the "Self-check express lanes" column indicates that the average number of self-check express lanes per store is 6.89. The only two stores with average customer ages between 34 and 36 are Store A and Store F, each of which has 8 self-check express lanes-more than the average number, 6.89. So in each store with an average customer age between 34 and 36, the number of self-check express lanes is above average.

The correct answer is True.

Sorting the table by the "Average customer age" column, we see that stores with higher average customer ages generally tend to have fewer self-check unlimited lanes. Thus, the table shows a negative correlation between average customer age and the number of self-check unlimited lanes.

The correct answer is True.

Sorting the table by the "Self-check express lanes" column, we see that all three stores with less than the average number of self-check express lanes have restaurants, whereas only one store of the six with more than the average number of self-check express lanes has a restaurant. Thus, stores with fewer self-check express lanes than average are more likely to have restaurants than are stores with more self-check express lanes than average, not less likely.

The correct answer is False.

PASSAGE 9

Would help explain	Would not help explain	Statements
✓		The proportion of the population of New Zealand that lives close to the ocean is larger than that of South Africa. Note that each youngster plays only one sport.
✓		Relative to other sports in South Africa, professional cricket players earn more money than any other professional sport players do.
	✓	People in coastal countries have a greater interest in water sports than those in inland countries.

45% plays cricket in South Africa which is greater than any other sports in SA so would help explain.

Australia is a coastal country but still, it has an almost equal proportion of sports interest while there is a different story for New Zealand so would not help explain

PASSAGE 10

True	False	
✓		A majority of the managers who oversaw an increase in sales over the previous year have an employee satisfaction rating higher than the median.
	✓	There is a positive correlation between the size of a branch's sales force and that branch's change in year-over-year sales.
✓		The branch that had the highest sales in the previous year has underground parking.

(a) Median of satisfactory rate should be 49-ish. Percent change over previous year - those with increases consists of 6 different managers. Majority would mean 4 out of 6. Turns out 4 out of 6 have satisfactory rate > 49. Answer True.

(b) No positive correlation as a decrease in year-over-year sales happens consistently even though sales force size increased. Answer False.

(c) Branch that had highest sales in previous year should be the ones around 100+ but yet with a -ve percent change in sales from the previous year, which means they dropped but still have the highest yearly sales (and the highest yearly sales is 100-ish). Stripley had a sales of 112.2 from the previous year which is the highest - it has underground parking. Answer True.

PASSAGE 11

Yes	No	Statements
✓		If range is taken into consideration, then humidity in Sanatcruz is more consistent than humidity in Colaba.
	✓	Median of temperature difference between maximum and minimum temperature in Santacruz is more than that in Colaba.
	✓	Mean maximum temperature of 1st June is lower than that of 2nd & 4th June.

First statement : If range is taken into consideration, then humidity in Sanatcruz is more consistent than humidity in Colaba.

My answer is (YES)

Range of humidity in Sanatcruz: 10

Range of humidity in Colaba: 13

Second statement : Median of temperature difference between maximum and minimum temperature in Santacruz is more than that in Colaba.

My answer is (NO)

temperature difference between maximum and minimum temperature in Santacruz: 5.9 5.4 7 6.6 6.4

Median: 6.4

temperature difference between maximum and minimum temperature in Colaba: 7.1 6.9 5.6 5.6 6.6

Median: 6.6

6.4 < 6.6

Third statement : Mean maximum temperature of 1st June is lower than that of 2nd & 4th June.

My answer is (NO)

Mean maximum temperature of 1st June: 35

Mean maximum temperature of 2nd June: 34.85 < 35

No need to check 4th June

PASSAGE 12

Yes	No	Statements
✓		The average (arithmetic mean) number of stations in the European subway systems is more than double the average (arithmetic mean) number of stations in the South American subway systems.
✓		The number of lines in the New York subway system exceeds the median number of lines by more than 13.
	✓	The London subway system has the greatest total length as measured by kilometers of lines.

(a) The arithmetic mean of the number of stations in the European subway systems

= (Paris, France) + (Madrid, Spain) + (London, England)

$= (302 + 301 + 270) = \frac{873}{3} = 291$

The arithmetic mean of the number of stations in the South American subway systems

= (Buenos Aires, Argentina) + (Santiago, Chile)

$= \frac{(118+86)}{2}$

Double this number is = (118 + 86) = 204

$291 > 204 \rightarrow$ YES

(b) Order the data by the Number of lines for this question. Then

The number of lines in the New York subway system = 25

The median number of lines = That of London = 11

$25 - 11 = 14 > 13 \rightarrow$ YES

(c) For this, keep the following formulae in mind

Average Line Length = (Total Line Length) / (Total Number of lines)

Then order the data by the Number of lines. Then

For London $\rightarrow 11 \times 36.55 = 402.05$

Examine the data. We can clearly see that for China, $20 \times 28.6 = 572$.

572 > 402. So Wrong $\rightarrow$ NO

PASSAGE 13

Would help explain	Would not help explain	Statements
✓		The proportion of the population of Brazil that lives within close proximity to at least one museum is larger than that of Russia.
✓		Of the countries/political unions in the table, Russia has the fewest natural history museums per capita.
	✓	Of the countries/political unions in the table, the three that spend the most money to promote their natural history museums are also those in which science is most highly valued.

RO1: Evaluate

If this statement is to be explanatory, it would likely be because, on average, people living closer to museums are also more likely to visit museums. Sorting on Natural history museum shows that, for the two museum categories (natural history and science/technology), a greater percentage of Brazil's population than of Russia's visits in a single year. Therefore, if, on average, Brazil's population lives closer than Russia's to museums, it could help explain information in the table.

The correct answer is Would help explain.

RO2: Evaluate

If this statement is to be explanatory, it would likely be because, among the countries/political unions listed in the table, the lowest average number of institutions per capita is associated with the lowest proportion of the population visiting such institutions. Sorting the table by Natural history museum shows that, among the countries/political unions shown, Russia has the smallest proportion of its population visiting natural history museums in a single year.

The correct answer is Would help explain.

RO3: Evaluate

If this statement is to be explanatory, it would likely be because the countries/political unions in which people are most likely to visit natural history museums are also those in which people are most likely to visit science/technology museums. However, sorting the table by Natural history museum and Science/technology museum shows that the country/political union with the fifth highest proportion of the population visiting natural history museums (China) has the second highest proportion visiting science/technology museums, a proportion that is higher than that of the countries/political unions with the first (US), third (European Union), and fourth (Japan) highest proportions in the natural history category.

The correct answer is would not help explain.

PASSAGE 14

Greater scores are better	Greater scores are worse	
✓		Test A
	✓	Test B
	✓	Test C

The scores when sorted by score A is seen to be in descending order, that is, the greater scores are better

The scores when sorted by score B is seen to be in ascending order, that is, the greater scores are worse

The scores when sorted by score C is seen to be in ascending order, that is, the greater scores are worse

PASSAGE 15

True	False	
✓		The ratio of the number of states served by the interstate with median length to the number of states served by the shortest interstate is equal to 4 to 3.
	✓	The ratio of the length of the Interstate that serves the fewest states to the length of the Interstate that serves the most states is approximately 1 to 5.
	✓	The Interstate with the median Interstate Number has a number of states served equal to the mode of the number of states served.

The ratio of the number of states served by the interstate with median length to the number of states served by the shortest interstate is equal to 4 to 3......True

IS with median length (ISML) is I-10. Number of states served = 8

IS with shortest length (ISSL) is I-20. Number of states served = 6

$$\frac{\text{ISML}}{\text{ISSL}} = \frac{8}{6} = \frac{4}{3}$$

The ratio of the length of the Interstate that serves the fewest states to the length of the Interstate that serves the most states is approximately 1 to 5......False

IS serving fewest states is I-20 (serves 6 states). Length **(ISFL)** = 1539

IS serving most states is I-90 (serves 13 states). Length **(ISML)** = 3021

$$\frac{\text{ISFL}}{\text{ISML}} = \frac{1539}{3021}$$ Is approximately equal to ½

The Interstate with the median Interstate Number has a number of states served equal to the mode of the number of states served......False

IS with median IS number is I-70. Number of states it serves = **10**

Mode of the number of states served = **8**

Chapter 3

Graphic Interpretation

PASSAGE 1

The figure below shows the growth of global deinopid museum collections from 1800 through 2019, by decade, a period in which no such collections were decommissioned.

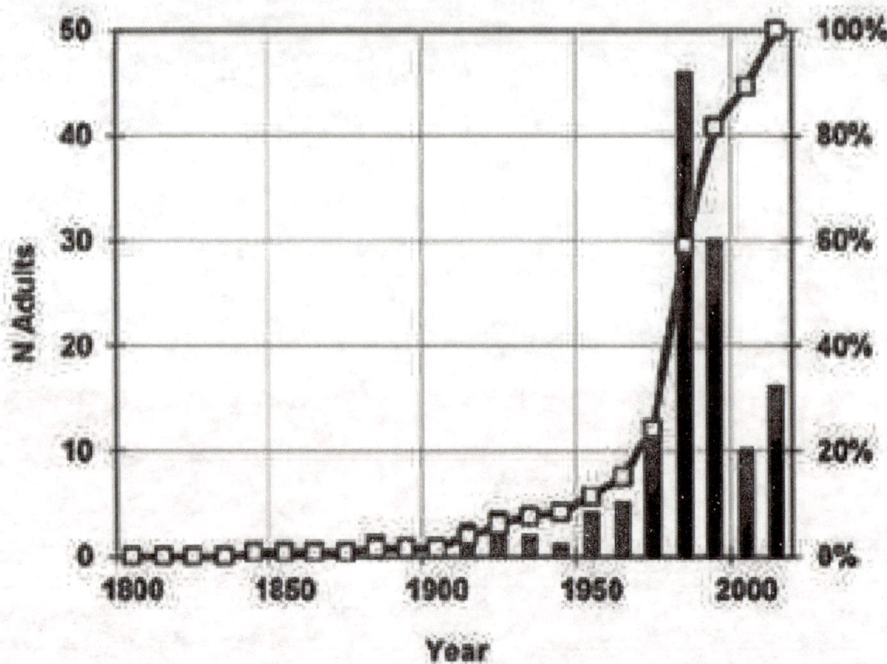

1. According to the figure, the total number of current deinopid museum collections is approximately __________.

A. 100

B. 105

C. 120

D. 135

E. 150

2. According to the figure, in the 1980s the number of global deinopid museum collections grew by approximately__________percent.

A. 30

B. 45

C. 50

D. 55

E. 60

PASSAGE 2

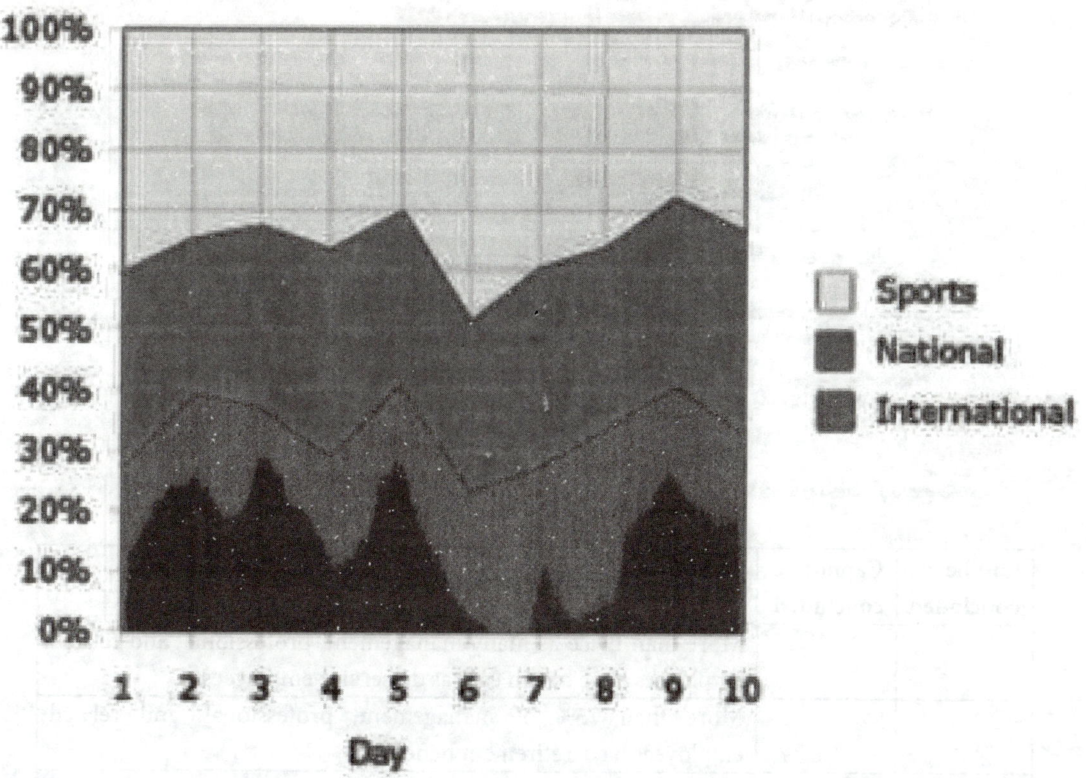

The graph is a stacked line graph that displays the proportion of visits to the three main news web pages of the Star news network. The x-axis represents the 10-day period during which the data was collected, while the y-axis represents the percentage of visits. The study did not differentiate between multiple visits by the same user on the same day or different days; it simply recorded the number of times the three websites were loaded

1. The news page whose percentage of hits was the most consistent over the 10 days measured was__________.

A. the international page

B. the national page

C. the sports page

2. If the total number of visits to Star doubled from Day 6 to Day 9, then the number of visits to the sports page__________ over the same period.

A. increased

B. remained constant

C. decreased

PASSAGE 3

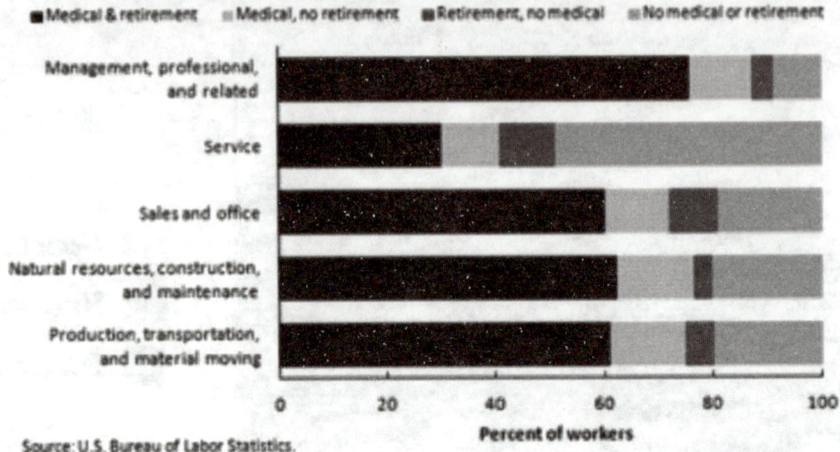

Can be concluded	Cannot be concluded	Statement
		More than twice as many management, professional, and related employees have health care as do service employees.
		More than 75% of management, professional, and related employees have retirement benefits.
		A higher percentage of natural resources, construction, and maintenance workers than of production, transportation, and material moving workers have some sort of retirement benefits.

PASSAGE 4

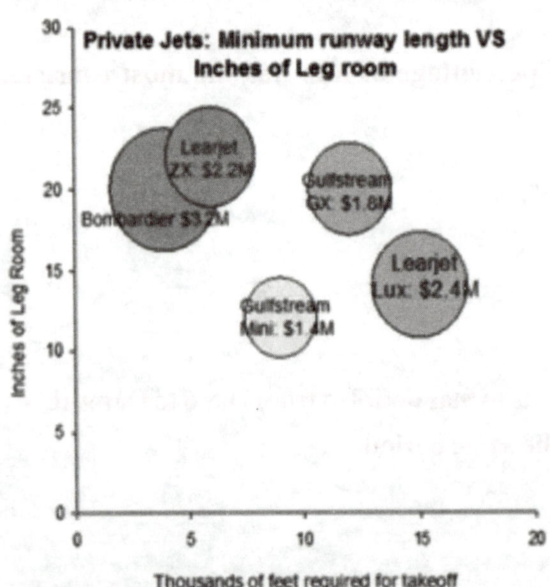

1. The business jet that offers the best value per inch of leg room is the____________.

A. Bombardier

B. Learjet ZX

C. Gulfstream Mini

D. Gulfstream GX

E. Learjet Lux

2. The owner of a Learjet Lux would have to pay____________more dollars per foot required for takeoff on a Bombardier?

A. 460$

B. 450$

C. 640$

D. 720$

PASSAGE 5

The graph illustrates how voters' initial stance on working-time reduction affects the likelihood of their final decision aligning with their initial preference. For each political party represented in the graph, less than 10% of their supporters initially opposed the idea of reducing working hours.

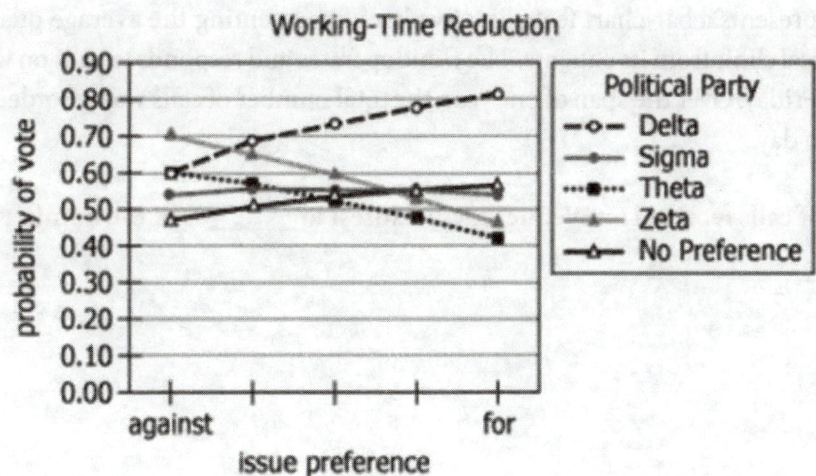

1. Members of the____________party are most apt to vote according to their previously stated preference regarding the issue of working-time reduction.

A. Sigma

B. Theta

C. Delta

D. Zeta

2. **Members of the ______________ party are most apt to vote against the issue of working-time reduction if their previously stated preference regarding the issue of working-time reduction was also against.**

A. Sigma

B. Theta

C. Delta

D. Zeta

PASSAGE 6

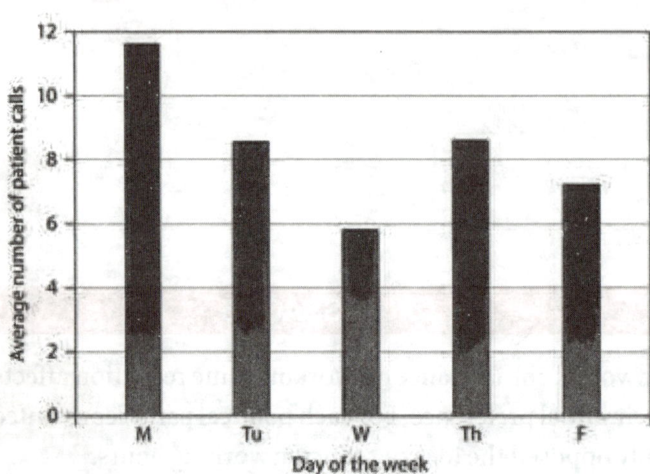

The given graph presents a bar chart featuring five bars, representing the average quantity of hourly calls received by a medical clinic from its patients. The clinic operates and responds to calls on weekdays, specifically Monday through Friday. Over the span of one year, the total number of calls was recorded and an average was calculated for each day.

1. **The number of calls received on Wednesdays is closest to ______% of the number of calls received on Mondays.**

A. 6

B. 12

C. 50

D. 60

E. 200

2. **The relationship between number of calls received and time since the beginning of the week is best described as __________.**

A. not meaningful

B. negative

C. positive

3. **Based on the information shown in the graph, if the clinic wishes to reduce the cost of maintaining its office staff while minimizing disruptions in service to its patients, it should cut down on the number of staff assigned to answer phone calls on __________.**

A. Mondays

B. Tuesdays

C. Wednesdays

D. Thursdays

E. Fridays

PASSAGE 7

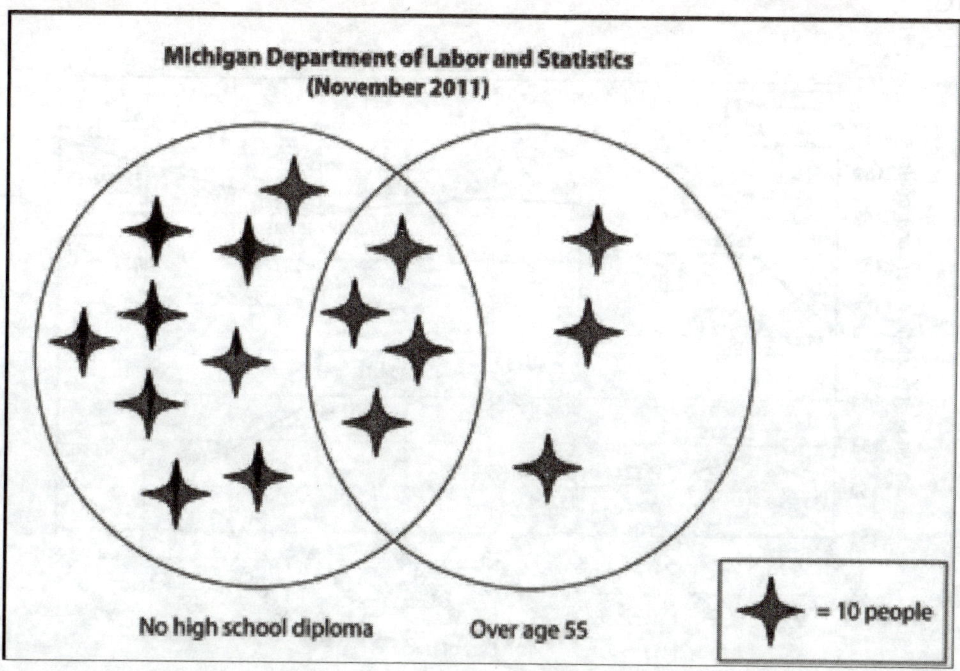

In a survey conducted with a sample of 1,000 individuals filing for unemployment, participants were asked to disclose details regarding their age and educational background. The Venn diagram above illustrates the survey findings, where each symbol represents a group of 10 individuals within the sample.

1. **Out of the entire sample, the probability that a randomly chosen person over age 55 has no high school diploma is __________.**

A. 1 out of 4

B. 3 out of 4

C. 4 out of 7

D. 7 out of 16

2. **Out of the entire sample, the probability that a randomly chosen person with no high school diploma is over the age of 55 is__________.**

A. 1 out of 4

B. 4 out of 9

C. 4 out of 13

D. 9 out of 16

PASSAGE 8

The given graph depicts the stock price trends over a period of 10 days for two competing shoe companies listed on the NASDAQ. The data represents the stock prices recorded between January 10th and January 20th in the year 2015. The upper line represents the stock prices for NKE, while the lower line represents the stock prices for AG.

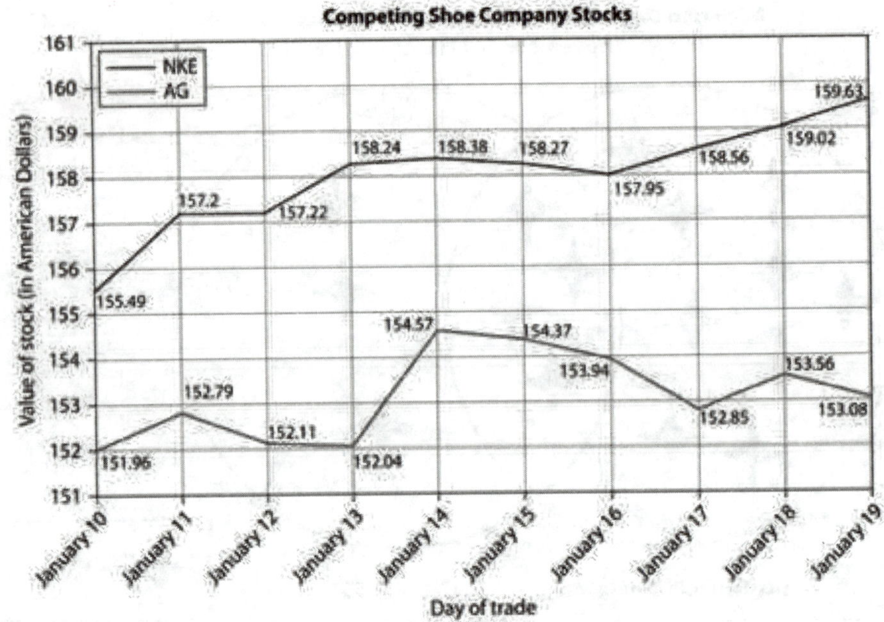

1. **The percent change in the value of NKE stock over the entire ten days is about _______ the percent change in the value of AG stock over that same period.**

A. equal to

B. 2 times

C. 4 times

2. **For the span between January 13th and January 16th, the average (arithmetic mean) value of AG stock falls approximately between _______ dollars.**

A. 151 and 153

B. 153 and 155

C. 157 and 159

PASSAGE 9

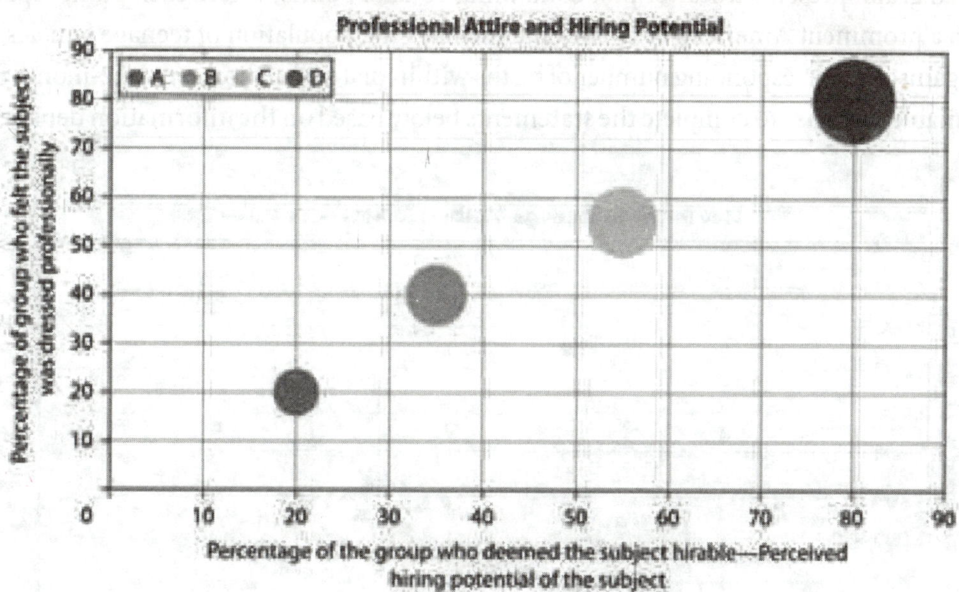

The provided graph illustrates the outcomes of a survey conducted among four distinct focus groups labeled A, B, C, and D. Each group was presented with a different image of the same man dressed in attire suitable for a professional job interview. The images varied in terms of the number of professional indicators, such as a tie, formal shoes, a briefcase, and other factors, with each subsequent image containing more professional markers than the previous one. Following the viewing of the image, focus group members were asked two questions: "Did you perceive the candidate as dressed professionally?" and "How likely is the candidate to be hired for the position?"

The positioning of each circle on the graph represents the perceived level of professionalism associated with the outfit in a particular photo, based on the percentage of focus group members who considered the attire as professional. The relative size of the circle indicates the extent to which focus group members indicated that the candidate would be hired for the job.

1. **The relationship between the percentage of the group who felt the subject was dressed professionally and the percentage of the group who believed the subject would be hired is ______.**

   A. negative

   B. zero

   C. positive

2. **The percentage of people in group B who felt the candidate was dressed professionally is closest to ______ times the percentage of people in group A who felt the candidate was dressed professionally.**

   A. 1.5

   B. 2

   C. 2.5

PASSAGE 10

The provided graph presents a scatter plot containing 35 data points, where each point represents the teen birth rate in a prominent American city. The data includes the population of teenage females, aged 15 to 19, measured against the corresponding number of births within that population over a 12-month period. Choose the most suitable response to complete the statements below based on the information depicted in the graph.

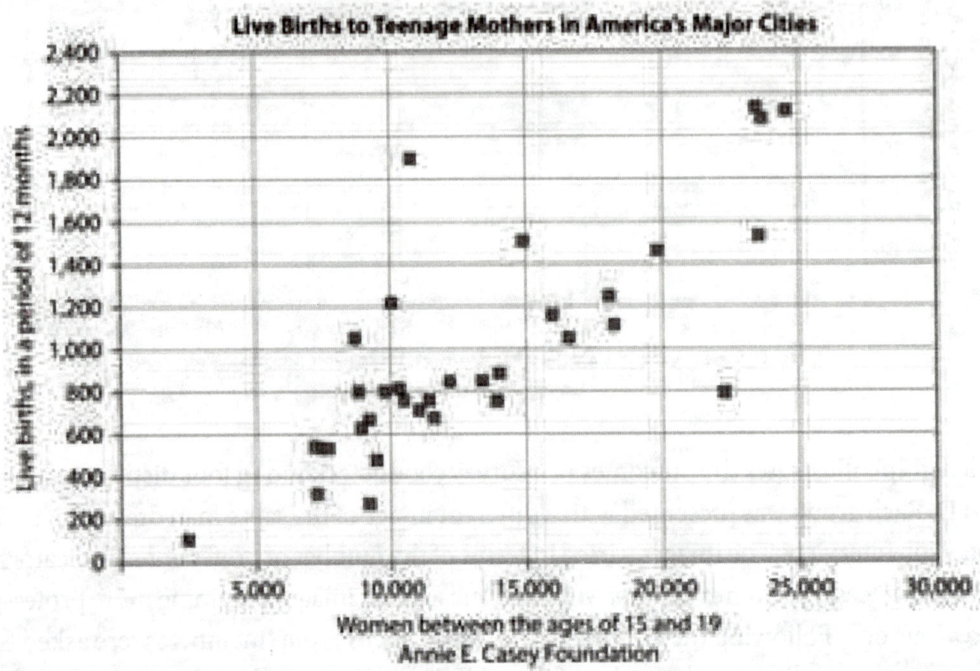

1. The city with the largest population of 15- to 19-year-old women had about _______ percent as many births in that age group as the city with the smallest population.

A. 5

B. 10

C. 21

D. 210

E. 2,100

2. The relationship between the number of women between 15 and 19 and the number of births within that population is ______.

A. negative

B. zero

C. positive

PASSAGE 11

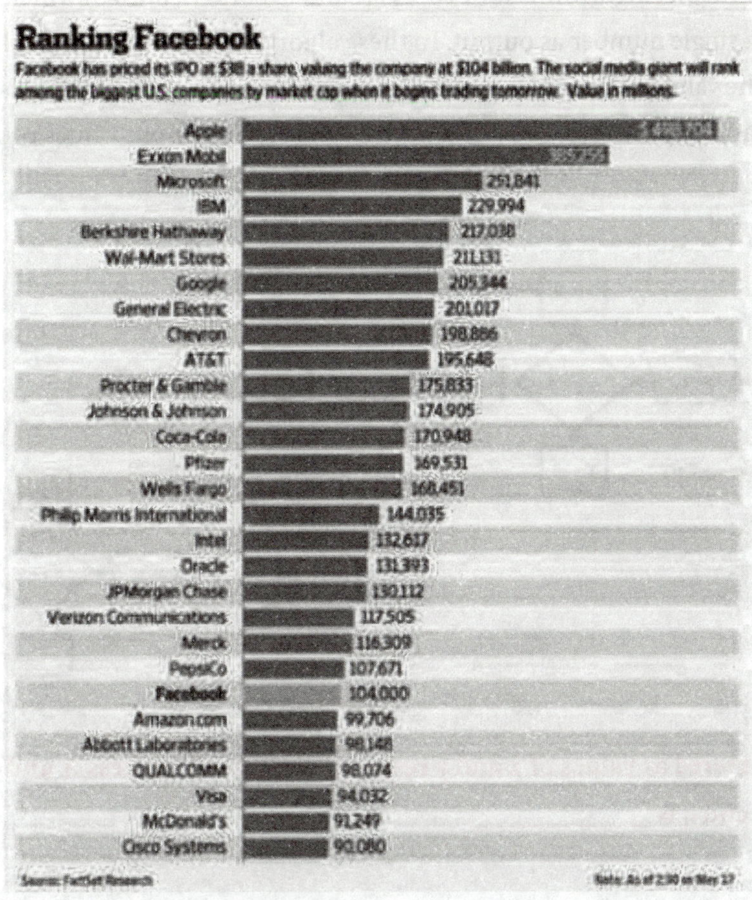

The graph shows the market capitalization value in millions of dollars for the largest companies in the market as of May 17, 2012. Facebook, priced at $38 for the IPO, is bolded and rankings in at $104 B market cap value.

1. Facebook's stock would have to increase to roughly_______________per share in order for Facebook's market capitalization value to reach the value of Apple's market cap.

A. 145$

B. 183$

C. 200$

2. Of the 29 companies listed, the top 10 make up_______________the remaining 19 companies combined.

A. More than

B. The same

C. Less than

PASSAGE 12

The given flowcharts depict algorithms for Process A and Process B, both of which require two integers as input and produce a single number as output. In these algorithms, the resulting values of variables p and q are determined by the values of variables x and y after undergoing a specific process. It is important to note that the values of x and y themselves are influenced by the original input values provided to the respective process.

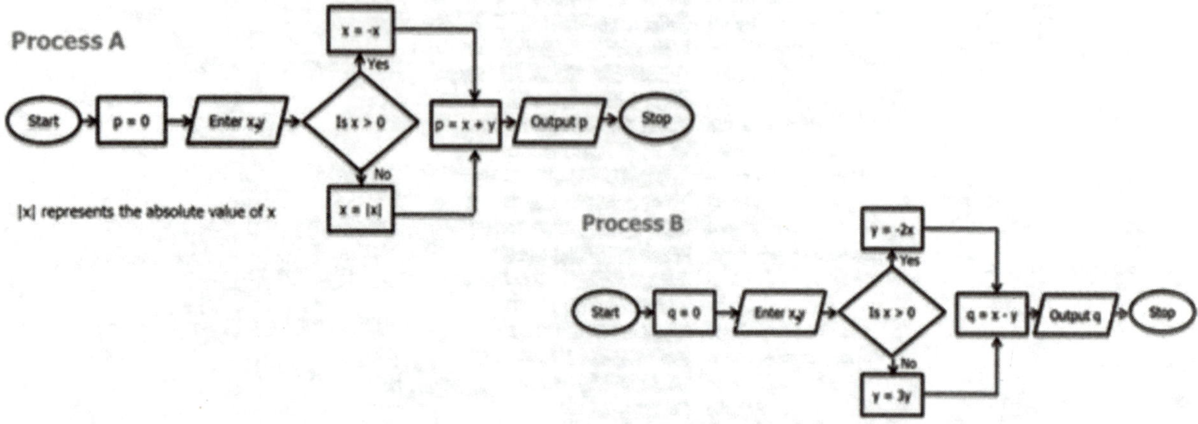

1. **If -2 and 1 are entered as values of x and y respectively in both Process A and Process B., the sum of output values p and q is ____________**

   A. –8

   B. –2

   C. 2

   D. 4

2. **If 2 and -3 are entered as values of x and y respectively in both Process A and Process B the value of |p-q| is ____________**

   A. 1

   B. 2

   C. 11

   D. 12

PASSAGE 13

Performance of a blue-chip company over 6 years has been represented in the chart below. Each circle indicates ratio of Revenue to Profit (value mentioned in the circle). The horizontal axis shows profits.

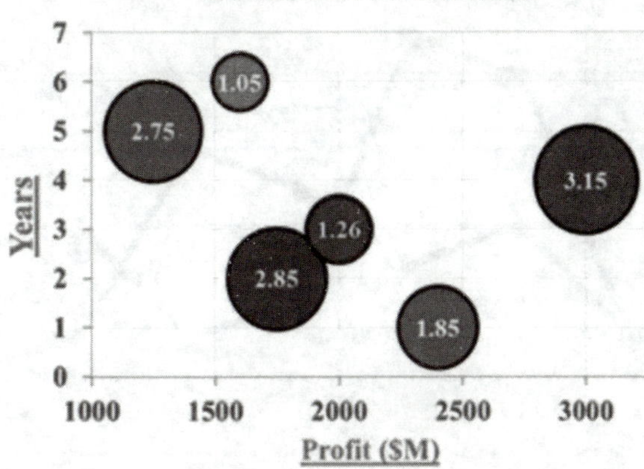

1. The highest profit comparative to revenue was in the year __________.

A. 1

B. 3

C. 4

D. 5

E. 6

2. Profit to expense ratio is least in the year __________.

A. 1

B. 2

C. 3

D. 4

E. 6

3. $ __________ M was the least expense incurred in the 6 year period.

A. 60

B. 80

C. 520

D. 800

E. 1250

PASSAGE 14

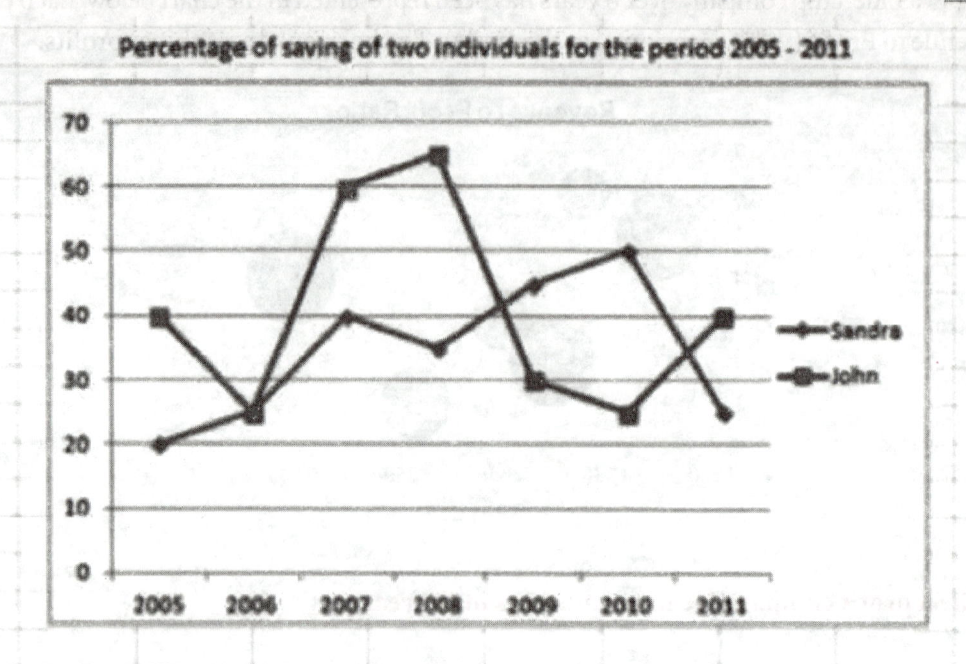

The figure above plots the percent of their incomes that John and Sandra each saved each year from 2005 to 2011.

1. If Sandra spent a total of $26000 in 2008, how much money did she save in 2008?

A. $4000

B. $14000

C. $18000

2. The incomes of Sandra and John in 2007 were in the ratio 4:5. What was the ratio of their expenses?

A. 4:5

B. 5:4

C. 6:5

3. If Sandra and John each saved $18000 in 2009, what was the difference in their incomes in that year?

A. $2700

B. $15000

C. $20000

PASSAGE 15

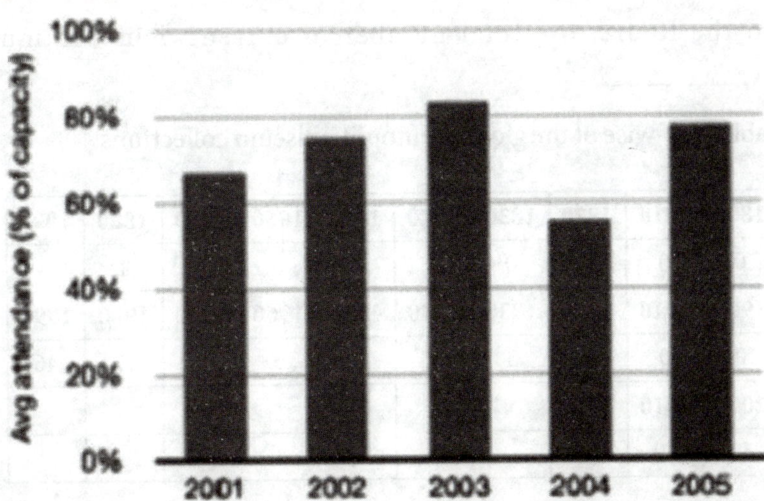

The attached chart graphs the average attendance per game for a certain sports franchise for 5 seasons, represented as percentage of stadium capacity. The stadium's capacity was increased from 60,000 seats to 90,000 seats before the 2004 season.

1. The franchise's highest average attendance occurred in ___________.

A. 2002

B. 2003

C. 2004

D. 2005

2. The highest total attendance for a season (the sum of individual game attendances) occurred in ___________.

A. 2002

B. 2003

C. 2004

D. It cannot be determined

3. From 2003 to 2004, the average attendance per game ___________.

A. Increased by more than 5%

B. Decreased by more than 5%

C. Stayed approximately the same

Answer Explanations

PASSAGE 1

1. According to the figure, the total number of current deinopid museum collections is approximately____________.

First make a table year-wise of the global deinopid museum collections

1800	1810	1820	1830	1840	1850	1860	1870	1880	1890
0	0	0	0	1	0	0	0	1	0
1900	**1910**	**1920**	**1930**	**1940**	**1950**	**1960**	**1970**	**1980**	**1990**
0	0	2	3	2.5	1	5	6	12	46
2000	**2010**	**2019**							
30	10	16							

Now Calculate for each year = 0 + 0 + 0 + 0 + 1 + 0 + 0 + 0 + 1 + 0 + 0 + 0 + 2 + 3 + 2.5 + 1 + 5 + 6 + 12 + 46 + 3 = +10 + 16 = 135.5 = D

Answer: D

2. According to the figure, in the 1980s the number of global deinopid museum collections grew by approximately____________percent.

To answer the second question add the global deinopid museum collections till the year 1970 and then compare it with the year 1980.

Global deinopid museum collections till the year 1970 = 21.5

Global deinopid museum collections till the year 1980 = 21.5 + 12 = 33.5

Percent change = 1221.5 = 55.81 = 1221.5 = 55.81% (33.5 – 21.5 = 12)(33.5 – 21.5 = 12)

Answer: D

PASSAGE 2

1. It is worth noting that the percentage of visits to a specific page on any given day is the size of the corresponding shade for that day. We observe that the size of "National" is more or less consistent (Decreases in "Sports" generally correspond to similar decreases in "International". Same for increases).

Answer: B

2. Percentages corresponding to "Sports" for the two days:

Day 6 : slightly less than 50%

Day 10 : slightly greater than 30%

30% of a quantity twice as large as another quantity is clearly larger than 50% of the smaller quantity.

Answer : A

PASSAGE 3

Can be concluded	Cannot be concluded	Statement
		More than twice as many management, professional, and related employees have health care as do service employees.
		More than 75% of management, professional, and related employees have retirement benefits.
		A higher percentage of natural resources, construction, and maintenance workers than of production, transportation, and material moving workers have some sort of retirement benefits.

More than twice as many management, professional, and related employees have health care as do service employees.....

Cannot Be Concluded

Almost 88%, of Management, Professional & Related employees have health care benefits, but only 42-43% of Service employees have those benefits. We can conclude that the %age of MP&R is twice that of Service employees, but since there are no details on the number of employees in each segment, this statement cannot be concluded.

More than 75% of management, professional, and related employees have retirement benefits.....

Can Be concluded

Employees in MP&R who have Medical & Retirement benefits are almost 78%, and those with Retirement and no Medical are almost 3-4%. Total MP&R with Retirement Benefits ~ 81%-82%. So, this statement can be concluded.

A higher percentage of natural resources, construction, and maintenance workers than of production, transportation, and material moving workers have some sort of retirement benefits.....

Cannot Be Concluded

%age of Natural Resource, Construction, and Maintenance workers with some sort of retirement benefits:

Medical & Retirement ~ 62%

Retirement & No Medical ~ 3%%

Total = 65%

%age of Production, Transportation, and Material moving workers with some sort of retirement benefits:

Medical & Retirement ~ 61%

Retirement & No Medical ~ 7%%

Total = 68%

PASSAGE 4

1. Gulfstream Mini = 1.4/12.5 = 0.112.

   Similarly for others :

   Learjet Lux = 0.184.

   Gulfstream GX-0.9.

   Learjet ZX-0.11

   Bombardier = 0.16.

   Hence Gulfstream GX

   Answer: D

2. Lear jet Lux = 2.4/15 = 0.16

   Bombardier = 3.2/4 = 0.8

   Difference in both = 0.8-0.16 = .64

   Now convert millioons and thousands of feet you get 640

   Answer: C

PASSAGE 5

1. Members of the______________party are most apt to vote according to their previously stated preference regarding the issue of working-time reduction.

   What's asked is which teams previously stated reference/actual preference is the highest, => which party voted for in the previously stated reference and in the actual preference.

   ⇒ the probability for such team would be highest.

   Thus, we can infer from the graph, that the probability is maximum for Delta party (~ 0.8).

   Answer C.

2. Members of the______________party are most apt to vote against the issue of working-time reduction if their previously stated preference regarding the issue of working-time reduction was also against.

   The party which would be most apt to vote against, would be which has a higher probability in against and a lesser one in for.

   From the graph,we can infer that the in case of against the Zeta has the highest probability which goes from 0.70 to 0.45, => Zeta's party members are most apt to vote against if their previous vote was also against.

   Answer D.

PASSAGE 6

1. Average Calls (Wednesday) / Average Calls (Monday) = 5.75 / 11.5 = 0.5 = 50%

   Answer C

2. No clear pattern (whether increasing / decreasing) over the week is deduced from the Graph

   Not Meaningful

   Answer A

3. Since the average number of calls (on Wednesdays) is the minimum, the clinic should cut the number of staff on Wednesdays

   Wednesdays

   Answer C

PASSAGE 7

For the given sample of 1000,

No High School Diploma; < 55 years = 90 ....(1)

No High School Diploma; > 55 years = 40 ....(2)

High School Diploma; > 55 years = 30 ....(3)

thus, High School Diploma; < 55 years = 1000– (90 + 40 + 30) = 840 ....(4)

Total sample = 1000

----

1. Persons over age 55 = 70

   > 55 years; No High School Diploma = 40

   Probability = 40/70 = 4/7

   Answer C

2. Persons No High School Diploma = 130 (ie, 90+40)

   No High School Diploma; > 55 years; = 40

   Probability = 40/130 = 4/13

   Answer C

PASSAGE 8

1. NKE stock → 155.49 to 159.63

   (% change) = (159.63 - 155.49) / 155.49

   = 4.14 / 155.49

   = 2.7 (approx)

AG stock → 151.96 to 153.08

(% change) = (153.08 - 151.96) /151.96

= 1.12 / 151.96

= 0.7 (approx)

Thus, the answer = 2.7 / 0,.7 = 4 times (approx)

Answer C

2. For the AG stock, stock prices for Jan 13 to Jan 16 = 152.04 , 154.57 , 154.37, 153.94

Hence, the mean = (152.04 + 154.57 + 154.37 + 153.94) / 4 = 153.73 (value between 153 and 155)

Answer B

PASSAGE 9

1. % of the group who felt the subject was dressed professionally → The position of each circle on the graph.

Degree to which focus group members indicated that the candidate would be hired for the job → The relative size of the circle.

For any particular group, say A/B/C/D,

As the % of the group who felt the subject was dressed professionally (indicated by the position shift to the right on the Y-axis of the graph) ie, increases, so does the Degree to which focus group members indicated that the candidate would be hired for the job (indicated by the relative size of the circle) increases.

Answer C

2. For the group B, the Graph shows % (Hired Professionally) = 40%

For the group A, the Graph shows % (Hired Professionally) = 20%

Answer B

PASSAGE 10

1. Using the Scatter Plot,

City with the smallest population (ie, 2500) ... No of Births = 100

City with the largest population (ie, 24000) ... No of Births = 2100

So, the 21 times (ie, 2100%)

Answer E

2. Using the Scatter Plot, it can be seen that number of women (increases to the right along X-axis), number of child births (increases to the top along Y-axis).

Thus, the Graph has a Positive slope.

Answer C

PASSAGE 11

1. Apple's market cap is ~ \$499B. Therefore, Apple's market cap is 498/104~500/100 = 5 times bigger than Facebook's. Hence, Facebook's share price would have to increase 5 times to match Apple's. \$38 × 5 = \$190. \$183 is closer to \$190 than \$200, thus \$183 is the answer.

   Answer B

2. The top 10 ~ (\$499+\$385+\$252+\$230+\$217+\$211+\$205+\$201+\$199+\$196)B = \$2.595T.

   The remaining 19 ~ (\$176 + \$175 + \$171 + \$170 + \$168 + \$144 + \$133 + \$131 + \$130 + \$118 + \$116 + \$108 + \$104 + \$100 + \$98 + \$98 + \$98 + \$94 + \$91 + \$91)B = \$2.514T. Hence top 10 make up more than remaining 19.

   Answer A

PASSAGE 12

1. In process A and B value entered is $x = -2$ and $y = 1$

   For process A $x = -2$, $X < 0$ then $x = |X|$ so value of x is changed to 2

   Value of $P = X + Y = 2 + 1 = 3$

   For process B $x = -2$, $X < 0$ then $y = 3y$ so value of y is changed to 3

   Value of $Q = x - y = -2-3 = -5$

   The sum of values of p and q is $-5 + 3 = -2$

   Answer B

2. In process A and B value entered is $x = 2$ and $y = -3$

   For process A- $x = 2$, $x > 0$ so value of x is converted to $-x$, so value of $x = -2$

   Value of $p = x + y = -3-2 = -5$

   For process B $x = 2$, $X > 0$ then $y = -2x$ so value of y is changed to -4

   Value of $Q = x - y = 2 + 4 = 6$

   value of $|p - q| = |-5 -6| = |-11| = 11$

   Answer C

PASSAGE 13

1. E
2. D
3. B

PASSAGE 14

1. From Graph, In 2008, Sandra saved 35% of income. Let her income be x.

   So she spent = x – 0.35x = 0.65x which is given as 26000

   ⇒ 0.65x = 26000

   x = 40000

   So Sandra saved 0.35x = 0.35*40000 = 14000

   Answer B.

2. Given : The incomes of Sandra and John in 2007 were in the ratio 4:5.

   Lets assume the income of Sandra as 4x and of John as 5x.

   From graph, In 2007, Sandra saved 40% of her income. So her expense was 60% of her income. Lets call it Es

   Es = 60% × sandra's income = 0.6 × 4x = 2.4x

   From graph, In 2007, John saved 60% of her income. So his expense was 40% of his income. Lets call it Ej

   Es = 40% × john's income = 0.4 × 5x = 2x

   Ratio of Sandra's Expenditure/ John's Expenditure is ⇒ 2.4x/2x = 1.2 ⇒ 6/5

   Answer C.

3. Given : Each saved 18000 in 2009.

   From graph, In 2009, Sandra saved 45% of her income. let her income be x

   45% × x = 18000

   ⇒ x = 40000

   From graph, In 2009, John saved 45% of her income. let his income be y

   30% × y = 18000

   ⇒ y = 60000

   difference in income is y – x = 60000 – 40000 = 20000

   Answer C.

PASSAGE 15

1. We got to compare highest average attendance (in absolute numbers)

   Now for years before 2004 and after 2003 we can compare directly via avg percent attendance as the base (total capacity) is same. Hence, we need to compare between 2003 and 2005

   for 2003: Avg attendance = ~82%

Avg attendance in absolute numbers: $0.82 \times 60000 = \sim 49000$

for 2005: Avg attendance = ~78%

Avg attendance in absolute numbers: $0.78 \times 90000 = \sim 72000$

Answer D

2. To calculate the total absolute attendance we will need the total number of games played in the season. Without this information we cannot compute the total attendance for a season.

   Although we can compare the total attendance among different years based on avg attendance:

   from 2002

   Answer D

3. %Increase in attendance = (Attendance in 2004-Attendance in 2003)/Attendance in 2003

Attendance in 2003 = %Attendance × capacity

$= (0.58 \times 90000 - 0.82 \times 60000)/0.82 \times 60000 \sim 6\%$

Answer A

Chapter 4

Two Part Analysis

PASSAGE 1

Steve is contemplating expanding his current rectangular garden, and he has two choices to consider. In the first option, he plans to extend the length of the existing garden by 5 meters while keeping the width the same. This expansion would result in an enlarged garden with an area twice that of the original garden. Alternatively, Steve could choose the second option, which involves increasing the width of the existing garden by 2 meters without altering the length. This adjustment would yield an enlarged garden with an area 1.5 times greater than that of the original garden.

From the Dimensions column in the following table, identify a length and a width, in meters, for Steve's existing garden that are consistent with Steve's two options. Make only two selections, one in for each column.

Length (m)	Width (m)	Dimensions
		3
		4
		5
		6
		7
		8

PASSAGE 2

At XYZ Inc., an employee will receive a verbal warning if they have accumulated 3 unexcused absences within a 365-day period. If the number of unexcused absences reaches 4, the employee will receive a written reprimand. The company defines the severity of an absence based on the duration of the missed work. Missing between 10 minutes and 2 hours counts as one-third of an absence, missing between 2 and 4 hours counts as half an absence, and missing more than 4 hours counts as a full absence. However, employees have the option to make up for up to 1 hour of an unexcused absence by staying late on the same day.

From the table provided, choose one description of an employee who met the criteria for a verbal warning, and select another employee who qualified for a written reprimand. Please make two selections, one from each column of the table.

Verbal warning	Written reprimand	Statements
		Absent all day on 5 Aprili 2010, 8 June 2010, 17 April 2011, and 14 June 2011
		Absent 4.5 hours but stayed 1 hour late on May 13 May 2010; absent all day on 2 June 2010, 1 May 2011, and 21 July 2011
		Absent 4.5 hours on 19 March 2010; stayed 1 hour late on 20 March 2010; absent all day on 8 and 9 February 2011; arrived 40 minutes late on 17 April 2011
		Absent 3.5 hours on 13 September 2010; absent 1 hour on 15 September 2010; absent 6 hours on 16 September 2010; absent 2.5 hours on 18 September 2010; absent 1 hour on 19 September 2010
		Absent 3 hours on 7 July 2010; absent 2.5 hours on 13 September 2010; absent all day on 31 January 2011 and 4 July 2011; absent 5 hours on 12 March 2011

PASSAGE 3

The events A and B are independent, and the probability that event A occurs is 0.4.

In the table below, choose the two numbers that are consistent with the information that is given. In the first column, select the row that shows the probability that at least one of the events A and B occurs, and in the second column, select the row that shows the probability that event B occurs.

Probability that at least one of the events A and B occurs	Probability that event B occurs	
		0.10
		0.25
		0.50
		0.55
		0.60
		0.80

PASSAGE 4

It is recommended that computer users employ distinct passwords for each of their online accounts to enhance security. These passwords should be strong, making them difficult for hackers to decipher. However, remembering multiple strong passwords can be challenging, particularly for users with numerous online accounts.

Fortunately, there are software solutions available at little or no cost that can securely store and encrypt passwords. Users only need to remember a single password to access all their stored passwords. By installing such software on a computer and entering the necessary information, users can comply with the recommendations of security experts. Some versions of this software can even be copied to portable devices like USB drives, enabling users to access their passwords from any compatible computer. For users with multiple accounts who would otherwise struggle to use different strong passwords for each account, following the advice of security experts may require making certain sacrifices in order to achieve significant gains in security.

Indicate by appropriate selections in the first and second column which of the items in the third column would describe a sacrifice for this user and which would be a gain. Make only two selections, one in each column.

Sacrifice	Gain	
		Money
		Computing Speed
		Security
		Number of online account
		Time

PASSAGE 5

Professor A : It is proposed that the aid industry should narrow its focus and allocate resources primarily towards primary schools located in the most impoverished regions. Additionally, there should be an emphasis on providing essential healthcare items like medicines and mosquito nets. Furthermore, attention should be given to a select number of significant agricultural initiatives.

Professor B : There is a belief that a substantial portion of education efforts has not yielded the desired outcomes. In cases where a village or town lacks adequate schooling, it is argued that providing infrastructure like roads might be more beneficial than solely focusing on hiring teachers. The rationale behind this perspective is that when local farmers are able to transport their produce to the market efficiently, their increased income can be utilized to support schools financially and ensure their long-term success.

Suppose that the professors' statements express their genuine opinions. Select statements (1) and (2) as follows : Professor A would likely disagree with (1) and Professor B would take (2) to present logical support for (1). Select only two statements, one per column.

(1)	(2)	Statements
		A. The aid industry should focus less on the areas of health and agriculture than it now does.
		B. The aid industry should focus more on primary education than it now does.
		C. The aid industry should focus its spending less on primary education than it now does.
		D. Projects in health and agriculture are more likely to be successful if they are not paid for by the aid industry.
		E. Projects in education are more likely to be successful if they are paid for by the aid industry.
		F. Projects in education are more likely to be successful if they are paid for by local people.

PASSAGE 6

Given the Eurostar's role as a high-speed train system, it offers rapid, efficient, and environmentally friendly transportation throughout Europe. When operating at a constant speed of T kilometers per hour (T km/hr), the Eurostar generates fuel emissions of CO_2 at a rate of E kilograms per kilometer (E kg/km) under typical travel conditions.

Choose the expression that represents the amount of CO_2 fuel emissions produced by the Eurostar during a one-hour journey at a constant speed, T, under normal travel conditions. Also, select the expression that represents the quantity of CO_2 emitted by the Eurostar while traveling at a constant speed, T, for a distance of 200 kilometers. Please make two selections, one from each column.

CO_2 emitted in 1 hour	CO_2 emitted in 200 kilometer	Expression
		$200E$
		$\frac{E}{200}$
		ET
		$\frac{T}{200}$
		$\frac{T}{E}$

PASSAGE 7

The following excerpt is from a fictitious article in a journal of psychiatric medicine about a fictitious mental health condition called diaemotiopluralism.

For psychiatrists studying the behavior of those suffering from diaemotiopluralism, there is critical significance in observing the subject both when alone and when interacting with his or her peers. Such observations allow researchers to study not only the normal or "base" state of the affected person, including the effect that being alone has on an individual, but also the effects of diaemotiopluralism on social interactions, position in social order, and ability to participate in constructive workplace relationships. Individuals who suffer from diaemotiopluralism are often susceptible to overstimulation, particularly in situations involving high levels of interpersonal contact.

Moreover, there are varying degrees of diaemotiopluralism, with different social situations affecting individuals in unique ways. It is interesting to observe not only the actual symptoms of the disorder but also the coping mechanisms that the individual develops in an attempt to compensate for, overcome, or manage his or her condition.

From the table provided, determine the scenario that would pose the greatest challenge for an individual with diaemotiopluralism, as defined above. Additionally, identify the scenario that a person experiencing diaemotiopluralism would find the least challenging to handle.

Most Difficult	Least Difficult	Scenarios
		Working in an office
		Riding alone in a car
		Having lunch at home with a spouse
		Watching television with a friend
		Sleeping

PASSAGE 8

The gardener is in the process of planning the layout for a garden, which consists of two rectangular beds named A and B. Each bed will accommodate a total of 5 different types of shrubs or flowers. The gardener has a choice of 6 types of annual flowers, 4 types of perennial flowers, and 7 types of shrubs to select from for each bed. Bed A must include precisely 1 type of shrub and exactly 2 types of annual flowers. On the other hand, Bed B is required to have precisely 2 types of shrubs and at least 1 type of annual flower. It should be noted that no flower or shrub will be utilized more than once in each bed.

Identify the number of possible combinations of shrubs and flowers for bed A and the number of possible combinations of shrubs and flowers for bed B. Make only two selections, one in each column.

Bed A	Bed B	
		520
		630
		756
		1,028
		2,242
		2,436

PASSAGE 9

An employee of a certain company is creating the smallest possible cubic box into which a spherical piece of art will be placed for an exhibit. The longest distance around the piece of art is ? (2/4 meters).

Select the approximate value, in meters, of the sphere's diameter d and select the desired value, in meters squared, of the area A of the box's interior base. Make only two selections, one in each column.

d	A	
		0.56
		0.62
		0.68
		0.75
		0.79
		0.83

PASSAGE 10

The arboretum has the intention of establishing three new groves, each consisting of four trees. Specifically, each grove should comprise two distinct conifer trees and two different flowering trees. It is a requirement that at least one of the groves includes both a hemlock and a crabapple tree. Additionally, it is stipulated that no two groves can contain more than one tree of the same type, and it is prohibited to plant the same type of tree in all three groves.

Grove 1

- hemlock (conifer)
- spruce (conifer)
- magnolia (flowering)

Grove 2

- crabapple (flowering)
- dogwood (flowering)
- larch (conifer)

Grove 3

- cherry (flowering)
- crape myrtle (flowering)
- hemlock (conifer)

Select a tree that must be added to one of the groves. Then select a tree that cannot be added to any grove. Make only two selections, one for each column.

Must be added to one of the groves	Cannot be added to any grove	
		Cedar (conifer)
		Hemlock (conifer)
		Crabapple (flowering)
		Cypress (conifer)
		Fir (conifer)
		Pine (conifer)

PASSAGE 11

Samantha is considering two different phone plans. Plan A has a monthly fee of $15 and a per-minute rate of $0.1. Plan B has a monthly fee of $30 and a per-minute rate of $0.02. Samantha estimates that she will use 500 minutes per month. Based on this information, select for Average cost for the average monthly cost Samantha will pay for Plan A, and select for Amount saved the average amount Samantha will save per month by choosing Plan B over Plan A. Make only two selections, one in each column.

Average cost	Amount saved	
		$25.00
		$35.00
		$45.00
		$55.00
		$65.00

PASSAGE 12

A grocery store provides a discount program where customers can enjoy discounts on specific items. The program offers a 15% discount on all dairy products and a 10% discount on all fruits and vegetables. During the previous month, a customer made purchases amounting to $120 for dairy products and $80 for fruits and vegetables. In addition, the customer bought $50 worth of other items that were not eligible for any discounts.

In the table below select the total amount paid by the customer for all purchases including discounts, and the total amount paid by the customer for all purchases, without any discounts. Make only one selection in each column.

Total amount with discount	Total amount without discount	
		$200
		$219
		$224
		$245
		$250
		$304

PASSAGE 13

A committee of k members was formed from the n members of a certain company's board of directors. Each member of the committee sent exactly one email summarizing his or her perspective on the committee's findings to each board member who was not a member of the committee, and to no one else. The total number of these email summaries sent was 35.

Select values for k and for n that are jointly consistent with the given information. Make only two selections, one in each column.

k	n	
		4
		5
		7
		10
		12

PASSAGE 14

The farmer possesses a piece of land that is bounded by two roads intersecting at a right angle, forming a right triangle. One of the roads has a length of 2 kilometers (km), while the length of the other road is b km. The longest side of the boundary measures c km, and the area enclosed by the land is represented by A km^2.

In the table, select the value that is closest to c and the value that is closest to A so that the values are jointly consistent with the given information. Make only two selections, one in each column.

C	A	
		2.0
		2.8
		4.0
		5.7
		8.0

PASSAGE 15

A group of friends wants to order a pizza for a dinner party. To accommodate everyone's preferences, one-half of the pizza must contain at least 1 but no more than 3 kinds of meat and at least 2 but no more than 5 kinds of vegetable; the other half of the pizza must contain at least 2 but no more than 4 kinds of meat and at least 3 but no more than 6 kinds of vegetable. Below is the menu of options for both meats and vegetables.

Meats:

- Bacon
- Ham
- Pepperoni
- Sausage

Vegetables:

- Artichokes
- Mushrooms
- Olives
- Onions
- Peppers
- Spinach
- Tomatoes

Select a combination of ingredients that the friends could order for Each half of the pizza and a combination of ingredients that they can order for Neither half of the pizza. Make only two selections, one in each column.

Each half	Neither half	
		Bacon, artichokes, mushrooms, pepperoni, olives and sausage.
		Artichokes, mushrooms, pepperoni, peppers, spinach, and tomatoes.
		Artichokes, ham, olives, onions, peppers, sausage, spinach, and tomatoes.
		Artichokes, mushrooms, olives, onions, peppers, sausage, and spinach.
		Artichokes, ham, mushrooms, olives, onions, pepperoni, and tomatoes.

Answer Explanations

PASSAGE 1

Length (m)	Width (m)	Dimensions
		3
	✓	4
✓		5
		6
		7
		8

RO1

For any rectangle, the area is equal to the length (L) times the width (W). In Steve's garden, a length 5 m longer would yield an area twice as large. In other words, (L + 5)W = 2LW. Distributing the W gives LW + 5W = 2LW, and subtracting LW from both sides gives 5W = LW.

We are also told that a width 2 m longer would yield an area 1.5 times as large. In other words, L(W + 2) = 1.5LW. Distributing the L gives LW + 2L = 1.5LW, and subtracting 1.5LW from both sides gives 2L = 0.5LW. Multiplying both sides of the equation by 2 gives 4L = LW.

Thus, 5W = LW and 4L = LW, so 5W = 4L. Dividing both sides of the equation by 5 gives W=4/5L. The following table shows what the width of Steve's garden would be for each of several possible lengths:

L	$\frac{4}{5}L$
3	2.4
4	3.2
5	4
6	4.8
7	5.6
8	6.4

The only value for the width that is one of the possible options is 4. The corresponding length is 5.

The correct answer is 5.

RO2

The table provided in the analysis of RO1 shows that if the length is 5, the corresponding width is 4.

The correct answer is 4.

PASSAGE 2

Verbal warning	Written reprimand	Statements
		Absent all day on 5 Aprili 2010, 8 June 2010, 17 April 2011, and 14 June 2011
		Absent 4.5 hours but stayed 1 hour late on May 13 May 2010; absent all day on 2 June 2010, 1 May 2011, and 21 July 2011
✓		Absent 4.5 hours on 19 March 2010; stayed 1 hour late on 20 March 2010; absent all day on 8 and 9 February 2011; arrived 40 minutes late on 17 April 2011
		Absent 3.5 hours on 13 September 2010; absent 1 hour on 15 September 2010; absent 6 hours on 16 September 2010; absent 2.5 hours on 18 September 2010; absent 1 hour on 19 September 2010
	✓	Absent 3 hours on 7 July 2010; absent 2.5 hours on 13 September 2010; absent all day on 31 January 2011 and 4 July 2011; absent 5 hours on 12 March 2011

Verbal warning: Absent 4.5 hours on 19 March 2010; stayed 1 hour late on 20 March 2010; absent all day on 8, 9, and 10 of February 2011; arrived 40 minutes late on 17 April 2011

So here the employee would have only 3.5 absence here since March 2010 - March 2011 will be the one year period considered, so verbal warning would be there

Written reprimand: Absent 3 hours on 7 July 2010(.5 absence); absent 2.5 hours on 13 September 2010 (.5 absence); absent all day on 31 January 2011 and 4 July 2011(2 absenced); absent 5 hours on 12 March 2011 (1 absence)

PASSAGE 3

Probability that at least one of the events A and B occurs	Probability that event B occurs	
		0.10
	✓	0.25
		0.50
✓		0.55
		0.60
		0.80

We're asked to find the probability that event B occurs, such that one of the answer choices reflects the probability of either A or B occurring-in other words, any outcome other than neither A nor B occurring.

Since the only outcome we want to exclude is neither A nor B occurring (see stimulus explanation, above), we can create an equation by subtracting that one undesired outcome from the total of 1:

Probability that at least one of A and B occurs $= 1 - [0.6(1 - b)]$

$$= 1 - (0.6 - 0.6b)$$

$$= 1 - 0.6 + 0.6b$$

$$= 0.4 + 0.6b$$

(Note that there are two other ways to set this equation up. We could add the three desired outcomes together to yield 0.4b + 0.4(1 - b) + 0.6b. Alternately, we could add the probabilities of A and B, then subtract the double-counted outcome of both occurring, yielding 0.4 + b - 0.4b. On Test Day, go with whichever approach feels most straightforward-all of these approaches simplify to 0.4 + 0.6b.)

Now let's consider the possible values given in the answer choice list. Thinking about the situation logically, we can determine that the probability that B occurs must be less than the probability that at least one of A or B occurs. We will therefore begin by plugging in the smaller values from our list for the variable b in the equation we set up above. If one of these values for b results in a probability for "at least one of the events A or B" that matches one of the given choices, we know we have found the correct answer.

If b were equal to 0.1, then the probability that at least one of A and B occurs would equal 0.46, which is not an answer choice. This strongly suggests that 0.25 is the probability that B occurs, since it is the only other small answer choice. A larger probability might be possible, since the probability of at least one of A and B might be as high as 0.8, but plugging in b = 0.25 is a reasonable next step.

We'll substitute b = 0.25 into our equation and see whether it produces one of the other answer choices. If it does, that pair will be correct. If it doesn't, we'll try a different value for b. Plugging b = 0.25 into our equation yields:

Probability that at least one of A and B occurs = 0.4 + 0.6(0.25)

= 0.4 + 0.15

= 0.55

This possible value matches one of the answer choices, so we have found the values that satisfy the conditions. Now, as always with Two-Part Analysis questions, we must be careful to select the correct answer choices in the appropriate columns; it would be a shame to do all the math correctly but lose the points for this question by mixing up the columns.

The correct response for the "probability that at least one of the events A and B occurs" is 0.55; the correct response for the "probability that event B occurs" is 0.25.

PASSAGE 4

Sacrifice	Gain	
		Money
		Computing Speed
	✓	Security
		Number of online account
✓		Time

In the second paragraph, the word "fortunately" suggests that the expert is recommending the special software as a way to solve the problems described in the first paragraph. The expert says the software is available at no cost, so no money need be sacrificed to use it. And the passage does not say or suggest anywhere that using the software would require sacrificing computing speed, security, or the user's number of online accounts. However, the passage does say it would take time to install the software and enter all the required information.

Thus, by recommending the software, the expert is effectively suggesting that users sacrifice some time in order to set it up.

The correct answer is Time.

The passage does not say or suggest anywhere that using the software would cause users to gain money, computing speed, or online accounts, nor that it would save them time. But the software does make it much easier for users to use a different strong password on every account even if they would not do so otherwise. The first paragraph says that this practice improves security. Thus, the expert is recommending the software as a way for users who would not otherwise use a different strong password on every account to gain security.

The correct answer is Security.

PASSAGE 5

(1)	(2)	Statements
		A. The aid industry should focus less on the areas of health and agriculture than it now does.
		B. The aid industry should focus more on primary education than it now does.
✓		C. The aid industry should focus its spending less on primary education than it now does.
		D. Projects in health and agriculture are more likely to be successful if they are not paid for by the aid industry.
	✓	E. Projects in education are more likely to be successful if they are paid for by the aid industry.
		F. Projects in education are more likely to be successful if they are paid for by local people.

The wording of the question suggests that the correctness of an answer for one of the response opportunities will depend on the correctness of the answer to the other. We are to find a statement such that the information indicates Professor A would likely disagree with the first statement and Professor B would take the second statement to present evidence against the first.

The only statement that the dialogue strongly suggests Professor A would disagree with is the third option. For example, if the relative distribution of spending by the aid industry between primary schools in the poorest areas, medicines and other basic supplies for health care such as mosquito nets, and the few key agricultural initiatives is maintained, while spending in other areas is drastically reduced, then the aid industry will thereby focus its spending more on primary education than it now does.

The correct answer is The aid industry should focus its spending less on primary education than it now does.

Given the answer above, the question requires identification of the statement that Professor B would take to be evidence for the statement that the aid industry should focus its spending less on primary education than it now does. The claims attributed to Professor B, in the context of the dialogue with Professor A, strongly suggest that she would take such evidence to be provided by the sixth option.

The correct answer is Projects in education are more likely to be successful if they are paid for by local people.

PASSAGE 6

CO_2 emitted in 1 hour	CO_2 emitted in 200 kilometer	Expression
	✓	200 E
		$\frac{E}{200}$
✓		ET
		$\frac{T}{200}$
		$\frac{T}{E}$

The total amount of CO_2 emitted equals the number of kilograms per kilometer times the number of kilometers. At a rate of T km/hr, the Eurostar travels T km in 1 hour, so the CO_2 emitted in that hour is E (the number of kilograms per kilometer) times T.

The total CO_2 emitted in 200 kilometers equals E (the number of kilograms per kilometer) times the number of kilometers, 200.

Answer:

CO_2 emitted in 1 hour: ET

CO_2 emitted in 200 kilometer: 200E

PASSAGE 7

Most Difficult	Least Difficult	Scenarios
✓		Working in an office
		Riding alone in a car
		Having lunch at home with a spouse
		Watching television with a friend
	✓	Sleeping

The correct answers are working in an office as most difficult to manage, and sleeping as least difficult to manage.

We know from the information given in the journal article that those with diaemotiopluralism have a problem with overstimulation from social interactions. Working in an office is the scenario in which there is likely to be the most social interaction to stimulate an individual. When sleeping, stimulation from outside sources would most likely not be an issue.

Answer:

Most Difficult: Working in an office

Least Difficult: Sleeping

PASSAGE 8

Bed A	Bed B	
		520
✓		630
		756
		1,028
		2,242
	✓	2,436

Bed A

For Bed A, we're told that the gardener must include exactly 1 type of shrub and exactly 2 types of annual flower. The problem also specifies that bed A must contain a total of 5 different types of shrubs or flowers, so bed A must also contain 2 types of perennial flower.

To choose 1 shrub from 7 possibilities, we calculate 7!/(1!6!) = 7. When choosing only 1, there is always the same number of possibilities as there is of items (7 possibilities, so 7 choices). To choose 2 annual flowers from 6 possibilities, we calculate 6!/(2!4!) = 15. To choose 2 perennial flowers from 4 possibilities, we calculate 4!/(2!2!) = 6. There are 7 possibilities for a shrub, 15 possibilities for the annual flowers, and 6 possibilities for the perennial flowers. In total, there are 7×15×6 = **630 possibilities for bed A.**

Bed B

For Bed B, we're told that the gardener must include exactly 2 types of shrub and at least 1 type of annual flower. This bed must also contain a total of 5 different types of shrubs or flowers.

To choose 2 shrubs from 7 possibilities, we calculate 7!/(5!2!) = 21.

Choosing bed B flowers is more tricky. We have three possible scenarios: the gardener chooses 1 annual flower (and therefore 2 perennials) OR the gardener chooses 2 annuals (and therefore 1 perennial) OR the gardener chooses 3 annuals (and therefore 0 perennials). We need to calculate the number of combinations for each and then add them together.

1 annual and 2 perennials: choosing 1 always matches the number of options, so there are 6 ways to choose the 1 annual flower. We calculated the number of possible combinations for 2 perennials when we did bed A: the number of possible combinations is 6. There are, therefore, 6 Ã- 6 = 36 possible ways to have 1 annual and 2 perennials.

2 annuals and 1 perennial: We calculated the number of possible combinations for 2 annuals when we did bed A above: the number of possible combinations is 15. For the perennials, we're choosing only 1, so there are 4 possible ways to choose a perennial. There are 15 A– 4 = 60 possible ways to have 2 annuals and 1 perennial.
3 annuals and 0 perennials: to have three annuals, we calculate 6!/(3!3!) = 20.

To have 1 OR 2 OR 3 annuals, we have 36 + 60 + 20 = 116 possible ways. In order to have this AND our 2 shrubs, we have 116 A– 21 = **2,436 possibilities for bed B.**

PASSAGE 9

d	A	
		0.56
	✓	0.62
		0.68
		0.75
✓		0.79
		0.83

Longest Area Around the spherical piece of art is its circumpherence i.e. $2\pi r$

so $2\pi r = \pi^2/4$

r comes as $\pi/8$ hence Diameter D = $\pi/4$ = 0.79

Area of Base A is D2 = 0.792 = 0.62

PASSAGE 10

Must be added to one of the groves	Cannot be added to any grove	
		Cedar (conifer)
	✓	Hemlock (conifer)
✓		Crabapple (flowering)
		Cypress (conifer)
		Fir (conifer)
		Pine (conifer)

Cedar (conifer) - It can be added in Grove 2 & 3 but it is not a Must be.

Hemlock (conifer) - It cannot be added to any groves as it has already been chosen for Grove 1 & 3. Adding it to Grove 2 will violate Condition-4

Crabapple (flowering) - It has to be added to Grove 1, so as to fulfill Condition-2. Grove 2 & 3 already has two flowering trees, so it cannot be added in these groves.

Cypress (conifer) - It can be added in Grove 1 or 3 but it is not a Must be.

Fir (conifer) - It can be added in Grove 1 or 3 but it is not a Must be.

Pine (conifer) - It can be added in Grove 1 or 3 but it is not a Must be.

Must be added to one of the groves - Crabapple (flowering)

Cannot be added to any grove - Hemlock (conifer)

PASSAGE 11

Average cost	Amount saved	
	✓	\$25.00
		\$35.00
		\$45.00
		\$55.00
✓		\$65.00

Plan A has a monthly fee of \$15 and a per-minute rate of \$0.1, so the total cost of 500 minutes

$$= 15 + (500 \times 0.1) = 65\$$$

Plan B has a monthly fee of \$30 and a per-minute rate of \$0.02, so the total cost of 500 minutes

$$= 30 + (500 \times 0.02) = 40\$$$

Average monthly cost Samantha will pay for Plan A = 65\$

The average amount Samantha will save per month by choosing Plan B = 65 – 40 = 25\$

PASSAGE 12

Total amount with discount	Total amount without discount	
		\$200
		\$219
✓		\$224
		\$245
	✓	\$250
		\$304

Without discount, the customer paid the following

Dairy product \$120

Fruits \$80

Other items \$50

Dairy product has a discount of 15%

Hence the discounted price $= 120 \times 0.85 = 102$

Fruits has a discount of 10%

Hence the discounted price $= 80 \times 0.9 = 72$

Total cost with discount $= 102 + 72 + 50 =$ \$224

Total amount with discount = \$224

Total amount without discount = \$250

PASSAGE 13

k	n	
		4
		5
✓		7
		10
	✓	12

number of board = n,

number of comittee = k (k person from n person) $\Rightarrow k < n$

each k send e-mail to board member who was not a member of the committee (n – k)

so total e-mail will be

$k \times (n - k) = 35 = 7 \times 5$

K = 7

N = 12

PASSAGE 14

C	A	
	✓	2.0
✓		2.8
		4.0
		5.7
		8.0

The sides of the plot's boundary that form the right angle of the triangle are 2 km and b km long, and the longest side is c km long. Using the Pythagorean Theorem, $c^2 = 2^2 + b^2 = 4 + b^2$ Taking the square root of each side gives $\sqrt{4+b^2}$. The area of the triangle, A km, can be found using the equation $\frac{1}{2}$ (bas)(height) $= \frac{1}{2}$(b)(2). Since A = b, A can be substituted into the previous expression:

$c = \sqrt{4+A^2}$ Using this equation, the value of c can be calculated for each possible value of A. The table below shows the calculations, rounded to the nearest tenth:

A	$c = \sqrt{4+A^2}$
2.0	2.8
2.8	3.4
4.0	4.5
5.7	6.0
8.0	8.2

The only one of these values of c that is among the options given is 2.8.

The correct answer is 2.8.

RO2

As shown in the table provided in the analysis for RO1, c = 2.8 corresponds to A = 2.0.

The correct answer is 2.0.

PASSAGE 15

Each half	Neither half	
		Bacon, artichokes, mushrooms, pepperoni, olives and sausage.
		Artichokes, mushrooms, pepperoni, peppers, spinach, and tomatoes.
		Artichokes, ham, olives, onions, peppers, sausage, spinach, and tomatoes.
	✓	Artichokes, mushrooms, olives, onions, peppers, sausage, and spinach.
✓		Artichokes, ham, mushrooms, olives, onions, pepperoni, and tomatoes.

1st Half :

Meat: Min-1; Max-2

Veg: Min-2; Max-5

2nd Half :

Meat: Min-2; Max-4

Veg: Min-3; Max-6

The Selection, which can be used for either half will contain 2 meat options (since it is the overlap) and 3/4/5 veg options.

The Selection, which can not be used for either half will have 1 meat option (as there are only 4 options available) and 6/7 veg options.

Bacon, artichokes, mushrooms, pepperoni, olives and sausage......3 meat and 3 Vegetables, Can be used only for 2nd half

Artichokes, mushrooms, pepperoni, peppers, spinach, and tomatoes......1 meat and 5 Vegetables, Can be used only for 1st half

Artichokes, ham, olives, onions, peppers, sausage, spinach, and tomatoes......2 meat and 6 Vegetables, Can be used only for 2nd half

Artichokes, mushrooms, olives, onions, peppers, sausage, and spinach......1 meat and 6 Vegetables, Cannot be used for any half

Artichokes, ham, mushrooms, olives, onions, pepperoni, and tomatoes......2 meat and 5 Vegetables, Can be used for either half

